McGraw-Hill's
GMAT
GRADUATE MANAGEMENT ADMISSION TEST
2010 Edition

McGraw-Hill's
GMAT
GRADUATE MANAGEMENT ADMISSION TEST
2010 Edition

James Hasik

Stacey Rudnick

Ryan Hackney

New York | Chicago | San Francisco | Lisbon
London | Madrid | Mexico City | Milan | New Delhi
San Juan | Seoul | Singapore | Sydney | Toronto

1 2 3 4 5 6 7 8 9 0 QPD/QPD 0 1 4 3 2 1 0 9

Book alone:
ISBN 978-0-07-162412-1
MHID 0-07-162412-0
ISSN 1943-5002

Book/CD set:
ISBN P/N: 978-0-07-162414-5 of set
　　　　　 978-0-07-162416-9

MHID P/N: 0-07-162414-7 of set
　　　　　 0-07-162416-3
ISSN 1943-7094

McGraw-Hill books are available at special quantity discounts for use as premiums and sales promotions, or for use in corporate training programs. For more information, please write to the Director of Special Sales, McGraw-Hill Professional, Two Penn Plaza, New York, NY 10121-2298. Or contact your local bookstore.

This publication is designed to provide accurate and authoritative information in regard to the subject matter covered. It is sold with the understanding that neither the author nor the publisher is engaged in rendering legal, accounting, or other professional services. If legal advice or other expert assistance is required, the services of a competent professional person should be sought.

—From a Declaration of Principles jointly adopted
By a Committee of the American Bar
Association and a Committee of Publishers.

GMAT is a registered trademark of Graduate Management Admission Council, which was not involved in the production of, and does not endorse, this product.

The authors wish to thank Judy Unrein for her contributions to the 2008, 2009, and 2010 editions.

Contents

PART THREE BEYOND THE GMAT

PART FOUR THE PRACTICE TESTS

Foreword

Congratulations! By purchasing this book, you are taking the first step to one of the best decisions you can make—an investment in yourself! In today's intensely competitive business environment, it is critically important that individuals who want to advance in their careers continue to learn—and obtaining an MBA degree is one of the most effective ways for you to strengthen your analytical and business acumen.

The MBA is a fantastic degree—it will prepare you to pursue a wide variety of career options—and even years after graduation the coursework you have completed in an MBA Program will have given you the breadth of business perspective to switch from marketing to consulting or vice versa, as well as to take on the broad responsibilities of a CEO!

As part of the application process to an MBA Program, you will need to take the Graduate Management Admissions Test (GMAT). As I'm sure you know, the GMAT is a challenging standardized test and therefore you owe it to yourself to present a GMAT score which represents your "best effort." While your GMAT score results will be but one factor that selective business schools consider when reviewing your application file, for many MBA Programs, and certainly the world's most selective business schools, your GMAT results are a key element in reviewing your application file. The other key factors in making an admissions decision are the quality of your work experience, academic record, recommendation letters and essays, as well as your interpersonal qualities, in particular your demonstrated leadership skills.

You should also know that a strong score on the GMAT can make a big difference, not only in whether or not you are admitted to a top-tier MBA Program, but that, if admitted, it can greatly enhance the probability that you will receive a scholarship. Essentially, a strong GMAT score, in combination with progressive work experience, solid undergraduate grades, and a positive interview can be the difference between admission to none of your desired MBA programs, and the chance to choose between several attractive MBA Program options.

McGraw-Hill's GMAT will provide you with a template to help you best prepare to take this challenging test. I urge you to make this investment in yourself—to pursue an MBA—and the first step along this path is to prepare wisely to take the GMAT. This book will give you the tools, techniques and *insight* into the design of the GMAT so that you can adequately prepare for the test. I have known Jim Hasik for many years and he is a bright and engaging GMAT preparatory teacher. However, what I have always admired most about Jim is that he takes a genuine interest in his students and this same approach is evident in his writings. Stacey Rudnick has contributed her considerable talents and expertise to this book as well. As an MBA career services professional, she brings a deep understanding of the MBA marketplace and a real appreciation for the skills set desired by the most selective MBA Programs and the most prestigious hiring firms. She has worked not only as a Brand Manager for Kodak but also in the career services office for two Top 20 MBA Programs. In addition, while an MBA student at Goizueta Business School, Stacey was one of our most talented student leaders. Co-author Ryan Hackney is a professional writer specializing in educational content. He has two degrees from Harvard University and has worked for the Boston Consulting Group and for an Internet startup.

Jim, Stacey, and Ryan have written this book in a straightforward and easy-to-read manner. It is not designed to teach you everything you ever wanted to know about the GMAT—but instead, is written to tell you everything that you *need to know* to most effectively prepare for the test. As you prepare to take the GMAT, *McGraw-Hill's GMAT* is an ideal place to start. In order to realize your best score, it is critically important that you know the following prior to taking the GMAT.

▶ Understand how the computer-based GMAT is designed and how the test will conform to your specific skill levels

▶ Understand the format of the verbal section questions and the types of analytical problems you will need to solve

▶ Understand the math concepts that you will need to know to perform well on the analytical sections

▶ Understand the structure of the writing assessment instrument and how you will be graded

This book will address all these issues and more. For individuals who completed few quantitative courses in college, or those who lack confidence about their math skills, the math review chapters will be especially important. You should know that MBA Admissions Committees at most top-tier MBA Programs place particular emphasis on an applicant's quantitative test results. Conversely, if verbal reasoning skills or reading comprehension are not your strong suit, you should spend more time preparing for those sections of the test.

In addition to the theoretical and analytical skills set that MBA studies teach, one of the most valuable aspects of the MBA degree is the lifelong friendships that the MBA Program experience offers. Whether you go to a full-time, part-time, or an Executive MBA Program, your classmates and teammates will make an indelible mark on your thinking—and many will become your lifelong friends. From my own personal experience, I know this to be true.

For the past 21 years, since my own graduation from the University of North Carolina's MBA Program, I have spent each Labor Day weekend with the six members of my MBA Program study group and their families—it is a time for renewing our friendship. In my 17 years at Emory's Goizueta Business School I have found the same to be true. I frequently speak with Goizueta alumni, and whether I'm in New York City or Seoul, they speak fondly of seeing classmates at weddings, of new business ventures developed with teammates, and of visiting alumni during their business and personal travels throughout the globe. The MBA Program experience is designed to change and stretch you beyond your comfort zone and it will definitely accomplish that objective. However, it is the network that you build through MBA studies that is the most rewarding aspect of the experience.

Good luck to you on the GMAT and in the MBA application process afterwards, and again, congratulations on your decision to make such a wise investment in yourself.

Sincerely,

Julie R. Barefoot

Associate Dean and Director of MBA Admissions

Goizueta Business School

Emory University

Atlanta, Georgia, USA

McGraw-Hill's GMAT: Introduction

WELCOME TO THE GMAT

Welcome to the GMAT. Were we saying this to you in person, we might duck after speaking those words. For many people, there's nothing remotely welcoming about the GMAT. To many business school applicants, the test appears to be the most painful hurdle they must clear in their admissions process, and the one for which their work experience has left them the least prepared.

Yet still they come: tens of thousands of people take the GMAT every year, subjecting themselves to three and a half hours of questions about linear equations, statistics, logic, English syntax, and just what the writer of that obscure passage meant by "shibboleth." The GMAT can be irritating, but like it or not, it's an unavoidable bump on the path to an MBA. And it doesn't have to be your enemy; a high score on the GMAT can help pave the way to a spot in a top business school, which could lead to a very lucrative and rewarding career in brand management, consulting, investment banking, starting your own business . . . but we're getting ahead of ourselves. You know why you have to take the GMAT. It's our business to help you make your GMAT score a strong point on your application.

The GMAT tests skills that you use all the time; it just tests them in ways that you probably never encounter in the real world. Every day of your life, you seek out information, analyze arguments, and compare quantities and values. If you've graduated from college, you should have been exposed at least once in your life to almost all of the mathematics and syntax concepts that are tested on the GMAT. Your success on the GMAT will be determined in large part by how well you can marshal these skills and half-forgotten concepts for the very specific types of problems presented by the GMAT. This book will help you do just that.

ATTAINING YOUR COMPETITIVE EDGE: McGraw-Hill's GMAT

Broadly speaking, success in business comes from effectively executing a strategy to attain a competitive edge. What you are looking for in your application to business school is a competitive edge; the GMAT is, after all, a competition between you and every other B-school candidate in the country. There can be a lot of winners in this competition, but you will be compared to each of them, so you must develop a strategy that will help you attain your competitive edge on this vital aspect of the application process. This book will help you develop two different strategies: first, a strategy of preparation for the days, weeks, or months before you take the test; and second, a strategy of execution for when you walk into the testing center and sit down at the keyboard.

McGraw-Hill's GMAT presents information tailored to those test takers who are hoping for a high score—a score in the mid-600s or higher that will open the doors to the top business schools. While this book presents information on the entire range of subjects and difficulty levels encountered in GMAT questions, we have placed special emphasis on addressing the more difficult question types that high-scoring test takers are more likely to see, such as combinatorics, Boolean mathematics, and parallel reasoning questions. We have observed that the majority of GMAT books on the market today are engineered to provide a medium-sized bump to a medium-range score, and they just don't get around to addressing the more difficult topics. This book seeks to help applicants develop a competitive edge in their quest to enter the most competitive business schools.

We have also gone a step further and provided you with four chapters to help with the rest of your B-school preparation process. We cover the questions you should ask in selecting a school, the preparation that is needed for the *rest* of your application (there is more to this than the GMAT), what to expect in graduate business school, and how to think about your job search from the vantage point of an applicant. MBA programs are more than graduate study—they're professional study—so the point of this, after all, is the rewarding and lucrative job that you will land on the other end.

MEET THE GMAT

Please allow us to introduce you to your new friend, the GMAT. The GMAT is a three-and-a-half-hour writing and multiple-choice test. For many years GMAT test forms were created by Educational Testing Service (ETS), a private company based in Princeton, New Jersey. ETS is famous as the creator of the SAT. However, since January 2006, creating new GMAT test forms has been the job of ACT, Inc., an Iowa-based company that also develops a well-known college admission exam. ACT designs the GMAT in coordination with the Graduate Management Admission Council (GMAC), a consortium of business schools with its headquarters in McLean, Virginia. GMAC provides ACT with guidelines about the type of information business schools are looking for from the GMAT, and ACT turns these guidelines into the test you are going to encounter in the near future.

Administering the test is the job of still another company, called Pearson VUE. This company is the electronic testing division of Pearson Education.

What You Will See

You will probably take the GMAT on a computer at a Pearson VUE test center. You'll get the specifics about where and when that will be when you register for the test (more on registration at the end of this chapter). The parts of the test are as follows:

Section	Number of Questions	Number of Minutes
Analytical Writing Assessment	1 "Analysis of an Issue"	30
Analytical Writing Assessment	1 "Analysis of an Argument"	30
Optional Break		10
Quantitative	37 Multiple-Choice ~15 Data Sufficiency ~22 Problem-Solving	75

Continued

Section	Number of Questions	Number of Minutes
Optional Break		10
Verbal	41 Multiple-Choice	75
	~12 Critical Reasoning	
	~14 Reading Comprehension	
	~15 Sentence Correction	

Each of these test sections is covered in detail in the chapters of this book. Add up the minutes and the number of different types of questions you're going to face. When you take the test, you will spend about four hours in the testing center furiously analyzing, writing, computing, reading, scribbling, reasoning, and, almost certainly, guessing. It's not an easy test—if it were, business schools wouldn't use it. But with the proper preparation, you can handle it and make your score work for you.

How the GMAT Is Scored

When you finish the multiple-choice sections of the GMAT, the computer will take about an eighth of a second to calculate your score on those sections. You will then have a choice of either seeing your score—in which case it will be official—or canceling your score without seeing it. Your full score will include:

1. Your quantitative score, from 0 to 60
2. Your verbal score, from 0 to 60
3. Your overall score, from 200 to 800, in increments of 10
4. Your score on the Analytical Writing Assessment, from 1 to 6 in half-point increments (this score requires a human grader, so it will arrive in the mail a few weeks after you take the GMAT)

Your overall score is the one that people generally think of as your "GMAT score." While it is the most important aspect of your GMAT score from a business school's perspective, admissions officials will almost certainly look at the other score components, the quantitative score in particular, in order to see how balanced a candidate you are. All four scores will also come with a corresponding percentile number indicating where your score stands in relation to those of all GMAT test takers.

The Computer-Adaptive GMAT

The computer-adaptive GMAT is not the same test as the old paper-based GMAT. When you take the test on a computer, the computer gives you different questions based on how many of the previous questions you have answered correctly. It begins by giving you a question of medium difficulty—which means that ACT expects roughly half of the test takers to answer it correctly and half to get it wrong—and if you answer it correctly, the computer will give you a harder question; if you answer it incorrectly, the computer will give you an easier question. As you answer more questions, the computer will refine its picture of the level of difficulty you are capable of handling. By the end of the test, it should, theoretically, present you with questions at a level of difficulty where you get about half the questions right and half wrong (unless you're heading for either a very high or a very low score). Obviously, the higher the level of difficulty at which you end a test section, the higher your score will be. *You want to see hard questions.*

There are a number of reasons why the test makers switched to the computer-adaptive test (hereafter CAT). First, it greatly expands the flexibility of time and place at which a person can take the test; under the old system, there were only a few opportunities per year to take the GMAT. Second, since each person receives what is essentially a unique test, there is much less concern about cheating. Third, the CAT is theoretically a more accurate measure of a test taker's abilities than the old paper-based test. There are some trade-offs, however, that make the CAT in some ways a more difficult test to prepare for than the old test.

The nature of the CAT means that you will need to employ different strategies to attain your desired score than you would have used for the paper test:

1. *The early questions are crucial.* On a paper test, all the questions are valued equally, but on the CAT, the earlier questions play a much larger role than the later questions in determining your score range. Answering the first five questions correctly is far more valuable to your score than answering the last five questions correctly, because by the end of the test the CAT has already pretty much decided the general area where your score is going to be. If, for example, you can answer eight or more of the first ten questions correctly, the CAT will peg you as a strong test taker and will give you more difficult questions for the rest of the test. *It is worthwhile to budget extra time for the early questions in order to get them right, even if this means you have to guess on some questions at the end.* More on guessing later.

2. *You can't skip.* The CAT gives you questions based on the results of prior questions, so it will not allow you to skip questions and go back to them later. Technically, you can just go past a question without answering it, but this will count against your score. For this reason, you are better off making your best guess and possibly getting the points for a correct answer. *It is in your best interests to answer every question in every section, even if this means you have to guess.*

3. *You can't write on the test.* You can use scratch paper, so you will need to train yourself to use scratch paper effectively. Using scratch paper is less efficient than writing and crossing out answers on the test paper itself, so *do not* allow yourself to get into the habit of writing on the tests provided in this or other books. In your practice, always try to recreate the conditions of the actual test as closely as possible. Many test takers find it is helpful to make an answer grid so that they can keep track of which answer choices they have eliminated. It could look like the following:

1	A̶	B̶	C̶	(D)	E̶
2	A̶	(B)	C̶	D̶	E̶
3	(A)	B̶	C̶	D̶	E̶
4	A̶	B̶	C	D	E
5	A	B	C	D	E
6	A	B	C	D	E
7	A	B	C	D	E

4. *You have to type the Analytical Writing Assessment essays.* This could be an advantage for you if you are a good typist, but it could be a handicap if you don't often type. See more in Chapter 11, "The Analytical Writing Assessment."

ACHIEVING YOUR GOALS ON THE GMAT

Your success on the GMAT will result from three separate types of skills, all of which can be improved through preparation:

1. *GMAT skills.* These are the combination of knowledge and ability that allows you to find the correct answers to GMAT questions. The chapters in this book give specific guidance on these skill areas, and the practice tests allow you to put these skills into action. GMAT skills include:
   a. Math skills: geometry, algebra, compound interest, and so on.
   b. Reading quickly and retaining information
   c. Breaking down arguments
   d. Grammar skills
   e. Writing skills, and so on; as we mentioned above, it's a long test

2. *Pacing and endurance.* The GMAT is both a sprint and a marathon. You have less than two minutes, on average, for each verbal question and barely two minutes for each quantitative question. With unlimited time, you, and most test takers, would get most of the questions right. You don't have unlimited time, however, so it is essential that you develop the ability to work through these questions very quickly so that you can put your GMAT skills to their best use. Speed, however, is not enough; at nearly four hours in length, the GMAT requires that you have extraordinary mental stamina so that you to stay focused throughout the test. The best way to prepare yourself for the pacing challenges of the GMAT is to take several practice tests while observing strict time limits.

3. *Guessing technique.* Everybody has to guess sometimes. You may not be sure about the mathematical point in question, you may not be able to figure out exactly what the question is trying to ask, or you may just run out of time. What differentiates good test takers from great test takers is the ability to guess in such a way as to maximize the chances for a correct answer. With some practice and some insight into how ACT writes its wrong answers, you can increase your odds of guessing correctly from the 20 percent of a completely random guess to 50 percent or higher.

So how do you develop these skills? Practice, practice, practice. The content chapters in this book will provide you with factual information about the GMAT skills you will need in order to answer questions on the test, as well as some valuable advice about how to approach pacing and guessing. The six practice tests in the book, as well as the six practice tests on the CD-ROM, will provide you with questions spanning the entire range of subject matter and difficulty you are likely to encounter on the GMAT. Reading about the GMAT can help you to a degree, but there is really no substitute for working through many, many GMAT problems.

Preparation Strategy

Your GMAT preparation strategy can differ dramatically based on how much time you have to prepare. A two-month preparation plan will be significantly different from a two-week plan. We have attempted to make *McGraw-Hill's GMAT* into a flexible tool that you can use in the way that works best for you. The one thing you can't get around, though, is time. The more time and energy you devote to preparation, the better your odds are of achieving your goals.

You should figure out now when you're going to take the test (if you haven't already), and customize one of the below action plans to meet your needs. To help you determine your schedule, you should figure out two things: (1) what score you're already making, and (2) what score you want to make.

To figure out what score you're already making, your first step is always to take a practice test. If you have bought the CD-ROM version of this book, take a GMAT CAT from the CD-ROM. Otherwise, take one of the practice tests printed in this book. Either test will give you the best idea of what to expect as you continue to practice. When you take practice tests, it's best to create as realistic a testing environment as possible, so clean up your work area, get out some scratch paper, turn off your phone, and let roommates and family members know you're not to be disturbed. Also, tell yourself that this is the real test so that you can have a similar adrenaline reaction to what you would have on test day. (For many testers, this actually helps their scores, but either way, your reaction is part of creating a realistic testing environment.)

To figure out what score you want to make, do some research on the schools that you would like to attend; find out what their average GMAT scores are and what other factors play into their admissions processes. Also, ask about how they use the GMAT in admissions. Many schools will tell you that no single GMAT score will guarantee you admission; many schools have a "baseline" GMAT score that is required, but among candidates who have reached that score, the GMAT is not used to further determine admission. For more information on choosing a program and the admissions process, read Chapters 12 and 13 in this book.

Of course, if you know where you want to go to school and your admission deadline is approaching, you may have no choice but to prepare for the GMAT in a couple of weeks. That can be done, but it will require hard work, and it's best if you can clear other commitments as much as possible before sitting the exam.

Be sure to actually schedule your exam at this time; you don't want to wait too long and then have to change your plans because your local testing center doesn't have an available test date that works for you. See the Registering for the GMAT section near the end of this chapter for more information.

Action Plan 1—If You Have Two Months

This is an adequate amount of study time for most people, but that depends on your work schedule and personal commitments. If you have a spouse and family, this is a good time to practice your skills at getting "buy-in" from your family members so that they will support your efforts to get a great score on the GMAT.

Two months until test day

▶ Examine your scores from the practice GMAT that you took. Since you have two months to prepare, you can probably focus on each area of the test in depth, but you should start with your weaknesses. Reading Comprehension in particular tends to require more long-term work, so it may be a good idea to start working on the Reading Comprehension chapter early. If there is any math content that consistently gives you trouble—geometry, perhaps, or quadratic equations—start brushing up on it as well. Similarly, certain question types may be problematic; Data Sufficiency questions are generally unfamiliar to most test-takers before taking the GMAT, so they may be a weakness. Identify three key areas to work on first.

- Schedule time over the following month to work on the chapters in this book that correspond to those three key areas. Be sure you read and review each whole chapter, in addition to working the drills at the end of each chapter. For the best retention, read the chapter and work half of the practice problems in one study session, then review the chapter and work the remainder of the practice problems in the next study session.
- Set aside time to take one of the practice tests in the book (or another if you have already taken one). Take the entire test in one sitting, if possible. If not, at least take a whole section at a time.

One month until test day

- Take another GMAT from the CD-ROM or from the tests in this book to check your progress. Chances are, you've improved in your weaker areas, but you still need to increase your overall speed.
- Schedule time in the next three weeks to complete the chapters you have not worked and take two more practice tests in the book. For chapters that cover material with which you are adept, start with the drills at the end of the chapter. Do half of them and check your accuracy. If you've made any mistakes, review the explanations and use the chapter to brush up on your knowledge and skills; then complete the rest of the end-of-chapter drills.

Two weeks until test day

- Take another GMAT from the CD-ROM or from the tests in this book to check your progress. If needed, re-evaluate your study schedule for this week to accommodate any additional areas you need to review or practice.

One week until test day

- Take another GMAT from the CD or from the tests in this book. This test will give you the best idea of what score to expect on test day.
- Call the test center if you have any final questions, make sure you have your required identification ready, and actually drive to the testing center so that you know exactly how to get there and how long it will take.
- To keep your mind focused and ready, schedule some review work every day, but don't cram. The idea is definitely not to get stressed out.

Action Plan 2—If You Have Two Weeks

Preparing for the GMAT in just a couple of weeks is ambitious, but it has been done. The more time and energy you can carve out for GMAT practice, the better.

Two weeks until test day

- Examine your scores from the practice GMAT you took from the CD or from the tests in this book. To make your preparation as efficient as possible, you really need to home in on your weaknesses at this point. You probably are not going to have time to study every area in depth, but you need to shore up your weak areas so that if one of those questions shows up in the first part of your verbal or quantitative section (which is likely), you can at least eliminate some wrong answers and make an educated guess. Choose which areas you're going to focus on first according to your primary weaknesses.

▶ Schedule time over the next week to do the chapters that focus on those areas. If possible, do an entire chapter and all the practice problems that go with it in one sitting.

One week until test day

▶ Take another GMAT from the CD-ROM or from the tests in this book to check your progress.

▶ Schedule time over the next week to address the remaining chapters that you need to cover. Try a few questions from the practice problems at the end of a chapter, then review what you need from the chapter to clear up any questions you might have, then do more practice problems.

▶ Alternate your study of the chapters with doing whole sections from the practice tests at the end of this book.

▶ Call the test center if you have any final questions, make sure you have your required identification ready, and actually drive to the testing center so that you know exactly how to get there and how long it will take.

Three or four days until test day

▶ If there is time, do another GMAT from the CD-ROM or from the tests in this book to check your progress and get more used to the testing procedure. By the time you take the actual test, you will know what to expect.

The Day Before the Test

No matter which preparation schedule you've chosen, your preparation on the day before the test should be the same.

▶ If at all possible, schedule some relaxing activity that will get you focused on something other than the test. A full-body massage would be nice, but if that isn't possible, a brisk walk is great for relieving stress too. The night before the test, watch your favorite comedy or action movie, play a video game, or even color in a coloring book to stay relaxed. Do things that do not tax your brain-power and choose activities that appeal to you.

▶ *Don't* cram, or stay up late, or don't do anything to dehydrate yourself (and drinking a lot of alcohol falls into this category), and stress yourself out about the test and your future plans.

Test-Day Strategy

Some day soon—probably sooner than you'd like—the day for your face-to-face encounter with the GMAT will arrive. Your test-day strategy should include the following:

▶ Stick to whatever *routine* will make you most comfortable when you walk into the test. For example, if you have coffee every morning, have it on the morning before you take the test; if you don't usually drink coffee, don't start on the day of the GMAT. It is a good idea to eat a light meal in the hours before the test. You don't want to get hungry, but you don't want to feel sluggish, either. You may want to bring a snack that you can eat during your two five-minute breaks.

▶ *Prepare your scratch paper ahead of time.* You will be able to start the test yourself at the testing center, so do everything you can to prepare during the time before the test begins. We've already talked about the importance of keeping track of the answer choices that you've eliminated for each question, but it's very easy to stop doing this during the test, out of fear that you're wasting time. So set up your scratch paper beforehand. One good way to do this is to use an answer grid (discussed and shown previously). This will give you plenty of room to make calculations, keep you organized so that you don't mix your calculations up between different problems, and save you time during the test.

▶ *Keep track of your pace during the test.* Remember that it is acceptable to budget extra time for the earlier questions, particularly the first five. *Do not* spend too much time on any particular question. You can afford to spend up to three minutes on several questions and still finish the test as long as you can make up time on other questions, but if you find yourself going much longer than three minutes on any question (except, possibly, for the first five), then you should make your best guess and move on. Once you've answered a question, do not give it any more thought. You have more questions to answer.

▶ Another factor to consider is the presence of *experimental questions*. More than 20 percent of the questions you see may not affect your score at all, but are just experimental questions that the test makers are testing out on you to see whether they will be good questions to use in the future. So if a question seems unusually hard or unusually easy, or you just can't crack it, there's a decent chance that the question won't count anyway. So whatever you do, *do not* waste four minutes on a question that is not going to help your score in the end.

▶ If you find yourself running short on time at the end—say you have five minutes and five questions remaining—then it is time to *start strategic guessing*. Even if you can't determine the answer in a single minute, you can almost certainly eliminate a few of the answers and substantially increase your chances of getting some of the questions correct. Guessing in this way can be uncomfortable, but it can substantially improve your score if you do it in a disciplined way. In order to know how to handle this situation if it happens to you on the test, it is important that you observe time limits when you take practice tests. Guessing well is a skill that comes with practice, so incorporate it into your practice plans.

If Something Goes Wrong at the Test

Sometimes the test does not go according to plan. Most likely, everything will go fine, but it is worth devoting a little thought ahead of time to how you would handle the following scenarios:

You freak out, your mind freezes up, or the test is *way* harder than you expected.

▶ If you really are not at your best during the test, then you can cancel your score at the end and retake the test another day. It happens—something might have happened in your personal life, you could be sick, or you might just be having an off day. If this happens, you can cancel your score and walk away. It will cost you another $250 to take the test again, and you will get your score a few weeks later. Before you cancel, though, be aware that on the day of the test, many people think that their performance was worse than it actually was. Remember, the test makers want to give you questions hard enough that you will miss some; difficult questions mean that you're heading for a high score. Cancel only if you are certain that your performance really was below your capabilities.

Something bizarre and distracting happens at the testing center.

▶ The designated testing centers are usually very well run, so the risk of outside distractions or computer malfunctions is low. These things are possible, though. If something outside of your control happens that you feel may affect your score, you should notify the staff at the testing center immediately. If the problem cannot be remedied, you can file an official complaint with the staff at the testing center, and then immediately after you leave the center, you should file a report by e-mail to ACT. If the test administrators support your claim, they might cancel your score and let you take the test again without charge.

REGISTERING FOR THE GMAT

One advantage of the CAT is that the GMAT is now far easier to register for than it was in the past. Just grab a credit card or your checkbook and either call up 1-800-717-GMAT or go online at www.mba.com. The registration fee as of early 2009 was $250. Call several weeks ahead of time in order to get the date and time of day you want. You can choose either a morning or an afternoon slot, so pick the time of day you think your mind will be at its best. GMAC will give you all the information you need to show up for your testing slot.

ADDITIONAL PRACTICE

If you seek additional practice on the GMAT, the first place to look is the source itself. On the Web site www.mba.com, you'll find some computer-based practice tests that use questions from old GMATs. These tests will provide you with a very authentic test experience.

SOME FINAL ADVICE

▶ Read all questions carefully.
▶ Give extra attention to the early questions.
▶ Keep track of your pace (average about two minutes per question).
▶ Use process of elimination to guess strategically if you run short on time.
▶ Practice!
▶ Keep calm!
▶ Good luck!

ACKNOWLEDGMENT

The authors wish to thank Judy Unrein for her contributions to the 2008, 2009, and 2010 editions.

James Hasik	Stacey Rudnick	Ryan Hackney
Austin, Texas	Austin, Texas	Houston, Texas

GMAT Information for International Test Takers

People from all over the world aspire to attend a U.S. business school. But the admissions process is distinctly different for applicants from outside the United States. The differences are apparent from the moment you begin preparing for the GMAT.

More and more people living outside of the United States are taking the GMAT. In fact, in the 2006–2007 academic year, 101,756 of the 219,077 GMAT test takers were from outside the United States. That's nearly half at 46 percent. The majority of international test takers came from India with 21,481. China followed with 13,048, and then Korea with 6,811, Canada with 6,400, Taiwan with 5,218, Japan with 3,417, Israel with 2,855, France with 2,420, Thailand with 2,091, Germany with 2,071, and the United Kingdom with 1,730.

REGISTERING FOR THE TEST

Since the end of 2005, test takers have been unable to walk into a test center and register on the spot. Nowadays, everyone—from abroad or the United States—has to register for the test in advance. You may register online at www.mba.com, by telephone, by fax, or by mail.

If you choose to register online, you must sign up as a registered user of the www.mba.com Web site. Be sure to enter your name and birth date exactly as they appear on the identification you will present at the test center. Fee payments can only be made by credit or debit card.

If you choose to register by telephone, you may do so by calling one of the following numbers. (You may want to check the www.mba.com Web site to see if any of these numbers have changed.)

In the Americas:
Telephone (toll-free within the United States and Canada only): 1-800-717-GMAT (4628), 7:00 a.m. to 7:00 p.m. Central Time
Telephone: 1-952-681-3680, 7:00 a.m. to 7:00 p.m. Central Time
Fax: 1-952-681-3681

Asia and Pacific Region:
Telephone: +603 8318-9961, 9:00 a.m. to 6:00 p.m. AEST
In India: +91 (0) 120 439 7830, 9:00 a.m. to 6:00 p.m. Indian Standard Time
Fax: +603 8319 1092

Europe/Middle East/Africa:
Telephone: +44 (0) 161 855 7219, 9:00 a.m. to 6:00 p.m. BST
Fax: +44 (0) 161 855 7301

To register for the GMAT by mail or fax, download the appropriate form from the www.mba.com Web site. Fax your completed form to the fax number listed for your region listed above or mail it to:

Pearson VUE

Attention: GMAT Program

PO Box 581907

Minneapolis, MN 55458-1907

USA

Be aware that it can take up to eight weeks for letters to reach the United States from some countries.

GMAC and other experts suggest registering for the GMAT well in advance. This is especially good advice if you plan to take the test outside the United States. First, it may take you some time to decide where exactly you will take the test. Also, the application process in general will take longer for you because of the necessary paperwork. Chad Troutwine, co-founder and co-owner of Veritas Prep in Malibu, California, warns that applicants in India and China will need even more time because the interest in taking the GMAT among people in those areas far outweighs the number of testing centers in those countries. In some cases, says Troutwine, people in India and China have had to wait three to five weeks to take the test.

Finally, you will want to start taking the GMAT earlier because you might want to retake the test before submitting your applications to U.S. business schools. International applicants, says Troutwine, tend to take the test more times than American students. The good news is, however, that you tend to do better than domestic test takers. The average score for non-U.S. test takers in the 2006–2007 academic year was 547, compared to 529 for U.S. test takers, according to GMAC.

FINDING A TEST CENTER

With permanent testing centers in major cities in countries such as Argentina, Australia, Bolivia, Botswana, Brazil, Colombia, Finland, throughout India, Hong Kong, Egypt, Tanzania, Thailand, and Zimbabwe to name a few, most applicants should not have any trouble finding a place to take the test. In fact, the GMAT is available in 98 countries. If there are no permanent centers near your home, you can travel to the next closest center. Just keep in mind that traveling will add to your bills.

When you register for the GMAT, you may schedule a test appointment at any testing center around the world. To locate a test center in your country or region, go to the www.mba.com Web site. There you will find a complete listing of worldwide testing centers. When you register online, you will find out which times are available at the testing center that you have chosen.

ON TEST DAY

On test day, you will be required to present proper identification in order to take your test. Your government-issued ID must have the following:

▶ Valid date (unexpired), legibility, and your name shown in the Roman alphabet exactly as you provided when you made your test appointment, including the order and placement of the names

▶ Your date of birth (must exactly match the date provided when you registered for your test appointment)

- ▶ A recent, recognizable photograph
- ▶ Your signature

In most cases, the following are the only forms of identification that will be accepted at the test center.

- ▶ Passport
- ▶ Government-issued driver's license
- ▶ Government-issued national/state/province identity card (including European ID card)
- ▶ Military ID card

Note that if you are taking the GMAT in **Bangladesh, China** (including **Hong Kong), India, Japan, Pakistan, Singapore**, or **South Korea**, you must present your passport as identification.

Testing centers around the world look the same, have the same layout and design, and implement the same procedures, according to GMAC. The goal is to provide the same standard and remove variables, so everyone is on an even playing field from the start. Everyone takes the test on a computer—gone are the days of the paper GMAT—but the computer skills required of test takers are minimal. You need to be able to use a mouse and word processor, enter responses, move to the next question, and access help. Keep in mind, however, that using the help function could steal valuable time from you during the test. If you need to learn these computer basics, your best bet is to do so before you take the actual test.

TEST PREPARATION FOR INTERNATIONAL TEST TAKERS

GMAC is very careful to make sure that the GMAT is not biased against international test-takers. The test makers pre-test all questions by including them in "experimental" test sections given to both U.S. and international test takers. If statistics prove that any of the new questions put the internationals at a disadvantage, those items never appear on the test, says Fanmin Guo, director for psychometric research at GMAC in McLean, VA. Still, international test takers face certain challenges.

The biggest and most obvious difficulty for international test takers is the language barrier. Many of the people from abroad who sign up to take the GMAT are non-native English speakers. The entire test, including instructions and questions, is in English. One-fourth of the test is focused on verbal skills and one-half is a writing test, which requires not only an understanding of the language but a command of it. "If you do not understand what is being asked, you will not be able to show your reasoning skills," says Guo. Your writing, reading comprehension, and grammar skills are directly tested on the GMAT. You'll need to think about how comfortable you are reading, writing, and understanding English—and how you can improve those skills.

Improving Your English

Most experts, including teachers at some of the most popular GMAT test prep courses in the United States, advise international students to read as much in English as they can in the months leading up to the test. If you can, read articles online to get used to absorbing English material while reading from a computer screen, which is how it will be on exam day. Guo suggests reading financial and business periodicals to get used to the business terminology that you'll likely see on the exam. He reminds test takers, however, that the test sometimes includes reading material from other subjects such as the humanities or sciences, but the majority is focused on business.

Other activities that might help you are creating and using flash cards with difficult English words on them and practicing your English by communicating with others who speak the language. Watching American TV shows in English (some of them are now available online) and studying grammar by filling out workbooks or taking online drills can also help. Keep a journal and express your thoughts about what you've read and seen in writing. Your goal should be to practice presenting evidence in a cohesive and interesting way to support your arguments in the writing section of the exam. When you read items from American publications, says Guo, pay particular attention to how the writers gather evidence and present it because there are often subtle cultural differences at play. Remember that the quantitative part of the GMAT is also in English. Tracy Yun, CEO of Manhattan Review test prep in New York, has her international students review both glossaries and math formulas in English. Frankly, all of these drills are good practice for business school itself because your courses will all be taught in English and you'll be expected to keep up.

Becoming Familiar with Standardized Tests

Getting acquainted with standardized tests is another must-do for international test takers. This type of exam is a part of the average American's educational experience but is not necessarily a cultural norm in other parts of the world. Often, people outside the United States are unfamiliar with multiple-choice questions. These are questions in which you are given from two to five choices for the correct answer. There are strategies for choosing the best one when you're not sure. For example, you can eliminate answers that you know are incorrect and then choose among the remaining choices. This is called "taking an educated guess," and it can improve your chances of picking the correct answer. You can learn how to do this by taking practice tests like the ones in this book. Even if you have to take sample paper tests as opposed to online ones, you should do it. Taking practice tests will also help you become familiar with the test format. In fact, the test makers say that learning the format can save internationals time during the exam because you won't have to bother focusing on the instructions in addition to all the other reading you will have to do.

Managing Time

Time is indeed very important on exam day. This can be difficult for international test takers. You'll be expected to understand a second language and complete the GMAT in the same amount of time as native English speakers. Keeping calm is the first step to overcoming the pressure. As you prepare, Yun suggests that you gain confidence in your skill level before you start timing yourself during practice tests. Once you feel reasonably comfortable with the language, format, and types of questions, you should then start timing yourself. You can make the material easier to understand, especially the reading comprehension items, says Troutwine, by breaking it up into sizable chunks.

Next, you'll need to prioritize. To best manage your time, Yun suggests being most prepared for the items that are most important, namely the verbal and quantitative sections of the test. The first part of the test is the Analytical Writing Assessment, where you will have to complete two separate writing tasks with 30 minutes for each. While the writing task is important, it is scored separately from the other two sections of the test and is not factored into your total test score.

Your focus as you prepare for the test should be the quantitative and verbal sections, which are the parts that count most toward your final score. In the quantitative section, you will have 75 minutes to answer 37 multiple-choice questions covering data sufficiency ("Do I have enough information to answer the question?") and problem solving. For the verbal section, you will have 75 minutes to complete 41 multiple-choice questions that test reading comprehension, critical reasoning, and your ability to correct English sentences. You will receive score ranges between 0 and 60 for each of these sections.

When you register for the GMAT, you will receive a free sample test. GMAC offers other free resources and information about the exam on its mba.com Web site. Books like this one are great prep tools because they pack in lots of information about the GMAT, often include practice exams or sample questions, and they're affordable. If you have the money, prep courses and private tutoring are offered by various companies around the world and online. Prices range from $100 to $1,500, depending on the type of instruction you choose.

ANOTHER HURDLE FOR INTERNATIONALS: THE TOEFL

Demonstrating your English language skills on the GMAT probably will not be enough for admissions committees. Most American MBA programs require non-native English speakers to also take the Test of English as a Foreign Language (TOEFL), an Internet- or paper-based standardized test that measures your English proficiency. Admissions committees use this score to judge your language skills and make sure you will be able to succeed in classes that are taught in English. In fact, more than 6,000 institutions and agencies in 110 countries rely on TOEFL scores, according to the Educational Testing Service (ETS), which creates the TOEFL exam.

ETS recently introduced a new Internet-based ("iBT") version of the test. The TOEFL iBT is available in the United States, Canada, France, Germany, Italy, and Puerto Rico. It is also available in many cities in Africa, the Americas, Eurasia, the Middle East, and North Africa, according to the ETS Web site (http://www.ets.org/toefl). A paper-based version of the test (TOEFL PBT) is still being offered in countries and test centers where the TOEFL iBT is not yet available.

What are the differences between the Internet and paper tests? First, of all, of course, the iBT is given on a computer and the PBT is given with a paper and pencil. There are also other differences. The TOEFL iBT, which takes about four and a half hours to complete, measures reading, listening, speaking, and writing skills, whereas the TOEFL PBT, which takes about three and a half hours to complete, measures listening, grammar, reading, and writing, according to ETS. Not surprisingly. You will have an easier time scheduling an appointment to take the iBT version because it is administered 30 to 40 times per year at test centers around the world, whereas the PBT is offered just six times per year at test centers where the TOEFL iBT is not available. The paper-based version of TOEFL costs $140, but the iBT costs $150.

The main reasons ETS launched the Internet-based version were to better measure the test taker's ability to communicate well in an academic environment, reflect how language is actually used, and keep up with best practices in language teaching, according to the ETS book, *The Official Guide to the New TOEFL iBT* (McGraw-Hill, 2007). "TOEFL iBT emphasizes integrated skills and provides better information to institutions about students' ability to communicate in an academic setting and their readiness for academic coursework," according to the ETS Web site. "With iBT, ETS can capture speech and score responses in a standardized manner."

Preparing for the TOEFL

GMAT preparation—especially if you focus on English as suggested—will help you prepare for the TOEFL. For both tests, you'll want to focus on any activities that will improve your English language fluency. Learning vocabulary and grammar are priorities. For the TOEFL iBT, you will have to also prove your speaking ability. Conversing and speaking in English out loud should help. Online language forums that would allow you to practice with others are also a good idea because they will force you to understand and be understood in English. With another person on the other end of the conversation, you will know whether you are making mistakes or succeeding with the language.

For both the TOEFL iBT and PBT, you will find practice tests online. Books, such as the McGraw-Hill-published *Official Guide to the New TOEFL iBT*, which includes a CD-ROM and sample tests, can also come in handy. There are preparation courses for the TOEFL exam as well.

Experts and ETS remind test takers that time is of the essence for the TOEFL exam just as it is for most standardized tests. Those taking the TOEFL iBT exam have from 60 to 100 minutes to complete the reading section, which includes three to five passages with 12 to 14 questions for each, and 60 to 90 minutes to finish the listening section, which includes four to six lectures with six questions each and two to three conversations with five questions each. The speaking and writing sections of the test combined account for 70 minutes. There is a five-minute break between the reading and listening sections and the speaking and writing sections.

Suggestions for pacing yourself include avoiding spending too much time on one question and remaining calm. A clock appears on the computer screen to show you how much time you have left. You can "hide" the clock if you find it distracting, but you should probably check it every so often. The computer clock will alert you when you have five minutes remaining in the listening and reading sections.

When you register for the PBT, ETS sends you free test-preparation materials including two paper-based tests, 68 minutes of listening material on one CD, scoring information, review material, and exercises for the Test of Written English (TWE), according to the ETS Web site. You will still want to learn to pace yourself. But one of the most important factors in the PBT is properly filling out your responses. Make sure that you use a soft-medium number 2 or HB black lead pencil, warns ETS on its Web site. You must fill in the entire circle next to your response, and be careful that you are choosing the circle from the correct row. If you decide to change answers or see pencil marks anywhere on the paper where they do not belong, erase them completely. If you are not careful about how you fill in the circles, the computer that corrects the exams could improperly score your test.

BUSINESS SCHOOL ADMISSIONS

People who live outside the United States but are considering American business schools often have lots of questions about the application process in general. At the forums on BusinessWeek.com (http://forums.businessweek.com/n/pfx/forum.aspx?webtag=bw-bschools&nav=start), international business school applicants frequently bring up issues that are on their minds as they try to find the best fit among the top American MBA programs. Here are four issues that come up very frequently.

Fact or Fiction? Certain parts of the business school application are weighed more than others by the admissions committee.

Fiction. The overwhelming majority of admissions directors will tell you that they—and their colleagues—read each application cover to cover. Every section is important. They want to get a sense of who the applicant is and what he or she brings to the table. Your GMAT score and GPA from undergraduate studies will tell them if you can handle the academic rigor of the institution. The TOEFL score will prove your English-language proficiency, a must if you are to participate in courses taught in English. Recommendations will provide evidence from an objective third party who knows you and your work well. Your work experience will shed light on what you've been doing with your time since earning an undergraduate degree or its equivalent. For insight into who you are as a person and the qualities you will bring to campus, the committee will look to your essays.

Here, again, you'll have to write well in English. There is no room for errors when writing your application essays. Spelling and grammar must be impeccable. Also, be sure you understand the questions being asked and that you are answering them directly. Admissions Committee members are constantly complaining that applicants—even native English-speaking ones—fail to answer the question that is being asked of them in the essays. If you're not sure what's being asked, pick up a phone or write an e-mail to someone in the admissions committee and ask. Most of them are happy to take queries from potential students.

You do not have to be fancy. Keep your essays straightforward and to the point. Use simple language and lots of examples that support your thesis to keep the reader interested. Be honest and genuine. Having someone read your essay and offer his or her opinion is advisable. But do not have someone write or rewrite the essay for you, and never plagiarize. Committing these violations shows a lack of understanding for the ethical standards to which most, if not all, American business schools adhere. Admissions committees will not look kindly on these breaches, and you will not get accepted.

Getting into business school on your own merits is far from impossible. If you take the necessary time to complete the application, choose your words for the essays thoughtfully, study for the TOEFL and GMAT, and ask the right people for letters of recommendation, you will have an excellent chance of getting into your top-choice business schools.

Fact or Fiction? To apply to graduate business school in the United States, you must have a four-year college degree or its equivalent.

Fact. You cannot even apply to an American MBA program without an undergraduate degree. However, many international applicants are stumped by the meaning of "four-year college degree." Admissions committees at top MBA programs realize that many countries have different standards and that four-year undergraduate programs might not exist in your home country. Each school to which you apply will have a different method for having you prove that the degree you earned is similar enough to the traditional American four-year degree for you to enter the program. The business schools are used to deciphering among the different countries and their diverse range of degrees, so you should have no problem. In other words, don't stress about this.

Fact or Fiction? American business schools only accept a certain number of applicants from each region. Therefore, if many people from my country or region apply to a particular business school, I have less of a chance at getting accepted, regardless of my application.

Fact and fiction. This subject comes up often on the BusinessWeek.com forums—and the conversations tend to stir debate. While the admissions committees constantly deny having any sort of quota system, they admit that they seek diversity when trying to put together the next class for their business school. But they see diversity as more than just being about ethnic, cultural, and racial groups. The schools are also looking for people in different industries and functions with different aspirations for the future.

Recently, applicants from India and China—where business is booming and there's a newfound demand for managers—have been abundant at American business schools. Many of these students, especially those from India in the IT sector, have expressed fear that they have to do twice or three times as well on the GMAT and other aspects of their application to stay in the running at top programs because there are so many others just like them who want a spot. There is no denying that this is partially true. Many more of them are applying, so they have to perform their very best to keep a competitive edge.

But admissions committees at American business schools encourage students who feel they could fit into their programs to turn in their application. Even if thousands of people from your region or country are applying to business school X, you still may be the one to get accepted. The important thing is to show why you deserve a seat in the next class. Worrying about your statistical chance of getting into a program wastes your time. Some of this is dependent on luck and what that particular school is looking for in a candidate, which is why you cannot really predict who will get accepted and rejected. The only choice you have is to do your best.

Fact or Fiction? You must write what you think the admissions committee wants to see in the application essays.

Fiction. Many international applicants mistakenly think that there is some sort of template or formula to writing an effective essay. While it is true that you must write in a straightforward, well-organized manner, you will fail if you try to write what you think the admissions committee members want to see. If you pick up a book of essays from applications that have been accepted and try to mimic what someone else wrote, you risk ending up in the toss pile. All school representatives really want to see is someone who has passion for their program and has a plan for his or her life and career. They want to know why you have chosen to apply to their school and how their school will help you accomplish your future goals. The more specific you can get about what you'd like to do, when, how, and what role the school will play in this plan, the happier they will be. Of course, they want to see your unique spin on the subject. Tell your story in an interesting way because they have to read hundreds—sometimes thousands—of these essays—and you want to keep them captivated. Authenticity combined with a dash of creativity will win every time.

THE BUSINESS SCHOOL INTERVIEW

Most American business schools require applicants to interview with someone from the school, usually an graduate, a current student who has been trained to conduct applicant interviews, or an administrator or admissions representative. Sometimes, you can request the interview and sometimes the school invites you. Every school is different, so you should look into this when you're filling out your application, so you know what to expect.

You already know how important it is for non-native English speakers to gain fluency before applying to business school in the United States. But knowing the rules of a language is not enough. You also need to carry out a conversation with native English speakers. This is particularly important when you are interviewing with business schools. Many of the interviews are behavioral, which means the school will be asking you questions about yourself, your experiences, and how you have handled particular situations. There are usually no trick questions. The interviewers simply want to know a little more about you and get a sense of the type of personality you will be bringing to campus.

Preparing for the Interview

To prepare for the interview, you should practice answering questions in English, preferably with an English-speaking person. You should probably think about specific examples of your leadership, management skills, and values. Seriously consider what drew you to this particular school, what its culture is like, why you would fit in there, and how the school can help you achieve your career goals. Also, come up with intelligent questions to ask about the school. Usually, the interviewer gives you a chance to interview him or her, too. Seize the opportunity. Refrain from asking questions whose answers will appear on the school's Web site, such as how many credits do I need to graduate, or what are the core requirements? Instead, ask about the work load you should expect or the events the school offers to unify the community. If you have heard about something specific, such as a project all first-year students at a particular school are required to complete, ask about that.

Face-to-Face vs. Telephone Interviews

Schools tend to prefer face-to-face interviews. But those are not always possible for international applicants. Sometimes, applicants from abroad have to participate in the interview via telephone. Be prepared for either situation. Realize that the school will not think any less of you if it has to talk to you via telephone because you live in a part of the world where there is no graduate or admissions representative. American business schools accept hundreds of international applicants in a given year, and they know that some of them live in more remote areas. In other words, you do not lose points for the phone interview.

If, however, you are planning a campus visit anyway, then you can try to schedule a face-to-face interview. To prepare for an in-person meeting, you should plan to dress in business attire. A traditional dark suit will suffice. Women should avoid showing too much skin and wearing exaggerated or loud accessories such as huge earrings or patterned tights. Keep it simple and conservative. When you greet your interviewer, shake his or her hand firmly and look him or her in the eye. This is a cultural norm in American business.

Depending on where you live in relation to the school, campus visits can get expensive. But you should reserve them for the schools you are most seriously considering attending. Your best bet—if you live very far away from the campus—is to wait until you have been accepted to schools and then decide which one or two interest you most. Then schedule visits only to those campuses to decide whether to put down a deposit. Make the most of campus visits and interviews. Consider these tasks another part of the research. Business school is a huge investment, and you want to make sure you choose the right school for you.

ONE LAST HURDLE: THE STUDENT VISA

One of the things that set international applicants apart from domestic students is their need for a visa to live in the United States. In the years following the September 11 terrorist attacks, there have been lots of rumors about visas, who gets them, and who does not. The biggest change has been that every student must be officially cleared by the government before receiving his or her visa. This does not really change the process for you, but you will need to give yourself enough time, so that the proper documents can get processed in a timely fashion. Once you have been accepted to business school and have chosen an institution to attend, the process of obtaining a student visa must begin.

Getting a student visa to study in the United States is not as hard as getting an H1-B visa to work in the country after graduation. Experts, including the United States government, suggest that students begin the student visa process as soon as possible. At the very least, you should get started three months before you need the visa, according to reporting on BusinessWeek.com. Besides needing the time to complete the requisite forms, you will also need to schedule an appointment for the required embassy consular interview, and the waiting times for this vary and can be lengthy.

Visa Requirements

During the student visa process, you are expected to prove that you have adequate financing to study in the United States, ties to your home country, and a likelihood that you will return home after finishing your studies, according to reporting by BusinessWeek.com. In addition, you will have to participate in an ink-free, digital fingerprint scan and provide a passport valid for travel to the United States and with a validity date at least six months beyond your intended period of stay. The school will provide you with an I-20 form to complete. Your school will use this to register you with the Student and Exchange Visitor Information System (SEVIS), an Internet-based system that maintains accurate and current information on non-immigrant students and exchange visitors and their families. If you have a spouse and/or children who will be joining you, then you must register them with SEVIS as well. You'll also need to submit a completed and signed nonimmigrant visa application with Form DS-156 and DS-158. A 2" by 2" photo that meets certain requirements, which you can find at the U.S. Department of State site (http://travel.state.gov/visa/temp/types/types_1268.html#apply) is necessary as is an MRV receipt to show payment of the visa application fee, a visa issuance fee if applicable, and a separate SEVIS I-901 fee receipt. At the U.S. Department of State site, you will find information on all this and more.

Transcripts, diplomas from previous institutions, scores from standardized tests such as the GMAT and TOEFL, and proof you can afford the school (think income tax records, original bank books, and statements) are things you should have on hand, according to the U.S. government. If you have dependents, you will also need documents that prove your relationship to your spouse and children (think marriage license and birth certificates).

Dealing with bureaucracy of this nature can get frustrating. It is important to stay calm and do your best to follow the instructions. Remember to call on your business school if you need help. Although meeting deadlines, starting early, and turning in all the paperwork does not guarantee that you will receive a visa, it does increase your chances of having an easier time. Anything you can do to streamline the application and entrance process into business school will serve you well as you move your life from one country to another.

PART ONE The Quantitative Section

CHAPTER 1

The Techniques of GMAT Problem-Solving

You are going to see more Quantitative Problem-Solving questions than any other type of question on the GMAT, around 22 out of the 37 Quantitative problems on the test. These questions cover a wide range of mathematical concepts that you almost certainly encountered in high school, but that you might not have studied since. A very easy Problem-Solving question could look like this:

1. A certain standardized test taken by business school applicants demands that the test takers answer 37 quantitative questions within 75 minutes. Which of the following is closest to the average amount of time the test takers can spend on each question?

    A. 1 minute, 58 seconds

    B. 2 minutes, 2 seconds

    C. 2 minutes, 5 seconds

    D. 2 minutes, 12 seconds

    E. 121.6 minutes

Word problems like this are common on the GMAT. The trick with any word problem is to work step-by-step, making sure you pay as much attention to the words as the numbers, because the words tell you how to do the problem. In this example, you can see from the answer choices that the answer will probably include seconds, so it might be a good idea to turn that 75 minutes into seconds from the start; the GMAT assumes that you know things like "there are 60 seconds in a minute." So, you have $75 \times 60 = 4{,}500$ seconds in which to complete 37 questions. 4,500 divided by 37 equals 121.62 . . . seconds (you can tell from the answer choices that you don't need to calculate any farther than that), which is closest to 2 minutes, 2 seconds, answer B.

Most problems can be solved in a number of different ways. If, for example, you don't like long division, you could approach this question in the following way: 75 minutes divided by 37 questions is 2 minutes per question with a remainder of 1 minute. That remainder means that you have 60 additional seconds divided up among 37 questions; you could divide 60 by 37, or you could reason that since 37 is close to 30, and 60 divided by 30 equals 2, then you have about 2 seconds more per question, which is answer choice B, 2 minutes, 2 seconds.

Ponder that answer for a moment. A period of 2 minutes, 2 seconds is plenty of time to calculate a simple arithmetic problem like this one, but would it be enough to calculate the volume of 2 right circular cylinders? Probably, if you dive right in and you remember that the volume of a right circular cylinder $= \pi r^2 h$, but almost certainly not if you need to scramble around in your head for an approach to the problem and a formula that may or may not be right.

Your task, then, is to brush up on your math and work enough practice problems that when you see a question like the following, you'll know how to answer it correctly in a short enough amount of time that you'll be able to get to all 37 questions.

2. A certain barrel, which is a right circular cylinder, is filled to capacity with 100 gallons of oil. The first barrel is poured into a second barrel, also a right circular cylinder, which is empty. The second barrel is twice as tall as the first barrel and has twice the diameter of the first barrel. If all of the oil in the first barrel is poured into the second barrel, how much empty capacity, in gallons, is left in the second barrel?

   A. There is no empty capacity.
   B. 100 gallons
   C. 300 gallons
   D. 700 gallons
   E. 800 gallons

The GMAT would consider this question medium difficult, so if you can solve it already, good for you. If not, don't sweat it. We will walk through the process.

The answer is D. You don't know what the actual dimensions of the first barrel are, but you know that the volume of a cylinder $= \pi r^2 h$ (r = radius and h = height), and in the case of the first barrel, $\pi r^2 h = 100$ gallons. You don't know the exact dimensions of the second barrel either, but you know that its height is twice that of the first barrel, so $2h$, and its diameter is twice that of the first barrel, and since the diameter of a circle is double the radius, it follows that the radius of the second barrel must be twice that of the first barrel as well, so $2r$. The volume of the second barrel, therefore, is $= \pi(2r)^2(2h) = 8\pi r^2 h = 8 \times (\pi r^2 h)$. Therefore, the second barrel has a volume eight times that of the first barrel, so 8×100 gallons = 800 gallons. If the 100 gallons in the first barrel are poured into the second barrel, then the remaining empty capacity of the second barrel is 800 gallons minus the 100 gallons, which equals 700 gallons.

THE ANSWERS: NOT NECESSARILY YOUR FRIENDS

The answers can be your friends under certain circumstances. If, for example, the answers to a certain question were as follows:

   A. -2π
   B. π
   C. 2π
   D. 4π
   E. 8π

then you would know that the number π has to be part of your answer, so you could be sure to include it in your calculations. Noticing this fact ahead of time could also keep you from attempting to make any calculations with an approximation of π, such as 3.14159. It always pays to look at the answers ahead of time to see what form the answer might take.

But, and this is a big old but, you should never trust the answers. They are treacherous and deceitful, and don't let anyone tell you otherwise. The GMAT test writers work through all of the wrong answers you could come up with—a misplaced decimal here, a misplaced negative sign there—and slip them into the answer choices to lead you astray. Consider the answer choices for our hypothetical barrels of oil:

A. There is no empty capacity: this is for the skeptics out there who assume that this must be a trick question.
B. 100 gallons: this is a number that is already in the question, and it is the answer choice someone would make if he figured that the second barrel is twice the size of the first barrel, or if he misread the question as asking how many gallons are now *in* the second barrel.
C. 300 gallons: this would be the correct answer if a person figured that the second barrel was twice as high and twice as wide, so therefore it is $2 \times 2 = 4$ times larger than the first barrel.
D. **700 gallons:** this is the correct answer.
E. 800 gallons: this is the capacity of the second barrel; a person could easily reach this second-to-last step, see this answer, and mark it down without actually finishing the question.

The GMAT test writers think up misleading answers for every question, and they test out different wrong answers on actual test takers to see which ones they are most likely to fall for. Yes, this is sneaky. And yes, it makes the test more difficult. The only ways to combat this sneakiness are to

1. Know your stuff, i.e., work lots of practice problems.
2. Read the questions very carefully and know what is being asked.
3. Check your work as you go.

Plugging in the Answers

There is one more situation in which the answers can be your friends, sort of. Sometimes you just can't work out the problem in a straightforward way. You've read the question three times, and you just can't figure out how to set up the equation. In this case, and particularly if there is algebra involved, you can *plug in the answers and see if one fits.* For example, say that you see the following question:

What number when multiplied by $\frac{4}{9}$ yields $\frac{2}{3}$?

A. $\frac{2}{9}$
B. $\frac{2}{3}$
C. $\frac{3}{2}$
D. $\frac{9}{4}$
E. $\frac{9}{2}$

The direct way to solve this problem is with algebra: $\frac{4}{9} \times n = \frac{2}{3}$, and solve for n. But what if all of the algebra you know, in the heat of the testing frenzy, immediately flies out of your brain? The GMAT has been known to do this to people. Should this happen to you, you have another option: simply multiply each of the answers by $\frac{4}{9}$ until one of them yields $\frac{2}{3}$. The answer, then, is simply a matter of reaching choice C and determining that $\frac{4}{9} \times \frac{3}{2} = \frac{12}{18} = \frac{2}{3}$.

You can solve quite a few problems in this reverse way. If the straightforward approach isn't working for you, take a few moments to see if you can work backward from the answers. We will explain several problems this way throughout the book, to help you learn and master the approach.

The Most Common Answer Theorem

This isn't really a theorem, in the formal sense. It is a technique for guessing if you can't eliminate more than one or two answer choices. It doesn't work all the time, but it works on Problem-Solving questions far more often than it probably should. Here's what you do: if you don't know which answer to choose, *pick the one with the most elements in common with the other answer choices.*

What does this mean? Consider the following answer choices:

A. $\dfrac{2x+3y}{7}$

B. $\dfrac{2x+3y}{x+y}$

C. $\dfrac{2x+3y}{xy^2}$

D. $2x+3y$

E. $7(2x+3y)$

If you don't have any idea which answer is correct, for this question you should pick choice A. Why? Because it has the most in common with the other answers. All of the choices involve the expression $2x+3y$, so that obviously is part of the answer. Three out of five choices involve fractions, so the correct answer probably contains a fraction. Two choices contain the number 7. There are no other similarities between the answer choices. Choice A combines the fraction and the number 7, so it has the most in common with the other answer choices. Therefore, it should be your choice.

Other elements of similarity to look for include the following:

▶ Are there more positive or negative answer choices?
▶ Are there more answer choices with fractions (or decimals) or integers?
▶ Do some answer choices contain exponents/square roots/a certain variable/π or some other element?

This technique does not work all the time, or even half of the time. You are still guessing. But it generally works more than 20% of the time, and any technique that can potentially improve your score is worth knowing. This technique is also helpful on Sentence Correction questions. It offers no help for Data Sufficiency questions.

The reason this technique works is that the question writers attempt to write incorrect answers that *look like the right answer.* As we stated earlier, the writers work through all of the mistakes that you could make and include answer choices that include those mistakes. These tempting-but-wrong answers tend to contain elements in common with the correct answer. Thus, the Most Common Answer Theorem works more often than it should. Sometimes, even when the answers try to be treacherous and deceitful, they wind up being our friends anyway.

PROBLEM-SOLVING TIPS

Keep the following tips in mind as you work through the GMAT.

▶ *As you proceed, check each step.* Do this quickly, but make sure that you check your work as you go. Take a page from manufacturing management: it's easier to build the quality into the process from the start than to inspect it in later. Keeping your calculations on track is a matter of arithmetic and algebraic practice, so if your day job doesn't involve math, you'll want to spend some time getting familiar with this sort of thing again. Work as quickly as you can, but not so quickly that your error rate increases. You should try to gauge your maximum effective rate through repetitive work with practice tests and problem sets.

▶ *Can you see clearly that the step is correct?* If not, you may have a problem. Many GMAT questions—for that matter, many standardized test questions in general—feature incorrect answer choices built around classic process errors. Move a decimal point when you shouldn't? That answer will show up. Assume that the diagram is to scale when it isn't? The result of that mistake will be in the list as well.

▶ *Can you prove that it is correct?* Proof is sometimes difficult to come by on the GMAT. Proving that something is correct is both satisfying and relieving. As long as you haven't committed some gross conceptual error, you will probably be able to move on to the next question with some peace of mind. The problem is that you won't always come away with this sense of finality. The "what is the next number in the sequence" problems are a good example of this. You may not be able to prove mathematically that the next number in the sequence is, say, answer choice B. With only two minutes in which to work, you won't want to try. Then again, comfort with analytical ambiguity is an important attribute of management consultants and financial managers, so get used to some level of ambiguity.

▶ *Did you use all the data?* Red herring is not just a name for an Internet business magazine; it's also the name for a misleading bit of information that seems useful, but that has no real use in solving a problem. (The term red herring may have derived from the red ink in which the disclaimers on securities prospectuses used to be written—the implication of the term was that the prospectus was valuable mostly as a way to wrap fish.) Red herrings occasionally appear on Problem-Solving questions, and they are the name of the game in Data Sufficiency. Since you'll be looking at both types of questions mixed together, you'll need to adjust your strategy as you go. In general, when working Problem-Solving quantitative questions, you will need to use all of the pieces of information the question gives you. If you have not used all the data, check over your work again. You may very well have worked the problem correctly, but it's worth another look.

Looking Back

The last task, if there is time, is to examine the solution that you have obtained. In the first five questions, you should absolutely check your answers, because these early questions carry a disproportionate weight on your score. Toward the end, if you're running short on time, you're probably better off trusting your work and moving on so that you'll have a chance on every question. If you have the time, here are some questions to ask:

▶ *Does the answer make sense?* In retrospect, was the answer obvious, or a little *too* obvious? Remember: those false answer choices are not picked randomly; they're the result of quite a bit of thought by people who get paid to think of ways to trip up test takers. If you found your answer very quickly, you may want to spend a little more time on the problem. And if the scope of your answer doesn't seem to make sense in the context of the question—for example, if an answer tells you that a convenience store sells its candy bars for $55 apiece—then you might want to check over your numbers.

▶ *Can you check the result?* Before you work through all your math again, try to find some quick check that could disprove your conclusion. Is the angle just too big for that triangle? Does the value fit into an earlier equation in your solution? If not, consider how much time it will take to start over again. If you can find the discrepancy quickly, then zoom in on it and get the right answer. If you spend 30 seconds gazing blankly at the question without any further insights, it's time to put down an answer and move on.

▶ *Can you derive the solution differently?* More than a few GMAT questions will be susceptible to more than one problem solving technique. After you've used one, the others may appear more obvious. If you can see another method, and can use it quickly, consider using it to check your answer.

CHAPTER 2

Data Sufficiency

INTRODUCTION

Data Sufficiency problems make up about two-fifths of the quantitative questions on the GMAT. These questions are probably not like any test problem you've encountered before, but they do involve thought processes you use all the time. They don't ask you to answer the question; instead, they ask you to determine *whether or not you can answer the question with the information given.* Consider the following question:

> What is the minimum GMAT score, on the 200–800 scale, that an applicant must have in order to gain acceptance to the UltraTech Management School, a prestigious, nonaccredited business school?
>
> (1) The UltraTech Management School charges $8,000 per semester for tuition.
> (2) The UltraTech Management School accepts any applicant that has taken the GMAT and paid the application fee.
>
> A. Statement (1) ALONE is sufficient, but statement (2) alone is not sufficient.
> B. Statement (2) ALONE is sufficient, but statement (1) alone is not sufficient.
> C. BOTH statements TOGETHER are sufficient, but NEITHER statement ALONE is sufficient.
> D. EACH statement ALONE is sufficient.
> E. Statements (1) and (2) TOGETHER are NOT sufficient.

So, how would you answer a question like this? First, you read the question stem—that's the part at the beginning that ends with a question mark:

> What is the minimum GMAT score, on the 200–800 scale, that an applicant must have in order to gain acceptance to the UltraTech Management School, a prestigious, nonaccredited business school?

So what is the question asking for? A single number, within the range of 200–800, that corresponds to the minimum GMAT score an applicant must have to get into the business school. If the information the question gives you allows you to determine that number, then the statement or statements containing the information are sufficient to answer the question. If a statement does not allow you to determine that number, then it is not sufficient. Most Data Sufficiency questions will ask either for a number, as this question does, or for a "yes" or "no" answer. If the information at hand can allow you to produce one and only one answer, or if it provides a definitive "yes" or "no" under all conditions, then it is sufficient. If the answer is "yes" under some conditions but "no" under others, then the information is insufficient.

AD or BCE

All Data Sufficiency questions offer you the same five answer choices—the choices provided for the question just given. You need to memorize these answer choices cold before you walk into the test. In fact, do it now.

Done? Good. Now, the fact that every Data Sufficiency question offers the same answer choices means that you can approach each one the same way. You read the question stem. You figure out what it is asking. Then you read statement (1). From here on, it's *AD or BCE*.

What this means is that if statement (1) is sufficient, then the answer to the question will be either

A. Statement (1) ALONE is sufficient, but statement (2) alone is not sufficient.

or

D. EACH statement ALONE is sufficient.

If statement (1) is sufficient, then A and D are the only possible answers. You can cross the others off your list right now. On the other hand, if statement (1) is not sufficient, then the answer *cannot* be A or D. Now, let's consider the question given. Is statement (1) sufficient?

(1) The UltraTech Management School charges $8,000 per semester for tuition.

Well, no. The amount of tuition has nothing to do with the minimum acceptable GMAT score for this school, so there is no way that statement (1) will allow you to determine the single number that the question stem requires. Therefore, the answer must be one of the following:

B. Statement (2) ALONE is sufficient, but statement (1) alone is not sufficient.

C. BOTH statements TOGETHER are sufficient, but NEITHER statement ALONE is sufficient.

E. Statements (1) and (2) TOGETHER are NOT sufficient.

Once you've determined whether or not statement (1) is sufficient, you move on to statement (2). We are now considering B, C, and E. Let's examine statement (2):

(2) The UltraTech Management School accepts any applicant that has taken the GMAT and paid the application fee.

Is this statement sufficient? It tells us that accepted applicants must have taken the GMAT, so therefore they must have a score somewhere on the 200–800 scale, but it does not explicitly identify a minimum score. But a minimum score is *implicitly* stated here, because if the school is willing to accept *anyone* who has taken the GMAT and paid the application fee, then it has a *de facto* minimum GMAT score of 200. There's the single number we were looking for—200. It doesn't really matter what the answer is, what matters is whether or not we can answer the question. Since we can find one and only one answer to the question, statement (2) is *sufficient* to answer the question. The answer to this particular Data Sufficiency question must be

B. Statement (2) ALONE is sufficient, but statement (1) alone is not sufficient.

If statement (2) alone is enough to answer the question, then the answer cannot be C or E. Each of these answer choices is mutually exclusive. Once you get the hang of these answer choices, you can develop a rhythm for approaching Data Sufficiency questions and dispatching them quickly and accurately.

Many test takers find it helpful to visualize the Data Sufficiency process as a decision tree:

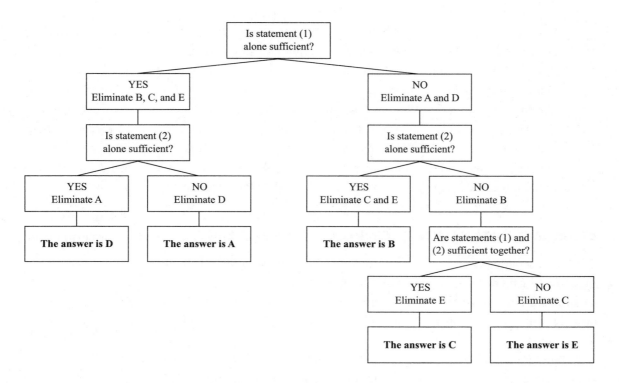

The Data Sufficiency Decision Tree

Every Data Sufficiency question should be answered with the same technique: by asking yourself the two or three questions listed in the flowchart. After you've practiced this technique on a few dozen questions, it should become second nature. We stress the importance of practice for all types of GMAT questions, but practice is doubly important for data sufficiency. People who have not internalized the Data Sufficiency decision tree tend to flounder around when they see these questions, and burn up precious minutes trying to figure out the answer choices instead of figuring out the questions themselves.

THE INTENT BEHIND THE QUESTION TYPE

Many people find Data Sufficiency questions to be strange and somewhat annoying. In some ways, though, they are more similar than Problem-Solving questions to the kinds of management problems people in business school and actual businesses face:

1. *In school* you will find yourself digging through vast piles of information. You may need, on any given night, to read several 16-page case studies, run a series of numbers several times,

write up position papers, and (if you're foolhardy enough to try a really serious finance program) then turn to several problem sets involving efficient frontiers and swap-pricing calculations. It can get insane at times. If, however, you have the ability to sort quickly through what is essential and what is not, you can manage the workload.

That's really what the Data Sufficiency questions are designed to uncover: whether you can manage workload time-efficiently without having to work through the details of every calculation. Some of the more challenging Data Sufficiency questions don't involve calculation at all, but rather demand that you glance at a problem and evaluate a series of standard questions accurately. That skill can really help you survive a top-flight MBA program.

2. *After school*, even if your quantitative workload decreases, you'll (hopefully) one day find yourself at the head of the mahogany conference table making the Big Decisions. Management jobs bring a wide breadth of responsibilities over areas where you'll have to listen to the answers generated by other people. When some consultant or engineer is explaining why this or that will work or can't happen, you probably will not have the time to run the numbers yourself, so you will have to have a sense of whether the numbers *could* or *could not* work out as described. A sense for the possibilities and constraints in numbers is an invaluable tool for any business executive.

WORKING DATA SUFFICIENCY PROBLEMS EFFICIENTLY

The key to working Data Sufficiency problems efficiently is to master the decision tree—remember, AD or BCE—and to work problems only as far as is necessary to determine their sufficiency. In some situations, such as those involving algebraic linear equations, you can tell that the problem is solvable even if it would take a long time to solve. We'll discuss these types of equations in the algebra material in Chapter 4.

There are a few useful things to know about how the test writers compose Data Sufficiency questions. For example, when a Data Sufficiency question starts with *is*, *are*, or *does*, you are trying to find a yes or no answer, rather than a number. A statement is sufficient as long as it gets you a definite yes or no; either one means you have enough information to answer the question. If you can get both a *yes* and a *no* depending on which numbers you use, that statement is not sufficient.

This is important to note because it is easy to confuse a *yes* answer with the statement being sufficient to answer the question. These questions may seem more complicated than other Data Sufficiency questions, so be sure to take your time and keep track of your work on your scratch paper. With practice, you will become used to this format and it will no longer seem confusing.

Also, when the answer to a question is D—"EACH statement ALONE is sufficient"—the answer provided by both statements will be the same; you should not see a situation in which one statement leads to a yes and the other statement to a no, or where one statement leads to a 6 and the other to a 7. There is no reason why ACT could not create a question in this way—the directions and the answer description for D would not disallow it—but past questions have generally followed this pattern of consistent answers.

Trickery

The test writers get tricky sometimes—well, most of the time—in the construction of the sufficiency statements. They might, for example, provide a partial but insufficient solution in statement (1) and then provide the missing pieces in statement (2), leading most test takers to pick C, "BOTH statements TOGETHER are sufficient, but NEITHER statement ALONE is sufficient." The tricky part is that the pieces provided in statement (2) may be sufficient on their own to solve the problem, so the answer is really B, but the test taker was primed from statement (1) to look for a specific piece of information in statement (2). Here is a simple example:

If x and y are nonzero integers, is $\frac{x}{y}$ an integer?
(1) $x = 5$
(2) $y = x$

A careless test taker might reason as follows: statement (1) alone is not sufficient because it says nothing about y, but it gives half of the puzzle. Statement (2) gives us the other half by allowing us to conclude that $y = 5$, and therefore $\frac{x}{y} = \frac{5}{5} = 1$, which is an integer. Therefore, the answer is C.

The problem here is that the answer is actually B. Statement (2) alone is sufficient to answer the question, because a nonzero integer divided by itself will always equal 1, which is an integer. It doesn't matter that statement (2) filled in the pieces for statement (1); what matters is that statement (2) alone is sufficient. This question is not mathematically difficult, but many test takers would incorrectly answer C, just as the test writers intended. The only way to guard against this sort of trickery is to evaluate each statement apart from the other before you ever consider how they might be combined.

Guessing

You should be able to avoid completely random guessing on Data Sufficiency questions. The decision tree is a formalized process of elimination that should substantially limit your choices if you can determine the sufficiency of just one statement.

If you do need to guess blindly, try to resist your initial impulse to pick C or E. Most test takers, when baffled by Data Sufficiency questions, tend to pick C or E because they look more complicated. ACT knows this, and designs the difficult questions with this in mind. Remember, difficult questions are just as likely to have A, B, or D as an answer. C or E might very well be the correct answer for a really puzzling question, but keep in mind that ACT might have crafted the question to steer you that way. Look through the statements again, and try to determine the sufficiency of at least one of them before you make a guess.

When It's Not AD vs. BCE

And speaking of guessing, what do you do if you can't tell whether statement (1) is sufficient? Should you just give up and pick E? Well, no . . . Now it's time for some extra credit. It is possible to start the decision tree with either statement (1) or statement (2), depending on which one is easier for you to evaluate. If you start with statement (2) and it *is* sufficient, the only possible answers are B and D (rather than A and D). If statement (2) *is not* sufficient, the only possible answers are A, C, and E (rather than B, C, and E).

If that sounds really confusing, just remember that if you ever have to start the decision tree with statement (2), just flip A and B.

Application Problems

Lest we scare you off of C and E answers entirely, we have to state that they still each make up about 20% of the Data Sufficiency answers, the same as the other answer choices. To show that we have no hard feelings against these answer choices, here are two application problems that demonstrate how you might encounter an answer of C or E.

1. $x + y = 8$. Does $x = 3$?

(1) $2x + z = 8$
(2) $3y - 4z = 7$

A. Statement (1) ALONE is sufficient, but statement (2) alone is not sufficient.
B. Statement (2) ALONE is sufficient, but statement (1) alone is not sufficient.
C. BOTH statements TOGETHER are sufficient, but NEITHER statement ALONE is sufficient.
D. EACH statement ALONE is sufficient.
E. Statements (1) and (2) TOGETHER are NOT sufficient.

Solution. So what's the answer? Start with the question stem. You're looking for a yes or no answer, does $x = 3$? Let's examine statement (1):

(1) $2x + z = 8$

Is it sufficient? No, because it does not give us a unique value for x. The statement could be true if $x = 1$ and $z = 6$, or if $x = 3$ and $z = 2$; the answer to the question might be yes or no—at this point we cannot say. So cross A and D off your list; it now has to be either B, C, or E. Let's move on to statement (2):

(2) $3y - 4z = 7$

Is it sufficient? No. If it gave us a unique value for y, that, in conjunction with the question stem, would be sufficient to answer the question yes or no, but statement (2) gives us no unique value for y. The statement could be true if $y = 5$ and $z = 2$, or if $y = 0$ and $z = -\frac{7}{4}$ (remember, the question stem never said that the variables were integers, whole numbers, or positive numbers; you should consider all possibilities). Therefore, statement (2) alone is insufficient, so the answer must be C or E. The step now is to consider whether the statements in combination, together with the question stem, can provide a definitive yes or no.

You now have three equations and three variables. Since none of the statements is a restatement of any of the others—which has to be true, since they all have different pairs of variables—you actually have enough information right now to solve for x. Since you know that you can solve for x, you know that you will be able to answer the question, so you could just stop here with the assurance that answer C is the correct answer. But since we haven't covered algebra yet, let's work it out here for fun.

First, let's get rid of the z, since it isn't in the question stem. If you multiply 4 times both sides of the equation in statement (1), $2x + z = 8$, you get the equation $8x + 4z = 32$, and if you then add both sides of this equation to the two sides of the equation in statement (2), $3y - 4z = 7$, you get the equation $8x + 3y = 39$.

$$
\begin{array}{rl}
(4)\,(2x+z) = (8)(4) \quad \rightarrow \quad & 8x + 0y + 4z = 32 \\
& \underline{+0x + 3y - 4z = 7} \\
& 8x + 3y = 39
\end{array}
$$

Now, multiply –3 times both sides of the equation in the question stem to get $-3x - 3y = -24$, and add both sides to both sides of our last equation:

$$(-3)\,(x{+}y) = (8)(-3) \quad \rightarrow -3x + -3y = -24$$

$$\begin{array}{r} +8x + \ 3y = \ 39 \\ \hline 5x \qquad = \ 15 \end{array}$$

The only solution to the equation $5x = 15$ is $x = 3$. So, although we technically did not have to arrive at this specific result, or even to know specifically whether the answer was yes or no as long as we knew that we *could find out*, we now have a definitive, resounding yes to the question, and a definitive and resounding C.

2. Is city A closer to city B than it is to city C?

    (1) City C is 197 miles from city A.
    (2) City C is 163 miles from city B.
    A. Statement (1) ALONE is sufficient, but statement (2) alone is not sufficient.
    B. Statement (2) ALONE is sufficient, but statement (1) alone is not sufficient.
    C. BOTH statements TOGETHER are sufficient, but NEITHER statement ALONE is sufficient.
    D. EACH statement ALONE is sufficient.
    E. Statements (1) and (2) TOGETHER are NOT sufficient

Solution. The first step is, look at the question stem. You need to compare two distances, and you're looking for a definitive yes or no: Is city A closer to city B than it is to city C? Now move on to statement (1):

    (1) City C is 197 miles from city A.

Is this statement sufficient to answer the question? No, because it gives us only one of the two distances we would need to answer the question. The other distance we need is the distance between city A and city B. Since statement (1) alone is insufficient, you can cross off answer choices A and D. Let's move on to statement (2):

    (2) City C is 163 miles from city B.

Is this statement sufficient? No, because it does not give us either of the two distances we would need to answer the question. So the answer cannot be B; the only options left now are C and E. What happens if we combine the statements? You could draw a diagram that looks like this:

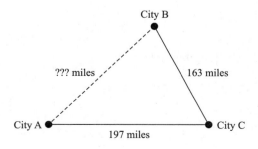

What do the laws of geometry tell us about this diagram? Without knowing any angles, they don't tell us very much. We could infer that the maximum possible distance between A and B is $163 + 197 = 360$ miles and that the minimum possible distance between A and B is $197 - 163 = 34$ miles. Clearly, city A could be closer to either city B or city C; we just can't tell with the information given. We have a name for the answer to questions like this. That name is E.

PRACTICE PROBLEMS

Now that you've gotten a little more confident, we're going to give you the opportunity to practice "without the training wheels." When you want to check your work, you can turn to the solutions at the end. If you aren't familiar with some of the mathematical concepts, make a note to pay particular attention to that chapter in this book; this practice set covers a wide range of topics tested on the GMAT.

On all data sufficiency problems, the answer choices are the same (as you've learned). We've put them here for your reference.

    A. Statement (1) ALONE is sufficient, but statement (2) alone is not sufficient.

    B. Statement (2) ALONE is sufficient, but statement (1) alone is not sufficient.

    C. BOTH statements TOGETHER are sufficient, but NEITHER statement ALONE is sufficient.

    D. EACH statement ALONE is sufficient.

    E. Statements (1) and (2) TOGETHER are NOT sufficient.

1. Is x an integer?

    (1) x is evenly divisible by $\frac{1}{2}$.

    (2) x is evenly divisible by 2.

2. What is the ratio of $2a$ to b?

    (1) $\frac{a}{b} = 2$

    (2) $a + b = 5$

3. What is the average of a list of n consecutive integers?

    (1) The smallest number in the list is 5.

    (2) $n = 8$

4. Is $s = r$?

    (1) $s^2 = r^2$

    (2) s is positive.

5. In triangle ABC, what is the length of AB?

    (1) The length of BC is 5 and the length of AC is 12.

    (2) Angle C = 90°.

6. If there are only red, blue, and green marbles in a jar, what is the ratio of red to blue marbles?

(1) The ratio of red to green marbles is 2:3.
(2) The ratio of green to blue marbles is 6:5.

7. Over a holiday weekend, a certain car dealer sold off $\frac{4}{5}$ of the cars on its lot. If the cars sold for an average of $6,000 each, how many cars were on the dealer's lot at the beginning of the weekend?

(1) The average value of the remaining cars on the lot is $5,000.
(2) The car dealer made $48,000 in car sales over the weekend.

8. What is the value of $\frac{fg}{h}$?

(1) $f = \frac{1}{2}h$
(2) $h = 5g$

9. Was the price of a certain stereo in March greater than its price in May?

(1) The price of the stereo in March was 80 percent of its price in April.
(2) The price of the stereo in April was 120 percent of its price in May.

10. If the square root of t is a real number, is the square root of t positive?

(1) $t > 0$
(2) $t^2 > 0$

11. If the ratio of brown cars to blue cars in a certain parking lot is 2:3, how many brown cars are in the lot?

(1) There are 15 blue cars in the lot.
(2) There are 25 cars total in the lot.

12. What is the value of $f^2 - g^2$?

(1) $f = -g + 8$
(2) $f = g - 2$

13. A shelf contains only books of poetry, short stories, and non-fiction. If Jana draws a book randomly off the shelf, what is the probability that the book will be non-fiction?

(1) There are 15 books on the shelf.
(2) There are 4 books of poetry and 5 books of short stories on the shelf.

14. A job opening was posted in September and again in January. In September, the number of applicants for the position was 60. What was the percent change in the number of applicants from September to January?

(1) The number of applicants in January was one-third the number of applicants in September.
(2) The number of applicants in January was 20.

15. Is $a^3 > 20$?

    (1) $a^4 > 80$

    (2) $a^5 > 200$

16. What is the length of a side of a certain cube?

    (1) The volume of the cube is 27.

    (2) The surface area of the cube is 54.

17. How many prime factors of x are also prime factors of y?

    (1) $x = 30$

    (2) y is a multiple of x.

18. Is $m > 0$?

    (1) $\dfrac{|m|}{2} = 2$

    (2) $m^3 = 64$

19. What is the value of $\dfrac{v}{w}$?

    (1) $\dfrac{w}{v} = -1.5$

    (2) $v > 0$

20. There are twenty students in a class, all of whom scored between 0 and 100 on their final exams. If the class average was 85, how many people scored below the average score on the exam?

    (1) Twelve people in the class scored higher than an 85.

    (2) The lowest eight scores added up to 640.

Solutions

1. **B.** A reminder: The question stem starts with *is*, so this is a *yes* or *no* problem. The first step is to determine whether statement (1) is sufficient, which we can do by trying out some real numbers. If x is 2, which is evenly divisible by $\frac{1}{2}$, then the answer would be *yes*. But if x were 1.5, which is also evenly divisible by $\frac{1}{2}$, then the answer would be *no*. Since you can get either *yes* or *no*, statement (1) is not sufficient and you should cross off A and D.

Now let's move on to statement (2). There are no non-integer numbers that are divisible by 2, so *yes* is the only possibility. Statement (2) is sufficient, so we can eliminate C and E, and the correct answer is B.

2. **A.** Statement (1) says that $\frac{a}{b} = 2$. We are looking for the ratio $\frac{2a}{b}$. If you substitute 2 for $\frac{a}{b}$ in that ratio, you get 2 times 2, which equals 4. Statement (1) is sufficient. Cross off B, C, and E.

How about statement (2)? Remember, you have to forget about the information you got from statement (1). Since there are several values for a and b that would add up to 5, let's try a couple of variations to see if we always get the same ratio. If *a* is 3 and *b* is 2, the ratio of $2a$ to *b* would be 6:2 or 3:1. But if we used $a = 2$ and $b = 3$ instead (and nothing tells us that we can't), the answer to the question stem becomes 4:3. When we can get different answers, we can tell the statement is not sufficient, so we can eliminate D. A is the correct answer.

3. C.   Statement (1) tells us the smallest number, but not how many numbers are in the list. It is not sufficient. Cross off A and D.

Statement (2) tells us the value of *n*, so the question becomes: *What is the average of a list of 8 consecutive integers?* Since those integers can be large, small, or even negative, we have no way to tell what the average is. Statement (2) is not sufficient, so we can eliminate B.

Now let's put the two statements together. If we know that 5 is the smallest number in a list of 8 consecutive numbers, then we can easily reconstruct the list and find the average. So the statements are sufficient when put together, and the answer is C.

4. E.   Here's another question that is looking for a *yes* or *no* answer. Statement (1) allows for both positive and negative values of both *s* and *r*, so we cannot tell if $s = r$. Statement (1) is not sufficient; cross off A and D.

Statement (2) just tells us that *s* is a positive number; we don't know anything about *r* at all and cannot tell if they are equal; statement (2) alone is not sufficient. Let's eliminate B.

What if we combine the two? Statement (2) tells us that *s* is positive, but *r* could still be either positive or negative. We still cannot tell if they are equal, so the answer is E.

5. C.   Statement (1) alone is tempting if you are familiar with the right triangles that tend to be tested over and over on the GMAT; however, we don't know from statement (1) that *ABC* is a right triangle, so we should cross off A and D.

With only statement (2), we certainly don't have enough information to answer the question, so B can be eliminated. Together, though, we can complete the picture of a right triangle with two known sides, which means we can figure out the third side using Pythagorean Theorem, and our answer is C. (Since the squares of the two legs add up to 169, the hypotenuse is 13.)

6. C.   Statement (1) doesn't give us any information about the number of blue marbles at all. It is not sufficient and we can cross off A and D.

Statement (2) doesn't give us any information about the number of red marbles, so we can eliminate B.

When we combine both statements, we have ratios that involve all three colors of marbles. Let's see what happens when we use some real numbers. If there are 6 green marbles, then there are 4 red marbles and 5 blue marbles, making the ratio of red to blue marbles 4:5. If we used a different number for the green marbles—say, 12—we would end up with the same ratio of red to blue. This happens frequently with relative numbers such as ratios, proportions, averages, and probability; keep in mind that you don't always have to know the actual numbers to know the ratios.

Statements (1) and (2) together are sufficient, so the answer is C.

7. B.   Given statement (1) alone, we only know average values of both the cars that were sold and the cars that remained; the dealer could have sold 4 cars and had 1 left, or sold 8 cars and had 2 left, or an infinite number of other options. So we can eliminate A and D.

With statement (2), we are able to find the number of cars sold by dividing the total sales by the average price. 48,000/6,000 = 8, so the dealer sold 8 cars. Since that is $\frac{4}{5}$ of the cars on the lot, the dealer started off with 10 cars. Statement (2) is sufficient, so the answer is B.

8. E.   Statement (1) doesn't tell us about g at all, so it is insufficient, and we can cross off A and D. Similarly, statement (2) doesn't tell us about f, so we can eliminate B. If we put the statements together, we have only two equations for our three variables, so we still cannot solve. Since the statements together are not sufficient, the answer is E.

9. C.   Again, this problem is looking for a *yes* or *no* answer. Statement (1) doesn't tell us anything about the May price, so it is not sufficient. We can cross off A and D.

Statement (2) doesn't tell us anything about March, so it is not sufficient and we can cross off B. With both statements together, we know relative prices, and no matter what numbers we were to assume, the May price ends up slightly higher than the March price. So the answer is definitely *no*, meaning that both statements together are sufficient, and the answer is C.

10. E.   This question is looking for a definite *yes* or *no* answer. Statement (1) is not sufficient since all it tells us is that t is a positive number. Unless the radical sign $\left(\sqrt{}\right)$ is used, a positive number has two square roots, a positive root and a negative root. For example, if t is 4, then it has two square roots, 2 and −2. So we can eliminate A and D.

With statement (2) alone, we don't get much more information; all it really tells us is that t is a positive number (it cannot be negative, since the square root of a negative number is a complex number, not a real number). So again, t could be 4, and its root could be either positive or negative. So we can eliminate B. Putting them both together doesn't tell us whether the square root of t is positive either, so our answer has to be E.

11. D.   When we evaluate statement (1), we can tell that there are 10 brown cars in the lot, because that's the only number that would give us a ratio of 2:3 if there are 15 blue cars. So we can eliminate B, C, and E.

Taking statement (2) alone, we can tell that we have 15 blue and 10 brown cars in the lot, because those are the only numbers that would add up to 25 and give a ratio of 2:3. So either statement is sufficient on its own, which means D is the correct answer.

12. C.   When we see a quadratic formula like $f^2 - g^2$, we almost always want to simplify it to see its parts better. This formula simplifies into $(f + g)(f - g)$, so if we can get values for each of those parenthetical statements, we can calculate the value of the whole. Statement (1) gives the value of $f + g$ when it is rearranged, but doesn't give the value of $f - g$. We can cross off A and D.

Statement (2) gives the opposite: the value of $f - g$ only. So it is not sufficient on its own—we can cross off B—but the two statements are sufficient together, so C is the correct answer.

13. C.   Statement (1) doesn't tell us anything about the breakdown of the different types of books, so we don't know how likely Jana is to draw a non-fiction book. Eliminate A and D.

Statement (2) alone doesn't tell us anything about the number of non-fiction books. So we can eliminate B.

Putting the statements together, we can tell that there are 6 non-fiction books on the shelf by subtracting 4 and 5 from 15. Therefore, Jana has a $\frac{6}{15}$ or $\frac{2}{5}$ probability of drawing a non-fiction book at random, and our answer is C.

14. D.   Statement (1) lets us find the number of January applicants (20) and then we can find that the percent change in applicants was $66\frac{2}{3}$%, so it is sufficient and we can eliminate B, C, and E.

Statement (2) tells us the same thing; it is also sufficient, so we can cross off A and we are left with D.

15. B.   Here's another question that is looking for a *yes* or *no* answer. Statement (1) allows for both positive and negative values of a, so it is not sufficient, and we can cross off A and D.

Statement (2), on the other hand, tells us that a is positive and must be a value of at least 3. If $a > 3$, then the answer to the question stem must always be *yes*. Therefore, statement (2) is sufficient, and our answer is B.

16. D.   Statement (1) tells us that the length of a side of the cube is 3, since the volume is just the length of one side cubed. So we can cross off B, C, and E.

Statement (2) is a little trickier, since surface area is generally a less familiar concept. If the surface area of the whole cube is 54, then the area of each one of the 6 faces is 9. That means each side is 3, so statement (2) is also sufficient, and our answer is D.

17. C.   Statement (1) tells us nothing about the prime factors of y, so it is not sufficient on its own. We can eliminate B, C, and E. We do know at this point, though, that the set of prime factors in question is {2, 3, 5}.

Statement (2) on its own tells us nothing about the prime factors of x, so it is not sufficient on its own. We can eliminate B.

Putting them together, we can see that all of the prime factors of x would also be prime factors of y, so they have those same three prime factors in common. Since the statements are sufficient together, then answer is C.

18. B.   Statement (1) is not sufficient because m could equal either 4 or –4, giving us either a *yes* or a *no*. So we can eliminate A and D.

Statement (2) tells us that m has to be positive 4, so it is sufficient, and our answer is B.

19. A.   Statement (1) tells us the value of the reciprocal of $\frac{v}{w}$ ... –1.5 or $-\frac{3}{2}$. That means $\frac{v}{w}$ has to equal $-\frac{2}{3}$, so statement (1) is sufficient and we can eliminate B, C, and E.

Statement (2) alone tells us nothing about w and very little about v, so it is not sufficient. A is our answer.

20. E.   Statement (1) is tricky because it implies that eight people scored lower than 85, but in fact, it is possible according to the question for some people to have scored exactly an 85, so it is not sufficient and we can eliminate A and D.

Statement (2) doesn't really give us any information; it tells us that the lowest eight scores had an average of 80, but we don't know how many of those scores were below 85. So we can eliminate B.

Putting the statements together, we can tell that 12 people made above an 85 and the 8 others had an average of 80, but we can't tell how many of the 8 were below an 85, so we have to eliminate C. E is our answer.

CHAPTER 3

Basic Principles of Numbers

INTRODUCTION

Almost all of the mathematical concepts tested on the GMAT were probably taught in your high school math classes. The good news about that is at one time you knew this stuff. The bad news is that, unless you're an engineer or financial analyst in your day job, you've probably forgotten some if not most of it. Don't worry, though. The GMAT tests a relatively small number of mathematical concepts, and does so in fairly predictable ways. With a modest amount of preparation, you can earn quite a good score, provided that your mathematics knowledge was sound in the first place. If your math background is weak, you should devote a substantial amount of time to preparation for the quantitative section.

The GMAT tests some very basic concepts that even people who are very good at math tend to forget over time. So, without further ado, let's move onto some basic concepts about numbers.

NUMBER TERMINOLOGY

Integers and Whole Numbers

Integers are generally called "whole numbers" in real life, but they're not technically the same thing. Basically, both of them can't have any decimals or fractions attached; they're the numbers you would use to describe things that aren't normally split into parts, like marbles, cars, and people. The only difference is that integers can be negative, while whole numbers are only positive or zero.

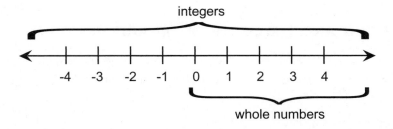

What's tricky about the GMAT, though, is paying attention to when the problem is asking for an integer and when it's asking for a number. When the problem asks for just a number, that number could be positive, negative, zero, a fraction, a decimal—literally any real number.

Rational and Irrational Numbers

You are not likely to be tested on the concept of rational versus irrational numbers, but it can be helpful to know the difference when you're studying, particularly when you're studying geometry. Rational numbers are any numbers that can be expressed as a fraction (or ratio) of any other numbers, so basically any integer or fraction, such as –3, 45.375, and 4/25. Irrational numbers extend out for many places behind the decimal, such as π or $\sqrt{2}$. We will look at those more closely in Chapter 6.

Real and Imaginary Numbers

All numbers tested on the GMAT are real numbers, unless a problem specifically states otherwise, which is extremely rare. So really all you need to know is that if you're calculating, and all of a sudden you're supposed to take an even root (square root, fourth root, etc.) of a negative number, such as $\sqrt{-100}$, you've started dealing with imaginary numbers and you need to check your calculations. The GMAT is not interested in your powers of imagination.

Prime Numbers

The GMAT is interested in prime numbers—very interested. A prime number has exactly two distinct factors: itself and 1. So the set of prime numbers includes {2, 3, 5, 7, 11, 13, 17, 19, 23, 29, . . . }. No number smaller than 2 is prime; not 1, not 0, and no negatives. No fractions or decimals are considered prime. It is worth memorizing the first 10 or so primes because they show up often on the GMAT, and trying to count the factors of 23, which is prime, is not something you want to take the time to do in the middle of the test.

Absolute Value

A number's absolute value is its distance from zero on the number line, and like any distance, it's always positive. So the absolute value of 3 is 3, and the absolute value of –3 is 3. This is expressed as $|3| = 3$, and $|-3| = 3$. It's not something you have to deal with every day, but it really is that simple; just take it slowly and be sure not to skip steps when you're dealing with absolute value. The only way the test writers can really make it more complex is to put a math problem inside the absolute value signs. In that case, just treat the absolute value signs like parentheses (more on that later): Work the math inside the signs and take the absolute value of the result.

ALGEBRAIC NOTATION AND THE ORDER OF OPERATIONS

A mastery of algebra is one of the most useful skills you can bring to the GMAT, because algebra applies not only to those problems that explicitly mention variables, such as

If $x \neq 3$ then $\dfrac{x^2(x-3) - x + 3}{x - 3} =$

but also to word problems with unknown variables:

If Jim's donut shop sold 220 donuts this morning for $121.00, how much, on average, did Jim charge for each donut?

The following chapter will deal with applying algebra to realistic GMAT problems. In this section, we will just review basic methods, notation, properties, and order of operations.

Variables are the first way you can tell you're dealing with an algebra problem. These stand in for unknown amounts, and are typically italicized letters on the GMAT, such as x, y, z, a, b, c, and n. They can be a little intimidating to deal with if you haven't used them in a while, but they really mean the same thing as the blanks you used to see in middle school math.

$$2 + x = 5$$

is the same as

$$2 + \underline{\quad} = 5$$

Solving for x is just a matter of figuring out what goes in that blank. For this problem, you just may just be able to tell that $x = 3$, but that is generally not going to be possible as the problems get more difficult, so it's worth it to learn the basics.

> ▶ **The Goal:**   Solve for x. Calculate the value of x. Figure out what x equals. Get x on one side of the equal sign and everything else on the other side. (There are some exceptions to this of course; sometimes problems will ask you to solve for xy, but the rules are the same in that case. The basic purpose of GMAT algebra is to figure out the value of the unknown.)

> ▶ **The Method:**   Whatever is being done to x, do the opposite thing to it. So if the problem has $2 + x$ on one side of the equal sign, subtract 2. Lather, rinse, repeat, and you will get x alone.

> ▶ **The Unbreakable Rule:**   *Whatever you do to one side of the equation, you must do the same thing to the other side.* That's right, algebraic equations are called *equations* because they have an equal sign, and whatever is on the left side of the equal sign has to be, well, *equal to* whatever is on the right side of the equal sign *at all times.*

So taking an example from above:

$$2 + x = 5$$

Subtract 2 from both sides:

$$2 + x - 2 = 5 - 2$$

Simplify:

$$x = 3$$

Voila! You have your answer: $x = 3$.

A few words about notation: Addition and subtraction are expressed as you would expect, with the + and − sign. Multiplication can be expressed a variety of ways:

- ▶ With a multiplication sign: 2×3, $2 \cdot 3$
- ▶ With parentheses: $2(3)$, $(2)(3)$
- ▶ With numbers and variables placed directly next to each other: $2x$, xy

Don't worry though; you will never see numbers placed directly next to each other to indicate multiplication. When you see "23," it will always mean the number 23, never 2×3.

It is possible to see division signs ($\div$), but generally division problems are expressed as fractions on the GMAT. So you will see $\dfrac{10x}{y}$, generally not $\div$.

The order of operations determines in which order you do anything in math, and it applies to algebra, as well. It's the same order of operations that your spreadsheet program uses, and the same one you learned in school: **PEMDAS** (aka Please Excuse My Dear Aunt Sally). What it really stands for is:

Parentheses Exponents Multiplication Division Addition Subtraction

More precisely, it's (1) Parentheses, (2) Exponents, (3) Multiplication and Division from left to right, and (4) Addition and Subtraction from left to right.

So, if you're given the expression $(2 + 3)x$, it equals $5x$, not $2 + 3x$, because the operations inside the parentheses take precedence.

There's also something else you need to know about parentheses: Whenever you have a parentheses being multiplied to something or divided by a number or variable, that operation must happen to all the terms (numbers or variables) inside the parentheses. This is called the *distributive property*. So,

$$x(y + z) = xy + xz$$

and

$$\frac{x+y}{z} = \frac{x}{z} + \frac{y}{z}$$

Okay, it doesn't look like there are parentheses on the division problem above, but that's just because it's being expressed as a fraction, as it normally will be on the GMAT. Whenever you have a collection of terms that are being added or subtracted in the numerator or denominator of a fraction, the parentheses are understood. So $\dfrac{x+y}{z}$ is really the same as $\dfrac{(x+y)}{z}$.

The distributive property does not apply to addition and subtraction, by the way. So $x + (y + z) = x + y + z$, not $(x + y) + (x + z)$.

A collection of two terms, such as $y + z$, is called a *binomial*, since it is composed of two terms. Three such terms (e.g., $x + y + z$) make up a *trinomial*, and any general collection of terms is called a *polynomial*. Multiplying two polynomials together requires multiplying every term in one polynomial by every term in the other. With binomials, the FOIL (First, Outside, Inside, Last) rule is a handy mnemonic:

$$(x + y)(w + z) = xw + xz + yw + yz$$

More often on GMAT questions, the binomials in a problem contain the same variables. Three common binomial expressions are

$$(x + y)(x + y) = (x + y)^2 = x^2 + 2xy + y^2$$
$$(x - y)(x - y) = (x - y)^2 = x^2 - 2xy + y^2$$
$$(x + y)(x - y) = x^2 - y^2$$

These binomial expressions are useful to know, as they have appeared on many GMAT problems in the past. Of these, the most useful is $(x + y)(x - y) = x^2 - y^2$, which is in general $(x^n + y^n)(x^n - y^n) = x^{2n} - y^{2n}$ for any integer n, because it allows us to simplify complex expressions. For example:

Which of the following is equivalent to $(x + y)(x^2 + y^2)(x^4 + y^4)(x - y)$?

A. $x - y$

B. $(x^2 - y^2)$

C. $(x^4 - y^4)$

D. $(x^8 - y^8)$

E. $x^8 - 4x^2y^2 + y^8$

You could multiply out a series of four polynomials like that, but it would take a long time. If you remember that $(x + y)(x - y) = x^2 - y^2$, you can combine the first and last binomials into the simpler expression of $(x^2 - y^2)$. You can then combine this with the next term and get

$$(x^2 - y^2)(x^2 + y^2) = (x^4 - y^4)$$

You can then combine this with the following and final term to get

$$(x^4 - y^4)(x^4 + y^4) = (x^8 - y^8)$$

And so the answer is D, $(x^8 - y^8)$.

As this problem shows, a familiarity with common binomial expressions can simplify your life, or at least the part of it dealing with the GMAT. For those of you who followed that problem and said, "Wait, what exactly did you do with those exponents?" it's time to get up to speed with the wonderful world of exponents.

EXPONENTS AND ROOTS

You will see many, many exponents on the GMAT quantitative section. An exponent signifies that a variable or constant is to be multiplied by itself a given number of times. Thus,

$$x^2 = (x)(x) \quad x^3 = (x)(x)(x) \quad x^4 = (x)(x)(x)(x) \quad \text{and so on.}$$

When you multiply an expression raised to an exponent by the same expression raised to an exponent, you add the exponents. Thus,

$$x^2 x^5 = \left[(x)(x)\right]\left[(x)(x)(x)(x)(x)\right] = x^{2+5} = x^7$$
$$3^2 \times 3^3 = 3^5$$

Likewise, if you divide an expression raised to an exponent by the same expression raised to an exponent, you subtract the exponent in the denominator (the bottom) from the exponent in the numerator (the top):

$$\frac{x^5}{x^2} = \frac{(x)(x)(x)(x)(x)}{(x)(x)} = x^{5-2} = x^3$$

$$\frac{3^3}{3^2} = 3^{3-2} = 3^1 = 3$$

$$\frac{y^3}{y^5} = y^{3-5} = y^{-2} \quad Note\text{: the exponent in the numerator is less than the exponent}$$

in the denominator; therefore, the exponent in the answer is negative.

When you see a number raised to an exponent raised to another exponent, you multiply the exponents:

$$(x^5)^2 = x^{5 \times 2} = x^{10} \quad \text{since} \quad (x^5)^2 = \left(x^5\right)\left(x^5\right) = x^{10}$$

$$\left(3^2\right)^3 = 3^{2 \times 3} = 3^6 \quad \text{since} \quad \left(3^2\right)^3 = \left(3^2\right)\left(3^2\right)\left(3^2\right) = \left(3^6\right)$$

Questions asking you to add, subtract, or multiply exponents are common on the GMAT. Less common, but certainly still possible, are questions that deal with exponents with negative values, fractional values, or a value of zero. However, you should know how to handle these cases. First of all, any real number raised to the zero power equals 1:

$$x^0 = 1$$
$$355^0 = 1$$
$$-17^0 = 1$$
$$0.00001^0 = 1$$

Nice and consistent, right? An expression raised to a negative exponent means that you put the expression raised to the positive exponent in the denominator of a fraction (i.e., on the bottom):

$$x^{-5} = \frac{1}{x^5}$$

$$3^{-3} = \frac{1}{3^3} = \frac{1}{27}$$

Any number greater than 1 raised to a negative exponent will result in a number that is greater than 0 but less than 1. Try out a few numbers to verify that. Now, a number raised to a fractional power is a much more wily phenomenon. Fractional exponents represent square roots, cube roots, and the like:

$$x^{\frac{1}{5}} = \sqrt[5]{x}$$

$$27^{\frac{1}{3}} = \sqrt[3]{27} = 3$$

What is a root? The square root of x is a number that when squared will equal x. The cube root of x is the number that when cubed will equal x. Thus,

$$\sqrt{4} = 2$$
$$\sqrt{9} = 3$$
$$\sqrt[3]{64} = 4$$
$$\sqrt[4]{625} = 5$$
$$\sqrt[5]{x^5} = x$$

Higher-level root problems are considered difficult, so you are not likely to see them unless you're earning a high score. The calculations for higher-level exponents and roots can get complicated in a hurry, so in order to make these problems possible, the GMAT tends to use the same numbers over and over. You should familiarize yourself with the exponent values that have appeared frequently on GMATs in the past:

$0^2 = 0, 0^3 = 0$ (0 to any power other than 0 is 0; $0^0 = 1$)

$1^2 = 1, 1^3 = 1$ (1 to any power is 1)

$2^2 = 4, 2^3 = 8, 2^4 = 16, 2^5 = 32, 2^6 = 64, 2^7 = 128, 2^8 = 256, 2^9 = 512, 2^{10} = 1{,}024$

$3^2 = 9, 3^3 = 27, 3^4 = 81, 3^5 = 243$

$4^2 = 16, 4^3 = 64, 4^4 = 256$

$5^2 = 25, 5^3 = 125, 5^4 = 625$

$6^2 = 36, 6^3 = 216$

$7^2 = 49, 8^2 = 64, 9^2 = 81, 10^2 = 100, 11^2 = 121, 12^2 = 144, 13^2 = 169$

It wouldn't be bad practice to do the calculations on all of these equations yourself in order to get your arithmetic skills up to speed. All of these numbers have appeared on GMAT problems in the past, and they will appear on them again. Note that the inverse of these equations provides you with square root values: $\sqrt{121} = 11$, $\sqrt[5]{32} = 2$, and so on.

FACTORING NUMBERS

The factors of a number are those numbers that can be multiplied together to produce the number in question. Thus, the factors of 12 are 1, 2, 3, 4, 6, and 12, because you can produce 12 in all of the following ways:

$$1 \times 12 = 12$$
$$2 \times 6 = 12$$
$$3 \times 4 = 12$$

But how can you come up with all those factors quickly and easily, without leaving any out? A factor T is a great way to do just that. So if you're coming up with the factors of 12, you would draw a T, and put 12 at the top (just to remind yourself which number you're finding factors of):

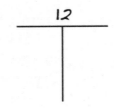

Now it's time to list out the factors. Listing them out systematically, in pairs, in the factor T helps ensure that you don't leave any out. Start with 1 on the left side, since 1 is a factor of any real number. Twelve divided by 1 is 12, so 12 is the corresponding factor on the right side. Then 2: 12/2 is 6, so 6 is also a factor. Then keep counting up, obviously skipping any numbers that don't divide evenly into 12.

$$
\begin{array}{c|c}
\multicolumn{2}{c}{12} \\
\hline
1 & 12 \\
2 & 6 \\
3 & 4 \\
\end{array}
$$

At this point, the next number on the left side would be 4, but 4 is already in the list, so listing it again would just be a duplication of effort. This is how you can tell you're done finding all the factors of any number.

Let's try this on a realistic GMAT problem:

Which of the following sets contains only factors of 45?

A. {1, 3, 5, 7}
B. {1, 5, 7, 13}
C. {1, 3, 5, 13, 15}
D. {3, 5, 9, 15}
E. {3, 5, 7, 45}

If you make a factor T, you will have all the factors of 45 at your fingertips:

$$
\begin{array}{c|c}
\multicolumn{2}{c}{45} \\
\hline
1 & 45 \\
3 & 15 \\
5 & 9 \\
\end{array}
$$

Answer choice D is the only one that has only factors of 45 in the set. It doesn't have all of them, but that's okay; the problem didn't specify that all of them had to be there. Choice D is the best answer.

Prime Factors

You will probably see a couple of problems on the GMAT that deal with prime factors. These are all the prime numbers that you would multiply together to make a single number, and each number has exactly one unique set of prime factors. They are not tough to calculate, but just like finding factors, it's best to have a simple, systematic method of finding them so that you don't spend too much time on the test making sure you've covered them all. Let's take this practice problem as an example:

What is the sum of the prime factors of 100?

A. 7
B. 10
C. 14
D. 25
E. 50

You're going to sketch out a prime factor tree (not a T this time). Start by just writing down the number you need to find prime factors of:

$$100$$

Now this is where it really comes in handy to have memorized the first ten or so prime numbers. The first prime number is 2, so if your original number is divisible by 2 (which 100 is), draw a couple of lines from the original number and put 2 at the end of one, and the result when you divide 100 by 2 (which would be 50) at the end of the other. The number 2 is prime, so it's done, finished, you can even draw a circle around it if you want. Now you're going to do the same thing with 50, and continue on down the tree. If 50 is divisible by 2, go ahead and divide it. If not, move on to the next prime number (which is 3), and if it's not divisible by 3, move on to the *next* prime number (which is 5). Repeat until you have all prime numbers at the ends of your "branches"—twos, threes, fives, sevens, elevens, and so on. The final prime factor tree for 100 looks like this:

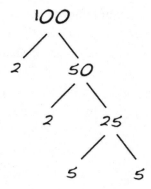

That means that the prime factors of 100 are: 2, 2, 5, and 5. The problem asks you to add them up, so 2 + 2 + 5 + 5 = 14, and C is the correct answer.

Careful; some problems will ask for *distinct* prime factors only. Distinct essentially means unique, so you would only list each prime factor once. The *distinct* prime factors of 100 are 2 and 5.

WORKING WITH NONINTEGERS

Integers are, generally speaking, easier to work with than nonintegers because the calculations necessary for manipulating them are shorter. But in the business world you have to deal with fractional numbers all the time. The price of a washer and dryer might be $899.99 with a 5% rebate. Interest rates on mortgages move up and down an eighth of a percentage point at a time, e.g., from 5.625% to 5.750%. Questions involving percentages, decimals, and fractions appear on the GMAT all the time. To ace this test, you need to be equally comfortable on both sides of the decimal point.

Percentages

Per cent is Latin for "by hundred," so percentages express numbers in hundredths. Thus,

$$45\% = 45/100 = 0.45$$

This can get confusing when we speak of decimal percentages:

$$0.45\% = 0.45/100 = 45/10,000 = 0.0045$$

There is a reasonable chance that a GMAT question will attempt to confuse you by putting a decimal within a percentage, so remember to watch for this. Coincidentally, decimal percentages are commonly used in finance, where hundredths of a percentage point are called basis points. Thus, to a banker,

$$0.45\% = 45 \text{ basis points}$$

Be very careful with questions asking about *percentage increases*. There is a difference between questions asking for the "percent increase" and the "percent of." When a number is doubled, it is *increased* by 100%, not 200%, but the resulting number is 200% of the original number (and the original number is 50% of the resulting number).

For example, if the price of an air conditioner increases from $300 to $600 over 10 years, the *percent increase* is 100% because the amount increased by $300. It is also true, however, when you are not talking about *percent increase* but are just discussing what percent $600 is of $300, $600 is 200% of $300 (and $300 is 50% of $600).

When a number is tripled, it is increased by 200%, and the resulting number is 300% of the original number. We can almost guarantee that one of the incorrect answer choices in a question involving percentage increases will feature a figure 100% greater than the correct choice.

Fractions

First, a little refresher terminology: The top of the fraction is called the *numerator* and the bottom is called the *denominator*. In this book we'll usually just call them the *top* and the *bottom,* for simplicity's sake.

One of the most important skills to have when dealing with fractions on the GMAT is reducing. Fractions are usually—though not always—best reduced as far as possible *before* they are multiplied by anything in GMAT questions. You could burn up a lot of time trying to work with a fraction like

$$\frac{210}{2772}$$

So the first step when you see a mean looking fraction is to figure out ways to simplify it. There are four rules that you can follow, generally in order:

1. Try to divide both the top and bottom by 2. This is called reducing the fraction by 2. Two is the first prime number, so it is always where you should start. If the number is even, then it's divisible by 2. Do this as many times as possible. In this case, that yields

$$\frac{210 \div 2}{2772 \div 2} = \frac{105}{1386}$$

2. Then try to divide both the top and the bottom by 3 (especially if reducing by 2 didn't work). A number will be divisible by 3 if the sum of its digits is a multiple of 3. In this case,

$$105: 1 + 0 + 5 = 6 \text{ and } 6 \text{ is a multiple of } 3, \text{ since } 6 \div 3 = 2$$
$$1386: 1 + 3 + 8 + 6 = 18 \text{ and } 18 \text{ is a multiple of } 3, \text{ since } 18 \div 3 = 6$$

So we know that 3 is a factor of both the numerator and the denominator; therefore, reducing by 3 yields

$$\frac{105 \div 3}{1386 \div 3} = \frac{35}{462}$$

3. Next, try to divide both the top and the bottom by 5. If a number ends in 5 or 0, it's divisible by 5. Here, we could take it out of the numerator:

$$\frac{35 \div 5}{462 \div 5} \text{ but } 462 \text{ is not divisible by } 5$$

4. Finally try to divide both the top and the bottom by 7:

$$\frac{35 \div 7}{462 \div 7} = \frac{5}{66}$$

And now we have a fraction that isn't so hard to work with.

If these four steps haven't reduced the number to a workable level, you could consider whether it is divisible by other primes, such as 11 or 13. If the number is that complicated, though, check over the answer choices to see whether you really need to reduce the fraction any further; if the answer choices themselves contain unwieldy fractions, then maybe further reduction is unnecessary. If the number is really messy, you also may consider whether there might be an easier way to solve the problem.

Decimals

There is a time to work with decimals, and a time to work with fractions. For example, if a question asks you:

If 37.5% of the 880 students at a certain college are enrolled in biology classes, how many students at the college are NOT enrolled in a biology class?

A. 110
B. 330
C. 550
D. 430
E. 880

You could multiply 0.375×880, but you could probably work the problem faster if you realize that

$$0.375 = \frac{3}{8}$$

then you could multiply

$$\frac{3}{8} \times 880 = \frac{3 \times 880}{8} = 3 \times \frac{880}{8} = 3 \times 110 = 330$$

Remember that the question asked how many students are NOT enrolled in a biology class, so don't forget to subtract:

$$880 - 330 = 550$$

which is answer choice C.

Either method, multiplying by a decimal or by a fraction, works; the key is that if the quicker method can save you a few seconds here, those seconds might be the difference between a right answer and a wrong answer on a harder question near the end of the test. The rule of thumb is that if the answer choices are in decimals, you should probably work the problem with decimals, and if the answer choices contain fractions, then you should stick with fractions. If the answer choices do not steer you in either direction, go with the one that appears simpler and faster.

There are some equivalences between fractions and decimals that can save you time if you remember them for the test:

1/8	=	0.125	1/100	=	0.01
1/4	=	0.25	1/50	=	0.02
3/8	=	0.375	1/25	=	0.04
1/2	=	0.5	1/20	=	0.05
5/8	=	0.625	1/10	=	0.1
3/4	=	0.75	1/3	=	0.3333
7/8	=	0.875	2/3	=	0.6666

Rounding

Occasionally a problem will involve a long string of digits to the right of a decimal point that are not particularly useful. Sometimes, rounding the number to a rough estimate will do the trick just as well. For example, a problem like the following has appeared on the GMAT:

Which of the following is closest to $\dfrac{4.0456 \times 9.9985^3}{201.73}$?

A. 4

B. 20

C. 40

D. 200

E. 2,000

You don't need to make the full calculation here, because the question asks you which number is "closest," and the answer choices don't have all of the decimal points that a really accurate answer would have. It is simpler to view the number as

$$\frac{4 \times 10^3}{200} = \frac{4,000}{200} = 20$$

Rounding can sometimes help you find answers much faster, or at least determine quickly which answer choices cannot be correct.

KEY CONCEPTS TO REMEMBER

▶ Three binomial relationships:

$$(x+y)(x+y) = (x+y)^2 = x^2 + 2xy + y^2$$
$$(x-y)(x-y) = (x-y)^2 = x^2 - 2xy + y^2$$
$$(x+y)(x-y) = x^2 - y^2$$

▶ Six rules about exponents and roots:

$$x^a x^b = x^{a+b}$$
$$\left(x^a\right)^b = x^{ab}$$
$$x^1 = x$$
$$x^0 = 1$$
$$x^{-a} = \frac{1}{x^a}$$
$$x^{1/a} = \sqrt[a]{x}$$

PRACTICE PROBLEMS

1. The sum of the non-prime numbers between 40 and 50, non-inclusive, is

A. 131
B. 176
C. 274
D. 405
E. 495

2. If $x = -2$, what is the value of $4x^3$?

A. −32
B. −24
C. −8
D. 8
E. 32

3. $\dfrac{3}{1/7} + \dfrac{7}{1/3} =$

A. $\dfrac{21}{58}$

B. $\dfrac{58}{21}$

C. 21
D. 42
E. 58

4. What is the decimal equivalent of $\left(\dfrac{1}{4}\right)^2$?

A. 0.0016
B. 0.0625
C. 0.16
D. 0.25
E. 0.5

5. What is the smallest integer k for which $64^k > 4^{14}$?

A. 4
B. 5
C. 6
D. 7
E. 8

6. If $x = -3$, then $\dfrac{x^2 + x}{-2x} =$

    A. −2

    B. −1

    C. $\dfrac{1}{2}$

    D. 1

    E. 2

7. If $(x - 1)^2 = 144$, which of the following could be the value of $2x$?

    A. −26

    B. −22

    C. −11

    D. 12

    E. 13

8. How many different positive integers are factors of 342?

    A. 9

    B. 11

    C. 12

    D. 20

    E. 22

9. If $27^p \times 3^2 = 3^4 \times 9^8$, what is the value of p?

    A. 3

    B. 6

    C. 8

    D. 15

    E. 16

10. 200 is what percent of 40?

    A. 0.2%

    B. 2%

    C. 5%

    D. 20%

    E. 500%

11. If f and g are distinct prime numbers less than 10, which of the following *cannot* be the product of f and g?

A. 6

B. 9

C. 10

D. 14

E. 15

12. What percent of 180 is 45?

A. 0.25%

B. 4%

C. 25%

D. 40%

E. 250%

13. $\dfrac{(0.5)^6}{(0.5)^3}$

A. 0.125

B. 0.25

C. 0.625

D. 12.5

E. 25

14. How many positive factors do 180 and 96 have in common?

A. 6

B. 12

C. 16

D. 18

E. 24

15. Which of the following is the closest approximation of $\dfrac{30.1 \times 1.98}{120.9}$?

A. $\dfrac{1}{6}$

B. $\dfrac{1}{4}$

C. $\dfrac{1}{2}$

D. 1

E. 5

16. Which of the following is equal to the cube of a non-integer?

    A. −64

    B. −1

    C. 8

    D. 9

    E. 27

The following data sufficiency problems consist of a question and two statements, labeled (1) and (2), in which certain data are given. You have to decide whether the data given in the statements are *sufficient* **for answering the question. Using the data given in the statements** *plus* **your knowledge of mathematics and everyday facts (such as the number of days in July or the meaning of** *counter-clockwise***), you must indicate whether**

    A. Statement (1) ALONE is sufficient, but statement (2) alone is not sufficient.

    B. Statement (2) ALONE is sufficient, but statement (1) alone is not sufficient.

    C. BOTH statements TOGETHER are sufficient, but NEITHER statement ALONE is sufficient.

    D. EACH statement ALONE is sufficient.

    E. Statements (1) and (2) TOGETHER are NOT sufficient.

17. If $s\sqrt{r} = t$, what is the value of r?

    (1) $r^2 = 625$

    (2) $\dfrac{t}{s} = 5$

18. Is $ab > 2$?

    (1) $a = 2$

    (2) $0 < \dfrac{a}{b} < 1$

19. Is $f < g$?

    (1) $f < g + 1$

    (2) $\dfrac{|f|}{|g|} < 1$

20. What is the value of $\dfrac{12}{5^p}$?

    (1) $p < 0$

    (2) $p^2 - 9 = 0$

Solutions

1. C.   The non-prime numbers between 40 and 50 are 42, 44, 45, 46, 48, and 49. (Remember, the *non-inclusive* means we don't include the 40 and 50.) Add them all up and we get 274.

2. A.   Remember to follow the order of operations and cube –2 first to give you –8; then multiply by 4 and you get –32.

3. D.   To divide by a fraction, just flip the top and bottom and multiply. So $\dfrac{3}{1/7} + \dfrac{7}{1/3}$ turns into $(3 \times 7) + (7 \times 3)$, or 21+21, which gives us 42.

4. B.   To square a fraction, we have to square both the numerator and the denominator, which gives us $\dfrac{1}{16}$. If you want to avoid the long division, you can just divide 1 by 2, which gives you $\dfrac{1}{2}$ or 0.5. Divide again and you get $\dfrac{1}{4}$ or 0.25. Keep going until you get to $\dfrac{1}{16}$, or 0.0625.

5. B.   If we don't want to do a lot of calculations, we're going to have to manipulate the exponents. The first step is to put the 64 and the 4 in the same terms, so let's make the $64 = 4^3$ instead. Now the question is looking for the smallest integer k for which $4^{3k} > 4^{14}$, which is the same as finding the smallest integer k for which $3k > 14$. The best answer is 5, or B.

6. D.   Be sure to follow the order of operations and plug in –3 for x. The equation becomes $\dfrac{(-3)^2 - 3}{-2(-3)}$, which becomes $\dfrac{6}{6}$, or 1.

7. B.   Since there are only two possible values of $2x$, it's easiest to start with them and find one that is also in the answer choices. Since $(x-1)^2$ could equal either 12 or –12, x could equal 13 or –11, which means that $2x$ could equal either 26 or –22. Of the answers, only B will work.

8. C.   From the answers we can see that the list of factors will be relatively small, so it's easiest just to list them out. The pairs of factors are 1 and 342, 2 and 171, 3 and 114, 6 and 57, 9 and 38, and 18 and 19. That makes 12 factors.

9. B.   Once we simplify $27^p \times 3^2 = 3^4 \times 9^8$, we get $(3^3)^p \times 3^2 = 3^4 \times (3^2)^8$, or $3^{3p} \times 3^2 = 3^4 \times 3^{16}$. That is the same as $3p + 2 = 4 + 16$, so p must equal 6.

10. E.   We can take this question directly into an equation, which would look like $200 = \dfrac{x}{100} \times 40$. When we solve, we get 500, choice E.

11. B.   The prime factors less than 10 are 2, 3, 5, and 7, so the product of any two of those cannot be correct. That eliminates choice A (the product of 2 and 3), C (the product of 2 and 5), D (the product of 2 and 7), and E (the product of 3 and 5). Since 9 is the product of 3 and 3, which are not distinct (or 1 and 9, which are not prime), B is the correct answer.

12. C.   This question can also be put directly into equation form: $\dfrac{x}{100} \times 180 = 45$. When we solve, we get 0.25, choice C.

13. A.   Simplifying gives us $(0.5)^3$, which is 0.125.

14. A.   The positive factor pairs for 180 are: 1 and 180, 2 and 90, 3 and 60, 4 and 45, 5 and 36, 6 and 30, 9 and 20, 10 and 18, and 12 and 15. The positive factor pairs for 96 are: 1 and 96, 2 and 48, 3 and 32, 4 and 24, 6 and 16, and 8 and 12. They have 1, 2, 3, 4, 6, and 12 in common for a total of 6 factors.

15. C.   Approximating the equation gives us $\dfrac{30 \times 2}{120}$, which simplifies to $\dfrac{1}{2}$.

16. D.   Of the answer choices, only 9 is not a "perfect" cube, which means that its cube root is a non-integer.

17. D.   Statement (1) tells us that $r = 25$ or -25, but when you look at the question stem, the radical sign for r is present, which only allows for a positive root. So $\sqrt{r} = 5$. Therefore statement (1) is sufficient and we can eliminate B, C, and E.

Statement (2) also gives us enough information to solve for r. If we rearrange the equation in the question stem, we can get $\frac{t}{s}$ on one side, giving us $\sqrt{r} = \frac{t}{s}$. Since $\frac{t}{s} = 5$, $\sqrt{r} = 5$. So statement (2) is also sufficient, and our answer is D.

18. C.   Statement (1) does not give us a definite *yes* or *no* answer, because b could be a lot of different numbers. So we can eliminate A and D.

Statement (2) is also not sufficient, as a and b could equal 1 and 2, or 0.5 and 2, or 2 and 4, or an infinite number of other variations in which a is smaller than b. So B is not correct.

Putting them together, we know that $a = 2$, and b must be larger than a to satisfy statement (2). ab then must be larger than 2 and the answer to the question is definitely *yes*. C is the correct answer.

19. E.   Statement (1) is not sufficient because f could be less than g or it could just be $g + 0.5$. We can cross off A and D.

Statement (2) is not sufficient because while the absolute value of f must be less than the absolute value of g, the actual value of g could still be negative while f could be positive. The statement doesn't give us enough information, so we can eliminate B.

Putting the statements together doesn't really give us any more information, so the correct answer is E.

20. C.   Because statement (1) just tells us that p could be any negative number, it is not sufficient to answer the question. A and D can be eliminated.

Statement (2) alone tells us that p could be either 3 or -3, which would give different values for $\frac{12}{5^p}$, so it is also not sufficient and we can eliminate B.

The statements together tell us that p must be -3, so we can solve for $\frac{12}{5^p}$ and C is the correct answer.

CHAPTER 4
Algebra

INTRODUCTION

Understanding algebra is essential for most rigorous business schools; therefore, algebra is included in large quantities on the GMAT. Unfortunately, though (or fortunately, depending on your point of view), GMAT problems don't necessarily test your algebra skills the same way business schools will test them — or the way you will need them in real life. So while you will want to make sure your algebra skills are sharp for school, and you will need basic manipulation skills for the GMAT (like those you studied in the last chapter), there are also some shortcuts you can take to get you in and out of problems efficiently on the test. Consider the following problem.

> Hector runs a one-product widget shop. Each month, his fixed costs, whether he produces anything or not, amount to x dollars. The marginal cost of producing and selling one widget is a constant y dollars, regardless of the number he produces. He generally can sell widgets for z dollars each. What is the minimum number of widgets he must produce, assuming he sells every widget he produces, to break even (neither make a profit nor incur a loss) in a given month?

A. $\dfrac{x}{(y-z)}$

B. $\dfrac{x}{(z-y)}$

C. x

D. $\dfrac{x}{z}$

E. $\dfrac{x}{y}$

The breakeven point is a very important concept in business (and business school), so it appears frequently on the GMAT. Thus you need to memorize the definition in case the problem doesn't define it: the breakeven point is the point at which the profit is zero, so the business is neither making nor losing money on the project or product line under discussion.

On a problem like this one, your first instinct is probably to take the given variables and write an algebraic equation, which you will then solve and hope that it looks like one of the answer choices. In theory, that sounds great, except that the test writers tend to make these problems extra-tricky by throwing in conversions that you may not notice or by changing around variables in an answer choice so that the correct answer doesn't look like the answer you come up with. That's what the writers get paid to do — make the problem hard enough to weed some people out. So to raise your score, you need tools that make the problems easier to work, or that make it possible for you to solve a greater number of difficult problems than you would otherwise. That's where substitution comes in.

Substitution: The Algebra-Killer

Let's use Hector's situation to learn about substituting real numbers. The first thing to notice is the answer choices. See how they have algebraic expressions in them? Algebraic expressions or single variables are sure signs that you can substitute numbers and make this problem easier.

Hector's fixed cost is x per month. Let's find an easy number to work with that you can use for x — say, 100. Write down $x = 100$. And suppose the cost of producing one widget is 2. (You can ignore all of the dollar signs, since you're working in dollars all the way through the problem.) So $y = 2$. And the price Hector can sell a widget for is 6 . . . $z = 6$. So let's make sure you have all of that on your scratch paper:

$x = 100$

$y = 2$

$z = 6$

And if you can't remember which numbers represent what, you can always take it a step further, like this:

fixed costs $= x = 100$

cost to produce 1 widget $= y = 2$

selling price of 1 widget $= z = 6$

Now, since you want to "break even" at 0, you basically have to figure out how many widgets you have to produce to cover the big cost — the fixed cost. Producing and selling one widget makes you a profit of 4, since $6 - 2 = 4$. How many widgets do you need to produce and sell to make up for the fixed cost of 100? Well, 100 divided by 4 is 25. You need to produce 25 widgets to break even; that is the answer.

But of course, all of the answers are variables and expressions, so you need to do some quick-but-careful work before you're done. Let's go through all of the answers, eliminating anything that doesn't equal 25. The variables keep the same values you assigned them before, of course — aren't you glad you wrote those down?

A. $100/(2-6) = -25$, which is not the same as 25. Eliminate A.
B. $100/(6-2) = 25$, so you can keep B.
C. 100 doesn't equal 25. Eliminate C.
D. $100/6$ doesn't equal 25. Eliminate D.
E. $100/2$ doesn't equal 25. Eliminate E.

Clearly, B is the only answer that works. But what if you hadn't chosen those specific numbers? Would you still get the same answer? Yes, you would. As long as you follow the rules in the problem (such as using positive integers when they tell you x and y must be positive integers), and use the same process, you will get the same answer. However, sometimes it is possible to get additional correct answers as well, simply because you *are* dealing with variables. Let's see this problem with a couple of different numbers substituted for the variables:

$x = 100$

$y = 5$

$z = 10$

The profit from producing one widget is 5, so you need to produce 20 widgets to make up for the fixed cost of 100. Therefore, 20 is the answer you're looking for in the answer choices.

    A. $100/(5-10) = -20$, which is not the same as 20. Eliminate A.

    B. $100/(10-5) = 20$, so you can keep B.

    C. 100 doesn't equal 20. Eliminate C.

    D. $100/10$ doesn't equal 20. Eliminate D.

    E. $100/5 = 20$, so you can keep E.

Uh-oh. See how the correct answer stayed correct, but an additional answer became correct as well? It's not too terribly big of a deal if this happens; all you have to do is pick some different numbers (again, making sure that you're following any rules set up in the problem), and narrow down among the answers that are left. The good news is that the ones that didn't work before stay wrong, so the second substitution is usually pretty quick and easy. You can also usually avoid this pitfall by avoiding using the same number twice (see how 5 is used twice in the second example?) and by avoiding using 1 and 0.

To avoid another pitfall, make sure your numbers are easy to work with. If you originally chose $x = 100$, $y = 2$, and $z = 5$, there's nothing really wrong with those numbers, but you will end up with an answer of 33 1/3 widgets, which simply isn't easy to work with. If you run into that situation, just change your numbers a little until things are easily divisible.

Substitution Using Answer Choices

Sometimes rather than having variables in the answer choices, you have five possibilities that represent an unknown in the problem itself. Often the easiest way to solve this kind of problem is to work backwards from the answer choices, substituting each one into the problem situation until you find the one that is correct. Be careful though: the urge to write an algebraic equation can be particularly strong with this question type, and it can get in the way of seeing how easy these problems really can be. Let's consider this depreciation problem:

Ace Transport has acquired two trucks to carry different types of cargo. One costs $70,000; the other costs $52,000. The company expects that the first will last 165,000 miles, after which it can be sold for salvage for about $4,000. The other will fetch the same salvage price, but will last 200,000 miles. The two trucks convoy together, so they always show the same mileage readings. If the value of each truck declines at different constant rates for every mile driven, at what mileage reading will the residual values of the two trucks be equal?

A. 87,500 miles

B. 100,000 miles

C. 107,750 miles

D. 112,500 miles

E. The residual values will never be equal.

Depreciation is another important concept for business and business school, so you will very likely see it on GMAT questions. The type of depreciation you will see on the GMAT will be straight-line depreciation, meaning that whatever is depreciating is depreciating at a constant rate, so there's no funny business like a car depreciating 10% as soon as you drive it off the lot and then a different percent per year afterwards.

This isn't an easy problem no matter what, but you don't have to spend time and effort writing equations for each truck and then graphing them. Instead, start by making just a few simple calculations.

The first truck will depreciate by $66,000 total, because 70,000 – 4,000 = 66,000. It is expected to drive 165,000 miles, so you need to calculate the amount it depreciates per mile. Dividing $66,000 by 165,000 gives $0.40, so the first truck depreciates by 40 cents per mile.

The second truck will depreciate by $48,000, because $52,000 – 4,000 = 48,000. It is expected to last 200,000 miles. Dividing $48,000 by 200,000 gives $0.24, so the second truck depreciates by 24 cents per mile.

The question asks at what mileage will the two trucks have the same residual — or remaining — value. At this point you have to ask yourself, would it be easier to go find the value (somewhere between 1 and 165,000), or would it be easier to just check the values listed in the answer choices? Clearly the math isn't super-simple either way, but at least the answer choices are a place to start, so let's go there. Typically, you want to start with the middle answer choice (choice C) because the answer choices are listed in ascending or descending order, so checking choice C allows you to eliminate other answers that are either too big or too small. But if there are some answer choices that are way easier to work (like choice B, in this case), it's perfectly okay to start there.

Choice B is 100,000 miles. Using the depreciation rates you found above, calculate how much each truck depreciates in 100,000 miles and see if the residual values are the same. Truck 1's original price is 70,000. It depreciates $0.40 per mile for 100,000 miles, so 70,000 – 0.4(100,000) = 70,000 – 40,000 = 30,000. Truck 2's original price is 52,000. It depreciates $0.24 per mile for 100,000 miles, so 52,000 – 0.24(100,000) = 52,000 – 24,000 = 28,000. The residual values are not equal, so choice B is not the correct answer. But can you do a little bit of ballparking to eliminate other answers? Yes. Since truck 1 is going to depreciate faster than truck 2, you know you need a higher number of miles for their residual values to be equal. So you can also eliminate choice A.

So where to go next? Since you need a higher number, either choice C or choice D would make sense. However, choice D is the more logical one to try because if it doesn't work, you will be able to tell whether C could be correct just based on the trends, or whether there is no point at which the residual values are equal. So let's try D.

D. Truck 1: 70,000 – 0.4(112,500) = 70,000 – 45,000 = 25,000
   Truck 2: 52,000 – 0.24(112,500) = 52,000 – 27,000 = 25,000

The residual values are equal, so D is correct. You don't need to try all of the answers on this type of problem because there are no variables. Once you find an answer choice that works, mark it and move on.

By the way, if you couldn't do the math on that one fairly quickly, it's time to do some brush-up on your computation skills. This level of non-calculator math will be tested on the higher GMAT math questions.

QUADRATICS

Another context in which you are very likely to deal with algebraic concepts is in working with quadratics. If you haven't dealt with quadratics in a few years, here is what you need for the GMAT. First of all, there are three basic formulas that you need to memorize cold. Here they are:

$$(x + y)^2 = x^2 + 2xy + y^2$$
$$(x - y)^2 = x^2 - 2xy + y^2$$
$$(x + y)(x - y) = x^2 - y^2$$

If you need to make flash cards, do it. The reason that you need to memorize these is that while we all know we *could* derive, factor, solve, FOIL, and whatnot, knowing these equations means that you won't have to do all that work for most of the quadratic problems on the test. You just recognize one of these forms and presto — you change it into the equivalent form.

Now, in the few cases in which you're not dealing with $(x + y)^2$, $(x - y)^2$, or $(x + y)(x - y)$, you may need to do some actual manipulation. In those cases, you're either going to be changing something from parenthetical form — $(x + y)^2$ — into an expression — $x^2 + 2xy + y^2$ — or the other way around. If you're starting off with parentheses, you FOIL. If you're starting off with an expression, you factor.

FOIL

FOIL stands for First, Outside, Inside, Last, and it's simply an order of operations to make sure that you do everything you need to do to get the form changed properly. For example, let's say you're starting with $(x + 5)(x - 3)$. You multiply one term from each set of parentheses, using FOIL as your order.

First terms: Multiply x and x to get x^2
Outside terms: Multiply x and -3 to get $-3x$
Inside terms: Multiply 5 and x to get $5x$
Last terms: Multiply 5 and -3 to get -15

So your terms are x^2, $-3x$, $5x$, and -15. You combine what you can and end up with $x^2 + 2x - 15$. Done!

Factoring

Factoring is also called finding the roots or solutions of an equation. The good news is that it always follows the same steps, much the same as FOIL. Let's say you have the expression $x^2 + 7x + 12$. First you draw the parentheses and put an x in each one:

$(x\quad)(x\quad)$

Now all you have to do is fill in the numbers and plus/minus signs. The trick is to find the *factors* of the last term — the one with no variable — in this case, 12. 12 has the following factors:

1 and 12

2 and 6

3 and 4

Now all you have to do is find the factor pair that you can combine to form the coefficient of the middle term (in this case, 7). 3 and 4 can be added to create 7, so that is your factor pair. You will leave both the 3 and the 4 positive because you need to create a positive 7.

$(x + 3)(x + 4)$

Sometimes factoring is all you need to do. For example, if you were looking at a problem with $x^2 + 7x + 12$ on the top of a fraction and $(x + 4)$ on the bottom, factoring the top expression would allow you to reduce the fraction and simplify the problem. But if the problem asks for the roots of the equation $x^2 + 7x + 12 = 0$, you would need to take it a step further.

Finding the roots or solutions means finding the numbers you could substitute for x to make the equation equal 0. So now you have solved to find that the two possibilities are $(x + 3) = 0$ and $(x + 4) = 0$. Therefore, the roots or solutions are $x = -3$ and $x = -4$ (*not* $x = 3$ and $x = 4$).

Let's do one more example that is a little more difficult, so that you get some practice dealing with variations.

What are the solutions to the equation $x^2 + (-2x) = -15$?

A. −5 and −3

B. 5 and −3

C. 5 and 3

D. −5 and 3

E. There are no solutions to the equation.

First of all, you want to get this equation looking like the one you've worked before, so manipulate it to get zero on the right and everything else on the left. That gives $x^2 + (-2x) + 15 = 0$. Now write your parentheses and fill in an x for each pair: $(x)(x)$. Now find the factors of 15:

1 and 15

3 and 5

Which pair can you manipulate to get a −2? Clearly, that's 3 and 5. Subtracting the 5 from the 3 would give you −2, so fill in your parentheses accordingly. You get $(x - 5)(x + 3)$. Setting each set of parentheses equal to 0 gives you your roots, 5 and −3. The correct answer is choice B.

Before moving on to the next chapter, work the sample problems. Brief solutions are provided after the problems.

PRACTICE PROBLEMS

1. Which of the following equations has a solution in common with $x^2 - 2x - 15 = 0$?

   A. $x^2 - 6x + 9 = 0$

   B. $x^2 + 2x - 15 = 0$

   C. $2x^2 + 9x + 9 = 0$

   D. $2x^2 + x - 3 = 0$

   E. none of the above

2. If $\dfrac{5+x}{x-3} = x$, then which of the following is a possible value of x?

   A. -3

   B. -2

   C. 1

   D. 5

   E. 7

3. In three years, Janice will be three times as old as her daughter. Six years ago, her age was her daughter's age squared. How old is Janice?

   A. 18

   B. 36

   C. 40

   D. 42

   E. 45

4. If apples cost x dollars per m dozen, how many dollars will it cost to buy n apples?

   A. $\dfrac{xn}{12m}$

   B. $\dfrac{xn}{m}$

   C. $\dfrac{m}{xn}$

   D. $\dfrac{12m}{xn}$

   E. $\dfrac{12mn}{x}$

5. Which of the following is a solution to the equation $x^2 - 4x - 32 = 0$?

   A. -12

   B. -8

   C. -4

   D. 4

   E. 12

6. Abby, Brandon, Cedric, and Deirdre are planning to attend a concert. If their friend Kim also goes with them, they will get a group discount on their tickets. If the total price of the tickets with the group discount is the same as the total price of the tickets without the group discount, how much is the discount?

A. 5%
B. 10%
C. 20%
D. 25%
E. 33%

7. Two boards are being cut for a construction project. If the total length of the boards is 100 inches and the shorter board is 5 inches less than half the length of the longer board, what is the length of the shorter board?

A. 25 inches
B. 30 inches
C. 35 inches
D. 65 inches
E. 70 inches

8. If the average (arithmetic mean) of a list of s integers is 18, what is the sum of the integers?

A. $9s$
B. $\dfrac{18}{s}$
C. $18s$
D. $\dfrac{9}{s}$
E. $18 + s$

9. What are the roots of the equation $x^2 - 12x = -27$?

A. $(18, 9)$
B. $(18, -9)$
C. $(-3, -9)$
D. $(-3, 9)$
E. $(3, 9)$

10. A group of hikers is planning a trip that will take them up a mountain using one route and back down using another route. They plan to travel down the mountain at a rate of one and a half times the rate they will use on the way up, but the time each route will take is the same. If they will go up the mountain at a rate of 4 miles per day and it will take them two days, how many miles long is the route down the mountain?

    A. 4

    B. 6

    C. 8

    D. 12

    E. 16

Solutions

1. C.   The equation in the question factors out to $(x - 5)(x + 3) = 0$; $x = 5$ or -3. The equations in the answer choices factor out to

    A. $x^2 - 6x + 9 = 0 = (x - 3)(x - 3)$; the solution is $x = 3$

    B. $x^2 + 2x - 15 = 0 = (x + 5)(x - 3)$; the solution is $x = 3, -5$

    C. $2x^2 + 9x + 9 = 0 = (2x + 3)(x + 3)$; the solution is $x = -3, -3/2$

    D. $2x^2 + x - 3 = 0 = (2x + 3)(x - 1)$; the solution is $x = -3/2, 1$

Of these choices, only C shares a solution, -3, with the equation in the question.

2. D.   This problem is solved easily enough by substituting numbers from the answer choices. Starting with choice C, you get $-3 = 1$, which clearly isn't true. If it isn't immediately clear whether to move up or down in the answer choices, don't spend a lot of time trying to save a little time — just move! Answer choice D gives you 5 on both sides of the equation, so it is correct.

3. D. This is another great problem to solve just by substituting answer choices instead of writing out a long equation. But you do have to make sure you're systematically keeping track of everything. The problem asks for Janice's age, so the answer choices are all possibilities for Janice's age.

    Starting with choice C, you know that Janice is 40, so in 3 years, she will be 43. She will be 3 times as old as her daughter at that point, so her daughter is . . . not an integer. That's actually a great indicator of a wrong answer when dealing with years, so let's move on.

    In answer choice D, Janice is 42, so in 3 years, she will be 45. She will be 3 times as old as her daughter, so her daughter will be 15. That means her daughter is 12 now. Six years ago, her age was her daughter's age squared. Do the numbers support that? Well, Janice was 36 and her daughter was 6, so yes, choice D works and is the correct answer.

4. A.   If we set up this problem as a proportion with dollars on top and apples on bottom, you get $\frac{x}{12m} = \frac{y}{n}$ (let's call the amount of money we're trying to solve for y). Cross-multiplying gives us $12my = xn$, and to get y alone, we would just divide by $12m$ on both sides, giving us $\frac{xn}{12m}$.

Why not substitute numbers on this one? Well, because the equation was set up for you and you only had to manipulate it. This problem wasn't as tricky as the ones in which you have to write your own equation. If you're more comfortable substituting numbers, though, it's still a great way to do the problem.

5. C.   The equation $x^2 - 4x - 32 = 0$ expands out into $(x - 8)(x + 4) = 0$, so the solutions are 8 and -4. Watch out for trap answers such as -8 and 4.

6. C.   This is a great problem to use the answer choices instead of writing a lot of complex equations. Let's say the price of a ticket without the discount is x. If the discount is 5%, then $4x = (5x) - 0.5(5x)$. We can simplify that and instead of finding the discount and subtracting it, we'll just take the percentage we would pay with the discount included. So, our new equation is $4x = 0.95(5x)$. That doesn't work out mathematically, and in fact, it's way off. So A is incorrect, and B is close to A, so let's skip B and try C. A 20% discount means that each person will pay 80% of the individual price, so the equation is $4x = 0.8(5x)$. That works out perfectly, so C is our answer!

7. B.   Again, this is a great problem to just try the answer choices. If the shorter board is "5 inches less than half" the longer board, we could just use the answer choices as the length of the shorter board, add five, and multiply by two. A doesn't work—if the shorter board is 25, the longer board would be 60, and those don't add up to 100. B works—a shorter board of 30 gives us a longer board of 70 (remember, add 5 then multiply by 2), and those add up to 100.

8. C.   Depending on how familiar you are with the theory behind averages, you may want to substitute real numbers in this problem. Let's make it simple and suppose $s = 2$. Your two numbers are 17 and 19, giving you an average of 18. Their sum is 36, and only answer choice C equals 36.

9. E.   First we have to manipulate the equation to get it into a standard form. By adding 27 to both sides, we get $x^2 - 12x + 27 = 0$ . . . something we're a little more used to seeing. Factoring this quadratic gives us $(x - 3)(x - 9) = 0$, so our roots are 3 and 9.

10. D.   The rate formula is a great help on problems like these, so remember $r = \frac{d}{t}$. For the trip down the mountain, the rate is 1.5 times the "up" rate of 4 miles per day, so the rate is 6 miles per day. The time is 2 days because it is equal to amount of time it takes to go up the mountain. Substituting those numbers in the formula allows you to solve for the distance, which is 12 miles.

CHAPTER 5

Probability and Statistics

INTRODUCTION

Probability and statistics are some of the most relevant quantitative skills tested on the GMAT. In your future life as a Master of Business Administration, you will probably do a lot of data forecasting and interpretation, and therefore you will do a lot of it in business school. The good news is that even if you don't work with this stuff on an everyday basis, the probability and statistics that you will see on the GMAT are not very hard mathematically; all you need is to brush up on a few math terms, a few formulas, and some pretty basic calculations.

> If the set S is composed of the following numbers {99, 100, 100, 105, 106, 116, 123}, which of the following is largest?
>
> A. The average (arithmetic mean) of set S
> B. The median of set S
> C. The mode of set S
> D. The range of set S
> E. The standard deviation of set S

A little ballparking takes you a long way on questions like this, and you may be able to discard two or even three answers the first time you read the problem. In the end though, there's no way you're going to get around knowing all this terminology if you really want a good score on the GMAT. So let's review.

THE MEAN

The *mean* is simply the average value of a set of numbers. On the GMAT this concept is usually written as "the average (arithmetic mean)," as in the preceding problem. To find the mean, sum the *values* of all the elements, and divide by the *number* of elements. So, for example, the mean of the set {99, 100, 100, 105, 106, 116, 123} is

$$\frac{99 + 100 + 100 + 105 + 106 + 116 + 123}{7} = \frac{749}{7} = 107$$

When dealing with this sort of calculation, there are two strategies:

1. *Just do it*. If the list is short and the numbers are relatively uncomplicated, then you shouldn't be averse to whipping out the pencil for a little addition and long division.
2. *Get clever*. The other approach is to look for a pattern, either among the numbers in the set or in the answer choices. The GMAT often makes this possible. Consider this example:

What is the average (arithmetic mean) of the set {105, 106, 107, 108, 109, 110, 111, 112, 113}?

  A. 108.5
  B. 109
  C. 110
  D. 968
  E. 981

You could definitely get this problem right by carefully adding up all the numbers and then dividing by the number of elements. $105 + 106 + 107 + 108 + 109 + 110 + 111 + 112 + 113 = 981$, and $981/9 = 109$, or answer choice B.

However, you could also look for a pattern. In arithmetic mean problems, if all the numbers in the list are evenly spaced—for example, if they're consecutive (as in the problem above) or if each one is 4 larger than the previous one—then the mean will just be the middle number. That's just how it works. If there is an even number of evenly spaced numbers in the list (such as 2, 4, 6, 8), you just take the mean of the middle two numbers (giving you 5 in this case).

You have to make sure that every number in the list follows the pattern, or the rule doesn't apply. However, if one number is slightly off, you may be able to do a little ballparking. For example, if you're asked to find the arithmetic mean of 28, 30, 32, 34, and 37, the mean clearly isn't going to be 32, but it's going to be just slightly larger than 32. One number getting slightly larger isn't going to change the mean all that much. (Go ahead, try it.)

If picking the middle number in an ordered list sounds familiar, that's because it's also how you calculate a median (more on that in a bit). So if you have an evenly-spaced list with an odd number of numbers, the middle number is both the mean and the median.

GMAT questions are often solvable by tricks like this because the GMAT actually wants to know whether you can spot these sorts of shortcuts. Knowing how to navigate through large data sets and complicated series of numbers quickly can make a big difference in, say, a complicated marketing case, so this sort of ability will be very important in your first year of MBA studies.

THE MEDIAN

The *median* is just the middle value in a set. By the middle value, we mean the value that has just as many elements in the set that are less than it as it has elements in the set that are greater than it. Returning to our set in the last example,

$$\{105, 106, 107, 108, 109, 110, 111, 112, 113\}$$

the median is 109, as 109 is the middle value, i.e., it is the fifth value in a set of nine. If we rearrange the order of the values to

$$\{113, 107, 111, 109, 108, 110, 106, 105, 112\}$$

the median is still 109, since four elements in the set are still less than 109 and four elements in the set are still greater than 109. Therefore, the order of values in a set does not affect the median. In this set the median coincides with the mean, but it does not have to.

Consider the following set:

$$\{99, 100, 100, 105, 106, 116, 123\}$$

The median is 105, because it is the middle number in a set of seven. If there is an even number of elements in the set, then the median is the number halfway between the two middle numbers. For example, in the set

$$\{105, 108, 110, 112, 114, 115\}$$

the median value is 111, since this is halfway between the two middle values, in other words, its average or arithmetic mean. If there are eight elements in a set, then the median is the average of elements four and five. If there are ten elements in a set, then the median is the average of elements five and six. Remember that a set can have only one median.

There's no real difficulty in calculating a median, but that doesn't mean the test writers can't make it tricky by presenting the numbers out of order or by making you create the list for them in some way. Just remember to create an ordered list and pick the middle number (or average the middle two numbers). For example:

A small car dealership charted its car sales for a two-week period on the chart below. For each number of cars sold, the dealership can now see on how many days they sold that many cars. What is the median number of cars sold on one day in the two-week period?

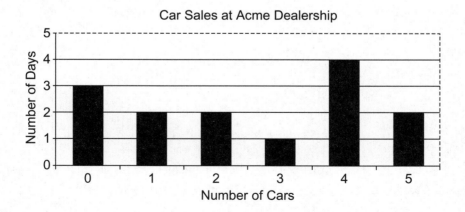

A. 2.5
B. 3
C. 3.5
D. 4
E. 5

To solve this problem, you have to create the list of numbers for yourself. The car dealership sold 0 cars on three separate days, so your list should have three zeroes: 0, 0, 0. The dealership sold 1 car on two separate days, so you can add two ones to the list: 0, 0, 0, 1, 1. And so on, until you have fourteen numbers in the list, one for each day in the two-week period. Your final list should look like this: 0, 0, 0, 1, 1, 2, 2, 3, 4, 4, 4, 4, 5, 5. Because there is an even number of numbers in the list, you would average the middle two (2 and 3) to get your median, which is 2.5.

THE MODE

The *mode* is just the most common element in a set. In the set

$$\{99, 100, 100, 105, 106, 116, 123\}$$

the mode is 100, because this number appears twice, while all other elements appear only once. Note that a set can have more than one mode. In the set

$$\{2, 2, 3, 3, 4, 5, 6, 7, 7, 8, 9\}$$

there are three modes: 2, 3, and 7. Each value appears twice.

The mode is not a difficult thing to calculate. If you encounter this sort of question, inspect the set, watch for tricks (like values out of order), pick the appropriate answer choice, and move on. If you are having trouble figuring out the mode, rewrite the elements in increasing order, just as you would do to find the median, and the mode (or modes) will become apparent.

THE RANGE

The *range* of a set is just the difference between the largest and smallest elements. If that seems simple, it is. For example, the range of the set

$$\{105, 106, 107, 108, 109, 110, 111, 112, 113\}$$

is 8, since $113 - 105 = 8$. Similarly, the range of the set

$$\{99, 100, 100, 105, 106, 116, 123\}$$

is 24, since $123 - 99 = 24$. The number of times that the smallest and largest elements appear is not relevant; what matters is that they are the smallest and largest elements.

CALCULATING THE STANDARD DEVIATION

Quickly, the standard deviation is the square root of the result of the summation of the squares of the differences between the individual values of the set and the mean, divided by the number of items in the set. Does that sound like something you could do in two minutes? No? Well, don't worry, because the GMAT won't ask you to. In plain English, the standard deviation tells us how spread out the values are in a set. A set with values that are tightly clustered together, such as

$$\{105, 106, 107, 108, 109, 110, 111, 112, 113\}$$

will have a small standard deviation, while a set with widely separated numbers, such as

$$\{2, 43, 187, 500, 1024\}$$

will have a large standard deviation, because the numbers *deviate* more from the *standard*. This means that you can get a sense of the standard deviation just by inspecting the elements in the set. There are really only two ways that the GMAT tends to test this concept. Try this example, which resembles some of the standard deviation questions that have appeared on past GMATs:

Which of the following sets has the largest standard deviation?

A. $\{107, 107, 108, 108, 109, 110, 110, 111, 111\}$
B. $\{105, 106, 107, 108, 109, 110, 111, 112, 113\}$
C. $\{101, 103, 105, 107, 109, 111, 113, 115, 117\}$
D. $\{106, 106, 107, 107, 108, 108, 109, 109, 1111\}$
E. $\{0, 106, 107, 108, 109, 110, 111, 112, 113\}$

The answer is D. Since standard deviation is a measure of the average deviation from the mean, clearly answer choices A, B, and C, which all have numbers clustered very closely together, will have small standard deviations. D and E both have "outlying" numbers that are farther away from the cluster of similar numbers (and therefore farther away from the mean). The 0 in answer choice E is about 100 away from the mean, but the 1111 in D is about 900 away, meaning the standard deviation of D will be much larger.

It is doubtful that you will ever have a problem on the GMAT that requires you to actually calculate the standard deviation instead of estimating, as we just did. If you want to be superprepared, though, here is how to do it: Mathematically, the standard deviation is

$$\sigma = \sqrt{\dfrac{\sum_{i=1}^{n}\left(\bar{x} - x_i\right)^2}{n}}$$

where $\bar{x}$ is the mean, and n is the number of elements.

To calculate this by hand,

1. Calculate the mean: ($\bar{x}$)
2. Subtract each value in the set from the mean (thus creating another set): ($\bar{x} - x_i$).
3. Square each of the values: $(\bar{x} - x_i)^2$
4. Add together all the values in this set (that is, sum the squares): $\sum_{i=1}^{n}(\bar{x} - x_i)^2$
5. Divide the sum by the number of values in the set: $\sum_{i=1}^{n}(\bar{x} - x_i)^2/n$
6. Take the square root of this value: $\sqrt{\sum_{i=1}^{n}(\bar{x} - x_i)^2/n}$

The other type of standard deviation question you might encounter on the GMAT provides you with the standard deviation for a set and tests whether you know what that means. A question could appear like the following:

> A set has an average (arithmetic mean) of 42 and a standard deviation of 1.8. Which of the following values is two standard deviations away from the mean?
>
> A. 36
> B. 38.4
> C. 40.2
> D. 43.8
> E. 75.6

Numbers that are one standard deviation away from the mean are simply the numbers you get by adding the standard deviation to the mean OR subtracting the standard deviation from the mean. So a number that is one standard deviation (1.8) away from a mean of 42 could either be 40.2 or 43.8.

To find a number that is two standard deviations from the mean, you just multiply the standard deviation by 2, and again, add or subtract from the mean. So when the standard deviation is 1.8, two standard deviations equal 3.6, and two standard deviations away from a mean of 42 would be 38.4 or 45.6. If you want to see that in equation form, it's $42 \pm 2(1.8) = 38.4$ and 45.6.

Pretty simple stuff when compared to actually calculating standard deviation, right? Well, the good news is that that's pretty much all you will need for solving standard deviation problems on the GMAT.

You should have enough information now to answer the question posed at the beginning of the chapter:

> If the set S is composed of the following numbers {99, 100, 100, 105, 106, 116, 123}, which of the following is largest?
>
> A. The average (arithmetic mean) of set S
> B. The median of set S
> C. The mode of set S
> D. The range of set S
> E. The standard deviation of set S

Let's start with choice A. We've calculated the mean, and we know that it is 107. This is larger than the median, which is 105; even if we had not calculated the mean exactly, we could estimate that the mean is greater than the median because the three numbers greater than the median are relatively farther away from 105 than the three numbers less than the median. We know that the mode is 100, which is less than 107. We know that the range is $123 - 99 = 24$, which is less than 107. And while we don't want to waste time calculating the standard deviation of this set, we can see that the numbers aren't too far apart, so we can assume that the standard deviation is a relatively small number (it's actually around 9). Therefore, the answer has to be A, the average of set S.

WHAT YOU NEED TO REMEMBER

The *mean*	is the average of a set, or the sum of its values divided by the number of elements.
The *median*	is the middle value of a set. Note that if there is an odd number of elements in the set, the median will be in the set, but if there is an even number of elements, the median will be the value halfway between the two middle-most elements.
The *mode*	is the most common element in the set. Note that there may be more than one mode.
The *range*	is the span of the set. It is the smallest value subtracted from the largest.
The *standard deviation*	is a measure of the degree to which the values in a set are spread out.

APPLICATION PROBLEMS—STATISTICS

The GMAT sometimes tests statistical concepts visually. The next several problems involve the data set at the right and the graph below. Each of the points at the right is plotted on the graph as an X-Y pair (the Xs run horizontally, and the Ys vertically). Since these are drill questions, they will differ a bit from those on the GMAT. While you can calculate the values by hand, you shouldn't need to do so, and you probably wouldn't be able to do so in the two minutes or so that you'll have for each question.

X	Y
22.3428	0.2141
7.6654	11.1677
8.5955	0.8881
14.3589	0.5454
17.6411	1.7067
6.4042	13.4480
21.6396	0.3005
19.4805	6.6545
12.9962	7.2681
10.5549	10.5108
18.3253	3.8199
19.0539	24.7435
6.7122	8.4796
11.9699	2.8641
7.9197	3.2149
9.7871	3.0499
11.0604	1.4132
4.3302	0.8355
5.6040	1.7807
8.5695	3.0499
2.5882	1.7312
1.0875	0.1513
3.1519	0.4525
0.7774	1.3067
0.9194	0.2024
0.0596	0.0367
0.8907	0.1811
2.8510	0.3191
1.9444	0.9149
0.5687	0.3620

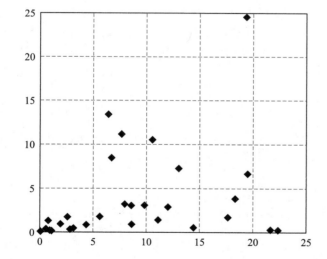

1. Which is greater, the mean of the Xs or the mean of the Ys?
2. Which is greater, the median of the Xs or the median of the Ys?
3. Which is greater, the range of the Xs or the range of the Ys?
4. Which is greater, the mode of the Xs or the mode of the Ys?

Solutions

1. **X.** The mean of the Xs is approximately 8.5, and the mean of the Ys is around 3.5. You could add up the sums by hand and then divide by 30 to get an exact figure, but if the GMAT gives you a distribution like this, you would be better off saving your time by estimating it visually. Six of the X values are over 15, while only one Y value is over 15, which is a pretty strong indicator that the Xs have a higher mean.

2. **X.** The median X is 7.7925, but the median Y is only 1.5600. You could line the numbers up from least to greatest, and then pull out the middle values, but that would take time. The quicker approach is to see where the weight lies along each dimension. The Xs appear to be reasonably evenly distributed along their axis, but the Ys clearly cluster toward the bottom.

   You might note that there are times when the mean of one set will be larger, but the median of the other will be the greater. That would be a fine observation; it's just not the case here.

3. **Y.** The range of the Xs is 22.2832, and the range of the Ys is 24.7068. Range is an easy value to calculate; you just need to identify the outliers for both X and Y and see which ones have the bigger range. You could also do this visually; there are both X and Y values very close to 0, but there is a Y value, 24.7435, that is clearly larger than the largest X value, 22.3428. Even without calculating an exact range, you could estimate that the range of the Ys would be about 2.5 larger than the range for the Xs.

4. **Y.** The Ys have two points with values of 3.0499, while the Xs have no repeat value. Since the Ys have a mode and the Xs do not, the Ys have the higher mode.

PROBABILITY

The GMAT tests your knowledge of probability in a number of different ways, but all of the questions boil down to the same concept. The probability that an event X will occur =

$$\frac{\text{The number of possible outcomes in which X occurs}}{\text{The total number of possible outcomes}}$$

If event X happens in every possible outcome, the probability is 100% or 1. If event X doesn't happen in any of the possible outcomes, the probability is 0% or simply 0. For example, if you reach into a bag that contains only 20 green jellybeans, the probability that you will pull out a green jellybean is 20/20, or 100%. The probability you will pull a purple jellybean out of the bag is 0/20 or 0, because there are 0 purple jellybeans out of the 20 jellybeans in the bag.

Of course, if we dealt only with certainties, it wouldn't be called "probability," so the test makers generally ask probability questions in which the probability of an event is somewhere between 0 and 1. A simple probability question might ask:

> A bag contains 26 purple jellybeans, 15 green jellybeans, and 9 yellow jellybeans; these jellybeans are the only items in the bag. If a person picks a jellybean at random out of the bag, what is the probability that the jellybean will be green?
>
> A. 15%
> B. 20%
> C. 25%
> D. 30%
> E. 35%

To get the answer, we divide the number of outcomes in which the desired event occurs by the total possible number of outcomes. If there are 15 green jellybeans out of a total of $26 + 15 + 9 = 50$ jellybeans, then the probability that one picked at random will be green is $15/50 = 0.3 = 30\%$, answer D.

The test makers make these problems more complicated by changing the number of items in the middle of the question and by asking the question from a different angle from what you may be expecting. A more difficult probability question might look like this:

> A bag contains 26 purple jellybeans, 15 green jellybeans, and 9 yellow jellybeans; these jellybeans are the only items in the bag. If a person reaches into the bag and picks out only purple jellybeans, how many jellybeans would the person have to pick out in order to double the probability that a jellybean picked out of the bag at random would be a green jellybean?
>
> A. 5
> B. 15
> C. 19
> D. 24
> E. 25

To solve this problem, you would first need to figure out what it means to double the probability of picking a green jellybean at random. Your first step would be to determine the initial odds of picking a green jellybean; we know from the last question that those odds are $15/50 = 0.3 = 30\%$. Doubled odds, therefore, are 60%, or 0.6. Since the person picking out the jellybeans in this question is picking only purple jellybeans, we know that the number of green jellybeans remains the same, 15. If x is the new total of jellybeans after the person picks out the purples, we can set up the equation:

$$0.6 = \frac{15}{x} \implies 0.6x = 15 \implies x = \frac{15}{0.6} = 25$$

So the new total of jellybeans must be 25. If the original total was 50, a person would have to pick out 50 − 25 = 25 purple jellybeans in order to double the probability of picking a green jellybean at random.

Or if equations aren't really your strong suit, you can just use the answer choices to help out. Knowing that you want a probability of 60% for the green jellybeans, let's say that you're going to take 19 purple jellybeans out of the bag (which is answer choice C). That would leave you with 7 purple + 15 green + 9 yellow = 31 jellybeans. The probability is 15/31, which is less than half, so you need to take out quite a few more jellybeans. Using answer choice E gives 1 purple + 15 green + 9 yellow = 25 total, and greens are 15/25, which equals 60%. Bingo.

This process may feel like it's taking a while, but it's a very reliable method for solving some probability problems that seem hard to approach otherwise, so it's a good tool to have.

Conditional Probabilities

Things get a little more complicated when you're asked to figure out the probability of two or more events happening. For example, let's take an example, hopefully not pulled from your life: Let's say the probability of your computer crashing on any given day at work is 1/5. The probability of your boss having a screaming fit on any given workday is 1/3. What is the probability of your computer crashing and your boss having a screaming fit on the same workday? To calculate the probability of separate events all happening, you just multiply the probabilities of the individual events together. So in this example, the probability of both events happening on the same workday is 1/5 × 1/3 = 1/15. That's great; you only have to look forward to one of those joyful days every three weeks or so!

That's what happens when calculating the probability of multiple events; because you're multiplying fractions, the probabilities start to get very small. And no matter how many events you have, you just keep multiplying the probabilities; so if your car also doesn't start on the first try about every one in four workdays, the probability of your computer crashing, your boss having a screaming fit, and your car not starting on the first try is 1/5 × 1/3 × 1/4 = 1/60. So that's pretty rare, thank goodness.

But what if you want to figure out the probability of event X OR event Y happening? For example, let's say you live in a city with great public transportation, and either the 37 bus or the 51 bus can take you to work from the bus stop right in front of your apartment. The 37 bus arrives every 5 minutes and the 51 bus arrives every 8 minutes. In any given minute that you stand at the bus stop, what is the probability of a bus arriving that can take you to work? Well, the probability of the 37 bus arriving is 1/5, because it will arrive during 1 minute of every 5 minutes. Similarly, the probability of the 51 bus arriving is 1/8. But you don't need both buses; either one would do. So you don't multiply; you add. If you're not very familiar with adding fractions, you can always convert to decimals and add from there. 1/5 is equal to 0.2 and 1/8 is equal to 0.125. (And if you didn't know those off the top of your head, go back to Chapter 3 to brush up on converting fractions to decimals.) So your addition problem is 0.2 + 0.125, which is 0.325.

If this were a set of real answer choices, how would you know which of them equals 0.325? Since it's a probability problem, the answer choices are going to be expressed as fractions, so all you have to do is divide the numerators by the denominators to figure out which one equals 0.325. And of course, don't forget to ballpark; you can completely eliminate answer choices that aren't close to 1/3. If you add fractions, you will get $1/5 + 1/8 = 13/40$.

Another concept you will need to know is the probability that something *won't* happen. It's not too tough to figure out, but sometimes more complex problems will be easier to figure out if you deal with the probability that something won't happen instead of the probability that something will happen. For instance, consider the following problem:

> A jar has three black marbles and three white marbles. If you draw four marbles, replacing each marble before drawing the next one, what is the probability that you will draw at least one white marble?
>
> A. $\dfrac{1}{16}$
>
> B. $\dfrac{1}{4}$
>
> C. $\dfrac{1}{2}$
>
> D. $\dfrac{3}{8}$
>
> E. $\dfrac{15}{16}$

First of all, there is an equal number of black and white marbles and that ratio will remain constant throughout, since you're replacing each marble you draw. So you can just treat this problem as if there are only two marbles: one black and one white.

Regardless of whether you use that shortcut, one way to do this problem is to create a probability tree. This is a good tool to use when there are relatively few possibilities; simply sketch them out, like so:

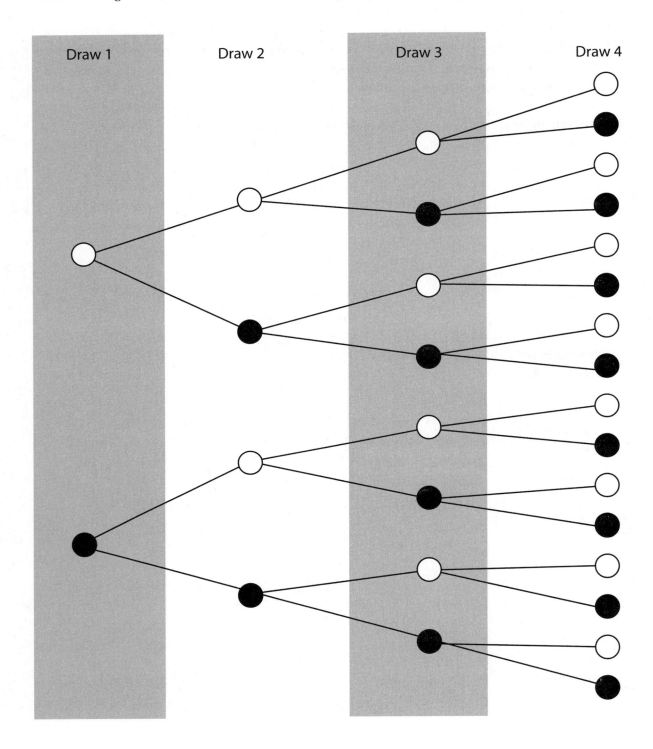

What the sketch represents is this: on draw 1, you have two possibilities: white or black. On draw 2, you also have two possibilities: white or black. And so on until draw 4 is complete. The number of possibilities in the final column is the total number of possibilities, which in this case is 16. That goes in the denominator of the fraction. But what goes in the numerator? Any set of draws that contains at least one white marble. Just follow the paths to see which possibilities those are. Fifteen of the paths have at least one white marble, so the answer is 15/16, or choice E.

If sketching isn't your preference, you can write out the possibilities, but it may be harder to systematically keep track of which possibilities you've already accounted for. This is how it would look to write out the possibilities:

WWWW	BWWW
WWWB	BWWB
WWBW	BWBW
WWBB	BWBB
WBWW	BBWW
WBWB	BBWB
WBBW	BBBW
WBBB	BBBB

Either way, you can see that there are sixteen possibilities, and fifteen of them contain at least one white marble. But what if instead of figuring out how many possibilities contained at least one white marble, you asked the opposite question: How many possibilities contain *all black* marbles? Then the problem gets easier to figure out; looking at either the sketch or the list, you can see that only one possibility in sixteen consists of all black marbles, meaning the remaining fifteen possibilities contain at least one white marble. But when we throw in another shortcut, it gets even easier. Ready?

When you're calculating the probability of multiple events and there is the same number of possibilities in each event, you can simply take the number of possibilities on each event, and raise it to the number of events, and you have the denominator of your fraction. Like this: If there are two different possibilities for each draw (black and white), and there are four draws, your fraction looks like this:

$$\frac{?}{2^4} = \frac{?}{16}$$

Now all you have to do to solve the problem is find the number of possibilities that meet the requirements that the problem is asking for. If there is only one possibility with all black marbles, that leaves fifteen possibilities with at least one white marble. So no matter which way you calculate it, the correct answer is 15/16.

At this point you may be asking, why can't we just give you one way to calculate probability? Well, we could, but probability is tested in so many different ways it actually works more to your advantage to know several different ways of calculating it. When it gets confusing though, remember that it all boils down to the basics. Write down the formula, figure out how many possibilities there are total, and then figure out how many of the possibilities are the ones the problem is asking for. If you need to, write it all out and get there by brute force; don't spend five minutes deciding which method would be quicker to use.

Finally, remember your ballparking skills. If you're calculating the probability that multiple things will happen, the result is going to get smaller the more fractions you multiply in there. If the requirements are easy to meet (such as "at least one white marble in four draws"), the result is going to be pretty close to 1. If the requirements are hard to meet (such as in "given a six-sided die that you roll twice, what is the probability you will end up with two rolls that add up to more than 10?") the result is going to be pretty close to zero.

So far, you have dealt with conditional probabilities that are *independent,* which means that what happens in one event has no effect on the next event. A coin is tossed and whether it's heads or tails has no effect on the outcome of the next toss. A die is rolled and no matter which number it lands on, each number has the same chance of coming up on the second roll that it did on the first roll: 1/6. You draw marbles out of a jar and put them back, so there is no change on the number of marbles in the jar for each draw.

But, what if the problem specifies that you keep the marbles out of the jar instead of putting them back? It's not difficult to deal with, but it is a situation you should be familiar with before you take the actual test. So let's look at an example problem:

A drawer contains four red socks, six blue socks, and five black socks. If you draw two socks from the drawer at random, what is the probability that both of them will be blue?

A. $\dfrac{16}{225}$

B. $\dfrac{1}{9}$

C. $\dfrac{1}{7}$

D. $\dfrac{4}{25}$

E. $\dfrac{53}{70}$

Drawing two socks out of a drawer at the same time is the same as drawing them one right after the other without putting them back, so we consider them two separate draws for the sake of easier math. On the first draw, there are six blue socks out of fifteen socks total, so your first draw is 6/15 (or 2/5 if you reduce, to make the rest of the calculation easier). On the second draw, there are five blue socks remaining, but this time it's out of 14 socks, not 15. So the fraction for the second draw is 5/14. Multiply them together and reduce to get your answer.

$$2/5 \times 5/14 = 10/70 = 1/7$$

$$\frac{2}{5} \times \frac{5}{14} = \frac{10}{70}$$

Reduce and you get 1/7, so choice C is the correct answer.

Now let's look at a more complex example, using a situation from real life in which otherwise ordinary people become consumed with the minutiae of conditional probability: the last two rounds of a hypothetical ACC basketball tournament. Duke is about to play North Carolina in the first game of the next-to-last round. After that, regardless of what happens in that game, Maryland (fear that turtle) will play Virginia. We'll assume that this year North Carolina has the strongest team, but that anything can happen when two teams meet on the court. Well, not quite: we'll include some probabilities in our model so that we can estimate, *ex ante*, what might happen. We'll use the table shown here as our compilation of those probabilities.

Example: ACC Tournament Matchups—Probability that the Team at Left will Win

	Duke	UNC	UVa	Maryland
Duke				
UNC	0.65			
UVa	0.45	0.50		
Maryland	0.30	0.35	0.45	

What is the probability, from the vantage point of the opening buzzer of the Duke–UNC game, that any of these teams will win the tournament? To determine that, the first thing to do is to lay out a probability tree. The tree has three stages:

1. The Duke–UNC game, with two possible outcomes. Duke has a 35 percent chance of winning, and (since the totals sum to one) UNC has a 65 percent chance of winning.
2. The Maryland–Virginia game, with (again) two possible outcomes. This part of the tree is replicated for each possible outcome of the Duke–UNC game. That's because there are four ways that this could play out:
   a. Duke could beat UNC, and Maryland could beat UVa.
   b. Duke could beat UNC, and UVa could beat Maryland.
   c. UNC could beat Duke, and Maryland could beat UVa.
   d. UNC could beat Duke, and UVa could beat Maryland.

In this case, the probabilities do not affect one another—the games are *independent events*.

3. Lastly, the winners of the two games will meet in the final. As with our four possible two-game outcomes, we'll have four corresponding possibilities for a final round:

   a. Duke plays Maryland
   b. Duke plays UVa
   c. UNC plays Maryland
   d. UNC plays UVa

Example: ACC Tournament—Probability Tree

	Penultimate Round		Final Round
	First Game	*Second Game*	

But how do you calculate the probability that those underdog Terrapins (i.e., Maryland) will win the tournament? By multiplying the probabilities, as you have done before.

Thus, the probability that Duke will beat UNC in the first game of the next to last round, that Maryland will beat Virginia in the second game, and that Maryland will then beat Duke in the finals is

$$0.35 \bullet 0.045 \bullet 0.30 = 0.0473 \text{ or } 4.73\%$$

That doesn't look so good, but there are other possibilities. As the following spreadsheet shows, we can multiply all of these triplets through to find the probability for any one specific outcome.

Example: ACC Basketball Tournament—Outcomes

Winner	Probability	Winner	Probability	Winner	Probability	Overall Probability
Duke	0.35	Maryland	0.45	Duke	0.70	0.1102
Duke	0.35	Maryland	0.45	Maryland	0.30	**0.0473**
Duke	0.35	UVa	0.55	Duke	0.55	0.1059
Duke	0.35	UVa	0.55	UVa	0.45	0.0866
UNC	0.65	Maryland	0.45	UNC	0.65	0.1901
UNC	0.65	Maryland	0.45	Maryland	0.35	**0.1024**
UNC	0.65	UVa	0.55	UNC	0.50	0.1788
UNC	0.65	UVa	0.55	UVa	0.50	0.1788
					Total	1.000

If you add the numbers in the rightmost column, you'll note that they actually add to 1.0001. That's rounding error—the point is that the probabilities actually sum to 1, or 100 percent, which is what we need to see. At this point, to find the probability that the Terrapins will go all the way, we add the probabilities of the two ways in which it could happen:

► Duke beats UNC, Maryland beats Virginia, Maryland beats Duke (4.73%).
► UNC beats Duke, Maryland beats Virginia, Maryland beats UNC (10.24%).

Thus there are two possible ways, with a combined probability of 14.97 percent, for Maryland to win the whole thing.

Please note that on the actual GMAT, you are very unlikely to see any questions dealing with actual sports teams, on the grounds that such questions would give an unfair advantage to those test takers who are well versed in the sport in question. So no, your time spent watching ESPN does not count as preparation for the GMAT.

PRACTICE PROBLEMS

1. Lottery balls numbered consecutively from 1 through 100 are placed in a spinner. If one ball is drawn at random, what is the probability that it will have the number 1 on it at least once?

A. $\dfrac{9}{100}$

B. $\dfrac{1}{10}$

C. $\dfrac{11}{100}$

D. $\dfrac{19}{100}$

E. $\dfrac{1}{5}$

Month	Noah's Landing	Bellaville
1	3	2
2	2	0
3	0	4
4	2	x
5	1	1

2. Monthly rainfall was recorded for two towns over a five-month period using the chart above. If the median rainfall in Noah's Landing was equal to the average (arithmetic mean) rainfall in Bellaville, what is the value of x?

A. 1

B. $\dfrac{8}{5}$

C. 2

D. 3

E. 10

3. If x is a positive, single-digit integer such that $\frac{4}{3}x$, $2x$, x, and $x+2$, and $3x-2$ form a non-ordered list of consecutive integers, which of the following could be the median of that list?

A. 3

B. 4

C. 5

D. 6

E. 8

4. If the sum of a list of five consecutive odd integers is 5, which of the following could be true?

   I. The average (arithmetic mean) of the list is equal to 5.

  II. The median of the list is equal to 5.

 III. The range of the list is equal to 5.

A. None

B. I only

C. II only

D. I and II

E. I and III

5. A jar contains only red, yellow, and orange marbles. If there are 3 red, 5 yellow, and 4 orange marbles, and 3 marbles are chosen from the jar at random without replacing any of them, what is the probability that 2 yellow, 1 red, and no orange marbles will be chosen?

A. $\dfrac{1}{60}$

B. $\dfrac{1}{45}$

C. $\dfrac{2}{45}$

D. $\dfrac{3}{22}$

E. $\dfrac{5}{22}$

Day	Price
Monday	17.94
Tuesday	18.19
Wednesday	18.06
Thursday	17.54
Friday	17.38

6. Closing prices for a certain stock were recorded each day for a week in the table above. If the monthly average (arithmetic mean) was 18.43 and the standard deviation was 0.27, how many days during this week did the closing price fall within two standard deviations from the average?

A. 1

B. 2

C. 3

D. 4

E. 5

7. A freight elevator can carry a maximum load of 1200 pounds. Sean, who weighs 200 pounds, is in the elevator with two packages weighing 150 pounds and 280 pounds. If he needs to fit three more packages in the elevator that weigh as much as possible without exceeding the elevator limit, what is the difference between their average and the average of the two packages already in the elevator?

A. 25

B. 85

C. 190

D. 215

E. 210

8. WINK, Inc. follows a certain procedure that requires two tasks to be finished independently in order for a job to be done. On any given day, there is a $\frac{7}{8}$ probability that task 1 will be completed on time, and a $\frac{3}{5}$ probability that task 2 will be completed on time. On a certain day, what is the probability that task 1 will be completed on time, but task 2 will not?

A. $\frac{1}{20}$

B. $\frac{3}{40}$

C. $\frac{13}{40}$

D. $\frac{7}{20}$

E. $\frac{13}{40}$

The following data sufficiency problems consist of a question and two statements, labeled (1) and (2), in which certain data are given. You have to decide whether the data given in the statements are *sufficient* for answering the question. Using the data given in the statements *plus* your knowledge of mathematics and everyday facts (such as the number of days in July or the meaning of *counter-clockwise*), you must indicate whether

    A. **Statement (1) ALONE is sufficient, but statement (2) alone is not sufficient.**

    B. **Statement (2) ALONE is sufficient, but statement (1) alone is not sufficient.**

    C. **BOTH statements TOGETHER are sufficient, but NEITHER statement ALONE is sufficient.**

    D. **EACH statement ALONE is sufficient.**

    E. **Statements (1) and (2) TOGETHER are NOT sufficient.**

9. Kara attends a university where students study for an average (arithmetic mean) of 13.4 hours per week. How many hours per week does Kara study?

    (1) The standard deviation of study time at Kara's school is 2.8.

    (2) Kara's study time is one standard deviation away from the mean.

10. The cards in a deck are numbered consecutively from 1 to 20. If some cards are red and some cards are black, what is the probability of drawing a red card?

    (1) The odd-numbered cards are all red.

    (2) The even-numbered cards are all black.

Solutions

1. E. The balls with the number 1 on them at least once are 1, 10, 11, 12, 13, 14, 15, 16, 17, 18, 19, 21, 31, 41, 51, 61, 71, 81, 91, and 100. Count them up and you get 20 balls out of 100, or 1/5.

2. D. Noah's Landing had a median rainfall of 2 inches, because if we put the numbers in an ordered list (0, 1, 2, 2, 3), the middle number is 2. That means Bellaville had a mean of 2 inches. Since the mean is just the total of the numbers divided by the number of numbers, and there are five numbers in the list, the total of that list must be 10. When we subtract the existing values from 10, we get $10 - 2 - 0 - 4 - 1 = 3$.

3. C. Since there are only nine single-digit, positive integers, and not all of them will yield integers when we use them in these algebraic expressions, let's start with trying to find a value for x that will give us a list of consecutive integers. 1 won't work, since $\frac{4}{3} \times 1$ is not an integer. Same with 2. When we use 3, though, we get $\frac{4}{3} \times 3 = 4$; that's an integer. The other expressions give us $2 \times 3 = 6$, 3, $3 + 2 = 5$, and $3 \times 3 - 2 = 7$. So our group includes 4, 6, 3, 5, and 7. They aren't in order, but they don't have to be according to the problem, and they are consecutive. But be careful! The problem asks for the median of the list, not the value of x. The median of the list 3, 4, 5, 6, 7 is 5.

4. A. Let's start by finding a list of five consecutive odd integers that add up to 5. −3, −1, 1, 3, and 5 is one such list. In fact, can you think of another? There isn't one, so now we just have to see which of the Roman numerals is true in this case. I isn't true—the mean is 1. II is also untrue—the median is also 1. And the range is 8, so none of the Roman numerals are possible, and A is our answer.

5. D. It doesn't really matter in which order we draw the marbles since they're really all drawn at once, but from a mathematical standpoint, it's much easier to take these probabilities one at a time. Let's first take the probability of drawing a yellow marble from the jar. Since there are 5 yellow marbles out of 12 marbles total, the probability of drawing a yellow marble is $\frac{5}{12}$. The probability of drawing a yellow marble after that is $\frac{4}{11}$, since one yellow marble is missing and one marble is missing from the total. Finally, the probability of drawing a red marble is $\frac{3}{10}$. So the probability of drawing the specified combination of marbles is $\frac{5}{12} \times \frac{4}{11} \times \frac{3}{10} = \frac{60}{1320}$. Once we reduce we get $\frac{1}{22}$. But since the order we draw in does not matter, we need to multiply this by the number of ways to arrange the three drawn marbles. It could be YYR, RYY, or YRY, for a total of 3 possible arrangements. So our total probability is $\frac{1}{22} \times 3$, or $\frac{3}{22}$.

6. C. Since two standard deviations away from the mean works out to 18.3 − 2.7 × 2 = 17.89, there are 3 days during which the stock prices fell between 17.89 and 18.3: Monday, Tuesday, and Wednesday. We really don't have to worry about prices above the mean, because there were none of them during this time frame.

7. A. Sean and the two packages in the elevator weigh 630 pounds together, so the three packages Sean wants to put into the elevator must weigh a maximum of 1200−630, or 570. If we divide that by 3, we get the average weight of each package, 190. The two packages already in the elevator weigh a total of 430 together, so their average weight is 215. Subtract 190 from 215 and we get the difference in the averages, or 25.

8. D. Task 1 has a $\frac{7}{8}$ probability of being completed on time, and task 2 has a $\frac{3}{5}$ probability of being completed on time, which can also be expressed as a $\frac{2}{5}$ probability of *not* being completed on time, which is what the problem asked for. Multiply the probabilities and we get $\frac{7}{8} \times \frac{2}{5}$, or $\frac{14}{40}$, which reduces to $\frac{7}{20}$.

9. E. Statement (1) alone tells us more about the student population, but nothing in particular about Kara, so it is not sufficient and we can cross off A and D.

Statement (2) alone tells us nothing because we don't know what the standard deviation is, so we can eliminate B. Together, the statements tell us that Kara studies for either 16.2 hours or 10.6 hours, but because we don't know whether she studies more or less than the mean, the statements are not sufficient together and our answer is E.

10. C. This is a very deceptive problem. Statement (1) tells us that 10 of the 20 cards are red, but it doesn't say that those are the *only* red cards in the deck, so it's not sufficient on its own and we can eliminate A and D.

The same thing applies to statement (2); it doesn't say that those are the *only* black cards in the deck. When we put the statements together, on the other hand, we see the whole picture and know that exactly 10 of the 20 cards are red. So our answer is C.

CHAPTER 6

GMAT Geometry

INTRODUCTION

Geometry is generally the least relevant content on the GMAT in terms of the math you do every day (and, for that matter, the math that you will do in business school). So geometry problems can be a little stress-inducing to future business school students, most of whom haven't studied it since high school (which was typically at least five years ago and often much more than that).

The good news, though, is that this material does come back with some review. The better news is that you're not going to be tested on nearly the breadth of material you were in high school. There aren't any proofs or theorems; just a limited set of geometric formulas and principles. These involve parallel lines, triangles, quadrilaterals, circles, and a few regular cylinders.

PARALLEL AND INTERSECTING LINES

Parallel lines are lines in the same plane that, if extended to infinity, would never intersect:

Most problems involving parallel lines will include either a geometric shape with parallel lines, such as a rectangle or parallelogram, or two parallel lines that are intersected by another line. The angles formed by the intersection of a line with two parallel lines have some interesting properties.

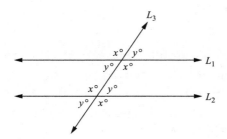

When lines intersect, the measures of the angles on opposite sides of the intersection are equal; these angles are called *vertical angles*. In the diagram, all of the angles labeled *x* have equal measures, and all of the angles labeled *y* have equal measures. The measures of the angles on the same side of a line, here represented as *x* and *y*, must add up to 180°; these are called *supplementary angles*. A line that intersects two *parallel* lines will produce angles of equal measure with both of the parallel lines, as shown by the *x* and *y* angles in the preceding diagram.

The GMAT tests this concept in a number of ways. Consider the following Data Sufficiency question:

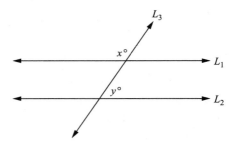

In the diagram above, if lines L_1 and L_2 are parallel, what is the value of *x*?

(1) $y = 70°$
(2) $x > 90°$

    A. Statement (1) ALONE is sufficient, but statement (2) alone is not sufficient.
    B. Statement (2) ALONE is sufficient, but statement (1) alone is not sufficient.
    C. BOTH statements TOGETHER are sufficient, but NEITHER statement ALONE is sufficient.
    D. EACH statement ALONE is sufficient.
    E. Statements (1) and (2) TOGETHER are NOT sufficient.

To answer this question, you need to recognize that if L_1 and L_2 are parallel, then all of the acute angles in this diagram are going to have a measure of $y°$ and all of the obtuse angles are going to equal $x°$, and that *x* and *y* are supplementary angles. Now consider statement (1):

(1) $y = 70°$

If *x* and *y* are supplementary, then $x° + y° = 180° \rightarrow x° = 180° - y° = 180° - 70° = 110°$. Thus, you can answer the question with statement (1) alone, so the answer to this question must be either A or D. Now consider statement (2):

(2) $x > 90°$

What does this tell you? Just that *x* is an obtuse angle. It could have a value anywhere between 90° and 180°. Therefore, statement (2) alone is not sufficient, so the answer must be A.

Parallel lines questions don't get much more difficult than this. Remember, when you have a line intersecting two parallel lines, and you know the measure of one of the angles, then you can determine the measures of all the other angles.

TYPES OF TRIANGLES AND THEIR ATTRIBUTES

Triangles figure very heavily in the GMAT because they are the simplest type of polygon (a polygon is a multisided figure). They are thus at once easy to understand, but also rich in mathematical detail.

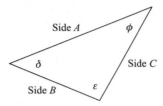

Angles, Sides, and Area

Every triangle has three sides, here denoted as A, B, and C, and three angles, here denoted as δ, ε, and ϕ (these names are arbitrary; the GMAT will identify sides and angles in a variety of ways). The sum of the lengths of the sides equals the perimeter, and the sum of the measures of the angles of any triangle is 180°:

$$A + B + C = P \text{ (perimeter)}$$

$$\delta + \varepsilon + \phi = 180°$$

Of the interior angles of a triangle or any polygon, an angle with a measure of less than 90° is called an *acute angle*, an angle with a measure of exactly 90° is called a *right angle*, and an angle with a measure of greater than 90° but less than 180° is called an *obtuse angle*. Since the angles of a triangle must add up to exactly 180°, in any triangle with a right or obtuse angle, the other two angles must be acute angles.

Another attribute of triangles is that no one side length can be greater than or equal to the sum of the lengths of the other two sides. Likewise, no side length of a triangle can be less than the difference of the remaining two side lengths. In the triangle in our example, A cannot be larger than $B + C$, and B cannot be smaller than $A - C$, i.e. $A < B + C$ and $B > A - C$.

Many of the triangle questions on the GMAT deal with the area of triangles. The most direct way to find the area of a triangle is to determine the height of the triangle and plug it into the following formula:

$$A = \frac{1}{2}bh$$

Here, b is the base, h is the height, and A is the area. We all remember from high school or earlier the "one-half the base times the height" mantra, but as shown here, it's not always obvious what the base should be. *Base* can be a misleading term, as it doesn't need to be on the bottom of the figure. The GMAT often will not include the height, also called the altitude, on the diagrams it provides, but usually you will have sufficient information to draw it in on your own diagram.

There is one more way to find the area of a triangle, though it isn't much used. Heron's Formula is handy when you know nothing more than the measures of the three sides. In this formula, the lengths of the sides are represented as *a*, *b*, and *c*, and *s* represents the semiperimeter, which is just half the perimeter. Heron's Formula is as follows:

$$A = \sqrt{s(s-a)(s-b)(s-c)} \quad \text{where } s = \frac{1}{2}(a+b+c)$$

It's not easy to remember, but it can be useful if finding that third side of a triangle is quicker for you than finding an altitude.

Isosceles Triangles

Triangles with two sides of equal length are called isosceles triangles. No, they aren't named after some Dead Greek Guy named Isosceles (yes, we've gotten this question before). *Isoskelos* is just Greek for "equal legs." There are two key things you need to remember about isosceles triangles:

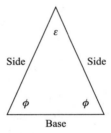

▶ Two of the sides are of equal length.
▶ The two angles opposite the sides of equal length are also of equal degree measure (e.g., in the diagram $\phi = \phi$).

Equilateral Triangles

Equilateral triangles are a special case of isosceles triangles in which all the sides are of equal length. From this it follows that all the angles are of equal measure as well, and *each of these angles measures 60°*. Identifying a triangle as equilateral on the GMAT can be very useful because you can then determine that any side can be immediately related to any other side, as can any angle to any other angle. There's also a special formula for the area of an equilateral triangle:

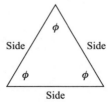

$$A = \frac{\sqrt{3}}{4}s^2 \quad \text{where } s \text{ is the length of any given side}$$

As an exercise, you can try to derive this using Heron's Formula.

Right Triangles

Right triangles are triangles in which one of the angles has a measure equal to 90°. The beauty of a right triangle is that the lengths of its sides relate to one another according to the Pythagorean Theorem. The Pythagorean Theorem has been invoked over and over by GMAT problems in the past. We're not sure who decided that mastering the Pythagorean Theorem was an important hurdle to clear for admission to an MBA program, but there it is. The good news is that you almost certainly knew it once, and if you don't remember it, it's easy to memorize again. The theorem states that, where A and B are the lengths of the legs of a right triangle and C is the length of the hypotenuse:

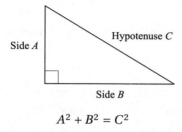

$$A^2 + B^2 = C^2$$

Pythagoras is a Dead Greek Guy, and his original proof is a beautiful thing to behold. Fortunately, you will never in your life be asked to reproduce it. As we noted earlier, however, you do need to be very careful in identifying just which are the sides, and what is the hypotenuse. There are a few problems from past GMATs in which those things have not been obvious.

You also need to be careful when applying the Pythagorean Theorem that you use the order of operations correctly. Remember to square A and square B separately and then add the results together. This is especially important to remember when you are solving for the length of the hypotenuse. A very common mistake made when using the Pythagorean Theorem is to "distribute" the square root over the $A^2 + B^2$:

$$\sqrt{A^2 + B^2} \neq A + B$$

Note that the little square at the vertex of sides A and B is meant to denote that the angle is a right angle (90°). That will be important on the GMAT, since the current test-writing regime uses the same notation. Note also that there are right triangles that are also isosceles triangles (as in the figure here), but that there are no right equilateral triangles. In the latter case, that's because we cannot (at least not in Euclidean space) have a triangle with three angles each of 90°. That would violate the rule that the measures of the three angles of a triangle must add up to 180°.

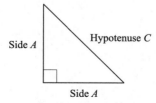

A special case of triangle that shows up frequently on GMAT questions is the *right isosceles triangle*. The three angles within right isosceles triangles have measures of 45°–45°–90°. For right isosceles triangles, the Pythagorean Theorem reduces to

$$C^2 = A^2 + A^2 \rightarrow C^2 = 2A^2$$

If you take the square root of this formula, you can determine the ratio of the length of the hypotenuse to the length of the sides in a right isosceles triangle:

$$\sqrt{C^2} = \sqrt{\left(2A^2\right)} \rightarrow C = \sqrt{2}A$$

Thus, if one of the legs of a right isosceles triangle has a length of 5, then you know that the other leg also has a length of 5 and the hypotenuse has a length of $5\sqrt{2}$.

Some Special Triangles

In addition to the right isosceles triangle, there are a few other special-case right triangles that appear frequently on GMAT questions.

The 3–4–5. The 3–4–5 triangle is a right triangle with side lengths in the ratio of 3 to 4 to 5. The lengths could be 3–4–5, or they could be 6–8–10, 9–12–15, and so on. The sides of the basic 3–4–5 triangle square through the Pythagorean Theorem as $9 + 16 = 25$, and the other triangles with this ratio square through as well (e.g., $36 + 64 = 100$, $81 + 144 = 225$, and so on). The GMAT frequently uses these ratios so that you can work through the calculations more quickly; if you know to expect them, you can work through them still more quickly.

The 5–12–13. The 5–12–13 triangle is a right triangle with side lengths in the ratio of 5 to 12 to 13. The sides square in the Pythagorean Theorem as $25 + 144 = 169$. This one appears in questions somewhat less frequently than the 3–4–5. Note that you could see a 10–24–26 triangle as well.

The 30°–60°–90°, a.k.a. the $1 - \sqrt{3} - 2$. If you see that a triangle has legs of 1 and $\sqrt{3}$, you can calculate that

$$1^2 + \left(\sqrt{3}\right)^2 = 1 + 3 = 4 = 2^2$$

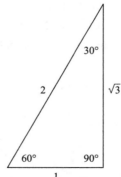

The 30° –60° –90°, or 1– $\sqrt{3}$ – 2 triangle

And therefore the hypotenuse has a measure of 2. Triangles with lengths of this ratio always have angles with the measures of 30°, 60°, and 90°, and triangles with angles of those measures always have sides with lengths in the ratio of 1 to $\sqrt{3}$ to 2 (i.e., they could be 5, $5\sqrt{3}$, and 10, or 8, $8\sqrt{3}$, and 16, and so on.). This kind of triangle appears in all sorts of GMAT problems involving geometry. For reference, $\sqrt{3}$ is approximately equal to 1.7, so it is greater than 1 but less than 2. It is important with these triangles to remember which angle corresponds with which side: the 30° angle is opposite the side with length 1, the 60° angle is opposite from the side with length $\sqrt{3}$, and the 90° is across from the side with length 2.

If you're having trouble remembering this, here's a good rule of thumb: the largest angle is always directly opposite the largest side, the smallest angle is always directly opposite the smallest side, and so on.

QUADRILATERALS

After triangles, the next most common polygon on the GMAT is the quadrilateral. A quadrilateral is a polygon with four sides. Occasionally you'll run into pentagons, hexagons, and octagons on the test, but these are rare.

Squares and Rectangles

Squares and rectangles are by far the most common quadrilaterals encountered on the GMAT. Both squares and rectangles have four right angles and two sets of parallel sides. All four sides of a square are of equal length, while a rectangle can have pairs of sides of different lengths:

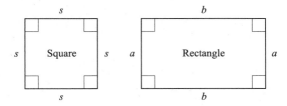

The area of a square, of course, is just the square of one of its sides (s^2), and the perimeter of a square is 4 times any side ($4s$). For a rectangle, things are only slightly more complicated:

$$P = 2a + 2b; A = ab \text{ (rectangle)}$$

A square is a special case of a rectangle. Note that a square divided along a diagonal makes two isosceles right triangles. Since the diagonal of the square is the hypotenuse of the isosceles right triangle, the diagonal of the square has a length of $\sqrt{2}s$. A rectangle divided along a diagonal makes two right triangles as well, and you can determine the length of a diagonal of a rectangle by means of the Pythagorean Theorem.

Rhombi and Parallelograms

A rhombus is a quadrilateral with sides of equal length and two sets of opposite angles with equal measures, but the measures of all four angles are not necessarily equal. If the measures of all four angles were equal, then you would have a square. A square is a special case of the rhombus in which all four angles are equal. A parallelogram is a quadrilateral with two pairs of parallel sides; the sides in each parallel pair are of equal length, but not necessarily the same length as the other pair of sides.

A rectangle is a special case of a parallelogram in which the measures of all of the angles are equal, a rhombus is a special case of a parallelogram in which all sides are of equal length, and a square is a special case of a parallelogram in which all sides are of equal length and all angles are of equal measure. In both rhombi and parallelograms, the angles on opposite sides of the figure have equal measures (i.e., the two acute angles have equal measures, and the two obtuse angles have equal measures). The diagram here shows not just the shapes, but also the beginning of an approach to calculate their areas:

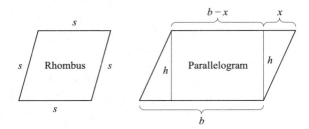

The area of a parallelogram is easy to deduce, if you just remember that it's basically composed of a rectangle and a pair of triangles. The area, then, is just

$$A = \left(b - x\right)h + 2\left(\frac{1}{2}xh\right) = bh - xh + xh = bh$$

That is, it's no different from the area of the analogous rectangle, but if you forget that, you can get it back quickly with a little geometric reasoning. You can work out the same relationship for the rhombus.

Once again, remember that the opposite sides in rhombi and parallelograms are parallel to each other. That is, after all, the meaning of "parallelogram."

Trapezoids

The last quadrilateral of note is the trapezoid, which has just one pair of parallel sides. In isosceles trapezoids, the other two sides have matching lengths—kind of like isosceles triangles do. The diagram here shows how to calculate its area. Divide the figure into a rectangle and two triangles, much as you would for a parallelogram. Then, add the areas of those components:

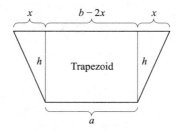

$$A = ah + 2\left(\frac{1}{2}xh\right) = ah + xh = h\left(a + x\right)$$

This means that *the area of a trapezoid is the height times the average of the lengths of the two parallel sides.*

CIRCLES

There is a small set of things to remember about circles for the GMAT. First, some notation:

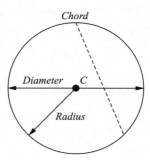

▶ The *radius* is generally, but not always, denoted with an *r*, and it is half the length of the *diameter*, which is generally (but again, not always) denoted with a *d*.

▶ The *center* is frequently labeled with a *C*.

▶ Unlike diameters and radii, not every line segment inscribed in a circle is anchored in the center. Those line segments that have their endpoints on the circle are called *chords*. (A diameter is a special case of a chord that crosses the center.)

Now, on to the few formulae to remember:

▶ The circumference is the distance around the circle (or what's called the perimeter in a polygon). It's also often denoted with a *c*, which can be confusing. You'll find it with the formula

$$c = \pi d = 2\pi r$$

Whether you use the diameter or the radius is just a matter of personal preference, or of which is more clearly provided in the question. As for π (otherwise known as "pi"), it is reasonably approximated by 3.14, though in many problems it will appear as itself in the answer choices. If it does, don't convert it to 3.14 in your calculations or you will waste a great deal of time. When dealing with circles, always check the answer choices first to determine whether you need π in your answer.

▶ The area of a circle is also found with π:

$$A = \pi r^2$$

It's generally not convenient to try to substitute the diameter into this formula. You're probably better off dividing it in half to find the radius, then plugging that number in. Most of the time, this is the more profitable route in GMAT geometry.

▶ Finally, there is one formula involving chords that you may need to know, since questions involving it have appeared a few times in the past. In the diagram shown here, the dotted line is a diameter, the solid line is a radius, and the dashed line is a chord. When the angle between a chord and a diameter is subtended by an angle between a radius and the same diameter, the measure of the second angle is twice that of the first. If that's a mouthful, just study the diagram. If you see that, remember that the inside angle is twice the outside angle. If you can't remember which is supposed to be larger, then just look to see which appears larger. This is probably the one place where the diagram will always be more or less drawn to scale.

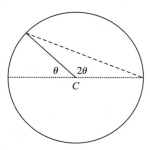

VOLUME OF BOXES AND RIGHT CIRCULAR CYLINDERS

Geometry questions can sometimes become more difficult conceptually when they extend into a third dimension. When the GMAT does ask about the volumes of solid figures, it tends to ask about either boxes—the three-dimensional forms of squares or rectangles—or right circular cylinders, as depicted in the figure. Calculating volumes is actually pretty easy: just find the area of the base and multiply that by the figure's height. The volume of a cube is the cube of a side, s^3. The formula for the volume of a box with a rectangular base is

$$\text{Volume} = \text{length} \times \text{width} \times \text{height}$$

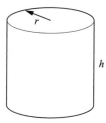

The volume of a right circular cylinder is likewise the area of the base times the height:

$$V = A_b h = \pi r^2 h$$

since the base of a right circular cylinder is a circle and the area of a circle is πr^2.

WHAT YOU NEED TO REMEMBER

The area of a triangle: $A_\Delta = \frac{1}{2} bh$

Heron's Formula for the area of a triangle: $A = \sqrt{s(s-a)(s-b)(s-c)}$, $s = 1/2(a+b+c)$

The area of an equilateral triangle: $A = \frac{\sqrt{3}}{4} s^2$

The Pythagorean Theorem: $A^2 + B^2 = C^2$

The 3–4–5 triangle: $3^2 + 4^2 = 5^2$

The 5–12–13 triangle: $5^2 + 12^2 = 13^2$

The 30°–60°–90° triangle: $1^2 + (\sqrt{3})^2 = 2^2$

The area of a parallelogram: $A_p = bh$

The area of an isosceles trapezoid: $A_T = h(a+x)$ or $= \frac{1}{2} h(a+b)$

The circumference of a circle: $c = 2\pi r$

The area of a circle: $A_o = \pi r^2$

The volume of a right circular cylinder: $V = \pi r^2 h$

PRACTICE PROBLEMS

1. In a right isosceles triangle, the lengths of the two nonhypotenuse sides are designated a. What is the area of the triangle in terms of a?

A. $\frac{1}{3} a^2$

B. $\frac{\sqrt{2}}{3} a^2$

C. $\frac{1}{2} a^2$

D. $\frac{\sqrt{3}}{2} a^2$

E. $\sqrt{2}a^2$

2. The U.S. Defense Department has decided that the Pentagon is an obsolete building and that it must be replaced with an upgraded version: the Hexagon. The Secretary of Defense wants a building that is exactly 70 feet high and 200 feet on a side, and that has a hexagonal bull's-eye cutout in the center (somewhat like the current one) that is 50 feet on a side. What will be the volume of the new building in cubic feet?

A. 3,937,500 cubic feet

B. 15,750 cubic feet

C. 11,550 $\sqrt{3}$ cubic feet

D. 15,750 $\sqrt{3}$ cubic feet

E. 3,937,500 $\sqrt{3}$ cubic feet

3. What is the area of the shaded figure?

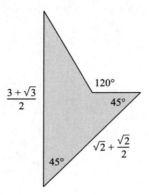

A. $\dfrac{(9 + \sqrt{3})}{8}$

B. $\dfrac{(5 + 3\sqrt{2})}{3}$

C. $\dfrac{9}{2}$

D. $\dfrac{3}{2} + \sqrt{3}$

E. $\dfrac{(9 + \sqrt{3})}{2}$

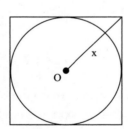

4. In the figure above, $x = 2$. What is the area of circle O?

A. $\sqrt{2}\pi$

B. 2π

C. $2\sqrt{2}\pi$

D. 4π

E. $4\sqrt{2}\pi$

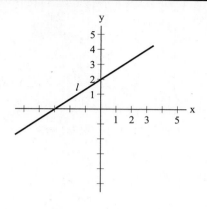

5. Which of the following could be the equation of line l in the figure above?

    A. $2x = 3y - 2$

    B. $2x = 3y - 6$

    C. $3x = 2y - 6$

    D. $\dfrac{2}{3}x = 2y - 2$

    E. $\dfrac{2}{3}2x = 3y - 6$

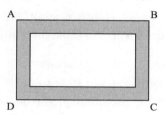

Note: figure not drawn to scale

6. In the rectangular figure above, the area of the shaded region is equal to the area of the non-shaded rectangle. If $AB = 6$, $BC = 4$, and the longer side of the non-shaded rectangle is an integer, what is one possible measurement for the shorter side of the non-shaded rectangle?

    A. $\dfrac{3}{4}$

    B. 1

    C. $\dfrac{3}{2}$

    D. $\dfrac{12}{5}$

    E. $\dfrac{16}{3}$

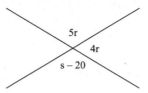

Note: figure not drawn to scale

7. In the figure above, what is the value of $2s - r$?

A. 60
B. 70
C. 100
D. 140
E. 220

The following data sufficiency problems consist of a question and two statements, labeled (1) and (2), in which certain data are given. You have to decide whether the data given in the statements are *sufficient* for answering the question. Using the data given in the statements *plus* your knowledge of mathematics and everyday facts (such as the number of days in July or the meaning of counterclockwise), you must indicate whether

A. Statement (1) ALONE is sufficient, but statement (2) alone is not sufficient.
B. Statement (2) ALONE is sufficient, but statement (1) alone is not sufficient.
C. BOTH statements TOGETHER are sufficient, but NEITHER statement ALONE is sufficient.
D. EACH statement ALONE is sufficient.
E. Statements (1) and (2) TOGETHER are NOT sufficient.

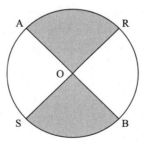

8. In the figure above, what is the area of the shaded region?

(1) $AB = 8$
(2) Angle $AOR = 45°$.

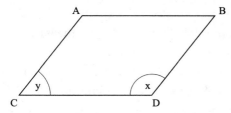

Note: figure not drawn to scale

9. In the figure above, what is the value of *x*?

    (1) $2y = 100$.

    (2) *ABCD* is a parallelogram.

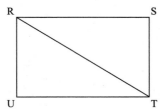

10. In the figure above, what is the length of *RT*?

    (1) $RU = 5$

    (2) $RS = 12$

Solutions

1. C. The formula for the area of a triangle is $1/2\, bh$. You can orient an isosceles right triangle so that the two equal sides form both the base and the height. If these sides are of length *a*, then plugging these values into the area formula gives us the result $1/2\, a^2$, which is answer C. The diagram shows how the equal sides form both the base and the height:

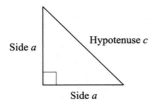

2. E.   This is very definitely a multi-step problem. First, you need to recognize that we're dealing with nothing more than an oddly-shaped cylinder: the base is a regular polygon, so by dividing it into a number of manageable pieces, we can calculate its area. However, before we do that, we'll need to figure out how to treat that hole in the middle of the six-sided doughnut. The easiest thing to do is to think about it as "negative area"—to calculate its area, and then subtract that area from the area of the larger, filled-in shape to find the area of the region around it. The following diagram below shows the three steps:

Step 1	*Step 2*	*Step 3*
Draw the Hexagon, including bull's-eye	Divide it into a solid part and a hole	Cut each of the resulting pieces into six smaller ones

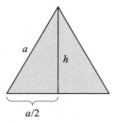

Next, we'll need to calculate the areas of those two different triangles. If you happen to remember the formula for the area of an equilateral triangle, great; skip to that step. If not, you'll need to derive it. That's not that hard: using the diagram that follows, you can divide the equilateral triangle into two right triangles, each with height h, hypotenuse a (there go those shifting variable names again), and base $a/2$. Since we don't know what h is, it would be nice to state that in terms of a as well. We'll do that first, by relying on the Pythagorean Theorem:

$$\left(\frac{a}{2}\right)^2 + h^2 = a^2 \rightarrow \frac{1}{4}a^2 + h^2 = a^2 \rightarrow h^2 = \frac{3}{4}a^2 \rightarrow h = \frac{\sqrt{3}}{2}a$$

Step 4: Calculate the area of the triangle

The area of the entire equilateral triangle is just twice the area of the right "half triangle" on either side:

$$A = 2\left(\frac{1}{2}bh\right) = 2\left(\frac{1}{2}\frac{a}{2}\frac{\sqrt{3}}{2}a\right) = \frac{\sqrt{3}}{4}a^2$$

Six of these form the whole of the large (outer) hexagon, so that area is

$$\alpha_{\text{hex}} = 6 \times \frac{\sqrt{3}}{4}a^2 = \frac{3\sqrt{3}}{2}a^2$$

Six of the smaller triangles form the whole of the hole in the middle. We'll need a different variable for these, since we're talking about a different a at this point. We can define these as the outer a_o and inner a_i sides:

The area of the Hexagon (minus the bull's eye) =

$$A_{\text{outer}} - A_{\text{inner}} = \frac{3\sqrt{3}}{2}a_o^2 - \frac{3\sqrt{3}}{2}a_i^2$$

Then, the height is a uniform 70 feet all around, so finding the volume is just a matter of multiplying through by that height:

$$V = h\left(\frac{3\sqrt{3}}{2}A_o^2 - \frac{3\sqrt{3}}{2}A_i^2\right) = h\left(\frac{3\sqrt{3}}{2}\right)\left(A_o^2 - A_i^2\right)$$

Of course, that doesn't look much like the answer choices, so we'll need to substitute the values for the variables:

$$V = 70\left(\frac{3\sqrt{3}}{2}\right)\left(200^2 - 50^2\right) = 35 \times 3\sqrt{3} \times \left(40,000 - 2,500\right) = 105\sqrt{3} \times 37,500 = 3,937,500\sqrt{3}$$

If you looked over the answer choices, you will know that $\sqrt{3}$ is an acceptable component of your answer; the thrust of this question is geometry, so the GMAT would not make you calculate a square root as part of the problem. The volume corresponds with answer choice E.

3. A.   This figure may look intimidating, but it's actually quite harmless. To tackle it, you must first recognize that it can be split into two smaller triangles, as shown in the diagram. Once you've separated the triangles, you can start labeling the lengths. The lower triangle has two 45° angles, so it is clearly a right isosceles triangle. That means that we should be able to find the area quickly. An intermediate step will be calculating the lengths of the (equal) sides, which we'll designate as x. That will also have a follow-on purpose. We'll be able to use the length x with the full length of the left side of the figure to calculate the length of the rising side of the smaller triangle. First, though, we'll get back to the lower triangle and the Pythagorean Theorem:

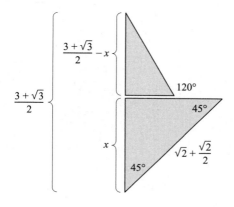

$$x^2 + x^2 = \left(\sqrt{2} + \frac{\sqrt{2}}{2} \right)^2 \rightarrow 2x^2 = \left(\sqrt{2} + \frac{\sqrt{2}}{2} \right)\left(\sqrt{2} + \frac{\sqrt{2}}{2} \right)$$

$$2x^2 = 2 + \frac{\sqrt{2}\sqrt{2}}{2} + \frac{\sqrt{2}\sqrt{2}}{2} + \frac{\sqrt{2}\sqrt{2}}{4} = 2 + 1 + 1 + \frac{1}{2}$$

$$2x^2 = \frac{9}{2} \rightarrow x^2 = \frac{9}{4} \rightarrow x = \frac{3}{2}$$

Now we can use the result for x to find that smaller length:

$$\frac{3 + \sqrt{3}}{2} - x = \frac{3 + \sqrt{3}}{2} - \frac{3}{2} = \frac{\sqrt{3}}{2}$$

The triangle may not look familiar yet, but the angle at the right is a giveaway. Since it's a 120° angle, the supplementary angle θ must be 60°. This is because interior and exterior angles along the same line segment must always sum to 180°. Since another angle in the triangle is right (90°), we now can assert that angle σ measures 30°, since all the angles inside a triangle must sum to 180° as well. This means that we have a 30°–60°–90° triangle. One needs to be careful at this point, as it is easy to misidentify the lengths in one of these. Remember, it is not that the lengths are always 1, $\sqrt{3}$, and 2; but that they are always in the ratio of 1: $\sqrt{3}$:2. If the long nonhypotenuse side has a length of one-half of $\sqrt{3}$, then the other sides should be halved as well. The short side will have length 1/2, and the hypotenuse will have length 1.

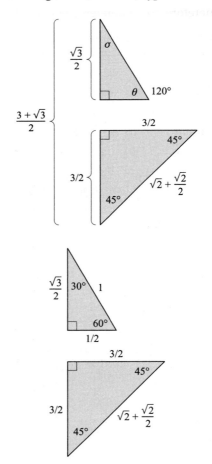

At this point, as shown in the last diagram, we can ignore all our calculations but those for a few lengths. The area of the original figure is found with just the four numbers in black:

$$A = A_{\Delta up} + A_{\Delta down} = \left(\frac{1}{2}b_{\Delta up}h_{\Delta up}\right) + \left(\frac{1}{2}b_{\Delta down}h_{\Delta down}\right)$$

$$= \left(\frac{1}{2} \times \frac{1}{2} \times \frac{\sqrt{3}}{2}\right) + \left(\frac{1}{2} \times \frac{3}{2} \times \frac{3}{2}\right) = \frac{\sqrt{3}}{8} + \frac{9}{8} = \frac{9 + \sqrt{3}}{8}$$

or answer choice A. That's about it. There are other ways of finding the area, but if you can handle the steps here, you should have little trouble with GMAT geometry.

4. B.   Since we are looking for the area of the circle, we really need to find the radius. The line segment from the center of the circle to the vertex of the square is 2, so we can use that to find the radius. If you extend line x to the opposite vertex of the square, you have drawn a diagonal of that square, which is also the hypotenuse of a 45°–45°–90° triangle. The diagonal measures 4. You normally multiply a leg of a 45°–45°–90° triangle by $\sqrt{2}$ to get the hypotenuse, so we have to divide the hypotenuse by $\sqrt{2}$ to get the leg (which is also the side of the square and the diameter of the circle). Therefore, the diameter is equal to $\frac{4}{\sqrt{2}}$ and the radius is equal to $\frac{2}{\sqrt{2}}$. But we're not done; we still have to find the area. The formula for the area of a circle is $A = \pi r^2$, so we have to substitute $\frac{2}{\sqrt{2}}$ in for r. Squaring both the top and bottom of the fraction, we get $\frac{4}{2}$, or 2. So the area of the circle is 2π.

5. B.   Since none of the answer choices are actually in the recognized form for an equation of a line, the best thing in this case is to figure out what the equation of the original line is in $y = mx + b$ form, and then figure out which of the answer choices can be manipulated to form that same equation. This line crosses the y axis at 2, so the y-intercept is 2 and our equation becomes $y = mx + 2$. Now we need to figure out the slope. Since the point goes through (0, 2) and (3, 4), the slope is $\frac{2}{3}$. The equation we're looking for is now $y = \frac{2}{3}x + 2$. If we manipulate the equations in the answer choices so that the y always has a coefficient of 1 and everything is on the correct side of the equal sign, B is the only correct answer.

6. D.   The larger rectangle has an area of 24, so the non-shaded rectangle must have an area of 12. Starting with the answer choices for the length of the shorter side, we can divide them into 12 until we find a valid length for the longer side. A would give us 16 for the longer side, which wouldn't work because that wouldn't fit inside another rectangle with 6 as the longest side. B would give us 12 for the longer side, which is still too big. C gives us 8, which is also too big. D gives us 5, which is possible and therefore is the correct answer.

7. E.   Since $4r$ and $5r$ form a straight line, which is 180 degrees, $4r + 5r = 180$. When we simplify that to $9r = 180$, we can solve to get $r = 20$. Therefore $5r = 100$, and $s - 20 = 100$. So we can tell that $s = 120$. Using those numbers, the equation $2s - r$ becomes $2(120) - 20$, which equals 220.

8. C.   Statement (1) alone lets us find the radius, which can tell us the area of the whole circle, but we still don't know what portion of the circle is made up by the shaded region, so we have to eliminate A and D. Statement (2) alone tells us what proportion of the circle is encompassed by the shaded region, but doesn't tell us the area of the whole circle, so we can eliminate B. Putting the statements together, we have both pieces of information, which we can use to find the area of the shaded region, so statements (1) and (2) are sufficient together, and our answer is C.

9. C.   Statement (1) is tempting, because the figure appears to be a parallelogram, but we don't really know that it is without some indication that there are two sets of parallel lines. So statement (1) is actually not sufficient, and we can eliminate A and D. Remembering that we have to take statement (2) alone, it is not sufficient by itself to solve for the value of x, so we eliminate B. Putting both statements together, we have the information we need: If the figure is a parallelogram, then the angles add to 360. If $2y = 100$, then $2x = 260$ and $x = 130$. So our answer is C.

10. E.   Statement (1) is not sufficient on its own, since you can never solve for one side of a triangle given only one other side. Let's eliminate A and D. Statement (2) is not sufficient for the same reason, so we can eliminate B. Putting the statements together, it appears that we have enough information to solve for the diagonal of the rectangle (also known as hypotenuse of a right triangle) . . . except that we don't have any indication that the figure is actually a rectangle. So the statements are still not sufficient and the answer is E.

CHAPTER 7

Boolean Problems and Combinatorics

INTRODUCTION

The GMAT contains a variety of logic problems dealing with set theory, number theory, binary categories, and combinatorics. While the technical terms for these categories seem a little daunting, most of the math involved is pretty basic; in fact, using math that is more complicated than necessary is a sure way to waste time and energy on the test.

BOOLEAN PROBLEMS ON THE GMAT

Boolean problems are those in which you are asked to determine whether a mathematical expression corresponds to one of two states. These questions could ask whether an expression is

- ▶ True or false
- ▶ Even or odd
- ▶ Positive or negative
- ▶ Integer or noninteger

Clearly, there's no way for any value to be *both* of either of these; x can't be both even and odd, or positive and negative. That's why the categories are "binary"; there are two distinct possibilities.

To answer this type of question efficiently, there are some rules that you absolutely, positively, must memorize if you haven't already. Here they are:

Even vs. Odd

- ▶ even × even = even
- ▶ odd × odd = odd
- ▶ even × odd = even

- ▶ even + even = even
- ▶ odd + odd = even
- ▶ even + odd = odd

Positive vs. Negative

- ▶ positive × positive = positive
- ▶ negative × negative = positive
- ▶ positive × negative = negative

- ▶ positive + positive = positive
- ▶ negative + negative = negative
- ▶ positive + negative = It depends!

When you add a positive and negative, the one with the larger absolute value (or distance from zero) wins. So if the positive number has the larger absolute value, the result will be positive, and vice versa.

Also, remember that subtracting a positive is the same as adding a negative, so if you see a subtraction sign, you can just change it to an addition sign, change the following number into its inverse, and follow the rules above.

Exponents

Exponents just continue all of the multiplication rules above. Therefore, assuming you're dealing with integer exponents . . .

▶ An *odd* raised to an exponent continues to yield an *odd* result, regardless of whether the exponent itself is even or odd: $3^2 = 9$, $3^3 = 27$, $3^4 = 81$, $3^5 = 243$.

▶ An *even* raised to an exponent continues to yield an *even* result, regardless of whether the exponent itself is even or odd: $2^2 = 4$, $2^3 = 8$, $2^4 = 16$, $2^5 = 32$.

▶ Any number raised to an *even* exponent will be *positive*: $-4^2 = 16$, $3^2 = 9$, $-\dfrac{1}{2}^2 = \dfrac{1}{4}$.

Integers vs. Non-integers

integer $\times$ integer = integer
non-integer $\times$ non-integer = non-integer
integer $\times$ non-integer = It depends!

When you multiply an integer and a non-integer, the result will be a non-integer *unless* the integer is a multiple of the non-integer's denominator. For example, $\frac{1}{2} \times 3 = \frac{3}{2}$ (a non-integer), but $\frac{1}{2} \times 2 = 1$ and $\frac{1}{2} \times 4 = 2$ (both are integers because 2 and 4 are multiples of the denominator 2). If that is confusing, remember that you can often use real numbers instead of rules to work these problems on the GMAT. And speaking of real numbers . . .

Other Tools for Working Problems Efficiently

Sometimes your knowledge of binary categories is enough to get you through a problem; other times, it's a good way to ballpark out a few answer choices. When problems get more complex, though, it's good to have a concrete way to deal with all of the abstract *stuff* they like to throw at you. That's why we recommend using real numbers when you can. Let's try a couple of examples using the rules you memorized above (because you did, right?) and plugging in real numbers when you need to.

If x, y, and z are integers, then x^2y^2z will be negative whenever

A. x is negative
B. y is positive
C. z is negative
D. xy is negative
E. It cannot be determined from the information given.

If you're totally on top of your Positive vs. Negative rules, including exponents, you may immediately recognize that anything raised to an even exponent such as 2 will be positive, so both x^2 and y^2 will be positive . . . which means your result is positive so far. Only making z negative will give the negative result the problem is looking for, so the answer must be choice C.

However, if any one of those rules escapes your mind in this very stressful testing situation, what do you do? Well, you can use real numbers based on what the answer choices tell you.

- **Choice A.** If $x = -2$, x^2 is positive. You know you need a *negative* result in order for this answer choice to be correct, but you also know that if you can play by the rules in the problem and still get a *positive* result, you can eliminate this answer choice. So let's try to get a *positive* result, substituting 2 for y and 3 for z (both positive numbers). Your final result is 4×4×3, and if you remember a few Positive vs. Negative rules, you don't even have to multiply any further to know that the result is positive. Eliminate choice A.
- **Choice B.** Now you can use essentially the same numbers, this time making y negative. How about $x = 2$, $y = -2$, and $z = 3$? Again, you get 4×4×3, a positive result. Eliminate choice B.
- **Choice C.** This time use positives for x and y, say 2 and 3. z must be negative, so you can use –2. Now your expression becomes 4×9×–2. You were able to get a negative result even using as many positive numbers as you could, so let's keep that one.
- **Choice D.** Either x or y has to be negative this time, because xy is negative. Well, you've already seen two examples in which either x or y was negative — answer choices A and B — and you were still able to get a positive result. So you can eliminate choice D.
- **Choice E.** Well, you *were* able to tell what would cause you to get a negative result, in answer choice C. This answer is here only to confuse you. Eliminate choice E.

That means choice C is right again, no matter whether you use the rules alone or in combination with using real numbers. Either way, though, you can see that knowing the rules allows you to make some shortcuts. Let's try another one.

x and y are positive integers. If $xy + x$ is odd, then which of the following must be even?

A. x
B. y
C. $x + y$
D. $xy - x$
E. $x^2 - y$

Chances are that knowledge of the rules alone can't take you all the way to the correct answer on this one, so let's try some substitution. This time, let's use a slightly different method for practice. We'll pick real numbers to start, say $x = 3$ and $y = 2$, so that $3(2) + 3 = 9$, which is an odd result like the problem tells you it needs to be. Now you're looking for answer choices that must be even.

- **Choice A.** $x = 3$, which is not even, so you can eliminate choice A.
- **Choice B.** $y = 2$, which is even, so you can keep choice B.
- **Choice C.** $3 + 2 = 5$, which is not even, so you can eliminate choice C.

- **Choice D.** $3(2) - 3 = 3$, which is not even, so you can eliminate choice D.
- **Choice E.** $3^2 - 2 = 7$, which is not even, so you can eliminate choice E.

Luckily, you found only one answer that works. Choice B. But think back to Chapter 4; if more than one answer choice had been even, you would have just quickly substituted a different x and y (still ones that made $xy + x$ odd) and kept narrowing down the answer choices that remained.

COMBINATORICS PROBLEMS: TWO APPROACHES

Combinatorics is the body of math that deals with combinations and permutations. Questions of this type are relatively rare on the GMAT, but you may see one, and if you are shooting for a high score, you will want to answer it correctly. Combinatorics problems tend to be conceptually difficult and time-consuming, so you need to approach them with a strategy if you don't want them to eat up all of your time.

There are two approaches you can take to a combinatorics problem. The first could be called "reasoned brute force": understand what is being asked, reason through the problem, and then write down every combination or permutation asked for. On the GMAT these questions tend to involve fewer than 30 or so permutations, so it may be possible for you work out a problem like this in little more than 2 minutes if you dive right in.

The second approach is to solve the problems using combinatorics formulas. These formulas can be mathematically difficult and hard to apply, but they can give you the answer to a particularly difficult question far faster than brute force. We'll discuss the brute force method first. Let's consider a question:

> In a family with 3 children, the parents have agreed to bring the children to the pet store and allow each child to choose a pet. This pet store sells only dogs, cats, and monkeys. If each child chooses exactly one animal, and if more than one child can choose the same kind of animal, how many different arrangements of animals could the family leave with?
>
> A. 6
> B. 8
> C. 9
> D. 10
> E. 12

The first step with a problem like this is to figure out what you're looking for. You're looking for combinations of three variables—let's call them D, C, and M—in groupings of three, in which a variable can be repeated more than once and in which order does not matter (i.e., DDC is the same as DCD). Let's look at all the combinations the children could choose involving dogs:

DDD
DDC
DDM
DCC
DMM
DCM

So there is 1 possibility involving 3 dogs, 2 possibilities involving 2 dogs, and 3 possibilities involving 1 dog. Since all possibilities involving dogs are exhausted, it should be easier to pick out all the remaining combinations involving the remaining two variables:

CCC
CCM
CMM
MMM

Can you think of any other possibilities? Let's hope not, because there are no others. The answer is 10, which is choice D. Note that this system would have worked just as well if you'd started with monkeys or cats. The trick is to start on a system that will inevitably exhaust all possibilities.

Brute force has its limitations, though. Say you encounter the following question:

A sock drawer contains seven socks, each one a different solid color. The colors of the socks are red, orange, yellow, green, blue, indigo, and violet. If the socks are laid next to each other, how many different arrangements of socks could be made?

A. 24
B. 240
C. 1,024
D. 2,520
E. 5,040

First, understand what is being asked. You're looking for permutations of seven variables—let's call them R, O, Y, G, B, I, and V—in groupings of seven, with no repeat variables in each grouping, and order in this case does matter (i.e., ROYGBIV is not the same as ROYGBVI). You could write out every possible permutation, starting like this:

ROYGBIV
ROYGBVI

ROYGVIB
ROYGVBI
ROYGIVB
ROYGIBV

ROYBGIV
ROYBGVI
ROYBVIG
ROYBVGI
ROYBIVG
ROYBIGV
ROYVBIG … and so on

As you can see, with some problems, the brute force method could take a very long time. On this particular problem, it might take you the whole test, as you might be able to guess by looking at the scope of the available answers. It is in problems like this one that combinatorics formulas come in handy.

Factorials

The key concept in combinatoric math is the *factorial*. The factorial of an integer n is the successive product of n times all the positive integers smaller than n, right down to 1. In practice, that means that

$$n! = n \times (n-1) \times (n-2) \times (n-3) \times \ldots \quad 1$$

Actually, the 1 is wholly unnecessary, but you get the point. The factorial function blows up rather quickly, so you'll not be asked to calculate a factorial much larger than these:

$0! = 1$ (it is simply defined that way)
$1! = 1$
$2! = 2 \times 1 = 2$
$3! = 3 \times 2 \times 1 = 6$
$4! = 4 \times 3 \times 2 \times 1 = 24$
$5! = 5 \times 4 \times 3 \times 2 \times 1 = 120$
$6! = 6 \times 5 \times 4 \times 3 \times 2 \times 1 = 720$
$7! = 7 \times 6 \times 5 \times 4 \times 3 \times 2 \times 1 = 5,040$

Before we move on to the formulas, let's consider how the concept of factorials alone could be used to solve the sock problem above. Suppose the question asked:

In how many different ways could you arrange a single red sock in a sock drawer if there are exactly 7 spaces for socks?

The answer, clearly, is 7. Now, what if the question asked:

In how many different ways could you arrange a single red sock and a single orange sock in a sock drawer if there are exactly 7 spaces for socks?

The answer is slightly more complicated this time. There are 7 ways you could arrange the red sock. Once the red sock is put in the drawer, there are now only 6 remaining spots in which to put the orange sock, so the total possible number of arrangements is $7 \times 6 = 42$. Now what if the question asked:

In how many different ways could you arrange a single red sock, a single orange sock, and a single yellow sock in a sock drawer if there are exactly 7 spaces for socks?

This time, we have 7 ways to put in the red sock, 6 places left to put in the orange sock, and then 5 remaining places left to put in the yellow sock. So the total number of possible arrangements is $7 \times 6 \times 5 = 210$ possible arrangements of these 3 socks in 7 spaces.

Hopefully you see where this is going. To find seven unique spaces for seven unique spots in which the order matters, we will have:

$$7 \times 6 \times 5 \times 4 \times 3 \times 2 \times 1 = 5,040 \text{ possible arrangements}$$

The answer to the question, therefore, is E. The factorial argument we just walked through is essentially a longhand version of the formulas we are about to discuss. The point of this explanation is that, even if you don't remember the specific formulas to use, you can combine the concept of the factorial with your own mathematic reasoning to work through most combination and permutation problems.

Combinations

When we refer to *combinations* instead of *permutations*, we are talking about groupings in which order does not matter, e.g., a red sock *and* a green sock instead of a red sock *and then* a green sock. In the following formula, C stands for the total number of possible combinations, n stands for the total number of elements involved (e.g., 7 socks), and k is the subset of unordered elements taken from n (e.g., 3 socks out of the 7):

$$_nC_k = \frac{n!}{k!(n-k)!}$$

This formula may look imposing, so let's apply it to a problem:

A sock drawer contains seven socks, each one a different solid color. The colors of the socks are red, orange, yellow, green, blue, indigo, and violet. If a person reaches into the drawer and pulls out two socks, how many different color combinations are possible in the selected pair of socks?

A. 12
B. 15
C. 21
D. 36
E. 42

You could write out every possibility and solve this problem that way, but it is almost certainly faster to use the formula. In this case, $n = 7$ and $k = 2$:

$$_nC_k = \frac{n!}{k!(n-k)!} = \frac{7!}{2!(7-2)!} = \frac{7!}{2!(5)!} = \frac{7 \times 6 \times 5 \times 4 \times 3 \times 2}{2 \times 5 \times 4 \times 3 \times 2} = \frac{7 \times 6}{2} = \frac{42}{2} = 21$$

Note that it was not necessary to calculate 7! out to 5,040. By canceling out common elements in the numerator and denominator, we were able to produce an equation that was quite simple to calculate. Most combination problems you see on the GMAT will work out smoothly like this; the test writers figure that if you can use this formula correctly, they don't need to test your multiplication skills.

Just for a visual verification, let's consider how we would have worked this problem by brute force:

RO

RY   OY

RG   OG   YG

RB   OB   YB   GB

RI   OI   YI   GI   BI

RV   OV   YV   GV   BV   IV

Add up the combinations: $6 + 5 + 4 + 3 + 2 + 1 = 21$. Clearly, either method works for a problem of this scope. One interesting thing to note with combinations is that picking 2 and leaving 5 behind is mathematically the same thing as picking 5 and leaving 2 behind. The formula for the latter situation would look like:

$$_nC_k = \frac{n!}{k!(n-k)!} = \frac{7!}{5!(7-2)!} = \frac{7!}{5!(2)!} = \frac{7 \times 6 \times 5 \times 4 \times 3 \times 2}{5 \times 4 \times 3 \times 2 \times 2} = \frac{7 \times 6}{2} = \frac{42}{2} = 21$$

Now let's move on to a slightly more complicated situation, in which the order of the elements matters.

Permutations

When order matters, the number of permutations is almost always larger than the equivalent number of unordered combinations. The formula for permutations, using the same variables of n for the total number of elements involved and k as the ordered subset of n, is as follows:

$$_nP_k = \frac{n!}{(n-k)!}$$

This is described as "n pick k," and it is always a larger number than "n choose k." Note that, as opposed to the combinations formula, there is no $k!$ on its own in the denominator. Let's apply the formula to an ordered variant of our previous example problem:

A sock drawer contains seven socks, each one a different solid color. The colors of the socks are red, orange, yellow, green, blue, indigo, and violet. A person reaches into the drawer, pulls out two socks, and puts a single sock on each foot. If each sock can fit either the left or the right foot, and if it matters whether a particular sock is on the left or the right foot, how many different sock fashion combinations could the person make from the seven socks?

A. 12

B. 15

C. 21

D. 36

E. 42

Applying the formula, with $n = 7$ and $k = 2$, yields the following:

$$_7P_2 = \frac{7!}{(7-2)!} = \frac{7!}{(5)!} = \frac{7 \times 6 \times 5 \times 4 \times 3 \times 2}{5 \times 4 \times 3 \times 2} = 7 \times 6 = 42$$

Working this problem by brute force would require writing down twice as many permutations as in the previous example if you wrote down every permutation, but you wouldn't necessarily need to. You could recognize that for each of the 21 combinations possible for pairing RO, RY, and so on, there is the mirror image form if the person switches the socks from right to left. In other words, for every RO there is an OR, for every RY there is a YR, and so on. Therefore, there must be exactly twice as many permutations as there are combinations, so $21 \times 2 = 42$.

Finally, let's consider how we would apply the permutation formula to a previous question:

> A sock drawer contains seven socks, each one a different solid color. The colors of the socks are red, orange, yellow, green, blue, indigo, and violet. If the socks are laid next to each other, how many different arrangements of socks could be made?
>
> A. 24
> B. 240
> C. 1,024
> D. 2,520
> E. 5,040

Applying the permutation formula, with $n = 7$ and $k = 7$ (since there is no subset), we get the following:

$$_7P_7 = \frac{7!}{(7-7)!} = \frac{7!}{0!} = \frac{7 \times 6 \times 5 \times 4 \times 3 \times 2 \times 1}{1} = 5,040$$

Clearly, knowing the formula allows you to sidestep the ugly process of writing out over 5,000 different permutations. If you don't feel that you can memorize the formulas, don't worry. As we stated earlier, combinatorics problems are rare on the GMAT.

PRACTICE PROBLEMS

1. An art gallery owner is hanging paintings for a new show. Of the six paintings she has to choose from, she can only hang three on the main wall of the gallery. Assuming that she hangs as many as possible on that wall, in how many ways can she arrange the paintings?

   A. 18
   B. 30
   C. 64
   D. 120
   E. 216

2. A composer's guild is planning its spring concert, and ten pieces have been submitted for consideration. The director of the guild knows that they will only have time to present four of them. If the pieces can be played in any order, how many combinations of pieces are possible?

   A. 40
   B. 210

C. 1,090

D. 5,040

E. 10,000

3. If x and y are odd integers, which of the following must always be a non-integer?

   A. xy

   B. $\dfrac{x}{y}$

   C. $\dfrac{y}{x}$

   D. $\dfrac{xy}{2}$

   E. $-xy$

4. Dan has a membership at a local gym that also gives classes three nights a week. On any given class night, Dan has the option of taking yoga, weight training, or kickboxing classes. If Dan decides to go to either one or two classes per week, how many different combinations of classes are available?

   A. 3

   B. 6

   C. 7

   D. 9

   E. 12

5. Terry is having lunch at a salad bar. There are two types of lettuce to choose from, as well as three types of tomatoes, and four types of olives. He must also choose whether or not to have one of the two types of soup on the side. If Terry has decided to have the salad and soup combo and he picks one type of lettuce, one type of tomato, and one type of olive for his salad, how many total options does he have for his lunch combo?

   A. 9

   B. 11

   C. 24

   D. 48

   E. 54

6. If r is negative and s is positive, which of the following *must* be negative?

   A. $\dfrac{|r|}{s}$

   B. $\dfrac{|s|}{r}$

C. $r^2 + s$

D. $r^2 s^2$

E. $-\dfrac{r}{s}$

Solutions

1. D. This problem asks for us to arrange the paintings, so it is a permutation. Using the $_nP_k = \dfrac{n!}{(n-k)!}$ formula and using 6 as our n and 3 as our k, we get the following: $\dfrac{6 \times 5 \times 4 \times 3 \times 2 \times 1}{3 \times 2 \times 1}$ When we cancel out, we get $6 \times 5 \times 4$, which is 120.

2. B. This problem is a combination, so we would use the formula $_nC_k = \dfrac{n!}{k!(n-k)!}$. Since 10 is our n and 4 is our k, the equation works out to $\dfrac{10 \times 9 \times 8 \times 7 \times 6 \times 5 \times 4 \times 3 \times 2 \times 1}{4 \times 3 \times 2 \times 1 \times 6 \times 5 \times 4 \times 3 \times 2 \times 1}$. Simplifying and multiplying gives us 210 combinations.

3. D. Since we know that x and y are odd, xy *must* always be odd. Therefore, $\dfrac{xy}{2}$ will always be a non-integer. None of the other answer choices has this relationship; in all of the other cases, it is possible to have values of x and y that would yield integer results.

4. D. This problem is best done by brute force. First, we must establish that Dan has the option of taking one or two classes per week. If he only takes one class, the three possibilities are Y, W, and K. If he takes two classes per week, the six possibilities are YY, KK, WW, YK, YW, and WK (because the problem is looking for combinations, not arrangements). So that adds up to nine possible combinations.

5. D. This is a relatively simple problem if you know the process—and you read carefully. All you have to do is multiply the number of options: 2 types of lettuce, 3 types of tomatoes, 4 types of olives, and 2 soup options. (You did remember the soup, didn't you?) $2 \times 3 \times 4 \times 2 = 48$, so 48 is our answer.

6. B. Based on the rules of positive and negative numbers, the only answer choice that must be negative is B, since it takes a positive and divides it by a negative. All other manipulations end up positive.

PART TWO
The Verbal and Writing Sections

CHAPTER 8

Critical Reasoning

INTRODUCTION

Many people find the GMAT Critical Reasoning section to be one of the more difficult parts of the test, mostly because the questions look different from any type of problem they have seen before. In casual reading you might come across something that looks like a Reading Comprehension passage, and you might notice grammatical errors like those in Sentence Correction questions, but you are not likely to encounter something that looks like a Critical Reasoning question. Don't worry, though. Critical Reasoning questions test the same thought processes you use every day.

Critical Reasoning questions test your skills in evaluating the strengths and weaknesses of arguments. This is something you do all the time, without necessarily realizing it. When you're buying a car, do you accept the salesperson's claim that *this is the car for you*, or do you examine the argument for potential weaknesses? If a co-worker approaches you with an idea about a new business direction, do you just stand there nodding, or do you consider the potential benefits and pitfalls of the idea? Obviously, in both cases you take the critical approach. You evaluate arguments every day of your life. Now, you must apply those same critical reasoning skills to the very specific format tested by the GMAT.

Approximately 12 of the 41 verbal questions you will see on the GMAT will be Critical Reasoning questions. Answering this type of question generally takes longer than the other types of verbal question, so ACT gives you a slightly smaller number of these questions. When you receive your first Critical Reasoning question, the instructions will look like this:

> For this question, select the best of the answer choices given.
> To review these directions for subsequent questions of this type, click on HELP.

These directions, obviously, don't tell you very much about what to expect. Here's what you can expect: You will see a brief reading passage, usually around 50 words long, that will present some form of argument. (ACT refers to these passages as a "stimulus.") Immediately after the passage will be a short question (the "question stem") that asks you to examine some aspect of the reasoning in the passage. As with all other GMAT question types, these questions give you five answer choices, of which only one is correct.

Critical Reasoning questions require you to quickly change gears between different topics and different kinds of convoluted logic. ACT will try to trip you up in logical traps and deceptive answers. To maximize your chances for getting the high score you want, you need to famil-iarize yourself with the basic structure and common patterns of Critical Reasoning questions, and you must approach the questions with an efficient and critical approach:

1. Read the question stem first, and determine what type of question you are facing.
2. Read the passage critically; analyze the basic components of the argument in light of the question.
3. Formulate a correct answer to the question in your head or on scratch paper.
4. Attack the answer choices until only one remains.

CRITICAL REASONING READING

The reading techniques most appropriate for Critical Reasoning questions are not the same as those best suited for Reading Comprehension questions. First, you will see only one or, rarely, two questions for each Critical Reasoning passage, so it is very beneficial to *read the question stem before reading the passage* so that you will know what to look for: assumptions, conclusions, structural elements, and so on. Second, every word in a Critical Reasoning passage could be significant to the answer, so you must read every word and understand every idea in the passage. The passages are short, so it is worth your time to read slowly and to understand fully the argument presented.

You must also *read critically*. What this means is to read with an eye toward the unstated assumptions in the argument, as well as toward its potential strengths and weaknesses. This is why it is important to read the question stem before reading the passage; you will know whether you are looking for a flaw in the argument, an unstated assumption, or a general understanding of the argument's logic. Reading with the question in mind will help you to identify the relevant parts of the argument with greater efficiency and accuracy.

Always try to formulate at least a rough answer before you look at the answer choices. The wrong answers are designed to confuse and mislead you, so don't look to the answers for help. If you have at least a vague idea of what the correct answer should look like, you will be able to distinguish more quickly between the correct and incorrect answer choices.

WHAT IS AN ARGUMENT?

Critical Reasoning passages are all arguments of one form or another. What *argument* means here is a statement in which a *premise*, or piece of information, is used to support a *conclusion*. Most ques-tions of this type include a premise or series of premises followed by a conclusion, although it is also fairly common for the conclusion to lead off the passage. An argument does not rest only on its stated premises, however, but also on the unstated *assumptions* that help support the conclusion. These unstated assumptions are the subject matter of most Critical Reasoning questions.

For example, an argument could look like the following:

Earthquakes often destroy houses that are not built according to the building code. Dora's house was built according to the building code, so it will survive the next earthquake.

In this argument, there are two premises:

Premise 1: Earthquakes often destroy houses that are not built according to the building code.

Premise 2: Dora's house was built according to the building code.

And one conclusion:

Therefore, Dora's house will survive the next earthquake.

The stated premises alone, however, are not sufficient to prove that the conclusion is correct. Stating that substandard houses are sometimes destroyed by earthquakes does not provide sufficient evidence to conclude that standard houses are never destroyed by earthquakes. In order for the argument to hold up, it must rely on one or more unstated assumptions. These assumptions could include the following:

▶ Buildings that comply with the building code will survive any earthquake.

▶ The next earthquake will not be so severe that it will destroy all buildings in the area.

▶ The building code in question is relevant to whether or not a building will survive an earthquake (as opposed to dealing exclusively with fire safety, flood safety, and so on).

This argument is somewhat simpler than that in most of the questions you will see on the GMAT, but its type of logic is representative. You could look at a Critical Reasoning argument as a kind of stool, with the conclusion as the seat held up by the legs of premises and assumptions. Most of these stools are slightly wobbly. GMAT questions may ask you to kick one of the legs (assumptions) out from under the stool to weaken the argument, or they may ask you to strengthen the stool by propping it up with another leg.

ASSUMPTION QUESTIONS

The most basic type of Critical Reasoning question asks you to identify an assumption of the argument. A question of this type might have the following wording:

▶ Which of the following is an assumption that enables the conclusion above to be properly drawn?

▶ Which of the following is an assumption made in drawing the conclusion above?

▶ The conclusion of the argument above cannot be true unless which of the following is true?

▶ Any of the following, if introduced into the argument above as an additional premise, makes the argument above logically correct EXCEPT

Assumption questions ask you to examine the relationship between the premise and the conclusion in an argument, and to determine what other conditions are necessary in order for the argument to be valid. In the example given about Dora's house surviving the earthquake, the correct answer will need to bridge the logical gap between the statement "Dora's house meets the building code" and the conclusion "Dora's house will survive the next earthquake." The answer will be some variant on

Houses that meet the building code will survive the next earthquake.

Note that the specific wording of the question will determine the specific wording that is acceptable for the answer. For example, if the question asks, "Which of the following is an assumption made in drawing the conclusion above?" then a statement like "The building code contains provisions that help protect houses from earthquake damage" could be sufficient. However, if the question asks, "Which of the following is an assumption that enables the conclusion above to be properly drawn?" then this relatively noncommittal statement would be insufficient, because it alone is not sufficient to prove that Dora's house necessarily will survive the earthquake. Critical Reasoning questions often hinge on the fine meaning of individual words, so always read the passages carefully, and read the question stems *very* carefully.

WEAKEN THE ARGUMENT

The most common type of Critical Reasoning question by far is the weaken-the-argument question. If the argument in the passage is a stool held up by assumptions, then this type of question asks you either to locate the spot where a leg is missing or to kick a leg out from under the stool. These questions could have the following wording:

▶ Which of the following, if true, would most weaken the conclusion above?
▶ Which of the following, if true, most severely undermines the argument presented above?
▶ Which of the following, if true, most clearly points to a flaw in the manufacturer's plan?

The thinking required here is very similar to that required for an assumption question, but you have to take it a step further. With these questions, you determine what assumptions have to be true in order for the argument to be true, and then find the answer that challenges one of those assumptions. In the example of Dora's house, a correct answer could look like one of these:

▶ When the last major earthquake occurred in the area, many houses that met the building code were destroyed.
▶ Geologists predict that the coming earthquake will be far more severe than any earthquake previously recorded in the area.
▶ The building code in Dora's area is designed exclusively to protect homes against flood and fire damage.

Each of these answers kicks at the assumptions holding up the conclusion, thereby weakening the argument. The thinking here is similar to the kind of thinking you use every day when you evaluate arguments: you look for flaws in the argument, and you consider ways in which the plan might not work exactly as promised.

When answering these questions, be careful not to pick an answer that actually strengthens the argument. These answers are tempting because they often deal with the same themes as answers that weaken the argument, but they use slightly different wording that produces the opposite effect. ACT usually puts at least one answer choice like this in every weaken-the-argument question.

STRENGTHEN THE ARGUMENT

Strengthen-the-argument questions use very similar thinking to weaken-the-argument questions, but instead of kicking the assumptions out from under the argument, you are asked to prop them up. This type of question comes up perhaps half as often as weaken-the-argument questions.

Strengthen-the-argument questions could have the following wording:

▶ Which of the following, if true, would most significantly strengthen the conclusion drawn in the passage?

▶ Which of the following, if true, offers the strongest support for the manager's conclusion that the locks were not at fault?

▶ Which of the following, if true, provides the strongest evidence in favor of the professor's hypothesis?

In the case of Dora's house and the earthquake, you must look for a statement that confirms one of the assumptions upon which the conclusion rests. Strengthening answers for that question might look like this:

▶ In the last earthquake, no buildings that met the building code were severely damaged, although several substandard buildings collapsed.

▶ Geologists predict that the next earthquake will be so minor that no damage is expected for any building in the area.

▶ The local building code was designed by architects who used data from previous earthquakes in the area to determine the best ways to protect homes from earthquake damage.

Each of these answers addresses potential flaws in the argument—the same flaws that a weaken-the-argument question would try to exploit. Remember, most of these arguments could go either way, and you need to be careful to make sure that the answer you choose points in the desired direction. As with weaken-the-argument questions, strengthen-the-argument questions almost always have at least one answer that deals with the correct subject matter, but in a way that is actually the opposite of what the question asks for. Don't be fooled.

Note that the correct answer to a strengthening question does not necessarily have to prove that the argument is correct. An answer that eliminates a single potential flaw in the argument could be the correct answer, as long as it is the best among the available answer choices.

INFERENCE QUESTIONS

Inference questions ask you to make a logical inference based on the information presented in the passage. The wording of these questions can vary widely, but the basic question behind them is the same: if the statements in the passage are true, what else has to be true? Assumption questions are actually a specific kind of inference question that asks: if the argument is valid, you can infer that which of the following assumptions must be true in order to logically connect the premise and the conclusion? The same type of critical thinking is used for both assumption and inference questions, but the nature of the inference is slightly different. The inferences discussed here are not necessarily vital components of the argument, but rather logical extensions from it; in the metaphor of the stool, if you kicked over one of these inferences, the stool would not necessarily topple over.

Inference questions might relate to the assumptions of an argument, to its premise, to its conclusion, or to its application to a related situation. Questions of this type might look like this:

▶ If the statements above are true, which of the following must be true?

▶ The statements above, if true, best support which of the following assertions?

▶ Which of the following can be correctly inferred from the statements above?

▶ If the statement above is true, then what outcome could be expected in a fight between a bear and a lion?

The key to answering these questions correctly is to keep your logic very tight. The writer of the argument can make unsupported assumptions, but you cannot. The correct answer will be a small logical hop, not a leap, from the statements in the passage. Many test takers are surprised by how reserved the correct answers for inference questions usually are, because they expect the correct answer to be a bolder statement. Do not expect a bold answer. The correct answer will usually be a very moderate statement, and it will be the only one that *has to be true if the statements in the passage are true.*

Let's consider an example with Dora's imperiled house:

Many houses that do not meet the building code will collapse in the next earthquake. The foundation of Dora's house contains the structural stabilizers required by the building code, so her house will survive the earthquake.

There are a few valid inferences that you can draw from this statement:

▶ Houses that do not meet the building code do not necessarily contain structural stabilizers.
▶ Structural stabilizers play a role in protecting houses from earthquake damage.
▶ Houses that do not contain structural stabilizers have a higher chance of being damaged in an earthquake than houses that contain these stabilizers.

Note that these inferences, while valid, do not all have to be true in order for the conclusion "Dora's house will survive the earthquake" to be true. Note also the moderate tone of the inferences. It is easier to establish that structural stabilizers "play a role in protecting houses" than that they "protect houses from all damage." Phrases like *not necessarily* and *have a higher chance* help create the weak claims that ACT tends to favor in this type of question. Remember, it is easier to prove that a weak claim must be true than that a strong claim must be true, so ACT usually relies on weak claims.

One method that many strong test takers use to evaluate answer choices for this type of question is to ask, *what if the opposite of this answer were true?* A correct answer will always make sense within the context of the passage, whereas the opposite of the statement generally will not. If a statement and its opposite both make equally good sense in the context of a sentence, then it probably is not the correct inference. Practice this technique with the inferences given earlier to see how it works; in every case, the opposite statement runs contrary to the sense of the passage.

LESS COMMON QUESTION TYPES

The previously discussed question types will make up the majority of the questions you see. If you master these question types, you can earn a good score on the Critical Reasoning section. If you want a great score, though, you should master the less common question types as well. There is a very good chance that at least a couple of the following question types will appear among the 12 or 50 Critical Reasoning questions you see on the GMAT.

Explain/Resolve the Discrepancy

Sometimes the arguments in Critical Reasoning passages will leave some ends clearly untied. They may present information that is confusing, or even contradictory, when taken on its own. The question will then ask you to provide a logical explanation that resolves the confusion. Questions of this type could look like this:

- ▶ Which of the following, if true, would best explain the sudden increase in productivity described above?
- ▶ Which of the following, if true, best accounts for the fact that ethanol is not widely used in internal combustion engines?
- ▶ Which of the following, if true, would help to explain the discrepancy described above?

The reasoning for these questions is actually quite similar to the reasoning used for assumption questions. Explanation questions often present you with a premise and a conclusion that seemingly do not work together, and you need to find the assumption that connects the two in a logical way. For example, consider the following passage:

Over the past year, Robert won several medals in running competitions. He was recently involved in a minor automobile accident, however, and as a result of his injuries, he currently is required to wear a cast. Despite this fact, he is favored to win the big race next month.

Which of the following would help to explain the apparent paradox described above?

You need to find the unstated assumption that could make the conclusion true in spite of the premise. A correct answer could be

- ▶ Robert wears a light cast on his wrist that does not slow him when he runs.
- ▶ The big race next month is a balloon race.
- ▶ The cast will be removed next week, and doctors expect Robert to be fully recovered before the big race occurs.

Each of these statements, if true, could account for Robert's favored status in the big race next month despite his cast and injuries. Before you look at the answers for a question of this type, always try to sketch out an idea of what the correct answer could look like. Jot down a short version of it on your scratch paper if that helps. The actual answer might take a very different direction from the one you sketched out, but the exercise of formulating an answer will help you to see the kinds of unstated assumptions that could fit between the premise and the conclusion.

Ask the Right Question

This variant on the explanation question asks you to take a step back and ask what else you would need to know in order to analyze or explain the situation. Questions of this sort could have the following wording:

- ▶ Which of the following must be studied in order to evaluate the argument presented above?
- ▶ Which of the following investigations is most likely to yield significant information that would help to evaluate the geologist's hypothesis?

▶ The answer to which of the following questions would be most useful in evaluating the significance of the experimental data described above?

Although these questions look somewhat different from the strengthen/weaken-the-argument questions discussed previously, the reasoning involved is not so different. The question/investigation/experiment in the correct answer should examine one of the premises or assumptions upon which the conclusion is based. You are not asked to strengthen or weaken the argument, but to provide a question for which the answer will strengthen or weaken the argument. Let's consider an example:

Many houses that do not meet the building code will collapse in the next earthquake. The foundation of Dora's house contains structural stabilizers designed to withstand any earthquake of 6 or lesser magnitude on the Richter scale. Consequently, Dora's house will survive the earthquake.

The answer to which of the following questions would be most useful in evaluating the accuracy of the conclusion above?

The answer you're looking for should be something on the order of, "What will be the magnitude of the next earthquake?" The answer to this question will tell you whether or not the argument can logically proceed from the premise—"Dora's house can withstand an earthquake of less than 6 magnitude"—to the conclusion—"Dora's house will survive the earthquake." The thinking is the same as that used when you look for the assumptions in an argument, only with this type of question, you need to take a step further back and ask the question that will validate or disprove a key assumption.

Parallel Reasoning

These questions ask you to analyze the logical structure of the passage, and then find the answer choice that displays the most similar reasoning. Questions of this type might look like one of the following:

▶ Which of the following is most like the argument above in its logical structure?
▶ Which of the following supports its conclusion in the same way as the argument above?
▶ The logical flaw in the reasoning above is most similar to that in which of the following statements?

What you need to do with these questions is break the argument down into its most basic parts. Critical Reasoning passages often contain convoluted wording and unnecessary details that obscure the main point of the passage. You need to look past these distractions and distill the basic argument. Consider the following question:

Over the past year, Robert won several medals in running competitions, including races of 400 meters and 800 meters. He was recently involved in a minor automobile accident, however, and as a result of his injuries, he currently is required to wear a cast. Consequently, when he competes in the big race next month, he will be unlikely to win.

Which of the following is most like the argument above in its logical structure?

A. The best runners are unlikely to be the best swimmers.
B. The student probably will not finish his paper on time because his computer is not working.

C. Jim's small frame and slow reflexes will prevent him from ever becoming a successful heavyweight boxer.

D. Maria accidentally fell down the stairs, leaving her with minor injuries and a cast on her arm.

E. Millions of people enter the state lottery every month, and consequently no individual ticket holder is likely to win.

These answer choices show some of the tricks ACT uses to make these questions difficult. Parallel reasoning questions almost always have a few answers that have surface similarities to the argument in the passage, but that do not actually demonstrate parallel reasoning. The mention of running in A and of a minor accident in D are designed to make you think that if the answer deals with similar subject matter, it must have a similar argument. This is not the case. In fact, *if you see an answer that contains very similar subject matter to the passage in question, you should be particularly suspicious of that answer.*

The best technique here is to distill the basic argument of the passage. It could be, "Robert is wearing a cast, so he is unlikely to win the race next month," or, even more basic, "Because Y is currently true, X is unlikely to happen." Remember, the specifics of the passage do not matter here, so stating the argument in terms of X and Y can help you focus on the reasoning. Now break down the reasoning in each of the answers and see if it is the same:

A. X is unlikely to be Y.
B. X is unlikely to happen because of the current situation Y.
C. X will not happen because of permanent condition Y.
D. X happened.
E. Because X is true, Y is unlikely to happen to Z.

Clearly, B has the most similar logical structure: because something is currently the case, a desired outcome dependent on that something is unlikely to happen. Restating arguments in terms of X and Y may not come naturally to you, so practice it on the tests in this book. When you take the test on the computer, write down your simplified statement of the argument on your scratch paper before you look at the answer choices. Remember, it is the job of the answer choices to mislead you, so make sure you know what you're looking for before you start on the answers.

Find the Conclusion

This question type is the counterpart to assumption questions. The passage will present you with a series of premises, and you will be asked to draw a logical conclusion from the information in the passage. Questions of this type could look like this:

▶ Which of the following conclusions can properly be drawn from the information above?

▶ The economist's argument, as presented above, is structured to lead to what conclusion?

The key to these questions is to choose the answer that *has to be true* if the premises in the passage are true. If you can think of a reasonable scenario in which an answer choice would not be true, then it is probably wrong. Keep your logic very tight here. The proper conclusion will require a logical hop, not a leap. It will most likely be consistent in content and tone with the premises in the passage.

Fill In the Blank

This type of question presents you with most of an argument, but leaves a blank space at the end, which you are asked to fill in. The blank space will usually represent the conclusion of the argument, but it could also represent a key premise. The wording for these questions will always be some variant of

▶ Which of the following best completes the passage below?

These questions are really quite straightforward. Examine the argument in the passage. Determine whether it is the conclusion or a premise that is missing. Formulate the answer in your head, then look through the answers for the one that fits. For example, if you see a question that looks like

Which of the following best completes the passage below?

Over the past year, Robert was unbeaten in running competitions at the distances of 400 meters and 800 meters. He was recently involved in a minor automobile accident, however, and as a result of his injuries he is required to wear a cast that will significantly restrict his movement for the next six months. Consequently, when an important running competition of 400 meters is held next month, _____.

The answer will be something on the order of "Robert will not be able to win the race" or, preferably, "Robert is unlikely to win the race"; the more moderate answer is usually the correct one. Look for the conclusion that the stated premises are directing you toward. In general, you should treat these questions the same as you would a find-the-conclusion question: keep your logic tight, and look for the answer that has to be true if the premises in the passage are true.

Boldface/Structure of the Argument

This is a relatively uncommon question type that has started to appear on the GMAT in recent years. It is somewhat different from all the question types described so far because it asks you to analyze the structure of an argument in addition to the argument's validity. A boldface question may look something like the following:

Many houses that do not meet the building code will collapse in the next earthquake. To meet the building code, houses must contain structural stabilizers sufficient to withstand an earthquake of 6 or lesser magnitude on the Richter scale. **Dora's house meets the building code**, so **Dora's house will survive the next earthquake.**

In the argument above, the two portions in **boldface** play which of the following roles?

A. The first portion is a conclusion that must be true based on the evidence; the second portion is a conclusion that is not necessarily true based on the evidence.
B. The first portion is a conclusion that must be true based on the evidence; the second portion is evidence in support of that conclusion.
C. The first portion is a conclusion that is not necessarily true based on the evidence; the second portion is evidence in support of that conclusion.

D. The first portion is evidence that supports the argument; the second portion is a conclusion that is not necessarily true based on the evidence.

E. The first portion is evidence that supports the argument; the second portion is a conclusion that must be true based on the evidence.

These questions, although different in structure from most Critical Reasoning questions, are still largely concerned with your ability to understand and appraise an argument. In this case, you should be able to read the passage and determine that the first portion in boldface—**Dora's house meets the building code**—is a premise, or "evidence that supports the argument," while the second portion—**Dora's house will survive the next earthquake**—is the conclusion. By determining these facts, you can eliminate choices A, B, and C. The difference between D and E is whether or not the conclusion must be true based on the evidence. In this case, the conclusion does not have to be true, since the argument is lacking a key assumption regarding the magnitude of the next earthquake. Therefore, the conclusion is not necessarily true, and D is the correct answer.

Remember, boldface questions, like all Critical Reasoning questions, test your ability to understand and evaluate arguments—and you understand and evaluate arguments every day of your life. This is just a different way of testing those skills. Read the passage slowly, determine which portion is the conclusion and which portions are premises, and evaluate the strength of the argument.

THE ART OF WRONG ANSWERS

ACT devotes four times as much effort to composing wrong answers as it does to creating the correct ones, so you should read any answer with a healthy dose of skepticism. ACT designs its wrong answers to look like right answers. The best way to avoid these trap answers is to formulate a clear idea of what the correct answer should look like before you approach the questions. Some of the techniques ACT frequently uses to create wrong answers are the following:

1. *Scope*. The correct answer must match the scope of the argument. Answer choices that are out of scope could be
   a. *Answers from left field*. These answers sound interesting, but do not actually address what the question asked.
   b. *Going too far*. These are very common. For example, if an argument relies on the assumption "Some Italian restaurants also serve Chinese food," it would be incorrect to choose an answer that states, "All Italian restaurants serve Chinese food." Always beware of absolute words like *all*, *none*, or *never*, because these very strong statements are often very hard to prove; GMAT arguments tend to rely instead on more qualified assumptions that include words such as *usually, could be, possible*, and so on.
   c. *Not far enough*. These answers make accurate statements that go part of the way toward answering the question, but are weaker than another answer that more fully answers the question. The key to avoiding these trap questions is to consider every answer choice carefully so that you don't fall for a half answer.
2. *True, but irrelevant*. ACT will give you statements that are most likely true in the context of the passage, but that don't answer the question. Always make sure you know exactly what is being asked.

3. *Restate the passage.* Unlike Reading Comprehension questions, Critical Reasoning questions are very unlikely to have a close paraphrase from the passage as the correct answer. Critical Reasoning questions ask for unstated assumptions, and they ask for conclusions only when the conclusion is not explicitly stated. The familiar wording of a restatement from the passage may look friendly, but it is almost certainly a trap.

4. *Value judgments/advocating positions.* ACT will often provide answer choices that advocate positions on the argument. These may be positions you agree with, but unless the question specifically asks for a value judgment, this is almost certainly the wrong answer. If any answer states that anyone or anything *should* be something—e.g., all homebuilders *should* build houses according to the building code—then you should probably keep looking for a better answer.

5. *Opposite.* For strengthen and weaken questions, ACT will almost always provide at least one answer that gives the *opposite* of what the question asked. A weaken-the-argument question might have one to four answers that actually strengthen the argument, and the same goes for strengthening questions. Read the question carefully so that you do not fall for this trap.

PRACTICE ARGUMENTS

The best way to prepare for the Critical Reasoning questions on the GMAT is to work through lots of practice questions. Before you dive into the Practice Problems at the end of this chapter (or the Practice Tests at the end of this book), it will be useful to practice the basic skills that apply to every Critical Reasoning question: breaking the argument into its component parts and evaluating the logic of the argument.

For each of the five following arguments, determine:

1. The premises
2. The conclusion
3. The assumptions
4. Two statements that weaken the argument
5. Two statements that strengthen the argument

The Arguments

1. The reticulated alligator is found in nature only in the coastal wetlands of North America. Unfortunately, because of urban expansion and industrial development, the coastal wetlands of North America are disappearing at a rate of 100,000 acres per year. With only two million acres of coastal wetlands left on the continent, it is inevitable that the reticulated alligator will become extinct within 20 years.

Premises: _____

_____

_____

Conclusion: _____

_____

_____

Assumptions: _____

_____

_____

Weaken: _____

_____

_____

Strengthen: _____

_____

_____

2. A state government is facing a budgetary shortfall in which expected income meets only half the costs of the projected budget. The state legislature has called an emergency session to address the fiscal crisis. One legislator, after reviewing the situation, concluded that the only way for the state to resolve the 50 percent shortfall in the budget is to double the state's personal income tax rate from 4 percent to 8 percent.

Premises: _____

_____

_____

Conclusion: _____

_____

_____

Assumptions: _____

_____

_____

Weaken: _____

_____

_____

Strengthen: _____

_____

_____

3. The MegaTek company has invested approximately $10 million in microphotonics product development in each of the last five years. Last year MegaTek's microphotonics products brought in revenues of $8 million, which was higher than the company had earned from these products in any previous year. The CEO, observing that in five years the microphotonics line had failed to ever yield a profit, concluded that canceling the microphotonics product line would be the correct economic decision for his company.

Premises: _____

_____

_____

Conclusion: _____

_____

_____

Assumptions: _____

_____

_____

Weaken: _____

_____

_____

Strengthen: _____

_____

_____

4. After experiencing disappointing sales results in the spring, a clothing company hired a consultant to analyze its sales data to determine how the company could boost its sales for the fall season. The consultant studied the sales data for the company's retail outlets in April and May and observed that during this period, the company sold 50 percent more pink sweaters than sweaters of any other color. The consultant concluded that the company should develop a whole line of pink clothes for the fall season.

Premises: _____

_____

_____

Conclusion: _____

_____

_____

Assumptions: _____

_____

_____

Weaken: _____

_____

_____

Strengthen: _____

_____

_____

5. The National Academy of Health has released findings that people who weigh over 200 pounds have a higher incidence of heart disease than do people weighing less than 200 pounds. A pharmaceutical company has developed a new drug called HeartApart, which improves the quality of life for people with heart disease. A representative from the pharmaceutical company has suggested to physicians that they should recommend HeartApart to their patients who weigh over 200 pounds in order to improve these patients' quality of life.

Premises: _____

_____

_____

Conclusion: _____

_____

_____

Assumptions: _____

_____

_____

Weaken: _____

_____

_____

Strengthen: _____

_____

_____

Solutions

Passage 1, the Reticulated Alligator

Premises: The reticulated alligator is found in nature only in the coastal wetlands of North America; coastal wetlands are disappearing at a rate of 100,000 acres per year; there are two million acres of coastal wetlands left in North America.

Conclusion: The reticulated alligator will become extinct within 20 years.

Assumptions: The reticulated alligator cannot survive anywhere other than the coastal wetlands of North America; the rate of disappearance of coastal wetlands will remain steady or increase until all the wetlands have disappeared.

Weaken: Viable populations of reticulated alligators have been maintained in captivity for decades. Reticulated alligators introduced into wetlands in Africa have thrived. Over a million acres of coastal wetlands have been declared permanent national wildlife preserves, which prohibit any form of building or industrial activity in the preserve.

Strengthen: The rate of destruction of coastal wetlands has increased in every decade of the twentieth century and has shown no signs of slowing down. Reticulated alligators kept in captivity have been found to be particularly vulnerable to diseases. The reticulated alligator population has already been diminished to the point that most biologists think the species will never recover.

Passage 2, State Budgetary Shortfall

Premise: A state government is facing a budgetary shortfall of 50 percent.

Conclusion: The only solution is to double the state's personal income tax rate.

Assumptions: Doubling the personal income tax rate will provide sufficient revenue to meet the 50% budget shortfall; there is no other source of revenue that can help address the budget shortfall; the problem cannot be addressed through reduced spending; it will be possible to double the personal income tax rate; doubling the personal income tax rate will actually result in twice as much personal income tax revenue.

Weaken: Personal income tax currently accounts for only one-third of the state's income. The majority of the state's income comes from excise taxes on natural resource production. The projected budget for this year is far higher than in previous years because it contains a provision to build a sports stadium to help lure a professional sports franchise to the state. Personal income tax rates in this state can be increased only through voter referendums, and the last three voter referendums to increase the personal income tax rate failed by large margins. Substantial increases in personal income tax rates often result in increased attempts by citizens to avoid paying taxes, up to and including the decision to leave the state.

Strengthen: The personal income tax accounts for 100 percent of the state government's income. Almost all of the state's annual budget is dedicated to fixed expenditures that cannot reasonably or legally be reduced. The citizens of the state are, in general, extremely happy to live there and would be willing to pay higher taxes in order to maintain the state services they have come to expect.

Passage 3, Microphotonics Product Development

Premises: MegaTek has invested $10 million in microphotonics in each of the last five years; last year microphotonics products brought in $8 million, which was greater than in any previous year; microphotonics products have not yielded a profit in any year.

Conclusion: Canceling the microphotonics product line is the correct economic decision.

Assumptions: MegaTek's microphotonics product line will not become sufficiently profitable in a sufficiently short span of time to justify further investment in the product line.

Weaken: MegaTek sold $1 million of microphotonics products two years ago, which was the first year in which MegaTek realized any sales from its microphotonics product line. (This answer suggests a rapid growth rate that could soon lead to profitability.) Industry experts consider MegaTek's microphotonics products to be the best products in a market that is expected to grow to over $5 billion per year within the next decade.

Strengthen: Industry experts do not believe that the microphotonics market will ever exceed $10 million. The introduction of nanophotonics technology last year made all microphotonics products obsolete. The $8 million MegaTek earned from its microphotonics product line last year was only marginally higher than the sum it earned from these products five years ago.

Passage 4, Pink Clothing Line

Premises: Spring sales for a clothing company were disappointing; in April and May the company sold 50 percent more pink sweaters than sweaters of any other color.

Conclusion: The company can increase sales by developing a whole line of pink clothes for the fall season.

Assumptions: The primary reason that the pink sweaters sold better than sweaters in other colors was that customers liked the color pink, and not some other factor involving these sweaters; the sales edge that the pink sweaters enjoyed will also apply in another season and on other articles of clothing.

Weaken: More than two-thirds of the sweaters offered in the spring at the company's retail outlets were pink. Because of a minor error that affected production of all of the company's pink sweaters in the spring but no other color of sweater, all pink sweaters were sold at a substantially lower price than sweaters of any other color. People tend to associate the color pink with springtime, but tend to favor earth tones in the fall.

Strengthen: People who have purchased pink sweaters are likely to buy other articles of clothing in the same color to match. Although the company's pink sweaters were priced slightly higher than the other colors of sweater sold in the spring, the company still sold out of pink sweaters by the end of May. The fashion trends that favored pink clothing in the spring continued to gather strength through the summer.

Passage 5, Heart Disease Drug

Premises: People who weigh over 200 pounds have a higher incidence of heart disease; HeartApart improves the quality of life for people with heart disease.

Conclusion: Doctors should recommend HeartApart to their patients who weigh more than 200 pounds in order to improve these patients' quality of life.

Assumptions: A sufficient percentage of the people who weigh more than 200 pounds have heart disease, that recommending the drug to the group in general is sensible; weight is the best criterion on which to recommend use of this drug to a group of people; the side effects of this drug are not so onerous that they will harm the quality of life of this group of people more than the drug will improve the group's quality of life.

Weaken: While heart disease is more prevalent among people who weigh more than 200 pounds than it is among people who weigh less than 200 pounds, only 5 percent of people who weigh more than 200 pounds currently have heart disease. HeartApart has been shown to induce side effects such as headaches and nausea in a significant percentage of people who take the drug. Epidemiological studies have shown that high blood pressure, a biometric that is approximately as easy to obtain as a patient's weight, is a far more reliable predictor of heart disease than weight alone.

Strengthen: HeartApart has no known side effects. HeartApart has been shown to prevent or delay the incidence of heart disease in people who are at risk for the disease but have not yet developed it. HeartApart offers such substantial benefits to people with heart disease that it will improve the average quality of life for a group even if only a minority of the group has heart disease.

PRACTICE PROBLEMS

Questions 1–2 are based on the following:

A community college is experiencing high turnover rates among its computer science faculty members. To rectify this problem, the computer science department head has proposed to the dean that beginning next year, starting salaries for computer science instructors be increased by 10 percent to provide a more competitive pay package.

1. Which of the following indicates a flaw in the department head's plan?

    A. Computer science faculty members generally indicate satisfaction with the number and type of classes they are given to teach.

B. The community college is in a relatively safe area of town with affordable housing.

C. Local technology companies provide good supplemental consulting work to many faculty members.

D. Yearly pay increases for instructors in all departments are set at a level below the current inflation rate.

E. There are several academic institutions nearby with similar pay structures to the department head's proposal.

2. Which of the following must be studied in order to evaluate the validity of the department head's plan?

A. What effects do changes in technology have upon the way classes are assigned?

B. Is the majority of turnover in the computer science department initiated by the faculty or the administration?

C. What factors are involved in recruiting the most talented computer science instructors?

D. What are the technological benefits to having advanced computer science classes taught on campus?

E. How would better turnover rates improve the quality of education offered by the community college?

Questions 3–4 are based on the following:

The Hanks Manufacturing Company has been receiving complaints about the quality of the products in the WWWidget product line. To eliminate these complaints, the operations director has decided to adopt a quality assurance program similar to that of WINK, Inc., which has a high customer satisfaction rate.

3. Which of the following may most reasonably be inferred from the statements above?

A. Products in the WWWidget line have been breaking shortly after being installed.

B. The WWWidget line is a relatively new line of products for The Hanks Manufacturing Company.

C. The operations director used to work for WINK, Inc. and is therefore familiar with the quality assurance program.

D. The WWWidget line is in danger of costing The Hanks Manufacturing Company its profitability.

E. The complaints about the WWWidget line indicate a customer satisfaction rate that is lower than that of the WINK, Inc.'s customer satisfaction rate.

4. Which of the following, if true, offers the strongest support for the operations director's plan?

A. The Hanks Manufacturing Company and WINK, Inc. both produce consumer-level Internet connectivity products and market them to similar target audiences.

B. The quality assurance program that the operations director is recommending will decrease the margins of the WWWidget line by 10%.

C. Despite the complaints about the WWWidget line, The Hanks Manufacturing Company still has a high customer satisfaction rate based on industry standards.

D. WINK, Inc. provides its customers with personal, onsite training on the use of its products.

E. The Hanks Manufacturing Company has been in business for over a decade longer than WINK, Inc.

Questions 5–6 are based on the following:

A survey was recently given to all high school students in a certain town to measure the effect of environmental factors on attitudes and behavior, and the results indicated that students who play a minimum of two hours per day of violent video games are more likely to engage in violent behavior in school and at home. Therefore, playing violent video games encourages violence among teens.

5. Which of the following is most like the argument above in its logical structure?

A. A developing country gained access to televisions on a widespread basis for the first time, and as a consequence, the population has become more entertainment-oriented.

B. A census report shows that more highly educated people live in areas of heavy pollution than in other areas; therefore, educated people are more likely to pollute.

C. A survey of homeowners indicated a strong preference for a reduction of property taxes; therefore, the upcoming proposal to reduce property taxes is likely to win.

D. A driver's education uses a video simulator to teach driving skills to students; only after passing the simulation can one obtain a learner's permit to drive an actual car.

E. A record company knows that most of its buyers are 18–25-year-old males; therefore, it markets its albums to stores where that target is most likely to shop.

6. Which of the following, if true, would most weaken the argument above?

A. The same survey was conducted in a neighboring town with similar results.

B. Playing violent video games keeps violent teenagers at home and prevents them from engaging in publicly aggressive behavior.

C. The survey used a standard question format that did not allow students to produce responses that could not be interpreted incorrectly.

D. Students who play violent video games often have a history of behavioral issues leading back to early childhood.

E. The survey was given over a period of days to ensure that all students attending the high school would participate.

Questions 7–8 are based on the following:

In the week before a local election, a news company polled registered voters in the area to ask them which candidate they planned to vote for. **Voters from a representative sample of genders, ages, races, and political affiliations were polled**, and 53% of them said they would vote for incumbent Jana Reyes for mayor over any other candidate. Based on the poll results, the news company concluded that Reyes would win the mayoral race.

7. Each of the following, if true, could weaken the conclusion presented above *except*:

   A. The news company conducted the poll by phone, mainly in the middle of the day over two weekdays.

   B. This race has been a particularly tumultuous one in which public opinion has often turned very quickly.

   C. In this town, any mayoral race in which the top candidate receives less than 55% of the vote will result in a runoff election.

   D. In the past, polls given by the news organization that showed more than a 5% lead by a particular candidate have predicted the outcome of the race with a high degree of accuracy.

   E. Due to an administrative error, Jana Reyes will be a write-in candidate on the ballot in the actual election.

8. In the argument above, the portion in boldface plays which of the following roles?

   A. It is a conclusion that must be proven in order for the argument to be valid.

   B. It is an assumption that provides little support for the conclusion of the argument.

   C. It is a premise that has questionable validity in the context of the argument.

   D. It provides evidence to support another premise of the argument.

   E. It provides evidence to support the news company's conclusion.

Questions 9–10 are based on the following:

Gary Johnson, a major star in track and field, advertises a certain brand of vitamin supplements for aspiring athletes. Alan runs cross country for his university and has decided to start a fitness regimen including the vitamins to improve his event rankings.

9. The statements above, if true, best support which of the following assertions?

   (A) The vitamins have been shown to improve stamina in scientific studies.

   (B) Alan's regimen also includes changes in his workout and diet.

   (C) Alan is not satisfied with some aspects of his current athletic performance.

   (D) Gary Johnson used the vitamins to become a major track and field star.

   (E) Alan has fallen victim to the marketing strategies of the company that manufactures the vitamins.

10. Which of the following, if true, most clearly points to a flaw in Alan's reasoning?

   (A) Gary Johnson runs the 400-meter dash, not cross country events.

   (B) The vitamins are designed to build muscles for shot put and discus throwers.

   (C) Alan's coach recommends a fitness program that includes vitamins and conditioning exercises.

   (D) While Alan's performance has remained steady over the last year, his event rankings have dropped because of the improved performance of his competitors.

   (E) The efficacy of the vitamins has mainly been tested on college-aged athletes.

Solutions

1. D.   The department head's plan states that a more competitive pay package will solve the turnover problem; therefore, the assumption is that the current pay package isn't adequate to keep faculty members there. If D is true, the value of the pay package will decrease over time, making it unlikely that the turnover problem won't return.

2. B.   The department head's plan also assumes that the faculty members have at least some choice in remaining at the school; otherwise, a competitive pay package wouldn't matter. So B brings up an issue that must be considered in order for the validity of the plan to be evaluated. By the way, did you notice the answer choices dealing with computers and technology? While they may bring up some issues that are peripherally important to computer science instructors, they are mostly distraction and not core to evaluating the plan.

3. E.   Since the operations director is recommending the quality assurance program as a way to eliminate the complaints, it is reasonable to infer that the company using that program has a higher rate of customer satisfaction than The Hanks Manufacturing Company. The other answer choices could very well be true and are, by and large, reasonable, but they can't be inferred from the information in the passage.

4. A.   Since the argument hinges on whether the two things being compared (the two companies) are actually comparable, anything that draws a similarity between them supports the operations director's proposal.

5. B.   The argument states that two phenomena are present; and assumes that one causes the other. It ignores the possibility that a separate factor causes both of those phenomena, and it also ignores the possibility that the cause and effect is actually reversed. The reasoning in B is similar. Again, notice the answers dealing with videos and other types of entertainment? They're just there to distract you from actually examining the structure of the argument.

6. D.   Again, the argument assumes that since two phenomena are there, one is actually the cause of the other and there is no alternate cause. Answer choice D attacks that assumption, so it weakens the argument.

7. D.   This argument, like many arguments that rest upon a poll or survey, assumes that the sample being polled is representative of the whole with respect to what is being asked about. The answers that weaken the argument either bring up ways in which the survey was not representative, or they introduce mitigating factors that would call the survey's validity into question. Answer choice D supports the conclusion of the survey because if Jana Reyes received 53% of the surveyed votes (and, according to the language of the survey, only one candidate could be chosen), then the most her nearest competitor could have received is 47%. That's a spread of more than 5%, so this survey falls into the category that the news organization typically predicts correctly.

8. D.   Since the statement in italic supports the survey results by saying the survey was representative with respect to some factors that may have influenced the results, it supports the conclusion. And since the statement was actually stated, it is a "premise" or "support," not an assumption.

9. C. If Alan is trying to improve his event rankings, it can be assumed that he is not satisfied with his current performance. Yes, this is a very wishy-washy statement, but remember, that means it is better supported by the argument than an extreme statement would be. And again, the rest of the answer choices may be reasonable, but they are not supported by the information in the argument.

10. B. Alan's plan assumes that the vitamins are appropriate for all track and field athletes, when their needs may actually be very different. Something designed for a heavy lifter who wants to build muscles may be entirely counterproductive for a runner like Alan.

CHAPTER 9
Sentence Correction

INTRODUCTION

ACT evaluates grammar and mechanics on two parts of the GMAT: the Sentence Correction questions and the Analytical Writing Assessment. There are about 15 Sentence Correction questions among the 41 Verbal questions, which means that Sentence Correction questions will make up a slightly larger part of your Verbal score than either Reading Comprehension or Critical Reasoning.

When you begin the Sentence Correction section of the computer-adaptive GMAT, you will see the following instructions:

> The question presents a sentence, part of which or all of which is underlined. Beneath the sentence you will find five ways of phrasing the underlined part. The first of these repeats the original; the other four are different. If you think the original is best, choose the first answer; otherwise choose one of the others.

> This question tests correctness and effectiveness of expression. In choosing your answer, follow the requirements of standard written English; that is, pay attention to grammar, choice of words, and sentence construction. Choose the answer that produces the most effective sentence; this answer should be clear and exact, without awkwardness, ambiguity, redundancy, or grammatical error.

> To review these directions for subsequent questions of this type, click on HELP.

Familiarize yourself with these instructions now so that you will not need to spend any time reading them on the day of the test.

As the instructions say, these questions test "correctness and effectiveness of expression" and your control of "standard written English." This is the English you were taught in high school, in which verbs agree with their subjects and modifiers are never misplaced. GMAT English is formal and dry; it sticks to the rules much more closely than we generally do when we're not taking a test.

You don't have to be a great writer to do well on the GMAT Sentence Correction questions. What you do have to do is figure out what makes a sentence incorrect. The English language is enormously complex, with thousands of stated and unstated rules of what makes a good sentence. Fortunately, your task will not require you to learn thousands of anything.

Most Sentence Correction questions are based on a handful of grammar points that you can quickly learn to recognize.

Here's how you should approach Sentence Correction questions:

1. Read the whole sentence, slowly and carefully. Don't just read the underlined part, because you need to determine what role the underlined part plays in the whole sentence.

2a. If there seems to be an error in the underlined part—and about 80 percent of the time there will be—try to identify what exactly is wrong. Do this before you look at the answer choices, because the test writers will try to hijack you with wrong answers that look correct. There are three basic ways in which an answer can be wrong:

    I. It violates a rule of grammar.

    II. It is worded in an unclear way.

    III. It is worded in a "nonstandard" way; i.e., it sounds funny.

2b. If the underlined section appears to be correct, note that to yourself, but remember that you still need to rule out every answer choice before you confirm that the original is correct.

3. Look at the answer choices one by one. If you found an error in the underlined part of the original sentence, eliminate answer choice A and any answer choice that repeats the same error. The test writers often repeat errors two or three times among the five answer choices, so identifying an error early and correctly can pay dividends in helping you get through the answer choices quickly. Look for additional errors that crop up in the answers and eliminate the answer choices where they crop up. With a little search-and-destroy work, you can be down to one answer choice much more easily and quickly than if you were trying to compare all five answer choices together.

If you never found an error in answer choice A, search for errors in the remaining answer choices so that you can eliminate those and hopefully, only have A remaining. It's much more reliable than just picking A because it sounds okay.

4. If you have two answer choices that seem okay, note differences between the two. The error or errors have to reside in something that is phrased differently in the two answers, or is included in one but not the other. Use the rest of the sentence to decide which one is correct. And once you're down to one answer choice, pick it and don't look back.

The trick to handling Sentence Correction questions quickly is to know the types of errors ACT is likely to throw at you. With some practice, you'll get the hang of it. The following seven error types encompass at least 95% of the Sentence Correction questions you are likely to see on the GMAT.

VERBS: WHERE THE ACTION IS

Verbs are the engines of English grammar, and as such they play an important role in differentiating between a good sentence and a bad one. Two of the major types of errors you will find in GMAT questions are subject–verb agreement and verb tense.

Subject–Verb Agreement

For any verb in a sentence, it must be clear who is the subject of the verb, and the verb must agree in number with the subject. For example, you might see a question that looks like this:

Leo, like most <u>babies, drink lots of milk.</u>

This sentence is incorrect, because the subject, "Leo," is a singular noun that requires the singular verb form "drinks." A correct answer could be "babies, drinks lots of milk" or "babies, enjoys drinking milk." Note that ACT will try to distract you by putting another noun or phrase between the subject and the verb so that you might think the plural noun "babies" is the subject of the sentence. Most people can catch errors of this sort pretty easily if the verb comes right after the subject, so the test writers employ a number of devices to complicate the subject–verb agreement:

1. Modifying phrases or clauses between the subject and the verb: "Leo, like most babies, drink lots of milk." (should be *drinks*).
2. Placing the verb before the subject in the sentence: "Drinks lots of milk does Leo, like most babies." (The verb error here is "Leo does drinks milk"; if it read "Drink lots of milk does Leo," it could be grammatically correct although stylistically ugly.)
3. Subject joined by *either . . . or* or *neither . . . nor*; although there are two nouns named, the true subject is *either* or *neither*, both of which require a singular verb: "Neither Leo nor the twins drink much milk" (should be *drinks*).
4. Collective nouns such as *audience, council, group, majority,* or *series.* Generally speaking, the number of a verb with a collective noun as its subject depends on the sense of the sentence, but on the GMAT this type of noun is usually treated as a singular noun. ACT also frequently uses singular collective pronouns: *each, everyone, everybody, nobody.* Example: "Each of the babies drink lots of milk" (should be *drinks*).

The key to handling this type of error is to determine what the subject is for each verb in the sentence.

Verb Tense

Tense errors are somewhat less common than subject–verb agreement errors on the GMAT, but they still appear often. The key to verb tenses is that they have to make sense. Actions that ended in the past cannot be happening in the present, and actions that are beginning in the present cannot be ongoing in the past. *For most questions, all of the verbs in the sentence should be in the same tense: past with past, present with present, and future with future.* This is a form of the principle of *parallelism,* which will be discussed later. If an underlined passage contains two different tenses, read it carefully to make sure that the chronology makes sense. Two verb tenses that the GMAT often uses in incorrect sentences are the conditional (used to describe actions that have not occurred but could occur) and the past perfect (used to describe actions in the past that ended in the past).

Here is an example of a verb tense question:

We dried off the car after <u>it would stop</u> raining.

A. it would stop
B. it will stop
C. it stops
D. it was stopping
E. it stopped

You should be able to tell quickly that A is incorrect, because it makes no sense to use the conditional tense for a past action. B is also incorrect because the future tense makes no sense here, nor does the present tense in C. The answer obviously needs to be in a past tense, but the past imperfect in D doesn't make sense because the *after* in the sentence suggests that there was a definite point in time at which the rain stopped, so the ongoing past action of D is illogical. Only the past tense in E makes sense.

Another kind of verb tense question could look like this:

After <u>it had stopped</u> raining, we will dry off the car.

A. it had stopped
B. it will be stopping
C. it stops
D. it was stopping
E. it stopped

The underlined passage uses the past perfect tense, which applies to past actions that terminated in the past. In the context of this sentence, the past perfect makes no sense, because the sentence clearly implies that the drying will occur in the future after the ongoing rain stops; the past tenses in A, D, and E, therefore, cannot be right. B and C are the only sensible choices in the chronology of the sentence. Of the two, C is the superior choice, because "After it stops raining, we will dry off the car" clearly conveys the intended meaning of the sentence, and because "After it stops raining" is more *idiomatic* than B, "After it will be stopping raining." *Idiomatic expression* errors will be discussed later, but the basic principle is that any verb form as awkward as "it will be stopping raining" is almost certainly not the right answer.

PRONOUNS: IN PLACE OF THE RIGHT ANSWER

A pronoun is a substitute word that takes the place of another noun. *He, she, it, they,* and *them* are all pronouns. ACT very frequently uses pronoun errors in Sentence Correction questions. The test writers introduce errors by using the wrong pronoun for the noun it replaces, or by using pronouns in such a way that it is not entirely clear to whom or what the pronoun is referring.

Pronoun Reference

The first type of pronoun error we are going to examine is called a *pronoun reference* error. In this type of error, a pronoun is used, but it is not perfectly clear to whom or what the pronoun refers. A pronoun reference error could look like this:

According to Albert, Amy and Philip both wanted to take Ben shopping for hats, <u>but he didn't know which one of them to choose.</u>

The problems here are that *he* could refer to either Albert or Ben, and *them* could refer either to Amy and Philip or to the hats. A correct answer for this question might look like:

> According to Albert, Amy and Philip both wanted to take Ben shopping for hats, *but Ben didn't know which one of the hats to choose.*

A variant on the pronoun referent error could be called a *missing referent* error. In this type of error, the underlined passage contains a pronoun that does not have a noun elsewhere in the sentence to replace. This type of error could look like:

> Although Wellington feared a French naval invasion, he was confident that the coastal defenses could handle anything <u>they could throw at them</u>.

The problem here is *they*; although you could infer that *they* refers to the French navy, there is no mention in the sentence of the French navy, the French, French ships, or any other plural noun that *they* could replace. Be on the lookout for any use of *it*, *they*, or *them* that lacks a referent.

Pronoun Number

Another common form of pronoun error is *pronoun number* errors, in which a plural pronoun replaces a singular subject, or vice versa. This type of error could look like this:

> Jim obviously loves his two hounds, Rose and Shasta, <u>but they do not walk the dogs as often as</u> the veterinarian recommends.

The pronoun *they* in this context can refer only to the hounds, but the context of the sentence demands that Jim be the one who is not walking the dogs. The proper pronoun here should be *he*.

MISPLACED MODIFIERS

Like the pronoun reference error, the problem with the misplaced modifier is that it makes the sentence unclear. A *modifier* here is a phrase that modifies the subject of another phrase. In general, the modifier should be right next to the subject it is modifying. A *misplaced modifier* is one that, because of its position in the sentence, could lead a reader to misinterpret what noun is being modified. A misplaced modifier could look like this:

> <u>Running on all four legs with startling speed, Sylvia quickly photographed the fleeing chimpanzee.</u>

Sylvia's position in the sentence immediately after the modifying phrase makes her the obvious subject of the phrase, but the context of the sentence makes this reading ridiculous; even if Sylvia could run on all fours with startling speed, she certainly couldn't photograph any fleeing chimps while doing so. A clearer version of this sentence might look like

> Sylvia quickly photographed the fleeing chimpanzee, *running on all four legs with startling speed.*

Or, even better:

Sylvia quickly photographed the chimpanzee *as it fled on all four legs with startling speed.*

Why is the second correction better than the first? Because it simplifies the sentence, replaces a participle with a declarative verb, and removes any chance of ambiguity from the modifying clause. But for our purposes here, the important thing is to recognize what a misplaced modifier looks like.

Here are some of the types of misplaced modifiers you might encounter:

1. A participial phrase (this means a phrase with an *–ing* word), such as

Running on all fours, Sylvia quickly photographed the fleeing chimpanzee.

2. A participial phrase introduced by a preposition

Upon returning to the mountain lake, the ice-cold water chilled Sylvia to the bone. (Sylvia is much more likely than the water to be returning to the mountain lake.)

3. Adjectives

Wet and cold, the fire of the camp had never looked so inviting to Sylvia. (It is Sylvia who is wet and cold, not the fire.)

4. Adjectival phrases

A photojournalist with an excellent international reputation, Sylvia's photographs of wildlife always bring in top-dollar commissions. (Sylvia is the respected photojournalist, not her photographs.)

How do you spot a misplaced modifier? Whenever you see a dependent clause (i.e., a clause that could not be a complete sentence on its own) set off by commas, identify which noun in the sentence it appears to modify. If it is unclear which noun is the subject of the clause, or if the apparent subject makes little sense in the context of the sentence, then you have a misplaced modifier on your hands. Read through the answer choices carefully to determine which choice offers the most logical reading.

PARALLELISM

One of the principles of standard English usage is that if a sentence presents multiple related items or phrases, then each of those items or phrases should be presented in *parallel* grammatical structures. There are a few ways in which this principle is tested on the GMAT. The most common way is when items are mentioned in a list, as in the following:

Harold, a fervent environmentalist, is angry about the loss of wetlands, the decrease in biodiversity, <u>and the destroying</u> of the rainforest.

The problem here is that the first two items in the list are nouns (*loss* and *decrease*), but the third item is a gerund (*destroying*). The parallel form would be *destruction*. A parallel construction error could also look like the following:

Harold, a dedicated father, is always bringing the kids to soccer practice, attending piano concerts, <u>and he reads stories</u> to the children at night.

For the final clause to be parallel with the previous two, it should take the participle form "*and reading stories* to the children at night." Note that the nonparallel form could appear anywhere in the sentence, so whenever you see a list, be on the lookout for parallel constructions.

The other common form of parallel construction tested on the GMAT is in a two-part sentence in which the grammatical construction of the first half creates an expectation that the second half will have a similar form. This sort of question could look like this:

To say that Harold is a dedicated father <u>is giving credit where</u> credit is due.

Since the first clause of the sentence (*To say that Harold is a dedicated father*) begins with an infinitive, it creates the expectation that the second clause will take the same grammatical form. The correct form of this sentence would be

To say that Harold is a dedicated father *is to give credit where* credit is due.

Parallel construction questions can be difficult for many test takers, because parallelism is one of the principles of formal grammar that people routinely violate in everyday speech. Don't worry, though; with a little practice, you can quickly recognize the types of questions that ACT uses to test this principle. Just be on the lookout for (1) any kind of lists and (2) any two-part sentence.

IDIOMATIC EXPRESSIONS

Idiomatic expression refers to the way in which we generally match words together. Idiom errors are both the easiest and the hardest errors to spot on the GMAT. They are the easiest because, if you've been speaking English your whole life, the wrong answers should naturally look wrong and the right answers should naturally look right. They are also the hardest questions because there are thousands of idiomatic constructions in English, and if you are not familiar with the idiom in question, then you are pretty much out of luck.

Fortunately, the GMAT generally tests only a limited set of idiomatic constructions with which most test takers are already familiar. After looking over the following list and working through the Sentence Correction questions in the practice tests, you should have a good idea of the types of constructions that appear on the test. With this type of question in particular, if an answer sounds awkward or overly wordy, it is probably wrong. An idiomatic expression question might look like:

Since I don't enjoy vegetables, I would like the mango <u>rather with</u> the broccoli.

- A. rather with
- B. rather than
- C. rather
- D. but not also
- E. but rather not

The answer is B, because *rather than* is idiomatic and *rather with* and the other answers are not. Your ear alone may not always be a reliable test for Sentence Correction questions, but when you *know* that no one would say, "I would like the mango but rather with the broccoli," you should trust your instincts.

Here are some of the idiomatic expressions that have appeared in Sentence Correction questions in the past:

according to	conclude that	not only . . . but also
appear to	contribute to	prohibit from
as great as	a debate over	rather than
as good as, or better than	defined as	regard as
attributed to	determined by	result of
based on	a dispute over	see . . . as
because of	different from	subject to
choose from	in danger of	think of . . . as

FALSE COMPARISONS: APPLES AND ORANGES

The test writers often compose questions that incorrectly compare two things that are not comparable. A false comparison could look like this:

The tomatoes in this bin are <u>bigger than the other bin</u>.

The intended meaning, obviously, is that the tomatoes in one bin are bigger than the tomatoes in the other bin, but what the statement actually compares is the size of the tomatoes with the size of the other bin. Tomatoes should be compared to tomatoes, apples to apples, and oranges to oranges. A correct version of this sentence might read:

The tomatoes in this bin are bigger than those in the other bin.

Sentence Correction questions sometimes test this concept by falsely comparing two actions, or, rather, by comparing an action with a noun:

After observing the race, we can all agree that greyhounds run <u>faster than bulldogs</u>.

Although in everyday usage most people would find this sentence acceptable, it actually draws a false comparison between an action—the running of greyhounds—and a type of dog—bulldogs. The answers ACT would accept here would be ". . . greyhounds run *faster than bulldogs run*," or ". . . greyhounds run *faster than do bulldogs*."

You should always be on the lookout for false comparisons when a Sentence Correction question contains words such as *like, as, than,* or *similar to*. Note that *like* can compare nouns or noun phrases, while *as* compares clauses (i.e. phrases containing verbs). This is a form of idiomatic expression: X is *like* Y, but X is to Y *as* Y is to Z.

QUANTITY

The test writers often throw in questions that test your knowledge of how standard English handles different quantities. These questions usually focus on the different terminology English uses to describe quantities of two and quantities of greater than two. For example, you choose *among* the five answer choices, but you choose *between* the two best choices, and the superior of two choices is the *better* choice, while the superior among five choices is the *best* choice. A GMAT quantity question might look like this:

Although I cannot tell which one is <u>better, Adam can always differentiate between</u> the four flavors.

Since this sentence is talking about four flavors, the proper wording would be:

Although I cannot tell which one is *best, Adam can always differentiate among* the four flavors.

The following table presents some of the quantity words that frequently appear on GMAT questions:

If Two Items	If More than Two Items
Better	Best
Between	Among
Less	Least
More	Most

Another type of quantity question that sometimes pops up is the distinction between *countable* and *noncountable* items. If you are talking about a quantity to which you would normally assign a whole number, such as six cars or eight loaves of bread, then it is a countable item; if you instead talk about the amount of something rather than its number, such as a lot of traffic or a little soup, then it is a noncountable item (but note that a *cup of soup* would be a countable item). The most common *countable quantity* question that appears on the GMAT involves the distinction between *fewer* and *less*:

Mother gave me <u>less biscuits than</u> she gave Madeleine.

This is the sort of error that people make frequently in everyday speech. *Biscuits* is a countable term, since they occur in discrete units that should be represented as a whole number, so the proper word to compare their quantity is not *less* but *fewer*. The sentence should read

Mother gave me *fewer biscuits than* she gave Madeleine.

Note that English is somewhat inconsistent on this point; if mother had given Madeleine a greater number of biscuits (countable) or a larger amount of soup (noncountable), in either case she would have gotten *more* than me. *More* is used with both countable and noncountable items.

Here are some of the *countable quantity* words that show up on the GMAT:

Countable	Noncountable
Fewer	Less
Many	Much
Number	Amount, Quantity

Another variant to watch out for is how you talk about the word *number*. Consider the following example:

The number of orangutans <u>was more than</u> the gorillas.

This sentence actually has two problems: first, it draws a false comparison by comparing a number (the number of orangutans) with a kind of animal (gorillas); second, while there were more orangutans than gorillas, the number of orangutans was *greater* than the number of gorillas. A number is not *more*, it is *greater*. The sentence should read

The number of orangutans *was greater than that of* the gorillas.

Any time you see numbers or quantities in a GMAT question, be on the lookout for the errors just described.

RARE ERRORS

The previous seven error types will encompass the majority of the errors you will see on the GMAT. Remember, though, that all grammatical rules are fair game, so ACT could always throw something uncommon at you. Reviewing grammar textbooks and working through many practice questions could help prepare you if ACT decides to do something unusual. Some grammar points that are occasionally seen on GMAT questions include the following:

1. *The subjunctive mood.* Almost all of the verbs we use are in the *indicative* mood, which indicates actions that have occurred, are occurring, or will occur. The *subjunctive* mood is used to express wishes or statements that are not actually true. Subjunctive verbs appear in the past tense or past perfect tense; *were*, the subjunctive verb you are most likely to encounter, is the subjunctive form of *was*. Here are some examples of the subjunctive in action:

    If she *were* tall, she could be a good basketball player. (The implication is that she is not tall.)
    I wish I *had given* you a present. (But I did not.)

The rules for the subjunctive voice are complicated and it is encountered rarely on the GMAT, so your valuable study time would probably be better spent on other more common topics. If you're gunning for a perfect score, though, and you have the time, check out a grammar book and familiarize yourself with the subjunctive.

2. *Possessives.* ACT sometimes tests whether you know how to form a possessive properly. Don't confuse a possessive with a contraction: *its* is the possessive of *it*, *it's* is the contraction of *it is*. Don't accept a double possessive: "That *friend of Larry's* is also a friend of mine." (It should be either *Larry's friend* or *friend of Larry*).
3. *Split infinitives.* Do not put a preposition between the "to" and the verb form when forming an infinitive: "*to boldly go* where no one has gone before" is stylistically incorrect. This principle will almost certainly not be the main error tested in any sentence, but if an answer choice includes a split infinitive, it is probably incorrect.
4. *Terminal prepositions.* Do not end a sentence with a preposition (i.e., *to, with, about*, and so on). This grammar point is also very unlikely to be the main error in any sentence, but if you see it in an answer choice, that choice is probably incorrect.

THE MOST COMMON TYPE OF ERROR

The most common question type you are going to see is—no error at all. In about 20% of the Sentence Correction questions you encounter, which means probably about 3 of 15 on the computer-adaptive test, the underlined passage will be the best answer. These can sometimes be the most difficult questions, because the test format leads us to doubt all of the answers, and because ACT tries to make the wrong answers look right and vice versa. So how do you approach these questions? If the underlined passage does not contain any of the error types just listed, then choices B through E almost certainly will. Read through them slowly to seek out the errors in these choices. Once you have confirmed that all of the other choices are incorrect, go with answer A.

HOW TO APPROACH A HARD QUESTION

For each section of the GMAT, ACT has produced questions that most people will get right and that most people will get wrong. To break into the upper echelon of scores, you will need to be able to take difficult questions in your stride. ACT can make Sentence Correction questions difficult in a number of ways:

1. Correct answers that look wrong
2. Incorrect answers that look right
3. Longer underlined passages with several possible errors in each one
4. Several choices that are grammatically correct, but with one choice more "standard" than the others

If you're working on a question and it appears that ACT is throwing one or more of these challenges at you, congratulations! If you are getting hard questions, then you probably have a good chance at a high score. If you have absorbed the information in this chapter and worked through the practice questions in the accompanying tests, you should be able to tackle these hard questions with at least a good shot at getting them right. We all get stumped sometimes, though. If that happens, here are some tips for improving your odds of choosing the right answer.

Not Necessarily Wrong, but Not Right Either

The test writers follow patterns when they write questions. There are certain verbal constructions that they frequently use to compose incorrect answers. Some markers of wrong answers include the following:

▶ *Any answer that includes being* if it isn't talking about a human being. Simple, declarative verbs are usually clearer and more direct than any verb form including *being*.

▶ *Unwieldy verb constructions* like *having been {verb}-ed* or *will have been {verb}-ing* are usually wrong; for example, if a question gives you a choice between something like "the document having been read by Jack . . ." and "after Jack read the document . . .," you should probably go with the simpler verb construction.

▶ *Passive verb forms when active verbs would work just as well;* see the previous example. ACT, like English teachers everywhere, maintains that the active voice is more forceful than the passive voice, and therefore preferable. Passive verbs are very likely to be incorrect if there is no actor specified in the sentence (i.e., "the book was moved," but the sentence doesn't say who moved it).

▶ *Words ending in* –ing *when there are simpler choices.* Be careful here, because gerunds and participles are often parts of the correct answer, but if you have a choice between *the founding* and *the foundation*, your odds are slightly better with *the foundation*. If you have a choice between *founding* or *to found*, you should probably go with *to found*. ACT generally prefers nouns and infinitives to gerunds and participles, so keep this in mind when sorting through the answer choices.

Note that these are guidelines, not rules. The correct answer to a question could be: "The human being, having been read the document, opted for reading the document himself." But it's just not very likely. Try out these guidelines on some practice questions and try to get a feel for how ACT composes incorrect answers. Once you get a feel for the patterns ACT uses commonly, you will have a much easier time identifying the incorrect choices when you take the test.

If You Have to Guess

Hopefully, the information presented in this chapter and your own knowledge of English grammar will allow you to seek out and destroy the errors in all 15 or so Sentence Correction questions you will see on the GMAT. Unfortunately, tests don't always go the way we plan, ACT sometimes throws curveballs, and some grammar points inexplicably disappear from our brains when we sit down in front of the computer. If these things happen, don't panic. As with all the sections of the GMAT, the best strategy is to eliminate the answers you know are wrong and then choose the answer that looks best among the remaining choices.

There are some strategies that you can use for guessing on Sentence Correction questions. Because of the way this type of question is written, there are two strategies that will substantially improve your chances of guessing the right answer, even if you cannot definitively eliminate a single choice.

1. Pick the Shortest Answer. GMAT English favors "effectiveness of expression," and this often translates into "the most concise way of saying something." This is a good principle to know for writing in general—that if you have two equally correct and clear ways of saying something, the shorter way is probably the better choice. Also, when the question writers think up their wrong answers, they often throw in unwieldy constructions that make the incorrect answers longer than the correct one.

Remember, this is a guideline, not a rule. The shortest answer is often wrong, and the longest answer is sometimes right. But, if you look at many GMAT questions, the shortest answer is the correct one much more often than is the longest answer.

Remember also that this strategy does *not* work on the other question types. Sorting answers by length is relevant only to Sentence Correction questions because of the specific way that ACT composes wrong answers. *Do not* use this strategy for Critical Reasoning questions.

2. Pick the "Most Common" Answer. What "most common" means in this context is the answer with the most elements in common with the other answer choices. The reason this strategy is effective is that ACT has to compose incorrect answers that look like the correct answer, so the writers will often compose answer choices that are mostly correct but have one or two elements (verb form, pronoun, preposition, and so on) that make them incorrect. So if one verb form appears in three of the answers and the other two offer different verb forms, the choices with the "more common" verb form are more likely to be the correct answer; if two answer choices use one preposition while the other three use different prepositions, the choices with the "more common" preposition are more likely to be the correct answer; the answer that contains the "more common" verb form and the "more common" preposition is the "most common" answer, and it is more likely to be correct than the other choices. For example:

Greg went to the bank <u>for speaking among</u> Carrie.

    A. for speaking among
    B. by speaking with
    C. to speak with
    D. to speak by
    E. to speak

The "most common" answer, C, combines the most common verb form—*to speak*—with the most common preposition ending—*with*.

Will this strategy always work? Absolutely not. It will probably give you the correct answer less than 50 percent of the time, but probably more than 20 percent of the time. It is also not a bad way to compare the grammar of the different answers; in the process of looking for the "most common" verb tense or pronoun among the choices, you might figure out the grammar point in question and choose the correct answer. Try out this strategy on some sample questions to see if it works for you.

This particular strategy is more effective on Sentence Correction than on the other Verbal question types. A similar strategy is effective for Problem Solving questions.

FURTHER STUDY

Working through practice tests is the best way to prepare for any GMAT question type, but you can also improve your performance on Sentence Correction questions by outside study. Any high school or college grammar text will present the same grammar rules that the test writers use when they compose questions. Some of the best books written on the subject of English usage are *The Elements of Style* by William Strunk, Jr., and E.B. White, and *The Chicago Manual of Style* by the staff of the University of Chicago Press. A little extra study on English usage will not be a waste of time in any event, because we can all improve our writing skills.

PRACTICE SENTENCES

The GMAT often complicates things by combining several types of errors in the same question. The following sentences provide some extreme examples of what the GMAT might throw at you. Read through the sentences, then list as many types of error as you can identify in the sentence. Don't rewrite them at this point, since you won't have the opportunity or responsibility for doing that on the test, and you don't want to get in the habit of wasting time. Answers and rewrites follow the practice sentences so that you can see how the sentences might be phrased correctly.

After the practice sentences, you will have the opportunity to practice on realistic GMAT-style problems.

1. Cottonseed oil, the cooking oil of choice <u>within fried-food fanatics, burn with the higher temperature than corn oil</u>.

Errors:_____

_____

_____

2. If you had to say who was the greatest painter <u>between the three greatest painters of the Renaissance, being Michelangelo, Leonardo, and Raphael, we would have to say that Leonardo is the better</u>.

Errors:_____

_____

_____

3. Colleen and Lauren, the daughters of Cindi, <u>was at the mall when Cindi's mother said hello to her, their grandmother</u>.

Errors:_____

_____

_____

4. After riding this bus for the last 15 years, <u>I had been accustomed with the fumes of gas, the rudeness of fellow passengers, and to search in vain for a seat</u>.

Errors:_____

_____

_____

5. <u>There was too many rats on the boats, so it was demanded for there to be less of them onboard before I board it</u>.

Errors:_____

_____

_____

Solutions

1. Errors: idiomatic expression ("cooking oil of choice within fried food fanatics" and "burn with the"); subject-verb agreement ("cottonseed oil ... burn"); false comparison (compares corn oil with the burning of cottonseed oil). A correct version could look like

Cottonseed oil, the cooking oil of choice *among fried-food fanatics, burns at a higher temperature than does corn oil.*

2. Errors: verb tense ("was the greatest . . . is the better"); parallelism ("if you had to say . . ., we would have to say"); quantity ("between the three . . . Leonardo is the better"); idiomatic expression

("being Michelangelo . . ."; also, the general principle that you should avoid answers that contain "being"). A correct wording could be

If you had to say who was the greatest painter *among the three greatest painters of the Renaissance—Michelangelo, Leonardo, and Raphael—you would have to say that Leonardo was the best.*

3. Errors: subject–verb agreement ("Colleen and Lauren . . . was"); pronoun reference or pronoun number ("Cindi's mother said hello to her"); misplaced modifier ("when Cindi's mother said hello to her, their grandmother"; Cindi's mother *is* their grandmother). A correct wording could be

Colleen and Lauren, the daughters of Cindi, *were at the mall when Cindi's mother, their grand-mother, said hello to them.*

4. Errors: verb tense ("after . . . the last 15 years, I had been accustomed"; the past perfect implies that this condition ended at a definite point in the past, but the logic of the sentence suggests that the author is still accustomed to these things); idiomatic expression ("accustomed with"); parallelism ("the fumes . . ., the rudeness . . ., and to search"). A correct wording might look like

After riding this bus for the last 15 years, *I have become accustomed to the fumes of gas, the rudeness of fellow passengers, and the vain search for a seat.*

5. Errors: subject–verb agreement ("there was . . . rats"); passive verb ("it was demanded"; the sentence does not say who demanded, or what "it" is); countable quantity ("less of them"; this could apply only to "rats" or "boats," both of which are countable); pronoun reference ("before I board it"; what is "it"?); idiomatic expression ("demanded for there to be"). A correct wording of this sentence might read

There were too many rats on the boats, so I demanded that there be fewer rats onboard before I board a boat.

PRACTICE PROBLEMS

1. Belgrade is widely known as the <u>capital city of Serbia, but it is also one of the oldest</u> cities in Europe and the largest in the territory formerly known as Yugoslavia.
   A. capital city of Serbia, but it is also one of the oldest
   B. capital city of Serbia, nevertheless also one of the oldest
   C. Serbia's capital city, and it is also one of the older
   D. Serbia's capital, but it is also one of the older
   E. capital city of Serbia, but it is also one of the older

2. Contrary to popular belief, not every snake with reddish or brownish scales is a <u>copperhead; a wide variety of perfectly harmless snakes that are frequently mistaken</u> for copperheads.

   A. copperhead; a wide variety of perfectly harmless snakes that are frequently mistaken
   B. copperhead; a wide variety of perfectly harmless snakes that are frequently mistook

C. copperhead; there is a wide variety of perfectly harmless snakes that people frequently mistook

D. copperhead; there is a wide variety of perfectly harmless snakes that people frequently mistake

E. copperhead; a wide variety of perfectly harmless snakes that people frequently mistake

3. The controversial amendment to generally accepted accounting principles will require companies <u>accounting for stock options as expenses at the time they are granted.</u>

A. accounting for stock options as expenses at the time they are granted
B. accounting for stock options expenses at the time they are granted
C. that accounted for stock options expenses when they are granted
D. to account for stock options expenses at the point of time they are granted
E. to account for stock options as expenses when they are granted

4. The structures designed by Ralph C. Harris were fifteen- and seventeen-story buildings, and for their <u>time, were some of the larger and more luxurious hotels and residences</u> in existence.

A. time, were some of the larger and more luxurious hotels and residences
B. era, they were some of the larger and more luxurious hotels and residences
C. era, were some of the largest and more luxurious hotels and residences
D. time, they were some of the largest and most luxurious hotels and residences
E. era, were some of the largely and more luxuriously hotels and residences

5. <u>Weishan Liu, her being one of the world's leading players of the guzheng instrument,</u> has accumulated a long list of honors, including recording soundtracks for movies such as *Dim Sum* and *Indiana Jones and the Temple of Doom.*

A. Weishan Liu, her being one of the world's leading players of the guzheng instrument
B. Weishan Liu, one of the world's leading players of a musical instrument called the guzheng
C. Weishan Liu, the guzheng being a top instrument for her
D. The guzheng, of which Weishan Liu is one of the top players in the world
E. The guzheng, Weishan Liu being one of the top players in the world

6. <u>The cooperative announced last week that due to increasing sales in the tri-county area,</u> it would distribute a quarterly dividend of more than twice the usual amount to all of its members.

A. The cooperative announced last week that due to increasing sales in the tri-county area
B. The cooperative announced that due to increasing sales last week in the tri-county area
C. Last week, the cooperative announced that due to sales increasing on a tri-county basis
D. Last week, the cooperative, which announced increasing sales in the tri-county area
E. Due to increasing sales in the tri-county area the cooperative announced last week

7. Farmers frequently plant a nurse crop such as oats to protect seedlings from overexposure to the sun, prevent soil erosion, and <u>it reduces growth of weeds.</u>

   A. it reduces growth of weeds

   B. reduce weed growth

   C. reduction of weeds

   D. reduces weeds from growing

   E. reduce the growing of weeds

8. Chorioretinitis is an inflammation of the eye that normally <u>effects only small children,</u> and it usually can be treated with antibiotics.

   A. effects only small children

   B. effects small children ordinarily

   C. affected small children

   D. affects small children

   E. affects only small children

9. Though most laypeople do not know the difference between classical and clinical homeopathy, practitioners assert that clinical homeopathy is directed toward particular organs and tissues, and <u>has contributed more to scientific research.</u>

   A. has contributed more to scientific research

   B. contributed to more scientific research

   C. it contributes more scientific research

   D. contribute to most scientific research

   E. had more scientific contributions to research

10. Unlike the <u>United States, the president of the Philippines are elected</u> to a six-year term in office.

   A. United States, the president of the Philippines are elected

   B. United States, the president of the Philippines is elected

   C. United States, the people of the Philippines elect a president

   D. the president of the United States, the people of the Philippines elect

   E. the president of the United States, the president of the Philippines is elected

11. Recent improvements in technology, such as lighting that mimics the pattern and intensity of natural sunlight, <u>have made working night shifts much safer and more productive.</u>

   A. have made working night shifts much safer and more productive

   B. have made those that work night shifts safer and more productive

   C. has made it safer and more productive to work at night

   D. has increased the productivity and safety of working at night

   E. had made working at night more safer and increased productivity

12. Though dentists recommend brushing one's teeth three times a day, many adult Americans <u>brush just twice a day and floss hardly never.</u>

    A. brush just twice a day and floss hardly never

    B. brush your teeth twice and never floss

    C. brush just twice but rarely floss at all

    D. brush twice daily but hardly ever floss

    E. only brush twice daily and rarely floss at all

Solutions

1. A. A is grammatically correct as written and doesn't introduce some of the awkward structure found in B. C,D, and E are problematic because they use the word "older," which clearly isn't appropriate when discussing the cities of Europe, of which there are more than two.

2. D. The part of the original sentence after the semicolon could not stand on its own, so A could not be correct. B and E repeat the same problem; B and C also have the incorrectly structured "mistook." Answer choice D has correct verb construction and sentence structure.

3. E. The idiom "require to" dictates that A, B, and C are incorrect. D introduces the wordy phrase "at the point of time," which E says more simply as "when."

4. D. The sentence as it is written leaves out a subject to the verb "were," as does C and E. The main difference between the remaining answer choices is the use of the superlatives (largest/most) versus comparatives (larger/more), and because it is reasonable to assume that the buildings are being compared to multiple others, D is the best answer.

5. B. "Her being" in the original sentence is awkward and an incorrect use of pronoun object case. C is also awkwardly structured, and D and E put the guzheng as the subject of the sentence. Since the guzheng itself cannot win honors and record soundtracks, B is the best choice.

6. A. Answer choices B and C are almost as good as A, but they change the meaning slightly and are a bit awkward. D and E create fragments and comma splices, so are not the best answers.

7. B. Items in a list must be phrased in a parallel way, so "reduce" must be the verb used, which narrows the choices down to B and E. "Weed growth" is more direct than "the growing of weeds", so B is the better choice.

8. E. One issue in this sentence is "affect" versus "effect." Since "affect" is correct as a verb, A and B are incorrect. C is in the past tense, which is not appropriate for this sentence, and D changes the meaning of the sentence.

9. A. This sentence tests verb tense, so you need to determine which tense is needed. Since the contribution is probably extending into the present, present perfect tense is most appropriate, making A the best choice.

10. E. The original sentence compares the United States to the president of the Philippines, which is not correct; a correct sentence would compare a president to a president or a country to a country. If you look at the remaining answer choices to see what is being compared, only E presents a proper comparison and is otherwise grammatically correct.

11. A. Since the subject of the sentence is "recent improvements," only A and B agree in number and are in the proper tense. B changes the meaning of the sentence and doesn't make much sense, so A is best.

12. E. "Hardly never" is incorrect construction. B changes the pronoun from the "one" already in the sentence to "you" and also changes the meaning of the last part with the word "never." The exclusion of the word "daily" in C changes the meaning of the sentence significantly! The conjunction "but" in C and D is improper since the sentence has no change in the direction of meaning. E is the only choice that makes sense and is grammatically correct.

CHAPTER 10
Reading Comprehension

INTRODUCTION

Imagine you're sitting in your office, and your boss walks in and throws a stack of papers on your desk. The papers are the 10-K filings for five companies in an industry related to yours. Your boss says, "Do we need to be worried about these guys? Read those and come by my office at 11, I need to meet with the Board at 11:30. Oh, and I need to know the total widget sales for each company for each of the last three quarters." He walks out. You now have several hundred pages of financial documents to go over in less than an hour. What do you do?

You read fast, obviously, but that's not enough. You have to read selectively, and you have to read aggressively. If you're going to have any hope of getting through the reading and still having time to think, you're going to need a strategy. You need to read for big ideas, and you need to read for specifics.

These are the skills that the GMAT Reading Comprehension questions test. Approximately 14 of the 41 questions you will see on the GMAT Verbal section will be Reading Comprehension questions. These questions will be preceded by a reading passage of around 300 words, followed by three or four questions that test different types of reading skills. Before you begin one of these passages, you will see instructions that look like this:

> The questions in this group are based on the content of a passage. After reading the passage, choose the best answer to each question. Answer all questions following the passage on the basis of what is stated or implied in the passage.

> To review these directions for subsequent questions of this type, click on HELP.

Familiarize yourself with these directions now so that you will not need to waste time on them when you take the test.

Reading Comprehension questions favor people who can read fast and have good short-term memories. If you have these attributes, great; if not, don't worry—you can still get a great score if you know how to approach the material in the right way. Having the right strategy can improve almost anyone's score; the fastest reader in the world could bomb the Reading Comprehension section if he or she doesn't understand how ACT distinguishes between correct and incorrect answers.

READING COMPREHENSION STRATEGY

The key to doing well on Reading Comprehension questions is to get the information you need in the least amount of time. Time management is probably more important on this type of question than on any other, because you could burn up minutes poring over unimportant details in the passage if you don't know where to look; if that happens, you will shortchange your time for Critical Reasoning and Sentence Correction. You need to read strategically. This does not mean speed reading, and it does not mean rushing your answer. There are parts of each passage that you should read slowly and deliberately, and each question deserves time for careful thought. The trick here is to focus on the information you need and to waste as little time as possible on information that will not help you answer any questions.

So how do you do this? You need to be prepared. The best test takers walk into the test with a clear idea of what they are going to encounter, and with a strategy for approaching the passage and questions. To achieve your goals on the GMAT Reading Comprehension questions, you need to

1. *Know your enemy.* Know what to expect from the passages and the questions. If you know what's coming, you can tackle the GMAT with greater confidence and speed. You will also have a better idea of what correct and incorrect answers look like.

2. *Read strategically.* First, read the passage strategically for "big-picture" ideas and structure. Then, once you start on the questions, focus on the specific text that is relevant to your question. The correct answers are always grounded in the text.

3. *Practice.* Work through practice questions until you master steps 1 and 2.

PASSAGE TOPICS

Reading Comprehension passages have covered a wide array of topics in the past, but you can probably expect to see at least one passage dealing with science or technology, one passage dealing with business or economics, and one passage dealing with the social sciences (history, sociology, political science, and so on). Some people naturally feel more comfortable with some topics than with others, but you should approach them all in the same way: read fast for the big picture, focus on the information you need to answer the questions, and don't bring in any outside knowledge that cannot be verified by the passage itself.

You can also expect that at least one of the passages you see will deal with either women or a minority ethnic group. ACT includes these passages in part as a response to long-term criticism that the specific subject matter of its tests provides an advantage to white males. The question of whether these minority-themed passages rectify this historical imbalance is outside the scope of this book, but what is relevant to this book is that these reading passages invariably present minority groups in a positive light. *If you see an answer choice that suggests something negative about a minority group, you can be sure that it is the wrong answer.*

PASSAGE STRUCTURES

GMAT reading passages come in a variety of shapes, although they are all pretty close to the same size—approximately 250 to 350 words. Some present the views of the author in the first person, while others discuss ideas and facts from a strictly third-person perspective. Some start off with a hypothesis that they then go on to support, while others start with a hypothesis that they then attempt to refute. A very common type of passage compares two opposing arguments. Other passages explore topics without stating much of an argument at all. You should practice with many different reading passages in order to get a feel for the range of structures.

Paragraphs in the passage will often have "structural signposts" near the beginning that signal how the paragraph fits into the structure of the passage. Some of these signal that the paragraph is going to continue the line of thought expressed in the preceding paragraph, while other words signal that the paragraph is going to express a different point of view. The structural signposts you are likely to encounter on GMAT passages are

Continuing a Line of Thought	Changing the Line of Thought
▶ In addition	▶ Although
▶ By the same token	▶ But
▶ Likewise	▶ Despite
▶ Similarly	▶ Even though
▶ This argument	▶ Except
▶ Therefore	▶ However
▶ Thus	▶ On the other hand
	▶ Nevertheless
	▶ Yet

A very common type of passage will contrast a conventional viewpoint with a new viewpoint. Any passage that begins with a phrase like *the conventional view, the commonly accepted belief, it has been widely accepted,* or *the majority of economists believe* is probably going to compare a conventional viewpoint with a new line of thinking.

Should you treat passages with different structures differently? Not really. But you will probably be more comfortable on the test day if all the passages you see have structures similar to passages that you've seen before. And once you've worked through several practice passages, you will get a feel for the kinds of words and phrases that signal whether the passage is going to explore a topic, advance a hypothesis, compare competing arguments, or do something else.

QUESTION TYPES

There are roughly six different types of Reading Comprehension questions that ACT composes.

1. *Main idea.* Main idea questions test your ability to capture the big picture. Main idea and supporting idea questions are the most common types of Reading Comprehension questions. Main idea questions are often the first question after the reading passage. A question of this type could have the following wording:

   ▶ Which one of the following most accurately summarizes the main point of the passage?
   ▶ Which of the following statements most accurately captures the central idea of the passage?
   ▶ Of the following titles, which would be most appropriate for the contents of this passage?
   ▶ The passage can best be described as which of the following?

In most cases, the main idea will be expressed in one or two sentences in the first paragraph, although it is occasionally expressed in the final paragraph or, rarely, in an interior paragraph. Sometimes the main idea is never stated explicitly . If you cannot locate a clear thesis statement, it is usually helpful to skim through the passage and determine how it gets from the ideas of the first paragraph to the ideas of the final paragraph. What is discussed, and why?

Since main idea questions are so common, it is often a good idea to summarize the main point to yourself after your initial reading of the passage and then write that idea down on your scratch paper. This way, you will be less likely to be hijacked by tempting but incorrect answer choices. Tempting answers include those that state the central idea but add an element that is not included in the passage, and those that state the main idea of a single paragraph or section of the passage accurately but fail to address the entire passage.

2. *Supporting idea.* You will encounter a number of supporting idea questions on the test. Questions of this type focus on specific ideas or pieces of information presented in the passage. They require a more focused reading than do main idea questions. A question of this type could look like

   ▶ According to the passage, Kutusov believes which of the following regarding interest rates?
   ▶ Which of the following statements best expresses the Federalists' response to Montesquieu's criticism, as presented in the passage?
   ▶ According to the passage, mitochondria play what role in the metabolic processes of cells?

The answers to this type of question are always grounded in the text. They are often close paraphrases of statements made in the passage. Determine the keywords in the question—*Kutusov* and *interest rates*, *Federalists* and *Montesquieu*, *mitochondria* and *metabolism*—and scan through the passage until you find these words in connection with one another. Read up and down a few lines from these keywords. You will usually find a statement in the passage that says essentially the same thing as one of the answer choices. Sometimes you need to scan a little further, and sometimes you need to combine pieces of information from separate sentences, but with this type of question, the answer will always come directly from a statement in the passage.

3. *Inference.* In contrast to supporting idea questions, inference questions deal with ideas that are *not* stated in the passage. Inference questions prompt you to make a logical jump from the statements expressed in the passage to a conclusion that should be true if the statements in the passage are all true. Inference questions might look like

   ▶ Based on the information given in the passage, it can be reasonably inferred that Huntington would approve of which of the following forms of government?
   ▶ The author of the passage would be most likely to agree with which of the following statements?
   ▶ Based on the contents of the passage, it can be inferred that a biologist would be LEAST likely to observe a moose in which of the following environments?

The trick to inference questions is to stick closely to the wording of the passage and to keep your logic tight. The correct answer will require a logical hop, not a leap. Do not make unwarranted assumptions or use your own knowledge of the topic. What you need to do is read the section of the passage that the question asks about and then figure out *which of the answer choices must be true if the statements in the passage are true.*

A related type of inference question asks about the *author's purpose* in writing the article. Authors often have an unstated agenda or goal in mind when they write something. Sometimes ACT asks you to infer what that agenda or goal might be. This sort of question might look like

▶ The author most likely mentions the case of the Peruvian condor for what purpose?

▶ From the presentation of information in the concluding paragraph, it can be reasonably inferred that the author believes which of the following about Skokalky's theory?

Inference questions dealing with the author's purpose may relate to the main idea of the passage, they may relate to specific comments that the author makes, they may deal with the structure of the passage as a whole, or they may rely primarily on the tone of the article. The key to these questions is to choose the most complete statement of the author's goal for which there is indisputable evidence. *Make sure that any answer choice you select has clear support in the text.*

4. *Applying information.* Like inference questions, applying information questions deal with topics that are not mentioned explicitly in the passage. This type of question asks you to take the information given in the passage and apply it logically to a context outside of the passage. An applying information question could look like

▶ Which of the following situations is most similar to the economic situation described in the second paragraph?

▶ The medical test described in the passage would most likely be helpful for which of the following individuals?

▶ Parker's argument, as presented in the passage, is most similar to which of the following lines of reasoning?

You should take the same approach to this type of question as you take with inference questions, except that you usually need to make a larger logical leap. These questions test your ability to recognize the structure of an argument or an idea, and then recognize the same structure in a different context. Test takers often find this type of question to be among the more difficult Reading Comprehension questions.

5. *Logical structure.* These questions examine your ability to analyze the structure of the passage and to determine what role specific components play in the whole. Logical structure questions may look like

▶ The second paragraph plays what role in the passage?

▶ Muellner's theorem is most likely mentioned in lines 10–12 for what purpose?

▶ Which of the following most accurately describes the structure of the passage?

Logical structure questions often blend "big-picture" reading and focused reading. If you read strategically, you should have a good idea of how to answer a question like this after your initial quick reading of the passage. If you have a good idea of what the passage as a whole is about and what role each paragraph serves in the passage, you should be able to sort quickly through the answers to determine which answer best describes the structure of the passage. Keeping track of structural signals like *however* and *on the other hand* will help you recognize the common structures of GMAT passages more quickly.

6. *Style and tone.* This type of question is somewhat less common than the others because many Reading Comprehension passages are too dry to permit a challenging question on matters of style and tone. There is a good chance, though, that at least one of the questions you see will ask you to draw a conclusion about the author or the passage based on the author's use of language. A style and tone question could look like

  ▶ The author's attitude toward international polio control efforts could best be characterized as which of the following?
  ▶ Which of the following best describes the tone of the passage in its presentation of the Heinrichs hypothesis?
  ▶ Based on the statements in lines 20–23, which of the following could be inferred about the author's attitude toward bulldogs?

The key to answering this type of question is to identify "tone words" in the passage. Words with positive connotations—"*fortunately*, the *brilliant* scientist had an *auspicious* beginning"—set a kind of tone, while words with negative connotations—"*sadly*, the *misguided* plan was an *utter failure*"— lend an entirely different tone. Style and tone are naturally subjective topics, so to avoid disputes on this type of question ACT includes a relatively small number of tone words that correspond closely with only one of the available answers. Note that the answer will almost always be moderate in nature; Reading Comprehension passages almost never take strong positions on topics, and they almost never take a tone that is overly anything. "The author is guardedly pessimistic about disease control efforts," for example, will almost always be a better choice than "The author is furious about the dismal failure of disease control efforts." This principle of moderate over extreme applies to most types of Reading Comprehension questions.

If there are no obvious tone words, you can still get a sense of the tone through the author's choices of what information to present and how to present it. For example, if an author compares two arguments and presents criticisms of only one of them, you can reasonably infer that the author favors the argument that is not criticized.

STRATEGIC READING

By now you should have a good idea of what you are going to face on the GMAT Reading Comprehension section. It's time to start putting that knowledge into practice.

Before you attempt to answer any of the questions, power-read the passage. *Spend between one and two minutes* reading over the passage very quickly to determine

1. What is the *main idea* of the passage?
2. What is the basic *structure* of the passage, and what role does each paragraph play?
3. What are the *keywords* : the handful of people, things, or ideas that the passage revolves around?

You do not need to understand every idea in the passage, and you do not need to note every detail—most of the details will not appear on a single question. Do not waste time and mental energy mastering information that will not help you score points. In this initial reading—skim, speed-read, power-read, whatever you want to call it—your main goal is to get a clear idea of the big picture of the passage so that when you start on the questions, you will know where to look for information to confirm your answers.

Keep your scratch paper at hand, because you will probably want to take notes. First, try to identify the thesis statement, if there is one. It's often in the first paragraph. If there isn't a clear statement of the main idea of the passage, you still should develop a clear statement of it yourself, because there is a very good chance that you will see a main idea question. Jot down a statement of this main idea on your scratch paper. Note down in a few words or a sentence the primary subject matter of each paragraph. Don't spend a lot of time making these notes—just enough to get a good mental picture of the passage.

Other things to keep a lookout for in your initial reading: *tone words* that suggest what the author thinks about the subject matter of the passage, and *structural signposts*, words and phrases like *however, on the other hand,* or *so-and-so disagrees,* which signal a change in the argument of the passage. Keep a mental note of where these words are so that you can find them quickly if they seem relevant to a question.

It's important to note that one technique that was very effective on the old paper GMAT will not work now. This was to read the questions before reading the passage so that you would know what keywords to look for in the passage. Unfortunately, this technique will not work on the computer-adaptive GMAT, because you see only one question at a time. Since you will not be able to use this technique on the actual test, do not use it while doing practice questions on paper.

ANSWERING THE QUESTIONS: FOCUSED READING

Strategic reading is a great way to tackle a passage, but on its own it earns you no points. It's time to start earning your high score. Dive into the questions with *focused reading*. Focused reading means that you now need to slow down and read the questions, the answer choices, and the relevant parts of the passage slowly and carefully. Make sure you understand exactly what the question is asking. When you look through the specific parts of the passage relevant to the question, make sure you understand what the passage is saying. The correct answer is always *grounded in the text*.

When you read a question, you should be able to recognize quickly which of the six question types described earlier the question is (although sometimes ACT is tricky and combines two question types). The different question types require somewhat different strategies, but in each case *you need to consider every answer choice* or ACT puts a lot of effort into making the wrong answers look right, so you need to eliminate every other answer before you can be sure that you have the right one.

When you see a main idea or logical structure question—a question that deals with the passage's big picture—you should have a fairly good idea of what the answer should look like from your initial strategic reading of the passage. If you identified a likely thesis statement, do a focused reading of the thesis statement and the surrounding sentences. Work through the answer choices one by one, and check back through the passage to confirm that your understanding of it is correct. Also, be open to changing your mind about the passage if one of the answer choices makes you think about it in a new way.

Supporting idea questions are almost always grounded in specific words or sentences in the text. Read the question stem carefully, identify the subject matter of the question, and then find the specific place or places in the passage where this subject matter is mentioned. Read a couple of lines up and down from the mention, and then *find the answer that corresponds as closely as possible to the statement in the text*. ACT has to make these questions indisputable, so the correct answer will almost always correspond closely with a specific phrase or sentence in the text.

Style and tone questions are also grounded in specific words in the text, but these words are often scattered throughout the passage. For this type of question, hopefully, you noted any strong tone words on your initial reading of the passage. Go back to the passage and examine how these tone words are applied. Examine the structure of the argument and consider whether the structure provides an element of tone. For example, if there are two arguments presented, is one presented in greater detail and in more positive terms than the other? And remember, for tone questions, *the correct answer will usually be moderate in tone*.

Inference and applying information questions require you to focus in on the text and then take a step back. You need to focus very closely on how the passage deals with the subject matter of the question. Once you have a firm understanding of the argument, principle, or situation described in the passage, apply your understanding to the answer choices with cold logic. With inference questions, *find the answer choice that has to be true if the statements in the passage are true*. With applying information questions, avoid surface similarities in the answer choices and look for the answer choice that matches most closely the fundamental dynamics of the specified situation.

THE ART OF THE WRONG ANSWER

Of all the GMAT question types, Reading Comprehension questions have the most potential for subjectivity. It is very easy for two people to interpret the same text in two different ways; this is why English professors and corporate lawyers have jobs. ACT, however, cannot offer questions with subjective answers, because if it did, it would face thousands of angry complaints on every question (as it is, it faces only hundreds). In their efforts to make answer choices that are indisputably incorrect, the test writers tend to follow certain patterns:

▶ *Going too far.* The best answer is the one that corresponds as closely as possible to the information presented in the text, and *only* the information presented in the text. If an answer is mostly correct but makes an additional statement about something that is not mentioned in the text (and if it is not an inference or applying information question), it is probably wrong. If an answer overstates the case, it is almost certainly wrong. *The GMAT values moderation*, and it values sticking very closely to the text. Don't get carried away with extreme answers.

▶ *Not going far enough.* These are answers that are partly correct, but not as comprehensive as they could be. They might state the central idea of a paragraph instead of the central idea of the passage. They might mention one of the important arguments presented in the text, but neglect to mention that there is another. They may closely paraphrase the text, but not address the question entirely. These questions are the reason you need to read *all* of the answer choices, because a partially correct and not obviously incorrect answer can look awfully tempting when the clock is running down. Mark it down as a weak possibility and keep looking for a better answer.

▶ *Answering the wrong question.* Some answer choices are tempting because they would be the answer to *another question.* An elegant statement of the passage's main idea may look like a good answer, but not when the question asks for a supporting idea instead. This is where your focused reading comes in. Read the question carefully so that you know exactly what it is asking for. Read the relevant part of the passage carefully so that you know exactly what it is saying.

▶ *Quoting the wrong part of the passage.* These can be tricky. If you know that an answer sounds very similar to something that you read in the passage, and it is related to the subject matter of the question, that answer can look very tempting when you're in a hurry, even if it does not really answer the question. This is why you need to combine strategic and focused reading in an effective way. Use your initial reading to learn what pieces of information are where, so that you can find the right information quickly when you need it. The whole point of strategic reading is to use your time wisely so that you will not be rushed into the wrong answer.

Theory is great, but there is no substitute for practice. Put your techniques to work on the following passages and on the passages in the practice tests. Master the material presented in this chapter, and then adapt it into a personal approach that bests suits your own style of reading. Good luck!

PRACTICE PROBLEMS

Since the 1994 introduction to supermarket shelves of Calgene's Flavr Savr tomato, the first genetically modified food item to be offered to consumers, transgenic foods have made a quiet transformation of the food production system in America. The amount of farmland planted with transgenic crops exploded from barely over 10,000 acres in 1994 to approximately 200 million acres in 2004. The Grocery Manufacturers of America estimate that transgenic crops—primarily corn and soybeans—now appear in approximately 75 percent of all processed foods found in grocery stores. While many in the industry applaud this transformation as a beneficial use of technology that will improve products and profits, many observers are concerned that the long-term effects of these transgenic foods are still poorly understood.

Humans have been modifying food since the dawn of agriculture. The difference between conventional selective breeding and biotechnology is that instead of relying on natural but targeted reproductive processes, biotechnology relies on the tools of recombinant DNA technology, primarily restriction endonucleases and ligase enzymes, to alter the genetic codes of organisms in ways that could not occur in nature. One transgenic food organism, the "Bt potato," combines the genetic code of a regular potato with that of the *Bacillus thuringiensis* bacterium, resulting in a potato that is poisonous to many types of insect pests, but still edible by humans.

Critics of bioengineering warn that we have no long-term studies on the effects of such manipulation of food organisms. Modified foods might have unintended consequences for the health of people who eat them. The modifications introduced into domesticated crops might spread into wild plant species, fundamentally altering the ecosystem. Many critics have argued that the introduction of bioengineered foods gives biotechnology companies undue power over the processes of food production, and thereby leaves small farmers and farmers in the developing world at the mercy of large corporations. Perhaps the most common criticism leveled at transgenic foods is that they are "not natural."

Despite these criticisms, the agricultural industry in America has continued to move ahead with further research into and planting of transgenic crops. Government regulatory agencies, such as the EPA, the FDA, and the Department of Agriculture, have essentially given biotechnology companies free rein as long as they can establish that transgenic crops are "substantially similar" to conventional crops, and biotechnology companies have so far successfully fought off all efforts to have transgenic foods labeled as such. To date, no confirmed case of harmful health effects from transgenic foods has been documented. American consumers, although they consistently voice doubts about transgenic foods when asked about them on surveys, are apparently unconcerned that they eat, on average, several genetically modified foods each week.

Questions 1–6 refer to the passage above.

1. Which of the following statements best summarizes the main idea of the passage?

    A. The tools of recombinant DNA technology have spurred a fundamental transformation in the way in which food is engineered and grown.

    B. A majority of Americans now eat transgenic foods because of the benefits in nutrition and cost offered by these new products.

    C. Despite the fact that transgenic foods have been proven unsafe for human consumption, biotechnology companies have quietly achieved widespread distribution of these foods.

    D. Genetically modified foods, although they face criticism from those who doubt their safety, have become a significant part of the American food production system.

    E. Biotechnology offers a solution to the growing levels of hunger and malnutrition in the developing world, although critics worry that transgenic foods may have unintended health consequences.

2. The passage mentions each of the following as concerns raised by critics of transgenic foods EXCEPT:

    A. Transgenic foods might affect the health of consumers in unforeseen ways.

    B. Transgenic foods may be more resistant to insect pests than conventional crops.

    C. An agricultural distribution system based on genetically modified food will leave small farmers dependent on biotechnology conglomerates.

    D. There is no data on what the health effects may be for humans who eat transgenic foods over a period of several decades.

    E. Plant species in the wild might become contaminated by genetically modified species.

3. Which of the following inferences drawn from the statements in the final paragraph, if accurate, might best explain the apparently contradictory finding that Americans voice concerns over transgenic foods in polls but consume these foods on a regular basis?

A. Government regulatory agencies have approved the sale of transgenic foods to consumers as long as the producers can establish that the transgenic foods are "substantially similar" to conventional foods.

B. American farmers planted over 200 million acres with transgenic crops in 2004, a substantial increase from the acreage planted with transgenic crops a decade earlier.

C. American consumers may be unaware that they are eating transgenic foods because of the biotechnology industry's success in preventing the labeling of these foods.

D. Critics of genetic engineering have been unsuccessful in their attempts to impose bans on transgenic food through the EPA and FDA.

E. As of the writing of the passage, no deaths or other adverse health effects had been documented in connection with the consumption of transgenic foods.

4. The relationship between a conventional potato and a "Bt potato" is most similar to which of the following?

A. The relationship between a conventional automobile and one that has been equipped with a revolutionary new engine technology that allows it to fly.

B. The relationship between a regular hamburger and one that has been made poisonous through the addition of bleach.

C. The relationship between a laptop computer and a similar computer that is twice as fast as the first computer because it has a more powerful central processing unit.

D. A wild chicken and a domesticated chicken that has been bred to gain weight three times faster than a wild chicken.

E. A boiled potato and a baked potato with all the fixings.

5. The second paragraph plays what role in the passage?

A. It presents the first of two arguments discussed in the passage.

B. It suggests that the hypothesis advanced in the first paragraph is incomplete.

C. It refutes an argument and suggests an area for further study, which is discussed in the rest of the passage.

D. It suggests a new way of looking at a topic that differs from the conventional view presented in the first paragraph.

E. It provides background information relevant to the topic discussed in the following paragraphs.

6. The author's attitude toward transgenic food can best be described as which of the following?

A. Angry and concerned.

B. Accepting and optimistic.

C. Enthusiastically ambivalent.

D. Interested but uncommitted.

E. Hopeful but suspicious.

The origins of tea as a beverage can be traced back more than 5,000 years. Chinese mythology first addresses the drink in 3,000BC, when the emperor Nin Song was said to have discovered it. Nin Song was something of a visionary. Among other innovations, he believed that water should be boiled before drinking as a health precaution. As the story goes, he was traveling with some members of the court when they stopped to rest. Some leaves from a bush fell into the water being boiled for the weary travelers, and thus was tea born.

In 800AD, a man named Lu Yu wrote the first known book on tea cultivation and preparation. The work, called the Ch'a Ching, melded Zen Buddhist teachings with the art and craft of tea, forever linking the drink to spirituality.

In 1191AD, the cultivation and brewing of the leaves spread to Japan when a monk named Yeisei returned from pilgrimage, bringing seeds back with him. Yeisei had observed tea being used in and enhancing meditation and spiritual awareness in China. He shared this discovery with his peers and the tradition quickly caught on—all the way to the highest levels of society, including the imperial court.

Tea was so well-received in Japan that it was elevated to an art form, culminating in the creation of the well-known Japanese Tea Ceremony. The ceremony evolved and grew both more intricate and more exclusive, with students of the art receiving years of practice and training before they were allowed to perform it.

The once-lowly leaf had been raised to the pinnacle of spiritual and social grace. In the words of Lafcadio Hearn, an historian and writer of Irish origin who emigrated to Japan in the late 19th Century, "The Tea ceremony requires years of training and practice to graduate in art . . . yet the whole of this art, as to its detail, signifies no more than the making and serving of a cup of tea. The supremely important matter is that the act be performed in the most perfect, most polite, most graceful, most charming manner possible."

Questions 7–10 refer to the passage above.

7. The main purpose of this passage is to

    A. Trace the historical progression of tea from its origins to the present day.

    B. Give brief highlights from the history of the cultivation of tea.

    C. Provide an anecdotal account how tea became a drink.

    D. Highlight some important elements of the history of preparing and drinking tea.

    E. Argue against the notion of tea drinking as a valid social art.

8. The last sentence of the first paragraph serves to illustrate which of the following about tea?

    A. The mistake that led to tea drinking's ultimate elevation as a social grace

    B. The accidental and fortunate nature of how tea was discovered

    C. The spreading seeds of the habit of drinking tea

    D. The link between tea and Zen Buddhist practice of pilgrimage

    E. The unusually rapid way that tea was developed into a beverage

9. Which of the following inferences may be drawn from the discussion of Lu Yu's work?

    A. Before 800AD, it was largely unknown how to cultivate tea.

B. Some people even today drink tea for reasons other than its physical benefits.

C. Drinking tea was primarily a Zen Buddhist practice until the late 700s.

D. The Ch'a Ching is one of the earliest works of Chinese origin that is concerned with agriculture.

E. Lu Yu was interested in popularizing tea in countries other than China.

10. Based on the passage, Lafcadio Hearn would have agreed with which of the following statements about Japanese Tea Ceremony?

A. It is needlessly complex and intricate.

B. It is important that students of the art spend many years mastering it.

C. It is the pinnacle of Japanese taste and culture.

D. It is both a simple act and one that is rich with cultural significance.

E. It is an inextricable part of Japanese history and spirituality.

Iguacu Falls, which sit on the border between Argentina and Brazil, are said to make Niagara look like a leaky faucet. The great cataracts stretch for two and a half miles across lushly foliaged rocky outcroppings before plunging a staggering two hundred and thirty feet into the river below.

The falls region is densely forested, and is home to a wide variety of plants and animals, including a number of endangered ones. It is a paradise where parrots dive and swoop through the spray, butterflies cavort among the tropical plants and coatis, and giant otters and anteaters amble through the trees. The foliage itself varies between tropical and deciduous with orchids blushing in the shade of pines and ferns nodding gracefully in the shadow of fruit trees.

Depending on rainfall and water flow, between 100 and 300 individual falls tumble over the cliffs creating a stunning panoply of churning water. Small wonder that this natural powerhouse attracted the attention of developers. At the top of the falls on the Parana River sits Itaipu Dam, the world's largest operational hydroelectric power plant. The dam is often numbered among the wonders of the modern world.

The falls' superlatives don't stop with technology. Many consider the cataract system itself one of the natural wonders of the world. In 1986, UNESCO (United Nations Educational, Scientific, and Cultural Organization) concurred when it declared the falls a World Heritage site in order to ensure its preservation in the face of continuing technological development.

Questions 11–14 refer to the passage above.

11. The comparison in the first sentence is meant to emphasize the

A. Abundant beauty of Niagara Falls.

B. Plumbing problems that can be caused by building in close proximity to a waterfall.

C. Smallness of Niagara Falls in relation to Iguacu Falls.

D. Distance of Iguacu Falls from civilization.

E. Fact that Niagara Falls is a less popular tourist destination than Iguacu Falls.

12. The author's attitude toward Iguacu Falls can best be described as which of the following?

   A. Overweening pride.
   B. Positive appreciation.
   C. Mild acceptance.
   D. Apathetic objectivity.
   E. Cautious optimism.

13. What can most reasonably be inferred from the information in the final two paragraphs?

   A. Iguacu Falls' success as a hydroelectric site could potentially cause a threat to its longevity.
   B. Conservationist efforts have made a tremendous impact in the maintenance of the Itaipu Dam hydroelectric power plant.
   C. Brazil and Argentina are two of the largest producers of hydroelectric power in the world.
   D. UNESCO considers the preservation of Iguacu Falls crucial to the balance of the world ecosystem.
   E. Developers consider any opportunity to invest in hydroelectric power a lucrative business venture.

14. The author of the passage is primarily concerned with

   A. Exalting the beauties of a variety of waterfall sites.
   B. Outlining the history of Iguacu Falls since its discovery.
   C. Portraying the positive aesthetic and economic aspects of a natural phenomenon.
   D. Describing Iguacu Falls in terms that would make sense to an American audience.
   E. Discussing the tension between economic development and natural conservation.

Solutions

1. D.   This is a standard main idea question. The first paragraph contains the main ideas of the passage, primarily in its last sentence: "While many in the industry applaud this transformation as a beneficial use of technology that will improve products and profits, many observers are concerned that the long-term effects of these transgenic foods are still poorly understood." The passage is concerned with discussing the expansion of the transgenic food business in America, while also stating the concerns of those who oppose this development. Answer choice A makes a correct statement, but it focuses primarily on the second paragraph and ignores the entire question of criticism, so it does not provide a good summary for the passage as a whole. Answer choice B is also too limited, and it is probably inaccurate in stating that "a majority . . . eat transgenic foods *because* of the benefits," when it is unclear that many Americans are aware that they are eating transgenic foods. Answer choice C is incorrect because it makes a statement "transgenic foods have been proven unsafe," that is not supported by the passage. Answer choice D, the correct answer, addresses the main themes of the passage in a balanced tone that is characteristic of the passage itself. Answer choice E focuses on a topic—the developing world—that is not a major focus of the passage.

2. B. This is a supporting idea question. With an "all of the following EXCEPT" question, you need to find the relevant passage in the text and then eliminate all of the answer choices until only one possibility is left. In this case, the phrase *concerns raised by critics* should lead you to the third paragraph, which deals exclusively with these concerns. Answer choice A is a relatively close paraphrase of "Modified foods might have unintended consequences for the health of people who eat them." *Unintended* and *unforeseen* are not exactly the same, but they are close enough that this is a very weak answer, so you should cross it off your list. Answer choice B is supported in the text by the example given in the previous paragraph, but this example is *not* given as a concern raised by critics; rather, it is an argument in favor of the efficacy of transgenic food organisms. Note this one as a likely correct answer, but you still need to eliminate the others to be sure. Answer choice C corresponds closely to, "Many critics have argued that the introduction of bioengineered foods . . . leaves small farmers and farmers in the developing world at the mercy of large corporations." The statement in Answer choice D is a more specific example of the general criticism leveled in the first sentence: "Critics of bioengineering warn that we have no long-term studies on the effects of such manipulation of food organisms." And Answer choice E restates the concern expressed in the sentence, "The modifications introduced into domesticated crops might spread into wild plant species, fundamentally altering the ecosystem." Answer choice B is clearly the strongest answer.

3. C. This is an inference question that requires you to make a logical connection between two statements in the text that are not explicitly connected. Since the question specifies the "statements in the final paragraph," you should focus on that paragraph and then determine which of the answers might best resolve the "apparently contradictory finding." Answer choice A is an accurate reflection of a statement in the final paragraph, but it does not directly address the question. Answer choice B is outside of the final paragraph and fails to address the apparent contradiction, so it is clearly wrong. Answer choice C draws a connection between the final sentence and the statement, "biotechnology companies have so far successfully fought off all efforts to have transgenic foods labeled as such [i.e., (as genetically modified)]" in a way that could resolve the contradictory finding; mark this one as a strong possibility and move on. Answer choice D mentions an attempted ban that is found nowhere in the passage, so it is out of bounds and incorrect. Answer choice E is tricky, because it provides evidence for why people might not need to be concerned about transgenic foods, but it does not establish that this positive track record is well known, and it does not explain away the statement that "American consumers . . . consistently voice doubts about transgenic foods when asked about them on surveys." Answer choice C is the strongest answer.

4. A. This is an applying information question. You have to determine what the relationship is between a conventional potato and a "Bt potato," and then see which of the answer choices presents a corresponding relationship. From the information in the second paragraph, we know that a Bt potato is a potato that has been modified through a new kind of technology so that it has a potentially useful attribute—it is poisonous to insect pests but not to humans—that is not normally found in potatoes. Answer choice A presents a parallel situation: a car has been modified by technology so that it possesses a potentially useful attribute—the ability to fly—that is not normally encountered in automobiles. This looks like a strong answer, but you need to eliminate the other answer choices. Answer choice B presents a partially parallel situation—an item has been modified so that it is poisonous—but the addition of bleach does not correspond well to the modifying new technology of the Bt potato, and a bleached hamburger, unlike a Bt potato, is a completely useless item. Overall, B is a weaker choice than A. Answer choice C is partially parallel in that the second item may be more useful than the first, but there is no mention that the first was modified to produce the second, and the distinguishing attribute of the second computer, greater speed, is a difference in degree, and does not represent an entirely new attribute. Answer choice D is incorrect on similar grounds; a fatter chicken is just a variant on the old kind of chicken, rather than a chicken with an entirely new attribute. Also, it could be argued that selective breeding, since it is an old technology, is not a good match for the new technology that produced the Bt potato. Answer choice E is a poor choice because boiling and baking simply represent two different ways to prepare a potato; there is no mention of modifying technology or new attributes. Choices B, C, D, and E are all weaker than A, so A is the best choice.

5. E. This is a standard logical structure question. In your initial reading of the passage, you may have noticed that the second paragraph takes a step back from the controversy mentioned at the end of the first paragraph—which is the chief concern of the last two paragraphs—in order to provide information about how the genetic engineering of food works and to provide an example of a transgenic product. This paragraph cannot be said to present an argument (Answer choice A), suggest that the hypothesis of the first paragraph is incomplete (Answer choice B), refute an argument (Answer choice C), or suggest a new way of looking at something (Answer choice D). The only answer choice that provides a reasonable description of the role of the second paragraph is E; the technical terms and example provided in E are relevant background information for the discussion of transgenic foods in the following two paragraphs.

6. D. This is a tone and style question. You can gauge an author's attitude by the use of tone words with strong positive or negative connotations. This passage, however, has very little in the way of tone words, so you have to gauge the author's attitude by the choice of information presented. The lack of overt tone words means that there is no reason to suspect that the author is "angry," as in answer choice A. On the other hand, the author presents several concerns voiced by critics without refuting them, so the unreservedly positive terms "Accepting and optimistic" in Answer choice B cannot be correct. Answer choice C, "Enthusiastically ambivalent," may not even be possible; in any event, the author does not seem truly enthusiastic about either of the sides in the argument. Answer choice D, "Interested but uncommitted," does appear to be an accurate description, because the author is clearly interested enough in the subject to have written the passage, but he or she does not explicitly commit to either side. The terms in answer choice E are too strong in both directions; the author seems somewhat accepting of the developments in agriculture, but does not make any statements that could be characterized as "hopeful." The author's decision to enumerate the concerns of critics without fully refuting them suggests that the author *could* be suspicious, but there is no clear evidence that the author is *necessarily* suspicious. Answer choice D is the best answer. Note that D is the most moderate of the answer choices; this is characteristic of tone questions. ACT rarely permits the authors of passages to express strong emotions. When you see emotional terms like *angry* or *enthusiastic* in answer choices for this type of question, those choices are usually wrong.

7. D.   This is a primary purpose question, which is similar to a main idea question. It is testing whether you can determine accurately the scope of the information presented and describe the way in which it was presented. Clearly the passage was about the origins of tea, but many of the answer choices contain that element, and it's up to you to eliminate the ones that have extra, contradictory, or out-of-scope information. Answer choice A says that the passage "traces" tea's history "to the present day," which does not happen; the latest event in the passage takes place no later than 1899. Answer choice B concentrates on the *cultivation* of tea, which, though it is mentioned, is not the primary focus of the passage. Answer choice C is similarly mentioned, but it's nowhere near the bulk of the passage. Answer choice E is incorrect based on the first word; the passage is not structured to argue against anything. Answer choice D matches the intent and scope of the passage, so it is the best answer.

8. B.   This is a logical structure question that asks what point a certain sentence illustrates in the passage. The sentence has to do with how tea became a drink, so we would expect the correct answer to focus on that point. While answer choice A is tempting in that it mentions a "mistake," it is off-base because its focus is on tea being elevated to a social grace, something not discussed at this point in the passage. Answer choice C is also not the focus of the sentence; it is about how the habit of drinking tea spread. Answer choice D is also not what the sentence was about, and in fact the words used are from a different part of the passage. Answer choice E also has the wrong focus. The sentence is not about speed. Only answer choice B focuses on how tea was accidentally discovered as a drink.

9. B.   This is an inference question that asks you to make a connection between the information in one part of the passage and one of the answer choices. Answer choice A is tempting because Lu Yu wrote the first book on cultivating tea, but that does not imply that people didn't know how to cultivate tea anyway. Answer choice C is simply not supported by the passage, and the same is true for D. E is reasonable, but not something that can be inferred from the information given. Answer choice B is the only one that is somewhat supported by the passage; the phrase "forever linking the drink to spirituality" supports the statement that people today may drink tea for other than physical reasons.

10. D.   This is an applying information question that asks you to make a decision based on the information given in the passage. After reading the quote by Lafcadio Hearn, we can see that he sees the Japanese Tea Ceremony as something of a contrast, particularly by the use of the sentence ". . . yet the whole of this art . . . signifies nothing more than the making and serving of tea . . ." Answer choice A, however, is too extreme to be supported by the quote; Hearn is not strongly negative about the practice of tea ceremony. Answer choice B is perhaps something that is believed by members of Japanese society, but we have no support that Hearn believes it is "important." Answer choice C is also extreme. It is a statement from elsewhere in the passage, but not an opinion expressed by Hearn. Answer choice E is somewhat supported by the passage, though the word "inextricably" is a little extreme; however, it is not necessarily Hearn's opinion. Only answer choice D expresses the contradiction that Hearn saw in the practice of Japanese Tea Ceremony, and expresses it in a non-extreme, non-offensive way.

11. C.   This is a logical structure question that asks what point is emphasized by the comparison in the first sentence. The sentence says that Niagara Falls, which is commonly regarded as a huge series of waterfalls, looks like a leaky faucet when compared to Iguacu Falls. This is certainly a negative comparison for Niagara and one that makes a point of how small Niagara is (and, potentially, how unattractive). So answer choice A is not a possibility, and B and C have nothing to do with the purpose of the comparison that we've just stated. That leaves C and E, and while E may be true or reasonable, the passage doesn't give us support for it, certainly not in the first sentence. So C is the best possible answer.

12. B.   This is a style/tone question asking for the author's general attitude toward Iguacu Falls. We can tell from the many positive things the author says about Iguacu in the passage that it is a positive attitude. C and E are not positive enough and D is not positive at all, so they should be eliminated. Answer choice A is strongly positive, but there is no indication that the author is *proud* of Iguacu; "pride" is not reasonable because we have no reason to think that the author had any responsibility for any of the events in the passage, so it can be eliminated. So though B is probably a little weaker than the tone of the passage, it is the best answer choice.

13. A.   This is an inference question focusing on the final two paragraphs. Answer choices B and C are reasonable enough to assume, but the passage doesn't give any support for them. Answer choice D is also reasonable, but it goes farther in scope than the passage supports by saying "crucial" and "world ecosystem." Answer choice E is not supported by the passage and the word "any" makes this an extreme, and therefore bad, answer. Answer choice A is the only good inference; if UNESCO elected to declare the falls a World Heritage Site for its protection, it is reasonable to infer that there might be a potential threat to its survival, particularly because of the large hydroelectric power site mentioned in the next-to-last paragraph.

14. C.   This is a primary purpose/main idea question. Answer choice A is too broad in scope; the only waterfall site the author could be said to exalt in this passage is Iguacu Falls. Answer choice B is not supported by the passage, as very little of Iguacu Falls' history was discussed. Answer choice D is somewhat supported because of the comparison to Niagara Falls at the beginning, but ultimately it is not the focus of the whole passage. Similarly, answer choice E is tempting because of the information in the last paragraph, but it is not the focus of the passage as a whole. Answer choice C is the best supported, as the author does spend the whole passage extolling the virtues of a natural phenomenon, Iguacu Falls.

CHAPTER 11

The Analytical Writing Assessment

INTRODUCTION

You don't have to be a great writer to be good at business. You do, however, have to be able to make a good argument and to communicate it effectively. These are the skills that the GMAT Analytical Writing Assessment aims to test.

The Analytical Writing Assessment is composed of two parts: "Analysis of an Issue" and "Analysis of an Argument." In each part, you will have 30 minutes to write a persuasive essay arguing a position on the topics the computer provides for you. You will type these essays using a simple word-processing program on the same computer on which you will take the computer-adaptive GMAT.

HOW THE ANALYTICAL WRITING ASSESSMENT IS USED

You will receive a score from 0 to 6 on the Analytical Writing Assessment (hereafter AWA). Business schools that receive your GMAT results will see this score, as well as copies of your essays. Conventional wisdom is that business school admissions personnel tend to place less importance on the AWA score than on your total GMAT score or on your admissions essays. What this means is that you do not need to be too stressed about this part of the test; stress wouldn't do you any good, anyway. What this does *not* mean is that you can blow it off.

On the one hand, a good score on the AWA could potentially help your application. On the other hand, a poor performance on the AWA could raise some flags among the admissions people that you do not want raised. One of the major reasons that ACT sends the AWA essays to business schools is to give them *a way to check whether applicants wrote their own admissions essays.* If your admissions essays are much better than your AWA, then you could make some people suspicious and wind up with your application tossed into the "not-so-promising" file. If both your admissions essays and your AWA essays are poor, then you need to work harder on your writing skills.

HOW TO APPROACH THE AWA

If you are not already a literary giant, there probably is not time between now and the test to turn yourself into one. Fortunately, that is not a problem. *The AWA tests a very specific type of writing and grades it in a very specific way.* As long as your writing is basically sound, you can prepare yourself to earn a good score on the AWA. The first step is to understand how ACT arrives at that 0 to 6 score.

HOW THE WRITING ASSESSMENT IS SCORED

ACT states that a 6-level essay demonstrates the following characteristics:

▶ Explores ideas and develops a position on the issue with insightful reasons and/or examples.
▶ Is clearly well written.
▶ Demonstrates superior control of language, including diction and syntactic variety.
▶ Demonstrates superior facility with the conventions (grammar, usage, and mechanics) of standard written English but may have minor flaws.

In other words, ACT wants a good essay. So who determines how well you have done in accomplishing this goal?

ACT makes sure that every essay is read at least twice. The graduate students that ACT employs to read through the essays the first time will be reading several hundred essays on exactly the same topic, devoting two minutes at most to each essay. And yes, you can safely assume that they will be heavily buzzed on caffeine to get through it all. The second reader will take even less time, and may literally be buzzing, because the second reader is a computer. ACT employs a specially designed computer program to scan your essay and give it a score based on predetermined criteria. If the computer and the initial human reader disagree, another human reader will be called in to arbitrate.

So what does all this mean? First of all, it means that your literary genius will not be discovered here, so you can cross that off your list of goals. Second, it means that you can substantially improve your chances of getting the score you want by *writing for your audience*. A dazed human reading very fast and a computer reading very, very fast are going to look for similar things: organization, logical points, and good syntax.

Organization

The first thing your readers will notice is the structure of your essay. Do you have a clear thesis statement? Is the essay one long, rambling paragraph, or is it a clearly organized set of paragraphs with distinct roles in your argument? Does the essay's structure make your argument easier or harder to follow?

There is no secret to composing a well-organized essay. Follow this simple pattern, and your essay will, at the very least, have the appearance of organization:

▶ Paragraph 1: Introduction
  ○ State your argument in a clear thesis statement.
  ○ Acknowledge that the opposite position has merits, but that for the following reasons (summarize your reasons), your position is the correct one.
▶ Paragraph 2: Reason 1, with supporting evidence
▶ Paragraph 3: Reason 2, with supporting evidence
▶ Paragraph 4: Reason 3, with supporting evidence

▶ Paragraph 5: Conclusion

  ◐ For the reasons previously stated, your argument is the correct one.

  ◐ The issue statement/argument would have been more persuasive if it _____.

This structure is basically what ACT is looking for, so give it what it wants. You can have as few as one supporting paragraph, as long as it makes a couple of well-argued points, or as many as five or six supporting paragraphs, as long as they maintain a consistent argument. Anything more than eight paragraphs in total will probably detract from the organization of your essay. *You should aim for four to six paragraphs in total.* Also, remember to put your strongest arguments in your first supporting paragraphs so that these arguments will not get shortchanged if you are pressed for time at the end.

Another important way to improve the organization of your essay is to *use structural words and phrases that let your readers know where in the argument they are.* These words and phrases could include "On the one hand …"; "While some people believe {blank}, I argue instead …"; "In the first place …"; "For example …"; "An illustration of this principle is …"; "Finally …"; "In conclusion …"; and so on. The information on structural words in the Reading Comprehension chapter is very relevant here. Using these words will give your essay a sense of flow that will give both your readers the impression that the argument holds together.

Note: Originality in argument structure, or any attempt to approach the question in "an entirely new way," is probably not a good idea. Conforming to the standards that the human and computer readers are expecting is the best way to get a good score, so don't try to be too creative. Don't write the essay in poetry form. Don't engage in metaphysical speculation about the nature of arguments. Give the readers what they are looking for, and they will reward you for it.

Logical Points

The main benefit of a well-crafted organizational structure is that it will showcase the points of your argument. The points you state will make or break your argument, so make them count. Before you type a word, decide what your argument is going to be. Choose between two and six main points that you are going to use to support your argument. For each point, develop an example/scenario/piece of evidence that supports the point, and present this supporting information along with your point.

Your readers will see that you've made some logical points, they will observe that you have provided supporting evidence, and your score will go up.

Good Syntax

Good syntax means that your sentences are grammatically correct and easy to read. The rules that apply to Sentence Correction questions all apply here, so you have an extra incentive to brush up on your grammar. *Your primary goal is to make your argument clear.* If you have any doubt that a reader skimming over your sentence will follow your point, then rephrase the sentence in a clearer way.

You will improve your score by using *varied vocabulary and sentence structure*. For example, you should not use the same verb in two consecutive sentences if you can avoid it; if you use *see* in one sentence, then use a synonym such as *observe* or *notice* in the following sentence. Also, mix up the length and structure of your sentences. If all of your sentences follow the same pattern of subject–verb–object, your essay will appear dull. Note: Do not take this too far and use complicated words that you don't normally use, or compose long and unwieldy sentences. *The whole point is to make your essay more readable.* If you have any doubt about a word or sentence, then stay on the safe side and keep it simple.

FACTORS THAT CAN HELP OR HURT YOUR SCORE

Your success in meeting the criteria just discussed will largely determine your score. There are, however, a few other issues that can push your score up or down.

Bonus Points

One way to kick your score up a notch is to impress your reader (the human one; the computer is incapable of being impressed). The way to do this is to put something in your essay that the reader has not seen in the 200 other essays he or she has read that day. The place to do this is in your supporting evidence. You can back up your logical points with

▶ Facts and statistics relevant to the topic at hand (e.g., "Saudi Arabia possesses 24 percent of proven world petroleum reserves")

▶ Well-known literary references (e.g., "Employees at the MegaTek Corporation can probably relate to the Dickens line, 'It was the best of times, it was the worst of times'")

▶ Relevant similes and metaphors (e.g. "The governor may soon look up to see the Sword of Damocles dangling over his head")

▶ Relevant historical examples (e.g., "people do not always recognize a major business development when they see it; when the modern computer was invented in the 1950s, its developers thought that there might be fewer than ten buyers worldwide")

When you spice up your essay with outside knowledge, that outside knowledge has to be *relevant*, so you can't really plan the facts or quotes that you are going to use on your essay. That being said, you almost certainly know dozens of facts, references, and examples that will be relevant to the topics ACT gives you. The challenge for you is to incorporate this knowledge into your essay in a way that will make the essay stand out.

Recognizing the Arguments of the Other Side

Your conclusion will appear much stronger if it appears that you have considered the arguments on the other side of the argument or issue. You *should* address these arguments briefly as a counterpoint to your own argument. You *should* expose the weaknesses of these opposing arguments as a way to strengthen your own argument. You *should not* take both sides, because then you aren't really making an argument. Show that you know what the other side is thinking, and then show why that view is wrong.

Length

ACT does not officially factor length into an essay's score, but that does not mean that length is irrelevant. The fact is, *essay length and essay scores show a high degree of correlation*; very short essays tend to get lower scores, and essays with high scores tend to be longer than average. This does not mean, however, that the people who write the most will always get the best scores. A very long but sloppy essay that someone has thrown together without any clear argument or structure will get a low score, while a relatively short but persuasively argued essay could earn a high score.

Your goal should be to write as much as you can while keeping your argument clear and structured. Another way of looking at it is that it doesn't matter how many words you write, but it does matter how many good points you make and how well you make them. In general, the more lines of reasoning and evidence that you can bring to your essay, as long as they are consistent, the better your essay will be.

In summary, *write the longest good essay that you can.*

Spelling

ACT does not factor spelling directly into the score, but the fact is that your human readers will probably be less impressed with your argument as a whole if they notice lots of misspellings. The situation with the computer reader is worse, because a misspelling could prevent it from understanding your argument and giving you credit for valid points.

It is unlikely that spelling will affect your score either way, but to minimize the chances of misspellings hurting your score, you should:

▶ Budget your time so that you can type at a comfortable pace.
▶ Reserve a minute or two at the end to proofread your essay for obvious typos.

Typing

The AWA provides you with a simple word-processing program with which to write your essay. Your keyboard will have the standard keyboard functions, such as *Backspace, Enter,* and *Delete.* In addition, on the screen you will see buttons for three specialized functions: *Cut* and *Paste,* which allow you to *cut* a selected block of text from one place and *paste* it into another place, and *Undo,* which will undo your latest typing. The GMAT will give you a short tutorial on the use of these functions. There is no spellchecker.

The unfortunate truth about the format of the AWA is that it favors people who can type well over those who cannot. A lot of typos can negatively affect your score, and if slow typing prevents you from making all the logical points you intended to make, then your score will probably suffer. Perhaps worst of all, if you are uncomfortable at a keyboard, you will waste time worrying about the stupid keys instead of composing a brilliant argument.

If you are a poor typist, and if you have the time, you should make an effort to improve your typing skills. Practice on word-processing programs. It would not be a waste to take a typing class or invest in some instructional software, because you will almost certainly need to type at some point in business school or in your career. If you don't have a lot of time for this sort of thing, and if you need to choose between studying for the regular GMAT questions or working on your typing, then of course you should spend your time mastering the regular questions. Your score on the 800 scale is the one that business schools really care about. But if you have the time, do what it takes to get comfortable with a keyboard before you walk into the testing center.

MAXIMIZING YOUR SCORE

Now that you know how your score will be assessed, it's time to incorporate that knowledge into a strategy that will help you maximize your score on the AWA. Good use of time is essential to getting the score you want, so think of your strategy in terms of allocation of time:

1. Read the issue or argument very carefully—1 minute.
2. Consider the issue, choose your argument, outline your essay—4–6 minutes.
3. Write!—22–24 minutes.
4. Proofread the essay for obvious typos—1–2 minutes.

This time allocation strategy will serve you well for both the Analysis of an Issue and Analysis of an Argument essays. The real key here is the time you spend before you type a single word. If you just read the question and dive right in, the odds are that your essays will be muddled and inconsistent. *It is crucial that you know what is being asked and what you are arguing.* Give yourself a good five minutes or more to plan out what you are going to say. Having a well-structured outline not only will improve the organization component of your score, but will improve other aspects of your essay as well. The exercise of creating the outline will help you to clarify your thoughts, and it will help you determine which supporting arguments to put where. Finally, if you are writing with a good outline, your writing itself—grammar, sentence structure, and style—will most likely be improved, because you will know where you're going and be more confident about it.

Pacing is crucial, so it is important that you run through a few *practice essays* so that you know how much of an outline you can put together in five minutes, and how long an essay you can type in twenty-five minutes. There are sample essay topics at the end of this chapter on which you can practice.

ANALYSIS OF AN ISSUE

Analysis of an Issue questions present you with a short statement about an issue and then ask you to take a position on that issue. The question could look like

> At the end of the day, the only meaningful measure of a company's success is whether or not it has made money for its shareholders.
>
> To what extent do you agree or disagree with the opinion expressed above? Support your position with reasons and/or examples from your own experiences, observations, or reading.

Step 1 is to read the statement and decide whether you are going to agree or disagree. It is probably best to argue the position that you personally side with, because you will probably write a more persuasive essay that way, but ultimately your score has nothing to do with how strongly you feel about the issue, and everything to do with how well you argue your case. If you don't have a strong preference for one side or the other, go with the position for which you think you can make the stronger case.

It is very helpful at this stage to brainstorm reasons for and against the statement. You can write down on your scratch paper your reasons for and against. For the issue of measuring a company's success, you could make a list something like

For	Against
Making money is what businesses are for	Definition of success is too restrictive
Shareholder value helps management focus on important goals	Other groups make business success possible: employees, customers, society at large
If a company doesn't make money for shareholders, it will go out of business and employees and customers will be out of luck	Focusing only on shareholder value encourages management decisions that may be bad for the company in the long run

Clearly, an argument could be made on either side. Remember that while it can be helpful to address the arguments of the other side, you need to choose one side and stick with it. Whichever side you choose, you have to incorporate your reasons into a persuasive argument for your position, with supporting evidence. Your next step should be to sketch an outline of what your essay will look like. An outline for this issue could look like

Paragraph 1: Statement makes an interesting point, but ultimately defines success too narrowly. A better definition will include other groups: employees, customers, society.

P2: Focusing on employees is important too; example in-house child-care program.

P3: No business without customers; example customer service quality.

P4: Obligations to society; example cleaning up environment.

P5: Many measures of success; attention to these factors benefits shareholders.

Writing a good outline is worth at least five minutes of your time, because the quality of your outline (or, more accurately, the quality of the thinking that goes into your outline) will play a large role in determining the effectiveness of your essay. On the other hand, don't get carried away with putting too many details into your outline, since an outline alone earns you no points. An investment of five minutes is certainly worth it, but anything more than eight minutes is eating dangerously into your writing time. Remember, it will not hurt your score to write a long essay and it will probably help it, so give yourself adequate time to make your argument.

An essay on this topic could look like this:

The problem with the statement above is that it defines business success in an overly limited way that fails to consider other equally valid measures of success. While I acknowledge that many of the business leaders who have embraced the mantra of "shareholder value" have produced impressive financial results, I would contend that a more comprehensive view of business success will result over the long run in healthier businesses. A comprehensive picture of success will also take into account the other parties that contribute to and benefit from businesses: employees, customers, and society at large.

First of all, to be successful a company must have a good relationship with its employees. Strict adherence to shareholder value promotes an environment in which companies try to gain the greatest amount of work from their employees for the least money. These companies would be reluctant to accept a needless expense, such as an in-house child-care program for employees, which could take money out of the shareholders' next dividend check. The flaw in this thinking is that those child-care programs can actually more than pay for themselves, because they lead both to reduced absenteeism of working parents and to greater loyalty and morale among employees. Happy employees work harder, which translates into greater shareholder value in the long run. And we should never forget that employees can be customers too; Henry Ford's shareholders in the early twentieth century probably thought he was crazy to raise assembly-line salaries to an unheard-of $5 a day, but Ford knew that he was creating an entire generation of loyal Ford buyers. Ford understood that no company whose employees are unhappy can truly call itself a success.

Too much focus on shareholders can take attention away from the most essential part of any successful business—the customers. Without customers, there is no business. Executives with an eye only to shareholder value might, for instance, replace expensive customer service employees with an automated service line in order to save money. The problem here is that this decision risks alienating the customers, who have come to expect personal customer service. Those customers might very well switch to another company that cares more about a high-quality experience and less about writing dividend checks. And in the end, the company with the expensive but good customer service may wind up with the fatter dividend checks anyway, because it took away all the customers from the stingy company.

My final point is that any business is a part of the society in which it operates, and a truly successful business will contribute to the success of society at large. If a company sponsors community youth soccer teams, then it will reap no immediate benefits to the bottom line, but it will receive the long-term benefit of community goodwill. If a company decides to clean up an environmental mess that it is not technically obligated to cleanup, it may decrease profits, but it will be fulfilling its responsibility to society. This type of responsibility to society can also help promote long-term financial success by promoting community loyalty and by heading off costly lawsuits down the rode.

In summary, there are many meaningful ways to evaluate a company's success that do not fall neatly into the category of "making money for shareholders." A truly successful company will also evaluate its success in terms of its employees, customers, and society at large. Moreover, appreciating the value of these comprehensive factors will help to promote the interests of the shareholders in the long run.

This essay would earn a high score in the 5 to 6 range. While acknowledging a strength of the issue statement—that business leaders who accept its philosophy have produced "impressive financial results"—the author clearly states that he objects to the statement on the grounds that it defines business success in a too limited way. He then explores three other possible measures of success and provides examples for each of them to support the argument. Finally, he ties these alternative measures of success back to the original statement by arguing that attention to these other measures will ultimately result in greater financial success for shareholders.

The organization of the essay makes the argument easy to follow. The essay also includes structural elements that help the reader follow the argument: a clear thesis statement in the first sentence; a summary of the essay's main points at the end of the first paragraph; and structural signposts like "First of all," "My final point," and "In summary." If your essay follows a logical organization and contains facilitating structural elements, both the human reader and the computer will know that your argument is easy to follow, whether or not they care to follow it (in the case of the human) or can follow it (in the case of the computer). The essay also features good syntax as well as varied vocabulary and sentence structure.

The essay is not perfect. It contains two typos: "esential" in the third paragraph and "rode" instead of "road" in the fourth paragraph. It also probably would be preferable to move the example of customers to the first supporting paragraph position if customers truly are "the most essential part of any successful business"; points in the middle paragraph tend to be overlooked in favor of those in the first and final supporting paragraphs. Finally, some of the sentences are a bit convoluted, and some of the supporting pieces of evidence could be stronger. But flaws of this nature are expected on a rough draft, and do not prohibit an essay from meeting ACT's stated standards for a superior essay.

ANALYSIS OF AN ARGUMENT

Remember all the skills you learned for tackling Critical Reasoning questions? Good, because you need them here, too. When you write this essay, the computer will present you with an argument, which you will then be asked to analyze. Like most of the arguments in Critical Reasoning questions, the arguments on the AWA are wobbly. They make sense up to a point, but they invariably contain one or more flaws in reasoning. A question could look like this:

> The following is a transcript of a statement made by a recording industry executive at an industry conference:
>
> "The music recording industry is suffering grave economic losses due to the widespread piracy of digital music. This fate was an inevitable result of the industry's misguided decision to switch from the analogue format of vinyl records to the digital formats used today on compact disks and computer files. Copying a vinyl record requires expensive and bulky machinery, whereas anyone with a computer and an Internet connection can start up a music piracy business. To boost music revenues, the recording industry should switch entirely back to the analogue format of vinyl records. Also, I can state with complete authority that music just sounds better on a vinyl record."
>
> Discuss how well reasoned you find this argument. In your discussion, be sure to analyze the line of reasoning and the use of evidence in the argument. For example, you may need to consider what questionable assumptions underlie the thinking and what alternative examples or counterexamples might weaken the conclusion. You can also discuss what sort of evidence would strengthen or refute the argument, what changes in the argument would make it more logically sound, and what, if anything, would help you better evaluate its conclusion.

All AWA arguments are followed by similar instructions—"Discuss how well reasoned" and so on—so read these instructions carefully now so that you will be familiar with them when you walk into the testing center.

The first step in this type of question is to understand exactly what the argument is saying. Approach it with the same critical stance that you use for Critical Reasoning questions: what is the conclusion, what are the premises, and what are the unstated assumptions? For this argument, we have

Premise 1: The music recording industry is suffering grave economic losses due to the widespread piracy of digital music.

Premise 2: This fate was an inevitable result of the industry's misguided decision to switch from analogue to digital, because copying a vinyl record requires expensive and bulky machinery, whereas anyone with a computer and an Internet connection can start up a music piracy business.

Premise 3: Music sounds better on vinyl.

Conclusion: To boost music revenues, the recording industry should switch entirely back to the analogue format of vinyl records.

Note that the conclusion came in the second to last line, while the last line was actually a somewhat tangential premise. You cannot write an effective Analytical Writing essay if you fail to identify the correct conclusion, so determine the conclusion based on the sense of the passage, not on the position of sentences in the passage. The conclusion will probably come last, but this is not guaranteed.

Okay, we know what the argument says, but is it persuasive? In order for the conclusion to be true, a number of assumptions would also have to be true:

1. The premises themselves are true.
2. Switching back to vinyl would actually solve the problem of digital music piracy.
3. Switching back to vinyl would not have other consequences that might hinder the goal of "boosting music revenues."

This argument is vulnerable on any of these grounds. Most AWA arguments are vulnerable to multiple lines of attack. Your job now is to write a cogent essay that assembles these lines of attack in a logical and persuasive way. You should begin by sketching an outline of what you are going to say. It could be something like this:

Paragraph 1: Argument is flawed. Although digital piracy is an important issue, the conclusion is not properly drawn because of the following:

P2: The premises are flawed.

"grave economic losses" due to piracy questionable

current situation not necessarily "inevitable result" of switch to digital

statement that "vinyl sounds better" is unsupported

P3: Stated solution won't solve problem; people can still make digital files from records.

P4: Conclusion is bad idea, because switching to vinyl will hurt record sales more than piracy does.

P5: Summary—conclusion not properly drawn. New technology would provide better solution.

Your outline could be less detailed than this one, or it could be more detailed, as long as you don't spend more than five minutes or so writing it. The key is to plan out what you are going to say so that you can choose your best arguments and give your essay a logical structure.

A good technique to use on Analysis of an Argument questions is to present a brief paraphrase of the argument's key premise and conclusion at the beginning of your essay in order to show that you understand the argument. This technique forces you to distill the essence of the argument, it provides you with a good way to start the essay, and it allows you to frame the argument in a way that best suits your own argument.

Here is what an essay on this argument might look like:

The recording industry executive argues that in order to stem the tide of economic losses due to digital music piracy, the music recording industry should abandon the digital format entirely in favor of the old analogue format of vinyl records. While the executive does address a significant current problem for the music industry, the logic of his argument and the conclusion he reaches are both fundamentally flawed. Not only do the premises of his argument fail to support adequately his conclusion, but his conclusion would, if implemented, do more harm to the music industry than is currently inflicted by piracy.

To begin with, his premises are flawed. It is inaccurate to characterize the effects of digital formats on the music industry as "grave economic losses" when in fact the music industry has reaped far higher revenues by selling music in digital format—primarily compact disks—than it ever earned in the old analogue days of vinyl. Also, his somewhat irrelevant statement that "music just sounds better on vinyl" is supported only by his personal authority, which in this context cannot reasonably be characterized as "complete." Finally, his assumption that switching to vinyl records will halt music piracy due to technical complications is inherently flawed, because those vinyl records could very easily be recorded onto digital formats and then distributed over the Internet. His chosen solution does not actually solve his specified problem.

The executive's most fundamental error, however, is his failure to distinguish between stopping piracy and boosting revenue. Although his plan of reverting to an obsolete technology might, in a small way, impede the efforts of those who would use digital music unethically, it is more likely that it would result in far greater economic losses to the industry than are currently inflicted by piracy. The industry has switched overwhelmingly to digital formats because they offer a number of benefits both to the industry and to the consumer. For the industry, digital music is easier to produce and far less costly to distribute than bulky vinyl records. For consumers, digital formats such as compact disks and MP3s are far easier to store, sort through, and carry around than older analogue formats. For the whole industry to switch back to vinyl records would be like cutting off its nose to spite its face.

For the reasons stated above, the executive's argument simply does not hold up. If he were truly serious about addressing the problem of digital music piracy, his time would be better spent investigating technological ways to make digital formats more resistant to piracy.

This essay would earn a high score in the 5 to 6 range. The writer shows that he understands the argument being presented, but is not convinced by it for a number of reasons. He goes on to point out a series of flaws in the argument, and then to suggest an alternative approach to the question. By pointing out two potentially fatal flaws—the executive's plan will not necessarily stop piracy, and it may harm the industry more than it can help it—the author presents a compelling case that the executive's argument is fundamentally flawed.

Structurally, the essay is easy to follow. It states the author's basic analysis at the very beginning, and then indicates the types of arguments that are going to follow: an attack both on the logic that was used to reach the conclusion and on the implications of the conclusion itself. The final paragraph summarizes the argument and suggests an alternative solution. The essay follows the basic pattern of

Paragraph 1: The argument says this, but it is flawed for the following reasons.

Paragraph 2: Reason 1, and supporting evidence.

Paragraph 3: Reason 2, and supporting evidence.

Paragraph 4: For the reasons above, the argument is clearly flawed. A better argument would have _____.

The essay also uses some structural words that help the reader follow the argument: "While," "Not only . . . but," "To begin with," "For the reasons stated above . . ." These kinds of words signal to the human and computer readers that the argument flows, regardless of what it actually says. The writing is easy to understand and is generally free of grammatical and spelling errors. The varied vocabulary and sentence structure make the essay relatively painless to read.

PRACTICE ESSAYS

You will definitely improve your chances of earning a high score on the AWA by running through a few practice essays before you take the test. Writing is a skill that can be improved through practice, and writing for the GMAT is a very specific skill that can be greatly improved through practice. Pacing is a crucial component of the AWA, so use the following essay topics to get a feel for how you will pace yourself on the test day.

Sample Issues

For the issues that follow, take five minutes for each topic to digest the issue and to sketch an outline of how you would address the topic in a thirty-minute GMAT essay. For at least one of the topics, *type an essay under timed conditions*. It is important that you practice under the most authentic conditions possible, so use a word processor and stick to the time limit. For each of the issues statements, your assignment is to

Discuss the extent to which you agree or disagree with the opinion stated above. Support your views with reasons and/or examples from your own experiences, observations, or reading.

1. The producers of movies and television programs have a responsibility to provide entertainment that educates the public and upholds societal standards.
2. Issues that affect many nations, such as drug trafficking or acid rain, are best addressed at a multinational level.
3. Although people today have substantially more material things than people did fifty years ago, real quality of life has not improved in that time.
4. Colleges and universities should view their students as customers, just as businesses do.
5. The busiest people are the happiest people.

Sample Argument

For the arguments that follow, take five minutes for each argument to digest the argument and to sketch an outline of how you would address it in a thirty-minute GMAT essay. For at least one of the arguments, *type an essay under timed conditions.* It is important that you practice under the most authentic conditions possible, so use a word processor and stick to the time limit. For each of the arguments, your assignment is to

> Discuss how well reasoned you find this argument. In your discussion, be sure to analyze the line of reasoning and the use of evidence in the argument. For example, you may need to consider what questionable assumptions underlie the thinking and what alternative examples or counterexamples might weaken the conclusion. You can also discuss what sort of evidence would strengthen or refute the argument, what changes in the argument would make it more logically sound, and what, if anything, would help you better evaluate its conclusion.

1. The following appeared in a letter by the principal of North Lake Academy to parents of students enrolled in the school.

"You are probably aware of the disappointing overall scores our students received on the latest standardized test. This performance was even more disappointing in light of the above-average performance on the same test of students at Riverside Academy. In order to improve our scores, we have studied the curriculum at Riverside Academy, which is known for the excellence of its foreign language programs, in particular ancient Greek. Well, if it was good enough for Socrates and Aristotle, it's good enough for us. From now on, all students at North Lake Academy will study ancient Greek."

2. The following appeared in the editorial page of a widely read newspaper.

"Everyone knows that we need to reduce our nation's dependence on foreign oil. Our nation has become so dependent on outside sources because we have not devoted sufficient resources to exploiting our own domestic oil reserves. We also need to reduce the regulatory barriers that are hindering development of new nuclear and coal-burning power plants. If we take these steps, we can secure the energy sources necessary to ensure the well-being of our citizens."

3. The following appeared in a management consultant's report to the Middlemarch Shoe Company.

"The Middlemarch Shoe Company is facing fierce competitive pressures from both high-priced prestige brands and from high-volume, low-cost shoe manufacturers. Although Middlemarch products are consistently deemed to be of high quality by footwear experts, the brand does not command the respect of the prestige brands, and therefore cannot reasonably charge the higher prices of those brands. Consequently, if Middlemarch wishes to increase its revenues, it needs to lower its prices so that it can compete directly with the discount shoe manufacturers."

4. The following appeared in an internal memo from the research and development division of a pharmaceutical company.

"After a safety trial of prospective appetite suppressant QR172 in 1,000 lab rats, we have concluded that QR172 is sufficiently safe to begin safety and efficacy trials on humans. Although 28 of the 1,000 rats died during the course of the experiment, this is within the 3.5 percent natural mortality rate that is considered normal for experiments of this length with this species of rat. It should be noted that 22 of the rats died of starvation, a very rare phenomenon for captive rats provided with an adequate diet. The committee determined, however, that the weight loss experienced by the dead rats, less than a pound in each case, would be essentially harmless in an adult human, so QR172 is still considered safe for testing on humans."

5. The following appeared in promotional materials from a telephone directory publisher encouraging local restaurants to purchase advertising in the local telephone directory.

"Telephone directory advertising works! If it didn't, why would 7 of the top 9 lawyers, 5 of the top 6 air conditioning installers, and 8 of the top 8 plumbers in the local area all purchase advertising in the local telephone directory? One plumber chose not to purchase an ad during his first year of business, thinking it was too expensive. After a year of disappointing results, he purchased an ad in his second year and enjoyed a threefold increase in business during that year. The truth is, you can't afford *NOT* to advertise in your local telephone directory!"

PART THREE

Beyond the GMAT

CHAPTER 12

Choosing the Right Program

INTRODUCTION

Preparing to take the GMAT is an important—no, a critical—step toward the pursuit of the MBA, but it is only the start of the battle. In the next several chapters, we'll help you determine where to apply, how to get in, what to do once you're there, and how to go about looking for a job.

CHOOSING A SCHOOL: CONSIDERING YOUR OBJECTIVES

Your first requirement in picking a school is to know your objective. Why are you applying? Why do you want to study for the MBA? All told, there are probably four main reasons for enduring two years of study for the MBA:

▶ *You want to know how business works.* There are perfectly good reasons aside from wanting to earn money for seeking advanced education in management. Charles Handy of London's Open University has described the MBA as virtually a prerequisite to being an effective manager of a commercial enterprise. This is an overstatement, but there's a kernel of truth in it. There aren't too many places where one can learn the finer points of queueing theory, the details of financial statement analysis, the importance of the *F*-test in statistics, and the ins and outs of the Buy-One-Get-One (BOGO) marketing ploy in just two short years. How's that for a sales pitch?

▶ *You want to advance your career.* The MBA is hardly a prerequisite for success, but it certainly helps, and it has been getting more important in recent years. Most MBA programs equip their graduates to understand how to deal with many of the important questions that their organizations will need to tackle over time, and that they will face in their careers. So, if you find yourself in a meeting with a crowd of people 10 years your senior, you may find that you're the only one who actually knows how to unlever the discount rate, who understands what is really meant by supplier qualification, or who can make attractive PowerPoint slides in his sleep.

▶ *You want to make an obscene amount of money.* You've looked at what you're making now, and at the starting salaries of those MBA graduates, and you've decided that you're in. Remember, though, that this is not a lottery: MBA programs spend a lot of time and money screening potential business managers, and those with the potential then spend a lot of time and money getting up to the high level of competence that is expected of them. So, they're generally worth what people pay for them. As a side note, you are also getting paid that much for a reason—you'll work hard for the money you earn.

► *You want to teach business administration.* This is a less common, but still obvious reason for attending graduate business school. The leading Ph.D. programs, however, are not necessarily the leading MBA programs—there is a big difference between teaching Master's candidates and grooming those who will teach them in the future. The Tuck School at Dartmouth, for example, does not even offer a Ph.D. in business. So, if you're interested in something a bit more advanced than the MBA, you'll need to reach beyond the rankings; it's best to look at who is getting hired where. Finally, remember that the teaching of business is the most lucrative academic job one can get these days. Not many other university professors can earn in the low six figures as relatively junior faculty.

A BRIEF TAXONOMY OF MBA PROGRAM TYPES

The next question is, what sort of program to attend. Broadly speaking, there are two options.

The Full-Time Option

The pursuit of the traditional two-year, full-time program is probably why most people would buy a book like this. A full-time MBA program is like none other. While leading part-time MBA programs (discussed next) offer many of the academic attributes of their full-time equivalents, the full-time program is, for most ranked programs, the flagship program for the school and the focus of the school's administration and budget. What full-time MBA programs offer through this total immersion process is unparalleled access to a wide range of faculty, speakers, contacts, recruiters, and alumni on a weekly, and even daily, basis. If you can afford to quit your day job (more on that later in this chapter), the experience, both academic and social, is worth it.

Part-Time, Evening, and Weekend Programs

For those who have jobs that they either can't or don't want to surrender, there are other excellent options. Part-time programs generally allow students three to five years to complete the course work that a full-time program expects to cover in just two. Some schools, however, insist that their evening or weekend programs are not part-time at all; while they may stretch out the length of schooling, they may also allow less flexibility in what courses are taken when. For details, you simply must check with every school in which you are interested. Also check access to key faculty for both core courses and your intended electives. The best professors do not always pull double duty for day and evening programs.

The perceived detractor in this case is quality. There is a widespread perception that degrees attained in evening and weekend programs are somehow not the equal of those attained during the conventional full-time programs. This is hard to assert convincingly. At many schools, the faculty that teaches core courses and popular electives teaches for both full-time and part-time programs. What is often true, however, is that the evening, weekend, and part-time programs have slightly lower admission standards, at least in the quantitative aspects of an application. Excellent job experience in a mid-career professional can often make up for a less-than-stellar GMAT score or undergraduate GPA.

That can help if you find yourself in that category, but many recruiters know the difference, and some shy away from relying too heavily on the résumé books of the evening classes.

Executive programs are a further twist on the MBA concept. These are usually shortened versions of the standard MBA courses that gloss over some of the more quantitatively challenging course work and focus instead on high-level case work. The objective is not just to suck in senior managers with money to spend but rusty calculators. At a certain point, most business managers shift from being producers of analysis to being consumers of analysis, so the focus of their graduate education should shift as well.

On the other hand, career services assistance is often less impressive for part-timers. At one time, many executive and part-time students were sponsored by large corporations, and many universities did not want to irritate these corporations by offering their employees avenues of escape. This, however, is changing as well. Check the school's policy on this matter. You will specifically want to know what level of access to campus recruiting and career services assistance is available relative to that for full-time students.

A BRIEF BIBLIOGRAPHY OF SCHOOL RATINGS LISTS

At this point, we need to start narrowing things down to an actual school. If you're interested in a high-powered MBA education, you've assuredly by now heard about the Top 10, Top 20, or whatever "top list" is being published by the business media this week. Don't get too worked up about that concept. One of us remembers a brief first meeting with a consultant who was a graduate of the Richard Ivey School of Business at the University of Western Ontario. When the question of schools came up, she launched a verbal preemptive strike: "Western Ontario—it's one of the top 10 schools in the world, you know." The real question, though, is, "Can you estimate that discount rate?" After that, where you went to school is a secondary question. Actually, Ivey (or Western, as only someone from Ontario could claim) is a great school.

There's an old adage that there are about 30 schools in the Top 20. That is, ask any three people which are the leading schools in the world, and you'll get varying answers. Not that plenty of serious people don't try to be authoritative about it.

▶ *BusinessWeek* issues its survey every other autumn, in even years, and a great deal of work goes into it. It also publishes rankings of the best schools in finance, marketing, management, and entrepreneurship. Some weeks after the edition hits the newsstands, *BusinessWeek*'s parent company (and our esteemed publisher), McGraw-Hill, publishes a book-length review of all the MBA programs that the magazine rates. *BusinessWeek* doesn't stop there: the magazine's MBA Web site (http://www.businessweek.com/bschools/) is expansive, constantly updated, and worth reading. This ranking includes both qualitative and quantitative factors and is the only one that surveys the students themselves (as well as recruiters). It's easy to understand why *BusinessWeek*'s rankings are the most closely watched in the business.

▶ *US News & World Report* has the most quantitative of all the surveys. An annual survey that arrives each spring, this ranking provides a brisk snapshot of the top schools by quantifying peer reviews, recruiter reviews, placement success, and selectivity (which includes average GMAT and GPA). If you like to quantify results, this is a good quick look, but recognize that many factors in selecting a school cannot be quantified. Our advice is to visit the schools in person to form your own opinion.

- *The Financial Times (FT)* issues its survey annually, in January. If you've not read London's *FT*, you should know that it's probably the second most important English-language business newspaper in the world (after, of course, the *Wall Street Journal*). The *FT* survey pays rather more attention to schools outside the United States, which is a nice feature for those considering shipping out to overseas destinations for school.
- *The Economist* ranks schools according to more or less the same criteria as the *FT*. The Economist Intelligence Unit, the magazine's affiliated research group, also publishes *Which MBA?*, an annual book-length expansion of the survey. As a publication based in London, it too pays rather more attention to schools outside of North America. The *Economist*'s editorial staff is particularly well regarded by the schools that it surveys, so its opinions might be given some weight.
- *The Wall Street Journal (WSJ)* has a narrow but deep approach, surveying corporate recruiters for their opinions about, and satisfaction with, recruiting at various schools. The downside of this approach is that it focuses on a single attribute of the schools: the recent experience of the companies that have recruited there. The upside is that this is one of the most important attributes to measure—graduate business schools are professional schools, so you probably wouldn't be going except for the job. Besides, if you want data on other aspects of the schools, there are plenty of other publications that rate those. The *WSJ* also divides schools by their regional and national recruiting strength. If you have a geographic focus to your full-time employment aspirations, you should pay attention to which schools place their graduates where. The *WSJ*'s survey is released annually, and it is absolutely worth picking up.

By now, you may have caught one of the major flaws in all these approaches, except for that of the *Wall Street Journal*. Current students may have important opinions about individual schools, but they are the last group whom one should survey systematically. MBA students have a financial incentive to overstate how much they like their school: if its rank rises in the next survey released, each student stands a better chance of prizing higher compensation out of his next employer or client.

SELECTING A PORTFOLIO OF SCHOOLS

So, we've demonstrated that you should be interested in what journalists think are the world's best schools, but that you also shouldn't get too hung up on their lists.

MBAs among new Fortune 1000 CEOs in 2004 and early 2005, and the 2004 *BusinessWeek* rankings of the schools attended.

MBA Program	CEOs	Rank
The University of Chicago	3	2
Northwestern University (Kellogg)	2	1
The University of Pennsylvania (Wharton)	2	3
Harvard University	2	5
Dartmouth College (Tuck)	1	10
The University of California-Berkeley (Haas)	1	17
University of Texas (McCombs)	1	19
Washington University (Olin)	1	23

Continued

MBA Program	CEOs	Rank
American Graduate School of International Management (Thunderbird)	1	—
Michigan State University (Broad)	1	—
Lake Forest Graduate School of Management	1	—
Northwestern State University of Louisiana	1	—
Drexel University (LeBow)	1	—
La Salle University	1	—
Georgia State University (Robinson)	1	—
Lehigh University	1	—
No MBA at all	70	—
Total	91	

Source: USA Today, April 7, 2005.

Specifically, does this mean that you should pay close attention to who is number 23 or higher on a rankings list? Far from it. When you look more closely at the list and dig below the surface, some interesting patterns start to emerge:

▶ The American Graduate School of International Management (AGSIM), better known as Thunderbird (after the former Air Force base on which the campus sits), resolutely focuses on preparing its students for careers in international business. This year, one of its graduates, William Perez, took over as CEO of Nike. There aren't too many U.S. companies with more international concerns, and it's likely that Mr. Perez picked up a few things about those concerns at AGSIM.

▶ Michigan State University's standout CEO placement this year was Michael Johnston, the new head honcho of Visteon, one of the largest automobile manufacturers in the United States (and the former parts division of Ford Motor Company). Michigan State's Broad School of Management drifts on and off the Top 25 lists from year to year, but it's an excellent school. It's arguably one of the best schools in the world for studying the automotive industry and supply chain management.

▶ Why only two Harvard hires? In 1998, according to headhunting firm Stuart Spencer, the fraction of large-company CEOs with Harvard MBAs stood at 28 percent. That was an outstandingly large number that speaks directly to the influence that Harvard Business School (HBS) once had in U.S. business. By 2005, however, that figure was down to 23 percent, and, as the chart notes, it was dropping quickly. That drop may actually create some value in the economy. In a 2003 study, hedge fund managers Victor Niederhoffer and Laurel Kenner analyzed the share price performance of the nine Nasdaq 100 firms then run by HBS alumni. Over the preceding five years, they had significantly underperformed firms run by the MBA alumni of the other Ivy League programs, Stanford, MIT, and the state universities as well.

It should be evident from all this that the number one school (whatever that really means) on anyone's list is usually a fine program, but it's not the right program for everyone. So how to choose? By considering a range of factors within the context of your own educational needs:

Geography Matters

First, consider where the school is located. The preceding example of Michigan State illustrates this point perfectly. If you are primarily interested in the automotive industry, then Michigan State, the

University of Michigan, and Carnegie Mellon should absolutely be on your list. They all have excellent reputations in that business, and they are all close to Detroit, the undeniable center of the industry in North America. If running an index fund is your next desired gig, MIT ought to be on your list: you'll be raked over the statistical coals in the classroom, and Boston is pretty much the North American center of fund management.

You should also be thinking about where you want to live when you graduate. Columbia University has an excellent school, particularly if you want to work on Wall Street, but looking for a job in southern California while studying in New York City is a difficult task. UCLA's Anderson School is probably worth a long look at that point. Most schools do place people worldwide, but nearly all have regional strength. In the world of recruiting, proximity and convenience matter—for both the employer and the employee. It just isn't cost efficient to recruit remotely if you can find great talent in your own backyard. Despite its national and international reputation, Stanford places almost two-thirds of its graduates in northern California. After two years in Palo Alto, leaving can be a hard thing. So, before placing a school high on your list, you may want to consider just how geographically flexible you can be.

Size Matters

Size matters, but we can't say exactly how it matters for you, since it matters in both directions. The intimate environment of a small school like Emory's Goizueta Business School or the University of North Carolina's Kenan-Flagler School can make for a rewarding and collegial experience. If you crave personal attention and small class sizes, and you don't need five electives in options pricing from which to choose, then you won't need a class of over 700 peers. On the other hand, recruiters have a slight tendency to gravitate disproportionately toward larger programs. Recruiting takes time (and therefore money), and small schools offer fewer choices of potential hires for them. Thus, if you are picking a small school, consider the location. Emory has a built-in advantage over UNC: Atlanta is a much larger city than even the metropolitan Raleigh–Durham–Chapel Hill area. On the other hand, it's easy to patrol the Research Triangle from UNC, and there's a good possibility that someone you will know on the faculty or get to know through an alumnus will have the right contact to get you in the door. (See how this gets back to location?)

Academics Matter

Every school has a particular focus and relative academic strengths—even those that tout general management. That's easy to see in the finance departments of places like the University of Chicago and the University of Pennsylvania's Wharton School. But while case-intensive programs like the University of Virginia's Darden School aim to train general managers who can tackle a wide range of problems, this is also a focus. Many of the surveying organizations release not just Top 10 lists, but Top 10 lists for individual disciplines—say, the best schools for finance, marketing, or entrepreneurship. All the same, you will need to dig down a layer below what the lists reveal. The McCombs School at the University of Texas has an excellent finance department, but it is arguably the *leading* place in the world to study energy finance. If you're looking to work in Houston for BP or want a finance job with ExxonMobil in northern Virginia, it's worth a look.

More specifically, have a look at who teaches what. At many institutions your first year will mostly be consumed by core classes. (There are exceptions; the University of Chicago is particularly renowned for its laissez-faire, sink yourself if you so choose approach.) If those core classes are typically handed off to the junior faculty on the "least impressive instructor" list, think twice. Use your on-site visits to sit in on multiple core class lectures so that you can evaluate teaching methods, instructions, and the classroom exchanges among students to see if these classes match your expectations and your needs.

Recruiters Matter

Before applying anywhere, scrutinize the list of companies that have hired students in the past few years, and especially the last year. (Many recruiting lists are a composite over several years, so it's better to investigate who really hired recently.) Check to see which companies hired more than one student (several surveys list top hiring firms). It's fine to want to work for Goldman Sachs, but if the bank does not recruit formally at the school you're thinking of attending, then working for that outfit will be considerably less likely. It can be done, but it may also require a great deal of work on your part.

Next, consider whether you are laser-focused on a single industry, or whether you'd like the opportunity to explore more than one thing in school. The breadth of the recruiting population is then important. If you're convinced that you want to work in banking in New York City, then the Stern School of Business at New York University is an excellent choice. Wall Street is not the first destination for graduates of the W. P. Carey School at Arizona State University, but the school has a widely regarded reputation for producing logistics managers. Generally speaking, however, the better ranked the school is on more lists, the better will be your access to the wider pool of recruiters. Then again, this is an easy matter to test by querying the school in question as well as the current students.

Alumni Matter

You should absolutely investigate who the school has placed into what sorts of jobs, and where they have gone since then. The rankings lists of prominent alumni are not necessarily the place to start. Jon Corzine, the governor of New Jersey (and formerly U.S. senator and managing director of Goldman Sachs), is arguably one of the most visible alumni of the University of Chicago's Graduate School of Business, but you're not likely to get much time on his calendar. More important would be the names of the recent mid-career and less exalted senior alumni who have important positions in the industries you are considering. Every school tracks this information for recruiting and development purposes, so you should feel free to ask how deep the alumni pool is for the companies you are targeting.

Career Management Matters

Finally, built into that hefty tuition fee you'll be paying will be the services of a professional career services staff. Ask how many people are on the staff, what their respective roles are, and how long they have been in their jobs. Expect some turnover—career services is a tough business, with demanding clients (MBA students on one side and corporate recruiters on the other), so the burnout rate is high. Ask what programs the school runs throughout the year for students to prepare them for the job search and interviews. Also inquire as to what trips the school conducts to destinations as part of its outreach strategy or as student trips.

CHAPTER 13
Getting Admitted

THE IMPORTANCE OF THE GMAT IN ADMISSIONS

Since you're reading this book, you're probably already aware that the GMAT is a big deal in MBA admissions, at least for the leading schools. There are two reasons for this, one good and one not-so-good.

GMATs Matter, so GMATs Matter

The not-so-good reason is that the schools are ranked in part by the average GMAT scores of their incoming classes. Every year, most of the major rankings bodies—basically the editorial staffs of *BusinessWeek, The Economist, The Financial Times*, and *US News & World Report*—latch onto quantitative factors to a greater or lesser extent, because, well, they're quantitative. Actually, *BusinessWeek* releases its figures only every other year, which is probably just fine, since graduate school reputations and rankings should not shift radically in a year unless something truly exceptional (like a new building) or catastrophic (like a really bad recruiting year) happens. As for the publications, *The Wall Street Journal* is alone among this group in simply polling recruiters, which produces a quite different list.

GMAT scores are an easy figure for prospective applicants to grasp, so everyone wants to know the averages. How smart your classmates will be is an important consideration, since a great deal of one's graduate school education is provided by one's peers. Admissions staffs know this, so they watch (or, perhaps more accurately, chase) the average GMAT scores of the incoming class. That applicant may have worked in the West Wing of the White House, but the National Security Advisor's endorsement on his recommendation may not be enough to make up for a 520 score. That would tank the average, and the school (horrors) could fall a point or two.

GMATs Are a Hygiene Factor

Rankings pressure aside, there is a perfectly valid reason that admissions staffs care about GMAT scores. Contrary to the conspiracy theorists and those who are trying to sell you books of test-taking tricks, standardized tests are reasonably reliable, at least in one respect (keep reading). On the one hand, several internal business school studies we have seen indicate that there is little correlation between high GMAT scores (say, over 700) and either high grade-point averages or starting salaries down the road. In fact, one very quiet study from a second-tier school (one with a regional, but not quite national, reputation) indicated a negative correlation—applicants with high GMAT scores tended to receive slightly lower starting salaries two years later. At least one possible explanation is easy to understand: if you scored 750 and you're getting your MBA at Cornfield State University, you either (1) didn't want to stray too far from home or (2) had something defective in your application that kept you out of MIT. A total lack of social skills would make even the most crass "GMAT whore" (as one admissions officer has described it to us) think twice about admitting you—and it won't get you a job at Goldman Sachs, except crunching numbers in the back office.

At the same time, a very low GMAT score has been correlated with significant academic difficulties in first-year quantitative classes. If you want to be a high-class MBA, you need to understand multiple regression and discounted cash flows (yes, even if you're a marketing major). For the top programs, GMAT scores much below the 600 mark get a bit hard to bear now that averages are at 675 and above. A "5" at the beginning of the score will definitely make Stanford (and a lot of other schools) think twice, and it should. This is particularly true of a low quantitative score, since it's the quantitative classes that seem to cause the biggest problems. This may be about the only correlation that has been repeatedly demonstrated, but it is an important one. Admissions officers don't knowingly want to admit students who they fear will struggle unduly with the academic rigor of the class. Aside from the unseemly vocational side of the MBA, let us not forget that this is still an advanced degree from an institution of higher learning. GMAT scores are thus, in statistical parlance, a hygiene factor. The floor can only be so clean, but below a certain point, it can be *really* dirty.

So, a low GMAT score will not terminate your candidacy everywhere, but it is something to be concerned about. (Fortunately, you're reading this book.) If standardized tests do cause you stress, that's unfortunate. Business school is stressful too, so the timed format is useful for differentiating among candidates. For that matter, life on Wall Street is stressful, even if that's theoretically outside the bounds of what the test is trying to measure. Perhaps that's why many bankers care so much about those GMAT scores (as we will discuss in Chapter 15).

THE IMPORTANCE OF YOUR PAST UNIVERSITY TRANSCRIPTS

If your scores are nothing pretty, there may yet be hope. A strong undergraduate transcript, or a strong transcript from another graduate program, will help. What is strong? Naturally, a high GPA is important (top programs typically post an average undergraduate GPA of 3.4 or above), but a high-class rank is also important—so many people at Harvard get As these days that they may not mean as much. A good GPA or class rank in a quantitatively intense program is even better, because it suggests that you will (1) conquer your options-pricing course, (2) go on to a high-paying job on Wall Street, and (3) ultimately donate an eight-figure sum for a new building on campus (with windows on three sides of the dean's office).

Another important factor is the quality of the subjects on your undergraduate transcript. After a certain point, once you have demonstrated basic quantitative ability, it is less absolutely important whether you have taken electrical engineering or political science. Both are incidentally useful in graduate business studies, though do bear in mind that most admissions staffs will strive for some diversity in the academic concentrations of the prospective matriculants that they admit. That said, know that partial differential equations will look better on your transcript than basket weaving. Prestige matters here, too, so an art history major from Rice University may still look better than an electrical engineer from Cornfield State College.

However, don't expect the admissions staff to have special knowledge of what works in the real world. Engineering majors usually thrive in finance classes—after all, what is the Black-Scholes model but a heat transfer equation in disguise? Those students, however, do not necessarily profit from that ability economically. One recent study from a leading MBA program in the United States indicates that those with liberal arts and social science bachelor's degrees actually outearn their engineering-trained classmates in their first jobs. Why? Qualitative feedback indicates that they are better interviewees, which indicates better social skills, which mean a lot in this world and for your future earnings potential. So, if you studied circuit design in college, lose the attitude about the liberal arts and figure out fast which one is the salad fork.

RESEARCHING THE PROGRAMS

You should make sure that your list of schools is internally consistent. Many admissions applications ask about the other schools to which you are applying. There are at least two reasons for this. First, admissions officers generally want to know who their competition is. When it starts its next round of marketing efforts, the University of North Carolina (Kenan-Flagler) wants to know whether it needs to highlight its relative advantages with respect to Duke (Fuqua) or Emory (Goizueta). The other reason is that admissions officers want to see whether you've thought about the career implications of your choices. Applying to the University of Chicago, MIT, and Carnegie Mellon suggests that you have an affinity for mathematics, and that you might be looking for a career in which you can apply it on a daily basis. Listing a scattershot pattern of schools with significantly different characteristics suggests that you haven't done your homework on the schools, or that you might lack focus in your future career plans. Listing several high-powered schools alongside Hometown University indicates to the people there that Hometown is your safety-valve choice. In short, know what you are signaling.

PREPARING YOUR RÉSUMÉ

You will need a résumé for your application, so you might as well write a decent one now. Even if you don't, you will need one by September of your first year: recruiting doesn't wait. Résumé books need to be published, and basic résumés need to be put into the school's campus recruiting system. Presentations for second-year recruiting generally start in October, and you may just meet someone into whose hands you'd like to thrust a business card or résumé, even if you're a lowly first-year. Fall career fairs, both on and off campus, typically take place in the mid-September to mid-October time frame to target second-year students and make early assessments of first-years for intern recruiting.

So before writing your résumé, you must understand the purpose of the document. In most contexts, it has but one: to land you an interview with the organization that employs the person reading it. Since each reader will have a different set of criteria in mind, you should ideally customize your résumé for every submission. As that can be very time-consuming, you may consider maintaining a set of slightly different résumés for every type of application that you are making (whether for schools or for jobs). Whoever your audience, there are three broad themes that you will want to reveal without being overly explicit:

▶ *Your mission.* Where are you trying to go with your career? *Ceteris paribus* (and you should learn what that means for your microeconomics classes, if you don't know already), anyone making judgments about your résumé will be looking to see whether you are indicating a consistent direction in your life. Your résumé should ideally *tell a story* about your goals *without a bald statement of objectives at the top.* A little subtlety shows maturity and self-possession, not to mention writing skill, which is almost a lost art in business today. Get good at this and you will outshine the competition.

▶ *Your strategy.* How will you get there? Your résumé should show a somewhat deliberate progression in your career, even if you have changed direction once or twice (your essays can fill in the less obvious rationales for movement). It is important to show that you have thought about your own advancement and skill set and that this is showcased in your résumé. What are your relevant and transferable skills? For most people, going to business school is about wanting to make either a switch from your current industry or function or a leap forward in your current industry or function. Your MBA education should—according to your well crafted essays—fill in the knowledge and skills gaps to get you there. Thus, your résumé is a first look at your strategy, the platform on which you are constructing your next career move. As with all construction projects, it is important that the foundation be firm. From an admissions standpoint, if you don't know where you're going, it may be hard to get there, even with an MBA. Moreover, some thorough reflection on where you have been is helpful in crafting the stories that you will need in order to explain your past, present, and future self to recruiters.

▶ *Your tactics.* What specifically are you planning to do? Your résumé should make it clear that you know what the next step is or, at a minimum, should give the reader a clue so that the essays don't catch her completely off guard. This is a subtle affair that requires tailoring the language and the formatting to the expectations of the industry into which you are flinging your eight-and-a-half-by-eleven calling card.

Once you know what message you want to convey, make your laundry list—that collection of notes about everything seemingly significant that you have done in your life. Then, in the next iteration, list the skills that you have amassed and the results that you have achieved at every stop along the way. Try to select those that are the most relevant to the school to which you are applying and/or the job you are seeking. You can then fill in some more details about each of these to create your résumé bullet points. Put these aside for the moment; you'll need them after a few preliminaries.

There are generally four sections to a résumé:

1. Identification

Use your common name, unless you are from the Far East and specifically wish to use an English-style name. In this case, list both your given name and your English nickname, such as

Qiongyi (Jane) Wang

For an address, consider including your permanent address for holiday communications or to illustrate geographic interest. Include a telephone number and a school or personal e-mail address. In general, the school's e-mail address is preferred.

2. Education

List your degrees in reverse chronology, starting with the school that you are attending (if you are already there) or the last one that you attended (if you are using your résumé to gain admission somewhere). If your school offers concentrations or majors, list the relevant ones. If the school doesn't (and some, such as the University of Virginia's Darden School, don't), then don't create one.

As we noted earlier, consider listing your GMAT score, but only if it is above 700. That would be impressive. A lower score is still an accomplishment, but McKinsey probably won't think so. As a guideline, don't list your GMAT on your résumé (except when requested) unless your score is nicely (say 25 points) above the school's average.

Clubs and activities are important to list, if only to indicate that you have a life outside school, work, and GMAT preparation. There are plenty of people who want to work with interesting co-workers, and this is the place to show that you are one of those. More to the point, your outside accomplishments indicate that you will have the bandwidth to stay up until 4 a.m. making briefing slides for that important client, and still find time to play in a string quartet. Multitasking is a critical skill, not just in business, but in business school survival. Showcase this.

Your past overall GPAs (one per institution) may be useful assets to list, particularly if they were high. This generally means that you can include your GPA if it is higher than the average GPA of the (incoming) class. Otherwise, you're just calling unwanted attention to yourself.

Any significant scholarships that you earned (including ROTC) are important, because they indicate that some other organization thought that you were sufficiently important that it should hand you money. Both schools and recruiters like the confirmation of another's opinion. If you have plenty of room (or if you need to fill up the page), include the basis of your scholarship, the number selected out of the number of applications, and the percentage of your tuition that it paid.

Finally, list your graduate degree(s) (if any) first, followed by your undergraduate degree(s).

3. Experience

List your experience in reverse chronological order. For graduate students, this is generally better than the alternative, the functional résumé. In each case, start with the name of the company, the division (if applicable), the location, your title, and the dates of employment (month/year is generally accepted). If you desire and have the room, you may want to include a general overview statement, particularly if the company is not a household name in the industry in which you are seeking a position. After that, you can provide an overview (if needed) of your basic job responsibilities, including their scale and scope, but make sure to put the description of the company before the description of your job.

The most important part of your experience, however, is your list of accomplishments. Use bullets (left justified only), and include at least two per job (a single bullet is a logically inconsistent concept, and it shows). You may omit this format with less recent jobs in order to conserve space. Keep most of these bullet points to no more than three lines; this is important for scannability, and it demonstrates your efficiency in writing. The bullet points should generally be listed in their order of importance, but a reverse chronological ordering may be required to maintain logical organization. You will need to make that call yourself.

In writing this section, it is very important to focus on projects, specific relevant skills, and accomplishments. Your bullets should specify the actions you took, and the results you achieved. You should avoid company terminology, acronyms, and jargon, unless you are certain that the admissions officer (or recruiter) will understand them. Your individual responsibilities should be accurately represented, with specific details that enhance the reader's understanding of your value to an organization. You may use the names of clients and customers (if this is appropriate), the number of people that you supervised, the size of your budget, and the titles of the people you advised. You should quantify (absolutely or relatively) your results wherever possible. Note how you increased revenue, decreased costs, or reduced cycle time. If you "increased customer satisfaction," try to explain how this was measured. Consider these two bullet points:

▶ *CO A Co., 1-66 AR, OIF.*
▶ *Commanded a tank company of 95 soldiers that seized one of Saddam Hussein's palaces during the 2003 war in Iraq.*

The first could be comprehensible only to someone who had been in the military, while the second might actually elicit some interest from a general reader. Frankly, this is one of the most difficult things in career services to get across to former military officers, engineers, and computer scientists: your experience may be valuable (or it may not), but it's valuable only if it can be related specifically to an organization's needs. Keep the jargon out, and give your résumé to someone who is not in your line of work to see if she or he can comprehend your résumé bullet points.

What is worth highlighting? As noted, quantitative results are best. "Increased divisional profits by 45 percent over two years" is much more compelling than the ubiquitous but generic "improved business performance." Qualitative statements are valuable as well, as long as they demonstrate worthwhile qualities in some testable way. Some examples are shown in the following table.

Quality	Sample Bullet Point
Teamwork and coordination	▶ Led a cross-functional team of 12 from marketing, sales, engineering, and finance to resolve successfully our second-largest customer's most significant quality issue.
Analytical and quantitative rigor	▶ Developed a new production cost reduction method for the firm, and successfully tested it in four client engagements.
Communication skills	▶ Wrote six speeches for Deputy Secretary of Defense Paul Wolfowitz.
Pattern of accomplishments	▶ Ranked among the top three sales associates (in a region with over 100) three years out of four.
Strategic thinking and planning	▶ Surveyed the automated widget market for potential acquisition candidates, and recommended the two that the firm subsequently acquired.
Global orientation (cross-cultural)	▶ Negotiated long-lead supply contracts with Brazilian aircraft parts manufacturers (in Portuguese).

4. Additional Information

If you made the Olympic Trials in the hurdles, climbed K2, or currently play in your municipal symphony orchestra, that's worth noting. That you "enjoy reading, art, and running" is not. It is shocking how frequently phrases of this type actually appear on résumés, and they are the kiss of death. Almost everyone likes those things, so what's the point? That you weren't a sufficiently compelling character to come up with something better?

So what is interesting? Specific activities, clubs, volunteer work, sports, professional affiliations and accreditations.

> ► *Enjoy reading presidential biographies, studying fifteenth-century Italian art, and running competitive 10Ks.*

You may include computer skills if these are real assets (that does not include Microsoft Office, as facility with this is pretty much expected of any MBA). You may include personal interests, but note that your political and religious affiliations may not appeal to everyone. (On the other hand, those are useful on a résumé if you are looking to work for the Republican National Committee or Catholic Charities.) Foreign language skills, including your degree of fluency, are almost always useful to note, particularly if the company to which you are applying needs someone who knows (for example) Brazilian Portuguese. On the other hand, fluency in Spanish is not interesting if your résumé states that you graduated from the University of Navarre—it's expected, so it's redundant, and besides, you're really a *native* speaker, then. Specifically, in no case should you note that you are fluent in the working language of the country in which you are seeking a position—if you are from a country with a different working language, it will only suggest that you may not be as fluent as you would like everyone to think. For example, citing on your résumé that you are "fluent in English" as a Chinese student studying in the United States gives the reader the impression you are anything but fluent.

Above all, avoid the general. Don't tell us what an analyst does at Merrill Lynch—we know about that. Tell us what *you* did. Remember, a résumé is not a job description, nor is it an anthology of everything you have ever done. It is a list of your greatest hits, and—here is the kicker—the greatest hits may change depending on who your listening audience is.

Finally, if your work experience or undergraduate institution lies outside the country in which you are seeking a position, be sure to note your work authorization. If you are a citizen or authorized resident of more than one country, and that fact would be relevant to the recruiter in question, then note it. Dual nationality and European Union work authorization can be sought-after commodities in the right contexts.

In light of the preceding, we do have a few pet peeves about résumés, and these are worth noting as well:

> ► *Résumés that read like job descriptions.* As we stated earlier, we all know what an analyst at a Wall Street bank does. Recounting the obvious is not just unnecessary; it's a waste of the precious space on your résumé. It's also a waste of the reader's time, and remember, the sole purpose of this one-page document is to convince the reader (whether a university admissions officer or a recruiter) that you merit consideration in his or her program.
>
> ► *"Actively managed," or "significantly increased."* As previously suggested, phrases like these are the height of generica: they don't tell us anything. Remember, you are competing for jobs

against the two classmates sitting on either side of you in the Buy-One-Get-One Strategies class. They are most likely claiming to have significantly increased something in their last jobs. More worrisome, they each probably increased sales by 30 percent in a year, or cut operations costs by 50 percent by firing the unproductive half of the staff in their departments. Your "significantly" won't cut much mustard next to that. Go back, do your homework, and get to a number. Ballpark it if you have to, or find another way to say what you did—just avoid the bland.

▶ *Random capitalization.* This is particularly problematic for former U.S. military officers and some international students. Know what does and does not need to be capitalized. If you don't know, please consult Strunk and White's *The Elements of Style*, which is a great reference book that you should have on your bookshelf anyway.

▶ *Hyperlinked e-mail addresses.* These are not as interesting as Bill Gates would like to think. Actually, it's really annoying to accidentally launch a Web browser by mousing over the wrong line in an electronic copy of your résumé. Since many e-mail addresses include underscores, the hyperlink can hide this small but relevant bit of data.

▶ *Ten-point fonts.* These are fine if you don't care whether that management consultant who is scanning your school's résumé book in the Comfort Inn in Fargo at 2 a.m. (after finishing yet one more deck of slides for his ungrateful client) is going blind reading your miniature type. Be kind to your reader—we've been there, and the incredibly detailed résumé is not as interesting to read as you might think. Use a font that is approximately the same size as Times New Roman 11 point.

Remember that formatting is important. The person reading your résumé may very well read several hundred the day that she reads yours, so make it easy for her. Keep your résumé to one page only, with ample white space. Use, at a minimum, an 11-point font and margins of at least 0.7 inch on each side. Part of your task is to showcase your talents succinctly. If you've ever spent time in business, you know that most executives expect one-page briefs before they get to the 100-page study or the 50-page PowerPoint deck. Learning to write succinctly is an important business skill, and your résumé is a great place to start. Your résumé will probably be a recruiter's first indication of your overall writing skill.

Try to avoid abbreviating, except for long numbers. In that case, consistently use B for billion, M for million, and K for thousand, unless you are looking for a finance position, in which case use MM for millions. In most of Europe, M is used as the abbreviation for thousands, since the Latin word for that is *mille*. Do not consider using ampersands (&) in order to save space. The ampersand is appropriately used in Johnson & Johnson, but it is not appropriate to save you the two spaces you need to clear a line on your résumé. Similarly, spell out numerals ("ten" versus "10") only where you have the room to do so. While that's not the best practice in standard written (American) English, this is a résumé, so some shortcuts may be taken and numbers (even 1 through 10) stand out nicely.

Remember that your résumé is not meant to be comprehensive, and that it is understood to be a piece of personal marketing collateral. Omitting information that the recruiter doesn't need, or that you don't want him to have, is perfectly acceptable. In particular, omit words that aren't strictly necessary for making your point. Use action verb phrases, not complete sentences for your résumé bullet points. Start with a verb, and omit articles (i.e., *the*, *an*, and *a*) as superfluous. That is, write

> ▶ *Managed purchasing division that procured $15M in parts for Ford Motor Co.*
> ▶ *I managed a purchasing division that procured approximately $15 million in automobile parts for the Ford Motor Company.*

Finally, remember that accuracy in grammar and spelling is even more important. Anything that signals an inattention to detail tells the reader (the person who might be offering you a job) that you just don't care that much. Worse, it can be confusing. For more on this, read Lynne Truss's *Eats, Shoots and Leaves* (Gotham, 2004), but for now, these are a few random tips.

SOLICITING THE RIGHT RECOMMENDATIONS

Your résumé is what you say about yourself. While everyone expects that you will not tell lies in it, few think that it's anything more than a piece of self-produced marketing collateral. This is why schools ask for recommendations. Don't be fooled: recommendations are given serious consideration. They are not just a way for some functionary in the Human Resources department of your last employer to demonstrate perfunctory due diligence. Rather, recommendations are the way in which admissions staffs ascertain whether the people for whom, or with whom, you worked actually think that you are on an upward career trajectory. Exercise extreme care in choosing whom you will ask to write your recommendations. Remember, the letters are generally sealed, and your recommender is under no obligation to show you the letter before she seals the envelope (though that has been known to happen).

So what could go wrong? Several things:

- ▶ It is just possible that your boss or co-worker deeply resents your trek off toward the six-figure earnings potential of MBA-dom, and will smile as he stabs your effort in the back with a flaming piece of hate mail ("has a tendency to carry unlicensed weapons to the office"). But don't get too hung up on that.

- ▶ It is possible that you will be damned with faint praise. Phrases like "Janet did everything that I ever asked her to" and "he works extremely well under close and frequent supervision" are not the path into Kellogg. To avoid this, try to be absolutely certain that your recommender is actually impressed with your work, likes you personally, is aware of your career aspirations, and has the ability to communicate this effectively to a school in a written format.

- ▶ After that, make sure that you are picking your recommender(s) from the right pay grade. If the CEO has heard your name, but has not spoken to you, and offers to endorse the letter that your boss writes, you might hesitate a bit. If your résumé doesn't indicate that you worked with him, then the letter will seem out of place. Some big shots are known to enjoy playing kingmaker, and admissions staffs know this. It actually won't help your case.

- ▶ On the other hand, make sure that you aren't soliciting letters from two co-workers and your junior high school music teacher. A peer review may be requested, but reviews by people for whom you have worked—and worked recently—will do a better job of making your case (if, of course, they are actually good reviews). However, even if you work in the family business, don't ask your dad to write a recommendation for you. It won't help much.

REQUESTING AN INTERVIEW

Interviewing is very important. If the school to which you are applying offers interviews, request one. If possible, interview on campus, not just with a local alumnus. Interviews with the admissions staff are generally held in higher esteem, since they provide apples-to-apples comparisons among the majority of applicants.

Admittedly, it is more the school's interview than yours, but the reason for requesting it is to make sure that you have every opportunity to state your case. Note that there is a fine line between the engaging and the overbearing, and that it doesn't fall in the same place for all interviewers. Gauge your interviewer's interest in what you're saying, and either perk up or shut up, depending on the signals you're getting. If your interviewer is not giving those signals, she's not a good interviewer, which can be the case.

What to say? In answering the questions, explain without the boilerplate why you want to work toward the MBA, why you want to attend the school in question (as opposed to any other school), and what you aspire to do in your career after school. This last question should primarily focus on near-term goals, as opposed to your CEO aspirations. If you do aspire to be a CEO, that is great, but it is still helpful to your interviewer to know what your plan is for the first few steps along that path. In short, have a purpose, and for goodness sake, don't tell the interviewer that you have no clue as to your career plans aside from wanting to make a pile of money. If necessary, make up something plausible. Just be sure that you walk away from your interview having clearly communicated the following three points: your reason for wanting an MBA, your future career aspirations, and your thoughts as to why attending that particular school will help you to achieve those goals. (On the last point, remember that it helps if you have done your research on the school in question.)

Finally, it is particularly important to remember that every interaction you have with a school and those affiliated with it has the potential to create an impression. Impress a member of a school's advisory board, and a low GMAT score might not seem that important (we have seen this happen). Scream at the admissions secretary about how irritated you are that she lost your file, and she is likely to tell her boss, the admissions director. Any interaction you have with the school, whether by phone or by e-mail, has the potential to be included as part of your application. Niceness is a quality that is in alarmingly short supply among MBA students, so try to be likable.

WRITING SOME COMPELLING ESSAYS

The essay-writing process provides an important opportunity to reflect on why you want that MBA. In one sense, the essays are just the written long form of the interview questions that you will encounter. In the interview, your answers are expected to be well thought out, compelling, and hopefully original, but also a bit off the cuff. In the case of the essays, they really need to be polished as well as original—there's just too much time available not to get it right.

First, try to think of some way to make your essay creative—you really should try to take pity on the admissions staffs, who read hundreds of these essays every week for months during the admissions cycle. More to your interest, an also-ran essay will not stick out in anyone's mind when the admissions people meet to decide whether to admit you or the gal who just got back from that stint setting up microcredit lending institutions in Nepal.

Next, remember that this is a writing sample. The school would like to know that its students are arriving with some degree of literacy and that your undergraduate degree was worth the four-year investment. Will you be able to write coherent essays for classes? Will you be able to write compelling cover letters to prospective employers? If you get that job, will you be able to write coherent memoranda and reports?

If your application reveals a notable weakness, you may wish to address it directly with an essay. There are two potential ways to do this. Many schools offer an optional essay—one featuring a question like, "Is there anything else that you would like to tell us?" This is an excellent venue for explaining that two-year gap in your résumé or that string of C's from your freshman year of college. If that isn't an option, and you can spin the weakness into a feat of self-awareness, you might consider addressing it in one of the required essays. The often-seen "tell us about a time you faced adversity" question is just such an opening. Admissions directors do understand that fate and personal circumstances can throw the best-laid career plans out the window. Additionally, MBA programs are filled with "late bloomers" who did not have their futures figured out right after college and who may have wandered a bit before heading in a particular direction. If you can adequately explain your past circumstances and show the reader your intended direction with some conviction, you are more likely to overcome the somewhat meandering route that has brought you to this point.

Lastly, and most important, your answer to any essay question should not be something that anyone else could write. A compelling application is not just about creativity—it's about uniqueness. If you could insert the name "Joe Bloggs" in place of yours, as you wax on for a few paragraphs about how you want to climb the corporate ladder at Amalgamated Acme and then run for the U.S. Senate, save it. Okay, if you actually do want to do that, fine, but try to show how what you have done over the past few years somehow relates to your career path. Fortunately, the process of writing your essays provides the opportunity for the self-reflection that will aid your job search as well. Your story has to make sense to the admissions staff. If you can't figure out how to make that happen, then you may want to rethink exactly why you are applying to an MBA program in the first place.

THINKING ABOUT YOUR CAREER PLAN DURING THE ADMISSION PROCESS

Remember, while it all starts with the GMAT, it all gets back to the job. We will discuss the job hunt in greater detail in Chapter 15, but we must briefly mention it now. In the past few years, the relationship between admissions and career services within business schools has gotten closer. At many leading institutions, the former now routinely asks the latter for opinions regarding candidates. Are his career goals realistic? Will she be difficult to place into an internship? What sort of recruiters will be interested in his profile, and does that match those that we expect to have on campus? Could a negative answer mean that she might turn out to be a previously unrecognized admissions error? The school will be assessing not just your past performance, but your future marketability, and the latter is arguably more important.

Career changers will face the most scrutiny on this dimension. Top-flight MBA programs are often destinations for career changers. During the long economic expansion of the 1990s, many recruiters were flocking to the leading programs to hire anyone they could, so many twenty-somethings who were dissatisfied with their current situation saw the MBA as a way out. Indeed, for many it was. The problem today is that recruiting has tightened a bit, and past work experience is now relatively more valued. So, if you are a career changer, you will have to explain what you want to do, and why you don't want to continue on your current path. If you're an accountant, you will need to explain why you want to be a marketer, but *without saying too many negative things about accounting*. You really don't want to come across as a malcontent. You will also need to show how your progression through your previous activities has prepared you for the shift that you are looking to make.

That said, as long as you have a backup plan, don't be afraid to make the switch, and to make the MBA the hinge that you rely on in the process. It's a fabulous and edifying experience, and there is no other place in the world where so many recruiters, from so many different industries, will pay so much attention to you in such a short period of time.

CHAPTER 14

Getting Ready to Survive B-School

CONCEPTS TO REMEMBER FROM YOUR GMAT PREPARATION

As you shift your focus from preparing for the GMAT to preparing your applications, you may start to wonder whether all that test preparation will have any residual utility. It will, in at least two areas:

▶ *Analytical writing.* While your score on this section isn't the most important part of your admissions package, your ability to write analytically and quickly is critical to your success as an MBA. Sure, you may graduate without it, but the electronic messages, memoranda, and briefing slides that will probably constitute a significant chunk of your productive output as an MBA (that's a thought, isn't it?) will show a lack of preparation.

▶ *Algebra.* It really all gets back to algebra. You can probably forget all the geometry you relearned for the GMAT, since it has almost no connection to what you will do in graduate school. On the other hand, you will need every bit of the algebra you've reviewed in this book, and a good bit more. If your algebra is not good, get yourself a book with which to review it, or consider math camp.

MATH CAMP

"Math camp" is the affectionate MBA term for the mathematics review course that many schools offer in July or August for students who, well, haven't really thought about algebra, statistics, or calculus since high school. It's a relatively embarrassment-free reintroduction to all of the math that you once knew, then forgot, but really need to know again, fast. Expect to cover everything in Chapters 3 and 4 of this book in less than a day. At that point, you'll probably move on to more sophisticated algebra, and cover a considerable amount of probability and statistics as well.

Math camp may go further than that. In Chapters 3 and 4, we stressed the importance of algebra. That's not quite all the mathematics you'll need for an MBA program, as you'll need to understand statistics very well before you finish. Depending on where you go to school, you may need to brush up on your calculus as well.

If you're not concentrating in finance, then there aren't that many situations in which you will need to use or understand more than basic calculus. The only one that is certain to arise is the monopoly-pricing problem in microeconomics. That is the question of what price an unregulated monopolist should charge to maximize his profit. While you are certain to have that problem, you may not need a rigorous understanding of calculus.

What do we mean? Calculus is essential to solving the problem in the general form, but only algebra is required once you have that formula. So, if you attend the University of Chicago or the Sloan School at MIT, you'll see the calculus in class. If you attend case study programs at the University of Virginia's Darden School or the Harvard Business School, you almost certainly won't. You'll be handed the formula after a review of the calculus, and you'll just memorize it, use it once or twice, and then look it up if you ever need it again.

That all changes if you want to study finance or business economics in any depth. By your third semester of microeconomics, calculus and differential equations are part and parcel of your work. Options pricing just can't be done without them. (Apparently, before Black and Scholes devised their famous formula—derived through the solution of a differential equation resembling that used in heat transfer calculations—options pricing was largely a matter of, "Hey, I saw that new Chevy on the drive in. It's sporty. Let's buy some GM options.") So, if you think that you want to study higher finance or economics, and you have never taken calculus, you're seriously out of luck until you correct that problem.

Note that many schools also offer a camp for the accounting-challenged. Double-entry accounting is hardly an intuitive concept, but the adage that "accounting is the language of business" is almost as true as it is old and shopworn. That means that you really can't have a meaningful discussion with your classmates if your head tilts over uncontrollably to the left when you hear terms like "ee-bit-dah." (EBITDA is Earnings Before Interest, Taxes, Depreciation, and Amortization, and it's a useful measure of the cash-generating potential of a business.) Why *that's* important you'll pick up in financial accounting, financial statement analysis, and corporate finance—but you really should consider a gentle introduction if you've never had accounting before.

ESSENTIAL TOOLS FOR THE MBA STUDENT

So suppose you've posted an excellent score on the GMAT, you've written some fabulous essays (that are even mostly true), you've been accepted to an outstanding MBA program, you've mailed in your deposit, you've secured some gigantic student loans, and you've loaded up the truck to move to Philadelphia, Chicago, Palo Alto, or elsewhere. Wait—that cramped student apartment that you've secured for two years won't hold half your stuff, so you sold most of it on eBay. Given the impending impoverishment of your lifestyle, are there any things that you can't do without? Absolutely. Every MBA student needs, at a minimum, the same four essential pieces of gear:

1. *The laptop computer.* Don't even think about a desktop; the lack of portability will hugely cramp your mobility when working in groups. Furthermore, pay no attention to what the kid at Circuit City tells you are the performance differences between the two types of machine at the same price point. A three-year-old laptop has more than enough processing power and memory for what you will need to do. The only thing driving improvements in the personal computers marketed to individuals these days is the need to see greater resolution in the blood pools in Quake III. That's a fine way to make a living in software (we suppose), but there's no need for that in an MBA program. Sure, it will run your regression analyses faster, but a few

seconds per day is not worth tying your work to your desk. That cramped student apartment is really going to irritate you after a few weeks. Your student loans are paying for the "free" wireless that the school just installed, so you might as well take advantage.

The question of whether you should get a Macintosh or Windows machine is almost immaterial, unless you like contracting computer viruses. (OK, one of us has a bias against Windows machines.) It's the same Microsoft Office, which is (of course) the most popular office software suite. Macs run Excel, which is the only vital piece of software that almost everyone needs. Minitab and SPSS run on both as well, and you'll need one of those (or something similar) if you're at a school that takes statistics seriously. Now that new Macs are Intel-based, they can run Windows and all Windows-based software, as well. That said, you will find that Windows machines are the most popular version in business schools, in part because they are the most popular machines in business. Our advice: consider where you will be working after school. If you prefer a start-up or a creative environment that allows you to choose your machine, pick what you like. If, however, you know that your employer of choice is running on a few thousand Dell laptops, then consider that fact. Many schools are bundling laptops as part of the tuition these days, so before you go and drop a few grand, see what each program offers.

2. *The financial calculator.* Yes, you have that laptop computer. Yes, it has Microsoft Excel, which is by default a really big calculator. You still need a calculator, because it's annoying to have to pull out that laptop every time you need to multiply a string of numbers. That said, there are a number of routes.

You probably don't need a graphing calculator (though do check with the school to confirm this). That's not to say that you won't be graphing; *au contraire*, you'll be graphing a great deal. It's just that you'll probably want to print or project those graphs onto something a bit larger than a calculator screen. However, if you have a graphing calculator that you like, and it has the financial functions you need, then it should be more than adequate.

You could purchase a Hewlett-Packard, Texas Instruments, Casio, or other financial calculator. They all pretty much have the same net present value functions, and that's the main thing for which you'll need the calculator. The HP 12C was once the favorite of financial analysts, but TI and others have great (and less expensive) machines these days as well.

Another excellent route is to just procure a software-based financial calculator for your handheld computer. Landware's FinCalc for the Palm OS is an excellent option. Put that on a Treo, and suddenly your phone can calculate the yield on a 10-year T-bill. That's slick.

3. *The mobile phone.* If you don't have one yet (we can't really imagine that, but we wanted to cover the bases just in case), get one with good coverage both on campus and in any city in which you plan to spend significant time job-hunting. As we note in Chapter 15, check your messages every day, and don't go to sleep until you've responded to every one of them (well, every one that's important). If you can go the route of the Treo or the Blackberry, that's all the better—you won't need to carry an organizer, a telephone, and a calculator in your backpack, and you won't need to fumble with all three in order to do business. For that matter, the electronic mail functionality will mean that you needn't bring your laptop everywhere you travel, which can be a great relief.

4. The Wall Street Journal *subscription*. This is absolutely indispensable if you are headed to a career in investment banking, but it's almost as important for everyone else. Our sniffy European friends tell us that *The Financial Times* (the "pink pages," because of the salmon color of the paper) is a most acceptable substitute. Whatever. Reading *The Wall Street Journal* every day gives you a ground-level reminder about the way things really function, and a daily short course in the lexicon of commerce. One of the worst interviewing experiences one of us had (as an interviewer) involved an MBA student who kept referring to the European Union's currency as the "Eurodollar." (For reference, Eurodollars are not units of currency; they are bonds issued in Europe but denominated in U.S. dollars. They're not as popular as they once were, and the EU's currency is the euro.) He probably wouldn't have made such a career-limiting move if he had read the *Journal* daily.

CHAPTER 15

Recruiting and Career Management

INTRODUCTION

This chapter marks the end of our story, and just the beginning of yours. As we noted in Chapter 12, the job that you will land after school is probably the main reason that you are thinking about pursuing an MBA. Before we get there, however, we need to warn you about one frightening fact:

You may have finished your school search, but the GMAT is not finished with you.

Ponder the unfairness of that for a moment, and then, like any good capitalist, pull yourself up by your own bootstraps and stop complaining about what's not fair. You'll have plenty of time to change the world—right now, just deal with it.

THE IMPORTANCE OF THE GMAT TO RECRUITERS

The GMAT was developed and is maintained to tell admissions staffs how well prospective students are likely to do in their introductory Masters-level business classes. That doesn't mean that the GMAT is used only for that. Many of the larger investment banks and management consultancies crave the quantified objectivity of a test like the GMAT, and ask their prospective hires to forward them copies of their scores along with their transcripts. If the MBA programs can use the numbers, they reason, there is no reason that they cannot as well. (Kurt Salmon Associates, a consultancy that is well known for its retailing and supply-chain management skills, even has job candidates take its own exam, which irritated MBA students have long termed the KSAT. Procter & Gamble's similar test is affectionately known as the P&GMAT.)

PLANNING YOUR JOB SEARCH

In fact, at the leading MBA programs, you stand a good chance of being asked about your GMAT score within a few weeks of your arrival. Full-time recruiting for second-year students begins at most schools by October, and the talent scouts generally don't overlook the first-years who look promising. Some second-years who interned at McKinsey, and whom the Firm has deputized to look for talent, may ask that question at the end of a conversation, saying something like, "You know, I should introduce you to Bob, the managing partner for global whatever . . . *and by the way, what was your GMAT?*"

Management consultants have a deservedly bad reputation for being at least that competitive, so don't be surprised. In fact, seize the opportunity to showcase your talent with any firm in which you are even slightly interested. The quality of your internship will have a significant effect on the outcome of your full-time job search, so getting an early start on mapping out your strategy—even before you arrive at school—is a good idea. Things will begin in earnest almost immediately upon your arrival:

Typical schedule for first-year MBA recruiting

September	Self-assessment, résumé development, marketing plans
October	Career fairs, company research, cover letters, networking and interview skills
November	Mock interviews, case interview training, trips to Wall Street for investment banking, first résumé submissions for campus recruiting
December	Informational interviews with alumni; refining job search strategies
January–February	Additional mock interviews, start of on-campus interviews for first-years

What's a *trek*? That's a fair question, but you'll be very familiar with the concept by the end of your first term. As an example, consider the McDonough School of Business at Georgetown University. It's an excellent school, but it's a long way from San Francisco. If working in northern California's software industry is your bag, but you have your heart set on Georgetown, you might face a very difficult recruiting problem. Three thousand miles and three time-zone changes are a lot to overcome when trying to do business on a personal level. That's where the treks come in. The career services offices of many schools organize several day- to week-long group trips to cities that would otherwise be long hauls for individuals to make alone. These treks often include opportunities to network with local alumni and act like mini-hiring conferences, giving the employers a detailed look at an intimate group of students (typically no more than 30). Conversely, this gives students an opportunity to see the company's employees in their natural environment. A lot can be learned about a company's culture on site, so take advantage of these trips to learn more about a company than you might in the standard hour-long campus presentation.

TOOLS FOR CAREER MANAGEMENT

Whether you're headed to California or New Jersey, there are only a few things that you will need to manage your MBA career search. While this list may seem obvious, you really will need to pay solid attention to each item on it.

▶ *A few good suits.* Wearing a plaid sport coat to the Merrill Lynch interview seems like an obviously stupid idea, but we've seen it happen. Get yourself several new suits that fit perfectly (this includes appropriate hems on skirts or cuffs on pants, and tailoring the length of the jacket sleeves). This will be easy to do, since custom tailors patrol the better MBA programs like ticket scalpers outside a Yankees game. If you are buying retail, don't go to the cheapest place; a good interview suit is just as much an investment as the degree is. First impressions count. Go for classic styles, good material, and the best tailoring you can get. One final note for men: wear a white shirt to the interview. Beige shirts look uniformly bad on everyone, and blue shirts can be reserved for second-round interviews. A white shirt signals formality, which is a nice touch now that nearly everyone has gone business casual. One final note for women: keep the length of your skirt at or below the knee. A skirt that is too short sends the wrong signals in a job interview.

▶ *A sense of what "business casual" means.* The business casual concept has definitely made shopping cheaper, but it has also introduced a requirement for serious thought into the morning routine. The mostly defunct firm Arthur Andersen used to tell its new recruits (the men at least) to buy five white shirts, two gray suits, two blue suits, and one tan one in case your client liked to cut loose on Friday. Since even IBM doesn't expect suits anymore, it's a different world. Fortunately, many MBA programs actually host events on how to dress for business. If you've never given this much thought, plan on attending one. Fashions change, and it is good to know something about this even if fashion is not your business.

▶ *Good hair, a solid stare, and a firm handshake.* Okay, the world is really not that simplistic, but your personal grooming and demeanor are critical components of both admissions and placement. Remember, this is not about who had the best grades in college or (gasp) even who has the highest GMAT score. It's about who will have the biggest positive impact in management, so you must do everything you can to convey that at an early date. When you greet your interviewer, smile. Shake hands gently but firmly (no one likes to have their hand crushed, either—this is not a contest of strength). Get a good haircut close to the interview date (for men). For women, make sure your hairstyle allows you to interview without fiddling with your hair or constantly brushing it out of your face. This is distracting during an interview. Two minor but often overlooked points of grooming for men: when it comes to eyebrows, there should be two, so don't think you should be above tweezing. On a related note, nose hair is an absolute no-no. Since you will be shaking hands, be sure to neatly trim and file your nails. Personal fragrance is a very personal preference. Interview rooms are usually small, so your best bet is to go unscented. Final point: carry breath mints.

▶ *Your telephone and its voicemail system.* You can't find a job if the recruiter can't find you. Make sure your home telephone works well. Make sure your mobile phone (and you will need a mobile phone) works well and has good coverage. If it also has a financial calculator and e-mail client (like a Blackberry or a Treo), that's all the better. Make sure you check your messages several times daily. Ensure that your outgoing message is professional on both your home and your mobile lines at all times. Promptly call back the people who call you. It's that simple.

▶ *The e-mail clients in your laptop and handheld computers.* Get good at managing your inbox, because sooner or later in your MBA life you will find 200 messages lingering in that inbox some morning (one of us faces that every morning). Try not to check the mail on your Blackberry while that Booz-Allen partner is staring at you during his presentation to the second-year class, but other than that, keep on top of your message traffic.

▶ *Your résumé.* This is your calling card. More than a business card, it provides a scannable introduction to who you are and what you can do. Its sole purpose is to open a channel for a conversation—if it does that, you've gotten your at bat, and you can't complain about its performance.

▶ *Your cover letters.* These provide the situation-specific introduction that your résumé doesn't. Since we covered the résumé in Chapter 13, we are left with these to discuss.

PREPARING YOUR COVER LETTERS

There are times when a naked résumé will suffice with a recruiter: a New York investment bank (these places are usually not long on grace) may request stacks of one-page this-is-my-life summaries from MBA programs, and specifically ask that cover letters not be sent. For all other contacts, however, a cover letter is an essential element of the conveyance of a résumé. There is nothing less impressive than a résumé shoved in an envelope and mailed to a recruiter. Sending out a thousand of those is so easy that sending one in that generic format is never notable, no matter how stellar the content. It shows that you cared only enough to be expeditious.

Therefore, always include a cover letter in a mailing (e-mail or hard copy) to a potential employer, even if the company or institution states that it is optional. It indicates that you can write intelligently, and that you care to do so. This is not to say that you will be engaging in some perfunctory exercise. The cover letter has but two purposes: to illustrate your fit with the organization, and to induce the reader to pay close attention to your résumé. The cover letter is an opportunity to communicate your story—how you came to this point in your career, and why you'd like to talk to the organization about taking things further. The letter should highlight accomplishments, relevant work experience, and skills specific to the organization, without simply repeating the content of the résumé. That may seem difficult, but that is part of the value of the writing assignment.

Content

The most important thing that you can convey in your cover letter is how your skills are transferable—that is, how they will enable you to move from industry to industry or career to career. The cover letter illustrates how you have done the sort of work that the organization in question requires at some point in the past, or how your past experiences have prepared you for what lies ahead (whether that is a job or a seat in the program). Your cover letters must indicate your transferable skills derived from accomplishments, work experience, at-work training, and education. This includes skills in areas such as managing people, projects, and budgets; leading teams; improving work processes; communicating to large groups; implementing technical advances; closing sales; analyzing complex data; hiring; firing; and training your eventual replacement.

Formats

While we can't spoon-feed you the content, we can definitely help with the format, as there are some rules that you can follow. To start with, there is at least one classic three-paragraph format for cover letters that can serve as a basic template. Other approaches are perfectly valid, but this works if you need a well-tested guide. Again, we phrase this in terms of answers to the questions that any good recruiter would ask:

Paragraph 1: *Who am I and why am I writing?* There's a good chance that your name won't be immediately recognizable. Even if you think that it will be, a brief and casual introduction ("you may remember . . . ") may be worth the trouble. In general, most cover letters will begin with a framing statement about where you come from (your school and year) and lead quickly into more personal information about your specific interest in the firm and any people you have spoken with or research you have done to validate that interest.

Paragraph 2: *What skills do I have to offer, and how can the company use them?* Here, include your experience in school and in your previous work. You may provide some bullet points that tie specific details to the organization's needs. Don't be too generic ("Dell thinks logistics is important. I took a class in logistics"), or you will appear not to have done your homework. All things being equal, a recruiter would much rather hire someone who seems to care enough to have researched the company in question.

Paragraph 3: *What do I want next?* Thank the contact, and by all means, propose some next steps. You'd like to meet him for lunch or coffee, or find him when he next to comes to campus. Try to advance your case without seeming cocky, overbearing, or overeager. Just don't be afraid to ask for what you want—a meeting, time to talk, or the opportunity to interview.

Please note, however, that this is just a suggestion. There is no single best way to write a cover letter. Some that we've read have been both very creative and very compelling. The best you can hope for is to know your audience and write the sort of letter to which it will respond most enthusiastically. Regardless of the framework you choose to use, we can offer some general but universal advice:

▶ *Experiment with different versions.* If you start to encounter difficulty in recruiting, it may be time to vary the composition of your cover letters. It's difficult to know why you are not hitting the mark, but it's probably a good idea to change *something*.

▶ *Be wary of cut and paste.* That means, at all costs, try to write every letter as a fresh effort, keeping in mind the changing audience. If you do otherwise, there are a number of ways that you can go wrong. You may find yourself using the name "IBM" in that letter to Dell, or you may find in your second year that you're sending out letters asking for internships. Numerous students do this every year. Let someone else serve as a bad example.

▶ *Use any examples as a guide.* We could tell you the story of the recruiter at IBM who got 40 letters one day from MBA students, all from the same school, who had all just finished the same professional development seminar in cover letter writing. Every one of them followed the same format: "let me tell you about (paragraph 1) my leadership abilities, (paragraph 2) my potential for teamwork, and (paragraph 3) my communication skills." But we won't—it's too painful. The short form is just that the seminar instructor had suggested that format as an example for an assignment. Unfortunately, she ran into an impressionable and (to some extent) lazy bunch of students who all had the same résumé drop ahead of them. So, even if you see a letter that you think is perfect, try to introduce some variation into the ones that *you* write. Sooner or later someone might see more than one of them.

▶ *Keep the length to just one page.* Remember, this is an advertisement, not an infomercial. The person to whom you are addressing the letter is probably not someone who has much time for advertisements. That means that he most certainly does not want to flip the page to read oh-so-much more about you.

▶ *Make sure that the font matches that in your résumé.* Almost anything else makes the combination look as though it doesn't fit together, which suggests that either you didn't care enough to check, or you have a really deficient sense of aesthetics. That's more important than you might think: if you're on an upward career trajectory, at some point you will need to deal, at least incidentally, with marketing matters.

- *Use simple stationery*. Blue paper is eye-catching, but that effect wears off quickly, leaving the reader to wonder whether you actually thought that you'd gain an advantage that way.

- *Send it to the right person*. That may be an MBA recruiter, a decision maker within a particular functional area, a decision maker in another functional area who may refer you to the right person, or even a non-decision maker who might be sufficiently taken with your cause to champion your candidacy (this is especially true of alumni). Whatever you say, remember that the addressee will be one of the first people to learn about your interest in the organization. You would do well to make a good first impression, whether on a company or a school.

Review

Finally, as we noted about your résumé in Chapter 13, you must not send out any cover letter without a thorough review. This is aimed at eliminating poor grammar and punctuation, misspelled words, and (in this case) direct repetition of the résumé. As before, check the visual appeal of the letter, and exercise care in using industry-specific jargon. Try to avoid being cute or clever, as this often backfires by giving an unprofessional appearance.

THANK-YOU NOTES

A brief discussion of thank-you notes is in order, if only because they're something that you should get accustomed to writing during your application process. Whether they're sent to a potential recruiter or an influential alumnus of a targeted school, thank-you notes have several valuable uses. They reaffirm your interest in an institution, remind the interviewer or contact of who you are, offer the opportunity to mention something you might have omitted during the interview, and demonstrate the follow-through that is expected of MBA graduates.

When are thank-you notes appropriate? Frequently—as in after every job interview, after every informational interview, and on any occasion when someone has done a favor for you (e.g., referred your résumé to someone else or given you a name to call). They should be sent as quickly as possible, preferably within 24 hours of the interview or meeting. Today, electronic mail is absolutely acceptable as a means of delivery, especially when the decision is time-critical, as in the interview process. If anyone tells you otherwise, check whether he is wearing wing-tips and a three-piece suit. If, however, the thank-you is not time sensitive, a handwritten note has a warm and personal touch that is a welcome change from e-mail.

What should the thank-you note contain? Not much. Thank-you letters should be short and to the point, thanking the interviewer for meeting with you, mentioning some things that you discussed in the interview that are of particular interest to you, possibly adding something that you may not have mentioned in the interview that you feel is relevant, and reaffirming your interest in the position and the company.

The usual point about thoroughly reviewing the letter for transgressions against rules of grammar, style, punctuation, and spelling applies, so we'll not repeat it in detail. There is, however, one other important point to make: do not send the same letter to everyone in the same organization. Sooner rather than later, recipients are bound to compare notes, if only inadvertently. This will not go well for you.

INTERVIEWS

Since you'll be interviewing for a spot in an MBA program (or at least trying to land an interview for one), you should start preparing now. Thinking about job interviews will help you get ready for school interviews, so we'll focus on those. There is a long list of good books on the topic, and you should definitely consider reading a few of them. For now, we'll cover the basics.

The typical interview lasts 30 to 45 minutes. Most firms that conduct campus recruiting programs provide two interviews. The first round is most often a screening interview to gauge interest, background, skills, and fit with the organization. Second-round interviews can involve greater depth of questioning, and are often focused on specific industry knowledge. The second round is frequently off-campus (either at the firm's local office or in a suitable hotel), and may consist of a series of interviews with various staff members at different levels within the organization.

Most interviews contain a combination of what are basically three types of interview questions. From the perspective of the uninitiated, these are the Good, the Bad, and the Ugly.

The Good—the Résumé Walk-Through

"Walk me through your résumé."

If this seems easy, it should. This is the softball question that many interviewers start with (particularly when they've been up until 4 a.m. the night before entertaining the delegation from the Tokyo office). Unfortunately, that doesn't mean that you can't fail here. Plenty of people have.

The way to practice this is to tell your story repeatedly, either to yourself or to a colleague or classmate. Your spiel about your résumé should validate your story, while you go on to explain why you made the choices that you made, highlight the accomplishments that you are most proud of, and showcase the skills acquired in each position. If you are interviewing for a position in, say, marketing, then you should focus on the aspects of your career that relate to marketing. The table that follows illustrates some of the areas of accomplishment and skill that you might highlight, depending on what you think your interviewer most wants to hear about.

Sample Points for Marketing Interview	Ability to Highlight in Each Functional Area
Advertising	Determining a promotional message and a channel to reach target customers
Brand management	Managing all aspects of marketing for a product, typically consumer packaged goods
Competitive analysis	Benchmarking the price, positioning, market share, or other metric against that of your competition
Consumer research	Determining the characteristics, trends, and needs of a given market
Customer relations	Developing and managing a relationship with customers by ensuring that their needs are met
Product management	Managing all aspects of marketing and development for a product category, typically high-tech consumer products, content, or software
Public relations and communication	Determining overall brand positioning and managing communications channels to generate publicity and influence public perceptions
Sales	Generating transactions

While this seems simple, there are ways to excel even here. As you prepare your story, ask yourself whether you connected the dots between the positions, whether you hit the highlights that are relevant to your targeted career, and whether your story was compelling and interesting. Overall, does your story have a point? Like any good story, we are looking for the happy ending. To an interviewer, your spiel should finish with a compelling close on how and why working for Company ABC is a logical and happy conclusion to this phase of your life's story. Be prepared for interrupting probes about specific jobs, strengths, weaknesses, goals, disappointments, and measurable accomplishments.

As with everything that's been done for too long in the MBA business, there are some clear pitfalls to avoid:

▶ *Reciting the résumé.* Don't do this. Instead, use the items on your résumé to explain *why* you've made the decisions that you have, why you're interviewing with Dell, and why you should be hired (implicitly, though not explicitly, instead of your classmate in the next interview room). If we frequently use the question *why,* it is for one reason—that is what the interviewer is listening for. The interviewer has already read your résumé and determined that there are some good reasons for bringing you in to interview. Now he wants to find out whether his assumptions about you are right. Answering the "why" questions is all about verifying that you are the right candidate for the job.

▶ *Pointing out every last thing you've ever done.* Instead, think about how to match what you've done to what the organization needs. Hit the highlights of your professional career that best fit the job description at hand. Provide a targeted story, skipping the irrelevant details that don't support your case. Figure out in advance how you will add value to the enterprise you are targeting—and boil that down to your top three key points.

▶ *The dry executive summary.* Rather, tell a relevant, intriguing story about your life that is personal, is creative, and shows your self-confidence. If you're not confident, figure out how to fake it. Résumés are by their very nature dry reading. An interview is a chance to show that you have more personality than an 8 1/2-by-11-inch piece of paper. Avoid being bland.

Finally, be prepared at the end for the standard "why" questions. Frankly, these may come at any time, but if you can't answer them, you'll be staying very firmly with the first-round crowd. They can cover a wide range of topics, but some of the more common ones include

▶ Why finance? Why this school?
▶ Why are you interested in investment banking?
▶ Why are you interested in our company?
▶ Why are you interested in this job?
▶ Why did you change jobs at that point?
▶ Why is there a gap on your résumé?

There isn't a great deal more to say about this, except that you should be able to get at least this far and that you should practice answers to even the most basic questions. You'd be surprised at how many candidates blow their interviews on a softball question like "Why did you choose Fuqua?" by answering that they liked the climate, it is close to home and convenient, or (our personal favorite) it was the only place they got into. This is an easy question to get right. Spend at least a few minutes creating a winning response to these questions so that your answer is more thoughtful than what may come to mind under stress. If you cannot speak intelligently about every item on your résumé for at least two to three minutes, then either (1) it shouldn't be on your résumé, or (2) you should get a new monologue. This includes the additional section at the end.

The Bad—Behavioral Interviews

"Tell me about a time when you overcame adversity in your career."

No one likes these questions, but human resources people seem to find them useful, so most of us have had to answer them at some point. Some organizations use them more than others, but enough use them that you should have a ready-made story for a wide selection of canned questions. To a great extent, behavioral interviewing is a game, but like the GMAT, it's something for which you need to be prepared, like it or not. These include questions like

- Tell me about a time when you
  - Had a good/bad team experience.
  - Had to make an unpopular/difficult decision.
  - Had to make a decision with little information.
  - Persuaded someone to buy into your idea.
  - Resolved a team conflict.
  - Demonstrated leadership, teamwork, creative problem solving.
  - Faced a challenging team situation.
  - Failed to meet a goal.
- What comes naturally to you? What doesn't?
- What makes a great leader?
- Which of those skills are you best at? Worst at?
- Tell me about
  - Your worst boss
  - A team member who didn't pull his weight
  - Your greatest weakness
  - A decision that you wish you could reconsider
  - A missed deadline
  - A situation in which you found yourself over your head
  - Your biggest mistake
  - A time when you needed to handle criticism
  - Your most difficult client
- Why should we hire you?
- Why should we hire you instead of one of your peers?

If this is starting to sound like an episode of *The Apprentice*, you're on the right track. The behavioral interview is supposed to be stress-inducing, at least in those who aren't prepared for it. Preparation, however, is not that hard, as long as you care to take the time. At a minimum, make sure that your stories are well prepared, relevant, interesting, concise, specific, comprehensive, and job-related.

Next, use the STAR format in your responses to those questions that require an illustration of actions you have taken. The STAR format consists of four sequential statements:

- *Situation.* Did you set up the situation or problem quickly and cleanly? Might the listener be bored before you get to the point? Did you use industry-specific geek talk that he couldn't possibly understand? Above all, keep the setup short and strip the story down to the essential point. Eliminate detail.

- *Task.* Did you specify the challenge, job, or project that you faced? Was it obvious, or did you have to work to identify the hidden task that really needed to be taken on? Was it the sort of thing that only a select group of people could handle?

- *Action.* Did you clarify your role in the job or project? Did you specify the action *you* took? Why it was important? What would have happened had no one acted?

- *Result.* Did you get to a result or describe the outcome? What did you learn from the results? Are your actions still having some effect? Have you repeated this experience since then? As with all things MBA, try to quantify the results.

For each story that you plan to relate, strive to

- *Make a purposeful transition from situation and task to action and result.* There is an art to these stories, and while the concept may seem affected and artificial, skill in relating accomplishments this way will help you, whether you are applying to graduate school, trying to land that job at Booz Allen, or angling to convince a venture capitalist that you're the one to entrust with her next $10 million. Thus, your stories must be well scripted without seeming scripted. In the end, you just need to know your own career and experience very, very well.

- *Create a balance between "we" and "I."* That said, it's not just about you. The stories you relate about yourself should walk a fine line between extolling your virtues and demonstrating your humility. Talk too much about yourself, and you'll come off as "not a team player." Talk too much about the team, and you'll appear to be a straphanger—just one more warm body loaded in the back of the airplane on the way to the target. See the difference?

- *Tell the story from the point of view of that functional area.* No experience in the software business? No problem, as long as your story plausibly relates to the issue at hand. Remember, the people to whom you're trying to sell your experience really don't care about your experience. They care about what you can do for them with that experience.

- *Tell a story they'd want to hear about.* Since they don't care, and they're going to need to listen to hundreds of these spiels over merlot and cheese squares, try to be engaging. Your story just might be the one that sticks out and saves the evening.

The Ugly—Case Interviews

These are the interviews that uninitiated MBA candidates dread. In actuality, preparing for them is not so difficult, since succeeding at them is mostly a matter of practice. There is a great deal to say about case interviews, and there is a small library of trade books and crib notes about how to deal with them. Since you are not likely to face this sort of interview during your admissions interviews, we will cover only the basics here.

What sort of questions might you face? The following table shows some examples; again, we use examples compiled from marketing interviews, just to stick with our theme. At one time, questions of this type were the exclusive province of consultancies, but today, you're increasingly likely to get them from packaged goods companies, so it's good to know what your consulting-bound classmates will be facing. Additionally, we find that finance and marketing firms are increasingly using case or mini-case questions as a part of the interview process, so it is important to add this to your skill set.

The key to case interviewing is being interactive: you must ask questions, take notes, and act as though you're actually solving a client's question. The interviewer will be trying to determine how well you think under pressure and how well you manage that intellectual workload on the fly. If you're working what's normally a 60-hour per week job, being intellectually inefficient could leave you with an 80-hour-per-week job, and that is just not sustainable over the long haul.

Lines of Case Interview Questioning in Marketing	Potential Questions
Market segmentation	How would you determine the target market for this product?
Share of market	How would you go about trying to increase the number of customers for this product?
Branding	How would you enhance the way customers perceive this brand? How would you increase brand awareness?
Price strategy	At what price would you sell this product? What discount would you grant this large customer?
Channels of distribution	What channel would be most profitable for bringing this product to its ultimate customers? What conflicts might this entail in the channel, or with other channels?
Product or services mix	Within this multiproduct company, what is the best way to organize your mix of products and service offerings?
Product development	What are the key attributes that this product should offer consumers?
Positioning	What are the most logical means of advertising for influencing how your product is perceived by target customers? How do you want them to perceive it?
Product launch	How would you go about determining whether this new product will be profitable?
Promotions	What communications and offers would you use to increase interest in this special event?
Customer acquisition and retention	What does this company need to do to shore up declining interest in this particular product?

How do you deal with these questions? There are plenty of ways to tackle them, but broadly speaking, case interviewing involves six steps:

▶ *Listening.* The interviewer will generally start by providing some general background information on the case. He probably will not give you all the information you need in order to answer the question at the start, and he may throw in a few red herrings just to make your life difficult (no one ever said that management consultants were nice people). All the same, you need to take in all the information provided, and quickly filter it to see what is important.

▶ *Clarifying.* You'll next have the chance to ask questions. This is the first point at which you can go astray in the process, since you'll need to ask the right questions to get the right information. This will not be spoon-fed to you, because knowing which questions to ask a client is one of the most important skills in management consulting.

▶ *Decomposing.* Most management problems can be broken down into manageable chunks that can be analyzed separately. You may need to estimate how many people frequent a lunch cart on Michigan Avenue, or how many shrimp boats in the Gulf of Mexico carry GPS receivers with charting software. Whatever the nature of the problem, you may find yourself at this point scratching out a diagram or a chart for ease of analysis and effect in presentation.

▶ *Hypothesizing.* At this juncture, you'll need to formulate a possible answer. It needn't be the right answer, just a plausible one. You might state that your client would succeed at penetrating the market if three conditions were met—you'll need to explain what those three conditions are, but you get the point.

▶ *Testing.* The next step is to advance some ideas as to how to test the hypothesis. Explain what sort of information you'll need in order to determine whether you're on the right track. If you're told that you're not, don't panic—you can recover by articulating a backup hypothesis, and then detailing how you would test that.

▶ *Summarizing.* This last step is very important. Clients don't pay expensive management consultants just for their analytical skills; they pay for consultants' communications skills as well. If the answer is complicated and difficult to relate, great—figuring out an easily understood way of explaining it is where you really earn your fees, so get some practice now.

Another sort of case interview question you may encounter is affectionately called the "wild card." One of us got this question during an interview with A. T. Kearney:

You've just been hired by a crazy Texas billionaire to fill the Sears Tower with shaving cream. How long will that take?

Only slightly more practical is

It's 2500BC, and the Pharaoh has hired you to build a pyramid. How long will that take?

If this seems intimidating at the start, good—it's supposed to. One of us got a deservedly bad reputation for repeatedly asking that question of prospective new hires. That said, the problem actually tests whether you can break down a managerial problem into its component parts, quickly make back-of-the-envelope estimates about the significant parameters, and then sum up the calculations in an easy-to-grasp format. That's an important skill in business planning.

FINISHING UP AND LOOKING BACK

At the end of an interview, you'll often hear one of two final questions:

▶ *"What questions do you have?"* Anticipating this, always keep something in reserve. Actually, keep a list of these questions in reserve, since you never know when some character will think that he's going to trap you by asking the question several times. There is a long list of possibilities, from the career structure of people in the position in question to the possibility of overseas postings in the rotational program. For that matter, consider reserving an intelligent question or two as an excuse to call him back, at least if the conversation went well and you think that a call would reinforce your case.

▶ *"Is there anything else you'd like to add?"* If there's nothing else, you can state calmly but enthusiastically that you'd like the job. Shake hands, ask for a business card, and thank the interviewer for his or her time.

Immediately after any interview, you'll want to take stock of how you thought you performed, even taking some notes if it's helpful. Consider the verbal signals you provided, including your tone, clarity, speed of speech, volume, use of . . . uh . . . filter language and jargon, the appropriateness and sophistication of your vocabulary, and the general organization of your thoughts and answers. Consider also your nonverbal signals, such as your eye contact, gesturing, expression, dress, appearance, and general level of comfort.

NETWORKING

Being ready for an interview and well debriefed is all well and good, but that's true only if your résumé finds its way into the right hands, if the reader is the right person to read it, and if she subsequently deigns to grant you an interview. Job hunting, however, is not a game of batting averages—you need only one long ball over the fence to get where you need to go. The key, then, is to get more at bats (land more interviews), and the best way to do that is through networking. (By the way, if you don't like the baseball analogy, don't ask your finance professor why "K" is the variable used to denote the strike price of an option.)

Our research indicates that over 60 percent of today's MBA job leads come through networking, as opposed to blind résumé drops and other on-campus schemes. However, even if *who* you know is as important as *what* you know, you will still need to know *how* to get to know these people. Networking involves a wide range of activities, from cold calling, to shaking hands at career fairs and school receptions, to informational interviewing, to having an uncle who just happens to know the governor. This means that luck plays an important part in the process, but fortune also favors the bold. Not too many people have landed jobs sitting on the couch watching TBS. To get started, we recommend a six-step process.

1. *Build your list of contacts.* First, do everything you can to expand your network. There are no good excuses here—any good MBA program offers a wealth of opportunities through which to do this. The alumni database, the business librarians, the faculty, guest lecturers, career services staff, and the consulting/marketing/finance and social clubs are all sources of names, numbers, and linkages to the school and potential company contacts. Mining these sources will quickly lead you off campus, to professional organizations, chambers of commerce, company directories, and influential people whom your friends knew in the third grade. They're all fair game.

2. *Prepare your personal narrative.* Next, develop a script, just as you did in preparing for behavioral interviews. Remember, as an overconfident, high-powered MBA, you are always interviewing, and every time you meet someone, you might be looking at the source of your next gig. Be ready to

identify yourself with the right level of formality, refer to your intermediate contact, and ask whether this is a good time to talk. Know how to state your specific purpose, provide a deeper introduction, ask your questions, indicate your thanks, and suggest a follow-up. It's not that difficult.

3. *Prepare for the initial contact.* There are plenty of barriers to cold calling in most people, whether nervousness, fear, a lack of language skills, or a lack of practice. Here, having a script helps, and your pitch should be customized for the individual. Don't be afraid to practice your speech with a classmate, or just in front of the mirror. Make sure that you've done the necessary background research on the person you're calling, to understand the professional and personal context that he is bringing to the conversation.

4. *Make calls to set up appointments.* Fortunately, working the telephone is easy; you can even do it in your underwear (although we don't recommend that approach). Remember, though, that body language is missing; you'll have no gestures, smiles, or expressions with which to convey additional meaning. Tone, therefore, has to take the place of physical indicators, but you can still put yourself through the paces of a face-to-face meeting. Smile when you talk; stand or situp if it helps. Be expressive, even gesturing as you would in person. Believe it or not, smiling and acting as though you were having a face-to-face conversation, even while on the phone, make a significant difference in your tone of voice, conveying more personality and likability than someone who is seated and unexpressive.

Naturally, despite your initial enthusiasm, you will be shunted to voicemail. Be prepared for this as well. What's worse than sounding idiotic on the telephone is sounding idiotic in a recording that can be forwarded with the group-send button. So, speak slowly and clearly. Make your message specific and brief. State the abbreviated version of your script, and by all means, state your telephone number slowly and repeat it at the end of the message. Staccato delivery of the call-back number just makes the poor guy on the other end replay the message four times to catch every digit. That won't win you friends. You might even consider keeping a written script with you so that you deliver your spiel flawlessly every time. All the while, remember to check your machine regularly. "I forgot to check my voicemail" is not an excuse that will get you to the boardroom.

If your means of contact is e-mail, use the same message, just in writing. The difference here is that you really need letter-perfect grammar and style, and appropriate salutations and closings. It may be electronic mail, but that does not give you an excuse to TYPE IN ALL CAPITALS and throw emoticons ;) into your message to the vice president of marketing.

Finally, have a goal for each call or contact. You're not just ringing the other person up to say hello. You will always need to have a next step on the path toward getting what you want, so try to advance the conversation in that direction without seeming unctuous or anxious.

5. *Develop a tracking system.* None of this, of course, will be worth much if you can't remember whether you called that alumnus who knows the chair of the marketing department, or if you fail to call the fellow at Boeing who went to school with your roommate's uncle. A tracking system is essential. If that's a copy of some commercially available software (e.g., Act!), that's great. If it's the stone-knives-and-bearskins equivalent (a notebook or card file), that's fine, too, as long as it works for you. Whatever you use, your tracking system should provide space for noting whom you contacted, what you said, what she said back, what follow-up action you took or plan to take, and what uncompleted actions you still have outstanding.

6. *Conduct the interview/meeting.* If you actually *do* land the chance to talk to someone important, remember what you are seeking, whether it is information, advice, ideas about what to do next, or a referral to the next important person in the chain. Remember also what you are *not* seeking: a job—at least not at this juncture. That's for later. For now, you are seeking information from an expert, and a smidgen of flattery won't hurt. Try to find out whether your assumptions about this career or this firm are true. Ask about a day in the life of (DILO) a typical person in the organization. Get current information on trends affecting the business. There are many, many questions you can ask to show interest without asking for a job:

▶ What career opportunities do you envision in this field/industry?
▶ Which of my skills do you see as most transferable?
▶ What courses would you advise I take to pursue this field/industry?
▶ What is the typical career progression in this field/industry? What was yours?
▶ What organizations do you recommend I target?
▶ What obstacles do you think I will encounter?
▶ What steps do you recommend I take to overcome them?
▶ What advice do you have for me as I make this career change?
▶ Do you have any suggestions for my résumé?

It's your meeting, so drive toward what you need. Since you are the one doing the interviewing here, be willing to ask the questions and define the agenda, but be prepared to listen as well. Ask for referrals, close the meeting, and make sure to follow up with a thank-you note.

SELECTING THE RIGHT OFFER

In the end, the whole reason that you will have gone to business school is the job that you will obtain at the other end—whether in commerce, government, nonprofit, or academia, it's still all about business. We could spend a few pages here talking about that process, but your career services office will do a better job than we can here.

Rather, we should just remind you to start your business school expedition with the end in mind. As you are thinking about

▶ Where to apply
▶ What essays to write
▶ What to say during your admissions interviews
▶ Which corporate presentations to attend
▶ Which classmates to glom up to
▶ What to do with your Christmas break
▶ Which recruiters to hassle
▶ Which alumni to solicit
▶ Which networks to penetrate
▶ Where to seek an internship

remember that the whole point is to find the right job

- ▶ At the right compensation
- ▶ With the right lifestyle
- ▶ With the right co-workers
- ▶ In the right industry
- ▶ In the right location, and
- ▶ With the right upward trajectory

That's a lot to get right, and it will naturally involve trade-offs. So, as you are planning your admissions strategy, consider which of those criteria are relatively more important to you, and which you can relatively sacrifice now for the right possibilities later.

WILL THE GMAT EVER HAUNT YOU AGAIN?

Since this is a book about the GMAT, we must end by talking about this all-important test. That said, we have good reason to do so anyway, since the GMAT is more than just a hurdle that you must clear in order to enter a top-flight MBA program. One of us remembers being asked about SAT scores when interviewing with the Boston Consulting Group. It's annoying, and it's not very sensible, but if you want a job in the tony corridors of BCG, then your SAT scores could be a subject of discussion. That's not quite reasonable, because for many people (though perhaps not the majority), intellectual ability and academic performance improve after leaving college. Perhaps the distractions are fewer, perhaps the beer flows less and the coffee more, or perhaps some people just come into their own with the right, challenging job.

Whatever the case, as we noted at the beginning of the chapter, a GMAT score is frequently requested by recruiters from the pricier investment banks and consultancies and is a nice flag to have on your résumé if you are in the upper echelons of the scoring. Since MBA programs consider it a handy tool for judging your raw mental horsepower, it stands to reason that some of the more noted employers of high-priced MBAs will do so as well. If nothing else, it's a reasonably objective measure, in that everyone takes (more or less, given its computer-adaptive nature) the same test.

The GMAT test, however, is more than just a test. The skills that you will develop in preparing for this test will serve you well in business. Granted, you'll probably never again need to recall the formula relating the area of a triangle to its semiperimeter, but there are plenty of other things that you'll use again. Two, in particular, stand out:

- ▶ *Algebra*. We can't sufficiently reiterate the importance of understanding algebra. It's the one aspect of mathematics that everyone in management needs to understand in order to succeed. If you don't get comfortable with it, you'll always be relying on someone else to feed you the numbers. Since information is power, try not to stray too far from the data stream.

- ▶ *Verbal style*. The world's disk drives are filled with millions of bad briefing slides crammed with clumsy and incomprehensible statements (not to mention that bald PowerPoint guy clutching the fistful of dollars) and unintelligible e-mail messages. Don't add to the pile. Even if English is not your first language, you will climb much further up the corporate ladder if your spoken and written words make sense than if they don't. Every essay you write and every sentence you analyze getting ready for the test is another way to improve your position.

In the end, your success in getting into business school should be closely correlated with your projected success in business. Much of your success in both venues will be determined by your skill in communication. A skilled business communicator can spin a tale, persuade an audience, write a brief, deliver a speech, give a slide presentation, promote an idea, and above all sell himself. Business school is a safe place in which to further develop these skills, but it helps if you can demonstrate some promise in advance.

PART FOUR The Practice Tests

Instructions for the GMAT Practice Tests

The following practice tests recreate the range of questions you are likely to encounter when you take the GMAT Computer-Adaptive Test. Working through these practice tests, as well as those on the accompanying CD-ROM (if you have bought the CD-ROM version of this book) and companion website, under the most authentic conditions possible will help you gain the knowledge and confidence you will need to achieve your goals on the GMAT.

Each of the practice tests is composed of four parts:

1. Analytical Writing Assessment: "Analysis of an Issue"— 30 minutes
2. Analytical Writing Assessment: "Analysis of an Argument"— 30 minutes
3. Quantitative section: 37 questions — 75 minutes
4. Verbal section: 41 questions — 75 minutes

Detachable answer sheets for each of the tests are included at the end of this book. If you have access to a word processor or typewriter, type your responses to the Analytical Writing Assessment questions.

In order to maximize the benefits you gain from these practice tests, you should make your practice experience as similar as possible to the conditions you will experience on the actual test:

▶ Find a quiet and comfortable place where you will not be interrupted.
▶ Take an entire test in one sitting if you can find the time; if not, try to clear time to complete an entire section in one sitting.
▶ Time yourself and stick to the time limit. If you run short on time, force yourself to make educated guesses; you may need to make guesses on the actual test.
▶ Have your testing materials—answer sheet, scratch paper, and pencils—in hand before you begin the test. Do not use a calculator!
▶ Answer the questions in order—you cannot skip around on the GMAT CAT, so do not get into the habit of doing so.
▶ Write on scratch paper, not on the test itself. You will not be able to write on the computer screen, so get into the habit of using scratch paper.

Good luck!

Practice Test 1

ANALYTICAL WRITING 1

Analysis of an Issue

TIME—30 MINUTES

DIRECTIONS: In this section, you will need to analyze the issue presented and explain your views on it. There is no "correct" answer. Instead, you should consider various perspectives as you develop your own position on the issue.

Read the statement and the instructions that follow it, and then make any notes that will help you plan your response. Write your response on a separate sheet of paper. If possible, type your essay on a word processor. Observe the 30-minute time limit.

The success of a company correlates directly with the average job satisfaction of its employees.

Discuss the extent to which you agree or disagree with the opinion stated above. Support your views with reasons and/or examples from your own experiences, observations, or reading.

ANALYTICAL WRITING 2

Analysis of an Argument

TIME—30 MINUTES

DIRECTIONS: In this section, you will be asked to write a critique of the argument presented below. You may, for example, consider what questionable assumptions underlie the thinking, what alternative explanations or counterexamples might weaken the conclusion, or what sort of evidence could help strengthen or refute the argument.

Read the argument and the instructions that follow it, and then make any notes that will help you plan your response. Write your response on a separate sheet of paper. If possible, type your essay on a word processor. Observe the 30-minute time limit.

The following letter was printed in a medical journal:

Many nonprescription drugs can cause serious side effects, particularly when taken in conjunction with other drugs or in large quantities. If these potentially harmful nonprescription drugs were sold only by prescription, then a doctor or pharmacist would be able to explain the possible side effects of the drug and would also be able to monitor the quantity of the drug purchased, thereby decreasing the chance that a person would take too much of the drug. Therefore, any drug with potentially serious side effects should be sold only by prescription.

Discuss how well reasoned you find this argument. In your discussion, be sure to analyze the line of reasoning and the use of evidence in the argument. For example, you may need to consider what questionable assumptions underlie the thinking and what alternative examples or counterexamples might weaken the conclusion. You can also discuss what sort of evidence would strengthen or refute the argument, what changes in the argument would make it more logically sound, and what, if anything, would help you better evaluate its conclusion.

Solve the problem and indicate the best of the answer choices given.

NUMBERS: All numbers used are real numbers.

FIGURES: A figure accompanying a problem-solving question is intended to provide information useful in solving the problem. Figures are drawn as accurately as possible EXCEPT when it is stated in a specific problem that its figure is not drawn to scale. Straight lines may sometimes appear jagged. All figures lie in a plane unless otherwise indicated.

1. Greg sells gaskets. On three sales, Greg has received commissions of $385, $70, and $190, and he has one additional sale pending. If Greg is to receive an average (arithmetic mean) commission of exactly $220 on the four sales, then the fourth commission must be:

A. $135
B. $155
C. $220
D. $235
E. $645

2. In an effort to plan out expenses, the Roberts family is representing its annual budget as a circle graph. Each sector of the graph is proportional to the amount of the budget it represents. If "clothes and shoes" takes up 54° of the chart, how much of the Roberts's $20,000 annual budget is dedicated to clothes and shoes?

A. $1,500
B. $3,000
C. $4,500
D. $5,000
E. $5,400

3. What is the value of $3x^2 - 1.8x + 0.3$ for $x = 0.6$?

A. −0.3
B. 0
C. 0.3
D. 1.08
E. 2.46

4. Over a three-week period, the price of an ounce of gold increased by 25% in the first week, decreased by 20% in the following week, and increased by 5% in the third week. If the price of gold was G dollars per ounce at the beginning of the three weeks, what was the price, in terms of G, at the end of the three weeks?

A. $0.95G$
B. G
C. $1.05G$
D. $1.1G$
E. $1.15G$

5. If a cube has a total surface area of 96, what is its volume?

A. 16
B. 36
C. 64
D. 81
E. 96

6. The table below shows the enrollment in various classes at a certain college.

Class	Number of Students
Biology	50
Physics	35
Calculus	40

Although no student is enrolled in all three classes, 15 are enrolled in both Biology and Physics, 10 are enrolled in both Biology and Calculus, and 12 are enrolled in both Physics and Calculus. How many different students are in the three classes?

A. 51
B. 88
C. 90
D. 125
E. 162

7. In a nationwide poll, P people were asked 2 questions. If $\frac{2}{5}$ answered "yes" to question 1, and of those $\frac{1}{3}$ also answered "yes" to question 2, which of the following represents the number of people polled who did not answer "yes" to both questions?

A. $\frac{2}{15}P$
B. $\frac{3}{5}P$
C. $\frac{3}{4}P$
D. $\frac{5}{6}P$
E. $\frac{13}{15}P$

The following data sufficiency problems consist of a question and two statements, labeled (1) and (2), in which certain data are given. You have to decide whether the data given in the statements are <u>sufficient</u> for answering the question. Using the data given in the statements <u>plus</u> your knowledge of mathematics and everyday facts (such as the number of days in July or the meaning of *counterclockwise*), you must indicate whether

A. Statement (1) ALONE is sufficient, but statement (2) alone is not sufficient.
B. Statement (2) ALONE is sufficient, but statement (1) alone is not sufficient.
C. BOTH statements TOGETHER are sufficient, but NEITHER statement ALONE is sufficient.
D. EACH statement ALONE is sufficient.
E. Statements (1) and (2) TOGETHER are NOT sufficient.

NUMBERS: **All numbers used are real numbers.**

FIGURES: **A figure accompanying a data sufficiency problem will conform to the information given in the question, but will not necessarily conform to the additional information given in statements (1) and (2). Lines shown as straight can be assumed to be straight, and lines that appear jagged can also be assumed to be straight. You may assume that the position of points, angles, regions, etc., exist in the order shown and that angle measures are greater than zero. All figures lie in a plane unless otherwise indicated.**

NOTE: **In data sufficiency problems that ask for the value of a quantity, the data given in the statements are sufficient only when it is possible to determine exactly one numerical value for the quantity.**

8. A certain salad dressing made only of oil and vinegar is premixed and sold in the grocery store. What is the ratio of oil to vinegar in the mix?

(1) An 18.6-ounce bottle of the salad dressing contains 12.4 ounces of vinegar.
(2) In a 32-ounce bottle of the salad dressing, there is half as much oil as there is vinegar.

9. At a certain pancake festival with 600 attendees in which every attendee ate at least 1 pancake, how many people had only 1 pancake?

(1) At the festival there were 1,200 pancakes served, and no person had more than 3 pancakes.
(2) Seventy-two percent of the attendees at the festival had 2 or more pancakes.

10. A rectangle is equal in area to a square with sides of length 12. Is the diagonal of the rectangle greater in length than 20?

(1) The rectangle has a length of 16.
(2) The rectangle has a width of 9.

11. A type of candy comes in two flavors, sweet and sour, and in two colors, yellow and green. The color and flavor of the individual pieces of candy are not related. If in a certain box of this candy $\frac{1}{4}$ of the yellow pieces and $\frac{5}{7}$ of the green pieces are sour, what is the ratio of the number of yellow pieces to the number of green pieces in the box?

(1) In the box, the number of sweet yellow pieces is equal to the number of sour green pieces.
(2) In the box, the number of green pieces is two less than the number of yellow pieces.

12. In isosceles triangle ABC, what is the value of $\angle C$?

(1) The measure of $\angle B$ is $47°$
(2) The measure of $\angle A$ is $96°$

Solve the problem and indicate the best of the answer choices given.

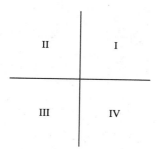

13. In the rectangular quadrant system shown above, which quadrant, if any, contains no point (x, y) that satisfies the equation $3x + 5y = -2$?

A. none
B. I
C. II
D. III
E. IV

14. If a copier makes 3 copies every 4 seconds, then continues at this rate, how many minutes will it take to make 9,000 copies?

A. 60
B. 100
C. 120
D. 200
E. 3,000

15. To be considered grade AA, an egg must weigh between 75 and 90 grams, including the shell. Shells of grade AA eggs weigh between 3 and 5 grams. What is the smallest possible mass, in grams, of a 12-egg omelet, assuming that only grade AA eggs are used, the shells are all discarded, and no mass is lost in the cooking process?

A. 800
B. 840
C. 864
D. 900
E. 1,080

16. $\dfrac{(0.2)^8}{(0.2)^5} =$

A. 0.0008
B. 0.001
C. 0.008
D. 0.04
E. 0.08

17. What is the ratio of $\left(\dfrac{1}{3}\right)^2$ to $\left(\dfrac{1}{3}\right)^4$?

A. 9
B. 3
C. 1
D. 1:3
E. 1:27

18. A group of 7 fishermen chartered a boat for a day to fish for flounder. The boat costs x dollars per day to rent. If the group can find 3 more fishermen on the docks who are willing to come aboard and share the rental costs, how much less will the rental cost be per person in terms of x?

A. $x/70$
B. $x/35$
C. $3x/70$
D. $3x/10$
E. $3x/7$

19. The size of a flat-screen television is given as the length of the screen's diagonal. How many square inches greater is the screen of a square 34-inch flat-screen television than a square 27-inch flat-screen television?

A. 106.75
B. 213.5
C. 427
D. 729
E. 1,156

The following data sufficiency problems consist of a question and two statements, labeled (1) and (2), in which certain data are given. You have to decide whether the data given in the statements are <u>sufficient</u> for answering the question. Using the data given in the statements <u>plus</u> your knowledge of mathematics and everyday facts (such as the number of days in July or the meaning of *counterclockwise*), you must indicate whether

A. Statement (1) ALONE is sufficient, but statement (2) alone is not sufficient.
B. Statement (2) ALONE is sufficient, but statement (1) alone is not sufficient.
C. BOTH statements TOGETHER are sufficient, but NEITHER statement ALONE is sufficient.
D. EACH statement ALONE is sufficient.
E. Statements (1) and (2) TOGETHER are NOT sufficient.

20. What is the value of n?

(1) $n^4 = 256$
(2) $n^3 > n^2$

21. An employee at a company was given the task of making a large number of copies. He spent the first 45 minutes making copies at a constant rate on copier A, but copier A broke down before the task was completed. He then spent the next 30 minutes finishing the task on copier B, which also produced copies at a constant rate. How many total minutes would the task have taken had copier A not broken down?

(1) Copier A produced twice as many copies in its first 5 minutes of operation as copier B produced in its first 15 minutes.
(2) Copier B produces 10 copies per minute.

22. If $ab \neq 0$, is c an integer?

(1) $c = 5a - 2b$
(2) $a = 2b$

23. $x = 0.57y9$. If y denotes the thousandth digit in the decimal representation of x above, what digit is y?

(1) If x were rounded to the nearest tenth, the result would be 0.6.
(2) If x were rounded to the nearest hundredth, the result would be 0.58.

24. Is integer $y > 0$?

(1) $-(2 + y) > 0$
(2) $(2 + y)^2 > 0$

Solve the problem and indicate the best of the answer choices given.

25. If 4 and 11 are the lengths of two sides of a triangular region, which of the following can be the length of the third side?

I. 5
II. 13
III. 15

A. I only
B. II only
C. I and II only
D. II and III only
E. I, II, and III

26. A certain truck uses 18 gallons of diesel fuel in traveling 270 miles. In order for the truck to travel the same distance using 10 gallons of diesel fuel, by how many miles per gallon must the truck's fuel mileage be increased?

A. 8
B. 9
C. 12
D. 15
E. 27

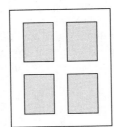

27. The figure above represents a window, with the shaded regions representing openings for glass and the pale regions representing the wood panels between and around the glass. If the window is 4.5 feet high by 2.5 feet wide, and if each of the wooden panels is exactly 4 inches thick, what is the total surface area, in square inches, of glass in the window? (1 foot = 12 inches; figure not drawn to scale)

A. 189
B. 378
C. 448
D. 756
E. 1,620

28. If $3(x^2 + x) - 7 = x^2 + 2(4 + x^2)$, then $x =$

A. 5
B. 6
C. 9
D. 15
E. 25

29. Suzie's Discount Footwear sells all pairs of shoes for one price and all pairs of boots for another price. On Monday the store sold 22 pairs of shoes and 16 pairs of boots for $650. On Tuesday the store sold 8 pairs of shoes and 32 pairs of boots for $760. How much more do pairs of boots cost than pairs of shoes at Suzie's Discount Footwear?

A. $2.50
B. $5.00
C. $5.50
D. $7.50
E. $15.00

30. For any 3 given numbers, which of the following is always equivalent to adding the 3 numbers together and then dividing the sum by 3?

  I. Ordering the 3 numbers numerically, from highest to lowest, and then selecting the middle number.
  II. Dividing each of the numbers by 3 and then adding the results together.
  III. Multiplying each number by 6, adding the resulting products together, and then dividing the sum by 9.

A. I only
B. II only
C. I and II only
D. II and III only
E. None of the above

31. A hat company ships its hats, individually wrapped, in 8-inch by 10-inch by 12-inch boxes. Each hat is valued at $7.50. If the company's latest order required a truck with at least 288,000 cubic inches of storage space in which to ship the hats in their boxes, what was the minimum value of the order?

A. $960
B. $1,350
C. $1,725
D. $2,050
E. $2,250

32. Chauncy, an English bulldog, received 1,618 votes in the Mr. Bulldog USA competition, giving him approximately 20 percent of the vote. Approximately what percent of the remaining votes would he have needed to receive in order to win 30 percent of the total votes?

A. 10%
B. 12.5%
C. 15%
D. 17.5%
E. 20%

The following data sufficiency problems consist of a question and two statements, labeled (1) and (2), in which certain data are given. You have to decide whether the data given in the statements are <u>sufficient</u> for answering the question. Using the data given in the statements <u>plus</u> your knowledge of mathematics and everyday facts (such as the number of days in July or the meaning of *counterclockwise*), you must indicate whether

A. Statement (1) ALONE is sufficient, but statement (2) alone is not sufficient.
B. Statement (2) ALONE is sufficient, but statement (1) alone is not sufficient.
C. BOTH statements TOGETHER are sufficient, but NEITHER statement ALONE is sufficient.
D. EACH statement ALONE is sufficient.
E. Statements (1) and (2) TOGETHER are NOT sufficient.

33. If 8 skiers raced down a course multiple times in one day, and each skier used a different pair of skis on each run, what is the total number of different skis used by the 8 skiers during the day?

(1) No skier shared any skis with any other skier.
(2) Each skier made exactly 12 runs during the day.

34. The symbol $\otimes$ represents one of the following operations: addition, subtraction, multiplication, or division. What is the value of $7 \otimes 4$?

(1) $4 \otimes 7 < 1$
(2) $4 \otimes 3 > 1$

35. Salespeople at a certain car dealership are paid a $250 commission on every car they sell up to their monthly quota, and $500 for every car they sell over the quota. What is the monthly sales quota at this dealership?

(1) One salesperson exceeded the quota by 8 cars and received a total monthly commission of $7,500.
(2) One salesperson achieved only half of the quota; he received a commission of $1,750 and a warning that he will be fired unless he meets the next month's quota.

36. If $a \neq -b$, is $\dfrac{a-b}{b+a} < 1$?

(1) $b^2 > a^2$
(2) $a - b > 1$

37. The hold of a fishing boat contains only cod, haddock, and halibut. If a fish is selected at random from the hold, what is the probability that it will be a halibut or a haddock?

(1) There are twice as many halibut as cod in the hold, and twice as many haddock as halibut.
(2) Cod account for 1/7 of the fish by number in the hold.

For the following questions, select the best of the answer choices given.

1. Studies have shown that companies that present seminars on workplace safety to their employees actually have higher rates of workplace accidents than do companies that do not present such seminars to their employees. Despite this finding, it is still in the best interests of companies and their employees for companies to present these seminars.

Which of the following, if true, provides the strongest support for the argument that the companies should continue to present these seminars?

A. Companies that present workplace safety seminars to their employees are likely to be in manufacturing industries or segments of the service sector that present more opportunities for workplace accidents than the average company.
B. A fast-food chain determined that the rate of workplace accidents remained the same at its franchises after all employees had viewed a 30-minute workplace safety video.
C. Workers are ultimately responsible for their own safety, and no amount of workplace education can alter their behavior.
D. A business research institute determined that workplace accidents reduce the productivity of manufacturing businesses by as much as 8 percent per year.
E. Many companies mistakenly believe that presenting workplace safety seminars to their employees relieves the company of legal liability in the event that employees are injured on the job.

2. For hundreds of years, pearl divers have gathered pearls directly from mollusks on the sea floor. This is an extremely risky profession, exposing the divers to risks of drowning, air embolism, and shark attacks. Still, as long as society demands authentic cultured pearls, these brave divers must continue to risk their lives.

Which of the following statements, if true, most seriously weakens the conclusion above?

A. Shark attacks on pearl divers have decreased steadily over the last three decades because of declining shark populations.
B. Cultured pearls are generally considered more beautiful than those made by artificial means.
C. Robotic pearl harvesters can gather pearls faster and at less cost than human divers, although they may disturb aquatic communities.
D. Part of the value of cultured pearls derives from the exotic way in which they are obtained.
E. With the proper equipment and training, a diver employing scuba gear can harvest three times as many pearls per hour as can a free air diver.

3. An electronics company's two divisions showed consistent performance over the last two years. In each year, the audiovisual department accounted for roughly 30 percent of the company's sales and 70 percent of the company's profits over the period, while the home appliance division accounted for the balance.

Which of the following statements regarding the last two years can be inferred from the statement above?

A. The audiovisual market is growing faster than is the home appliance division.
B. The home appliance division has realized lower profits per dollar of sales than has the audiovisual division.
C. Total dollar sales for each division has remained roughly constant for the last five years.
D. The company has devoted more money to research and development efforts in the audiovisual division than in the home appliance division.
E. To maximize profitability, the company should focus its resources on the home appliance division.

4. Gastric bypass surgery has been shown to be effective at helping extremely obese people lose weight. Some patients have lost as much as 300 pounds after undergoing the surgery, thereby substantially prolonging their lives. Despite the success of the treatment, most doctors have not embraced the surgery as a weight loss option.

Which of the following statements, if true, best accounts for the lukewarm reaction of the medical community to gastric bypass surgery?

A. Gastric bypass surgery carries a high risk of serious complications, including death.
B. Obesity is one of the leading contributors to heart disease and hypertension, two leading causes of death.
C. Obesity rates among the American population have been increasing consistently for the last three decades.
D. Many patients report that losing weight through diets is ineffective, since they usually gain the weight back within six months.
E. Most health insurance plans will cover the cost of gastric bypass surgery for morbidly obese patients at high risk of heart disease.

The questions in this group are based on the content of a passage. After reading the passage, choose the best answer to each question. Answer all questions following the passage on the basis of what is <u>stated</u> or <u>implied</u> in the passage.

While most people agree that the Golden Age of comic books began with the introduction of Superman in 1938 in *Action Comics #1*, there is less agreement about when exactly the Golden Age ended. There is a general consensus, however, about the factors that brought the Golden Age to a close: the rise of the horror comic book in the late 1940s, and the resulting backlash against comic books in the early 1950s.

Superhero comic books reached their peak of popularity in the early 1940s because of all the GIs in Europe and Japan who eagerly read about Superman, Batman, and The Spirit. When these soldiers came home, they still wanted to read comic books, but they sought out more adult content. William Gaines of EC Comics was happy to meet the market demand with such grim and gritty titles as *Weird Fantasy* and *The Crypt of Terror*. The creators of superhero comic books, not wanting to be left behind, responded by matching their protagonists against darker criminals in more violent encounters.

These darker comic books aroused the anger of child psychologist Fredric Wertham, who believed that comic books were leading the nation's youth into crime, violence, and drug abuse. Wertham's book, *The Seduction of the Innocent*, was a national best-seller that helped bring about congressional investigations into the corrupting influence of comic books. The Senate committee that reviewed Wertham's charges decided to create the Comics Code Authority, a regulatory body that prohibited comic books from mentioning sexuality, alcohol, drugs, criminal behavior, or any themes related to the horror genre.

These regulations had a numbing effect on the industry. EC Comics was nearly driven out of the comics business, and the other major players canceled many of their most prominent titles. The comics business did not recover until the Marvel revolution of the early 1960s ushered in the Silver Age.

5. This passage is primarily interested in which of the following?

   A. Investigating the factors that brought about the Marvel revolution and the Silver Age of comic books

   B. Reviewing the factors that brought about the end of the Golden Age of comic books

   C. Comparing and contrasting two eras in the history of comic books

   D. Condemning the horror comic book for its corrupting influence on the nation's youth

   E. Evaluating the historical legacy of William Gaines's EC Comics

6. According to the passage, which of the following was true of the creators of superhero comic books in the postwar years?

   A. They sought to head off the censorship of the Comics Code Authority by voluntarily prohibiting stories dealing with sexuality, drugs, or criminal behavior.

   B. They introduced characters such as Superman and The Spirit.

   C. They unintentionally laid the groundwork for the transition from the Golden Age of comic books to the Silver Age.

   D. They focused increasingly on flashy artwork and less on well-developed stories.

   E. They responded to the competitive pressure from horror comic books by increasing the amount of violence in their stories.

7. According to the passage, what can we infer to be the central message of Fredric Wertham's *The Seduction of the Innocent*?

   A. Adults reading violent comic books were as likely to be corrupted by them as young people were.

   B. The horror comic books of the late 1940s were inferior to the superhero comic books that gained popularity during World War II.

   C. Comic books were leading the nation's youth into crime, violence, and drug abuse.

   D. Creating a regulatory board to censor the comic book industry would drive the worst offenders out of the business.

   E. Comic books would never be able to convey stories of any serious literary merit.

8. According to the final paragraph of the passage, what may we infer about the comic book companies of the Silver Age?

   A. They were able to create popular comic books despite the regulations of the Comics Code Authority.

   B. They achieved commercial success because of the popularity of characters such as Spider-Man, the Hulk, and the Fantastic Four.

   C. They repeated the same mistakes as the comic book companies of the Golden Age.

   D. They failed to succeed because of the numbing effect of the Comics Code Authority regulations.

   E. Marvel Comics was the only major comic book company to survive from the Golden Age into the Silver Age.

9. In what light does the passage depict the efforts by Fredric Wertham to bring about regulation of the comic book industry?

   A. As a fanatical crusade brought about by Wertham's inner demons

   B. As a witch-hunt roughly analogous to the concurrent anti-Communist hearings by the House Committee on Un-American Activities

   C. As a reasonable response to an industry that had gone too far

   D. As an angry response to a trend in the subject matter of the comic book industry

   E. As an inappropriate response to a phenomenon that was not actually hurting anyone

10. According to the passage, which of the following statements can be made about the content of *Weird Fantasy* and *The Crypt of Terror*?

   A. Their adult-oriented content was not suitable for young readers.

   B. Their grim and gritty content was a market response to the demands of soldiers home from World War II.

   C. They frequently depicted violence and criminal behavior, but shied away from sexuality or drug abuse.

   D. Their sales surpassed those of previous best-selling titles such as Superman or Batman.

   E. The publication of *Weird Fantasy #1* coincided with the end of the Golden Age of comic books.

The following questions present a sentence, part of which or all of which is underlined. Beneath the sentence, you will find five ways of phrasing the underlined part. The first of these repeats the original; the other four are different. If you think the original is best, choose the first answer; otherwise choose one of the others.

These questions test correctness and effectiveness of expression. In choosing your answer, follow the requirements of standard written English; that is, pay attention to grammar, choice of words, and sentence construction. Choose the answer that produces the most effective sentence; this answer should be clear and exact, without awkwardness, ambiguity, redundancy, or grammatical error.

11. The way in which the mighty blue whale and the other baleen whales—the finback, gray, humpback, and right whales—<u>eats was discovered by</u> careful observation by biologists.

  A. eats was discovered by
  B. eat was discovered through
  C. eats were discovered by means of
  D. eat were discovered by
  E. eat was discovered resulting from

12. The eighteenth-century author Jonathan Swift once suggested in a satiric essay <u>Irish farmers could eat their children to address the twin problems of overpopulation and lack of food</u>.

  A. Irish farmers could eat their children to address the twin problems of overpopulation and lack of food
  B. that the twin problems of overpopulation and lacking food could be addressed by the eating of children by Irish farmers
  C. of the twin problems of Irish farmers, overpopulation and a lack of food, could be addressed by the eating of their children
  D. that Irish farmers could address the twin problems of overpopulation and lack of food by eating their children
  E. that Irish farmers, facing overpopulation and lacking food, could address the twin problems through eating their children

13. The stock market collapse of 1929 had far-reaching consequences for the national economy, causing a nationwide collapse in home values, putting millions out of work, <u>and by erasing</u> the investment savings of one-fifth of the population.

  A. and by erasing
  B. and erasing
  C. and having erased
  D. and erased
  E. by erasing

14. <u>No less remarkable than the invention of nuclear power</u> has been the way the technology has prompted governments to reevaluate the nature of international relations.

  A. No less remarkable than the invention of nuclear power
  B. What was as remarkable as the invention of nuclear power
  C. Inventing nuclear power has been none the less remarkable than
  D. The invention of nuclear power has been no less remarkable as
  E. The thing that was as remarkable as inventing nuclear power

15. <u>Unlike the recognition of ethical lapses in others, many people are disinclined to perceive the same flaws in themselves.</u>

  A. Unlike the recognition of ethical lapses in others, many people are disinclined to perceive the same flaws in themselves.
  B. Unlike the perception of ethical flaws in themselves, many people are willing to recognize these same flaws in others.
  C. Many people, willing to recognize ethical lapses in others, are disinclined to perceive the same flaws in themselves.
  D. Many people are disinclined to perceive the same flaws in themselves, but are willing to perceive ethical lapses in others.
  E. Although willing to recognize ethical lapses in others, many people in themselves are disinclined to perceive the same flaws.

For the following questions, select the best of the answer choices given.

16. The Elk City garbage dumps are so full that Elk City has been forced to pay a large sum to Caribou City to accept much of Elk City's garbage. The Elk City mayor has proposed paying for this garbage relocation by imposing a tax on manufacturing businesses in Elk City. MegaCorp, the largest manufacturing business in the area, protests that this tax is unfair because businesses should not have to pay for a garbage problem that has been created by homeowners.

Which of the following, if true, most weakens MegaCorp's argument?

A. MegaCorp already pays more than $10,000 per year in taxes and fees to Elk City.
B. MegaCorp employs more than 60 percent of the employed residents of Elk City.
C. A recycling program would address the garbage problem more effectively by reducing the overall quantity of waste.
D. MegaCorp's manufacturing processes produce more than 90 percent of the total waste that goes into Elk City's garbage dumps.
E. Caribou City is happy to receive the extra garbage because the fees it collects from Elk City have helped to address a shortfall in education funding.

17. There are Congressmen who say that the development of a space-based missile defense system will provide economic benefits only to military contractors. This claim is not true. A space-based missile defense system, even if it has no current applications for civilian businesses, will still benefit civilian businesses because those businesses will be able to find profitable uses for the government-developed technology in the future.

Which of the following statements, if true, provides the most support for the argument that a space-based missile defense system could provide future economic benefits for civilian businesses?

A. Several new materials developed for the Apollo space program were later adapted to provide basic components of the modern computer and electronics industries.
B. The missile defense system in question will not require the development of any new technologies.
C. Space-based missile defense programs may be the only way to defend civilian populations against preemptive nuclear attacks.
D. Space-based missile defense programs, although more expensive than traditional land-based systems, are theoretically more effective than traditional land-based systems.
E. The scientists employed on the project could make extraordinary advances in the capabilities of intercontinental ballistic missiles used by the army.

18. The commissioner of a professional sports league dictated that teams could not put players on the field who had a greater than 20 percent chance of suffering a career-ending spinal injury during competition. The commissioner justified this decision as a way to protect players from injury while protecting the league from lawsuits.

Which of the following, if true, would most undermine the effectiveness of the commissioner's new policy?

A. Spinal injuries can result in paralysis, loss of fine motor skills, and even death.
B. The previous year, more than seven players in the league suffered career-ending spinal injuries.
C. The players' union agrees that the risk of injury is an inevitable part of playing the game at a professional level.
D. There is no scientifically valid method for determining the likelihood of any player suffering a career-ending spinal injury at any given time.
E. Players barred from playing because of this new regulation will be entitled to compensation for lost wages at a level determined by the commissioner's office.

19. There are few things worse for a new parent than listening to a baby scream in hunger while a bottle of formula slowly warms up in a bowl of hot water. So why not just pop the bottle in the microwave and zap it in 20 seconds? Because microwaves heat fluids unevenly, and a hot pocket in the formula could seriously injure the baby.

Which of the following is presupposed in the argument against heating formula in the microwave?

A. Babies generally refuse to eat formula that has been heated in a microwave.
B. Microwave radiation might break down some of the proteins in formula that are vital to a baby's health.
C. Different microwaves use different amounts of power, and consequently some models could heat a bottle to scalding temperature faster than others.
D. Parents cannot be expected to consistently even out the temperature of a microwaved bottle by shaking it vigorously before giving it to the baby.
E. Once formula has been heated, any leftover formula should be discarded, because otherwise the formula could spoil between feedings and make the baby sick.

20. Charlie's Chainsaw Company has reason to believe that one of its models of saw is defective. A recall of all of the saws would cost more than $5 million, and would probably result in a loss in market share over the next quarter because of bad publicity. Still, a recall is the right economic decision.

Which of the following, if true, most supports the conclusion above?

A. Defective chainsaws can seriously injure or even kill the people who use them.
B. Charlie's chief rival has recalled two of its products within the past year.
C. Product recalls often result in a perception by customers that a given product is permanently defective, even after the defect has been remedied.
D. The stocks of publicly traded companies that announce product recalls often drop upon the announcement, but they generally return to the pre-announcement level within 12 months.

E. Three years ago a rival company went out of business because of large punitive damages awarded to a plaintiff who had been injured by a defective chainsaw.

21. A dog enthusiast took home two puppies from the dog shelter. He fed one of the puppies super-premium canned dog food, while he fed the other a generic brand from the grocery store. The dog fed on the generic brand gained weight twice as fast as the dog fed the super-premium brand. Because of the difference in these results, the dog enthusiast concluded that the generic brand actually provided nutrition superior to that of the super-premium brand.

Each of the following, if true, would weaken the evidence for the dog enthusiast's conclusion except for which of the following?

A. A dog will sometimes gain more weight when eating inferior-quality food because he must eat more of it to obtain the nutrients he needs.
B. The dogs were of mixed breeds and appeared to be descended from dogs of different sizes.
C. Both dogs ate all of the food given to them at each serving.
D. The dog enthusiast did not give the two dogs equal amounts of their respective foods.
E. The dog who received the super-premium dog food suffered from a digestive system disorder that hindered his growth.

The following questions present a sentence, part of which or all of which is underlined. Beneath the sentence, you will find five ways of phrasing the underlined part. The first of these repeats the original; the other four are different. If you think the original is best, choose the first answer; otherwise choose one of the others.

These questions test correctness and effectiveness of expression. In choosing your answer, follow the requirements of standard written English; that is, pay attention to grammar, choice of words, and sentence construction. Choose the answer that produces the most effective sentence; this answer should be clear and exact, without awkwardness, ambiguity, redundancy, or grammatical error.

22. A council of ecologists in Hawaii <u>have concluded that much of the currently uncontrolled invasive species on the island chain were arriving</u> in the holds of cargo ships.

- A. have concluded that much of the currently uncontrolled invasive species on the island chain were arriving
- B. has concluded that many of the currently uncontrolled invasive species on the island chain arrived
- C. have concluded that many of the currently uncontrolled invasive species on the island chain have arrived
- D. concluded that many of the currently uncontrolled invasive species on the island chain would arrive
- E. has concluded that much of the currently uncontrolled invasive species on the island chain had arrived

23. Some people say that the answer to crime is to build more prisons, but more sensitive observers argue that instead we should address the sources of crime <u>through reduced poverty, a cut off supply of illicit drugs, and by focusing on keeping kids in school.</u>

- A. through reduced poverty, a cut off supply of illicit drugs, and by focusing on keeping kids in school
- B. by the reduction of poverty, cutting off the supply of illicit drugs, and to focus on keeping kids in school
- C. by reducing poverty, cutting off the supply of illicit drugs, and focusing on keeping kids in school
- D. by means of reducing poverty, cutting off the supply of illicit drugs, and through focusing on keeping kids in school
- E. to reduce poverty, cut off the supply of illicit drugs, and to focus on keeping kids in school

24. <u>As automobiles replaced horses as the primary means of transportation, it was widely anticipated that</u> the time spent in transit by the average traveler would decrease.

- A. As automobiles replaced horses as the primary means of transportation, it was widely anticipated that
- B. Insofar as automobiles replaced horses as the primary means of transportation, it was anticipated widely
- C. With horses being replaced by automobiles as the primary means of transportation, there was wide anticipation that
- D. As the primary means of transportation replaced horses with automobiles, many anticipated that
- E. Automobiles replacing horses as the primary means of transportation produced anticipation widely that

25. Intrigued by the new rules that favored quickness over strength, <u>the decision of the coach was to give more playing time to the team's smaller athletes</u>.

- A. the decision of the coach was to give more playing time to the team's smaller athletes
- B. the coach decided to give the team's smaller athletes more playing time
- C. it was decided by the coach to give the team's smaller athletes more playing time
- D. the team's smaller athletes were given more playing time by the coach
- E. more playing time was given to the team's smaller athletes by the coach

26. At ground level, nitrous oxides are bad enough, <u>but when up high, atmospherically they</u> bond with free ions to create dangerous smog particles.

- A. but when up high, atmospherically they
- B. however, it is in the upper atmosphere in which it may
- C. but in the upper atmosphere, they
- D. however, but once in the upper atmosphere it is known to
- E. as in the upper atmosphere they

For the following questions, select the best of the answer choices given.

27. Paleontologists hypothesize that modern birds evolved from the family of dinosaurs that included *Tyrannosaurus rex*. This hypothesis would be strongly supported if evidence that dinosaurs from this family had a body covering resembling feathers could be found, but so far no such evidence has been found.

Which of the following, if true, would most help the paleontologists explain why no evidence of feathered dinosaurs has yet been found?

A. Fossilized dinosaurs have shown many birdlike characteristics, such as bone structure and winglike arms.
B. If birds are in fact the descendants of dinosaurs, then it can be argued that the dinosaurs never really died out.
C. Flying dinosaurs such as the *Pteranodon*, which is not thought to have been related to modern birds, do not appear to have had feathers.
D. Soft tissues such as skin and feathers do not fossilize like bones, and therefore are far less likely to have left permanent evidence in the fossil record.
E. The thousands of dinosaur fossils excavated by paleontologists represent only a tiny fraction of the billions of dinosaurs that once lived.

28. Bob and Linda are tired of the freezing cold days in Glenmont, so they are considering retiring to either Sunny Glen or Buena Vista. Bob points out that Sunny Glen has an average annual temperature 8 degrees Fahrenheit higher than that of Buena Vista. Linda insists, however, that Buena Vista would be the better choice.

Which of the following, if true, best accounts for Linda's preference for Buena Vista?

A. Different people experience cold in different ways, so what seems cold to Linda may seem pleasantly cool to Bob.
B. Sunny Glen has a somewhat higher risk of hurricanes than does Glenmont.
C. Buena Vista has a range of cultural offerings, including an opera, a ballet, and three jazz clubs.
D. Living in a place that gets very hot, such as Sunny Glen, can have as many health risks as living in a place that gets very cold.
E. While Sunny Glen is warmer than Buena Vista in the summer, it also has more freezing cold days in the winter.

29. Although many people would not believe it, the mosquito is actually the most dangerous animal in Africa. While the bite of the black mamba is invariably lethal when untreated, this dreaded snake kills only a few dozen people per year. Hippopotami, with their immense strength and foul dispositions, kill hundreds of people per year in rivers and lakes, but the mosquito is still more dangerous. Mosquitoes bite hundreds of millions of people in Africa every year, and they infect over a million each year with malaria, a disease that is often fatal.

Which of the following questions would be most useful in evaluating the claim made above regarding the mosquito?

A. Could a person survive an attack by a black mamba if that person received prompt medical attention?
B. What criteria are used to determine which animal is the "most dangerous" animal?
C. Could the incidence of mosquito bites be decreased through the judicious use of pesticides and insect repellent?
D. Does malaria kill more people per year in Africa than tuberculosis?
E. How does the percentage of people who survive hippopotamus attacks in Africa each year compare with the percentage of people who survive mosquito bites?

The questions in this group are based on the content of a passage. After reading the passage, choose the best answer to each question. Answer all questions following the passage on the basis of what is <u>stated</u> or <u>implied</u> in the passage.

Although hard statistics are difficult to come by, there is substantial anecdotal evidence that use of performance-enhancing drugs, or doping, is rampant in professional sports. Of perhaps greater significance to society are the estimated 1.5 million amateur athletes who use steroids, either to improve their appearance or to emulate the performance of their favorite professional athletes. This chemical epidemic is a pernicious threat to both the nation's health and our collective sense of "fair play."

Nonprescription anabolic steroids have been illegal in the United States since 1991, and most professional sports leagues have banned them since the 1980s. These bans are partly a matter of fairness—a talented athlete trained to the peak of her ability simply cannot compete with an equivalent athlete using steroids—but also based on issues of health. Anabolic androgenic steroids ("anabolic" means that they build tissues; "androgenic" means that they increase masculine traits) have been linked to liver damage, kidney tumors, high blood pressure, balding, and acne. They function by increasing the body's level of testosterone, the primary male sex hormone. In men, this dramatic increase in testosterone can lead to the shrinking of testicles, infertility, and the development of breasts; in women, it can lead to the growth of facial hair and permanent damage to the reproductive system. Steroids have also been linked to a range of psychological problems, including depression and psychotic rage.

The punishments for getting caught using steroids are severe, and the serious health consequences are well documented. Despite this, millions of professional and amateur athletes continue to use performance-enhancing drugs. Why is this?

One clear pattern is that many athletes will do whatever it takes to get an edge on the competition. Since the 1950s, Olympic athletes have played a cat-and-mouse game with Olympic Committee officials to get away with doping, because the drugs really do work. Athletes who dope are simply stronger and faster than their competitors who play fair. Professional athletes in football and baseball have found that steroids and human growth hormone can give them the edge to score that extra touchdown or home run, and in the modern sports market, those results can translate into millions of dollars in salary. For the millions of less talented athletes in gyms and playing fields across the country, drugs seem like the only way to approach the abilities of their heroes in professional sports.

The other clear pattern, unfortunately, is that it has been all too easy for abusers to get away with it. Steroid abuse is often regarded as a "victimless crime." One of the favored ways to trick the testers is to use "designer" steroids. There are thousands of permutations of testosterone, such as THG, that can be produced in a lab. Chemists have discovered that they can create new drugs that produce androgenic effects but do not set off the standard doping tests. Other methods have been to use the steroids but stop a few weeks before testing, to use other chemicals to mask the traces of steroids, or to switch

in a "clean" sample of urine at the testing site. Other athletes use steroid precursors, such as androstenedione, that have androgenic effects similar to those of steroids but are not illegal because they are not technically steroids. The sad fact is that unless the government and professional sports organizations are willing to get tough on the steroid problem, the use of performance-enhancing drugs in sports is not going to end.

30. What appears to be the primary purpose of this passage?

    A. To educate readers about the health threats involved in the use of performance-enhancing drugs

    B. To analyze the ways in which professional athletes have eluded attempts to screen for performance-enhancing drugs

    C. To discuss the reasons why performance-enhancing drugs are a dangerous and persistent problem for society

    D. To complain about the inadequate efforts by government and professional sports organizations to eliminate the problem of performance-enhancing drugs

    E. To argue that athletes, both professional and amateur, should not use performance-enhancing drugs on the grounds that they are both dangerous and unfair

31. According to the passage, all of the following are known potential consequences of steroid use except for which of the following?

    A. Damage to reproductive organs
    B. Decreased blood pressure
    C. Increases in the user's strength and speed
    D. Kidney tumors
    E. Increased risk of depression

32. The author's attitude toward the problem of steroid abuse is best described as which of the following?

    A. Cautious but optimistic
    B. Judgmental but supportive
    C. Ambivalent but resigned
    D. Curious but subjective
    E. Concerned but pessimistic

33. Which of the following can be inferred about a long-distance race in which both athletes who use performance-enhancing drugs and those who do not use these drugs compete?

A. The athletes using the drugs will be caught by the proper authorities and ejected from the race.
B. The athletes using the drugs will have a better chance of winning the race.
C. The athletes using the drugs will use steroid precursors that produce effects similar to those of androgenic drugs but are not technically steroids.
D. The athletes using the drugs are more likely to be professionals in their sport than the athletes who do not use such drugs.
E. The athletes using the drugs will be more likely to use any means possible to win the race, including intentional sabotage of the other racers' equipment.

34. The relationship of an athlete who does not use performance-enhancing drugs to an athlete who does use such drugs is most similar to which of the following?

A. The relationship of a farmer selling milk from cows that have been given bovine growth hormone, a legal drug that promotes greater than normal milk production, to a farmer selling milk from cows that have not been given bovine growth hormone
B. The relationship of a chess player to a competitor who uses psychological tricks in order to gain an advantage
C. The relationship of a boxer in the lightweight class to a boxer in the heavyweight class
D. The relationship of a person taking a standardized test according to the rules to a person taking the same test while using an illegal hidden calculator
E. The relationship of a person entering a pig in an agricultural contest to a person entering a guinea pig in the same contest

35. According to the passage, which of the following can be inferred about the "designer" steroid THG?

A. It can increase masculine traits in users without setting off standard doping tests.

B. It does not cause the health problems associated with traditional anabolic steroids.
C. Even if professional sports organizations could detect THG, they would take no action against those who use it.
D. It is a chemical permutation of progesterone, a hormone that has powerful effects on the human body.
E. Because it is a "designer" steroid, it is more expensive than generic steroids.

36. Which of the following best expresses the role of the third paragraph in the overall structure of the passage?

A. It redirects the theme of the passage from presenting a problem to explaining the reasons for the problem's severity.
B. It introduces a new concept that defines the rest of the passage.
C. It provides an answer to a question posed in the first two paragraphs.
D. It refutes the central hypothesis of the second paragraph and poses a question that is answered in the following paragraphs.
E. It narrows the focus of the passage from the general themes of the first two paragraphs to the more specific themes of the last two paragraphs.

The following questions present a sentence, part of which or all of which is underlined. Beneath the sentence you will find five ways of phrasing the underlined part. The first of these repeats the original; the other four are different. If you think the original is best, choose the first answer; otherwise choose one of the others.

These questions test correctness and effectiveness of expression. In choosing your answer, follow the requirements of standard written English; that is, pay attention to grammar, choice of words, and sentence construction. Choose the answer that produces the most effective sentence; this answer should be clear and exact, without awkwardness, ambiguity, redundancy, or grammatical error.

37. His opponent having sprained his wrist, Andrew could have won by exploiting this weakness, but he chose not to do it.

A. His opponent having sprained his wrist, Andrew could have won by exploiting this weakness, but he chose not to do it.
B. Andrew could have won by exploiting this weakness after his opponent sprained his wrist, but he chose not to do so.
C. Choosing not to do so, Andrew could have won after his opponent sprained his wrist by exploiting this weakness.
D. After his opponent sprained his wrist, Andrew could have won by exploiting this weakness, but he chose not to do so.
E. After his opponent sprained his wrist, Andrew could have, but chose not to do it, won by exploiting this weakness.

38. Since the average test score of students enrolled in charter schools were rising 7.5 percent in the spring, many educators concluded that the system was working.

A. Since the average test score of students enrolled in charter schools were rising 7.5 percent in the spring, many educators concluded
B. As the average test score of students enrolled in charter schools rose 7.5 percent in the spring, with many educators concluding
C. Because the average test score of students enrolled in charter schools rose 7.5 percent in the spring, many educators concluded
D. Because the average test score of students enrolled in charter schools were up 7.5 percent in the spring, many educators concluded
E. With average test scores rising by 7.5 percent among students enrolled in charter schools, and many educators concluded

39. The police chief argued that first-time offenders who have no high school diploma but who have families with a record of crime will probably break the law again.

A. who have no high school diploma but who have families with a record of crime

B. without a high school diploma and families having a criminal record
C. without a high school diploma whose families have a record of crime
D. whose families have criminal records and lacking high school diplomas
E. lacking high school diplomas and also having families having criminal records

40. Like the power-generating apparatus of a conventional car, that of a hybrid car depends on a combustible fuel to generate power.

A. that of a hybrid car depends on
B. hybrid cars depend on
C. hybrid cars' power-generating apparati are dependent on
D. that of a hybrid car's is dependent on
E. that of hybrid cars depend on

41. Since red flags are likely to be raised at the IRS by the reporting of gambling income, business owners who declare their income as business revenue is less likely to receive an audit.

A. Since red flags are likely to be raised at the IRS by the reporting of gambling income, business owners who declare their income as business revenue is less likely to receive an audit.
B. Because the reporting of gambling income is likely to raise red flags at the IRS, business owners can reduce their chances of receiving an audit by declaring that income as business revenue.
C. Business owners can reduce their chances of receiving an audit by declaring the income as business revenue, since the reporting of gambling income is likely to raise red flags at the IRS.
D. Their chances of receiving an audit are reduced by business owners who report that income as business revenue, because the reporting of gambling income is likely to raise red flags at the IRS.
E. The reporting of that income as business revenue can reduce the chances of business owners of receiving an audit, because of the red flags not having been raised at the IRS by the reporting of gambling income.

Practice Test 2

Analysis of an Issue

TIME—30 MINUTES

DIRECTIONS: In this section, you will need to analyze the issue presented and explain your views on it. There is no "correct" answer. Instead, you should consider various perspectives as you develop your own position on the issue.

Read the statement and the instructions that follow it, and then make any notes that will help you plan your response. Write your response on a separate sheet of paper. If possible, type your essay on a word processor. Observe the 30-minute time limit.

Because of research priorities at the national and academic levels, we know more about the surface of the moon than we do about the ocean floor of our own planet, despite the central role the oceans play in global transportation, food production, and climate. It would be more sensible to reallocate those resources dedicated to space research to the exploration of our oceans.

Discuss the extent to which you agree or disagree with the opinion stated above. Support your views with reasons and/or examples from your own experiences, observations, or reading.

ANALYTICAL WRITING 2

Analysis of an Argument

TIME—30 MINUTES

DIRECTIONS: In this section, you will be asked to write a critique of the argument presented below. You may, for example, consider what questionable assumptions underlie the thinking, what alternative explanations or counterexamples might weaken the conclusion, or what sort of evidence could help strengthen or refute the argument.

Read the argument and the instructions that follow it, and then make any notes that will help you plan your response. Write your response on a separate sheet of paper. If possible, type your essay on a word processor. Observe the 30-minute time limit.

A spokesman for a dairy company issued the following statement:

Many consumers buy organic milk because they are concerned about the consequences of the widespread use of recombinant bovine growth hormone and antibiotics in the conventional dairy industry. These concerns, however, are unfounded. While bovine growth hormone has been shown to produce significant developmental effects in cattle, no study has ever shown that its presence in commercial milk has had any developmental effects on human consumers. Regarding antibiotics, while it has been argued that large-scale, preemptive use of antibiotics in cattle feed can interfere with the animals' immune systems and can lead to the proliferation of antibiotic-resistant strains of bacteria, neither of these effects affect the quality of the milk produced by cattle that are fed antibiotics. Therefore, there is no reasonable justification for a consumer to pay $5 for a gallon of organic milk when a perfectly good gallon of conventional milk can be had for half the price.

Discuss how well reasoned you find this argument. In your discussion, be sure to analyze the line of reasoning and the use of evidence in the argument. For example, you may need to consider what questionable assumptions underlie the thinking and what alternative examples or counterexamples might weaken the conclusion. You can also discuss what sort of evidence would strengthen or refute the argument, what changes in the argument would make it more logically sound, and what, if anything, would help you better evaluate its conclusion.

Quantitative

Solve the problem and indicate the best of the answer choices given.

NUMBERS: All numbers used are real numbers.

FIGURES: A figure accompanying a problem-solving question is intended to provide information useful in solving the problem. Figures are drawn as accurately as possible EXCEPT when it is stated in a specific problem that its figure is not drawn to scale. Straight lines may sometimes appear jagged. All figures lie in a plane unless otherwise indicated.

1. Jim's Taxi Service charges an initial fee of $2.25 at the beginning of a trip and an additional charge of $0.35 for each 2/5 of a mile traveled. What is the total charge for a trip of 3.6 miles?

A. $3.15
B. $4.45
C. $4.80
D. $5.05
E. $5.40

2. If the area of a square with sides of length 8 centimeters is equal to the area of a rectangle with a width of 4 centimeters, what is the length of the rectangle, in centimeters?

A. 4
B. 8
C. 12
D. 16
E. 18

3. A certain lab experiments with white and brown mice only. In one experiment, 2/3 of the mice are white. If there are 13 brown mice in the experiment, how many mice in total are in the experiment?

A. 39
B. 33
C. 26
D. 21
E. 10

4. If $x = \dfrac{a}{3} + \dfrac{b}{3^2} + \dfrac{c}{3^3}$, where a, b, and c are each equal to 0 or 1, then x could be each of the following EXCEPT:

A. $\dfrac{1}{27}$

B. $\dfrac{1}{9}$

C. $\dfrac{4}{27}$

D. $\dfrac{2}{9}$

E. $\dfrac{4}{9}$

Score	Number of Applicants
5	2
4	12
3	21
2	7
1	8

5. Fifty applicants for a job were given scores from 1 to 5 on their interview performance. Their scores are shown in the table above. What was the average score for the group?

A. 2.79
B. 2.86
C. 2.91
D. 2.99
E. 3.03

The following data sufficiency problems consist of a question and two statements, labeled (1) and (2), in which certain data are given. You have to decide whether the data given in the statements are <u>sufficient</u> for answering the question. Using the data given in the statements <u>plus</u> your knowledge of mathematics and everyday facts (such as the number of days in July or the meaning of *counterclockwise*), you must indicate whether

A. Statement (1) ALONE is sufficient, but statement (2) alone is not sufficient.
B. Statement (2) ALONE is sufficient, but statement (1) alone is not sufficient.
C. BOTH statements TOGETHER are sufficient, but NEITHER statement ALONE is sufficient.
D. EACH statement ALONE is sufficient.
E. Statements (1) and (2) TOGETHER are NOT sufficient.

NUMBERS: All numbers used are real numbers.

FIGURES: A figure accompanying a data sufficiency problem will conform to the information given in the question, but will not necessarily conform to the additional information given in statements (1) and (2). Lines shown as straight can be assumed to be straight, and lines that appear jagged can also be assumed to be straight. You may assume that the position of points, angles, regions, etc., exist in the order shown and that angle measures are greater than zero. All figures lie in a plane unless otherwise indicated.

NOTE: In data sufficiency problems that ask for the value of a quantity, the data given in the statements are sufficient only when it is possible to determine exactly one numerical value for the quantity.

6. Carrie, Lisa, and Betty all make purchases at a music store that sells all records for a certain price and all CDs for a certain price. How much does Carrie pay for 1 record and 2 CDs?

(1) Lisa bought 3 records for $22.50.
(2) Betty bought 2 records and 4 CDs for $55.00.

7. N and P are points on the number line below 20. Is P closer to 10 than N is?

(1) P is greater than the average of 10 and N.
(2) $\frac{P}{N} = 3$

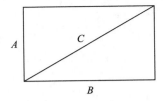

8. What is the area of the rectangular region depicted above with sides A and B and diagonal C?

(1) $C^2 = 9 + A^2$
(2) $A + B = 7$

9. Do at least 20 percent of the people in country X who are over the age of 25 possess a college diploma?

(1) In country X, among the population over the age of 25, 26 percent of the male population and 16 percent of the female population possess college diplomas.
(2) In country X, women account for 55 percent of the total population.

10. If $C = \frac{5r}{2s}$ and $s \neq 0$, what is the value of C?

(1) $r = 4s$
(2) $r = \frac{2}{5}$

Solve the problem and indicate the best of the answer choices given.

11. If $8a = 9b$ and $ab \neq 0$, what is the ratio of $\frac{a}{9}$ to $\frac{b}{8}$?

A. $\frac{64}{81}$
B. $\frac{8}{9}$
C. 1
D. $\frac{9}{8}$
E. $\frac{81}{64}$

12. Two hundred multiples of seven are chosen at random, and 300 multiples of eight are chosen at random. Approximately what percentage of the 500 selected numbers are odd?

A. 20%
B. 25%
C. 40%
D. 50%
E. 80%

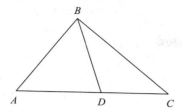

13. In triangle *ABC* above, if ∠*BAD* and ∠*ADB* have measures of $4n°$, ∠*ACB* has a measure of $n°$, and ∠*DBC* has a measure of $45°$, what is the measure of ∠*ABC*? (Figure not necessarily drawn to scale.)

A. $45°$
B. $60°$
C. $90°$
D. $105°$
E. $120°$

14. A coed soccer team has *W* women and *M* men on the team. If 4 women and 2 men are added to the team roster, and if one person on the team is selected at random to serve as team captain, then the probability that the team captain will be a woman can be represented as

A. $\dfrac{W+4}{W+M+6}$
B. $\dfrac{W+4}{W+M+2}$
C. $\dfrac{W+4}{M+2}$
D. $\dfrac{W+4}{W+M}$
E. $\dfrac{W}{M}$

15. What is the twenty-third decimal to the right in the fraction $\dfrac{23}{24}$?

A. 1
B. 2
C. 3
D. 4
E. 5

16. If Scott has earned *x* dollars by working 3 days a week at a constant daily rate for *w* weeks, which of the following represents his daily wage?

A. $3xw$
B. $\dfrac{3w}{x}$
C. $\dfrac{w}{3x}$
D. $\dfrac{xw}{3}$
E. $\dfrac{x}{3w}$

17. $\left(\dfrac{1}{3} - \dfrac{1}{2}\right) - 1 =$

A. $\dfrac{-7}{6}$
B. $\dfrac{-5}{6}$
C. $\dfrac{-1}{6}$
D. $\dfrac{5}{6}$
E. $\dfrac{7}{6}$

18. In a certain conservative mutual fund, 70 percent of the money is invested in bonds, and of that portion, 40 percent is invested in highly rated corporate bonds. If at least $1.4 million in this fund is invested in highly rated corporate bonds, what is the smallest possible total value for the mutual fund?

A. $4 million
B. $5 million
C. $6 million
D. $7 million
E. $8 million

19. If the diameter of a circle is 14, then the area of the circle is

A. 7π
B. 14π
C. 28π
D. 49π
E. 196π

The following data sufficiency problems consist of a question and two statements, labeled (1) and (2), in which certain data are given. You have to decide whether the data given in the statements are <u>sufficient</u> for answering the question. Using the data given in the statements <u>plus</u> your knowledge of mathematics and everyday facts (such as the number of days in July or the meaning of *counterclockwise*), you must indicate whether

A. Statement (1) ALONE is sufficient, but statement (2) alone is not sufficient.
B. Statement (2) ALONE is sufficient, but statement (1) alone is not sufficient.
C. BOTH statements TOGETHER are sufficient, but NEITHER statement ALONE is sufficient.
D. EACH statement ALONE is sufficient.
E. Statements (1) and (2) TOGETHER are NOT sufficient.

20. If a is an integer, is b an integer?

(1) The average (arithmetic mean) of a and b is an integer.
(2) The average (arithmetic mean) of a, b, and $b + 4$ is a.

21. Did Alberto pay more than N dollars for his new stereo, excluding the sales tax?

(1) The price Alberto paid for the stereo was $1.05N$, including the sales tax.
(2) Alberto paid $35 in sales tax on the purchase of his new stereo.

22. Is $r < 1$?

(1) $r > 0$
(2) $r^2 < 1$

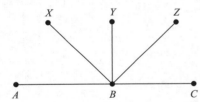

23. In the figure above, with B a point on the line AC, what is the measure of $\angle XBZ$? (Figure not necessarily drawn to scale.)

(1) BX bisects $\angle ABY$, which is a right angle, and BZ bisects $\angle YBC$.
(2) $\angle ABX = \angle XBY = \angle YBZ = \angle ZBC$

24. If P and Q are both positive, what is the value of P?

(1) PQ is a positive multiple of 5.
(2) 300 percent of P equals 500 percent of Q.

25. MegaTech and UltraCorp are considering a merger to form the MegaUltraTech Corporation. Does MegaTech have more employees than UltraCorp?

(1) The average (arithmetic mean) age of UltraCorp employees is 32.8, while the average age of MegaTech employees is 27.2.
(2) If the merger goes through and all employees from both companies remain employed, the average (arithmetic mean) age of the MegaUltraTech employees will be 31.4.

Solve the problem and indicate the best of the answer choices given.

26. In a sample of 800 high school students in which all students are either freshmen, sophomores, juniors, or seniors, 22 percent are juniors and 74 percent are not sophomores. If there are 160 seniors, how many more freshmen than sophomores are there among the sample of students?

A. 42
B. 48
C. 56
D. 208
E. 256

27. The time it took car P to travel 600 miles was 2 hours less than the time it took car R to travel the same distance. If car P's average speed was 10 miles per hour greater than that of car R, what was car R's average speed, in miles per hour?

A. 40
B. 50
C. 60
D. 70
E. 80

28. For any numbers a and b, $a \cdot b = ab(3 - b)$. If a and $a \cdot b$ both represent positive numbers, which of the following could be a value of b?

A. −5
B. −2
C. 2
D. 4
E. 7

29. Marcella has 25 pairs of shoes. If she loses 9 individual shoes, what is the greatest number of matching pairs she could have left?

A. 21
B. 20
C. 19
D. 16
E. 15

30. If Finn was 18 months old one year ago, how old was he, in months, x months ago?

A. $x - 30$
B. $x - 12$
C. $18 - x$
D. $24 - x$
E. $30 - x$

31. A restaurant orders 150 kg of pumpkins from the farmer's market. The farmer fills the order with 23 pumpkins. The average mass of the first 20 pumpkins is 6.5 kg. What must be the minimum average mass of the remaining 3 pumpkins to fill the order?

A. 5.5 kg
B. 5.67 kg
C. 6.67 kg
D. 7 kg
E. 11.5 kg

32. The square root of 636 is between which set of integers?

A. 24 and 25
B. 25 and 26
C. 26 and 27
D. 27 and 28
E. 28 and 29

33. In a forest 150 deer were caught, tagged with electronic markers, then released. A week later, 50 deer were captured in the same forest. Of these 50 deer, it was found that 5 had been tagged with the electronic markers. If the percentage of tagged deer in the second sample approximates the percentage of tagged deer in the forest, and if no deer had either left or entered the forest over the preceding week, what is the approximate number of deer in the forest?

A. 150
B. 750
C. 1,250
D. 1,500
E. 2,500

The following data sufficiency problems consist of a question and two statements, labeled (1) and (2), in which certain data are given. You have to decide whether the data given in the statements are <u>sufficient</u> for answering the question. Using the data given in the statements <u>plus</u> your knowledge of mathematics and everyday facts (such as the number of days in July or the meaning of *counterclockwise*), you must indicate whether

A. Statement (1) ALONE is sufficient, but statement (2) alone is not sufficient.
B. Statement (2) ALONE is sufficient, but statement (1) alone is not sufficient.
C. BOTH statements TOGETHER are sufficient, but NEITHER statement ALONE is sufficient.
D. EACH statement ALONE is sufficient.
E. Statements (1) and (2) TOGETHER are NOT sufficient.

34. If $5a = 9b = 15c$, what is the value of $a + b + c$?

(1) $3c - a = 5c - 3b$
(2) $6cb = 10a$

35. Stanley has gained 8 pounds a year ever since he turned 18. How much weight has Stanley gained since he turned 18?

(1) Stanley now weighs twice what he weighed when he turned 18.
(2) Stanley is now twice the age he was when he turned 18.

36. What is the value of the greater of two numbers if one of the numbers is three times the smaller number?

(1) One of the numbers is 12.
(2) The sum of the two numbers is 16.

37. If $\sqrt{r}$ is a positive integer, what is the value of r?

(1) $r < 70$
(2) $\sqrt{r} > 7$

41 QUESTIONS

Verbal

TIME—75 MINUTES

The following questions present a sentence, part of which or all of which is underlined. Beneath the sentence, you will find five ways of phrasing the underlined part. The first of these repeats the original; the other four are different. If you think the original is best, choose the first answer; otherwise choose one of the others.

These questions test correctness and effectiveness of expression. In choosing your answer, follow the requirements of standard written English; that is, pay attention to grammar, choice of words, and sentence construction. Choose the answer that produces the most effective sentence; this answer should be clear and exact, without awkwardness, ambiguity, redundancy, or grammatical error.

1. The gap in the ozone layer over the North Pole can expand each summer enough that it exposes regions as far south as Sweden by heightened UV radiation, also increasing rates of skin cancer in the northern regions by as much as 50 percent.

   A. that it exposes regions as far south as Sweden by heightened UV radiation, also increasing
   B. that regions as far south as Sweden have been exposed to heightened UV radiation, as well as having increased
   C. to expose regions as far south as Sweden to heightened UV radiation, increased
   D. to expose regions as far south as Sweden to heightened UV radiation and increase
   E. that exposure to heightened UV radiation in regions as far south as Sweden, as well as increasing

2. In winning the 1998 Kentucky Derby, Swiftilocks showed a burst of speed as that of Man o'War, who won 20 of 21 races in 1919 and 1920.

   A. as that of Man o'War, who won
   B. not unlike that of Man o'War, who won
   C. not unlike Man o'War, who won
   D. like that of Man o'War for winning
   E. like Man o'War and his winning

3. Rising tides of unemployment claims across the state has led the governor to declare the economy to be in a state of emergency.

   A. Rising tides
   B. Because the rising tide
   C. The tide is rising
   D. The rising tide
   E. The rising of the tide

4. Seeking to decrease the incidence of tooth decay, the American Dental Association is to spend $45 million over the next seven years promoting good dental hygiene.

   A. the American Dental Association is to spend $45 million over the next seven years promoting good dental hygiene
   B. the American Dental Association will spend $45 million over the next seven years to promote good dental hygiene
   C. over the next seven years the American Dental Association is to spend $45 million promoting good dental hygiene
   D. good dental hygiene will be promoted by the American Dental Association, which is spending $45 million over the next seven years
   E. $45 million will be spent by the American Dental Association over the next seven years on the promotion of good dental hygiene

5. Some paleontologists claim that the discovery of what appear to be feathers in the fossil of an Archosaur could force a revision of current theories on the phylogeny of Archosaurs, alter conceptions of dinosaur skin surfaces, and <u>require scholars to credit birds with a far earlier origin than previously thought</u>.

A. require scholars to credit birds with a far earlier origin than previously thought
B. scholars may be required to credit birds with a far earlier origin than previously thought
C. require a crediting by scholars of birds with a far earlier origin than previously thought
D. compared to what was previously thought, require scholars to credit birds with a far earlier origin
E. crediting birds with a far earlier origin than scholars had previously thought

For the following questions, select the best of the answer choices given.

6. Covington College has four full-time Classics professors, but only 12 Classics majors. This three-to-one student-to-professor ratio is the lowest in the college. Since the college is facing financial difficulties, and since the tuition fees from just 12 students is not sufficient to pay the salaries of 4 full-time professors, the college should cancel the Classics program to reduce expenses.

Which of the following, if true, most weakens the conclusion above?

A. Professors in the Classics department teach popular language and literature classes that are attended by hundreds of students who are not Classics majors.
B. Students at Covington College pay, on average, $22,500 per year in tuition and fees, while the average professor of humanities receives a salary of $61,500 per year.
C. A well-regarded Classics program adds prestige to a college or university.
D. The Classics department has already decreased in size from six full-time professors 10 years ago.
E. The study of classical literature and languages is increasingly irrelevant to the high-tech workplace of today.

7. A pharmaceutical company tested a new diet drug over a two-month period. The test group of 100 dieters lost an average of five pounds per person during the first month, but gained an average of two pounds per person in the second month.

All of the following could help explain the results of the experiment except:

A. The second month of the test occurred during a holiday season, when people are more likely to gain weight.
B. The diet drug has unpleasant side effects, causing many of the subjects to stop using the drug after the first month.
C. The pharmaceutical company provided low-calorie diets to the test subjects in the first month, but let the dieters choose their own food in the second month.
D. The pharmaceutical company selected for the test people who were 20 to 40 pounds over their ideal weights.
E. The diet drug relies on a metabolic effect that loses efficacy the longer a person takes the drug.

8. The Tricounty Bridge was supposed to relieve traffic in East Countway County. Although the bridge was opened last year, traffic in the county has gotten worse over the last year. To relieve the traffic situation in East Countway, therefore, the traffic commission should order the Tricounty Bridge closed.

Which of the following, if true, gives the most support to the conclusion of the passage above?

A. The increased traffic seen in East Countway over the last year is largely attributable to a large casino and resort hotel that opened for business shortly after the opening of the Tricounty Bridge.
B. The Tricounty Bridge allows inhabitants of heavily populated West Countway County to reach East Countway in less than a half-hour, as opposed to the two hours the trip required before the opening of the bridge.
C. The bridge is only open for the periods 7–9 a.m. and 3–5 p.m. on weekdays.
D. Ship captains on the Countway River have complained that the bridge disrupts shipping on the river, thereby hurting the local economy.
E. The bridge is unlikely ever to pay for itself with the current low toll payment.

9. Alcohol-control advocates argue that television advertising plays a large role in leading teenagers to drink. In Hungary, however, where television advertising of alcoholic beverages has been prohibited since 1980, teenage alcohol use is higher than in some other European countries where such advertising is allowed.

Which of the following statements draws the most reliable conclusion from the information given above?

A. Hungarian culture, in general, views alcohol use more positively than do most other European cultures.
B. Television advertising is the most effective way to encourage consumers to try a new alcoholic beverage.
C. Television advertising cannot be the only factor that affects the prevalence of teenage drinking.
D. Alcohol use among Hungarian teenagers has increased in recent years.
E. Alcohol abuse is the greatest threat facing Hungarian teenagers.

The questions in this group are based on the content of a passage. After reading the passage, choose the best answer to each question. Answer all questions following the passage on the basis of what is <u>stated</u> or <u>implied</u> in the passage.

The complex life cycle of the *Plasmodium* protozoan, the causative agent of malaria, has contributed to the difficulty of devising effective public health measures to combat the disease. It took scientists centuries to deconstruct the basic relationship between protozoan, mosquito vector, and human host. Modern physiologists and epidemiologists are still working out the intricacies of malarial infection.

The disease is transmitted by the bite of a female *Anopheles* mosquito infected with the *Plasmodium* parasite. Only *Anopheles* mosquitoes are capable of transmitting the disease, and only females take blood meals from humans. To become infected with *Plasmodium*, the female mosquito takes a blood meal from a human carrying the parasite in his or her blood. Once ingested, the parasite matures in the mosquito's gut for approximately a week, after which it migrates to the insect's salivary glands. By mixing with the mosquito's saliva, the parasite facilitates its transmission to a human host when the mosquito bites that human.

Once in a human's bloodstream, the parasite travels to the human's liver. At this initial stage, the *Plasmodium* parasite is called a sporozoite. Within the liver, the sporozoite can form 30,000 to 40,000 daughter cells, called merozoites, which are released into the host's bloodstream at a later date, sometimes within a week of the initial infection and sometimes as much as several months later. The merozoites seek out and attach themselves to red blood cells, in which they incubate 8 to 24 daughter cells over the next two days. When the daughter cells are mature, the red blood cell ruptures and the new parasites are released into the bloodstream to seek out red blood cells of their own. Some of the new merozoites become male and female gametocytes; if these gametocytes are ingested by a mosquito feeding on the host's blood, they will fertilize in the mosquito's gut to produce new sporozoites, and the cycle will continue.

The symptoms that we associate with malaria—a high, recurring fever; joint pain; a swollen spleen—are caused by toxins released from the red blood cells ruptured by merozoites. The human spleen can destroy these infected blood cells, but the *Plasmodium* parasite counters this effect by increasing the stickiness of proteins on the blood cells' surfaces so that the cells stick to the walls of blood vessels. If the sticky surface proteins affect a particularly large number of cells, the malaria can transform into a hemorrhagic fever, the most deadly form of malaria.

A further complicating factor in the natural history of malaria is the many variants of the *Plasmodium* protozoan. Scientists now recognize that malaria is caused by at least six different species: *P. falciparum, P. vivax, P. ovale, P. malariae, P. knowesli,* and *P. semiovale.* Of these species, *P. falciparum* accounts for the majority of infections and approximately 90 percent of malarial deaths in the world.

10. The passage is primarily concerned with which of the following?

A. Describing the life cycle of the *Plasmodium* protozoan as it relates to the disease malaria
B. Comparing and contrasting the life cycles of the six variants of the *Plasmodium* protozoan known to cause malaria
C. Addressing the public health implications of the life cycle of the *Plasmodium* parasite
D. Providing information on how a person can avoid infection with malaria
E. Describing the life cycle of the *Anopheles* mosquito as it relates to the transmission of the *Plasmodium* protozoan to humans

11. Which of the following most accurately states the role of the first paragraph in relation to the passage as a whole?

A. It summarizes two theories, the relative merits of which are debated in the passage.
B. It puts forth an argument that the rest of the passage is devoted to refuting.
C. It introduces a new concept that the rest of the passage expands upon.
D. It frames the background and relevance of the material to follow.
E. It outlines the major themes of each of the four paragraphs to follow.

12. If a mosquito were to bite a person, and that person were later to develop malaria and die of the disease, it is most likely that the person was infected with which of the following?

A. *Anopheles gambiae*
B. *Anopheles semiovale*
C. *Plasmodium malariae*
D. *Plasmodium vivax*
E. *Plasmodium falciparum*

13. The relationship of a merozoite to a sporozoite is most like which of the following?

A. A mother to a daughter
B. A brother to a sister
C. One of several subsidiaries spun off from a large corporation
D. A computer program to a computer
E. Orange juice to an orange tree

14. Based on the information given in the passage, which of the following would be most effective in preventing a person infected with malaria from developing a hemorrhagic fever?

A. Surgical removal of the spleen
B. A medicine that prevents changes to the surface proteins of red blood cells
C. An effective vaccine against malaria
D. A potent pesticide that reliably kills the *Anopheles* mosquito without producing any negative consequences for the environment or for human health
E. A small infusion of a weaker variant of the *Plasmodium* protozoan that will then compete with the existing parasitic infection

For the following questions, select the best of the answer choices given.

15. In fisheries in general, when a large harvest is taken one year, there will be fewer fish available to be harvested in the following year, leading to decreasing yields of most fish species over time. The Maine lobster is an anomaly, however. Even though the vast number of lobster traps covering the New England coast pull in more lobsters every year, the number of lobsters in the water has shown no signs of decreasing.

Which of the following, if true, most helps to explain the apparent anomaly concerning the number of Maine lobsters?

A. The decline of other fish species in the region has deprived the lobster of its natural food source of scavenged fish.
B. The bait in lobster traps provides abundant food for young lobsters, which are still small enough to swim out of the traps, leading to much higher survival rates among young lobsters than would be expected in nature.
C. As global warming heats the waters of the Atlantic coastline, the Maine lobster has extended its northern range to well past Nova Scotia.
D. The ever-increasing demand for lobsters in seafood restaurants and steakhouses across the country has driven a corresponding increase in the supply of the product.
E. The increased lobster harvest has resulted in many juvenile lobsters but very few breeding-age lobsters, which could result in a crash in lobster numbers in the near future.

16. Federal tax evasion is a serious crime that places an unfair tax burden on those members of society who pay their fair share. To reduce the incidence of tax evasion, the government needs to prosecute a few high-profile individuals whose cases will receive substantial media attention.

The argument above relies on which of the following assumptions?

A. The tax system is so complicated that even people who try to comply with it may inadvertently not pay some of their taxes.

B. The average citizen will be less likely to evade taxes after he or she sees a high-profile individual prosecuted for tax evasion.

C. Tax revenues collected from high-profile tax evaders will help to alleviate the unfair tax burden on honest citizens.

D. Although it is difficult to secure a conviction on a charge of tax evasion, if the government focuses its efforts on a small number of high-profile individuals, the odds of obtaining a conviction will increase.

E. While there is no universal measure for determining whether a taxation system is "fair" or "unfair," the current system was constructed by Congress to represent the societal priorities and values of the American people.

17. Adam's dog, a golden retriever named Hans, can respond to over 150 different commands. Adam cites this fact as evidence for his claim that Hans can understand the English language.

Which of the following, if true, casts the most doubt on Adam's claim that Hans can understand the English language?

A. Each of the 150 commands to which Hans responds involves both a spoken word in English and a distinctive hand sign.

B. Hans does not respond to the same commands when spoken to him by Adam's French and Italian friends in their own languages.

C. Scientists have demonstrated conclusively that canine vocal chords are incapable of replicating many of the sounds used in the English language.

D. Animal behaviorists have demonstrated that even very young dogs surpass both wolves and chimpanzees—animals that are thought to be more intelligent than dogs—in the ability to understand human nonverbal communication.

E. The golden retriever is widely considered to be less intelligent than the border collie, and no border collie has ever been shown to truly understand the English language.

18. The Comfocar company manufactures a sedan that can drive comfortably at 80 miles per hour. A rival company, Turbocar, recently introduced a comparably equipped sedan that can drive comfortably at up to 110 miles per hour. Turbocar claims that its sedan will outsell Comfocar's sedan because the Turbocar sedan can get customers to their destinations in comfort much faster than can the Comfocar sedan.

Which of the following, if true, casts the most doubt on Turbocar's claims?

A. Customers in surveys consistently rank comfort among the most important criteria in purchasing a car.

B. Many road surfaces are engineered to allow comfortable driving at speeds up to 120 miles per hour.

C. Automotive safety experts state that it is not safe for any car to be driven faster than 100 miles per hour.

D. Comprehensive research has determined that while the Turbocar model has faster acceleration and a higher top speed than the Comfocar sedan, both cars show approximately the same fuel efficiency.

E. Nowhere in the main marketing areas for these two car companies is it legal or practical to drive faster than 70 miles per hour.

The following questions present a sentence, part of which or all of which is underlined. Beneath the sentence, you will find five ways of phrasing the underlined part. The first of these repeats the original; the other four are different. If you think the original is best, choose the first answer; otherwise choose one of the others.

These questions test correctness and effectiveness of expression. In choosing your answer, follow the requirements of standard written English; that is, pay attention to grammar, choice of words, and sentence construction. Choose the answer that produces the most effective sentence; this answer should be clear and exact, without awkwardness, ambiguity, redundancy, or grammatical error.

19. <u>Blues musician Paul "Poboy" Smith, born in Tupelo, Mississippi, in 1936, has since 1958 been a fixture on the southern blues scene after the release of his debut album in that year.</u>

   A. Blues musician Paul "Poboy" Smith, born in Tupelo, Mississippi, in 1936, has since 1958 been a fixture on the southern blues scene after the release of his debut album in that year.

   B. Being born in 1936 in Tupelo, Mississippi, blues musician Paul "Poboy" Smith released his debut album in 1958 and has been a fixture on the southern blues scene since then.

   C. Born in Tupelo, Mississippi, in 1936, blues musician Paul "Poboy" Smith has been a fixture on the southern blues scene since the release of his debut album in 1958.

   D. Having been a fixture on the southern blues scene since 1958 when he released his debut album, Paul "Poboy" Smith is a blues musician who was born in 1936 in Tupelo, Mississippi.

   E. Since the release of his debut album in 1958, blues musician Paul "Poboy" Smith has been a fixture on the southern blues scene; he was born in Tupelo, Mississippi in 1936.

20. SEC regulations require that <u>a public company disclose to their</u> potential investors any legal, technological, or financial complications that could endanger their investments.

   A. a public company disclose to their
   B. a public company discloses to its
   C. a public company disclose to its
   D. public companies disclose to its
   E. public companies have disclosed to their

21. The genius of Beethoven can be seen in the widely observed phenomenon that his music has the same appeal to an illiterate shepherd wandering the steppes of <u>Kazakhstan as to</u> a professional musician sipping her latte in Paris.

   A. Kazakhstan as to
   B. Kazakhstan, just as to
   C. Kazakhstan; just as it would to a
   D. Kazakhstan, as it would to a
   E. Kazakhstan as a

22. <u>Mary, just as did the other students, objected to</u> the squash casserole.

   A. Mary, just as did the other students, objected to
   B. Like the other students, Mary was objectionable to
   C. Mary, like the other students, objected to
   D. Mary objected, in the manner of the other students, to
   E. Mary, as the other students, objected

23. At the MegaTek Corporation, an inexperienced financial analyst mistook the <u>rising cost of semiconductors as a seasonal fluctuation</u> in the market.

   A. the rising cost of semiconductors as a seasonal fluctuation
   B. rise in price of semiconductors as a seasonal fluctuation
   C. rising cost of semiconductors for a seasonal fluctuation
   D. rising of the cost of semiconductors for a fluctuation by season
   E. rise of semiconductors in price to a seasonal fluctuation

The questions in this group are based on the content of a passage. After reading the passage, choose the best answer to each question. Answer all questions following the passage on the basis of what is <u>stated</u> or <u>implied</u> in the passage.

    The collapse of the stock "bubble" of Internet-related companies in 2000–2001 has resulted in more than its fair share of analysis, hand-wringing, and finger-pointing. A panel discussion at a recent Technology Today conference in Santa Monica produced a heated debate between two former luminaries of the dot.com world: investment banker Pat Verhofen and Sue Mickelson, founder and CEO of Internet retailer Frizbeez.com.

    Verhofen fired the opening shot by placing blame for the collapse of Internet stocks on the shoulders of Internet entrepreneurs who aggressively promoted ideas without viable business models. These entrepreneurs were both irresponsible and deceptive, Verhofen argued, to take investors' money to fund operations that could not reasonably turn a profit, such as giving computers away for free or selling bulky objects, such as dog food or furniture, over the Internet. Many of these companies, he suggested, were little more than arrangements of smoke and mirrors designed to separate investors from their money.

Mickelson responded that Verhofen was like a fox in a henhouse blaming the rooster for all the dead chickens. Entrepreneurs cannot be blamed, she argued, for trying to make money for themselves and other people, because that is what entrepreneurs do. She also stated that you cannot know what ideas will or will not work until you try them; contemporaries of the Wright brothers said that a heavier-than-air aircraft could never work, and look at the skies today.

Mickelson instead placed the blame on the unscrupulous bankers and fund managers who hyped Internet stocks in order to cash in on fees from IPOs and trades. In contrast to entrepreneurs, these financial types actually do have a responsibility to offer only sound financial advice to their clients. If anyone should bear the blame, she argued, it should be people like Pat Verhofen.

Indigo Smith, the moderator of the panel, responded that perhaps the true fault lay with the common investors, who should not have invested in technology stocks in the first place if they lacked the knowledge to do so properly. While she expressed sympathy for those elderly investors who lost substantial portions of their retirement savings on flimsy Internet stocks, she observed that no one forced them to invest in those stocks.

24. Which of the following best describes the structure of the passage?

A. It mentions a puzzling situation, and then describes three approaches people have taken to help understand that situation.

B. It presents an argument for why something took place, and then offers a refutation of that argument.

C. It introduces a past phenomenon and then presents three explanations for why the phenomenon took place.

D. It describes a problem, offers a solution to the problem, and then offers reasons why the solution could not work.

E. It offers three explanations for a phenomenon and then summarizes what all three have in common.

25. Which of the following statements presents the strongest conclusion one could draw based on the information given in the passage?

A. The collapse of the Internet stock "bubble" drove thousands of investors into bankruptcy.

B. People involved with the Internet do not all agree on which party bears the most responsibility for the collapse of the Internet stock "bubble."

C. Of all parties involved with the Internet, financial professionals such as investment bankers and fund managers derived the most profits from the stock "bubble."

D. The Internet stock "bubble" could not have occurred if entrepreneurs had been honest about the true financial prospects of their companies.

E. The average investor has no one to blame but himself or herself if he or she invested in an Internet stock without adequately understanding the true financial prospects of the companies in question.

26. Which of the following best captures the meaning of the simile attributed to Mickelson that Verhofen "was like a fox in a henhouse blaming the rooster for all the dead chickens"?

A. As an entrepreneur, Mickelson understands that similes and other figures of speech can help convey complex ideas to audiences.

B. Verhofen, as an investment banker, was personally responsible for promoting businesses that he knew were not viable from a long-term perspective.

C. Foxes, unlike roosters, have no legitimate business in henhouses, and are far more likely than roosters to kill chickens.

D. As an investment banker, Verhofen was more likely to be the culprit of the crime than those he identified as responsible.

E. Entrepreneurs cannot be blamed for trying to make money for themselves and other people because that is what they do.

27. If Mickelson had not used the example of the Wright brothers in her argument, what other example might have illustrated her point as well?

  A. Despite widespread public opinion that the sun revolves around the earth, Galileo Galilei published findings showing that the earth revolved around the sun; he later retracted this assertion as a result of pressure from the Church.

  B. A tobacco company chose to market cigarettes to children despite widespread public opinion that such marketing is unethical; over the following decade, the company expanded its share of the tobacco market.

  C. A home electronics company devoted substantial development resources to eight-track audio technology despite widespread industry opinion that cassette tapes were the wave of the future; eight-tracks were soon replaced by cassette tapes, which in turn were replaced by compact disks.

  D. A newspaper chose to publish a story that government lawyers said it could not print; the newspaper won its case against the government lawyers in a federal court, and the writer of the story won a Pulitzer Prize.

  E. A computer company initiated research into manufacturing a computer for home use when widespread public opinion held that computers could be useful only for large corporations or government agencies; personal home computers became a multibillion-dollar market.

28. If Verhofen's arguments and statements are all correct, which of the following statements can accurately be inferred?

  A. Biotechnology executives who aggressively raise investment capital for bioengineered products with no conceivable market should be held responsible if biotechnology stocks crash.

  B. Investors should make financial decisions only with the advice of qualified financial advisors, such as investment bankers or fund managers.

  C. If people lose money on investments that they inadequately researched, they have only themselves to blame.

  D. If insurance companies provide home insurance for homes built in a hurricane zone and those homes are subsequently all destroyed by a major hurricane, the insurance company should be blamed for any investment losses suffered by its shareholders.

  E. The collapse of Internet stocks would not have occurred if companies had not attempted to sell bulky items, like dog food, over the Internet.

The following questions present a sentence, part of which or all of which is underlined. Beneath the sentence, you will find five ways of phrasing the underlined part. The first of these repeats the original; the other four are different. If you think the original is best, choose the first answer; otherwise choose one of the others.

These questions test correctness and effectiveness of expression. In choosing your answer, follow the requirements of standard written English; that is, pay attention to grammar, choice of words, and sentence construction. Choose the answer that produces the most effective sentence; this answer should be clear and exact, without awkwardness, ambiguity, redundancy, or grammatical error.

29. While some military planners claimed that it would be possible to win a war fought with nuclear weapons, many scientists argued that such a war could not truly be won, because the fallout from nuclear warfare would create a nuclear winter and <u>it also would be rendering the earth uninhabitable</u>.

  A. it also would be rendering the earth uninhabitable

  B. rendering the earth uninhabitable

  C. might have uninhabitably rendered the earth

  D. render the earth uninhabitable

  E. would also have rendered the earth uninhabitable

30. Providing adequate public health-care facilities is a crucial task in a county like Travis, <u>where more than 60 percent of household incomes are</u> below the poverty line.

A. where more than 60 percent of household incomes are
B. where more than 60 percent of household income is
C. which has more than 60 percent of the household incomes
D. where they have more than 60 percent of household income
E. where more than 60 percent of them have household incomes

31. Noted for its tenacity and courage, <u>the English bulldog, having originally been bred for the brutal sport of bull-baiting, but now is cherished</u> as a loyal animal companion.

A. the English bulldog, having originally been bred for the brutal sport of bull-baiting, but now is cherished
B. English bulldogs were originally bred for the brutal sport of bull-baiting, but they are now cherished
C. English bulldogs were originally bred to bait bulls in a brutal sport, but it is now cherished
D. the English bulldog was originally bred for the brutal sport of bull-baiting, but it is now cherished
E. the English bulldog, originally bred to bait bulls for a brutal sport, is now being cherished

32. Advanced market research for the MegaTek Corporation predicts that launching a MegaTek Superstore in a given city <u>would only succeed should the density of repeat customers have been greater than</u> 200 per square mile.

A. would only succeed should the density of repeat customers have been greater than
B. will succeed only should the density of repeat customers be more numerous than
C. will succeed only if the density of repeat customers is greater than
D. should only succeed with a repeat customer density of greater than
E. will succeed only with repeat customer density being greater than

For the following questions, select the best of the answer choices given.

33. In order to increase revenues, a cell-phone company has decided to change its fee structure. Instead of charging a flat rate of $20 per month and $0.05 for every minute over 200 minutes, the company will now charge $50 per month for unlimited usage.

Which of the following is a consideration that, if true, suggests that the new plan will not actually increase the company's revenues?

A. A rival company, which charges no start-up fee, offers an unlimited calling plan for $40 per month.
B. Two-thirds of the company's customers use less than 500 minutes per month.
C. Studies have shown that customers using unlimited calling plans will increase their monthly usage of minutes by over 50 percent.
D. One-fifth of the company's customers use in excess of 1,000 minutes per month.
E. In recent months the company has received several complaints of insufficient signal strength and poor customer service.

34. A real estate developer in Florida, desiring to protect his high-rise apartment building on the beach from hurricane damage, has planted sea oats in two rows in front of his building in order to encourage the development of sand dunes between the water and his building.

Which of the following, if true, casts the most doubt on the probable effectiveness of the developer's plan?

A. Sand dunes provide little protection for tall buildings against the wind, which is sufficiently powerful even in minor hurricanes to cause serious damage to buildings.
B. Sand dunes have been shown to provide effective protection against the storm surge, the pounding waves driven by hurricane-force winds onto dry land.
C. Although sea oats will lead to the growth of sand dunes over many years, it would be far faster to build concrete bunkers between the building and the water.
D. Hurricane insurance has become so expensive that many owners of beachfront property choose not to buy it.
E. The developer has invested in reinforced steel girders and shatterproof glass as a way of minimizing damage to his building in the event that a hurricane hits the area.

35. According to local tradition, Sultan Abu ibn al-Hasan founded the East African trading state of Kilwa in the mid-tenth century. Professor Ascalon, however, argues that Sultan al-Hasan did not rule in Kilwa until at least a century later.

Which of the following, if true, provides the strongest support for Professor Ascalon's position?

A. The Hunsu Kubwa Palace, the largest stone structure in sub-Saharan Africa prior to the eighteenth century, dates to the rule of Sultan Sulaiman in the fourteenth century.

B. The oldest mosque on the island, which has traditionally been attributed to the reign of Abu ibn al-Hasan, has a foundation dating to ca. 800 C.E.

C. The Kilwa Chronicle, a document based on Kilwa oral history that has been shown to be unreliable on matters of chronology, dates the rise to power of Sultan al-Hasan to the year 957 C.E.

D. Silver and copper coins bearing the name of Abu ibn al-Hasan have been found in archeological sites dating from the late eleventh to the fourteenth centuries, but none have been found in sites dating earlier than the late eleventh century.

E. Archeological records suggest that the island of Kilwa enjoyed a period of economic prosperity beginning in the mid-eleventh century.

36. In theory, Ecuador could be a major exporter of shrimp. In actuality, it is not. The explanation is that 80 percent of the country's rich estuaries are owned by the government. This hurts Ecuador's shrimp production, because the government does not have the flexibility necessary for efficient shrimp farming that private industry possesses.

The answer to which of the following questions would be most relevant to evaluating the adequacy of the explanation given above?

A. Who owns the 20 percent of estuaries that are not owned by the government?

B. What percentage of Ecuador's production of shrimp is consumed domestically?

C. Has the government stated any plans to sell any of its estuaries to private industry, provided that the price is sufficient?

D. Is Peru, Ecuador's neighbor to the south, actually better suited for commercial shrimp farming than Ecuador, which is a substantially smaller country?

E. How does Ecuador's shrimp production on government-owned estuaries compare to that on comparable land owned by private industry?

The questions in this group are based on the content of a passage. After reading the passage, choose the best answer to each question. Answer all questions following the passage on the basis of what is <u>stated</u> or <u>implied</u> in the passage.

One of the best sources modern scholars have for learning about Hellenistic Egypt is the large supply of papyrus fragments that have turned up in the Egyptian desert over the last century. Papyrus is a thick type of paper made from a reedy plant found in Egypt. Papyrus is much tougher than the wood-pulp paper used in modern society; whereas a book produced today will most likely fall apart within a century, there are papyrus fragments that are still legible over 2,000 years after scribes wrote on them.

It is primarily by accident that any of these fragments have survived. Most of the surviving fragments have been found in ancient garbage dumps that were covered over by the desert and preserved in the dry heat. The benefit of this type of archeological find is that these discarded scraps often give us a more accurate picture of the daily lives of ancient Egyptians—their business affairs, personal correspondence, and religious pleas—than the stone engravings and recorded texts that were intended to be passed down to later generations.

One of the most important papyrus discoveries of recent years was the revelation in 2001 that a scrap of papyrus that had been discarded and used to wrap a mummy contained 110 previously unknown epigrams (short, witty poems) by the Hellenistic poet Posidippus (ca. 280–240 B.C.). Posidippus lived in Alexandria and benefited from the support of King Ptolemy II Philadelphos (ruled 284–246 B.C.). These new epigrams have yielded fascinating insight into the court culture and literary sensibilities of early Hellenistic Egypt.

King Ptolemy, of course, was also a sponsor of the famous library of Alexandria, the greatest depository of knowledge in the ancient world. According to the twelfth-century Byzantine writer John Tzetzes, the ancient library contained nearly half a million papyrus scrolls. If that library had not burned down, maybe archeologists today would not have to spend so much of their time sorting through ancient trash!

37. The author's primary intention in this passage appears to be which of the following?

A. To shed light on the underappreciated work of the Hellenistic poet Posidippus

B. To compare the relative merits of papyrus and wood-pulp paper as media for recording information

C. To discuss the ways in which papyrus fragments help scholars learn about Hellenistic Egypt

D. To answer the questions regarding the burning of the library of Alexandria, one of the great mysteries of the ancient world

E. To suggest possibly fruitful paths for future archeological research into Hellenistic Egypt

38. Which of the following would best illustrate how a discarded fragment of papyrus might give us a more accurate picture of the daily lives of ancient Egyptians than a record intended to be permanent?

A. A poet such as Posidippus may have composed rough drafts of his epigrams on papyrus fragments prior to writing them in their final form.

B. Grocery lists, which give insights into the diets of ancient people, would never be included in stone inscriptions but could be scribbled on scraps of papyrus.

C. The Hellenistic monarchs employed some of the finest historians of the Greek world to provide chronicles of their reigns.

D. Some papyrus fragments may have been used for purposes other than writing, such as binding wounds or wrapping small packages.

E. Stone inscriptions describing military events often embellish the truth to favor whoever is paying for the inscription.

39. The mention of the discovery of 110 previously unknown epigrams by the poet Posidippus serves what purpose in the passage?

A. Revealing insights into the nuances of court culture in Hellenistic Egypt

B. Demonstrating how durable a material papyrus can be

C. Arguing for a greater appreciation of this little-known Hellenistic poet

D. Highlighting the importance of royal patronage in the development of arts and literature in the Hellenistic world

E. Illustrating the kind of discovery that can be made from researching papyrus fragments

40. According to information given in the passage, which of the following locations would probably yield the highest probability of finding a previously undiscovered papyrus fragment?

A. The ship of a royal messenger that sank off the Egyptian coast of the Mediterranean Sea in the third century B.C.

B. The charred remnants of an ancient Egyptian palace that was burned by Roman troops in the first century B.C.

C. The refuse heap of an ancient Egyptian town that was buried in the desert in the fifth century A.D.

D. The private collections of French and British explorers from the nineteenth century A.D. who first uncovered many of the principal sites of Egyptian archeology

E. The library of a Hellenistic fishing village that sank into the marshes of the Nile Delta in the third century A.D.

41. What does the author imply by the final statement: "If that library had not burned down, maybe archeologists today would not have to spend so much of their time sorting through ancient trash!"?

A. The author implies that if the library had not burned down, archeologists would be able to appreciate the full cultural legacy of King Ptolemy II Philadelphos.

B. The author implies that if the library had not burned down, scholars today would have not only the full works of Posidippus, but also those of Aeschylus, Sophocles, and Euripides.

C. The author implies that if the library had not burned down, the scrolls contained within the library would have decomposed before modern times in any event, because they would not have been preserved in the dry heat of the desert.

D. The author implies that if the library had not burned down, it might have contained more complete details about the life and culture of Hellenistic Egypt than can be found in the papyrus fragments from ancient refuse dumps.

E. The author implies that if the library had not burned down, the cultural awakening of the Renaissance might have occurred centuries earlier.

Practice Test 3

Analysis of an Issue

TIME—30 MINUTES

DIRECTIONS: In this section, you will need to analyze the issue presented and explain your views on it. There is no "correct" answer. Instead, you should consider various perspectives as you develop your own position on the issue.

Read the statement and the instructions that follow it, and then make any notes that will help you plan your response. Write your response on a separate sheet of paper. If possible, type your essay on a word processor. Observe the 30-minute time limit.

People value things more when they have suffered for them.

Discuss the extent to which you agree or disagree with the opinion stated above. Support your views with reasons and/or examples from your own experiences, observations, or reading.

ANALYTICAL WRITING 2

Analysis of an Argument

TIME—30 MINUTES

DIRECTIONS: In this section, you will be asked to write a critique of the argument presented below. You may, for example, consider what questionable assumptions underlie the thinking, what alternative explanations or counterexamples might weaken the conclusion, or what sort of evidence could help strengthen or refute the argument.

Read the argument and the instructions that follow it, and then make any notes that will help you plan your response. Write your response on a separate sheet of paper. If possible, type your essay on a word processor. Observe the 30-minute time limit.

A speaker at an electronic entertainment conference made the following statement:

Video games have been widely criticized for having a negative effect on the nation's youth. If one looks at the facts, however, over the last 25 years, the period in which the use of video games became common among the nation's youth, math scores on the most commonly used college aptitude test have risen consistently, and entry-level salaries for college graduates have also risen significantly. This evidence suggests that video games are actually providing young people with the skills they need to succeed in college and in the workplace.

Discuss how well reasoned you find this argument. In your discussion, be sure to analyze the line of reasoning and the use of evidence in the argument. For example, you may need to consider what questionable assumptions underlie the thinking and what alternative examples or counterexamples might weaken the conclusion. You can also discuss what sort of evidence would strengthen or refute the argument, what changes in the argument would make it more logically sound, and what, if anything, would help you better evaluate its conclusion.

The following data sufficiency problems consist of a question and two statements, labeled (1) and (2), in which certain data are given. You have to decide whether the data given in the statements are sufficient for answering the question. Using the data given in the statements plus your knowledge of mathematics and everyday facts (such as the number of days in July or the meaning of counterclockwise), you must indicate whether

A. Statement (1) ALONE is sufficient, but statement (2) alone is not sufficient.
B. Statement (2) ALONE is sufficient, but statement (1) alone is not sufficient.
C. BOTH statements TOGETHER are sufficient, but NEITHER statement ALONE is sufficient.
D. EACH statement ALONE is sufficient.
E. Statements (1) and (2) TOGETHER are NOT sufficient.

NUMBERS: All numbers used are real numbers.

FIGURES: A figure accompanying a data sufficiency problem will conform to the information given in the question, but will not necessarily conform to the additional information given in statements (1) and (2). Lines shown as straight can be assumed to be straight, and lines that appear jagged can also be assumed to be straight. You may assume that the position of points, angles, regions, etc., exist in the order shown and that angle measures are greater than zero. All figures lie in a plane unless otherwise indicated.

NOTE: In data sufficiency problems that ask for the value of a quantity, the data given in the statements are sufficient only when it is possible to determine exactly one numerical value for the quantity.

1. If x is an integer, is $\dfrac{18 + 54}{x}$ an integer?

   (1) $18 < x < 54$
   (2) x is a multiple of 18

2. If $a > 0$ and $b > 0$, is $\dfrac{a}{b} > \dfrac{b}{a}$?

   (1) $a = b - 2$
   (2) $\dfrac{a}{4b} = \dfrac{1}{5}$

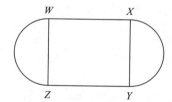

3. The figure above shows the shape of a flowerbed. If arcs WZ and XY are semicircles and $WXYZ$ is a square, what is the area of the flowerbed?

   (1) The perimeter of square $WXYZ$ is 24.
   (2) The diagonal $WY = 6\sqrt{2}$.

4. A total of 72 passengers are on a ship, and they go out on an excursion in boats R and Q. How many of the ship's passengers are female?

   (1) There are 13 females on boat Q.
   (2) There are equal numbers of women on boats R and Q.

5. In the xy plane, is the point $(4, -2)$ on the line l?

(1) Point $(1, 1)$ is on line l.
(2) The equation $x = 2 - y$ describes line l.

Solve the problem and indicate the best of the answer choices given.

NUMBERS: All numbers used are real numbers.

FIGURES: A figure accompanying a problem-solving question is intended to provide information useful in solving the problem. Figures are drawn as accurately as possible EXCEPT when it is stated in a specific problem that its figure is not drawn to scale. Straight lines may sometimes appear jagged. All figures lie in a plane unless otherwise indicated.

6. A type of extra-large SUV averages 12.2 miles per gallon (mpg) on the highway, but only 7.6 mpg in the city. What is the maximum distance, in miles, that this SUV could be driven on 25 gallons of gasoline?

A. 190
B. 284.6
C. 300
D. 305
E. 312

7. The ratio of 2 quantities is 5 to 6. If each of the quantities is increased by 15, what is the ratio of these two new quantities?

A. 5:6
B. 25:27
C. 15:16
D. 20:21
E. It cannot be determined from the information given

8. $\sqrt{6^2 + 8^2 - 19} =$

A. $3\sqrt{2}$
B. 8
C. 9
D. 10
E. $\sqrt{119}$

9. In an animal behavior experiment, 50 tagged white pigeons and 200 tagged gray pigeons were released from a laboratory. Within one week, 88 percent of the white pigeons and 80.5 percent of the gray pigeons had returned to the laboratory. What percent of the total number of pigeons returned to the laboratory?

A. 80.5
B. 82
C. 82.5
D. 85
E. 86.5

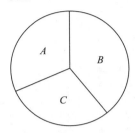

10. In the circular region shown above, sections A and B represent $\frac{3}{8}$ and $\frac{5}{11}$, respectively, of the area of the circular region. Section C represents what fractional part of the area of the circular region?

A. $\frac{15}{88}$
B. $\frac{2}{11}$
C. $\frac{5}{22}$
D. $\frac{45}{88}$
E. $\frac{73}{88}$

11. At the wholesale store you can buy an 8-pack of hot dogs for $1.55, a 20-pack for $3.05, and a 250-pack for $22.95. What is the greatest number of hot dogs you can buy at this store with $200?

A. 1,108
B. 2,100
C. 2,108
D. 2,124
E. 2,256

The following data sufficiency problems consist of a question and two statements, labeled (1) and (2), in which certain data are given. You have to decide whether the data given in the statements are <u>sufficient</u> for answering the question. Using the data given in the statements <u>plus</u> your knowledge of mathematics and everyday facts (such as the number of days in July or the meaning of *counterclockwise*), you must indicate whether

A. Statement (1) ALONE is sufficient, but statement (2) alone is not sufficient.
B. Statement (2) ALONE is sufficient, but statement (1) alone is not sufficient.
C. BOTH statements TOGETHER are sufficient, but NEITHER statement ALONE is sufficient.
D. EACH statement ALONE is sufficient.
E. Statements (1) and (2) TOGETHER are NOT sufficient.

12. What was the percent decrease in the price of MegaTek (MGTK) stock during the market decline of March 1, 2001, to March 1, 2002?

(1) The price of MGTK was $56.20 on March 1, 2001.
(2) The price of the stock on January 1, 2002, was only one-quarter of its price as of March 1, 2001.

13. Greg's long-distance telephone plan charges him $0.50 for the first 4 minutes of a call, and $0.07 per minute for each subsequent minute. Greg made a call to Carrie for x minutes, where x is an integer. How many minutes long was Greg's call?

(1) The last 7 minutes of Greg's call cost $0.22 less than the first 7 minutes of the call.
(2) The call did not cost more than $1.05.

14. If x and y are both positive numbers, is x greater than 75% of y?

(1) $5x > 4y + 1$
(2) $x = 6$

15. Is $xyz = 1$?

(1) $x(y^z) = 1$
(2) $5z = 0$

16. What is the average (arithmetic mean) of x and y?

(1) The average of $x + 3$ and $y + 5$ is 14.
(2) The average of x, y, and 16 is 12.

Solve the problem and indicate the best of the answer choices given.

17. One day a car rental agency rented 2/3 of its cars, including 3/5 of its cars with CD players. If 3/4 of its cars have CD players, what percent of the cars that were not rented had CD players?

A. 10%
B. 35%
C. 45%
D. 66.7%
E. 90%

18. If x is 20 percent greater than 88, then $x =$

A. 68
B. 70.4
C. 86
D. 105.6
E. 108

19. A farmer with 1,350 acres of land had planted his fields with corn, sugar cane, and tobacco in the ratio of 5:3:1, respectively, but he wanted to make more money, so he shifted the ratio to 2:4:3, respectively. How many more acres of land were planted with tobacco under the new system?

A. 90
B. 150
C. 270
D. 300
E. 450

20. $\sqrt{144} + \sqrt{225} + \sqrt{324} =$

A. 18
B. 33
C. 36
D. 42
E. 45

21. What is the perimeter of a square with area $\dfrac{9P^2}{16}$?

A. $\dfrac{3P}{4}$
B. $\dfrac{3P^2}{4}$
C. $3P$
D. $3P^2$
E. $\dfrac{4P}{3}$

22. If a three-digit number is selected at random from the integers 100 to 999, inclusive, what is the probability that the first digit and the last digit of the integer will both be exactly two less than the middle digit?

A. 1:900
B. 7:900
C. 9:1,000
D. 1:100
E. 7:100

23. Which of the following inequalities is equivalent to $-4 < x < 8$?

A. $|x - 1| < 7$
B. $|x + 2| < 6$
C. $|x + 3| < 5$
D. $|x - 2| < 6$
E. None of the above

24. $\dfrac{80 - 6(36 \div 9)}{\frac{1}{4}} =$

A. 416
B. 224
C. 188
D. 104
E. 56

25. Three different lumberjacks can chop W amount of wood in 30 minutes, 45 minutes, and 50 minutes according to their different levels of skill with the axe. How much wood, in terms of W, could the two fastest lumberjacks chop in 2 hours?

A. $6\frac{2}{3}\ W$
B. $6\ W$
C. $4\frac{2}{3}\ W$
D. $3\ W$
E. $2\frac{2}{3}\ W$

The following data sufficiency problems consist of a question and two statements, labeled (1) and (2), in which certain data are given. You have to decide whether the data given in the statements are **sufficient** for answering the question. Using the data given in the statements **plus** your knowledge of mathematics and everyday facts (such as the number of days in July or the meaning of *counterclockwise*), you must indicate whether

A. Statement (1) ALONE is sufficient, but statement (2) alone is not sufficient.
B. Statement (2) ALONE is sufficient, but statement (1) alone is not sufficient.
C. BOTH statements TOGETHER are sufficient, but NEITHER statement ALONE is sufficient.
D. EACH statement ALONE is sufficient.
E. Statements (1) and (2) TOGETHER are NOT sufficient.

26. In what year was Edward born?

(1) In 1988, Edward turned 17 years old.
(2) Edward's sister Lisa, who is 14 months older than Edward, was born in 1970.

27. Is $rs = rx - 2$?

(1) r is an odd number
(2) $x = s + 2$

28. A CEO is building an extra-wide garage in which to park his limousines. The garage is x feet wide, and at least 2 feet of space is required between each two cars and between the cars and the walls. Will all 9 limousines fit in the garage?

(1) The average width of the limousines is the square root of x.
(2) $x = 100$.

29. If $q + r + s = 45$, what is the value of qr?

(1) $q = r = s$
(2) $q - r - s = -15$

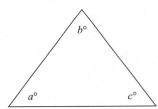

30. Is the triangle depicted above isosceles? (Figure not necessarily drawn to scale.)

(1) $180° - (a + c) = 60°$
(2) $a = 2b - c$

Solve the problem and indicate the best of the answer choices given.

31. Last year Jackie saved 5% of her annual salary. This year, she made 10% more money than last year, and she saved 8% of her salary. The amount saved this year was what percent of the amount she saved last year?

A. 56%
B. 76%
C. 158%
D. 176%
E. 188%

	P	Q	R	S
P	0	144	171	186
Q	144	0	162	X
R	171	162	0	Y
S	186	X	Y	0

32. The table above shows the one-way driving distance, in miles, between four cities: P, Q, R, and S. For example, the distance between P and Q is 144 miles. If the round trip between S and Q is 16 miles further than the round trip between S and R, and the round trip between S and R is 24 miles less than the round trip between S and P, what is the value of X?

A. 174
B. 182
C. 186
D. 348
E. 364

33. If 35 percent of 400 is 20 percent of x, then $x =$

A. 200
B. 350
C. 700
D. 900
E. 1,400

34. $(2^3 - 1)(2^3 + 1)(2^6 + 1)(2^{12} + 1) =$

A. $(2^{24} - 1)$
B. $(2^{24} + 1)$
C. $(2^{48} - 1)$
D. $(2^{96} + 1)$
E. $2^6(2^{12} - 1)$

35. To be considered for "movie of the year," a film must appear in at least ¼ of the top-10-movies lists submitted by the Cinematic Academy's 765 members. What is the smallest number of top-10 lists a film can appear on and still be considered for "movie of the year"?

A. 191
B. 192
C. 193
D. 212
E. 213

36. In a sample of associates at a law firm, 30 percent are second-year associates, and 60 percent are not first-year associates. What percentage of the associates at the law firm have been there for more than two years?

A. 10
B. 20
C. 30
D. 40
E. 50

37. Which of the following fractions has the greatest value?

A. $\dfrac{48}{(2^5)(3^2)}$

B. $\dfrac{12}{(2^4)(3^3)}$

C. $\dfrac{6}{(2^3)(3^2)}$

D. $\dfrac{144}{(2^4)(3^4)}$

E. $\dfrac{81}{(2^3)(3^5)}$

Verbal

The questions in this group are based on the content of a passage. After reading the passage, choose the best answer to each question. Answer all questions following the passage on the basis of what is <u>stated</u> or <u>implied</u> in the passage.

Forget hostile aliens. According to a forthcoming book by noted astrophysicist Egbert Larson, the intrepid humans who first attempt interstellar space travel will face far more daunting challenges before they ever meet the Little Green Men.

Larson begins with the problem of relativistic time dilation. If you travel all the way to Alpha Centauri, you'd like to come back and tell your friends about it, right? It's not too likely to happen, though. If Mr. Einstein was right about relativity—and we're not going to say he wasn't—then time slows down when you approach the speed of light. A person traveling at any velocity near the speed of light will age only days for every week, month, or even year that passes on earth. Relativity does not present a problem for interstellar space travel, per se, but it does mean that interstellar civilizations or even just interstellar communications will require a mind-boggling amount of calendar juggling.

Did we mention that you'd have to travel at near the speed of light? That's because the distance between stars is so vast that even if you could travel at the speed of light—which, Larson reminds us, you can't—it would take more than four years to reach our closest star neighbors, Alpha Proxima and Alpha Centauri, and decades or centuries to reach the other stars in our "immediate neighborhood." And if you tried to accelerate directly to the speed of light like they do in the movies, you'd be instantly splattered on the back of your theoretical spacecraft. Achieving anything close to light speed will require sustained acceleration at a level that human bodies can withstand—say, a crushing two gravities—for over a year. Better hope somebody brings some chips.

Speaking of chips, food is going to be a problem. Since it is economically, if not physically, impossible to accelerate 200 years' worth of food to nearly the speed of light, and since you're not likely to find any grocery stores along the way, someone will have to figure out how to make food in space. Keeping a crew alive on the way turns out to be the trickiest part of all. Once you've got the nearly impossible physics of space travel worked out, you still have to figure out the chemistry and biology of keeping your air and water clean and keeping your crew fed and safe from radiation and infection, and—did we mention the 200 years?—you'll probably need several generations of crew members to complete the trip. Ever been on a bus for more than 24 hours? It's not a pretty picture.

We applaud Larson for his insightful writing and his scrupulous attention to scientific detail. For those of you seeking a cold, hard look at the reality of interstellar space travel, this is a stellar read. But be warned: Larson doesn't let you down gently. For those of you sincerely hoping to beam up with Scotty—and you know who you are—you might want to give this one a pass.

1. Which of the following would make the most appropriate title for this passage?

   A. Going Boldly Where No One Has Gone Before: The Promise and Peril of Interstellar Space Travel
   B. The Day the Earth Stood Still: Why Interstellar Space Travel Is Essential to Human Survival
   C. The Wrath of Larson: Egbert Larson's Quest to Build an Interstellar Spacecraft
   D. Busted Flat in Beta Regulus: The Crushing Challenges of Interstellar Space Travel
   E. Say It Isn't So, Mr. Einstein: Egbert Larson's Challenge to the Theory of Relativity

2. Based on the tone and content of the passage, it is most likely which of the following?

   A. A book review in a journal intended for astrophysics professionals
   B. A movie review in an entertainment industry publication
   C. A book review in a science magazine aimed at a general audience
   D. A book review in a newspaper
   E. A transcript of a talk given at a science fiction convention dedicated to "The poetry of space"

3. The passage implies that all except which of the following could be threats to human health during extended interstellar voyages?

   A. Meteor impact
   B. Radiation poisoning
   C. Accelerating too fast
   D. Starvation
   E. Old age

4. According to the passage, which of the following will present the most difficult challenge for humans attempting interstellar space travel?

   A. Achieving velocities near the speed of light
   B. Withstanding the acceleration necessary for traversing interstellar distances
   C. Maintaining clean air and water on a journey that could last centuries
   D. Accommodating the effects of relativistic time dilation
   E. Enabling the humans on board to survive during the journey

5. According to the information given in the passage, if two 20-year-old twins lived on earth, and one of them left on a journey for Alpha Centauri at very close to the speed of light, then managed to survive the journey and return to earth having aged 40 years during the journey, what could she expect to find upon her return to earth?

   A. Her great-grandmother
   B. Her twin at the age of 20
   C. Her twin at the age of 40
   D. Her twin at the age of 60
   E. Her twin's great-grandchildren

6. Which of the following inventions, if it could be perfected and manufactured at a viable cost, would address the most challenges to human interstellar space travel, as presented in the passage?

   A. A ram-scoop drive that can accelerate a spacecraft of any size to four-fifths of the speed of light within 24 hours
   B. A cold-sleep capsule that essentially halts the passage of time for human inhabitants while protecting them from all physical harm
   C. A sustainable biosphere that reliably generates healthy food and automatically cleans air and water
   D. A neutrino-based communications system that permits instantaneous communication across any distance without any relativistic time dilation
   E. An impervious force field that protects the ship and its inhabitants from radiation, meteor strikes, or hostile alien attacks

7. The author of the passage most likely mentions "Little Green Men" in the first paragraph for what purpose?

A. To poke fun at the ignorance of most science fiction readers

B. To introduce a daunting challenge that will have to be addressed before human interstellar space travel can become possible

C. To draw a comparison between the attempts of humans to voyage in space and the more successful attempts of other civilizations

D. To draw an amusing distinction between a supposed danger of space travel, as presented in the popular media, and the actual challenges posed by interstellar space travel, as perceived by scientists

E. To suggest that the concept of human interstellar space travel is as much of a myth as the "Little Green Men" that appear in science fiction movies and television programs

For the following questions, select the best of the answer choices given.

8. A wholesale fruit distributor, in an effort to increase its profit margins, has proposed cutting the tops off of the pineapples it ships in order to increase the number of pineapples it can ship in a standard-size truck.

Which of the following, if true, gives the strongest evidence that the fruit distributor's plan will increase its profit margins?

A. Pineapples with the tops cut off have been shown to rot three times faster than uncut fruit.

B. Customers buy whole pineapples in part because of their exotic, spiky appearance.

C. Cutting the tops off of pineapples may inadvertently remove some of the fruit within.

D. The fruit distributor ships primarily to a fruit canning company that has no use for pineapple tops.

E. Pineapple juice has been shown to be an even more potent source of vitamin C than orange or cranberry juice.

9. A brand of cough syrup comes with a measuring cup attached so that customers can measure the proper dosage. A consultant has pointed out that this cup is unnecessary, since most customers have measuring cups at home. Since the cups increase the cost of packaging the cough syrup and reduce the total number of units that can be shipped in a standard package, the consultant advises that the company can increase its net revenue on this product (total revenue minus total costs) by selling the cough syrup without the measuring cups.

Which of the following, if true, provides the strongest evidence that the company should not follow the consultant's advice?

A. Studies have shown that customers who use cough syrup without a measuring cup frequently take either too little or too much of the medicine, rendering the dosage either ineffective or, in cases of overdose, dangerous.

B. The company has included a measuring cup with each bottle of cough syrup for the last 18 years.

C. Studies have shown that 85 percent of consumers possess at home either a measuring cup, a set of measuring spoons, or both.

D. Many customers neglect to follow the recommended dosage of cough syrup even when the measuring cup is packaged along with the bottle of cough syrup.

E. Shipping the cough syrup bottles without the measuring cups will provide a marginal improvement in the number of cough syrup bottles that can be shipped in a standard package.

The following two questions are based on the following passage:

A study by a group of dentists has concluded that regular use of a certain brand of mouthwash is as effective as flossing in preventing gum disease. The mouthwash company has released a television ad suggesting that people who do not like flossing can now rely solely on mouthwash and brushing to maintain good dental health. A leading manufacturer of dental floss brought a lawsuit against the mouthwash company demanding that the advertisement be discontinued on the grounds that it is misleading.

10. Which of the following, if true, provides the strongest support for the dental floss company's claim that the advertisement is misleading?

A. The dental floss manufacturer is concerned that it will lose market share in the dental health market because the advertisement encourages people to switch from dental floss to mouthwash.

B. The dental floss company claims in its own advertisements that brushing and flossing after every meal is the most effective way to maintain good dental health.

C. Although mouthwash is an effective deterrent to gum disease, it is less effective than dental floss at removing plaque and preventing cavities between teeth.

D. Per usage, mouthwash is three times more expensive than dental floss, if the recommended amounts of both products are used.

E. The dentists who conducted the study on the effectiveness of mouthwash in preventing gum disease obtained their funding for the study from a company that manufactures mouthwash.

11. Which of the following, if true, most supports the mouthwash company's defense that its advertisement promotes greater public health?

A. Since the dental floss company is protesting the advertisement only to protect its own economic self-interest, it cannot be seen as representing greater public health.

B. Greater public health is best served if people use both mouthwash and dental floss, a combination that has been shown to be more effective than either method used alone.

C. Many people object to flossing because it is painful and causes their gums to bleed.

D. Since, on average, people are twice as likely to use mouthwash regularly as to floss regularly, the advertisement will increase the number of people who take effective action against gum disease, a serious public health problem.

E. Gum disease has been proven to have links with the early onset of heart disease, one of the top three threats to public health in terms of mortality.

12. An electrical appliance company has submitted a new model of washing machine for stress and durability testing. After the conventional round of tests, 26 of the 90 machines tested no longer functioned. Observing these results, the company determined that the washing machine model was acceptable for the consumer market.

Which of the following, if true, most strongly supports the company's decision regarding the washing machine?

A. When the number one rated washing machine was submitted for stress and durability testing, 96 out of 100 machines were still functioning at the end of the test.

B. Because of the extreme stress of the testing process, any model that has more than two-thirds of its machines functioning at the end of the test process is considered sufficiently durable for the consumer market.

C. Most consumers will tolerate a washing machine that functions only 64 times out of 90 attempts.

D. Although the model tested is less durable than other models on the market, its projected price is considerably lower than that of the most durable models.

E. The electrical failure that brought down most of the 26 washing machines that ceased functioning could probably be avoided if the machine were redesigned.

The following questions present a sentence, part of which or all of which is underlined. Beneath the sentence, you will find five ways of phrasing the underlined part. The first of these repeats the original; the other four are different. If you think the original is best, choose the first answer; otherwise choose one of the others.

These questions test correctness and effectiveness of expression. In choosing your answer, follow the requirements of standard written English; that is, pay attention to grammar, choice of words, and sentence construction. Choose the answer that produces the most effective sentence; this answer should be clear and exact, without awkwardness, ambiguity, redundancy, or grammatical error.

13. Having accounted for only 13 percent of the student body at Northlake High, students who attended Megalopolis Middle School dominate the Northlake High student government.

   A. Having accounted for
   B. With
   C. Despite having been
   D. Although accounting for
   E. As

14. Because the key witness died just prior to the start of the trial, <u>Detectives Mack and Smith were not able in determining the extent of</u> administrative corruption.

   A. Detectives Mack and Smith were not able in determining the extent of
   B. therefore the detectives, Mack and Smith, were unable to determine the extent of
   C. Mack and Smith, the detectives, were not able of determining the extent to
   D. Detectives Mack and Smith were not able to determine the extent of
   E. the extent was unable to be determined by Detectives Mack and Smith of

15. Health Department statistics demonstrate that children <u>reading high on glucose with family histories of diabetes</u> are twice as likely as the general population to develop diabetes.

   A. reading high on glucose with family histories of diabetes
   B. with high glucose readings whose families have a history of diabetes
   C. with high glucose readings and who have a diabetic history in the family
   D. having high glucose readings and also having histories of diabetes in their family
   E. with a history of diabetes running in the family and with high glucose readings

16. Medical experts have amassed evidence concluding that users of smokeless tobacco <u>be more prone to heart disease, hypertension, and mouth cancers</u> than people who do not use smokeless tobacco.

   A. be more prone to heart disease, hypertension, and mouth cancers
   B. are proner to heart disease, hypertension, and mouth cancers
   C. are more prone to heart disease, hypertension, and mouth cancers
   D. experience heart disease, hypertension, and mouth cancers at heightened rates
   E. suffer heart disease, hypertension, and mouth cancers at a higher risk

17. Chef Sylvia Bostock's eclectic offerings at her new restaurant, Sylvia's, range from an Asian-inspired tuna tartelette in a soy-ginger demiglace <u>with</u> a succulent cowboy rib-eye served atop a small mountain of fried onions.

   A. with
   B. to
   C. in addition to
   D. and
   E. and to

18. The governing board of the new league has modified its rules so that preexisting teams can stay together even though <u>not all their members meet the new minimum age requirement</u>.

   A. not all their members meet the new minimum age requirement
   B. the new minimum age requirement has not been met by all their members
   C. not all their members have met the new minimum age, as required
   D. all their members have not met the new minimum age requirement
   E. all their members do not meet the new minimum age requirement

For the following questions, select the best of the answer choices given.

19. Since 1960, the fast-growing town of Hotstone, Arizona, has drawn water from the Gray River, which feeds Lake Mudfish. If the town's water use continues to grow at its present rate, in about 20 years the water level of Lake Mudfish will inevitably decrease to the point that it can no longer support its biologically fragile population of fish.

The prediction above is based on which of the following assumptions?

A. As the town's water requirements grow, it will not be able to meet those requirements by drawing on water sources other than the Gray River.
B. Since 1960, the lake's population of fish has become more biologically fragile.
C. The amount of water that the lake loses to evaporation each year will increase over the next two decades.
D. There are multiple sources of water besides the Gray River that feed into Lake Mudfish.
E. The town of Hotstone will be able to reverse its trend of increasing water use if it implements an aggressive water conservation program.

20. Public protests can cause even the most powerful companies to change their policies. For example, an activist group recently staged a demonstration in front of the HydraBore corporate headquarters to protest the company's use of the chemical Ectomazathol. Within three months of the demonstration, HydraBore replaced Ectomazathol in its production plants with another chemical.

Which of the following, if true, casts the most doubt on the connection between the public protest and the decision of the company to change chemicals?

A. Preliminary studies show that the new chemical may be more carcinogenic than Ectomazathol.
B. The recently introduced chemical that is replacing Ectomazathol is less expensive and more effective in its industrial application than Ectomazathol.
C. HydraBore devoted no publicity efforts to announce its switch from Ectomazathol to the new chemical.
D. As protests against HydraBore have become more frequent, the company has subsequently increased its public relations budget.
E. The activist group that staged the demonstration has been linked to illegal acts of theft and sabotage within other corporate headquarters.

21. A recent spate of art thefts at a major museum has led to a drastic increase in the insurance premiums that the museum must pay to insure its collection. Many art fans are concerned that the museum, which traditionally has charged no entrance fee, will be forced to charge a high entrance fee in order to pay for the increased insurance premiums.

Which of the following, if true, would most alleviate the concern of the art fans that the museum will be forced to charge high entrance fees?

A. Law enforcement officials recently apprehended the Belgian Bobcat, a notorious art thief who has been linked to at least 20 art heists.
B. Citing a dispute with the insurance company over the terms of its coverage, the museum has chosen to cancel its insurance policy.
C. The majority of visitors to the museum are schoolchildren, who could not reasonably be expected to pay a high entrance fee.
D. The museum pays for the majority of its total expenses from its large endowment, which is earmarked specifically for purchasing new art.
E. The museum recently installed a state-of-the-art burglar alarm system that will make future thefts almost impossible.

22. Which of the following, if true, best completes the passage below?

The traditional view of Homer is that of a blind bard who wrote down the epic poems known as the *Iliad* and the *Odyssey* in the eighth century B.C.E. We know now, however, that this picture cannot be true. The language used in the epic poems contains elements of the Greek language dating from the twelfth to the eighth centuries B.C.E., but the Greek writing system was not developed until the late seventh century, when it was used to record clerical notes. A more accurate statement regarding Homer, therefore, is that, if he existed, he most likely _____.

A. wrote the poems down in the fifth century B.C.E., using a preexisting oral tradition of Greek epic poetry.
B. was involved in the recording of clerical notes in Greek in the seventh century.
C. composed the poems orally in the eighth century and then dictated them to a scribe in the late seventh century.
D. composed the poems orally in the twelfth century, using a predecessor of the Greek language.
E. composed the poems orally in the eighth century, using elements of preexisting Greek epic poetry.

The questions in this group are based on the content of a passage. After reading the passage, choose the best answer to each question. Answer all questions following the passage on the basis of what is <u>stated</u> or <u>implied</u> in the passage.

One of the biggest questions facing the art world today is the dilemma over the repatriation of cultural treasures. Although the subject has not been widely noted by the general public, in recent decades museums and art dealers have repeatedly faced off against the representatives of nations and ethnic groups whose cultural legacies have been robbed by the rapacious collecting of these so-called art experts. Advocates of repatriation have argued that cultural treasures should be returned to their nations of origin, both because of basic fairness and because the artwork and cultural artifacts in question are best understood within their local context.

Several prominent museums, most notably the British Museum in London and the Louvre in Paris, have defended themselves on the grounds that they can better protect and preserve these cultural treasures than can the developing nations and impoverished ethnic groups that frequently seek their return. They further argue that more people can see the treasures if they are proudly displayed in a major museum, as opposed to some poorly funded national museum in a backwater country; evidently, the quantity of viewers is more important than the relevance of the art and artifacts to the viewer.

The arguments of the museum curators fall apart in an instance such as the Elgin Marbles. These majestic marble sculptures, which once graced the Parthenon on the Acropolis in Athens, were stolen by Lord Elgin in the nineteenth century and given to the British Museum, which holds them to this day. The people of Athens have built a beautiful, modern museum on the Acropolis to display the Elgin Marbles and other treasures from the Greek cultural heritage, so there can be no valid argument that the Greeks are unable to house the sculptures properly. Furthermore, more people visit the Acropolis every day than visit the British Museum.

23. Of the following, the most appropriate title for the passage above would be:

A. The Elgin Marbles: Timeless Symbols of the Glory That Was Greece
B. The Role of Great Museums in the Preservation of Cultural Artifacts
C. Repatriation of Cultural Treasures: The British Museum's Dirty Little Secret
D. The Value of Cultural Treasures in Defining National Identity
E. A Curious Curator: Lord Elgin and the Rise of the British Museum

24. The third paragraph plays what role in the passage?

A. It summarizes all the points expressed in the first two paragraphs.
B. It raises new arguments that expand on those previously expressed.
C. It suggests a possible area for useful research in the future.
D. It rejects the arguments expressed in the first paragraph.
E. It provides concrete evidence against arguments expressed in the second paragraph.

25. The situation involving the repatriation of the Elgin Marbles to Athens is most similar to which of the following?

A. A Native American tribe in Oregon requests that a museum in Chicago return some ceremonial masks that could help in fundraising efforts to build a proposed museum in Portland.

B. The nation of Peru in South America threatens the nation of Ecuador with military action if Ecuador does not hand over various gold artifacts of the Inca Empire, which originated in Peru.

C. The National Archeology Museum of Cairo in Egypt requests that the Louvre return eight mummies from the time of Ramses the Great for the Cairo Museum's new exhibit hall dedicated to artifacts from Ramses' court.

D. The nation of Greece requests the nation of Turkey to provide Greek archeologists with free access to ancient Greek sites on the Ionian coast of Turkey, and to transfer any cultural artifacts found there to the National Archeology Museum in Athens.

E. A museum in Baton Rouge, Louisiana, requests that the Texas History Museum in Austin, Texas, send the original "Lone Star" flag to Baton Rouge for a new exhibit entitled, "Texas: Our Neighbor to the East."

26. What is the purpose of the final sentence of the passage?

A. To express pride in the cultural treasures of Athens

B. To refute the argument that more people can see the Elgin Marbles at the British Museum than at the Acropolis

C. To comment on the relative number of tourists at two of Europe's most famous tourist attractions

D. To express concern that the large number of tourists on the Acropolis will damage the Elgin Marbles, should they be returned

E. To provide an appropriate end to a rousing debate

27. The author's attitude toward museum curators who oppose the repatriation of cultural treasures is best summarized as what?

A. Righteous indignation
B. Bemused sarcasm
C. Seething anger
D. Condescending approval
E. Grudging admiration

28. Which of the following, if true, would best support the position taken by the advocates of repatriation, as expressed in the first paragraph?

A. Of seven gold Inca statues sent from the Field Museum in Chicago to the National Archeology Museum in Lima, Peru, four were stolen within six months of being put on display.

B. Mummies taken from the dry heat of Egypt and relocated to the damp climate of London have shown disturbing signs of decay.

C. Operating a first-rate art and archeology museum is financially unfeasible for most developing nations, which face a difficult enough challenge feeding their people.

D. A type of sculpture from central Africa appears dull and nondescript in a museum setting, but when placed in the region of its origin can clearly be seen to replicate the colors and shapes of local rock formations.

E. British colonists in India in the nineteenth century felt that it was their right to claim the nation's artistic treasures as their own in exchange for importing the benefits of a modern industrial society.

The following questions present a sentence, part of which or all of which is underlined. Beneath the sentence, you will find five ways of phrasing the underlined part. The first of these repeats the original; the other four are different. If you think the original is best, choose the first answer; otherwise choose one of the others.

These questions test correctness and effectiveness of expression. In choosing your answer, follow the requirements of standard written English; that is, pay attention to grammar, choice of words, and sentence construction. Choose the answer that produces the most effective sentence; this answer should be clear and exact, without awkwardness, ambiguity, redundancy, or grammatical error.

29. According to government health statistics, <u>Americans born before 1925 develop obesity by the age of 65 only 8 percent of the time, but 35 percent of those born since 1950 did so by age 35.</u>

A. Americans born before 1925 develop obesity by the age of 65 only 8 percent of the time, but 35 percent of those born since 1950 did so by age 35.
B. only 8 percent of Americans born before 1925 developed obesity by the age of 65; if they are born since 1950, 35 percent develop obesity by the age 35.
C. only 8 percent of Americans born before 1925 developed obesity by the age of 65; of those born since 1950, 35 percent developed obesity by the age of 35.
D. obesity develops by the age of 65 in only 8 percent of Americans born before 1925, and by 35 by the 35 percent born since 1950.
E. of Americans born before 1925, only 8 percent of them have developed obesity by the age of 65, but 35 percent of those born since 1950 do by the age of 35.

30. In his groundbreaking work on special relativity, Albert Einstein displayed an intellectual boldness in the face of a reluctant scientific establishment that was <u>not unlike that of Galileo Galilei, who refused</u> to accept the intellectual limits placed on him by the censors of the Church.

A. not unlike that of Galileo Galilei, who refused
B. like Galileo Galilei and his refusal
C. not unlike Galileo Galilei, who refused
D. like that of Galileo Galilei for refusing
E. as that of Galileo Galilei, who refused

31. <u>The rising of the rate</u> of tardiness among MegaTech employees has generated concern among management that the employees are not sufficiently focused on increasing shareholder value.

A. The rising of the rate
B. Rising rates
C. The rising rate
D. Because of the rising rate
E. Because the rising rate

32. Increasingly over the last few years, corporations involved in patent litigation <u>have</u> <u>opted to settle the lawsuit rather than facing</u> the protracted legal expenses of a court battle.

A. have opted to settle the lawsuit rather than facing
B. have opted settling the lawsuit instead of facing
C. have opted to settle the lawsuit rather than face
D. had opted for settlement of the lawsuit instead of facing
E. had opted to settle the lawsuit rather than face

33. The ManStop, Boston's hot new men's clothing store, offers a selection that <u>is on range from</u> conservative pin-striped suits for that day at the office to stylish cashmere pullovers for that night on the town.

A. is on range from
B. ranging from
C. ranges to
D. ranges from
E. having ranged from

For the following questions, select the best of the answer choices given.

34. An agricultural cooperative wants to sell more of its less popular vegetables, zucchini in particular. A consultant has suggested that the cooperative's farmers should attempt to market a purple form of zucchini instead of the conventional green form, because people generally dislike green-colored vegetables.

Which of the following, if true, casts the most doubt on the accuracy of the consultant's assertion?

A. Broccoli and green peas, which are both green vegetables, are among the most popular vegetables in the country.
B. Grapes and eggplants, which both have purple skin, are popular among consumers of all ages.
C. Summer squash, a yellow-colored cousin of the zucchini, is one of the most popular summer vegetables.
D. Green tomatoes are far less popular than red tomatoes.
E. A chewing gum company reports that its purple-colored grape gum is less popular than its green-colored sour apple flavor.

35. Homely Hotels has a customer loyalty program in which for every four nights a customer spends at a Homely Hotel, he or she receives a coupon good for one free night at any Homely Hotel. Recently people have begun selling these coupons on the Internet for less than the cost of a night at a Homely Hotel. This marketing of coupons has resulted in decreased revenue for the Homely Hotel chain.

To discourage this undesirable trade in free-stay coupons, it would be best for Homely Hotels to restrict:

A. The number of coupons a customer can receive in one year.

B. Use of the coupons to the specific hotel in which they were issued.

C. The valid dates of the coupons to only the month immediately following the date of issue.

D. Use of the coupons to the recipient or people with the same last name.

E. Use of the coupons to Homely Hotel franchises that charge an equal or lesser nightly rate than the franchise that issued the coupon.

36. An American manufacturer of space heaters reported a 1994 fourth-quarter net income (total income minus total costs) of $41 million, compared with $28.3 million in the fourth quarter of 1993. This increase was realized despite a drop in U.S. domestic retail sales of space-heating units toward the end of the fourth quarter of 1994 as a result of unusually high temperatures.

Which of the following, if true, would contribute most to an explanation of the increase in the manufacturer's net income?

A. In the fourth quarter of 1994, the manufacturer paid its assembly-line workers no salaries in November or December because of a two-month-long strike, but the company had a sufficient stock of space-heating units on hand to supply its distributors.

B. In 1993, because of unusually cold weather in the Northeast, the federal government authorized the diversion of emergency funding for purchasing space-heating units to be used in the hardest-hit areas.

C. Foreign manufacturers of space heaters reported improved fourth-quarter sales in the American market compared with their sales in 1993.

D. During the fourth quarter of 1994, the manufacturer announced that it would introduce an extra-high-capacity space heater in the following quarter.

E. In the third quarter of 1994, a leading consumer magazine advocated space heaters as a cost-effective way to heat spaces of less than 100 square feet.

The following questions present a sentence, part of which or all of which is underlined. Beneath the sentence, you will find five ways of phrasing the underlined part. The first of these repeats the original; the other four are different. If you think the original is best, choose the first answer; otherwise choose one of the others.

These questions test correctness and effectiveness of expression. In choosing your answer, follow the requirements of standard written English; that is, pay attention to grammar, choice of words, and sentence construction. Choose the answer that produces the most effective sentence; this answer should be clear and exact, without awkwardness, ambiguity, redundancy, or grammatical error.

37. Archeological excavations of Roman ruins on the Greek island of Crete show that securing control over the maritime trade routes of the Eastern Mediterranean was a primary goal of the Romans, as it was of the Greeks in preceding centuries.

A. as it was of the Greeks

B. like that of the Greeks

C. as that of the Greeks

D. just as the Greeks did

E. as did the Greeks

38. The family's mood, which had been enthusiastic at the beginning of the trip, sank as the temperature has risen, dramatically, but not enough for calling off the whole trip.

A. has risen, dramatically, but not enough for calling

B. has risen, but not dramatically enough to call

C. rose, but not so dramatically as to call

D. rose, but not dramatically enough to call

E. rose, but not dramatically enough for calling

39. Although no proof yet exists <u>of the electromagnetic disturbances observed being the results of nuclear weapons testing</u>, diplomats are treating the situation with utmost delicacy.

   A. of the electromagnetic disturbances observed being the results of nuclear weapons testing

   B. regarding the observed electromagnetic disturbances having been the results of nuclear weapons testing

   C. that the electromagnetic disturbances observed were the results of nuclear weapons testing

   D. that nuclear weapons testing resulted in the electromagnetic disturbances having been observed

   E. that the electromagnetic disturbance observed were resulting from nuclear weapons testing

40. Hip dysplasia is more common among German shepherds <u>than</u> dogs of other breeds.

   A. than

   B. than is so of

   C. compared to

   D. in comparison with

   E. than among

41. <u>The only lucid arguments printed in the newspaper concerning the new bond proposal was put forth by the high school principal who wrote a series of letters to the newspaper's editor.</u>

   A. The only lucid arguments printed in the newspaper concerning the new bond proposal was put forth by the high school principal in a series of letters to the newspaper's editor.

   B. The principal of the high school wrote a series of letters to the newspaper's editor that put forth the only lucid argument concerning the new bond proposal that was printed in the newspaper.

   C. In a series of letters to the newspaper's editor, the principal of the high school put forth the only lucid argument concerning the new bond proposal to be printed in the newspaper.

   D. The high school's principal's series of letters to the newspaper's editor lucidly put forth the only arguments concerning the new bond proposal to be printed in the newspaper.

   E. Putting forth the only lucid arguments concerning the new bond proposal to be printed in the newspaper, the series of letters to the newspaper's editor were written by the high school's principal.

Practice Test 4

ANALYTICAL WRITING 1
Analysis of an Issue

TIME—30 MINUTES

DIRECTIONS: In this section, you will need to analyze the issue presented and explain your views on it. There is no "correct" answer. Instead, you should consider various perspectives as you develop your own position on the issue.

Read the statement and the instructions that follow it, and then make any notes that will help you plan your response. Write your response on a separate sheet of paper. If possible, type your essay on a word processor. Observe the 30-minute time limit.

> Since unhealthy people increase health-care costs for all of society, society should impose greater penalties on those people who voluntarily indulge in unhealthy activities, such as smoking, excessive drinking, or overeating.
>
> Discuss the extent to which you agree or disagree with the opinion stated above. Support your views with reasons and/or examples from your own experiences, observations, or reading.

ANALYTICAL WRITING 2

Analysis of an Argument

TIME—30 MINUTES

DIRECTIONS: In this section, you will be asked to write a critique of the argument presented below. You may, for example, consider what questionable assumptions underlie the thinking, what alternative explanations or counterexamples might weaken the conclusion, or what sort of evidence could help strengthen or refute the argument.

Read the argument and the instructions that follow it, and then make any notes that will help you plan your response. Write your response on a separate sheet of paper. If possible, type your essay on a word processor. Observe the 30-minute time limit.

The following statement appeared in a consumer magazine:

A fear of crime has led many homeowners to purchase monitored burglar alarm systems, but these people are wasting their money. The primary benefit of any burglar alarm system is one of deterrence, and this effect can be achieved just as well by having a sign in front of the house suggesting that the house is equipped with an alarm, whether or not the alarm system is monitored or even exists. Moreover, if a sign fails to deter burglars from entering a house, there is very little chance that the guards who monitor the alarm system will arrive at the home in time to catch the burglars, since the burglars will surely leave as soon as the alarm sounds. Therefore, while it makes sense to have a sign suggesting that a house has a monitored alarm, and it may make sense to have an audible alarm, there is no reason to pay the high monthly fee for a monitored system.

Discuss how well reasoned you find this argument. In your discussion, be sure to analyze the line of reasoning and the use of evidence in the argument. For example, you may need to consider what questionable assumptions underlie the thinking and what alternative examples or counterexamples might weaken the conclusion. You can also discuss what sort of evidence would strengthen or refute the argument, what changes in the argument would make it more logically sound, and what, if anything, would help you better evaluate its conclusion.

The following data sufficiency problems consist of a question and two statements, labeled (1) and (2), in which certain data are given. You have to decide whether the data given in the statements are sufficient for answering the question. Using the data given in the statements plus your knowledge of mathematics and everyday facts (such as the number of days in July or the meaning of counterclockwise), you must indicate whether

A. Statement (1) ALONE is sufficient, but statement (2) alone is not sufficient.
B. Statement (2) ALONE is sufficient, but statement (1) alone is not sufficient.
C. BOTH statements TOGETHER are sufficient, but NEITHER statement ALONE is sufficient.
D. EACH statement ALONE is sufficient.
E. Statements (1) and (2) TOGETHER are NOT sufficient.

NUMBERS: All numbers used are real numbers.

FIGURES: A figure accompanying a data sufficiency problem will conform to the information given in the question, but will not necessarily conform to the additional information given in statements (1) and (2). Lines shown as straight can be assumed to be straight, and lines that appear jagged can also be assumed to be straight. You may assume that the position of points, angles, regions, etc., exist in the order shown and that angle measures are greater than zero. All figures lie in a plane unless otherwise indicated.

NOTE: In data sufficiency problems that ask for the value of a quantity, the data given in the statements are sufficient only when it is possible to determine exactly one numerical value for the quantity.

1. In the figure above, is $AB > BC$? (*Note*: Figure not necessarily drawn to scale.)

   (1) $AB > CD$
   (2) $(AD - AB) > (AD - BC)$

2. A box contains 90 jelly beans, of which some are orange, some are purple, and some are black. How many black jelly beans are in the box?

   (1) There are 27 orange jelly beans.
   (2) There are twice as many purple jelly beans as orange jelly beans.

3. Is 3^x greater than 100?

   (1) $9x = 36$
   (2) $\frac{1}{3^x} > 0.01$

4. How many more dogs than cats are in the veterinarian's office?

   (1) There is a total of 30 dogs and cats in the office.
   (2) The number of cats is the square root of the number of dogs.

5. If p is a positive integer, and $p \neq 0$, is $\dfrac{p^2 + p}{2p}$ an integer?

    (1) p is an even number.
    (2) p is a multiple of 3.

Solve the problem and indicate the best of the answer choices given.

NUMBERS: All numbers used are real numbers.

FIGURES: A figure accompanying a problem-solving question is intended to provide information useful in solving the problem. Figures are drawn as accurately as possible EXCEPT when it is stated in a specific problem that its figure is not drawn to scale. Straight lines may sometimes appear jagged. All figures lie in a plane unless otherwise indicated.

6. A certain prosthodontist specializes in implanting gold and silver teeth in his patients' mouths. He charges $650 for a gold tooth and $325 for a silver tooth. If his total fees for implanting gold and silver teeth last week were $15,925 in total, and he implanted five more gold teeth than silver teeth, how many teeth in total did he implant over the week?

    A. 31
    B. 32
    C. 33
    D. 34
    E. 35

7. What is the ratio of 3/7 to the product 3(7/3)?

    A. 3:7
    B. 1:3
    C. 3:21
    D. 1:7
    E. 3:49

8. If the average (arithmetic mean) of a and b is 110, and the average of b and c is 160, what is the value of $a - c$?

    A. −220
    B. −100
    C. 100
    D. 135
    E. It cannot be determined from the information given

9. A travel company wants to charter a plane to the Bahamas. Chartering the plane costs $8,000. So far, 18 people have signed up for the trip. If the company charges $300 per ticket, how many more passengers must sign up for the trip before the company can make any profit on the charter?

    A. 7
    B. 8
    C. 13
    D. 27
    E. 45

10. If $x^2 + 9x - 3 = 3x^2 + 2x(4 - x)$, then $x^2 =$

    A. 2
    B. 3
    C. 4
    D. 9
    E. 16

11. The pilot of a small aircraft with a 40-gallon fuel tank wants to fly to Cleveland, which is 480 miles away. The pilot recognizes that the current engine, which can fly only 8 miles per gallon, will not get him there. By how many miles per gallon must the aircraft's fuel efficiency be improved to make the flight to Cleveland possible?

    A. 2
    B. 4
    C. 12
    D. 40
    E. 160

12. A circle graph shows how the MegaTech corporation allocates its Research and Development budget: 14% microphotonics; 24% home electronics; 15% food additives; 29% genetically modified microorganisms; 8% industrial lubricants; and the remainder for basic astrophysics. If the arc of each sector of the graph is proportional to the percentage of the budget it represents, how many degrees of the circle are used to represent basic astrophysics research?

    A. 8°
    B. 10°
    C. 18°
    D. 36°
    E. 52°

The following data sufficiency problems consist of a question and two statements, labeled (1) and (2), in which certain data are given. You have to decide whether the data given in the statements are <u>sufficient</u> for answering the question. Using the data given in the statements <u>plus</u> your knowledge of mathematics and everyday facts (such as the number of days in July or the meaning of *counterclockwise*), you must indicate whether

A. Statement (1) ALONE is sufficient, but statement (2) alone is not sufficient.
B. Statement (2) ALONE is sufficient, but statement (1) alone is not sufficient.
C. BOTH statements TOGETHER are sufficient, but NEITHER statement ALONE is sufficient.
D. EACH statement ALONE is sufficient.
E. Statements (1) and (2) TOGETHER are NOT sufficient.

13. If $x + y = 36$, what is the value of xy?

   (1) $y - x = 14$
   (2) $y = 2x + 3$

14. A hotdog vendor sold $45 worth of hotdogs at lunchtime Tuesday. Each hotdog cost $1.50. What percentage of his day's stock of hotdogs did the vendor sell at lunchtime?

   (1) The vendor started the day with 120 hotdogs.
   (2) The vendor sold twice as many hotdogs at dinnertime as he sold at lunchtime.

15. For real numbers a, b, and c, is $ab = bc + 3$?

   (1) $ab = 3b$
   (2) $b + 3 = c$

16. What is the number of male employees at the factory?

   (1) If the factory were to hire 150 more employees and 2/3 of them were female, the ratio of male to female employees would be 8:3.
   (2) The factory has at least twice as many male employees as female employees, and it employs at least 150 females.

Solve the problem and indicate the best of the answer choices given.

17. An engineer designed a ball so that when it was dropped, it rose with each bounce exactly one-half as high as it had fallen. The engineer dropped the ball from a 16-meter platform and caught it after it had traveled 46.5 meters. How many times did the ball bounce?

   A. 5
   B. 6
   C. 7
   D. 8
   E. 9

The following two questions refer to the following diagram:

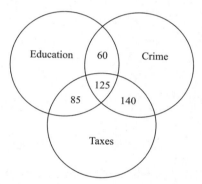

A newspaper polled 1,000 likely voters about which of the following issues, if any, played an important role in their decision-making process for an upcoming election: education, crime, and/or taxes. Of the voters surveyed, a total of 495 named education, 490 named crime, and 440 named taxes. In the figure above, the overlapping areas between two circles represent the people who named only those two items; the overlapping area between the three circles represents those people who named all three issues.

18. What percentage of those polled named only education or only crime but no other issue?

   A. 25.5%
   B. 31.5%
   C. 39%
   D. 55%
   E. 98.5%

19. How many of the 1,000 people polled responded "none of the above" to the questions?

A. 140
B. 110
C. 80
D. 20
E. 0

20. The equation $\dfrac{R-3}{28} = \dfrac{S+8}{35}$ relates the values of two linked currencies, where R is the value in dollars of one currency and S is the value in dollars of the other currency. Which of the following equations can be used to convert dollar values from the R currency to the S currency?

A. $S = \dfrac{5R-47}{4}$

B. $S = \dfrac{4R+47}{5}$

C. $S = \dfrac{5R+17}{4}$

D. $S = \dfrac{4R-17}{5}$

E. $S = \dfrac{5R}{4} - 12$

21. If x is a positive number and 1/2 the square root of x is the cube root of x, then $x =$

A. 64
B. 32
C. 16
D. 4
E. 1

22. If Josh, Doug, and Brad have a total of $72 among them, and Josh has three times as much money as Brad but only three-fourths as much as Doug, how much money does Doug have?

A. $8
B. $9
C. $27
D. $32
E. $36

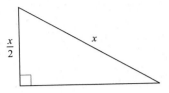

23. The flat triangular lot depicted above is available for development. If $x + \dfrac{x}{2} = $ 150 meters, what is the area of the lot in square meters?

A. 125
B. $150\sqrt{3}$
C. 1,500
D. $1,250\sqrt{3}$
E. $2,500\sqrt{3}$

24. For any numbers w and z, $w \cdot z = w^3 z(8 - w^2)$. If both z and $w \cdot z$ are positive numbers, which of the following could be a value of w?

A. 9
B. 3
C. 0
D. −2
E. −9

25. $\dfrac{\frac{1}{4} + \frac{1}{5}}{\frac{1}{8}} =$

A. $\dfrac{2}{5}$

B. $\dfrac{9}{20}$

C. $\dfrac{9}{8}$

D. $\dfrac{9}{5}$

E. $\dfrac{18}{5}$

26. Last year's receipts from the sale of greeting cards during the week before Mother's Day totaled $189 million, which represented 9 percent of total greeting card sales for the year. Total greeting card sales for the year totaled how many million dollars?

A. 17,010
B. 2,100
C. 1,890
D. 1,701
E. 210

27. What is the value of $5x^2 - 1.9x - 3.7$ for $x = -0.3$?

A. −4.72
B. −3.82
C. −3.58
D. −2.68
E. 0.57

The following data sufficiency problems consist of a question and two statements, labeled (1) and (2), in which certain data are given. You have to decide whether the data given in the statements are <u>sufficient</u> for answering the question. Using the data given in the statements <u>plus</u> your knowledge of mathematics and everyday facts (such as the number of days in July or the meaning of *counterclockwise*), you must indicate whether

A.   Statement (1) ALONE is sufficient, but statement (2) alone is not sufficient.
B.   Statement (2) ALONE is sufficient, but statement (1) alone is not sufficient.
C.   BOTH statements TOGETHER are sufficient, but NEITHER statement ALONE is sufficient.
D.   EACH statement ALONE is sufficient.
E.   Statements (1) and (2) TOGETHER are NOT sufficient.

28. Two cyclists are racing up a mountain at different constant rates. Cyclist A is now 50 meters ahead of cyclist B. How many minutes from now will cyclist A be 150 meters ahead of cyclist B?

(1) 5 minutes ago, cyclist A was 200 meters behind cyclist B.
(2) Cyclist A is moving 25% faster than cyclist B.

29. Is integer x divisible by 48?

(1) x is divisible by 16.
(2) x is divisible by 12.

30. Is $3 < \sqrt{x} < 5$?

(1) $x < 20$
(2) $x > 5$

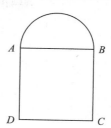

31. The figure above shows the shape of a brick patio. If arc AB is a semicircle and $ABCD$ is a square, what is the perimeter of the patio?

(1) The radius of the semicircle described by arc AB is 4.
(2) The perimeter of the square $ABCD$ is 32.

32. A call to Rosie's Psychic Hotline costs \$5.99 for the first 2 minutes and \$1.99 for each additional minute. Stuart called the hotline for x minutes, where x is an integer. How many minutes long was the call?

(1) The total charge for the call was \$11.96.
(2) The charge for the last 3 minutes of the call was \$0.01 less than half the total cost of the call.

33. If Z is represented by the decimal $0.W7$, what is the digit W?

(1) $Z > \dfrac{2}{3}$
(2) $Z > \dfrac{9}{10}$

Solve the problem and indicate the best of the answer choices given.

34. If a cube has a volume of 125, what is the surface area of one side?

A. 5
B. 25
C. 50
D. 150
E. 625

35. An investor bought 200 shares of stock in ABCD company in 1990. By 1992, the investment was worth only $\frac{2}{3}$ of its original value. By 1995, the 200 shares were worth only $\frac{1}{2}$ of their value in 1990. By what percent did the value of the investment drop from 1992 to 1995?

A. $16\frac{2}{3}\%$

B. 25%

C. $33\frac{1}{3}\%$

D. 50%

E. $66\frac{2}{3}\%$

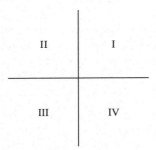

36. In the rectangular quadrant system shown above, which quadrant, if any, contains no point (x, y) that satisfies the equation $x^2 - 2y = 3$?

A. none
B. I
C. II
D. III
E. IV

37. Which of the following cannot be the median of five positive integers a, b, c, d, and e?

A. a

B. $d + e$

C. $b + c + d$

D. $\dfrac{b + c + d}{3}$

E. $\dfrac{a + b + c + d + e}{5}$

For the following questions, select the best of the answer choices given.

1. Companies that advertise on television complain that digital television recording (DTR) services make it possible for consumers to watch television programs without viewing the commercials that these advertisers have paid the television networks to broadcast. The DTR service providers respond that their services may actually help the advertisers, because without their service, many consumers would not have been able to watch the programs—or the commercials in them—in the first place.

Which of the following, if true, offers the most support to the advertisers' claims that the DTR services are currently hurting their businesses?

A. Even the best commercials are usually less entertaining than the programs that consumers choose to watch for themselves.
B. DTR services charge such high rates that only a small percentage of consumers subscribe to them.
C. The average per-second cost of advertising on television has risen every year for the past two decades.
D. More than 90 percent of subscribers to DTR services opt to use a setting that automatically edits out commercials.
E. DTR services alter the television viewing experience by allowing customers to view the program of their choice at the time of their choosing.

2. When airlines were deregulated in the 1970s, the average price of a ticket was $135. Three decades later, the average price is $275, there are twice as many in-air collisions, fliers in small markets are at the mercy of predatory carriers, and air rage is at an all-time high. It is time to re-regulate the air travel industry.

All of the following statements, if true, weaken the above argument except for which statement?

A. Because of inflation, a $275 ticket today is actually 10 to 20 percent less expensive than a $135 ticket was in 1975.
B. Deregulation has increased the choices available to fliers in terms of both time of flight and carrier.
C. Airlines are currently flying more than five times as many passenger miles per year as they did in 1975.
D. Compared with passengers in large urban areas, passengers in small markets pay, on average, twice as much per mile flown on domestic flights because their airports are generally served by fewer airlines.
E. Psychologists have been able to determine no connection between the deregulation of the airline industry and the onset of increased levels of air rage.

3. Skilled blacksmiths who could forge useful items out of iron used to play a central role in American life. The onset of industrialization and the mass production of iron products, however, have made the blacksmith's traditional role mostly obsolete. Still, there will always be a job available for a good blacksmith.

Which of the following, if true, provides the most support for the conclusion that a job will always be available for a good blacksmith?

A. Many people are willing to pay considerably more for tools hand-crafted by a blacksmith than for tools created by a machine.
B. Blacksmiths cannot produce iron products with the speed or consistency of machines.
C. Blacksmiths traditionally apprenticed to a master blacksmith for seven or more years before entering business independently.
D. The cowboy never would have conquered the West without the horseshoes crafted by blacksmiths.
E. As skilled craftsmen, blacksmiths traditionally served as community leaders throughout North America and Europe.

4. When unscrupulous people shoplift, a vicious cycle results. Retailers must raise their prices in order to make up for the lost sales, and the higher prices encourage more people to shoplift. This vicious cycle hurts honest consumers worst of all, because they have to pay higher prices.

The vicious cycle described above could not happen unless which of the following is true?

A. Shoplifters usually steal only items that they need but cannot afford.
B. Retailers do not take shoplifting losses into account when they initially set their prices.
C. The best way for retailers to address shoplifting is by punishing shoplifters to the fullest extent of the law.
D. Some people would shoplift no matter how low retailers set their prices.
E. It costs retailers more to pay security guards to prevent shoplifting than just to absorb the cost of occasional losses due to theft.

5. When Brad offered his old wooden desk at a garage sale, no one bought it, even though he offered it for only $10. When he offered it at the local auction house, however, someone bought it for $850.

Which of the following, if true, best explains why Brad was able to sell the desk for a high price at the auction while he could not sell it for a much lower price at the garage sale?

A. Brad advertised that the proceeds of the garage sale would benefit a local charity, while he made no such claims for the proceeds from the auction.
B. One of the legs of the desk was shorter than the other three, producing an unbalanced writing surface.
C. The auction house specializes in selling antique furniture, which is generally valued more highly than the discarded furniture sold at garage sales.
D. Brad insisted that anyone who bought the desk had to use it as an actual workspace.
E. Prospective buyers at auctions are often more interested in the auction process than in the items up for bid.

The following questions present a sentence, part of which or all of which is underlined. Beneath the sentence, you will find five ways of phrasing the underlined part. The first of these repeats the original; the other four are different. If you think the original is best, choose the first answer; otherwise choose one of the others.

These questions test correctness and effectiveness of expression. In choosing your answer, follow the requirements of standard written English; that is, pay attention to grammar, choice of words, and sentence construction. Choose the answer that produces the most effective sentence; this answer should be clear and exact, without awkwardness, ambiguity, redundancy, or grammatical error.

6. Four Dynacorp Optimall Omniprocessors were shipped in the fourth quarter, <u>and it brought</u> to 13 the number of these ultra-high-capacity processors shipped during the year.

A. and it brought
B. by bringing
C. and brings
D. having brought
E. bringing

7. After his 1962 season, in which he set a record for on-base percentage, Mitch McAlister left his old team and signed with the Springfield <u>Argonauts, with an annual salary of $550,000 and was the</u> highest salary in professional baseball at that time.

A. Argonauts, with an annual salary of $550,000 and was the
B. Argonauts, earning $550,000 per year and it was the
C. Argonauts for a yearly wage of $550,000, being the
D. Argonauts, with annual pay of $550,000 per year, which was the
E. Argonauts for an annual salary of $550,000, the

8. Nile perch, voracious predators that will eat anything smaller than themselves, <u>are natives of northern Africa but were introduced to Tanzania's Lake Victoria in a foolhardy attempt during the 1960s of boosting</u> the local sport-fishing industry; since their introduction, these sturdy fish have decimated most other aquatic species in the lake.

A. are natives of northern Africa but were introduced to Tanzania's Lake Victoria in a foolhardy attempt during the 1960s of boosting
B. are native in northern Africa but were introduced to Tanzania's Lake Victoria during the 1960s as foolhardy attempts to boost
C. are native to northern Africa but were introduced to Tanzania's Lake Victoria during the 1960s in a foolhardy attempt to boost
D. had been native to northern Africa but during the 1960s were introduced to Tanzania's Lake Victoria in a foolhardy attempt to boost
E. are native to northern Africa but were introduced to Tanzania's Lake Victoria as a foolhardy attempt of boosting

9. No giant squid has ever survived in captivity because these giant animals of the <u>deeps require extremely high water pressure for the purpose of maintaining its</u> internal osmotic balance.

A. deeps require extremely high water pressure for the purpose of maintaining its
B. deep requires extremely high water pressure to maintain its
C. deep require extremely high water pressure in order to maintain their
D. deeps requires extremely high water pressure so that it can maintain its
E. deep require for maintenance extremely high water pressure for their

10. The state medical review board is considering a new regulation <u>that physicians practicing in state facilities with past malpractice suits having been filed against them are required to disclose any such suits to prospective patients.</u>

A. that physicians practicing in state facilities with past malpractice suits having been filed against them are required to disclose any such suits to prospective patients
B. that requires physicians practicing in state facilities to disclose any past malpractice suits filed against them to prospective patients
C. to require physicians with past malpractice suits filed against them and who practice in state facilities to disclose these to prospective patients
D. for physicians that practice in state facilities requiring them to have disclosed to prospective patients past malpractice suits filed against them
E. requiring physicians who practice in state facilities to disclose to prospective patients any past malpractice suits filed against them

For the following questions, select the best of the answer choices given.

11. Our criminal justice system is inherently flawed because it relies on amateur juries of decent citizens, who lack the perspective to understand the criminal mind. To have an effective criminal justice system would require professional juries, who would be able to deal with these criminals in a way that gets results.

The argument above depends on which of the following assumptions?

A. Professional jurors will be more reliable than amateur jurors because they will not attempt to avoid jury duty.

B. Professional jurors will not be burdened by the biases against race, gender, and religion that amateur jurors bring into the courtroom.

C. Dealing with criminals in a way that gets results requires an understanding of the criminal mind.

D. No amount of professional training can impart the perspective of the criminal mind necessary to run an effective criminal justice system.

E. Jurors possessing the perspective to understand the criminal mind are unfit to serve on a jury, because they are likely to be criminals.

12. Advertisement: The most flavorful olives in the world are kalamata olives. The more kalamata olives used to make a bottle of olive oil, the more flavorful the oil, and no company buys more kalamata olives than Zorba's Olive Oil. Therefore, when you buy Zorba's Olive Oil, you're buying the most flavorful olive oil available today.

The reasoning presented in the advertisement is flawed because it overlooks the possibility that:

A. Not all of Zorba's competitors use kalamata olives in their oil.

B. Zorba's sells more olive oil than any other company.

C. The most flavorful olive oil is not necessarily the best olive oil.

D. Because of bulk discounts, Zorba's pays less per kilogram of kalamata olives than does its competitors.

E. The number of kalamata olives harvested every year is far less than the number of Spanish olives harvested every year.

13. The cypress trees of the Louisiana wetlands are threatened by the exploding population of nutria, a type of South American rodent introduced into the area in the 1930s in hopes of starting a nutria fur industry. Unfortunately, no one wanted the fur, and now the rodents number in the millions. A park ranger has suggested introducing the South American jaguar, the nutria's natural predator, into the Louisiana wetlands as a way to control the nutria population.

Which of the following, if true, casts the most doubt on the ranger's plan to introduce jaguars as an effective way to control the nutria population?

A. Past attempts to control the nutria population through traps and poison have resulted in limited and temporary population reductions.

B. A program in Florida found that the best way to conserve the root systems of wetland trees such as cypresses is to surround the trees' roots with tough plastic barriers.

C. The jaguar is a large and deadly predator that, if introduced, could kill livestock, pets, or even humans that it encounters in the Louisiana wetlands.

D. During the past year an unusually cold winter killed an estimated 35 percent of the nutria population in the Louisiana wetlands.

E. The South American jaguar is a predator of the ferret, which is currently the chief predator of the nutria in the Louisiana wetlands.

The questions in this group are based on the content of a passage. After reading the passage, choose the best answer to each question. Answer all questions following the passage on the basis of what is <u>stated</u> or <u>implied</u> in the passage.

Pretty much everybody agrees that clean air is a good thing, right? Evidently not so. Since the 1960s, when people started talking about clean air in the first place, the American energy industry, which includes coal companies, oil companies, and utility companies, has dragged its heels on every initiative to improve the quality of the air we breathe. Even after the Clean Air Act of 1970 and its amendments in 1977 and 1990 made it clear that controlling air pollution is a national priority, these companies have found tricks and loopholes to avoid compliance.

Perhaps the most egregious loophole is the one that allows older power plants to disregard limits on sulfur dioxide emissions until they undergo a major renovation, at which point they have to comply. Sulfur dioxide from coal-burning power plants is the primary cause of acid rain in North America. The Clean Air Act states that when coal-burning power plants upgrade their equipment, they must then comply with sulfur dioxide limitations by either installing scrubbing equipment that cleans the emissions or using fuel with lower sulfur content. The law tied the timing of compliance to major renovations in order to give power plants a grace period in which to comply. Many power plants, however, have exploited a loophole in this law by instituting a series of "minor" renovations that, in effect, upgrade their equipment without requiring them to comply with the Clean Air Act. Some plants have cheated the system by undergoing "minor" renovations for decades.

The power companies claim that they have to resort to these underhanded measures because the cost of compliance with the Clean Air Act is too high. And if everyone else is cheating the system, why should they have to install costly sulfur dioxide scrubbers?

This cost argument falls apart upon scrutiny. Since 1977, more than 400 power plants across the country have managed to comply with the restrictions and are still making money. The sulfur dioxide scrubbing equipment has turned out to be far less expensive than the power industry naysayers claimed it would be. Many power plants have even complied with the emissions limits *and* reduced their operating costs by switching from high-sulfur Appalachian coal to the low-sulfur coal produced in western states such as Wyoming and Idaho. Western coal is not only cleaner than eastern coal, but also, because it is generally closer to the surface, as much as 30 percent less expensive to extract.

Clearly, the costs of compliance with the Clean Air Act can be justified, but if these companies were honest, such justifications would not have to be made. If they were honest, they would acknowledge

the costs of *not* complying: the health costs of increased rates of asthma and lung cancer in high-emissions areas; the environmental costs of acid-scarred forests and lakes; the aesthetic costs of a haze of sulfur dioxide cutting visibility across the eastern United States to only half of what it was in pre-industrial times. When you look at the true costs you have to ask, is any cost too high for clean air?

14. Which of the following best expresses the purpose of this passage?

A. To explain how a loophole in the Clean Air Act allows power plants to avoid compliance with emissions restrictions
B. To raise awareness of the problems caused by sulfur dioxide emissions from coal-burning power plants
C. To argue against a specific implementation of the Clean Air Act that relates to greenhouse gas emissions
D. To argue that companies should not exploit a loophole in the Clean Air Act concerning an atmospheric pollutant
E. To advocate the passage of a new Clean Air Act that places limits on sulfur dioxide emissions

15. The author's tone can best be described as which of the following?

A. Angry and subjective
B. Calm and objective
C. Analytic and ambivalent
D. Grim and self-satisfied
E. Tentative and biased

16. The author most likely begins and concludes the passage with questions for what reason?

A. To suggest possible areas for current and future research
B. To pose a question that is answered in the body of the passage, and then to formulate a question that arises naturally out of the discussion
C. To gain the readers' attention and encourage their agreement with the arguments in the passage
D. To suggest through rhetorical questions that the problems described in the passage do not actually have answers
E. To test the readers' knowledge of the material discussed in the passage

17. According to information given in the passage, which of the following statements presents the most accurate comparison of an average ton of coal from Wyoming with an average ton of coal from the Appalachian range in West Virginia?

A. The former is cheaper and has higher sulfur content than the latter.
B. The latter is found closer to the surface and contains more sulfur than the former.
C. The former can help coal-burning power plants meet limits on sulfur dioxide emissions and costs more than the latter.
D. The latter generates more energy per pound of coal than the former.
E. The former is found closer to the surface than the latter and helps coal-burning power plants meet limits on sulfur dioxide emissions.

18. According to the information given in the passage, sulfur dioxide emissions are linked to all except which of the following phenomena?

A. Reduced visibility in the eastern United States
B. Damage to the ozone hole
C. Increased rates of asthma
D. Acid rain
E. Damaged forests

19. In the fourth paragraph, the passage mentions the "400 power plants" for what purpose?

A. To provide concrete evidence that many power plants have complied with the Clean Air Act provisions without undergoing ruinous financial hardship
B. To demonstrate the size and influence of the energy industry in the United States
C. To demonstrate that only a fraction of the power plants in the country have complied with the Clean Air Act, while hundreds of others have avoided compliance through tricks and loopholes
D. To demonstrate that companies can both comply with the Clean Air Act and achieve reductions in their operating costs by employing new, more efficient technologies
E. To suggest that those companies that have not complied are in the minority

20. Which of the following statements, if true, would provide the strongest argument for a utility company spokesman wishing to refute the arguments expressed in the passage?

A. Over the last decade, the energy industry has funded an environmental initiative that has planted more than 200,000 new trees.
B. The dangers of acid rain to human health have been wildly exaggerated by environmental extremists who seek to scare the general public.
C. The specifications of the Clean Air Act, although well intentioned, in practice require power plants to adopt less efficient technologies that increase emissions of atmospheric pollutants other than sulfur dioxide that have been linked to equally serious problems.
D. A substantial upgrade to a coal-burning power plant that includes the installation of sulfur dioxide scrubbing equipment can cost hundreds of millions of dollars, although companies can often recoup most of these costs over the following years as a result of efficiency benefits from the upgrade.
E. The scientific data upon which the Clean Air Act was based have not been corroborated by the scientists at the Center for Atmospheric Truth, a research group funded by a consortium of energy companies.

The following questions present a sentence, part of which or all of which is underlined. Beneath the sentence, you will find five ways of phrasing the underlined part. The first of these repeats the original; the other four are different. If you think the original is best, choose the first answer; otherwise choose one of the others.

These questions test correctness and effectiveness of expression. In choosing your answer, follow the requirements of standard written English; that is, pay attention to grammar, choice of words, and sentence construction. Choose the answer that produces the most effective sentence; this answer should be clear and exact, without awkwardness, ambiguity, redundancy, or grammatical error.

21. Although he played several musical instruments <u>while being a child,</u> Maestro Macintosh did not begin playing the piano until he was 23 years old.

A. while being a child
B. as a child
C. as in childhood
D. at the time of his childhood
E. at the time when he was a child

22. Unless the conservator can find a way to protect the photographs in the archives from light and air, these precious historical documents <u>have deteriorated and will continue to do so</u> both in color and in fine detail.

A. have deteriorated and will continue to do so
B. will continue to deteriorate
C. have been and will continue to deteriorate
D. will continue to deteriorate, as they already have
E. will be deteriorating yet more

23. Under SEC guidelines, a company in this situation is required either to submit revised financial statements or <u>that they withdraw their plans</u> for a public stock offering.

A. that they withdraw their plans
B. to withdraw its plans
C. that it withdraw planning
D. to have been withdrawn from their plans
E. it should withdraw its plans

24. Unless I am greatly mistaken, any apparent <u>connection between my dog and the destroying of</u> your petunias is purely coincidental.

A. connection between my dog and the destroying of
B. connection between my dog and the destruction of
C. connection of my dog with the destruction of
D. connection between my dog and the destroying to
E. connection from my dog with the destruction to

25. Nutritionists say that you cannot eat enough fruits and vegetables, arguing <u>that it provides nutrition</u> essential to health.

A. that it provides nutrition
B. that they provides nutrition
C. they provide the nutrients
D. it provides the nutrients
E. that they provide the nutrients

For the following questions, select the best of the answer choices given.

26. In theory, the Habbendorf rotary engine could be a great racing engine, but in practice, it is not. The reason is that the available fuels do not have sufficient octane to obtain maximum performance from the engine.

The answer to which of the following questions would be most relevant to evaluating the adequacy of the explanation given above for why the Habbendorf rotary engine is not a great racing engine?

A. If the Habbendorf rotary engine were to operate at maximum performance levels, how would its performance compare to that of an engine recognized as a great racing engine?
B. At what level of octane in its fuel does the Habbendorf rotary engine achieve maximum performance?
C. What levels of speed, acceleration, and efficiency must an engine display in order to be considered a "great racing engine"?
D. Could a Habbendorf rotary engine be modified so that it is able to achieve maximum performance with the fuels currently available?
E. If a car equipped with a Habbendorf rotary engine were to race against a comparable car equipped with a great racing engine, by how much would the performance of the great racing engine surpass that of the Habbendorf rotary engine?

27. Government deregulation of the long-distance telephone business has resulted in increased competition among telephone carriers, thus resulting in lower prices for consumers. This process, however, will ultimately result in lower-quality service for consumers, because as the telephone carriers drop their prices to compete with one another for customers, they will be forced to cut corners on nonessential items like customer service.

Which of the following, if true, casts the most doubt on the argument that government deregulation of the telephone business will result in lower-quality customer service?

A. Technological advances have decreased the cost of providing long-distance telephone service to less than one-half of its cost prior to deregulation.

B. In a customer survey regarding the electric utility business, another industry that recently went through deregulation, surveyors found that customer dissatisfaction with service was 30 percent higher than prior to deregulation.

C. Customers have listed poor customer service as their number one reason for switching from one long-distance telephone service provider to another.

D. Some companies have decreased the cost of customer service by installing automated telephone response systems that eliminate the need for expensive live employees.

E. The greatest competition for long-distance telephone service providers will come not from traditional telephone companies, but from cellular telephone service providers.

The next two questions refer to the following passage:

A pharmaceutical company tested a new painkiller on 1,000 lab rats that were fed large doses of the painkiller for a two-month period. By the end of the experiment, 39 of the rats had died. The company concluded that the painkiller was sufficiently safe to test on humans.

28. Which of the following, if true, provides the most support for the pharmaceutical company's conclusion?

A. The amount of painkiller fed to the rats was substantially greater, in relation to body mass, than the dosage any human would take under normal circumstances.

B. Because of the different body chemistry of humans and rats, some compounds can be dangerous for rats but safe for humans, and vice versa.

C. Tests of this same painkiller on dogs showed that 3 out of 50 dogs developed lesions on their livers during the course of the experiment.

D. The researchers found that during the experiment, the rats showed a significantly lower sensitivity to pain than rats do under normal circumstances.

E. In an experiment of this length with this number of rats, it is not unusual for up to 50 rats to die during the experiment for reasons unrelated to the experiment itself.

29. Which of the following, if true, would cast the most doubt on the pharmaceutical company's conclusion?

A. Fifteen of the 39 dead rats were later found to have died of a rare form of liver cancer that is generally seen in only 1 out of 600,000 lab rats.

B. The director of the experiment, although a respected scientist, is not a medical doctor, and therefore will not be able to continue as director of the experiment once it switches from animal to human trials.

C. Although the painkiller in question has been shown to block certain forms of pain, its duration of efficacy is less than that of other painkillers currently on the market.

D. Human trials of another drug produced by this pharmaceutical company were called off after 30 out of 1,000 rats died of heart failure during the animal testing phase of the experiment.

E. The pharmaceutical company is eager to introduce new drugs to the market because its best-selling product, a drug that reduces blood pressure, will soon lose its patent protection.

The questions in this group are based on the content of a passage. After reading the passage, choose the best answer to each question. Answer all questions following the passage on the basis of what is <u>stated</u> or <u>implied</u> in the passage.

James Joyce revolutionized the novel, the short story, and modern literature as we know it. He was born in Dublin, the first of 10 children in a Catholic family. His father was a civil servant whose poor financial judgment left the family impoverished for much of Joyce's youth. Young James attended Dublin's fine Jesuit schools, which gave him a firm grounding in theology and classical languages—subjects that appeared repeatedly in his later work. The story of his early life and his intellectual rebellion against Catholicism and Irish nationalism are told in the largely autobiographical novel *A Portrait of the Artist as a Young Man*.

In 1902, at the age of 20, Joyce left Dublin to spend the rest of his life in Paris, Trieste, Rome, and Zurich, with only occasional visits back home. Despite this self-imposed exile, Dublin was the setting for most of his writings. *Dubliners* (1914), Joyce's most accessible work, is a collection of short stories describing the paralyzing social mores of middle-class Catholic life. "The Dead," the final story in the collection, is frequently listed as one of the finest short stories ever written.

Joyce's next book, *Ulysses*, took seven years to write; once he finished writing it, he almost couldn't find anyone to publish it. Upon the novel's publication, both Ireland and the United States immediately banned it as obscene. Despite these obstacles, *Ulysses* has come to be generally recognized as the greatest twentieth-century novel written in English. The novel was revolutionary in many ways. The structure was unique: Joyce recreated one full day in the life of his protagonist, Leopold Bloom, and modeled the actions of the story on those of Ulysses in the *Odyssey*. In recounting Bloom's day, Joyce mentions everything that happens to Bloom—including thoughts, bodily functions, and sexual acts—providing a level of physical actuality that had never before been achieved in literature. To provide a psychological insight comparable to the physical detail, Joyce employed a then-revolutionary technique called stream of consciousness, in which the protagonist's thoughts are laid bare to the reader.

From 1922 until 1939, Joyce worked on a vast, experimental novel that eventually became known as *Finnegan's Wake*. The novel, which recounts "the history of the world" through a family's dreams, employs its own "night language" of puns, foreign words, and literary allusions. It has no clear chronology or plot, and it begins and ends on incomplete sentences that flow into each other. Many of

Joyce's supporters thought he was wasting his time on the project, although the playwright Samuel Beckett, who later won the Nobel Prize for Literature, helped Joyce compile the final text when his eyesight was failing. Today, *Finnegan's Wake* is viewed as Joyce's most obscure and possibly most brilliant work.

30. Which of the following would make the most appropriate title for this passage?

   A. The Long Way Home: *Ulysses* and *Finnegan's Wake*
   B. James Joyce, *Ulysses*, and the Battle against Censorship
   C. The Works of James Joyce, Ireland's Literary Genius
   D. The Hidden Value of James Joyce's Great Novels
   E. A Portrait of James Joyce as a Young Man

31. Based on the information in the passage, which of the following would be the most accurate statement about *Dubliners* and *Finnegan's Wake*?

   A. *Dubliners* contains one of the greatest short stories in the English language, and *Finnegan's Wake* is the greatest story in the English language.
   B. Many of the chief characters in *Finnegan's Wake* were earlier introduced in *Dubliners*.
   C. The linguistic experimentation of *Dubliners* paved the way for the "night language" of *Finnegan's Wake*.
   D. *Dubliners* is a longer book than *Finnegan's Wake*.
   E. *Dubliners* is a more accessible book than *Finnegan's Wake*.

32. Joyce's works helped introduce all except which of the following literary elements into modern English literature?

   A. Narration through second-person address
   B. Novel structure based on real-time chronology
   C. Linguistic experimentation
   D. Literary realism concerning physical reality
   E. Stream of consciousness

33. According to the passage, in what year was Joyce born?

A. 1880
B. 1882
C. 1885
D. 1902
E. 1914

34. The author most likely mentions James Joyce's childhood, family, and education to serve what purpose?

A. To suggest that he had to write in order to make a living
B. To suggest that he became a writer because of his father's influence
C. To provide the background and cultural context for his literary work
D. To provide evidence that his literary genius was present when he was a child
E. To explain his opposition to Catholicism and socialism in his later life

35. Who is the most likely intended audience for this passage?

A. Insurance professionals at a company seminar
B. University professors of English literature at a symposium on twentieth-century Irish playwrights
C. High school students in Ireland studying their nation's traditional folklore
D. College students studying twentieth-century English literature
E. Elementary school students studying the *Odyssey*

36. Which of the following can be inferred about Joyce's attitude toward Catholicism as practiced in Ireland at the end of the nineteenth century?

A. He felt that it repressed intellectual freedom and individual expression.
B. He viewed it as the central component of the Irish national psyche.
C. He feared that it was impeding the Irish nationalist movement.
D. He felt that it forced him to leave Dublin for Paris, Trieste, Rome, and Zurich.
E. He believed that Dublin's Jesuit schools provided the finest education in all of Ireland.

The following questions present a sentence, part of which or all of which is underlined. Beneath the sentence you will find five ways of phrasing the underlined part. The first of these repeats the original; the other four are different. If you think the original is best, choose the first answer; otherwise choose one of the others.

These questions test correctness and effectiveness of expression. In choosing your answer, follow the requirements of standard written English; that is, pay attention to grammar, choice of words, and sentence construction. Choose the answer that produces the most effective sentence; this answer should be clear and exact, without awkwardness, ambiguity, redundancy, or grammatical error.

37. Many doctors direct their patients to name-brand drugs, but smart consumers know that generic drugs cost half as much as buying name-brand drugs.

A. generic drugs cost half as much as buying name-brand drugs
B. buying generic drugs costs half as much as name-brand drugs
C. generic drugs cost half as much as name-brand drugs
D. buying generic drugs cost half as much as buying name-brand drugs
E. to buy generic drugs costs half as much as buying name-brand drugs

38. Usually found in pools of stagnant water or mud, crawfish are esthetically unappealing arthropods, except if they are boiled, at which point it yields a tasty treat.

A. crawfish are esthetically unappealing arthropods, except if they are boiled, at which point
B. crawfish are esthetically unappealing arthropods, but after a proper boiling
C. the crawfish is an esthetically unappealing arthropod, in contrast to after being properly boiled
D. the crawfish is an arthropod that does not appeal esthetically, but subsequent to having been boiled properly
E. the crawfish is an esthetically unappealing arthropod, although after a proper boiling

39. While the new health insurance regulations may be onerous for large corporations, <u>it can potentially be disastrous for small business owners, who</u> in many cases will have to lay off employees in order to pay for the extended coverage.

A. it can potentially be disastrous for small business owners, who
B. they are potential disasters for small business owners, since
C. potentially they will be disastrous for small business owners, whom
D. for small business owners it is a potential disaster, because
E. they are potentially disastrous for small business owners, who

40. <u>After leaving the Pentagon, MacTaggart could have profited from his connections with defense contractors, but he refused to do so.</u>

A. After leaving the Pentagon, MacTaggart could have profited from his connections with defense contractors, but he refused to do so.
B. MacTaggart could have profited from his connections with defense contractors after leaving the Pentagon, but he refused to do it.
C. MacTaggart could have profited after leaving the Pentagon from his connections with defense contractors, but he refused to do so.
D. Having left the Pentagon, MacTaggart could have used his connections with defense contractors to profit, but he refused to do it.
E. Refusing to profit from his connections with defense contractors, MacTaggart could have done so after leaving the Pentagon.

41. Product marketing jobs at MegaCorp are difficult to fill because they require specialized skills, <u>demand great responsibility, but also</u> barely any vacation time.

A. demand great responsibility, but also
B. great responsibility, and also
C. great responsibility, and with
D. carry great responsibility, and
E. carry great responsibility, and offer

Practice Test 5

ANALYTICAL WRITING 1

Analysis of an Issue

TIME—30 MINUTES

DIRECTIONS: In this section, you will need to analyze the issue presented and explain your views on it. There is no "correct" answer. Instead, you should consider various perspectives as you develop your own position on the issue.

Read the statement and the instructions that follow it, and then make any notes that will help you plan your response. Write your response on a separate sheet of paper. If possible, type your essay on a word processor. Observe the 30-minute time limit.

> Real-world experience is more useful in business than anything that can be learned in school.
>
> Discuss the extent to which you agree or disagree with the opinion stated above. Support your views with reasons and/or examples from your own experiences, observations, or reading.

ANALYTICAL WRITING 2
Analysis of an Argument
TIME—30 MINUTES

DIRECTIONS: In this section, you will be asked to write a critique of the argument presented below. You may, for example, consider what questionable assumptions underlie the thinking, what alternative explanations or counterexamples might weaken the conclusion, or what sort of evidence could help strengthen or refute the argument.

Read the argument and the instructions that follow it, and then make any notes that will help you plan your response. Write your response on a separate sheet of paper. If possible, type your essay on a word processor. Observe the 30-minute time limit.

The MegaTek Corporation's vice president of marketing made the following statement to the company's board of directors:

MegaTek has been losing market share to UltraCorp for three years straight. Customer surveys suggest that consumers perceive UltraCorp products to be of higher quality than those produced by MegaTek. MegaTek spends more annually on research and development than UltraCorp does, and it pays its employees a higher average salary, so we do not believe that our products are actually inferior; rather, the perception is due to the fact that UltraCorp charges higher prices and spends more money on advertising. In order to regain the lost market share from UltraCorp, MegaTek should raise its prices and devote more money to advertising.

Discuss how well reasoned you find this argument. In your discussion, be sure to analyze the line of reasoning and the use of evidence in the argument. For example, you may need to consider what questionable assumptions underlie the thinking and what alternative examples or counterexamples might weaken the conclusion. You can also discuss what sort of evidence would strengthen or refute the argument, what changes in the argument would make it more logically sound, and what, if anything, would help you better evaluate its conclusion.

Solve the problem and indicate the best of the answer choices given.

NUMBERS: **All numbers used are real numbers.**

FIGURES: **A figure accompanying a problem-solving question is intended to provide information useful in solving the problem. Figures are drawn as accurately as possible EXCEPT when it is stated in a specific problem that its figure is not drawn to scale. Straight lines may sometimes appear jagged. All figures lie in a plane unless otherwise indicated.**

1. Sam is training for the marathon. He drove 12 miles from his home to the Grey Hills Park and then ran 6 miles to Red Rock, retraced his path back for 2 miles, and then ran 3 miles to Rock Creek. If he is then n miles from home, what is the range of possible values for n?

A. $1 \leq n \leq 23$
B. $3 \leq n \leq 21$
C. $5 \leq n \leq 19$
D. $6 \leq n \leq 18$
E. $9 \leq n \leq 15$

2. Amber works 20 days a month at d dollars per day for m months out of the year. Which of the following represents her monthly pay?

A. $\dfrac{m}{20d}$
B. $20d$
C. $\dfrac{10md}{6}$
D. $\dfrac{20d}{m}$
E. $20md$

3. There are 450 birds at a small zoo. The number of birds is 5 times the number of all the other animals combined. How many more birds are there than nonbird animals at the zoo?

A. 400
B. 360
C. 270
D. 180
E. 90

4. If x, y, and z are positive integers, and $4x = 5y = 6z$, then the least possible value of $x + y + z$ is

A. 15
B. 28
C. 37
D. 42
E. 60

5. Three hundred multiples of three are picked at random, and three hundred multiples of four are picked at random. Approximately what percentage of the six hundred selected numbers are even?

A. 100%
B. 75%
C. 66%
D. 50%
E. 33%

Score	Number of students
92	4
91	6
?	3
83	7
71	5

6. The incomplete table above shows a distribution of scores for a class of 25 students. If the average (arithmetic mean) score for the class is 83, what score is missing from the table?

A. 75
B. 77
C. 81
D. 84
E. 86

7. $\dfrac{(5^2)(2^6)(3^4)}{72^2} =$

A. $\dfrac{5}{2}$

B. $\dfrac{25}{3}$

C. 25

D. 50

E. 150

The following data sufficiency problems consist of a question and two statements, labeled (1) and (2), in which certain data are given. You have to decide whether the data given in the statements are <u>sufficient</u> for answering the question. Using the data given in the statements <u>plus</u> your knowledge of mathematics and everyday facts (such as the number of days in July or the meaning of _counterclockwise_), you must indicate whether

A. Statement (1) ALONE is sufficient, but statement (2) alone is not sufficient.
B. Statement (2) ALONE is sufficient, but statement (1) alone is not sufficient.
C. BOTH statements TOGETHER are sufficient, but NEITHER statement ALONE is sufficient.
D. EACH statement ALONE is sufficient.
E. Statements (1) and (2) TOGETHER are NOT sufficient.

NUMBERS: All numbers used are real numbers.

FIGURES: A figure accompanying a data sufficiency problem will conform to the information given in the question, but will not necessarily conform to the additional information given in statements (1) and (2). Lines shown as straight can be assumed to be straight and lines that appear jagged can also be assumed to be straight. You may assume that the position of points, angles, regions, etc., exist in the order shown and that angle measures are greater than zero. All figures lie in a plane unless otherwise indicated.

NOTE: In data sufficiency problems that ask for the value of a quantity, the data given in the statements are sufficient only when it is possible to determine exactly one numerical value for the quantity.

8. What is the value of y?

(1) $y^2 + 8y + 16 = 0$
(2) $y < 0$

9. The integer x is how much greater than 4?

(1) $\dfrac{1}{10^x} = 0.000001$
(2) $10^x = 1{,}000{,}000$

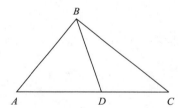

10. In triangle ABC above, if $\angle BAD$ and $\angle ADB$ have measures of $2n°$, and if $\angle ACB$ has a measure of $n°$, what is the length of side AB? (Figure not necessarily drawn to scale.)

(1) $n = 25°$
(2) $CD = 4$

11. A dairy farmer has two milk pails, M and P. Milk pail M is 1/3 full. How much milk is in P relative to M?

    (1) If M is poured into P, P will be full.
    (2) Milk pail P is smaller than M.

12. Is y between 1 and 2, exclusive?

    (1) y^2 is less than y
    (2) $y^2 + y$ is between 1 and 2, exclusive

Solve the problem and indicate the best of the answer choices given.

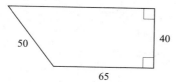

13. What is the perimeter of the figure above?

(Note, figure not necessarily drawn to scale)

    A. 155
    B. 185
    C. 220
    D. 235
    E. 250

14. In a certain growth fund, 3/5 of the investment capital is invested in stocks, and of that portion, 1/3 is invested in preferred stocks. If the mutual fund has $846,000 invested in preferred stocks, what is the total amount of money invested in the fund?

    A. $1,974,000
    B. $2,538,000
    C. $3,264,000
    D. $3,826,000
    E. $4,230,000

15. $(3^2+1)(81^2+1)(9^2+1)(3^2-1)=$

    A. 81^4+1
    B. 9^9-1
    C. $3^{16}-1$
    D. $3^{32}-1$
    E. $3^{96}+1$

16. If the area of a circle is 81π, then the diameter of the circle is

    A. 9
    B. 18
    C. 36
    D. 9π
    E. 18π

17. A standard Veggiematik machine can chop 36 carrots in 4 minutes. How many carrots can 6 standard Veggiematik machines chop in 6 minutes?

    A. 36
    B. 54
    C. 108
    D. 216
    E. 324

18. $\dfrac{(0.0063)(0.117)}{(0.03)(0.007)(0.0003)} =$

    A. 117,000
    B. 11,700
    C. 3,900
    D. 1,170
    E. 390

19. In a sample of patients at an animal hospital, 30 percent are cats and 60 percent are not dogs. What fraction of those patients who are not cats are dogs?

    A. $\dfrac{1}{7}$
    B. $\dfrac{1}{3}$
    C. $\dfrac{2}{5}$
    D. $\dfrac{3}{5}$
    E. $\dfrac{4}{7}$

20. Two dogsled teams raced across a 300-mile course in Wyoming. Team A finished the course in 3 fewer hours than did team B. If team A's average speed was 5 miles per hour greater than that of team B, what was team B's average speed, in miles per hour?

    A. 12
    B. 15
    C. 18
    D. 20
    E. 25

The following data sufficiency problems consist of a question and two statements, labeled (1) and (2), in which certain data are given. You have to decide whether the data given in the statements are <u>sufficient</u> for answering the question. Using the data given in the statements <u>plus</u> your knowledge of mathematics and everyday facts (such as the number of days in July or the meaning of *counterclockwise*), you must indicate whether

A.   Statement (1) ALONE is sufficient, but statement (2) alone is not sufficient.
B.   Statement (2) ALONE is sufficient, but statement (1) alone is not sufficient.
C.   BOTH statements TOGETHER are sufficient, but NEITHER statement ALONE is sufficient.
D.   EACH statement ALONE is sufficient.
E.   Statements (1) and (2) TOGETHER are NOT sufficient.

21. In a club for left-handed people that also admits the ambidextrous, are more than 1/3 of the members ambidextrous?

  (1) Exactly 50 percent of the male members of the club are ambidextrous.
  (2) The number of females in the club is exactly 1 fewer than half the number of male members.

22. If $a \neq 0$, is b greater than zero?

  (1) $a + b = 10$
  (2) $ab = 24$

23. A truck driver wants to load as many identical cylindrical canisters of olive oil as can fit into the 3-meter × 4-meter × 9-meter storage space of his truck. How many canisters can he load into the truck?

  (1) Each canister has a volume of $62,500\pi$ cubic centimeters.
  (2) The height of each canister is four times the radius.

24. In the figure above, what is the length of WZ?

  (Note, figure not necessarily drawn to scale)

  (1) $xy = 64$
  (2) $x^2 = y^2$

25. Over the course of a year, a certain house appreciated in value by 10 percent while the house next door decreased in value by 10 percent as a result of foundation damage. At the end of the year, the reduced price of the second house was what percentage of the increased price of the first house?

  (1) The amount by which the first house increased in value was half as much as the amount by which the second house decreased in value.
  (2) At the end of the year, the second house was worth $70,000 more than the first house.

Solve the problem and indicate the best of the answer choices given.

26. Of 40 applicants for a job, 32 had at least 5 years of prior work experience, 24 had advanced degrees, and 16 had at least 5 years of prior work experience and advanced degrees. How many of the applicants had neither 5 years of prior work experience nor advanced degrees?

  A. 0
  B. 2
  C. 4
  D. 8
  E. 16

27. If $a \neq 0$, and $a - \dfrac{3a^2 + 15}{a} = \dfrac{b}{a}$, then $b =$

  A. $(5-a)(3+a)$
  B. $(3-a)(5+a)$
  C. $2a^2 - 15$
  D. $-3a^2 + a - 15$
  E. $15 - 2a^2$

$$\begin{array}{r} 2\Delta7 \\ \times\varnothing14 \\ \hline 80,698 \end{array}$$

28. If Δ and $\varnothing$ represent single digits in the correctly worked computation above, what is the value of Δ times $\varnothing$?

A. 6
B. 10
C. 12
D. 15
E. 18

29. A retailer sells 5 shirts. The first 2 he sells for $64 and $39. If the retailer wishes to sell the 5 shirts for an overall average price of over $50, what must be the minimum average price of the remaining 3 shirts?

A. $49.00
B. $49.67
C. $50.00
D. $51.33
E. $55.50

30. The MegaTek Corporation is displaying its distribution of employees by department in a circle graph. The size of each sector of the graph representing a department is proportional to the percentage of total employees in that department. If the section of the circle graph representing the manufacturing department takes up 72° of the circle, what percentage of MegaTek employees are in manufacturing?

A. 20%
B. 25%
C. 30%
D. 35%
E. 72%

31. If $x * y = \dfrac{(2x - y)}{(2y - x)}$ for all integers x and y, then $(-5) * 2 =$

A. -12
B. $\dfrac{-4}{3}$
C. $\dfrac{-8}{9}$
D. $\dfrac{4}{3}$
E. 12

32. If x, y, and z are positive integers and $x^2 = y^2 + z^2$, which of the following must be true?

I. $x > z$
II. $x = y + z$
III. $y^2 + z^2$ is a positive integer

A. I only
B. II only
C. III only
D. I and II only
E. I and III only

The following data sufficiency problems consist of a question and two statements, labeled (1) and (2), in which certain data are given. You have to decide whether the data given in the statements are <u>sufficient</u> for answering the question. Using the data given in the statements <u>plus</u> your knowledge of mathematics and everyday facts (such as the number of days in July or the meaning of *counterclockwise*), you must indicate whether

A. Statement (1) ALONE is sufficient, but statement (2) alone is not sufficient.
B. Statement (2) ALONE is sufficient, but statement (1) alone is not sufficient.
C. BOTH statements TOGETHER are sufficient, but NEITHER statement ALONE is sufficient.
D. EACH statement ALONE is sufficient.
E. Statements (1) and (2) TOGETHER are NOT sufficient.

33. If M is a set of five numbers p, q, r, s, and t, is the range of numbers in M greater than 5?

(1) The average (arithmetic mean) of p, q, r, s, and t is 5.
(2) $p - r > 5$.

34. Of the 3,600 registered voters in Smith County who took part in the county referendum on altering the property tax exemption, 2,400 were Democrats and 1,200 were Republicans. What was the total number of female voters who voted in favor of the exemption?

(1) The number of female Democrats who voted in favor of the exemption was three times the number of female Republicans who voted in favor of the exemption.

(2) The 150 male Republicans who voted in favor of altering the exemption represented 2/5 of all Republicans who voted in favor of altering the exemption.

35. Is the value of $x^3y - x^2y^2 + xy^3$ equal to 0?

(1) $x = 0$

(2) $y = 0$

36. Is the positive integer y a prime number?

(1) $80 < y < 95$

(2) $y = 3x + 1$, where x is a positive integer

37. What is the area of square floor X?

(1) The perimeter of the floor is a whole-number multiple of 10.

(2) The diagonal of the floor measures $5\sqrt{2}$.

The questions in this group are based on the content of a passage. After reading the passage, choose the best answer to each question. Answer all questions following the passage on the basis of what is <u>stated</u> or <u>implied</u> in the passage.

Congressman Hastings has proposed that Congress should abolish the Electoral College system for electing the president and replace it with a system of direct popular election. The Electoral College system is flawed, he argues, because it runs directly counter to the democratic principle that every citizen's vote should count equally.

Because of the winner-take-all system in which the candidate who receives the most popular votes in a state receives all of that state's electoral votes, the citizens who voted for the losing candidate are effectively disenfranchised from the national election, even if their candidate lost the state by only a handful of votes. Moreover, because each state's number of electors is the same as its number of members of Congress, the citizens of small states get a disproportionately larger vote than citizens of more populous states. In the 1988 election, for example, the combined voting-age population of the six least populous states—Alaska, Delaware, North Dakota, South Dakota, Vermont, and Wyoming—was 3,119,000. These six states held 21 electoral votes among them. Florida, with a voting-age population of 9,614,000, also had 21 electoral votes. Because of inequities of this nature, there have been four presidential elections in which the candidate who won the Electoral College actually lost the popular vote: 1824, 1876, 1888, and 2000.

Congressman Markham has argued that Hastings's proposed changes are unnecessary and even dangerous. First of all, he argues, the Electoral College system, whatever its flaws, has resulted in a stable democratic government for more than 200 years, which shows that it is doing something right. Second, the winner-take-all system helps create decisive majorities in the Electoral College, thereby reducing the problem of disputed elections that we might see in the event of direct popular elections. Third, the current system of allocating electors helps protect the interests of small states, which would be largely neglected in favor of large states if the Electoral College were based entirely on population. Protecting these states' rights is essential to upholding the principle of federalism (in which the states and the federal government maintain distinct powers).

When the Electoral College system was first formalized by the Twelfth Amendment in 1804, a direct popular vote would have been impossible to implement, and the Electoral College was probably the best way to approximate the will of the people. Advances in technology and communication, however, now mean that a direct popular vote would be as simple, if not simpler, to administer than the current Electoral College system. Alternative ways to reform the system would be to do away with the winner-take-all system of state electors, to base the numbers of electors strictly on state populations, or to have a direct popular election but to weight the votes from different states differently in order to preserve the influence of small states.

1. The passage is primarily concerned with which of the following?

   A. Evaluating the merits of the Electoral College system as a means of protecting federalism
   B. Examining the impact of the Twelfth Amendment on the history of the American presidency
   C. Disputing the validity of the American democratic process
   D. Presenting arguments regarding the best way to elect the president of the United States
   E. Comparing arguments regarding the nature of democratic processes

2. Which of the following best describes the structure of the passage?

   A. It presents a critique of an institution, then provides a defense of that institution, and then offers possible compromises between the two positions.
   B. It presents an argument, lists problems with that argument, and then ultimately refutes the argument.
   C. It discusses both sides of a controversial topic and then chooses the side with the stronger arguments.
   D. It analyzes flaws in a traditional institution and then provides a series of steps to remedy the flaws.
   E. It presents two competing viewpoints and then shows the logical errors in both positions.

3. From the information provided in the paragraph, what can be inferred about the election of 1892?

   A. Its result was disputed on the grounds that smaller states had a disproportionate influence on the outcome.
   B. The winner of the election received more popular votes than his opponent.
   C. The winner-take-all system of state electoral votes led to a decisive majority for the winner in the Electoral College.
   D. Reforming the Electoral College system was an issue of contention in this election.
   E. This election led to the formalization of the Electoral College by the Twelfth Amendment.

4. Hastings's response to Markham's argument that the history of the American government "shows that it [the Electoral College] is doing something right" would most likely be which of the following?

   A. Under the current system, each voter in Alaska has proportionately three times as much voting power as each candidate in Florida.
   B. We do not know whether or not the American government would have been equally stable had the president been elected by a direct popular election since the beginning.
   C. If the candidate who lost the popular election won the presidency four times in 200 years, there is something wrong with the system.
   D. Maintaining a strong federal system is less important than upholding the principle that each vote should count equally.
   E. A process that maintained the Electoral College but removed the winner-take-all system would substantially reduce the disenfranchisement that occurs under the current system.

5. According to the passage's presentation of Markham's sentiments regarding federalism, which of the following systems for electing the president would be most objectionable to him?

   A. An Electoral College system identical to the one currently in use
   B. An Electoral College in which each state's number of electors was based strictly on population, but the winner-take-all system was maintained
   C. An Electoral College in which each state's number of electors was based strictly on that state's number of members of Congress, but in which the winner-take-all system was replaced by a divided electoral vote proportional to the state's popular vote
   D. A direct popular election in which the votes from citizens of smaller states were given more weight than citizens from larger states
   E. A direct popular election

6. Which of the following examples from international politics, if true, would give Markham the most support in his argument against Hastings?

A. A nation in Africa that modeled its government on the American governmental system after achieving independence from a European colonial power recently entered into a civil war that has effectively ended any true democratic processes.

B. The ancient city-state of Athens had a form of direct popular election in the fifth century B.C.E., but this government fell as a result of the Peloponnesian War that Athens fought against Sparta.

C. A South American nation that deposed its long-standing military dictatorship and instituted in its place a democratic government with a president elected through a direct popular election has experienced both economic growth and improved relations with the international community.

D. A nation in Central Europe that recently changed its government from a long-standing parliamentary monarchy to a government led by a popularly elected premier was recently thrown into chaos when the popularly elected premier declared a dictatorship.

E. The system of proportional power sharing by the members of the European Union has resulted in a number of thorny disputes between member states that will probably grow more severe as new nations from Eastern Europe enter the EU.

7. According to the information given in the passage, which of the following statements about Florida and South Dakota is most accurate?

A. Florida is a larger state in area than South Dakota.

B. South Dakota has a larger population than Florida.

C. The ratio of members of Congress to electors in the Electoral College is lower for the state of Florida than it is for South Dakota.

D. South Dakota has more members of Congress per voting-age citizen than Florida does.

E. A higher percentage of the voting-age population in South Dakota exercises its constitutional right to vote than is observed among the voting-age population of Florida.

The following questions present a sentence, part of which or all of which is underlined. Beneath the sentence, you will find five ways of phrasing the underlined part. The first of these repeats the original; the other four are different. If you think the original is best, choose the first answer; otherwise choose one of the others.

These questions test correctness and effectiveness of expression. In choosing your answer, follow the requirements of standard written English; that is, pay attention to grammar, choice of words, and sentence construction. Choose the answer that produces the most effective sentence; this answer should be clear and exact, without awkwardness, ambiguity, redundancy, or grammatical error.

8. Although it has not been confirmed <u>such proteins in whole milk are inducing in children under 12 months milk allergies</u>, most pediatricians advise waiting until the child is one year old before introducing whole milk into his or her diet.

A. such proteins in whole milk are inducing in children under 12 months milk allergies

B. that under 12 months the proteins in whole milk can induce milk allergies in children

C. of proteins in whole milk inducing milk allergies in children under 12 months

D. the proteins in whole milk can induce milk allergies in children under 12 months

E. that the proteins in whole milk can induce milk allergies in children under 12 months

9. The tango club, which appeared moribund five years ago, has picked up a new <u>step;</u> <u>its numbers are now three times more than</u> when the club president decided to bring in a live band.

  A. step; its numbers are now three times more than

  B. step; its numbers are now three times greater than

  C. step, their numbers now threefold that which they had been

  D. step; now with numbers three times greater than

  E. step, now with three times the number they had

10. During the bronze sculpture boom of the late 1950s, more than 20 tons of bronze were shipped to the SoHo district of Manhattan <u>so as they might sculpt</u> countless bronze statues, busts, abstract shapes, and whimsical figurines.

  A. so as they might sculpt

  B. in order that they might be sculpted into

  C. so that there could be sculpted

  D. for the sculpting of

  E. such that they could be sculpted into

11. <u>James Watson, who later headed the Human Genome Project, along with Englishman Francis Crick discovered the double helix in 1953, the basic structure of DNA, when the two were young scientists.</u>

  A. James Watson, who later headed the Human Genome Project, along with Englishman Francis Crick discovered the double helix in 1953, the basic structure of DNA, when the two were young scientists.

  B. The double helix, the basic structure of DNA, was discovered in 1953 by two young scientists, the Englishman Francis Crick and James Watson, who later headed the Human Genome Project.

  C. The basic structure of DNA, the double helix, was discovered in 1953 by the Englishman Francis Crick and James Watson, later head of the Human Genome Project, two young scientists.

  D. The Englishman Francis Crick and James Watson, later heading the Human Genome Project, were the young scientists who discovered the basic structure of DNA in 1953, which was the double helix.

  E. The basic structure of DNA, the double helix, was discovered by James Watson, later head of the Human Genome Project, along with another of two young scientists, the Englishman Francis Crick, in 1953.

12. Atmospheric scientists in recent years have observed increasing concentrations of chlorofluorocarbons in the tertiary layer of the stratosphere, <u>findings consistent with the documented growth in chlorofluorocarbon emissions from industrial activity</u>.

  A. findings consistent with the documented growth in chlorofluorocarbon emissions from industrial activity

  B. which are consistent with the documented growth in chlorofluorocarbon emissions from industrial activity

  C. a finding consistent with growth in chlorofluorocarbon emissions from industrial activity, as documented

  D. finding documented growth consistent with chlorofluorocarbon emissions from industrial activity

  E. which findings are consistent with industrial activity's documented growth in chlorofluorocarbon emissions

13. The medical board, <u>concerned by the drop in insurance payments and the failure of the accounting department to obtain</u> the anticipated funds, resolved to pursue legal action against the insurance company.

  A. concerned by the drop in insurance payments and the failure of the accounting department to obtain

  B. concerning the drop in payments by insurance and the failure of the accounting department to obtain

  C. because of its concern for the dropping insurance payments and the accounting department's failure at obtaining

  D. in its concern that the drop in insurance payments and the failure of the accounting department to obtain

  E. being concerned about the drop in insurance payments and the accounting department failing to obtain

14. The number of violent crimes committed in the greater metropolitan area of Sao Paolo, Brazil, <u>more than doubled</u> from 1975 to 1990 by the influx of drugs.

    A. more than doubled
    B. increased by more than twice
    C. increased more than two times
    D. was increased more than double
    E. was more than doubled

For the following questions, select the best of the answer choices given.

15. One of the biggest threats to a company's productivity is absenteeism. Studies have shown that companies with in-house child-care programs see fewer absences among their employees who are parents than companies without such programs. Therefore, many companies could boost their productivity by starting in-house child-care programs.

Which of the following, if true, most weakens the above argument?

    A. Companies that reimburse outside child-care programs actually see less absenteeism among working parents than companies with in-house programs.
    B. In-house child-care programs create distractions for nonparents that can harm their productivity.
    C. Absenteeism is not a serious problem for companies that impose harsh penalties on employees who miss work.
    D. Studies have shown that employees with children are more likely than those without children to remain in the same job for more than five years.
    E. Potential employees generally view companies with in-house child-care programs as more desirable places to work than companies without such programs.

16. A taxi driver purchased four tires of the Toughgrip brand for his cab. Within six months of his purchasing these tires, three of them suffered irreparable blowouts. Despite the poor track record of these tires, the driver replaced all three of the damaged tires with new Toughgrip tires.

Which of the following, if true, does NOT support the driver's decision to replace the damaged tires with new Toughgrip tires?

    A. Toughgrip tires are the only tires the driver can afford.
    B. The driver feels obligated to buy tires from his brother, who sells only Toughgrip tires.
    C. One of the tires was slashed by a rival driver, while the other two blew out in traffic because of material defects.
    D. The Toughgrip Company offered to replace all of the tires free of charge because the tires were covered under a 60,000-mile warranty.
    E. The taxi company for which the driver works has endorsed Toughgrip as the official tire of their company's cars.

The following two questions are based on the following passage:

An automaker is facing financial difficulties. The vice president of marketing has determined that the root of the company's problems is low brand loyalty. The vice president proposes, therefore, that the company begin an aggressive advertising campaign focused on children aged from three to eight years. By securing strong brand recognition with this demographic, he argues, the company will have an advantage when these customers reach an age when they can buy cars.

17. Which of the following, if true, provides the strongest support for the vice president's proposal?

    A. Federal law prohibits the advertising of alcohol or tobacco on any medium for which the primary audience is under 21 years of age.
    B. Children aged three to eight, even if they had the money to purchase a car, will not legally be able to drive one for several years.
    C. The cost of advertising on children's programs is comparable to the cost of advertising on adult special-interest programs.
    D. Focus groups have consistently observed that the automaker's brand is associated with "tradition" and "older" drivers.
    E. Studies have shown that lifelong customers of certain products, such as particular brands of toothpaste or peanut butter, frequently credit their brand loyalty to exposure to the product at an early age.

18. Which of the following, if true, raises the most serious doubts about the vice president's proposal?

  A. Studies have shown that children are an important factor in the car-buying decision for 75 percent of parents with children under 18 years of age.
  B. The financial difficulties facing the company will result in the company's declaring bankruptcy within five years if the difficulties are not addressed effectively.
  C. The company's most recent advertising campaign, focused on the theme of "Rev up your life," has received positive ratings from the demographic aged 18 to 29.
  D. Children are accustomed to viewing ads for car toys while watching their favorite television programs, so ads for actual cars will appeal to them.
  E. The vice president who made the proposal has only one year of experience in the automotive industry, but has spent more than 20 years in the financial services and children's entertainment industries.

The questions in this group are based on the content of a passage. After reading the passage, choose the best answer to each question. Answer all questions following the passage on the basis of what is <u>stated</u> or <u>implied</u> in the passage.

Dear Sirs,

  Given all the coverage that the emergence of hybrid cars has received in your pages in recent months, your readers may be interested to learn that gasoline-electric hybrids are not a new phenomenon at all, but rather the latest incarnation of an idea that has been kicking around for over a century. Indeed, the hybrid car has been around almost as long as the automobile itself.

  At the turn of the twentieth century, as the automotive age dawned, three power-generating technologies competed for dominance: steam, gasoline, and electricity. In the year 1900, steam was well known as the power source of the industrial revolution, and electricity was widely regarded as the power source of the future, so it was not at all obvious that internal combustion engines burning a fractional distillate of crude petroleum would have any particular edge in this race for the powertrains of America. Indeed, when engineer H.

Piper filed the first patent application for a gasoline-electric hybrid motor in 1905, his intention was to use the gas to give a little kick to his perfectly serviceable electric engine. His goal: an engine that could accelerate from 0 to 25 miles per hour in 10 seconds.

  Piper achieved his goal. Electric and hybrid-electric engines powered more than 35,000 vehicles sold in 1912. These cars were perfectly adequate for the time, but over the following decade they mostly disappeared from the market, through no fault of their own. The cause of their decline was the spectacular improvements in the cost and performance of gasoline-powered cars. An onslaught of fast and cheap internal combustion cars from Ford, General Motors, and Buick essentially buried the electric and electric-hybrid motors by the 1920s.

  Continuing performance improvements in internal combustion engines and inexpensive gas pretty much kept hybrids buried until the oil crises of 1973 and 1979 gave Americans a reason to start thinking about fuel efficiency. Engineers had the motivation to think about fuel-efficient hybrids, but they still lacked the means to make hybrids economically competitive with gas-powered cars, because the performance of gas-electric engines lagged far behind that of gas-powered engines in acceleration, top speed, and cruising range.

  Dramatic improvements in electronics and computer technology during the 1990s, however, finally made the hybrid a reality. Advances in battery performance and, most importantly, computer-guided electric power transfer created a car that could drive like a regular car, but do so on half the tank of gas. As another century dawns, perhaps we are entering into a new automotive age.

19. Based on the tone and content of the passage, the author of the passage is most likely which of the following?

  A. An automotive engineer writing to his company management
  B. An enthusiast of automotive history writing to the editors of a car magazine
  C. A college engineering student writing to a car manufacturer
  D. A history professor writing to a television producer of historical documentaries
  E. An environmental activist writing to the editors of a newspaper

20. The purpose of the article could best be summarized as which of the following?

A. To correct a mistaken impression about the performance of gasoline-electric hybrid cars

B. To educate readers about the economic and technological potential of hybrid cars

C. To refute a factually inaccurate statement made previously in the publication regarding the history of hybrid cars

D. To acquaint readers with the history of gasoline-electric hybrid cars

E. To educate readers about technological innovations at the dawn of the automotive age

21. According to the passage, electric and hybrid cars failed to capture the American automotive market in the early twentieth century because of what factor?

A. The improvement in cost and performance of gasoline-powered cars

B. The superior fuel efficiency of hybrid cars

C. The substandard performance of steam-powered cars

D. Consumer fear of being electrocuted by gasoline-electric hybrids

E. Government subsidies for gasoline- and coal-powered cars

22. According to the information given in the passage, which of the following best characterizes the different motivations behind the earliest experiments with gasoline-electric hybrids and the experiments going on in modern times?

A. The earliest experiments with hybrids sought to improve the fuel efficiency of electric engines, while modern experiments seek to improve the performance of gas-burning engines.

B. The earliest experiments with hybrids sought to improve the fuel efficiency of gas-burning engines, while modern experiments seek to improve the performance of electric engines.

C. Modern experiments with hybrids seek to improve the fuel efficiency of gas-burning engines, while the earliest experiments sought to improve the performance of electric engines.

D. Modern experiments with hybrids seek to improve the cruising range of gas-powered cars, while earlier experiments sought to improve the handling and safety of electric cars.

E. The earliest experiments with hybrids sought to combine the power of steam with the efficiency of electricity, while modern experiments seek to combine the efficiency of electricity with the power of gas.

23. The passage lists which of the following as a reason for the resurgence of interest in the gasoline-electric hybrid engine?

A. The onslaught of fast and inexpensive internal combustion cars from Ford, General Motors, and Buick

B. Advances in battery performance and electricity transfer

C. The Iranian hostage crisis of 1979

D. Dramatic improvements in computer technology

E. The oil crisis of 1973

24. Which of the following examples of business and technology bears the most similarity to the history of the hybrid car, as presented in the passage?

A. American aerospace companies in the 1960s created working prototypes of supersonic passenger aircraft that could complete intercontinental flights in half the time of conventional aircraft, but these projects were canceled because of concerns that the high-altitude craft posed too great a threat to the integrity of the ozone layer.

B. Although oil companies first attempted deep-sea drilling in the Gulf of Mexico in the 1930s, these deep-sea projects could not compete with land-based drilling projects until advances in drilling technology and the rising price of oil made deep-sea drilling economically viable in the late twentieth century.

C. Automakers in the 1980s, after concluding that the average driver could not be relied on to use seat belts consistently, chose to adopt airbags as a standard safety feature.

D. Lighter-than-air craft, such as Zeppelins, made up a substantial part of total air traffic in the early twentieth century, but they rapidly fell out of favor after airplanes proved to be a faster and safer form of transportation.

E. Although railroads carried more than 90 percent of all land-based commercial cargo in the United States in 1910, by 1980 railroads had been surpassed by trucks in total cargo carried, because of the greater speed and flexibility offered by the heavy truck as compared with the railroad.

25. Based on the information given in the passage, which of the following can be inferred about an electric-gasoline hybrid car in 1950?

A. It would have been difficult to find a power supply for such a car.

B. Its acceleration would have been roughly comparable to that of a gasoline-burning car that cost less than half as much as the hybrid car.

C. It would have been viewed as "the car of the future."

D. Its performance would have been limited by contemporary battery technology.

E. Had it been produced, it would have sold more than 35,000 units per year.

For the following questions, select the best of the answer choices given.

26. Drug use among teens concerns many people in California. Advocates of the "Stop Drugs Now" program, which was piloted in public schools in five California counties last year, argue that the program should be used throughout the state to decrease drug use among teenagers.

Which of the following statements, if true, would most strengthen the argument of the advocates of "Stop Drugs Now" that the program should be expanded statewide?

A. School programs are far less important than parental messages in influencing a teenager's decision to use drugs.

B. Drug use among teens in the five counties where the "Stop Drugs Now"

program was piloted has been dropping steadily for over a decade.

C. Teenagers at the public schools where the "Stop Drugs Now" program was piloted reported higher average levels of drug use than did teenagers at private schools in the same counties where the program was not piloted.

D. There is evidence that teenagers who start smoking at an early age are more likely to experiment with illegal drugs than teenagers who do not smoke.

E. The percentage of teenagers who reported using drugs at the schools where the "Stop Drugs Now" program was piloted dropped more in the last year than in any other year over the last decade.

27. A car manufacturer periodically discounts certain car models to its dealers to coincide with intensive advertising campaigns focused on those cars. After analyzing the results of this program, the manufacturer found that sales of the discounted cars were strong, but it also concluded that it could reap greater profits if it did not hold promotions in this way.

Which of the following statements, if true, best accounts for the manufacturer's conclusion about profitability?

A. Some consumers worry that discounted cars are more likely to be defective.

B. The car manufacturer had not been effective in controlling the production costs of the cars, and these rising costs ate into the manufacturer's profits.

C. Although dealers requested large numbers of the cars at discounted prices, they generally sold the cars at the normal retail price, thereby keeping more of the profit for themselves.

D. Many consumers buy large-ticket items, such as cars, only when they are on sale.

E. The manufacturer's intensive advertising campaign did not sufficiently emphasize the cars' high levels of performance on road tests.

28. Advertisement:

We at Vesuvius Vacuums always give our customers what they deserve, and they deserve the very best. That's why we use only SuperTec air filters.

Which of the following, if true, would most undermine the argument expressed in the advertisement?

A. In a test of three leading air filters, the SuperTec air filter performed at the same level as one of the filters and at a higher level than the other.
B. The SuperTec air filter is the only kind of air filter that will fit in the model of vacuum sold by Vesuvius Vacuums.
C. In a national study by a prominent consumer group, Vesuvius Vacuums gained a "superior" rating for product quality.
D. The customers of Vesuvius Vacuums have expressed no preferences concerning the type of air filter used in the product.
E. The specific air filter used in a given vacuum makes only a small difference in the long-term performance of that vacuum.

29. Oil is a nonrenewable resource, whereas sunshine is limitless. So why not run cars on solar power? Because a car powered by solar collecting panels would be fine on a sunny day, but as soon as the sun went behind a cloud, the car would no longer function.

Which of the following is presupposed in the argument against running a car on solar power?

A. Solar power is cleaner than fossil fuels, and it involves less geopolitical risk.
B. In most of the northern hemisphere, it can be expected that more than 150 days a year will be cloudy.
C. No system exists for storing solar energy for a car's use when the car is not in direct sunlight.
D. No one has yet introduced a commercially viable process for mass-producing solar cells that convert more than 10 percent of incoming sunlight into usable energy.
E. Consumers accustomed to the rapid acceleration of gasoline-powered cars will not accept the weak acceleration of solar-powered cars.

The following questions present a sentence, part of which or all of which is underlined. Beneath the sentence, you will find five ways of phrasing the underlined part. The first of these repeats the original; the other four are different. If you think the original is best, choose the first answer; otherwise choose one of the others.

These questions test correctness and effectiveness of expression. In choosing your answer, follow the requirements of standard written English; that is, pay attention to grammar, choice of words, and sentence construction. Choose the answer that produces the most effective sentence; this answer should be clear and exact, without awkwardness, ambiguity, redundancy, or grammatical error.

30. Chauncy, like most bulldogs, has a fondness for meat and gravy.

A. like most bulldogs, has
B. as most bulldogs, have
C. like many bulldogs, have
D. like most bulldogs, having
E. as with many bulldogs, has

31. Last season, oranges from South Florida were as bountiful as, if not more bountiful than, oranges from the normally more bountiful northern region.

A. as bountiful as, if not more bountiful than, oranges
B. equally bountiful, if not more so, to oranges
C. as bountiful, if not bountifuller, than oranges
D. so bountiful, and maybe more bountiful, than oranges
E. as bountiful, if not more bountiful, as oranges

32. Every lawyer knows that it is difficult to prove culpability in technically complicated lawsuits if there is a lack of some expert to testify about the complicated technical aspects.

A. if there is a lack of some expert to testify
B. unless there will be an expert who might testify
C. should there be no testimony from an expert
D. without an expert's testimony
E. lacking some expert to testify

33. To be a great salesman <u>requires strong personal skills, the ability to think fast, and demands</u> a can-do attitude.

A. requires strong personal skills, the ability to think fast, and demands

B. requires strong personal skills, the ability to think fast, and

C. requires strong personal skills, demands the ability to think fast, and

D. requiring strong personal skill, an ability to think fast, and demands

E. demands strong personal skills, an ability to think fast, but with

34. The tremendous insight of Einstein was that the passage of time does not appear the same <u>while standing still as it does to a person traveling</u> at a substantial portion of the speed of light.

A. while standing still as it does to a person traveling

B. to a person standing still as to a person traveling

C. to a person who is standing still as a person who is traveling

D. while standing still as to traveling

E. to a person standing still as to a person who travels

35. Professor Markham's theory fails to explain the extent <u>to which savings from personal income has shifted</u> to short-term bonds, money-market funds, and other near-term investments by the instability in the futures market.

A. to which savings from personal income has shifted

B. of savings from personal income that has been shifted

C. of savings from personal income shifting

D. to which savings from personal income have shifted

E. to which savings from personal income have been shifted

36. <u>Approximately $120 billion in venture capital is estimated as having poured into technology stocks during the late 1990s, creating</u> a valuation bubble that burst in 2000.

A. Approximately $120 billion in venture capital is estimated as having poured into technology stocks during the late 1990s, creating

B. During the late 1990s approximately $120 billion in venture capital is estimated to have poured into technology stocks and created

C. During the late 1990s it is estimated that there was approximately $120 billion in venture capital that was poured into technology stocks, creating

D. It is estimated that during the late 1990s, approximately $120 billion in venture capital poured into technology stocks, creating

E. It is estimated that there was approximately $120 billion in venture capital that poured into technology stocks during the late 1990s and created

37. Jim Smyth may be a charismatic speaker, but it seems to be counterproductive to have a high school dropout as mayor in a town <u>where illiteracy functionally affects 37 percent of the electorate</u>.

A. where illiteracy functionally affects 37 percent of the electorate

B. in which functionally the electorate is 37 percent illiterate

C. where 37 percent of the electorate are functionally illiterate

D. which has 37 percent of the electorate functionally illiterate

E. where, of the electorate, 37 percent of them functionally are illiterate

For the following questions, select the best of the answer choices given.

38. The decline in the price of biotech stocks has hurt many institutions that had invested heavily in biotech companies. Last year the state university added 200,000 shares of a biotech stock to its holdings. The stock in question has declined in value by more than 90 percent over the last 12 months. The college, however, did not purchase the stock, but received it as a gift. Therefore, the price decline will not harm the university's finances.

Which of the following, if true, casts the most doubt on the conclusion that the price decline of biotech stocks will not harm the university's finances?

A. The biotech sector is volatile; some stocks that lose 90 percent of their value in one year may regain all of their value and more in the following year.
B. The university needs to pay capital gains taxes only on a stock sale that results in a gain; stocks sold at a loss will incur no tax penalty.
C. Although the biotech sector is down, the overall health-care sector, in which the university has invested heavily, is up for the year.
D. The biotech company in question has a promising new drug in development that could revolutionize the treatment of type II diabetes.
E. The university began construction of a new laboratory last year that the provost had expected to pay for with the proceeds from the sale of the biotech stock in question.

39. A city councilman has proposed a controversial new plan to increase city revenues from the parking places downtown. He has proposed that instead of charging $1.20 per hour for parking in these spots, the city should make all parking spots five-minute loading zones, and then assess $15 parking fines on anyone who parks in the spots for more than five minutes.

Which of the following, if true, provides the strongest argument that the councilman's plan will not increase the city's revenue?

A. A system that promotes parking fines will anger citizens, and they will consequently vote the councilman out of office if the plan goes through.
B. The city owns only 14 parking spots in the downtown area.
C. The costs of assessing and collecting the parking fines will surpass the revenues likely to be collected from the new plan.
D. Ray's parking garage, the only competition for the city-owned parking places downtown, charges $18 per day for its parking places.
E. It has been observed that on an average day, approximately three different cars park in each of the city-owned parking spots downtown.

40. Over the last five years, Eagle Trust Bank has seen the number of its retail customer accounts drop by over 40 percent. Over this same period, the price of Eagle Trust stock has increased by more than 80 percent. This phenomenon has perplexed certain investors, who believe that a bank's stock should drop if its number of customer accounts drops.

Which of the following, if true over the last five years, best accounts for the observed movement in the price of Eagle Trust stock?

A. Two years ago Eagle Trust was investigated by the Securities and Exchange Commission for accounting irregularities, but last year the company was cleared of all charges.
B. Eagle Trust recently implemented a highly publicized program for no-fee home mortgages.
C. Eagle Trust is in the process of switching its customer base from retail customers to commercial customers, which now account for over 75 percent of the bank's revenues.
D. There have been many aggressive new entrants into the retail customer banking business over the last five years.
E. Eagle Trust is known for offering one of the best employee benefits packages in the industry.

41. Recent scientific studies have proven that ulcers are caused, at least in part, by the heliobacter bacterium. Dr. Redding has hypothesized that a natural way to prevent and cure ulcers is to eat large amounts of raw broccoli, which contains potent organic compounds that are beneficial to gastric health.

All of the following statements support Dr. Redding's hypothesis, EXCEPT:

A. It has been shown that people who consume raw broccoli on a regular basis have a 65 percent lower chance of developing ulcers than do the general population.

B. One of the organic compounds found in broccoli has been shown to have an antibiotic effect on the heliobacter bacterium.

C. Dr. Redding conducted a study in which groups of patients suffering from ulcers either ate large quantities of broccoli or ate a diet that included no vegetables; several of the patients who ate the large quantities of broccoli showed marked improvement in their conditions.

D. Broccoli is one of the most potent dietary sources of antioxidants, the organic compounds shown to combat the free radicals that are thought to cause cancer.

E. Test animals with chemically induced ulcers showed some signs of improvement when raw broccoli was incorporated into their diets.

Answer Key

1 QUANTITATIVE	1 VERBAL
1. D	1. A
2. B	2. C
3. C	3. B
4. C	4. A
5. C	5. B
6. B	6. E
7. E	7. C
8. D	8. A
9. B	9. D
10. D	10. B
11. A	11. B
12. B	12. D
13. B	13. B
14. D	14. A
15. B	15. C
16. C	16. D
17. A	17. A
18. C	18. D
19. B	19. D
20. C	20. E
21. A	21. C
22. E	22. B
23. E	23. C
24. A	24. A
25. B	25. B
26. C	26. C
27. D	27. D
28. A	28. E
29. B	29. B
30. B	30. C
31. E	31. B
32. B	32. E
33. C	33. B
34. C	34. D
35. D	35. A
36. A	36. A
37. D	37. D
	38. C
	39. C
	40. A
	41. B

PRACTICE TEST 2

Answer Key

2 QUANTITATIVE	2 VERBAL
1. E	1. D
2. D	2. B
3. A	3. D
4. D	4. B
5. B	5. A
6. B	6. A
7. E	7. D
8. C	8. B
9. E	9. C
10. A	10. A
11. C	11. D
12. A	12. E
13. D	13. C
14. A	14. B
15. C	15. B
16. E	16. B
17. A	17. A
18. B	18. E
19. D	19. C
20. D	20. C
21. E	21. A
22. B	22. C
23. D	23. C
24. E	24. C
25. C	25. B
26. B	26. D
27. B	27. E
28. C	28. A
29. B	29. D
30. E	30. A
31. C	31. D
32. B	32. C
33. D	33. A
34. B	34. A
35. B	35. D
36. B	36. E
37. C	37. C
	38. B
	39. E
	40. C
	41. D

Answer Key

3 QUANTITATIVE	3 VERBAL
1. C	1. D
2. D	2. C
3. D	3. A
4. C	4. E
5. B	5. E
6. D	6. B
7. E	7. D
8. C	8. D
9. B	9. A
10. A	10. C
11. B	11. D
12. E	12. B
13. C	13. D
14. A	14. D
15. B	15. B
16. D	16. C
17. E	17. B
18. D	18. A
19. D	19. A
20. E	20. B
21. C	21. B
22. B	22. E
23. D	23. C
24. B	24. E
25. A	25. C
26. A	26. B
27. E	27. A
28. C	28. D
29. A	29. C
30. E	30. A
31. D	31. C
32. B	32. C
33. C	33. D
34. A	34. A
35. B	35. D
36. C	36. A
37. A	37. A
	38. D
	39. C
	40. E
	41. C

PRACTICE TEST 4

Answer Key

4 QUANTITATIVE	4 VERBAL
1. B	1. D
2. C	2. D
3. D	3. A
4. C	4. B
5. A	5. C
6. A	6. E
7. E	7. E
8. B	8. C
9. B	9. C
10. D	10. E
11. B	11. C
12. D	12. B
13. D	13. E
14. A	14. D
15. C	15. A
16. E	16. C
17. A	17. E
18. C	18. B
19. B	19. A
20. A	20. C
21. A	21. B
22. E	22. B
23. D	23. B
24. E	24. B
25. E	25. E
26. B	26. A
27. D	27. C
28. A	28. E
29. C	29. A
30. E	30. C
31. D	31. E
32. D	32. A
33. B	33. B
34. B	34. C
35. B	35. D
36. A	36. A
37. C	37. C
	38. E
	39. E
	40. A
	41. E

Answer Key

5 QUANTITATIVE	5 VERBAL
1. C	1. D
2. B	2. A
3. B	3. B
4. C	4. C
5. B	5. E
6. A	6. D
7. C	7. D
8. A	8. E
9. D	9. B
10. B	10. D
11. E	11. B
12. D	12. A
13. E	13. A
14. E	14. E
15. C	15. B
16. B	16. C
17. E	17. E
18. B	18. B
19. E	19. B
20. D	20. D
21. C	21. A
22. C	22. C
23. C	23. E
24. C	24. B
25. A	25. D
26. A	26. E
27. E	27. C
28. D	28. B
29. A	29. C
30. A	30. A
31. B	31. A
32. E	32. D
33. B	33. B
34. C	34. B
35. D	35. E
36. C	36. D
37. B	37. C
	38. E
	39. C
	40. C
	41. D

PRACTICE TEST 1
Answers and Explanations
QUANTITATIVE

1. Greg sells gaskets. On three sales, Greg has received commissions of $385, $70, and $190, and he has one additional sale pending. If Greg is to receive an average (arithmetic mean) commission of exactly $220 on the four sales, then the fourth commission must be:

   A. $135
   B. $155
   C. $220
   D. $235
   E. $645

   ANSWER: D   For the average of four commissions to be $220, the total must be $220 \times 4 = 880$. 880 minus the sum of the three listed commissions ($385 + 70 + 190 = 645$) equals $235.

2. In an effort to plan out expenses, the Roberts family is representing its annual budget as a circle graph. Each sector of the graph is proportional to the amount of the budget it represents. If "clothes and shoes" takes up 54° of the chart, how much of the Roberts's $20,000 annual budget is dedicated to clothes and shoes?

   A. $1,500
   B. $3,000
   C. $4,500
   D. $5,000
   E. $5,400

   ANSWER: B   54° is 15 percent of the 360° in a circle; 15 percent of $20,000 is $3,000.

3. What is the value of $3x^2 - 1.8x + 0.3$ for $x = 0.6$?

   A. −0.3
   B. 0
   C. 0.3
   D. 1.08
   E. 2.46

   ANSWER: C   The equation $3(0.6 \times 0.6) - 1.8(0.6) + 0.3 = 1.08 - 1.08 + 0.3 = 0.3$

4. Over a three-week period, the price of an ounce of gold increased by 25% in the first week, decreased by 20% in the following week, and increased by 5% in the third week. If the price of gold was G dollars per ounce at the beginning of the three weeks, what was the price, in terms of G, at the end of the three weeks?

   A. $0.95G$
   B. G
   C. $1.05G$
   D. $1.1G$
   E. $1.15G$

   ANSWER: C   At the end of the first week, the price was $1.25 \times G = 1.25G$. At the end of the second week, it was $0.8 \times 1.25G = G$. At the end of the third week, the price was $1.05 \times G = 1.05G$.

5. If a cube has a total surface area of 96, what is its volume?

   A. 16
   B. 36
   C. 64
   D. 81
   E. 96

   ANSWER: C   A cube has six sides, so if the total surface area is 96, then the surface area of a square side is $96/6 = 16$. The area of a square is the square of the length of its sides, so the length of a side is the square root of $16 = 4$. The volume of a cube is the cube of the length of its sides, so $4 \times 4 \times 4 = 64$.

6. The table below shows the enrollment in various classes at a certain college.

Class	Number of Students
Biology	50
Physics	35
Calculus	40

Although no student is enrolled in all three classes, 15 are enrolled in both Biology and Physics, 10 are enrolled in both Biology and Calculus, and 12 are enrolled in both Physics and Calculus. How many different students are in the three classes?

A. 51
B. 88
C. 90
D. 125
E. 162

ANSWER: B   To find the total number of students, you must separate them into nonoverlapping groups so that no one is counted twice. The students taking only Biology are the 50 students minus the 15 also taking Physics and the 10 also taking Calculus, so there are 25 students taking just Biology. Using this same method, the number of students taking just Physics is $35 - 15 - 12 = 8$, and the number taking just Calculus is $40 - 10 - 12 = 18$. The total number, then, is $25 + 8 + 18 + 10 + 15 + 12 = 88$.

7. In a nationwide poll, P people were asked 2 questions. If 2/5 answered "yes" to question 1, and of those 1/3 also answered "yes" to question 2, which of the following represents the number of people polled who did not answer "yes" to both questions?

A. 2/15 P
B. 3/5 P
C. 3/4 P
D. 5/6 P
E. 13/15 P

ANSWER: E   The people who answered "yes" to both questions are 1/3 of 2/5 P, so 2/15 P. Therefore, the people who did not answer "yes" to both questions are $P - 2/15\ P = 13/15\ P$.

8. A certain salad dressing made only of oil and vinegar is premixed and sold in the grocery store. What is the ratio of oil to vinegar in the mix?

(1) An 18.6-ounce bottle of the salad dressing contains 12.4 ounces of vinegar.

(2) In a 32-ounce bottle of the salad dressing, there is half as much oil as there is vinegar.

ANSWER: D   (1) alone is sufficient, because if there are 12.4 ounces of vinegar, then there are $18.6 - 12.4 = 6.2$ ounces of oil; $6.2/12.4 = 1{:}2$. (2) alone is sufficient because it tells you directly that the ratio of oil to vinegar is $1{:}2$.

9. At a certain pancake festival with 600 attendees in which every attendee ate at least 1 pancake, how many people had only 1 pancake?

(1) At the festival there were 1,200 pancakes served, and no person had more than 3 pancakes.
(2) Seventy-two percent of the attendees at the festival had 2 or more pancakes.

ANSWER: B   (1) alone is not sufficient, because there could have been 300 people who had 1 pancake and 300 people who had 3 pancakes, or 600 people who had 2 pancakes. (2) alone is sufficient, because you can directly infer from the statement that $100 - 72 = 28$ percent of attendees, or 168, had only 1 pancake.

10. A rectangle is equal in area to a square with sides of length 12. Is the diagonal of the rectangle greater in length than 20?

(1) The rectangle has a length of 16.
(2) The rectangle has a width of 9.

ANSWER: D   Both (1) and (2) independently allow you to infer both the length and the width of the rectangle, because if the rectangle is equal in area to a square with sides of length 12, then its area $= 12 \times 12 = 144$, and so the width is $144/16 = 9$ and the length is $144/9 = 16$. By the Pythagorean theorem, we can determine that the diagonal is equal to the square root of $9^2 + 16^2 = 337$. You do not have to determine the actual square root of 337 to determine that it is less than 20, because $20 \times 20 = 400$.

11. A type of candy comes in two flavors, sweet and sour, and in two colors, yellow and green. The color and flavor of the individual pieces of candy are not related. If in a certain box of this candy $\frac{1}{4}$ of the yellow pieces and $\frac{5}{7}$ of the green pieces are sour, what is the ratio of the number of yellow pieces to the number of green pieces in the box?

(1) In the box, the number of sweet yellow pieces is equal to the number of sour green pieces.

(2) In the box, the number of green pieces is two less than the number of yellow pieces.

ANSWER: A   (1) alone is sufficient because it sets up a ratio between the colors and flavors; if $\frac{1}{4}$ of the yellow pieces are sour, then $\frac{3}{4}$ of the yellow pieces are sweet, and if 5/7 of the green pieces are sour, then 2/7 of the green pieces are sweet; if the number of sweet yellow pieces is equal to the number of sour green pieces, then $\frac{3}{4}$ of the number of yellow pieces is equal to 5/7 of the number of green pieces; if y represents the number of yellows and g represents the number of greens, then the ratio can be represented as $3y/4 = 5g/7$, which can be restated as $21y = 20g$, or $y/g = 20/21$. Statement (2) alone is not sufficient because it does not give sufficient information to determine the total number of either the greens or the yellows.

12. In isosceles triangle ABC, what is the value of $\angle C$?

(1) The measure of $\angle B$ is 47°

(2) The measure of $\angle A$ is 96°

ANSWER: B   (1) alone is insufficient, because $\angle C$ could be the matching angle of the isosceles triangle with $\angle B$ at 47°, or it could match with $\angle A$ at 66.5°, or it could be the nonmatching angle at 96°. (2) alone is sufficient, because if $\angle A$ is 96°, then it cannot be one of the matching angles of the isosceles triangle because two 96° angles cannot fit in a triangle, so $\angle C$ must be one of two 47° angles.

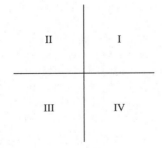

13. In the rectangular quadrant system shown above, which quadrant, if any, contains no point (x, y) that satisfies the equation $3x + 5y = -2$?

A. none
B. I
C. II
D. III
E. IV

ANSWER: B   The equation describes a line that crosses the x axis at −2/3 and crosses the y axis at −2/5, so it never passes through quadrant I. You can plug in points from each axis to verify.

14. If a copier makes 3 copies every 4 seconds, then continues at this rate, how many minutes will it take to make 9,000 copies?

A. 60
B. 100
C. 120
D. 200
E. 3,000

ANSWER: D   At 3 copies every 4 seconds, the copier will finish the batch in (9,000/3) × 4 seconds, or 12,000 seconds. There are 60 seconds in a minute, so 12,000/60 = 200 minutes.

15. To be considered grade AA, an egg must weigh between 75 and 90 grams, including the shell. Shells of grade AA eggs weigh between 3 and 5 grams. What is the smallest possible mass, in grams, of a 12-egg omelet, assuming that only grade AA eggs are used, the shells are all discarded, and no mass is lost in the cooking process?

A. 800
B. 840
C. 864
D. 900
E. 1,080

ANSWER: B   The smallest omelet will result from 75-gram eggs with shells of 5 grams each, resulting in 70 grams per egg added to the omelet. 70 grams/egg × 12 eggs = 840 grams.

16. $\dfrac{(0.2)^8}{\left(0.2\right)^5} =$

A. 0.0008
B. 0.001
C. 0.008
D. 0.04
E. 0.08

ANSWER: C $\dfrac{(0.2)^8}{\left(0.2\right)^5} = \left(0.2\right)^3 = 0.008$

17. What is the ratio of $\left(\frac{1}{3}\right)^2$ to $\left(\frac{1}{3}\right)^4$?

   A. 9
   B. 3
   C. 1
   D. 1:3
   E. 1:27

ANSWER: A $\left(\frac{1}{3}\right)^2$ equals $\frac{1}{9}$, while $\left(\frac{1}{3}\right)^4$ equals $\frac{1}{81}$. $\frac{1}{9}$ is nine times larger than $\frac{1}{81}$, so the ratio is 9:1.

18. A group of 7 fishermen chartered a boat for a day to fish for flounder. The boat costs x dollars per day to rent. If the group can find 3 more fishermen on the docks who are willing to come aboard and share the rental costs, how much less will the rental cost be per person in terms of x?

   A. $x/70$
   B. $x/35$
   C. $3x/70$
   D. $3x/10$
   E. $3x/7$

ANSWER: C   The difference in cost is the difference between $x/7$ and $x/10$. $x/7 - x/10 = (10x - 7x)/70 = 3x/70$.

19. The size of a flat-screen television is given as the length of the screen's diagonal. How many square inches greater is the screen of a square 34-inch flat-screen television than a square 27-inch flat-screen television?

   A. 106.75
   B. 213.5
   C. 427
   D. 729
   E. 1,156

ANSWER: B   The question specifies that the televisions are square, so the diagonals are part of 45–45–90 triangles. This means that the side of such a television is the diagonal divided by $\sqrt{2}$. This would be an awkward number to deal with, but the question calls for areas, so you need to square the length of a side in order to get the area of the screen, thereby removing the square root. Set up the equation

$$\left(\frac{34}{\sqrt{2}}\right)^2 - \left(\frac{27}{\sqrt{2}}\right)^2 = \frac{1{,}156 - 729}{2} = \frac{427}{2} = 213.5$$

20. What is the value of n?

   (1) $n^4 = 256$
   (2) $n^3 > n^2$

ANSWER: C   (1) alone is insufficient because n could equal either 4 or −4. (2) alone is insufficient, because although it tells us that $n > 1$, it does not give a value for n. If the statements are combined, $n = 4$ is the only solution to the stated criteria.

21. An employee at a company was given the task of making a large number of copies. He spent the first 45 minutes making copies at a constant rate on copier A, but copier A broke down before the task was completed. He then spent the next 30 minutes finishing the task on copier B, which also produced copies at a constant rate. How many total minutes would the task have taken had copier A not broken down?

   (1) Copier A produced twice as many copies in its first 5 minutes of operation as copier B produced in its first 15 minutes.
   (2) Copier B produces 10 copies per minute.

ANSWER: A   (1) alone is sufficient because it gives the relative rates of the two machines; if copier A can produce twice as many copies as copier B can produce in three times the time, then it could have finished the task in one-sixth the time it took copier B, or 5 minutes. (2) alone is insufficient because it does not allow you to determine the relative speeds of the two machines.

22. If $ab \neq 0$, is c an integer?

   (1) $c = 5a - 2b$
   (2) $a = 2b$

ANSWER: E   (1) alone is insufficient because it could give values for c that are both integers and nonintegers. (2) alone is insufficient because it says nothing about c. If the statements are combined, a and b could still take values that make c either an integer (e.g., 1, 2) or a noninteger (e.g., 1/3, 1/6).

23. $x = 0.57y9$. If y denotes the thousandth digit in the decimal representation of x above, what digit is y?

(1) If x were rounded to the nearest tenth, the result would be 0.6.

(2) If x were rounded to the nearest hundredth, the result would be 0.58.

ANSWER: E (1) alone is insufficient because it gives us no new information about y. (2) alone is insufficient because it tells us only that $y \geq 5$, which is not sufficient to answer the question. Combining the statements yields no new information.

24. Is integer $y > 0$?

(1) $-(2 + y) > 0$

(2) $(2 + y)^2 > 0$

ANSWER: A (1) alone is sufficient because this statement means that $y < -3$, which means that y is not greater than 0. (2) alone is insufficient, because the statement could work for values of y that are both greater and less than 0, such as 1 and −1.

25. If 4 and 11 are the lengths of two sides of a triangular region, which of the following can be the length of the third side?

I. 5
II. 13
III. 15

A. I only
B. II only
C. I and II only
D. II and III only
E. I, II, and III

ANSWER: B A leg of a triangle cannot be greater than or equal to the sum of the other two legs. This principle eliminates both I ($11 > 5 + 4$) and III ($4 + 11 = 15$). Therefore, II is the only acceptable length.

26. A certain truck uses 18 gallons of diesel fuel in traveling 270 miles. In order for the truck to travel the same distance using 10 gallons of diesel fuel, by how many miles per gallon must the truck's fuel mileage be increased?

A. 8
B. 9
C. 12
D. 15
E. 27

ANSWER: C If the truck travels 270 miles on 18 gallons, it is getting 270/18 = 15 miles per gallon. To travel 270 miles on 10 gallons, it would need to get 27 miles per gallon. 27 − 15 = 12.

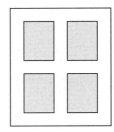

27. The figure above represents a window, with the shaded regions representing openings for glass and the pale regions representing the wood panels between and around the glass. If the window is 4.5 feet high by 2.5 feet wide, and if each of the wooden panels is exactly 4 inches thick, what is the total surface area, in square inches, of glass in the window? (1 foot = 12 inches; figure not drawn to scale)

A. 189
B. 378
C. 448
D. 756
E. 1,620

ANSWER: D For this problem, you could calculate the dimensions of each of the four pieces of glass, but it is probably simplest to calculate the area of glass as if the four pieces were just one rectangular area of glass. If the window is 4.5 feet high, then it is $4.5 \times 12 = 54$ inches high. 54 inches minus the 3×4 inches for the wooden panels means that the glass in the window is $54 - 12 = 42$ inches high. The window is 2.5 feet wide = 30 inches; 30 inches minus 12 inches for the panels means that the glass is 18 inches wide. $42 \times 18 = 756$ square inches. Note that the figure is not drawn to the dimensions given in the question.

28. If $3(x^2 + x) - 7 = x^2 + 2(4 + x^2)$, then $x =$

A. 5
B. 6
C. 9
D. 15
E. 25

ANSWER: A You can restate the equation as $3x^2 + 3x - 7 = 3x^2 + 8$, so $3x = 15$, and $x = 5$.

29. Suzie's Discount Footwear sells all pairs of shoes for one price and all pairs of boots for another price. On Monday the store sold 22 pairs of shoes and 16 pairs of boots for $650. On Tuesday the store sold 8 pairs of shoes and 32 pairs of boots for $760. How much more do pairs of boots cost than pairs of shoes at Suzie's Discount Footwear?

A. $2.50
B. $5.00
C. $5.50
D. $7.50
E. $15.00

ANSWER: B   One approach to this question is to set up the two equations and then eliminate one variable to solve for the other. If s represents the prices of shoes and b represents the price of boots, then $22s + 16b = 650$ and $8s + 32b = 760$. To eliminate b, multiply both sides of the first equation by 2 and then subtract the second equation from the modified first equation, and you get $44s - 8s + 32b - 32b = 1,300 - 760$; therefore, $36s = 540$, and shoes cost $15. Plug this value into one of the equations and you get $b = 20. $20 - $15 = 5.

30. For any 3 given numbers, which of the following is always equivalent to adding the 3 numbers together and then dividing the sum by 3?

I. Ordering the 3 numbers numerically, from highest to lowest, and then selecting the middle number.
II. Dividing each of the numbers by 3 and then adding the results together.
III. Multiplying each number by 6, adding the resulting products together, and then dividing the sum by 9.

A. I only
B. II only
C. I and II only
D. II and III only
E. None of the above

ANSWER: B   Choose any three numbers and test them on statements I, II, and III. You will quickly find that I and III are not always true. II is always true, because mathematically it and the process in the question are doing the same thing—summing the numbers and dividing by 3.

31. A hat company ships its hats, individually wrapped, in 8-inch by 10-inch by 12-inch boxes. Each hat is valued at $7.50. If the company's latest order required a truck with at least 288,000 cubic inches of storage space in which to ship the hats in their boxes, what was the minimum value of the order?

A. $960
B. $1,350
C. $1,725
D. $2,050
E. $2,250

ANSWER: E   An $8 \times 10 \times 12$-inch box contains 960 cubic inches. 288,000 total cubic inches divided by 960 cubic inches per box equals 300 boxes. 300 boxes times $7.50 per hat equals $2,250.

32. Chauncy, an English bulldog, received 1,618 votes in the Mr. Bulldog USA competition, giving him approximately 20 percent of the vote. Approximately what percent of the remaining votes would he have needed to receive in order to win 30 percent of the total votes?

A. 10%
B. 12.5%
C. 15%
D. 17.5%
E. 20%

ANSWER: B   If 1,618 was 20 percent of the vote, then there were approximately 8,090 votes (1,618/0.2 = 8,090). 30 percent of 8,090 would be 2,427. 2,427 − 1,618 = 809 additional votes that Chauncy would have needed in order to reach 30 percent. $\dfrac{809}{8,090 - 1,618} = 0.125 = 12.5\%$.

33. If 8 skiers raced down a course multiple times in one day, and each skier used a different pair of skis on each run, what is the maximum number of different skis used by the 8 skiers during the day?

(1) No skier shared any skis with any other skier.
(2) Each skier made exactly 12 runs during the day.

ANSWER: C   (1) alone is insufficient because it doesn't say how many times each skier raced the course. (2) alone is insufficient because it does not exclude the possibility of sharing; there could have been 12 pairs of skis shared among the 8 skiers, or there could have been a total of $12 \times 8 = 96$ skis, or any number in between. If the statements are combined, we see that the number has to be $12 \times 8 = 96$ skis.

34. The symbol $\otimes$ represents one of the following operations: addition, subtraction, multiplication, or division. What is the value of $7 \otimes 4$?

(1) $4 \otimes 7 < 1$
(2) $4 \otimes 3 > 1$

ANSWER: C   (1) alone is insufficient, because the statement could be true if the symbol represents either subtraction or division. (2) alone is insufficient, because the statement could be true if the symbol represents multiplication, division, or addition. If the statements are combined, the only common operation is division, so the answer is 7/4.

35. Salespeople at a certain car dealership are paid a $250 commission on every car they sell up to their monthly quota, and $500 for every car they sell over the quota. What is the monthly sales quota at this dealership?

(1) One salesperson exceeded the quota by 8 cars and received a total monthly commission of $7,500.
(2) One salesperson achieved only half of the quota; he received a commission of $1,750 and a warning that he will be fired unless he meets the next month's quota.

ANSWER: D   (1) alone is sufficient; we know the 8 cars over the quota will receive a total of $4,000 in extra commission ($8 \times 500), so divide the remaining money by $250 per car to determine the quota—$3,500/$250 = 14 cars. (2) alone is sufficient; $1,750 at $250 per car means that he sold 7 cars, and if 7 is half of the quota, then the quota is 14.

36. If $a \neq -b$, is $\dfrac{a-b}{b+a} < 1$?

(1) $b^2 > a^2$
(2) $a - b > 1$

ANSWER: A   (1) alone is sufficient; it states that the absolute value of b is greater than the absolute value of a, which means that $\dfrac{a-b}{b+a}$ is a negative number regardless of whether a and b are both positive, both negative, or a mix of positive and negative (plug in numbers to verify); since $\dfrac{a-b}{b+a}$ is a negative number, the answer to the question has to be "yes." (2) alone is insufficient, because if (a, b) equals $(4, 2)$ then $\dfrac{a-b}{b+a} = \dfrac{1}{3}$ and the answer is "yes," but if (a, b) equals $(4, -3)$ then $\dfrac{a-b}{b+a} = 7$, and the answer is "no."

37. The hold of a fishing boat contains only cod, haddock, and halibut. If a fish is selected at random from the hold, what is the probability that it will be a halibut or a haddock?

(1) There are twice as many halibut as cod in the hold, and twice as many haddock as halibut.
(2) Cod account for 1/7 of the fish by number in the hold.

ANSWER: D   (1) alone is sufficient because it means that if there is one cod, there are two halibut and four haddock, so halibut and haddock account for 6/7 of the fish in the hold, giving a probability of 6/7 of selecting one of these fish. (2) alone is sufficient, because the probability of selecting a cod is the inverse of the probability of selecting one of the other two fish, or 6/7.

Answers and Explanations

1. Studies have shown that companies that present seminars on workplace safety to their employees actually have higher rates of workplace accidents than companies that do not present such seminars to their employees. Despite this finding, it is still in the best interests of companies and their employees for companies to present these seminars.

Which of the following, if true, provides the strongest support for the argument that the companies should continue to present these seminars?

A. Companies that present workplace safety seminars to their employees are likely to be in manufacturing industries or segments of the service sector that present more opportunities for workplace accidents than the average company.

B. A fast-food chain determined that the rate of workplace accidents remained the same at its franchises after all employees had viewed a 30-minute workplace safety video.

C. Workers are ultimately responsible for their own safety, and no amount of workplace education can alter their behavior.

D. A business research institute determined that workplace accidents reduce the productivity of manufacturing businesses by as much as 8 percent per year.

E. Many companies mistakenly believe that presenting workplace safety seminars to their employees relieves the company of legal liability in the event that employees are injured on the job.

ANSWER: A   To strengthen the argument, the answer must refute the apparent connection between workplace safety seminars and higher rates of accidents; answer A provides a plausible explanation for this phenomenon.

2. For hundreds of years, pearl divers have gathered pearls directly from mollusks on the sea floor. This is an extremely risky profession, exposing the divers to risks of drowning, air embolism, and shark attacks. Still, as long as society demands authentic cultured pearls, these brave divers must continue to risk their lives.

Which of the following statements, if true, most seriously weakens the conclusion above?

A. Shark attacks on pearl divers have decreased steadily over the last three decades because of declining shark populations.

B. Cultured pearls are generally considered more beautiful than those made by artificial means.

C. Robotic pearl harvesters can gather pearls faster and at less cost than human divers, although they may disturb aquatic communities.

D. Part of the value of cultured pearls derives from the exotic way in which they are obtained.

E. With the proper equipment and training, a diver employing scuba gear can harvest three times as many pearls per hour as can a free air diver.

ANSWER: C   This answer provides an alternative means by which society can obtain cultured pearls without exposing divers to risk.

3. An electronic company's two divisions showed consistent performance over the last two years. In each year, the audiovisual department accounted for roughly 30 percent of the company's sales and 70 percent of the company's profits over the period, while the home appliance division accounted for the balance.

Which of the following statements regarding the last two years can be inferred from the statement above?

A. The audiovisual market is growing faster than the home appliance division.
B. The home appliance division has realized lower profits per dollar of sales than has the audiovisual division.
C. Total dollar sales for each division has remained roughly constant for the last five years.
D. The company has devoted more money to research and development efforts in the audiovisual division than in the home appliance division.
E. To maximize profitability, the company should focus its resources on the home appliance division.

ANSWER: B   If the home appliance division accounted for 70 percent of sales but only 30 percent of profits, it is clearly generating less profit per dollar of sales than is the audiovisual division.

4. Gastric bypass surgery has been shown to be effective at helping extremely obese people lose weight. Some patients have lost as much as 300 pounds after undergoing the surgery, thereby substantially prolonging their lives. Despite the success of the treatment, most doctors have not embraced the surgery as a weight loss option.

Which of the following statements, if true, best accounts for the lukewarm reaction of the medical community to gastric bypass surgery?

A. Gastric bypass surgery carries a high risk of serious complications, including death.
B. Obesity is one of the leading contributors to heart disease and hypertension, two leading causes of death.
C. Obesity rates among the American population have been increasing consistently for the last three decades.
D. Many patients report that losing weight through diets is ineffective, since they usually gain the weight back within six months.
E. Most health insurance plans will cover the cost of gastric bypass surgery for morbidly obese patients at high risk of heart disease.

ANSWER: A   This answer provides a substantial reason—the operation's risk of serious complications and death—for doctors to refrain from recommending the gastric bypass surgery.

5. This passage is primarily interested in which of the following?

A. Investigating the factors that brought about the Marvel revolution and the Silver Age of comic books
B. Reviewing the factors that brought about the end of the Golden Age of comic books
C. Comparing and contrasting two eras in the history of comic books
D. Condemning the horror comic book for its corrupting influence on the nation's youth
E. Evaluating the historical legacy of William Gaines's EC Comics

ANSWER: B   The introductory paragraph brings up the subject of the factors that brought the Golden Age to an end, and the next three paragraphs discuss these factors.

6. According to the passage, which of the following was true of the creators of superhero comic books in the postwar years?

A. They sought to head off the censorship of the Comics Code Authority by voluntarily prohibiting stories dealing with sexuality, drugs, or criminal behavior.
B. They introduced characters such as Superman and The Spirit.
C. They unintentionally laid the groundwork for the transition from the Golden Age of comic books to the Silver Age.
D. They focused increasingly on flashy artwork and less on well-developed stories.
E. They responded to the competitive pressure from horror comic books by increasing the amount of violence in their stories.

ANSWER: E   The passage states, "The creators of superhero comic books, not wanting to be left behind, responded by matching their protagonists against darker criminals in more violent encounters."

7. According to the passage, what can we infer to be the central message of Fredric Wertham's *The Seduction of the Innocent*?

A. Adults reading violent comic books were as likely to be corrupted by them as young people were.
B. The horror comic books of the late 1940s were inferior to the superhero comic books that gained popularity during World War II.
C. Comic books were leading the nation's youth into crime, violence, and drug abuse.
D. Creating a regulatory board to censor the comic book industry would drive the worst offenders out of the business.
E. Comic books would never be able to convey stories of any serious literary merit.

ANSWER: C   The sentence preceding the mention of Wertham's book states that he believed that comic books "were leading the nation's youth into crime, violence, and drug abuse."

8. According to the final paragraph of the passage, what may we infer about the comic book companies of the Silver Age?

A. They were able to create popular comic books despite the regulations of the Comics Code Authority.
B. They achieved commercial success because of the popularity of characters such as Spider-Man, the Hulk, and the Fantastic Four.
C. They repeated the same mistakes as the comic book companies of the Golden Age.
D. They failed to succeed because of the numbing effect of the Comics Code Authority regulations.
E. Marvel Comics was the only major comic book company to survive from the Golden Age into the Silver Age.

ANSWER: A   The last paragraph states that the CCA regulations had a numbing effect on comic book publishers, but it concludes with the statement that the industry recovered in the Silver Age. Since the passage did not state that the CCA regulations were repealed, we can infer that the companies succeeded despite the regulations.

9. In what light does the passage depict the efforts by Fredric Wertham to bring about regulation of the comic book industry?

A. As a fanatical crusade brought about by Wertham's inner demons
B. As a witch-hunt roughly analogous to the concurrent anti-Communist hearings by the House Committee on Un-American Activities
C. As a reasonable response to an industry that had gone too far
D. As an angry response to a trend in the subject matter of the comic book industry
E. As an inappropriate response to a phenomenon that was not actually hurting anyone

ANSWER: D   The passage describes the trend toward horror comics in neutral terms, and it states that horror comics "aroused the anger" of Wertham.

10. According to the passage, which of the following statements can be made about the content of *Weird Tales* and *The Crypt of Terror*?

A. Their adult-oriented content was not suitable for young readers.
B. Their grim and gritty content was a market response to the demands of soldiers home from World War II.
C. They frequently depicted violence and criminal behavior, but shied away from sexuality or drug abuse.
D. Their sales surpassed those of previous best-selling titles such as Superman or Batman.
E. The publication of *Weird Tales #1* coincided with the end of the Golden Age of comic books.

ANSWER: B   The second paragraph states: "When these soldiers came home, they still wanted to read comic books, but they sought out more adult content. William Gaines of EC Comics was happy to meet the market demand with such grim and gritty titles as *Weird Fantasy* and *The Crypt of Terror*."

11. The way in which the mighty blue whale and the other baleen whales—the finback, gray, humpback, and right whales—<u>eats was discovered by</u> careful observation by biologists.

A. eats was discovered by
B. eat was discovered through

C. eats were discovered by means of
D. eat were discovered by
E. eat was discovered resulting from

ANSWER: B The two subject-verb phrases in question here are "The way . . . was discovered" and "whales . . . eat"; only B and E present these verb forms properly. The construction "discovered resulting from" in E is awkward and unidiomatic; B is the best answer.

12. The eighteenth-century author Jonathan Swift once suggested in a satiric essay <u>Irish farmers could eat their children to address the twin problems of overpopulation and lack of food</u>.

A. Irish farmers could eat their children to address the twin problems of overpopulation and lack of food
B. that the twin problems of overpopulation and lacking food could be addressed by the eating of children by Irish farmers
C. of the twin problems of Irish farmers, overpopulation and a lack of food, could be addressed by the eating of their children
D. that Irish farmers could address the twin problems of overpopulation and lack of food by eating their children
E. that Irish farmers , facing overpopulation and lacking food, could address the twin problems through eating their children

ANSWER: D A and C fail to conform to the idiomatic construction "{subject} suggested that . . ."; B is awkward and is weakened by its use of the passive voice. In E, it is unclear that "twin problems" necessarily refers to overpopulation and lack of food. D is the clearest statement.

13. The stock market collapse of 1929 had far-reaching consequences for the national economy, causing a nationwide collapse in home values, putting millions out of work, <u>and by erasing</u> the investment savings of one-fifth of the population.

A. and by erasing
B. and erasing
C. and having erased
D. and erased
E. by erasing

ANSWER: B To maintain a parallel structure with "causing" and "putting," the verb in the final clause should be "erasing" without "by";

the presence of "by" in the phrase does not make sense with the rest of the sentence. B is the clearest and most idiomatic choice.

14. <u>No less remarkable than the invention of nuclear power</u> has been the way the technology has prompted governments to reevaluate the nature of international relations.

A. No less remarkable than the invention of nuclear power
B. What was as remarkable as the invention of nuclear power
C. Inventing nuclear power has been none the less remarkable than
D. The invention of nuclear power has been no less remarkable as
E. The thing that was as remarkable as inventing nuclear power

ANSWER: A A is grammatically correct and idiomatic, and it is stylistically preferable to the other choices.

15. <u>Unlike the recognition of ethical lapses in others, many people are disinclined to perceive the same flaws in themselves</u>.

A. Unlike the recognition of ethical lapses in others, many people are disinclined to perceive the same flaws in themselves.
B. Unlike the perception of ethical flaws in themselves, many people are willing to recognize these same flaws in others.
C. Many people, willing to recognize ethical lapses in others, are disinclined to perceive the same flaws in themselves.
D. Many people are disinclined to perceive the same flaws in themselves, but are willing to perceive ethical lapses in others.
E. Although willing to recognize ethical lapses in others, many people in themselves are disinclined to perceive the same flaws.

ANSWER: C A and B incorrectly compare "people" with "recognition" and "perception," respectively. In D, it is unclear what "the same flaws" is referring to. The construction "many people in themselves" in E is unidiomatic. C is the best answer.

16. The Elk City garbage dumps are so full that Elk City has been forced to pay a large sum to Caribou City to accept much of Elk City's garbage. The Elk City mayor has proposed paying for this garbage relocation by imposing a tax on manufacturing businesses in Elk City. MegaCorp, the largest manufacturing business in the area, protests that this tax is unfair because businesses should not have to pay for a garbage problem that has been created by homeowners.

Which of the following, if true, most weakens MegaCorp's argument?

A. MegaCorp already pays more than $10,000 per year in taxes and fees to Elk City.

B. MegaCorp employs more than 60 percent of the employed residents of Elk City.

C. A recycling program would address the garbage problem more effectively by reducing the overall quantity of waste.

D. MegaCorp's manufacturing processes produce more than 90 percent of the total waste that goes into Elk City's garbage dumps.

E. Caribou City is happy to receive the extra garbage because the fees it collects from Elk City have helped to address a shortfall in education funding.

ANSWER: D   If MegaCorp produces the majority of the waste that goes into the overfull garbage dumps, the company cannot validly claim that the problem was "created by homeowners."

17. There are Congressmen who say that the development of a space-based missile defense system will provide economic benefits only to military contractors. This claim is not true. A space-based missile defense system, even if it has no current applications for civilian businesses, will still benefit civilian businesses because those businesses will be able to find profitable uses for the government-developed technology in the future.

Which of the following statements, if true, provides the most support for the argument that a space-based missile defense system could provide future economic benefits for civilian businesses?

A. Several new materials developed for the Apollo space program were later adapted to provide basic components of the modern computer and electronics industries.

B. The missile defense system in question will not require the development of any new technologies.

C. Space-based missile defense programs may be the only way to defend civilian populations against preemptive nuclear attacks.

D. Space-based missile defense programs, although more expensive than traditional land-based systems, are theoretically more effective than traditional land-based systems.

E. The scientists employed on the project could make extraordinary advances in the capabilities of intercontinental ballistic missiles used by the army.

ANSWER: A   The example given demonstrates that a past technology developed by the government that did not have immediate civilian economic applications was later adapted to provide important economic benefits.

18. The commissioner of a professional sports league dictated that teams could not put players on the field who had a greater than 20 percent chance of suffering a career-ending spinal injury during competition. The commissioner justified this decision as a way to protect players from injury while protecting the league from lawsuits.

Which of the following, if true, would most undermine the effectiveness of the commissioner's new policy?

A. Spinal injuries can result in paralysis, loss of fine motor skills, and even death.

B. The previous year, more than seven players in the league suffered career-ending spinal injuries.

C. The players' union agrees that the risk of injury is an inevitable part of playing the game at a professional level.

D. There is no scientifically valid method for determining the likelihood of any player suffering a career-ending spinal injury at any given time.

E. Players barred from playing because of this new regulation will be entitled to compensation for lost wages at a level determined by the commissioner's office.

ANSWER: D If there is no valid way to determine which players have a 20 percent chance of suffering such an injury, there will be no way to enforce the commissioner's new policy.

19. There are few things worse for a new parent than listening to a baby scream in hunger while a bottle of formula slowly warms up in a bowl of hot water. So why not just pop the bottle in the microwave and zap it in 20 seconds? Because microwaves heat fluids unevenly, and a hot pocket in the formula could seriously injure the baby.

Which of the following is presupposed in the argument against heating formula in the microwave?

A. Babies generally refuse to eat formula that has been heated in a microwave.
B. Microwave radiation might break down some of the proteins in formula that are vital to a baby's health.
C. Different microwaves use different amounts of power, and consequently some models could heat a bottle to scalding temperature faster than others.
D. Parents cannot be expected to consistently even out the temperature of a microwaved bottle by shaking it vigorously before giving it to the baby.
E. Once formula has been heated, any leftover formula should be discarded, because otherwise the formula could spoil between feedings and make the baby sick.

ANSWER: D If parents could be expected to consistently even out the temperature of microwaved bottles, then the concern about hot pockets in the bottle would be unfounded.

20. Charlie's Chainsaw Company has reason to believe that one of its models of saw is defective. A recall of all of the saws would cost more than $5 million, and would probably result in a loss in market share over the next quarter because of bad publicity. Still, a recall is the right economic decision.

Which of the following, if true, most supports the conclusion above?

A. Defective chainsaws can seriously injure or even kill the people who use them.

B. Charlie's chief rival has recalled two of its products within the past year.
C. Product recalls often result in a perception by customers that a given product is permanently defective, even after the defect has been remedied.
D. The stocks of publicly traded companies that announce product recalls often drop upon the announcement, but they generally return to the pre-announcement level within 12 months.
E. Three years ago a rival company went out of business because of large punitive damages awarded to a plaintiff who had been injured by a defective chainsaw.

ANSWER: E Answer E suggests that the company has a justifiable concern that if the product is not recalled, the company could be involved in a damaging lawsuit that could even lead the company into bankruptcy; this concern provides a strong economic incentive to recall the chainsaws. Answer A could be correct if the passage referred to a "moral decision" or just "the right decision," but since the passage specifically refers to an "economic decision," answer E is the best choice.

21. A dog enthusiast took home two puppies from the dog shelter. He fed one of the puppies super-premium canned dog food, while he fed the other a generic brand from the grocery store. The dog fed on the generic brand gained weight twice as fast as the dog fed the super-premium brand. Because of the difference in these results, the dog enthusiast concluded that the generic brand actually provided nutrition superior to that of the super-premium brand.

Each of the following, if true, would weaken the evidence for the dog enthusiast's conclusion except for which of the following?

A. A dog will sometimes gain more weight when eating inferior-quality food because he must eat more of it to obtain the nutrients he needs.
B. The dogs were of mixed breeds and appeared to be descended from dogs of different sizes.
C. Both dogs ate all of the food given to them at each serving.
D. The dog enthusiast did not give the two dogs equal amounts of their respective foods.

E. The dog who received the super-premium dog food suffered from a digestive system disorder that hindered his growth.

ANSWER: C All of the other answers provide alternative reasons that the dogs might show different growth rates, but C offers no explanation for the observed difference in growth.

22. A council of ecologists in Hawaii <u>have concluded that much of the currently uncontrolled invasive species on the island chain were arriving</u> in the holds of cargo ships.

A. have concluded that much of the currently uncontrolled invasive species on the island chain were arriving
B. has concluded that many of the currently uncontrolled invasive species on the island chain arrived
C. have concluded that many of the currently uncontrolled invasive species on the island chain have arrived
D. concluded that many of the currently uncontrolled invasive species on the island chain would arrive
E. has concluded that much of the currently uncontrolled invasive species on the island chain had arrived

ANSWER: B The subject of the sentence is "council," so the plural verb "have concluded" in A and C is incorrect. The use of the conditional "would arrive" to describe species that are already "currently" on the island is illogical, so D is incorrect. E incorrectly uses "much" to describe the countable noun "species"; countable nouns require "many" instead of "much."

23. Some people say that the answer to crime is to build more prisons, but more sensitive observers argue that instead we should address the sources of crime <u>through reduced poverty, a cut off supply of illicit drugs, and by focusing on keeping kids in school.</u>

A. through reduced poverty, a cut off supply of illicit drugs, and by focusing on keeping kids in school
B. by the reduction of poverty, cutting off the supply of illicit drugs, and to focus on keeping kids in school
C. by reducing poverty, cutting off the supply of illicit drugs, and focusing on keeping kids in school

D. by means of reducing poverty, cutting off the supply of illicit drugs, and through focusing on keeping kids in school
E. to reduce poverty, cut off the supply of illicit drugs, and to focus on keeping kids in school

ANSWER: C The best answer should present each of the three points in the same grammatical construction, if possible. C presents each point as a gerund modified by a single adverb, which is grammatically correct and stylistically superior to the other options.

24. <u>As automobiles replaced horses as the primary means of transportation, it was widely anticipated that</u> the time spent in transit by the average traveler would decrease.

A. As automobiles replaced horses as the primary means of transportation, it was widely anticipated that
B. Insofar as automobiles replaced horses as the primary means of transportation, it was anticipated widely
C. With horses being replaced by automobiles as the primary means of transportation, there was wide anticipation that
D. As the primary means of transportation replaced horses with automobiles, many anticipated that
E. Automobiles replacing horses as the primary means of transportation produced anticipation widely that

ANSWER: A The underlined passage is grammatically correct and stylistically superior to the other choices.

25. Intrigued by the new rules that favored quickness over strength, <u>the decision of the coach was to give more playing time to the team's smaller athletes.</u>

A. the decision of the coach was to give more playing time to the team's smaller athletes
B. the coach decided to give the team's smaller athletes more playing time
C. it was decided by the coach to give the team's smaller athletes more playing time
D. the team's smaller athletes were given more playing time by the coach
E. more playing time was given to the team's smaller athletes by the coach

ANSWER: B   The introductory phrase "Intrigued by the new rules" makes sense only when it is applied to the coach, so B is the best answer.

26. At ground level, nitrous oxides are bad enough, <u>but when up high, atmospherically they</u> bond with free ions to create dangerous smog particles.

A. but when up high, atmospherically they
B. however, it is in the upper atmosphere in which it may
C. but in the upper atmosphere, they
D. however, but once in the upper atmosphere it is known to
E. as in the upper atmosphere they

ANSWER: C   The passage refers to "nitrous oxides" plural, so B and D are incorrect because they use the pronoun "it." Answer E does not make sense given the preceding clause, and A is awkwardly worded, so C is the best choice.

27. Paleontologists hypothesize that modern birds evolved from the family of dinosaurs that included *Tyrannosaurus rex*. This hypothesis would be strongly supported if evidence that dinosaurs from this family had a body covering resembling feathers could be found, but so far no such evidence has been found.

Which of the following, if true, would most help the paleontologists explain why no evidence of feathered dinosaurs has yet been found?

A. Fossilized dinosaurs have shown many birdlike characteristics, such as bone structure and winglike arms.
B. If birds are in fact the descendants of dinosaurs, then it can be argued that the dinosaurs never really died out.
C. Flying dinosaurs such as the *Pteranodon*, which is not thought to have been related to modern birds, do not appear to have had feathers.
D. Soft tissues such as skin and feathers do not fossilize like bones, and therefore are far less likely to have left permanent evidence in the fossil record.
E. The thousands of dinosaur fossils excavated by paleontologists represent only a tiny fraction of the billions of dinosaurs that once lived.

ANSWER: D   D provides an answer for the question of why, if feathered dinosaurs did exist, no evidence of their feathers has ever been found. Answer E also provides a partial answer—that the fossil record of dinosaurs is incomplete—but it is a weaker answer than D because it does not directly address the question of feathers.

28. Bob and Linda are tired of the freezing cold days in Glenmont, so they are considering retiring to either Sunny Glen or Buena Vista. Bob points out that Sunny Glen has an average annual temperature 8 degrees Fahrenheit higher than that of Buena Vista. Linda insists, however, that Buena Vista would be the better choice.

Which of the following, if true, best accounts for Linda's preference for Buena Vista?

A. Different people experience cold in different ways, so what seems cold to Linda may seem pleasantly cool to Bob.
B. Sunny Glen has a somewhat higher risk of hurricanes than does Glenmont.
C. Buena Vista has a range of cultural offerings, including an opera, a ballet, and three jazz clubs.
D. Living in a place that gets very hot, such as Sunny Glen, can have as many health risks as living in a place that gets very cold.
E. While Sunny Glen is warmer than Buena Vista in the summer, it also has more freezing cold days in the winter.

ANSWER: E   The passage specifically states that Bob and Linda are seeking to avoid freezing cold days, and answer E states that Buena Vista has fewer freezing cold days than Sunny Glen; this fact accounts for Linda's preference for Buena Vista, despite Sunny Glen's higher average temperature.

29. Although many people would not believe it, the mosquito is actually the most dangerous animal in Africa. While the bite of the black mamba is invariably lethal when untreated, this dreaded snake kills only a few dozen people per year. Hippopotami, with their immense strength and foul dispositions, kill hundreds of people per year in rivers and lakes, but the mosquito is still more dangerous. Mosquitoes bite hundreds of millions of people in Africa every year, and they infect over a million each year with malaria, a disease that is often fatal.

Which of the following questions would be most useful in evaluating the claim made above regarding the mosquito?

A. Could a person survive an attack by a black mamba if that person received prompt medical attention?
B. What criteria are used to determine which animal is the "most dangerous" animal?
C. Could the incidence of mosquito bites be decreased through the judicious use of pesticides and insect repellent?
D. Does malaria kill more people per year in Africa than tuberculosis?
E. How does the percentage of people who survive hippopotamus attacks in Africa each year compare with the percentage of people who survive mosquito bites?

ANSWER: B   The claim about mosquitoes is that "the mosquito is actually the most dangerous animal in Africa." The argument then provides examples of other dangerous animals, but suggests that the mosquito is more dangerous because it attacks more people and infects a very large number of them with a potentially fatal disease. The answer to the question in choice B would allow us to determine whether the quantitative argument in the passage actually does make the mosquito the "most dangerous animal in Africa." If it was determined that the "most dangerous animal" was the one most likely to kill a person in a single encounter, then the black mamba or the hippopotamus might be considered more dangerous than the mosquito. Choice E could be a follow-up to the question in B, but on its own it is less useful than B for evaluating the claim in the passage.

30. What appears to be the primary purpose of this passage?

A. To educate readers about the health threats involved in the use of performance-enhancing drugs
B. To analyze the ways in which professional athletes have eluded attempts to screen for performance-enhancing drugs
C. To discuss the reasons why performance-enhancing drugs are a dangerous and persistent problem for society
D. To complain about the inadequate efforts by government and professional sports organizations to eliminate the problem of performance-enhancing drugs
E. To argue that athletes, both professional and amateur, should not use performance-enhancing drugs on the grounds that they are both dangerous and unfair

ANSWER: C   The passage has two themes: presenting the dangers of performance-enhancing drugs, and then discussing the reasons why the problem is so hard to eliminate. The answer needs to address both of these themes. A and E address only the first of these themes, while B and D address only the second. C offers the most complete description of the passage's purpose.

31. According to the passage, all of the following are known potential consequences of steroid use except for which of the following?

A. Damage to reproductive organs
B. Decreased blood pressure
C. Increases in the user's strength and speed
D. Kidney tumors
E. Increased risk of depression

ANSWER: B   The article specifically states in the second paragraph that steroids "have been linked to . . . high blood pressure." This is the opposite of what B suggests. There is support for all of the other answers in the passage.

32. The author's attitude toward the problem of steroid abuse is best described as which of the following?

A. Cautious but optimistic
B. Judgmental but supportive
C. Ambivalent but resigned
D. Curious but subjective
E. Concerned but pessimistic

ANSWER: E   The author is clearly concerned by the problem of steroid abuse; this attitude is seen in a statement such as: "This chemical epidemic is a pernicious threat to both the nation's health and our collective sense of 'fair play.'" The author's pessimism is seen in the final sentence: "The sad fact is that unless the government and professional sports organizations are willing to get tough on the steroid problem, the use of performance-enhancing drugs in sports is not going to end." A is incorrect because the author is not optimistic; B is incorrect because the author is not supportive; C is incorrect because the author is not ambivalent; and D does not capture the tone of the article.

33. Which of the following can be inferred about a long-distance race in which both athletes who use performance-enhancing drugs and those who do not use these drugs compete?

A. The athletes using the drugs will be caught by the proper authorities and ejected from the race.
B. The athletes using the drugs will have a better chance of winning the race.
C. The athletes using the drugs will use steroid precursors that produce effects similar to those of androgenic drugs but are not technically steroids.
D. The athletes using the drugs are more likely to be professionals in their sport than the athletes who do not use such drugs.
E. The athletes using the drugs will be more likely to use any means possible to win the race, including intentional sabotage of the other racers' equipment.

ANSWER: B   The passage states: "the drugs really do work. Athletes who dope are simply stronger and faster than their competitors who play fair." There is no substantial evidence for any of the other answers.

34. The relationship of an athlete who does not use performance-enhancing drugs to an athlete who does use such drugs is most similar to which of the following?

A. The relationship of a farmer selling milk from cows that have been given bovine growth hormone, a legal drug that promotes greater than normal milk production, to a farmer selling milk from cows that have not been given bovine growth hormone
B. The relationship of a chess player to a competitor who uses psychological tricks in order to gain an advantage
C. The relationship of a boxer in the lightweight class to a boxer in the heavyweight class
D. The relationship of a person taking a standardized test according to the rules to a person taking the same test while using an illegal hidden calculator
E. The relationship of a person entering a pig in an agricultural contest to a person entering a guinea pig in the same contest

ANSWER: D   D is the best answer because in both situations, the latter is using illegal means to gain an advantage over the former.

35. According to the passage, which of the following can be inferred about the "designer" steroid THG?

A. It can increase masculine traits in users without setting off standard doping tests.
B. It does not cause the health problems associated with traditional anabolic steroids.
C. Even if professional sports organizations could detect THG, they would take no action against those who use it.
D. It is a chemical permutation of progesterone, a hormone that has powerful effects on the human body.
E. Because it is a "designer" steroid, it is more expensive than generic steroids.

ANSWER: A   Referring to "designer" steroids, in the fifth paragraph the passage states: "Chemists have discovered that they can create new drugs that produce androgenic effects but do not set off the standard doping tests." In the second paragraph, the passage states: "'androgenic' means that they increase masculine traits." There is no substantial support in the passage for any of the other answers.

36. Which of the following best expresses the role of the third paragraph in the overall structure of the passage?

- A. It redirects the theme of the passage from presenting a problem to explaining the reasons for the problem's severity.
- B. It introduces a new concept that defines the rest of the passage.
- C. It provides an answer to a question posed in the first two paragraphs.
- D. It refutes the central hypothesis of the second paragraph and poses a question that is answered in the following paragraphs.
- E. It narrows the focus of the passage from the general themes of the first two paragraphs to the more specific themes of the last two paragraphs.

ANSWER: A By posing the question "Why is this?" the third paragraph shifts the focus of the passage from a presentation of the problems caused by steroids to explanations of why large numbers of people use them despite the risks. Answer A captures this role best.

37. His opponent having sprained his wrist, Andrew could have won by exploiting this weakness, but he chose not to do it.

- A. His opponent having sprained his wrist, Andrew could have won by exploiting this weakness, but he chose not to do it.
- B. Andrew could have won by exploiting this weakness after his opponent sprained his wrist, but he chose not to do so.
- C. Choosing not to do so, Andrew could have won after his opponent sprained his wrist by exploiting this weakness.
- D. After his opponent sprained his wrist, Andrew could have won by exploiting this weakness, but he chose not to do so.
- E. After his opponent sprained his wrist, Andrew could have, but chose not to do it, won by exploiting this weakness.

ANSWER: D The problem with A is that it is unclear what the "it" at the end applies to: winning or exploiting the weakness. E has the same problem. The statements in B and C are presented in an illogical order, so it is more difficult to understand the meaning of the sentence. Of the choices, D is the clearest and conforms best to standards of written English.

38. Since the average test score of students enrolled in charter schools were rising 7.5 percent in the spring, many educators concluded that the system was working.

- A. Since the average test score of students enrolled in charter schools were rising 7.5 percent in the spring, many educators concluded
- B. As the average test score of students enrolled in charter schools rose 7.5 percent in the spring, with many educators concluding
- C. Because the average test score of students enrolled in charter schools rose 7.5 percent in the spring, many educators concluded
- D. Because the average test score of students enrolled in charter schools were up 7.5 percent in the spring, many educators concluded
- E. With average test scores rising by 7.5 percent among students enrolled in charter schools, and many educators concluded

ANSWER: C "Score" is a single noun, so the statements "score . . . were rising" in A and "score . . . were up" in D suffer from noun-verb agreement errors. The constructions "as . . ., with" in B and "with . . ., and" in E do not convey the causal relationship between the first and second clauses of the sentence that the statements imply, so these choices are inferior to C, which is grammatically and stylistically acceptable.

39. The police chief argued that first-time offenders who have no high school diploma but who have families with a record of crime will probably break the law again.

- A. who have no high school diploma but who have families with a record of crime
- B. without a high school diploma and families having a criminal record
- C. without a high school diploma whose families have a record of crime
- D. whose families have criminal records and lacking high school diplomas
- E. lacking high school diplomas and also having families having criminal records

ANSWER: C C is the clearest and most concise choice. A is less concise, and it is unclear why "but" is used here; B implies that the offenders lack both diplomas and families; D implies that the families lack diplomas; and E is awkwardly worded.

40. Like the power-generating apparatus of a conventional car, <u>that of a hybrid car depends on</u> a combustible fuel to generate power.

    A. that of a hybrid car depends on
    B. hybrid cars depend on
    C. hybrid cars' power-generating apparati are dependent on
    D. that of a hybrid car's is dependent on
    E. that of hybrid cars depend on

ANSWER: A **A is grammatically and stylistically correct, and is superior to any of the alternatives.**

41. <u>Since red flags are likely to be raised at the IRS by the reporting of gambling income, business owners who declare their income as business revenue is less likely to receive an audit.</u>

    A. Since red flags are likely to be raised at the IRS by the reporting of gambling income, business owners who declare their income as business revenue is less likely to receive an audit.

    B. Because the reporting of gambling income is likely to raise red flags at the IRS, business owners can reduce their chances of receiving an audit by declaring that income as business revenue.
    C. Business owners can reduce their chances of receiving an audit by declaring the income as business revenue, since the reporting of gambling income is likely to raise red flags at the IRS.
    D. Their chances of receiving an audit are reduced by business owners who report that income as business revenue, because the reporting of gambling income is likely to raise red flags at the IRS.
    E. The reporting of that income as business revenue can reduce the chances of business owners of receiving an audit, because of the red flags not having been raised at the IRS by the reporting of gambling income.

ANSWER: B **A is incorrect because it makes an error of number—"business owners . . . is less likely." C, D, and E are all confusing because they do not specify what kind of income (gambling income) they are referring to until late in the sentence. B is grammatically correct and presents the information in the most logical order.**

1. Jim's Taxi Service charges an initial fee of $2.25 at the beginning of a trip and an additional charge of $0.35 for each 2/5 of a mile traveled. What is the total charge for a trip of 3.6 miles?

    A. $3.15
    B. $4.45
    C. $4.80
    D. $5.05
    E. $5.40

    ANSWER: E **3.6 miles divided by 2/5 equals 9, so the total charge is $2.25 + (9 × $0.35) = $5.40.**

2. If the area of a square with sides of length 8 centimeters is equal to the area of a rectangle with a width of 4 centimeters, what is the length of the rectangle, in centimeters?

    A. 4
    B. 8
    C. 12
    D. 16
    E. 18

    ANSWER: D **The square has an area of 8 × 8 = 64, so the length of the rectangle is 64/4 = 16 (the area of a rectangle is its width times its length).**

3. A certain lab experiments with white and brown mice only. In one experiment, 2/3 of the mice are white. If there are 13 brown mice in the experiment, how many mice in total are in the experiment?

    A. 39
    B. 33
    C 26
    D 21
    E 10

ANSWER: A **Brown mice make up 1/3 of the mice in the experiment, so the total number of mice is $13 \times 3 = 39$.**

4. If $x = \dfrac{a}{3} + \dfrac{b}{3^2} + \dfrac{c}{3^3}$, where a, b, and c are each equal to 0 or 1, then x could be each of the following EXCEPT:

    A. $\dfrac{1}{27}$
    B. $\dfrac{1}{9}$
    C. $\dfrac{4}{27}$
    D. $\dfrac{2}{9}$
    E. $\dfrac{4}{9}$

    ANSWER: D **The most direct way to address this problem, since there are only eight possible values for x, is to determine all the possible values and then check them against the possible answers. x could equal 0, 1/27, 3/27 (= 1/9), 4/27, 9/27 (= 1/3), 10/27, 12/27 (= 4/9), or 13/27. The only answer not among these choices is D, 2/9.**

Score	Number of Applicants
5	2
4	12
3	21
2	7
1	8

5. Fifty applicants for a job were given scores from 1 to 5 on their interview performance. Their scores are shown in the table above. What was the average score for the group?

    A. 2.79
    B. 2.86
    C. 2.91
    D. 2.99
    E. 3.03

    ANSWER: B **You can calculate this average score exactly the same way you would calculate**

a GPA—multiply each of the scores by the number of applicants with that score, add them all up, and divide the sum by 50. 10 + 48 + 63 + 14 + 8 = 143; 143/50 = 2.86.

6. Carrie, Lisa, and Betty all make purchases at a music store that sells all records for a certain price and all CDs for a certain price. How much does Carrie pay for 1 record and 2 CDs?

(1) Lisa bought 3 records for $22.50.
(2) Betty bought 2 records and 4 CDs for $55.00.

ANSWER: B (1) alone is insufficient because it tells you only the price per record, and does not give the price of CDs. (2) alone is sufficient, because the quantity of items is twice that of Carrie's purchase, so the purchase price is therefore half of what Betty paid—$27.50.

7. N and P are points on the number line below 20. Is P closer to 10 than N is?

(1) P is greater than the average of 10 and N.
(2) $\frac{P}{N} = 3$

ANSWER: E Both statements alone and combined are insufficient, because, for example, the values (9, 3) for (P, N) meet all the conditions and yield an answer of "yes," while the values (18, 6) meet all the conditions and yield a "no."

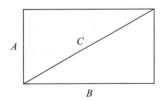

8. What is the area of the rectangular region depicted above with sides A and B and diagonal C?

(1) $C^2 = 9 + A^2$
(2) $A + B = 7$

ANSWER: C You need to know the product of A and B to solve this question. (1) alone is insufficient because it does not give the value for A, although you can infer from the Pythagorean theorem that B = 3. (2) alone is insufficient because (A, B) could be (1, 6) or it could be (3, 4), there is no way to tell. If the

statements are combined, you can take the value that B = 3 and determine from the equation in statement 2 that A = 4; therefore, the area of the rectangle is 12.

9. Do at least 20 percent of the people in country X who are over the age of 25 possess a college diploma?

(1) In country X, among the population over the age of 25, 26 percent of the male population and 16 percent of the female population possess college diplomas.
(2) In country X, women account for 55 percent of the total population.

ANSWER: E (1) is insufficient because it does not tell what percentage of the population over 25 is female; if the gender split is 50/50, then the answer to the question is "yes," if the gender split is 25/75 with more females, then the answer is "no." (2) alone is insufficient, and although it appears to address the insufficiency in statement (1), it actually does not, because we cannot infer that the gender split for the total population is the same as the gender split for the population over 25.

10. If $C = \frac{5r}{2s}$ and $s \neq 0$, what is the value of C?

(1) $r = 4s$
(2) $r = \frac{2}{5}$

ANSWER: A In order to answer this question, you need to remove both variables so that a numerical answer is left. (1) is sufficient because it allows you to restate the equation as $C = \frac{20s}{2s} = 10$. (2) is insufficient, because a variable remains in the equation.

11. If $8a = 9b$ and $ab \neq 0$, what is the ratio of $\frac{a}{9}$ to $\frac{a}{8}$?

A. $\frac{64}{81}$
B. $\frac{8}{9}$
C. 1
D. $\frac{9}{8}$
E. $\frac{81}{64}$

ANSWER: C The ratio of these numbers is $(a/9)/(b/8)$; you can substitute in the ratios from the question, so $a = 9b/8$; the ratio then is $(9b/72)/(b/8)$; divide b from both sides of the ratio, and multiply 8 times both sides of the ratio, and you wind up with 72/72 = 1.

12. Two hundred multiples of seven are chosen at random, and 300 multiples of eight are chosen at random. Approximately what percentage of the 500 selected numbers are odd?

   A. 20%
   B. 25%
   C. 40%
   D. 50%
   E. 80%

   ANSWER: A   All multiples of 8 are even, and half of the multiples of 7 are odd; the multiples of 7 make up 2/5 of the total, so if $^1/_2$ of those multiples of 7 are odd, then 1/5 of the total will be odd, or 20%.

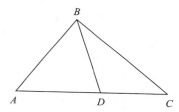

13. In triangle *ABC* above, if ∠*BAD* and ∠*ADB* have measures of $4n°$, ∠*ACB* has a measure of $n°$, and ∠*DBC* has a measure of 45°, what is the measure of ∠*ABC*? (Figure not necessarily drawn to scale.)

   A. 45°
   B. 60°
   C. 90°
   D. 105°
   E. 120°

   ANSWER: D   The principle to remember here is that an exterior angle of a triangle—such as ∠*ADB*—is equal to the sum of the remote interior angles of the triangle, in this case ∠*DBC* and ∠*DCB* (=∠*ACB*) of triangle *BDC*. Thus, ∠*DCB* + ∠*DBC* = $4n$, or ∠*DBC* = $3n = 45°$, and therefore $n = 15°$ and $4n = 60°$. The three angles of a triangle must equal 180°, so ∠*ABC* = 180° − 60° − 15° = 105°.

14. A coed soccer team has *W* women and *M* men on the team. If 4 women and 2 men are added to the team roster, and if one

person on the team is selected at random to serve as team captain, then the probability that the team captain will be a woman can be represented as:

   A. $\dfrac{W + 4}{W + M + 6}$

   B. $\dfrac{W + 4}{W + M + 2}$

   C. $\dfrac{W + 4}{M + 2}$

   D. $\dfrac{W + 4}{W + M}$

   E. $\dfrac{W}{M}$

   ANSWER: A   The probability is equal to the new number of women, i.e., $W + 4$, divided by the new total, which is $W + M + 6$. The answer, therefore, is $\dfrac{W + 4}{W + M + 6}$.

15. What is the twenty-third decimal to the right in the fraction $\dfrac{23}{24}$?

   A. 1
   B. 2
   C. 3
   D. 4
   E. 5

   ANSWER: C   This would be an unreasonably difficult question except that the fraction in question is the nonterminating decimal $0.958333\overline{3}$, so the number to the right of anything after the third decimal is 3.

16. If Scott has earned *x* dollars by working 3 days a week at a constant daily rate for *w* weeks, which of the following represents his daily wage?

   A. $3xw$

   B. $\dfrac{3w}{x}$

   C. $\dfrac{w}{3x}$

   D. $\dfrac{xw}{3}$

   E. $\dfrac{x}{3w}$

   ANSWER: E   His daily wage can be determined by dividing his total income by the total number of days he has worked. x is his income, and $3w$ is the total number of days he has worked, so $\frac{x}{3w}$ is his daily wage.

17. $\left(\frac{1}{3} - \frac{1}{2}\right) - 1 =$

A. $\frac{-7}{6}$

B. $\frac{-5}{6}$

C. $\frac{-1}{6}$

D. $\frac{5}{6}$

E. $\frac{7}{6}$

ANSWER: A   The statement $\left(\frac{1}{3} - \frac{1}{2}\right)$ equals $\frac{-1}{6}$; $\frac{-1}{6} - 1 = \frac{-7}{6}$.

18. In a certain conservative mutual fund, 70 percent of the money is invested in bonds, and of that portion, 40 percent is invested in highly rated corporate bonds. If at least $1.4 million in this fund is invested in highly rated corporate bonds, what is the smallest possible total value for the mutual fund?

A. $4 million
B. $5 million
C. $6 million
D. $7 million
E. $8 million

ANSWER: B   If 40 percent of the amount invested in bonds is invested in highly rated corporate bonds, then the total amount invested in bonds is $1.4 million times 10/4 = $3.5 million. $3.5 million in bonds is 70 percent of the total fund, so the total fund is $3.5 million times 10/7 = $5 million.

19. If the diameter of a circle is 14, then the area of the circle is

A. 7π
B. 14π
C. 28π
D. 49π
E. 196π

ANSWER: D   The diameter of a circle is twice its radius, so if the diameter is 14,

then the radius is 7. The formula for the area of a circle is πr^2, so the area of this circle is 49π.

20. If a is an integer, is b an integer?

(1) The average (arithmetic mean) of a and b is an integer.
(2) The average (arithmetic mean) of a, b, and $b + 4$ is a.

ANSWER: D   (1) alone is sufficient; the statement can be restated as $(a + b)/2$ is an integer; no noninteger divided by an integer—in this case, 2—is going to yield an integer, so $a + b$ must be an integer, and therefore b must be an integer. (2) alone is sufficient; the statement can be restated as $a + 2b + 4 = 3a$, so $b + 2 = a$; we know that a is an integer, and any integer plus 2 is an integer, so b must be an integer.

21. Did Alberto pay more than N dollars for his new stereo, excluding the sales tax?

(1) The price Alberto paid for the stereo was $1.05N$, including the sales tax.
(2) Alberto paid $35 in sales tax on the purchase of his new stereo.

ANSWER: E   (1) alone is insufficient because the answer could be "yes" or "no" depending on the percentage of the sales tax. (2) alone is insufficient because it gives no information about the price of the stereo relative to N. Combining the two statements yields no useful information, since neither the sales tax percentage nor the total purchase price is known, so the question cannot be resolved.

22. Is $r < 1$?

(1) $r > 0$
(2) $r^2 < 1$

ANSWER: B   (1) alone is insufficient because r could equal any positive number, which could give either an affirmative or a negative response to the question. (2) is sufficient, because the only values of r for which the statement is true are those between -1 and 1, exclusive, which means that the answer is "yes," $r < 1$.

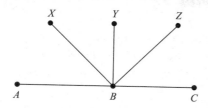

23. In the figure above, with B a point on the line AC, what is the measure of $\angle XBZ$? (Figure not necessarily drawn to scale.)

(1) BX bisects $\angle ABY$, which is a right angle, and BZ bisects $\angle YBC$.
(2) $\angle ABX = \angle XBY = \angle YBZ = \angle ZBC$

ANSWER: D (1) alone is sufficient, because if $\angle ABY$ is a right angle, then $\angle YBC$ must also be a right angle, and since both right angles are bisected, $\angle XBY$ and $\angle YBZ$ must both be equal to 45°, and therefore $\angle XBZ = 90°$. (2) alone is sufficient, because if all four of those angles are equal, and there can be only 180° on one side of a line, then each angle must equal 45°, and therefore $\angle XBZ = 90°$.

24. If P and Q are both positive, what is the value of P?

(1) PQ is a positive multiple of 5.
(2) 300 percent of P equals 500 percent of Q.

ANSWER: E Neither (1) nor (2) is sufficient, because there is an infinite number of values for P and Q that could meet either or both conditions [e.g., (5, 3), (10, 6), (15, 9), etc.].

25. MegaTech and UltraCorp are considering a merger to form the MegaUltraTech Corporation. Does MegaTech have more employees than UltraCorp?

(1) The average (arithmetic mean) age of UltraCorp employees is 32.8, while the average age of MegaTech employees is 27.2.
(2) If the merger goes through and all employees from both companies remain employed, the average (arithmetic mean) age of the MegaUltraTech employees will be 31.4.

ANSWER: C (1) alone is insufficient, because it gives us no information about the number of employees at either company. (2) alone is insufficient for the same reason. If the two statements are combined, we are able to infer that there are more employees at UltraCorp than at MegaTech, because the average age of the employees of the combined company is closer to the previous UltraCorp average than to that of MegaTech.

26. In a sample of 800 high school students in which all students are either freshmen, sophomores, juniors, or seniors, 22 percent are juniors and 74 percent are not sophomores. If there are 160 seniors, how many more freshmen than sophomores are there among the sample of students?

A. 42
B. 48
C. 56
D. 208
E. 256

ANSWER: B 22 percent are juniors, $100 - 74 = 26$ percent are sophomores, $160/800 = 20$ percent are seniors, and therefore $100 - (22 + 26 + 20) = 32$ percent are freshmen. 32 percent of 800 = 256 freshmen; 26 percent of 800 = 208 sophomores; 256 freshmen – 208 sophomores = 48 more freshmen than sophomores.

27. The time it took car P to travel 600 miles was 2 hours less than the time it took car R to travel the same distance. If car P's average speed was 10 miles per hour greater than that of car R, what was car R's average speed, in miles per hour?

A. 40
B. 50
C. 60
D. 70
E. 80

ANSWER: B You could set this up algebraically and eliminate a variable, but it might be faster to just set up a simple equation and plug in the answers until one fits the statements in the question. If car R is traveling at answer A's 40 miles per hour, then it will travel the 600 miles in 15 hours, while car P traveling at 50 mph will cover the 600 miles in 12 hours; this does not meet the 2-hour difference mentioned. If car R is traveling at answer B's 50 mph, then it will take 12 hours to cover 600 miles, while car P will cover it in 10 hours at 60 mph; this meets the 2-hour difference specified in the question, so B is the correct answer.

28. For any numbers a and b, $a•b = ab(3 − b)$. If a and $a•b$ both represent positive numbers, which of the following could be a value of b?

A. −5
B. −2
C. 2
D. 4
E. 7

ANSWER: C The most direct approach to this sort of problem is to plug in the answers and see which one works. Choices A and B are out because any negative value for b would result in a negative value for $a•b$ if a is positive. C works because it gives the result $a•b = 2a$, which has to be positive. D and E do not work because they result in negative values for $a•b$. Therefore, C is the only answer that provides a possible value for b.

29. Marcella has 25 pairs of shoes. If she loses 9 individual shoes, what is the greatest number of matching pairs she could have left?

A. 21
B. 20
C. 19
D. 16
E. 15

ANSWER: B The greatest number of matching pairs remaining will occur when the greatest number of lost shoes are part of matching pairs; if four matching pairs and one other individual shoe were lost, then Marcella would still have 20 matching pairs left.

30. If Finn was 18 months old one year ago, how old was he in months, x months ago?

A. $x − 30$
B. $x − 12$
C. $18 − x$
D. $24 − x$

E. $30 − x$

ANSWER: E If Finn was 18 months old 1 year ago, then he is now $18 + 12 = 30$ months old. $30 − x$ represents his age x months ago.

31. A restaurant orders 150 kg of pumpkins from the farmer's market. The farmer fills the order with 23 pumpkins. The average mass of the first 20 pumpkins is 6.5 kg. What must be the minimum average mass of the remaining 3 pumpkins to fill the order?

A. 5.5 kg
B. 5.67 kg
C. 6.67 kg
D. 7 kg
E. 11.5 kg

ANSWER: C The remaining three pumpkins must make up the difference between 150 kg and (20 pumpkins × 6.5 kg =) 130 kg, so 20 kg. For three pumpkins to fill 20 kg, each must have a minimum mass of 20 divided by 3, which equals $6^2/3$, which is best expressed here as 6.67 kg.

32. The square root of 636 is between which set of integers?

A. 24 and 25
B. 25 and 26
C. 26 and 27
D. 27 and 28
E. 28 and 29

ANSWER: B The best solution here is to plug in the numbers from the answers until you find one that works. $24 × 24 = 576$, $25 × 25 = 625$, $26 × 26 = 676 . . .$ therefore, the square root of 636 is between 25 and 26.

33. In a forest 150 deer were caught, tagged with electronic markers, then released. A week later, 50 deer were captured in the same forest. Of these 50 deer, it was found that 5 had been tagged with the electronic markers. If the percentage of tagged deer in the second sample approximates the percentage of tagged deer in the forest, and if no deer had either left or entered the forest over the preceding week, what is the approximate number of deer in the forest?

A. 150
B. 750
C. 1,250
D. 1,500
E. 2,500

ANSWER: D   5 out of 50 deer is 10 percent. If this is representative of the percentage of tagged deer in the forest, then the 150 tagged deer are 10 percent of the 1,500 total deer in the forest.

34. If $5a = 9b = 15c$, what is the value of $a + b + c$?

(1) $3c - a = 5c - 3b$
(2) $6cb = 10a$

ANSWER: B   Statement (1) alone is insufficient; you can restate the equation as $3b = 2c + a$; if you multiply both sides of the equation by 3, you get $9b = 6c + 3a$; you can determine from the equation $5a = 15c$ that $a = 3c$, so all this restated equation tells you is that $9b = 15c = 5a$, which tells you nothing about the actual value of a or b. Statement (2) is sufficient. If you divide both sides of the equation by 2, you get $3cb = 5a$; you know that $5a = 9b$, so you can form the equation $3cb = 9b$, which you can reduce to $c = 3$. With this value you can determine that $a = 1$ and $b = 1.8$, and you can thereby find a definitive answer to the question posed.

35. Stanley has gained 8 pounds a year ever since he turned 18. How much weight has Stanley gained since he turned 18?

(1) Stanley now weighs twice what he weighed when he turned 18.
(2) Stanley is now twice the age he was when he turned 18.

ANSWER: B   (1) alone is insufficient because it does not tell us what Stanley weighed when he turned 18. (2) alone is sufficient, because it tells us that he has aged 18 years since then, meaning that he has gained 18×8 pounds = 144 pounds.

36. What is the value of the greater of two numbers if one of the numbers is three times the smaller number?

(1) One of the numbers is 12.
(2) The sum of the two numbers is 16.

ANSWER: B   (1) alone is insufficient because the two numbers could be 4 and 12 or 12 and 36. (2) alone is sufficient because the only two numbers that meet the stated conditions are 4 and 12.

37. If $\sqrt{r}$ is a positive integer, what is the value of r?

(1) $r < 70$
(2) $\sqrt{r} > 7$

ANSWER: C   (1) alone is insufficient because r could be several numbers less than 70, such as 64 or 49. (2) alone is insufficient because r could be several numbers greater than 49, such as 64 or 81. When the statements are combined, the only number that meets both criteria is 64, so the answer is C.

Answers and Explanations

VERBAL

1. The gap in the ozone hole over the North Pole can expand each summer enough <u>that it exposes regions as far south as Sweden by heightened UV radiation, also increasing</u> rates of skin cancer in the northern regions by as much as 50 percent.

   A. that it exposes regions as far south as Sweden by heightened UV radiation, also increasing
   B. that regions as far south as Sweden have been exposed to heightened UV radiation, as well as having increased
   C. to expose regions as far south as Sweden to heightened UV radiation, increased
   D. to expose regions as far south as Sweden to heightened UV radiation and increase
   E. that exposure to heightened UV radiation in regions as far south as Sweden, as well as increasing

   ANSWER: D   The construction "exposes . . . by heightened UV radiation" in A is unidiomatic. In B, the construction "that regions . . . have been exposed" makes "regions" the subject of the clause, and this does not work with the following clause, where it appears that the regions, rather than the radiation, are increasing rates of skin cancer. C and E both form sentence fragments. D is the clearest and most standard statement of the information.

2. In winning the 1998 Kentucky Derby, Swiftilocks showed a burst of speed <u>as that of Man o'War, who won</u> 20 of 21 races in 1919 and 1920.

   A. as that of Man o'War, who won
   B. not unlike that of Man o'War, who won
   C. not unlike Man o'War, who won
   D. like that of Man o'War for winning
   E. like Man o'War and his winning

   ANSWER: B   A is incorrect because "like" rather than "as" should be used to compare two noun phrases. C and E are incorrect because they erroneously compare Man o'War to Swiftilocks's burst of speed. D fails to make clear whether Swiftilocks or Man o'War won the 20 races. B provides the clearest statement of the information.

3. <u>Rising tides</u> of unemployment claims across the state has led the governor to declare the economy to be in a state of emergency.

   A. Rising tides
   B. Because the rising tide
   C. The tide is rising
   D. The rising tide
   E. The rising of the tide

   ANSWER: D   A is incorrect because "tides" does not agree in number with "has led." B and C create sentence fragments. E is less idiomatic and concise than D. D is the best answer.

4. Seeking to decrease the incidence of tooth decay, <u>the American Dental Association is to spend $45 million over the next seven years promoting good dental hygiene</u>.

   A. the American Dental Association is to spend $45 million over the next seven years promoting good dental hygiene
   B. the American Dental Association will spend $45 million over the next seven years to promote good dental hygiene
   C. over the next seven years the American Dental Association is to spend $45 million promoting good dental hygiene
   D. good dental hygiene will be promoted by the American Dental Association, which is spending $45 million over the next seven years

E. $45 million will be spent by the American Dental Association over the next seven years on the promotion of good dental hygiene

ANSWER: B "the American Dental Association" is the subject of the introductory phrase "Seeking to decrease the incidence of tooth decay," so it should come immediately after that phrase; C, D, and E incorrectly place other phrases between the introductory phrase and its subject. D and E also unnecessarily use passive verb constructions. The construction "is to spend . . . promoting" in A is less idiomatic and forceful than "will spend . . . to promote" in B, because, in general, use of a declarative active verb is more forceful than use of a "to be" verb, and infinitives are generally more forceful than gerunds. B is the best answer.

5. Some paleontologists claim that the discovery of what appear to be feathers in the fossil of an Archosaur could force a revision of current theories on the phylogeny of Archosaurs, alter conceptions of dinosaur skin surfaces, and <u>require scholars to credit birds with a far earlier origin than previously thought</u>.

A. require scholars to credit birds with a far earlier origin than previously thought
B. scholars may be required to credit birds with a far earlier origin than previously thought
C. require a crediting by scholars of birds with a far earlier origin than previously thought
D. , compared to what was previously thought, require scholars to credit birds with a far earlier origin
E. crediting birds with a far earlier origin than scholars had previously thought

ANSWER: A A is grammatically correct and idiomatic, so it is the best choice. To maintain parallel structures with the other clauses in this sentence with an understood connection to the verb "could," the sentence should read "could force . . . , [could] alter . . . , and [could] require . . . "; thus, A and C are the only choices. The construction "require a crediting by scholars of birds" in C is awkward and confusing, so A is the best answer.

6. Covington College has four full-time Classics professors, but only 12 Classics majors. This three-to-one student-to-professor ratio is the lowest in the college. Since the college is facing financial difficulties, and since the tuition fees from just 12 students is not sufficient to pay the salaries of 4 full-time professors, the college should cancel the Classics program to reduce expenses.

Which of the following, if true, most weakens the conclusion above?

A. Professors in the Classics department teach popular language and literature classes that are attended by hundreds of students who are not Classics majors.
B. Students at Covington College pay, on average, $22,500 per year in tuition and fees, while the average professor of humanities receives a salary of $61,500 per year.
C. A well-regarded Classics program adds prestige to a college or university.
D. The Classics department has already decreased in size from six full-time professors 10 years ago.
E. The study of classical literature and languages is increasingly irrelevant to the high-tech workplace of today.

ANSWER: A This answer directly counters the argument that the Classics professors are not cost-justified to the college, because their salaries are supported not only by Classics majors, but by hundreds of nonmajors as well.

7. A pharmaceutical company tested a new diet drug over a two-month period. The test group of 100 dieters lost an average of five pounds per person during the first month, but gained an average of two pounds per person in the second month.

All of the following could help explain the results of the experiment except:

A. The second month of the test occurred during a holiday season, when people are more likely to gain weight.
B. The diet drug has unpleasant side effects, causing many of the subjects to stop using the drug after the first month.
C. The pharmaceutical company provided low-calorie diets to the test subjects in the first month, but let the dieters choose their own food in the second month.
D. The pharmaceutical company selected for the test people who were 20 to 40 pounds over their ideal weights.
E. The diet drug relies on a metabolic effect that loses efficacy the longer a person takes the drug.

ANSWER: D   This answer provides no explanation for the difference in weight loss experienced by the test subjects over the first and second months, while all of the other answers provide explanations.

8. The Tricounty Bridge was supposed to relieve traffic in East Countway County. Although the bridge was opened last year, traffic in the county has gotten worse over the last year. To relieve the traffic situation in East Countway, therefore, the traffic commission should order the Tricounty Bridge closed.

Which of the following, if true, gives the most support to the conclusion of the passage above?

A. The increased traffic seen in East Countway over the last year is largely attributable to a large casino and resort hotel that opened for business shortly after the opening of the Tricounty Bridge.
B. The Tricounty Bridge allows inhabitants of heavily populated West Countway County to reach East Countway in less than a half-hour, as opposed to the two

hours the trip required before the opening of the bridge.
C. The bridge is only open for the periods 7–9 a.m. and 3–5 p.m. on weekdays.
D. Ship captains on the Countway River have complained that the bridge disrupts shipping on the river, thereby hurting the local economy.
E. The bridge is unlikely ever to pay for itself with the current low toll payment.

ANSWER: B   This answer provides an explanation for the increase in traffic after the opening of the bridge, and supports the assertion that closing the bridge would reduce traffic in East Countway because it would discourage inhabitants of West Countway from entering the county.

9. Alcohol-control advocates argue that television advertising plays a large role in leading teenagers to drink. In Hungary, however, where television advertising of alcoholic beverages has been prohibited since 1980, teenage alcohol use is higher than in some other European countries where such advertising is allowed.

Which of the following statements draws the most reliable conclusion from the information given above?

A. Hungarian culture, in general, views alcohol use more positively than do most other European cultures.
B. Television advertising is the most effective way to encourage consumers to try a new alcoholic beverage.
C. Television advertising cannot be the only factor that affects the prevalence of teenage drinking.
D. Alcohol use among Hungarian teenagers has increased in recent years.
E. Alcohol abuse is the greatest threat facing Hungarian teenagers.

ANSWER: C   If teenagers in Hungary drink more alcohol than teenagers in some countries that do permit advertising of alcoholic products, clearly there are other factors influencing the situation.

10. The passage is primarily concerned with which of the following?

   A. Describing the life cycle of the *Plasmodium* protozoan as it relates to the disease malaria
   B. Comparing and contrasting the life cycles of the six variants of the *Plasmodium* protozoan known to cause malaria
   C. Addressing the public health implications of the life cycle of the *Plasmodium* parasite
   D. Providing information on how a person can avoid infection with malaria
   E. Describing the life cycle of the *Anopheles* mosquito as it relates to the transmission of the *Plasmodium* protozoan to humans

   ANSWER: A   The first three paragraphs are all directly addressed to the life cycle of the *Plasmodium* protozoan, and the last two paragraphs discuss the implications of the parasite's life cycle for malaria in humans. Answer C is partially accurate, but the passage is certainly more focused on describing the life cycle of *Plasmodium* than on describing its public health implications, so A is the better answer.

11. Which of the following most accurately states the role of the first paragraph in relation to the passage as a whole?

   A. It summarizes two theories, the relative merits of which are debated in the passage.
   B. It puts forth an argument that the rest of the passage is devoted to refuting.
   C. It introduces a new concept that the rest of the passage expands upon.
   D. It frames the background and relevance of the material to follow.
   E. It outlines the major themes of each of the four paragraphs to follow.

ANSWER: D   The first paragraph mentions the background of the effort to understand the life cycle of the malaria parasite ("It took scientists centuries to deconstruct the basic relationship between protozoan, mosquito vector, and human host"), and it provides relevance to the following passage by linking the topic to human health ("has contributed to the difficulty of devising effective public health measures to combat the disease").

12. If a mosquito were to bite a person, and that person were later to develop malaria and die of the disease, it is most likely that the person was infected with which of the following?

   A. *Anopheles gambiae*
   B. *Anopheles semiovale*
   C. *Plasmodium malariae*
   D. *Plasmodium vivax*
   E. *Plasmodium falciparum*

   ANSWER: E   The passage states, "Of these species, *P. falciparum* accounts for the majority of infections and approximately 90 percent of malarial deaths in the world."

13. The relationship of a merozoite to a sporozoite is most like which of the following?

   A. A mother to a daughter
   B. A brother to a sister
   C. One of several subsidiaries spun off from a large corporation
   D. A computer program to a computer
   E. Orange juice to an orange tree

   ANSWER: C   The passage states, "Within the liver, the sporozoite can form 30,000 to 40,000 daughter cells, called merozoites, which are released into the host's blood stream at a later date," so the relationship should be that of descent from the latter to the former, and of many from one, which answer C captures. Answer A could be correct if the order were reversed.

14. Based on the information given in the passage, which of the following would be most effective in preventing a person infected with malaria from developing a hemorrhagic fever?

A. Surgical removal of the spleen
B. A medicine that prevents changes to the surface proteins of red blood cells
C. An effective vaccine against malaria
D. A potent pesticide that reliably kills the *Anopheles* mosquito without producing any negative consequences for the environment or for human health
E. A small infusion of a weaker variant of the *Plasmodium* protozoan that will then compete with the existing parasitic infection

ANSWER: B   The passage states, "If the sticky surface proteins affect a particularly large number of cells, the malaria can transform into a hemorrhagic fever, the most deadly form of malaria." Answer C is incorrect because a vaccination would not help an already infected person.

15. In fisheries in general, when a large harvest is taken one year, there will be fewer fish available to be harvested in the following year, leading to decreasing yields of most fish species over time. The Maine lobster is an anomaly, however. Even though the vast number of lobster traps covering the New England coast pull in more lobsters every year, the number of lobsters in the water has shown no signs of decreasing.

Which of the following, if true, most helps to explain the apparent anomaly concerning the number of Maine lobsters?

A. The decline of other fish species in the region has deprived the lobster of its natural food source of scavenged fish.
B. The bait in lobster traps provides abundant food for young lobsters, which are still small enough to swim out of the traps, leading to much higher survival rates among young lobsters than would be expected in nature.
C. As global warming heats the waters of the Atlantic coastline, the Maine lobster has extended its northern range to well past Nova Scotia.

D. The ever-increasing demand for lobsters in seafood restaurants and steakhouses across the country has driven a corresponding increase in the supply of the product.
E. The increased lobster harvest has resulted in many juvenile lobsters but very few breeding-age lobsters, which could result in a crash in lobster numbers in the near future.

ANSWER: B   Answer B provides an explanation—the food in lobster traps leading to a higher survival rate among young lobsters—for the apparent anomaly that the lobster harvest can increase every year without decreasing the total population of lobsters.

16. Federal tax evasion is a serious crime that places an unfair tax burden on those members of society who pay their fair share. To reduce the incidence of tax evasion, the government needs to prosecute a few high-profile individuals whose cases will receive substantial media attention.

The argument above relies on which of the following assumptions?

A. The tax system is so complicated that even people who try to comply with it may inadvertently not pay some of their taxes.
B. The average citizen will be less likely to evade taxes after he or she sees a high-profile individual prosecuted for tax evasion.
C. Tax revenues collected from high-profile tax evaders will help to alleviate the unfair tax burden on honest citizens.
D. Although it is difficult to secure a conviction on a charge of tax evasion, if the government focuses its efforts on a small number of high-profile individuals, the odds of obtaining a conviction will increase.
E. While there is no universal measure for determining whether a taxation system is "fair" or "unfair," the current system was constructed by Congress to represent the societal priorities and values of the American people.

ANSWER: B Since prosecuting "a few high-profile individuals" can have little direct impact on the overall picture of federal tax collection, the only way in which this plan can meaningfully "reduce the incidence of tax evasion" is if it creates a widespread indirect impact by deterring a large number of citizens from attempting to evade taxes.

17. Adam's dog, a golden retriever named Hans, can respond to over 150 different commands. Adam cites this fact as evidence for his claim that Hans can understand the English language.

Which of the following, if true, casts the most doubt on Adam's claim that Hans can understand the English language?

A. Each of the 150 commands to which Hans responds involves both a spoken word in English and a distinctive hand sign.
B. Hans does not respond to the same commands when spoken to him by Adam's French and Italian friends in their own languages.
C. Scientists have demonstrated conclusively that canine vocal chords are incapable of replicating many of the sounds used in the English language.
D. Animal behaviorists have demonstrated that even very young dogs surpass both wolves and chimpanzees—animals that are thought to be more intelligent than dogs—in the ability to understand human nonverbal communication.
E. The golden retriever is widely considered to be less intelligent than the border collie, and no border collie has ever been shown to truly understand the English language.

ANSWER: A A provides an alternative explanation for the dog's ability to understand the 150 commands, suggesting that the dog may be responding to the "distinctive hand signs" instead of the English words.

18. The Comfocar company manufactures a sedan that can drive comfortably at 80 miles per hour. A rival company, Turbocar, recently introduced a comparably equipped sedan that can drive comfortably at up to 110 miles per hour. Turbocar claims that its sedan will outsell Comfocar's sedan because the Turbocar sedan can get customers to their destinations in comfort much faster than can the Comfocar sedan.

Which of the following, if true, casts the most doubt on Turbocar's claims?

A. Customers in surveys consistently rank comfort among the most important criteria in purchasing a car.
B. Many road surfaces are engineered to allow comfortable driving at speeds up to 120 miles per hour.
C. Automotive safety experts state that it is not safe for any car to be driven faster than 100 miles per hour.
D. Comprehensive research has determined that while the Turbocar model has faster acceleration and a higher top speed than the Comfocar sedan, both cars show approximately the same fuel efficiency.
E. Nowhere in the main marketing areas for these two car companies is it legal or practical to drive faster than 70 miles per hour.

ANSWER: E If it is neither legal nor practical for either of the sedan models to be driven faster than 70 miles per hour, then it is not true that the Turbocar will be able to get customers to their destinations faster than can the Comfocar.

19. Blues musician Paul "Poboy" Smith, born in Tupelo, Mississippi, in 1936, has since 1958 been a fixture on the southern blues scene after the release of his debut album in that year.

A. Blues musician Paul "Poboy" Smith, born in Tupelo, Mississippi, in 1936, has since 1958 been a fixture on the southern blues scene after the release of his debut album in that year.
B. Being born in 1936 in Tupelo, Mississippi, blues musician Paul "Poboy" Smith released his debut album in 1958 and has been a fixture on the southern blues scene since then.
C. Born in Tupelo, Mississippi, in 1936, blues musician Paul "Poboy" Smith has been a fixture on the southern blues scene since the release of his debut album in 1958.
D. Having been a fixture on the southern blues scene since 1958 when he released his debut album, Paul "Poboy" Smith is a blues musician who was born in 1936 in Tupelo, Mississippi.
E. Since the release of his debut album in 1958, blues musician Paul "Poboy" Smith has been a fixture on the southern blues scene; he was born in Tupelo, Mississippi in 1936.

ANSWER: C   A is flawed because it is unclear what "that year" refers to and because the combination of "since" and "after" is redundant. B presents a bizarre chronology by referring to Smith's birth in 1936 in the present perfect "being born" and then using the simple past for a later event in 1958; also, the "has been a fixture ... since then" is awkward. D is somewhat redundant in identifying Smith as a "blues musician" after identifying him as a "fixture on the southern blues scene," and it presents the information in an illogical order by introducing Smith's name so late in the sentence. E awkwardly separates the final clause from the rest of the sentence, so that there is really no reason why these should not be separate sentences. C is the most concise and idiomatic of the answer choices, and it presents the information in the most logical way.

20. SEC regulations require that a public company disclose to their potential investors any legal, technological, or financial complications that could endanger their investments.

A. a public company disclose to their
B. a public company discloses to its
C. a public company disclose to its
D. public companies disclose to its
E. public companies have disclosed to their

ANSWER: C   The subject and possessive pronoun of the underlined clause should agree in number, so A and D are out. B is incorrect because the construction "require that a public company disclose" must be in the subjunctive voice, and therefore must be "disclose" instead of "discloses." In E, it does not make sense here to use the past tense when talking about "potential investors." C is the clearest and most standard statement.

21. The genius of Beethoven can be seen in the widely observed phenomenon that his music has the same appeal to an illiterate shepherd wandering the steppes of Kazakhstan as to a professional musician sipping her latte in Paris.

A. Kazakhstan as to
B. Kazakhstan, just as to
C. Kazakhstan; just as it would to a
D. Kazakhstan, as it would to a
E. Kazakhstan as a

ANSWER: A   A is grammatically correct and reflects standard English usage of the construction "[subject] is the same to X as to Y." The other options are all less idiomatic than A, so A is the best answer.

22. Mary, just as did the other students, objected to the squash casserole.

A. Mary, just as did the other students, objected to
B. Like the other students, Mary was objectionable to
C. Mary, like the other students, objected to
D. Mary objected, in the manner of the other students, to
E. Mary, as the other students, objected

ANSWER: C "Just as did the other students" is a less standard construction than answer C, which is the clearest and most concise of the choices.

23. At the MegaTek Corporation, an inexperienced financial analyst mistook <u>the rising cost of semiconductors as a seasonal fluctuation</u> in the market.

- A. the rising cost of semiconductors as a seasonal fluctuation
- B. the rise in price of semiconductors as a seasonal fluctuation
- C. the rising cost of semiconductors for a seasonal fluctuation
- D. the rising of the cost of semiconductors for a fluctuation by season
- E. the rise of semiconductors in price to a seasonal fluctuation

ANSWER: C The proper construction is "mistook . . . for," not "mistook . . . as." Of the two answers with this construction, C and D, D is awkwardly worded, so C is the correct answer.

24. Which of the following best describes the structure of the passage?

- A. It mentions a puzzling situation, and then describes three approaches people have taken to help understand that situation.
- B. It presents an argument for why something took place, and then offers a refutation of that argument.
- C. It introduces a past phenomenon and then presents three explanations for why the phenomenon took place.
- D. It describes a problem, offers a solution to the problem, and then offers reasons why the solution could not work.
- E. It offers three explanations for a phenomenon and then summarizes what all three have in common.

ANSWER: C The passage introduces the past phenomenon of the Internet stock collapse in the first paragraph and then presents three alternative explanations of who was responsible for that collapse. C is better than A because the stated positions are better characterized as "explanations" than as "approaches," and C is better than E because the passage provides no summary of what the three explanations have in common.

25. Which of the following statements presents the strongest conclusion that one could draw based on the information given in the passage?

- A. The collapse of the Internet stock "bubble" drove thousands of investors into bankruptcy.
- B. People involved with the Internet do not all agree on which party bears the most responsibility for the collapse of the Internet stock "bubble."
- C. Of all parties involved with the Internet, financial professionals such as investment bankers and fund managers derived the most profits from the stock "bubble."
- D. The Internet stock "bubble" could not have occurred if entrepreneurs had been honest about the true financial prospects of their companies.
- E. The average investor has no one to blame but himself or herself if he or she invested in an Internet stock without adequately understanding the true financial prospects of the companies in question.

ANSWER: B The passage provides three opposing viewpoints on this very question, so clearly this is an accurate statement based on the passage. Answers A and C might be true, but there is inadequate support for them in the passage. Answers D and E present opinions similar to those of Verhofen and Smith, respectively, in the passage, but the question does not state that the opinions expressed in the passage are necessarily true, so these statements cannot be taken as "strong conclusions." B is the best answer.

26. Which of the following best captures the meaning of the simile attributed to Mickelson that Verhofen "was like a fox in a henhouse blaming the rooster for all the dead chickens"?

A. As an entrepreneur, Mickelson understands that similes and other figures of speech can help convey complex ideas to audiences.

B. Verhofen, as an investment banker, was personally responsible for promoting businesses that he knew were not viable from a long-term perspective.

C. Foxes, unlike roosters, have no legitimate business in henhouses, and are far more likely than roosters to kill chickens.

D. As an investment banker, Verhofen was more likely to be the culprit of the crime than those he identified as responsible.

E. Entrepreneurs cannot be blamed for trying to make money for themselves and other people because that is what they do.

ANSWER: D   The passage states that Verhofen is an investment banker and that Mickelson places blame for the Internet collapse on "unscrupulous bankers." Her metaphor implies that an investment banker blaming entrepreneurs is, like a fox found among a group of dead chickens, a more likely culprit than those he blamed. D captures this idea. B captures part of this idea, but it does not address the aspect of blaming others.

27. If Mickelson had not used the example of the Wright brothers in her argument, what other example might have illustrated her point as well?

A. Despite widespread public opinion that the sun revolves around the earth, Galileo Galilei published findings showing that the earth revolved around the sun; he later retracted this assertion as a result of pressure from the Church.

B. A tobacco company chose to market cigarettes to children despite widespread public opinion that such marketing is unethical; over the following decade, the company expanded its share of the tobacco market.

C. A home electronics company devoted substantial development resources to eight-track audio technology despite widespread industry opinion that cassette tapes were the wave of the future; eight-tracks were soon replaced by cassette tapes, which in turn were replaced by compact disks.

D. A newspaper chose to publish a story that government lawyers said it could not print; the newspaper won its case against the government lawyers in a federal court, and the writer of the story won a Pulitzer Prize.

E. A computer company initiated research into manufacturing a computer for home use when widespread public opinion held that computers could be useful only for large corporations or government agencies; personal home computers became a multibillion-dollar market.

ANSWER: E   The answer should describe a business or technological innovation that a person or company pursued despite widespread opinion that the idea could not work, and that then turned out to be a great success. The example of personal home computers in E captures all of the relevant themes. C is wrong because the innovation failed, and B and D are wrong because people said that the idea *should* not be done, not that it *could* not be done. A is a weak answer because it is talking about a concept rather than a business or technological innovation, and because Galileo retracted his cosmological statements. E is the best answer.

28. If Verhofen's arguments and statements are all correct, which of the following statements can accurately be inferred?

A. Biotechnology executives who aggressively raise investment capital for bioengineered products with no conceivable market should be held responsible if biotechnology stocks crash.

B. Investors should make financial decisions only with the advice of qualified financial advisors, such as investment bankers or fund managers.

C. If people lose money on investments that they inadequately researched, they have only themselves to blame.

D. If insurance companies provide home insurance for homes built in a hurricane zone and those homes are subsequently all destroyed by a major hurricane, the insurance company should be blamed for any investment losses suffered by its shareholders.

E. The collapse of Internet stocks would not have occurred if companies had not attempted to sell bulky items, like dog food, over the Internet.

ANSWER: A A provides the most similar circumstances to those of Verhofen's argument, in which Internet entrepreneurs "who aggressively promoted ideas without viable business models" should be blamed for the collapse of Internet stocks. B and C have no support in the text, D provides a different type of example that does not coincide well with Verhofen's argument, and E overstates Verhofen's position, since he identified companies that sell bulky items as one of the causes of the Internet stock collapse, but not the only cause. A is the best answer.

29. While some military planners claimed that it would be possible to win a war fought with nuclear weapons, many scientists argued that such a war could not truly be won, because the fallout from nuclear warfare would create a nuclear winter and <u>it also would be rendering the earth uninhabitable</u>.

A. it also would be rendering the earth uninhabitable
B. rendering the earth uninhabitable
C. might have uninhabitably rendered the earth
D. render the earth uninhabitable
E. would also have rendered the earth uninhabitable

ANSWER: D The correct answer should provide a parallel construction to "create a nuclear winter," since both phrases follow "nuclear warfare would"; answer D is parallel to "create a nuclear winter," and it is the most succinct of the available choices.

30. Providing adequate public health-care facilities is a crucial task in a county like Travis, <u>where more than 60 percent of household incomes are</u> below the poverty line.

A. where more than 60 percent of household incomes are
B. where more than 60 percent of household income is
C. which has more than 60 percent of the household incomes
D. where they have more than 60 percent of household income
E. where more than 60 percent of them have household incomes

ANSWER: A Answer A is grammatically and stylistically correct.

31. Noted for its tenacity and courage, <u>the English bulldog, having originally been bred for the brutal sport of bull-baiting, but now is cherished</u> as a loyal animal companion.

A. the English bulldog, having originally been bred for the brutal sport of bull-baiting, but now is cherished
B. English bulldogs were originally bred for the brutal sport of bull-baiting, but they are now cherished
C. English bulldogs were originally bred to bait bulls in a brutal sport, but it is now cherished
D. the English bulldog was originally bred for the brutal sport of bull-baiting, but it is now cherished
E. the English bulldog, originally bred to bait bulls for a brutal sport, is now being cherished

ANSWER: D The answer has to refer to "the English bulldog" singular, because the final phrase refers to "a loyal animal companion" singular; therefore, B and C are out. Answer A is incorrect because the "but now" does not work with the phrasing of the sentence. Between D and E, the wording of E is somewhat awkward in that "is now being cherished" is less standard than the simpler "is now cherished"; D is the best answer.

32. Advanced market research for the MegaTek Corporation predicts that launching a MegaTek Superstore in a given city <u>would only succeed should the density of repeat customers have been greater than</u> 200 per square mile.

A. would only succeed should the density of repeat customers have been greater than
B. will succeed only should the density of repeat customers be more numerous than
C. will succeed only if the density of repeat customers is greater than
D. should only succeed with a repeat customer density of greater than
E. will succeed only with repeat customer density being greater than

ANSWER: C Since the underlined passage is what "the MegaTek Corporation predicts," the underlined passage should take the future tense "will" rather than "would" or "should." Of the choices B, C, and E, C presents the most standard English construction.

33. In order to increase revenues, a cell-phone company has decided to change its fee structure. Instead of charging a flat rate of $20 per month and $0.05 for every minute over 200 minutes, the company will now charge $50 per month for unlimited usage.

Which of the following is a consideration that, if true, suggests that the new plan will not actually increase the company's revenues?

A. A rival company, which charges no start-up fee, offers an unlimited calling plan for $40 per month.
B. Two-thirds of the company's customers use less than 500 minutes per month.
C. Studies have shown that customers using unlimited calling plans will increase their monthly usage of minutes by over 50 percent.
D. One-fifth of the company's customers use in excess of 1,000 minutes per month.

E. In recent months the company has received several complaints of insufficient signal strength and poor customer service.

ANSWER: A If a rival company offers an apparently comparable plan for 20 percent less, it is likely that customers will switch to that rival company's plan, thereby reducing the company's revenue.

34. A real estate developer in Florida, desiring to protect his high-rise apartment building on the beach from hurricane damage, has planted sea oats in two rows in front of his building in order to encourage the development of sand dunes between the water and his building.

Which of the following, if true, casts the most doubt on the probable effectiveness of the developer's plan?

A. Sand dunes provide little protection for tall buildings against the wind, which is sufficiently powerful even in minor hurricanes to cause serious damage to buildings.
B. Sand dunes have been shown to provide effective protection against the storm surge, the pounding waves driven by hurricane-force winds onto dry land.
C. Although sea oats will lead to the growth of sand dunes over many years, it would be far faster to build concrete bunkers between the building and the water.
D. Hurricane insurance has become so expensive that many owners of beachfront property choose not to buy it.
E. The developer has invested in reinforced steel girders and shatterproof glass as a way of minimizing damage to his building in the event that a hurricane hits the area.

ANSWER: A Answer A describes a form of hurricane damage—wind damage—that the developer's plan can do little to prevent.

35. According to local tradition, Sultan Abu ibn al-Hasan founded the East African trading state of Kilwa in the mid-tenth century. Professor Ascalon, however, argues that Sultan al-Hasan did not rule in Kilwa until at least a century later.

Which of the following, if true, provides the strongest support for Professor Ascalon's position?

A. The Hunsu Kubwa Palace, the largest stone structure in sub-Saharan Africa prior to the eighteenth century, dates to the rule of Sultan Sulaiman in the fourteenth century.
B. The oldest mosque on the island, which has traditionally been attributed to the reign of Abu ibn al-Hasan, has a foundation dating to ca. 800 C.E.
C. The Kilwa Chronicle, a document based on Kilwa oral history that has been shown to be unreliable on matters of chronology, dates the rise to power of Sultan al-Hasan to the year 957 C.E.
D. Silver and copper coins bearing the name of Abu ibn al-Hasan have been found in archeological sites dating from the late eleventh to the fourteenth centuries, but none have been found in sites dating earlier than the late eleventh century.
E. Archeological records suggest that the island of Kilwa enjoyed a period of economic prosperity beginning in the mid-eleventh century.

ANSWER: D   Answer D does not provide proof that Sultan al-Hasan ruled in the eleventh century, but it does provide results that are consistent with that hypothesis. Moreover, the results cited answer exactly the sort of question that archeologists would ask in order to disprove the professor's hypothesis. None of the other answers offer support for the hypothesis, so D is the best answer.

36. In theory, Ecuador could be a major exporter of shrimp. In actuality, it is not. The explanation is that 80 percent of the country's rich estuaries are owned by the government. This hurts Ecuador's shrimp production, because the government does not have the flexibility necessary for efficient shrimp farming that private industry possesses.

The answer to which of the following questions would be most relevant to evaluating the adequacy of the explanation given above?

A. Who owns the 20 percent of estuaries that are not owned by the government?
B. What percentage of Ecuador's production of shrimp is consumed domestically?
C. Has the government stated any plans to sell any of its estuaries to private industry, provided that the price is sufficient?
D. Is Peru, Ecuador's neighbor to the south, actually better suited for commercial shrimp farming than Ecuador, which is a substantially smaller country?
E. How does Ecuador's shrimp production on government-owned estuaries compare to that on comparable land owned by private industry?

ANSWER: E   The explanation in the passage hinges on the assumption that shrimp farming on government-owned estuaries will be less productive than shrimp farming on estuaries owned by private industry. E directly questions whether that assumption is correct, and, if it is, to what degree government ownership is holding back the potential production of Ecuador's estuaries.

37. The author's primary intention in this passage appears to be which of the following?

A. To shed light on the underappreciated work of the Hellenistic poet Posidippus
B. To compare the relative merits of papyrus and wood-pulp paper as media for recording information
C. To discuss the ways in which papyrus fragments help scholars learn about Hellenistic Egypt
D. To answer the questions regarding the burning of the library of Alexandria, one of the great mysteries of the ancient world
E. To suggest possibly fruitful paths for future archeological research into Hellenistic Egypt

ANSWER: C   The first sentence of the passage is: "One of the best sources modern scholars have for learning about Hellenistic Egypt is the large supply of papyrus fragments that have turned up in the Egyptian desert over the last century." Each of the first three paragraphs addresses this topic directly, while the fourth paragraph addresses it tangentially.

38. Which of the following would best illustrate how a discarded fragment of papyrus might give us a more accurate picture of the daily lives of ancient Egyptians than a record intended to be permanent?

   A. A poet such as Posidippus may have composed rough drafts of his epigrams on papyrus fragments prior to writing them in their final form.
   B. Grocery lists, which give insights into the diets of ancient people, would never be included in stone inscriptions but could be scribbled on scraps of papyrus.
   C. The Hellenistic monarchs employed some of the finest historians of the Greek world to provide chronicles of their reigns.
   D. Some papyrus fragments may have been used for purposes other than writing, such as binding wounds or wrapping small packages.
   E. Stone inscriptions describing military events often embellish the truth to favor whoever is paying for the inscription.

ANSWER: B   **A grocery list provides the kind of information that could be important to archeologists today who want to learn about the daily lives of people in Hellenistic Egypt, but Hellenistic scribes would not have thought that information of this sort was important enough to mention in records intended for posterity.**

39. The mention of the discovery of 110 previously unknown epigrams by the poet Posidippus serves what purpose in the passage?

   A. Revealing insights into the nuances of court culture in Hellenistic Egypt
   B. Demonstrating how durable a material papyrus can be
   C. Arguing for a greater appreciation of this little-known Hellenistic poet
   D. Highlighting the importance of royal patronage in the development or arts and literature in the Hellenistic world
   E. Illustrating the kind of discovery that can be made from researching papyrus fragments

ANSWER: E   **The passage mentions the Posidippus discovery in order to give an example of the kind of new material that is** being found in these discarded papyrus fragments. Statements A, B, C, and D may be accurate to an extent, but they do not address how the mention of Posidippus relates to the overall theme of the passage.

40. According to information given in the passage, which of the following locations would probably yield the highest probability of finding a previously undiscovered papyrus fragment?

   A. The ship of a royal messenger that sank off the Egyptian coast of the Mediterranean Sea in the third century B.C.
   B. The charred remnants of an ancient Egyptian palace that was burned by Roman troops in the first century B.C.
   C. The refuse heap of an ancient Egyptian town that was buried in the desert in the fifth century A.D.
   D. The private collections of French and British explorers from the nineteenth century A.D. who first uncovered many of the principal sites of Egyptian archeology
   E. The library of a Hellenistic fishing village that sank into the marshes of the Nile Delta in the third century A.D.

ANSWER: C   **The passage states: "Most of the surviving fragments have been found in ancient garbage dumps that were covered over by the desert and preserved in the dry heat." The location described in answer C conforms closely with the type of place mentioned in the passage as where "most" of the fragments have been found, so this type of location will probably be the most fruitful place to look for more fragments.**

41. What does the author imply by the final statement: "If that library had not burned down, maybe archeologists today would not have to spend so much of their time sorting through ancient trash!"?

   A. The author implies that if the library had not burned down, archeologists would be able to appreciate the full cultural legacy of King Ptolemy II Philadelphos.

B. The author implies that if the library had not burned down, scholars today would have not only the full works of Posidippus, but also those of Aeschylus, Sophocles, and Euripides.

C. The author implies that if the library had not burned down, the scrolls contained within the library would have decomposed before modern times in any event, because they would not have been preserved in the dry heat of the desert.

D. The author implies that if the library had not burned down, it might have contained more complete details about the life and culture of Hellenistic Egypt than can be found in the papyrus fragments from ancient refuse dumps.

E. The author implies that if the library had not burned down, the cultural awakening of the Renaissance might have occurred centuries earlier.

ANSWER: D   The passage previously stated that the papyrus fragments, which are generally found in ancient refuse dumps, provide insights into daily life that cannot be found in more permanent sources. To reduce the need for archeologists to search for these papyrus fragments, the lost collection of the library would have to provide more complete information of the type found in the fragments than can be found in the fragments themselves; answer D suggests that the library would have contained such information.

Answers and Explanations

1. If x is an integer, is $\dfrac{18+54}{x}$ an integer?

(1) $18 < x < 54$
(2) x is a multiple of 18

ANSWER: C (1) alone is insufficient, because if $x = 36$, then the answer is "yes," but if $x = 37$, then the answer is "no." (2) alone is insufficient, because if $x = 36$, then the answer is "yes," but if $x = 180$, then the answer is "no." If the statements are combined, however, then the only value of x that meets all the conditions is 36, for which the answer is "yes."

2. If $a > 0$ and $b > 0$, is $\dfrac{a}{b} > \dfrac{b}{a}$?

(1) $a = b - 2$
(2) $\dfrac{a}{4b} = \dfrac{1}{5}$

ANSWER: D (1) alone is sufficient because it tells us that b is a larger number than a, which means that the answer to the question must be "no." (2) alone is sufficient; the statement can be simplified to $5a = 4b$, which means that b is larger than a, so the answer to the question must be "no."

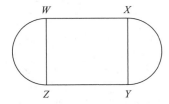

3. The figure above shows the shape of a flowerbed. If arcs WZ and XY are semicircles and $WXYZ$ is a square, what is the area of the flowerbed?

(1) The perimeter of square $WXYZ$ is 24.
(2) The diagonal $WY = 6\sqrt{2}$.

ANSWER: D (1) alone is sufficient; if the perimeter of the square is 24, then the length of each side is $24/4 = 6$, and the radius of each of the semicircles is $6/2 = 3$. The area of the square is $6 \times 6 = 36$, and since the formula for the area of a circle is πr^2, the area of the semicircles is $2 \times \frac{1}{2}[\pi(3 \times 3)] = 9\pi$; $36 + 9\pi$ is the area of the flowerbed. (2) alone is sufficient; the side of a square is the diagonal divided by $\sqrt{2}$ (this is derived from the Pythagorean theorem), so the sides are equal to 6; by following the same process used with statement (1), we can determine the area of the flowerbed.

4. A total of 72 passengers are on a ship, and they go out on an excursion in boats R and Q. How many of the ship's passengers are female?

(1) There are 13 females on boat Q.
(2) There are equal numbers of women on boats R and Q.

ANSWER: C (1) alone is insufficient because it gives no information about the number of females on boat R. (2) alone is insufficient because it does not give the number of women on either boat. If the statements are combined, we see that there are 13 women on each boat, or 26 in all.

5. In the xy plane, is the point $(4, -2)$ on the line l?

(1) Point $(1, 1)$ is on line l.
(2) The equation $x = 2 - y$ describes line l.

ANSWER: B (1) alone is insufficient because it offers information about only one point on the line. (2) alone is sufficient, because the line it describes includes the point $(4, -2)$.

6. A type of extra-large SUV averages 12.2 miles per gallon (mpg) on the highway, but only 7.6 mpg in the city. What is the maximum distance, in miles, that this SUV could be driven on 25 gallons of gasoline?

A. 190
B. 284.6
C. 300
D. 305
E. 312

ANSWER: D   The SUV will reach its maximum distance only if driven only on the highway; $25 \times 12.2 = 305$.

7. The ratio of 2 quantities is 5 to 6. If each of the quantities is increased by 15, what is the ratio of these 2 new quantities?

A. 5:6
B. 25:27
C. 15:16
D. 20:21
E. It cannot be determined from the information given

ANSWER: E   With no idea of what the quantities actually are, there is no way to tell how adding 15 to each of them will affect their ratio; for example, if the quantities were 5 and 6, the new ratio would be 20:21, but if the quantities were 10 and 12, the ratio would be 25:27.

8. $\sqrt{6^2 + 8^2 - 19} =$

A. $3\sqrt{2}$
B. 8
C. 9
D. 10
E. $\sqrt{119}$

ANSWER: C $\sqrt{6^2 + 8^2 - 19} = \sqrt{36 + 64 - 19} = \sqrt{81} = 9$

9. In an animal behavior experiment, 50 tagged white pigeons and 200 tagged gray pigeons were released from a laboratory. Within one week, 88 percent of the white pigeons and 80.5 percent of the gray pigeons had returned to the laboratory. What percent of the total number of pigeons returned to the laboratory?

A. 80.5
B. 82
C. 82.5
D. 85
E. 86.5

ANSWER: B   88% of 50 is 44, and 80.5% of 200 is 161. 44 + 161 = 205. 205/250 total pigeons = 0.82 = 82%.

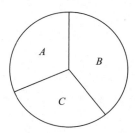

10. In the circular region shown above, sections *A* and *B* represent 3/8 and 5/11, respectively, of the area of the circular region. Section *C* represents what fractional part of the area of the circular region?

A. $\frac{15}{88}$
B. $\frac{2}{11}$
C. $\frac{5}{22}$
D. $\frac{45}{88}$
E. $\frac{73}{88}$

ANSWER: A   Section *C* is equal to $1 - (3/8 + 5/11) = 1 - (33/88 + 40/88) = 15/88$.

11. At the wholesale store you can buy an 8-pack of hot dogs for $1.55, a 20-pack for $3.05, and a 250-pack for $22.95. What is the greatest number of hot dogs you can buy at this store with $200?

A. 1,108
B. 2,100
C. 2,108
D. 2,124
E. 2,256

ANSWER: B   You should start with the 250-packs, because that is the best value, with each hot dog costing less than 10 cents. Rounding 22.95 to 23 for simplicity, you can determine that you can afford 8 of the 250-packs, for a total of $183.60. The 20-packs are the next best value at around 15 cents per hot dog, so with the remaining $16.40 you can buy 5 of the 20-packs for $15.25, leaving $1.15. $1.15 isn't enough for an 8-pack, so the total number of hot dogs is $8 \times 250 + 5 \times 20 = 2,100$.

12. What was the percent decrease in the price of MegaTek (MGTK) stock during the market decline of March 1, 2001, to March 1, 2002?

(1) The price of MGTK was $56.20 on March 1, 2001.
(2) The price of the stock on January 1, 2002, was only one-quarter of its price as of March 1, 2001.

ANSWER: E **(1) alone is insufficient because it gives only the value at the starting point of the period in question. (2) alone is insufficient because the price as of January 1, 2002, is irrelevant to the question. Combining the two statements yields no new insights.**

13. Greg's long-distance telephone plan charges him $0.50 for the first 4 minutes of a call, and $0.07 per minute for each subsequent minute. Greg made a call to Carrie for x minutes, where x is an integer. How many minutes long was Greg's call?

(1) The last 7 minutes of Greg's call cost $0.22 less than the first 7 minutes of the call.
(2) The call did not cost more than $1.05.

ANSWER: C **(1) alone is insufficient; we know that the first 7 minutes cost $0.50 + 3 × $0.07 = $0.71; the least the last 7 minutes could cost is 7 × $0.07 = $0.49, which is exactly $0.22 less than the first 7 minutes, so we know that the last 7 minutes did not include the first 4 minutes, but that is all we can tell. (2) alone is insufficient, because the call could have lasted any length of time under 12 minutes (12 minutes = $1.06, 11 minutes = $0.99). If the two are combined, the only value that meets all the conditions is 11 minutes.**

14. If x and y are both positive numbers, is x greater than 75% of y?

(1) $5x > 4y + 1$
(2) $x = 6$

ANSWER: A **(1) states that x is greater than 80% of y (the easiest way to confirm this is to plug in numbers), so the question is answered in the affirmative and (1) alone is sufficient. (2) is insufficient without providing any information about the relative value of y, so the answer is A.**

15. Is $xyz = 1$?

(1) $x(y^z) = 1$
(2) $5z = 0$

ANSWER: B **(1) alone is insufficient, because x, y, and z could be (1, 1, 1) or (1, 1, 0) or other values, which give different answers to the question. (2) alone is sufficient, because if $z = 0$, it does not matter what the values are for x and y; $xyz = 0 \neq 1$.**

16. What is the average (arithmetic mean) of x and y?

(1) The average of $x + 3$ and $y + 5$ is 14.
(2) The average of x, y, and 16 is 12.

ANSWER: D **(1) alone is sufficient; the statement could be restated to say that $x + y + 3 + 5 = 14 \times 2$, or $x + y = 20$; therefore, the average of x and y is 10. (2) alone is sufficient; the statement could be restated as $x + y + 16 = 12 \times 3$, or $x + y = 20$; therefore, the average of x and y is 10.**

17. One day a car rental agency rented 2/3 of its cars, including 3/5 of its cars with CD players. If 3/4 of its cars have CD players, what percent of the cars that were not rented had CD players?

A. 10%
B. 35%
C. 45%
D. 66.7%
E. 90%

ANSWER: E **One way to approach this problem is to think of the fractions as actual cars. Since the given denominators are 3, 4, and 5, imagine that there are 60 cars. In this case, the agency rented 40 cars (2/3), 45 of the total cars have CD players (3/4), and 27 of its cars with CD players were rented (3/5 of 3/4). From these numbers, we can determine that 20 cars in total were not rented, and 18 cars with CD players were not rented. 18 out of 20 is 90 percent.**

18. If x is 20 percent greater than 88, then $x =$

A. 68
B. 70.4
C. 86
D. 105.6
E. 108

ANSWER: D **20 percent of 88 is 17.6. 88 + 17.6 = 105.6.**

19. A farmer with 1,350 acres of land had planted his fields with corn, sugar cane, and tobacco in the ratio of 5:3:1, respectively, but he wanted to make more money, so he shifted the ratio to 2:4:3, respectively. How many more acres of land were planted with tobacco under the new system?

A. 90
B. 150
C. 270
D. 300
E. 450

ANSWER: D The numbers in both sets of ratios add up to 9, so you can look at each of the ratios in terms of ninths of 1,350. In the original planting system, tobacco accounted for 1/9 of the total, so 1,350/9 = 150. In the new system, tobacco accounts for 3/9, or 450. 450 − 150 = 300.

20. $\sqrt{144} + \sqrt{225} + \sqrt{324} =$

A. 18
B. 33
C. 36
D. 42
E. 45

ANSWER: E The statement can be restated as $12 + 15 + 18 = 45$.

21. What is the perimeter of a square with area $\frac{9P^2}{16}$?

A. $\frac{3P}{4}$

B. $\frac{3P^2}{4}$

C. $3P$
D. $3P^2$
E. $\frac{4P}{3}$

ANSWER: C The area of a square is the square of its sides, so one of the sides of this square is $\sqrt{\frac{9P^2}{16}} = \frac{3P}{4}$. The perimeter of a square is its side times 4, so the perimeter is $3P$.

22. If a three-digit number is selected at random from the integers 100 to 999, inclusive, what is the probability that the first digit and the last digit of the integer will both be exactly two less than the middle digit?

A. 1:900
B. 7:900
C. 9:1,000
D. 1:100
E. 7:100

ANSWER: B There are exactly 7 digits out of the 900 for which this statement is true: 131, 242, 353, 464, 575, 686, 797; that equals a probability of 7 out of 900.

23. Which of the following inequalities is equivalent to $-4 < x < 8$?

A. $|x - 1| < 7$
B. $|x + 2| < 6$
C. $|x + 3| < 5$
D. $|x - 2| < 6$
E. None of the above

ANSWER: D $|x - 2| < 6$ also represents all of the values for x between −4 and 8. A is equivalent to $-6 < x < 8$, B is equivalent to $-8 < x < 4$, and C is equivalent to $-8 < x < 2$.

24. $\dfrac{80 - 6(36 \div 9)}{1/4} =$

A. 416
B. 224
C. 188
D. 104
E. 56

ANSWER: B The statement is equivalent to $4[80 - 6(4)] = 4(56) = 224$.

25. Three different lumberjacks can chop W amount of wood in 30 minutes, 45 minutes, and 50 minutes according to their different levels of skill with the axe. How much wood, in terms of W, could the two fastest lumberjacks chop in 2 hours?

A. $6\frac{2}{3}\ W$

B. $6\ W$

C. $4\frac{2}{3}\ W$

D. $3\ W$

E. $2\frac{2}{3}\ W$

ANSWER: A The fastest lumberjack can chop W in 30 minutes, so in 2 hours = 120 minutes, he will chop $4W$. The next fastest can chop W in 45 minutes, so he will be able to chop $\frac{120}{45}\,W = 2\frac{2}{3}\,W$; $4W + 2\frac{2}{3}\,W = 6\frac{2}{3}\,W$.

26. In what year was Edward born?

(1) In 1988, Edward turned 17 years old.
(2) Edward's sister Lisa, who is 14 months older than Edward, was born in 1970.

ANSWER: A (1) alone is sufficient because it gives 1971 as the only answer. (2) alone is insufficient, because the conditions stated could apply to either 1971 or 1972.

27. Is $rs = rx - 2$?

(1) r is an odd number
(2) $x = s + 2$

ANSWER: E (1) alone can neither prove nor disprove the equation above because there are infinite values of r, s, and x for which the equation could be true or false. (2) alone is not sufficient. By plugging in $s + 2$ for x, you can determine that you can answer the question when $r = 1$, but you don't actually know that r does, in fact, equal 1. Putting both statements together, you still don't have enough information to answer the question, as there are values that could give you either true or false answers. So E is the correct answer.

28. A CEO is building an extra-wide garage in which to park his limousines. The garage is x feet wide, and at least 2 feet of space is required between each two cars and between the cars and the walls. Will all 9 limousines fit in the garage?

(1) The average width of the limousines is the square root of x.
(2) $x = 100$.

ANSWER: C (1) alone is insufficient because it gives us no actual measurements. (2) alone is insufficient because it gives us the width of the garage, but not the width of the cars. If the two are combined, we see that the cars cannot fit in the garage. The square root of $100 = 10$, so the 9 cars will require 90 feet of space, but the additional space required between and around the cars will be another 18 feet, so the cars will not fit in the garage.

29. If $q + r + s = 45$, what is the value of qr?

(1) $q = r = s$
(2) $q - r - s = -15$

ANSWER: A (1) alone is sufficient, because the only value for q, r, and s that meets the conditions of the question and the statement is 15; thus, we can determine the value of qr. (2) alone is not sufficient; although it would work for the values $(q, r, s) = (15, 15, 15)$, it would also work for $(q, r, s) = (15, 14, 16)$.

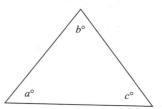

30. Is the triangle depicted above isosceles? (Figure not necessarily drawn to scale.)

(1) $180° - (a + c) = 60°$
(2) $a = 2b - c$

ANSWER: E A triangle is isosceles if two of its angles are equal. (1) tells us that $(a + c) = 120°$, which is not sufficient to prove whether or not the triangle is isosceles. (2) can be altered to $(a + c) = 2b$, which is not sufficient to prove whether or not the triangle is isosceles. If the two are combined, we have $2b = 120°$, and therefore $b = 60°$. Knowing the measure of one angle is still insufficient, since a could equal $59°$ and c could equal $61°$, so the question remains unresolved.

31. Last year Jackie saved 5% of her annual salary. This year, she made 10% more money than last year, and she saved 8% of her salary. The amount saved this year was what percent of the amount she saved last year?

A. 56%
B. 76%
C. 158%
D. 176%
E. 188%

ANSWER: D For simplicity, assume that she earned $100 last year and saved $5. This year she earned $110 and saved $110 \times 0.08 = \$8.80$. $8.80/5 = 1.76$.

	P	Q	R	S
P	0	144	171	186
Q	144	0	162	X
R	171	162	0	Y
S	186	X	Y	0

32. The table above shows the one-way driving distance, in miles, between four cities: P, Q, R, and S. For example, the distance between P and Q is 144 miles. If the round trip between S and Q is 16 miles further than the round trip between S and R, and the round trip between S and R is 24 miles less than the round trip between S and P, what is the value of X?

   A. 174
   B. 182
   C. 186
   D. 348
   E. 364

ANSWER: B   To find X, the distance between S and Q, start with a number you know; the distance between S and P is 186 miles, and the round trip therefore is 372 miles; 372 = the SR round trip + 24 miles, so SR round trip = 348 miles; SQ round trip = SR round trip −16 miles, so SQ round trip = 364. X is the one-way SQ distance, so 364/2 = 182.

33. If 35 percent of 400 is 20 percent of x, then $x =$

   A. 200
   B. 350
   C. 700
   D. 900
   E. 1,400

ANSWER: C   First, 35% of 400 = 140. If 140 = 0.2x, then x = 140/0.2 = 700.

34. $\left(2^3 - 1\right)\left(2^3 + 1\right)\left(2^6 + 1\right)\left(2^{12} + 1\right) =$

   A. $(2^{24} - 1)$
   B. $(2^{24} + 1)$
   C. $(2^{48} - 1)$
   D. $(2^{96} + 1)$
   E. $(2^{12} - 1)$

ANSWER: A $(2^{24}-1)$ is equal to $(2^{12}-1)$ $(2^{12}+1)$, which is equal to $(2^{12} + 1)$ $(2^6 + 1)$ (2^6-1), which is equal to $(2^{12} + 1)$ $(2^6 + 1)$ $(2^3 - 1)(2^3 + 1)$.

35. To be considered for "movie of the year," a film must appear in at least 1/4 of the top-10-movies lists submitted by the Cinematic Academy's 765 members. What is the smallest number of top-10 lists a film can appear on and still be considered for "movie of the year"?

   A. 191
   B. 192
   C. 193
   D. 212
   E. 213

ANSWER: B   765 times 1/4 equals 191.25, but the question states "at least 1/4," so the movie must appear on 192 lists.

36. In a sample of associates at a law firm, 30 percent are second-year associates, and 60 percent are not first-year associates. What percentage of the associates at the law firm have been there for more than two years?

   A. 10
   B. 20
   C. 30
   D. 40
   E. 50

ANSWER: C   The answer must be a subset of the 60 percent of associates that are not first-year associates. Of these, you must subtract the 30 percent that are second-year associates, leaving only 30 percent, so the answer is C.

37. Which of the following fractions has the greatest value?

   A. $\dfrac{48}{\left(2^5\right)\left(3^2\right)}$

   B. $\dfrac{12}{\left(2^4\right)\left(3^3\right)}$

   C. $\dfrac{6}{\left(2^3\right)\left(3^2\right)}$

   D. $\dfrac{144}{\left(2^4\right)\left(3^4\right)}$

   E. $\dfrac{81}{\left(2^3\right)\left(3^5\right)}$

ANSWER: A   This problem becomes much easier if you recognize that all of the fractions include $\dfrac{1}{\left(\left(2^3\right)\left(3^2\right)\right)}$; for purposes of comparison, you can multiply each of the fractions by $(2^3)(3^2)$ to simplify things. This leaves you with the following values: A = 12, B = 2, C = 6, D = 8, and E = 3; A is the greatest value.

Answers and Explanations

1. Which of the following would make the most appropriate title for this passage?

   A. Going Boldly Where No One Has Gone Before: The Promise and Peril of Interstellar Space Travel
   B. The Day The Earth Stood Still: Why Interstellar Space Travel Is Essential to Human Survival
   C. The Wrath of Larson: Egbert Larson's Quest to Build an Interstellar Spacecraft
   D. Busted Flat in Beta Regulus: The Crushing Challenges of Interstellar Space Travel
   E. Say It Isn't So, Mr. Einstein: Egbert Larson's Challenge to the Theory of Relativity

   ANSWER: D   An ideal title would capture the idea that this is a review of a book by Egbert Larson concerning the daunting challenges of interstellar space travel. C and E both appear to be attractive choices because they mention Larson and they mention issues addressed in the passage, but they are both incorrect because they focus on topics that are *not* in the passage: there is no mention in the passage of Larson's building a spacecraft, and his work seems to build on the theory of relativity rather than challenging it. B is mostly off topic. A and D both address the central issue of the difficulty of space travel, but A is incorrect because it introduces the concept of "the promise" of space travel, which is not addressed in the passage. D is the best answer.

2. Based on the tone and content of the passage, it is most likely which of the following?

   A. A book review in a journal intended for astrophysics professionals
   B. A movie review in an entertainment industry publication
   C. A book review in a science magazine aimed at a general audience
   D. A book review in a newspaper
   E. A transcript of a talk given at a science fiction convention dedicated to "the poetry of space"

   ANSWER: C   The passage is clearly talking about a book, so B is out. The passage assumes some knowledge of science—as shown by its reference to "Mr. Einstein" without any further identification that it is talking about the physicist Albert Einstein—but it does not assume a comprehensive knowledge of physics, as shown by its explanation of relativistic time dilation, a concept that no professional astrophysicist would need to have explained. Thus the very general audience of D and the very specific audience of A are both out. E is not obviously wrong, but the fact that the passage makes no mention of "poetry" and the fact that C specifically mentions a "book review" makes C the stronger choice.

3. The passage implies that all except which of the following could be threats to human health during extended interstellar voyages?

A. Meteor impact
B. Radiation poisoning
C. Accelerating too fast
D. Starvation
E. Old age

ANSWER: A   The passage mentions the dangers of B, D, and E in the fourth paragraph (the statement that the mission will need several generations implies that the first generation will die of old age), and C is addressed with the statement: "And if you tried to accelerate directly to the speed of light like they do in the movies, you'd be instantly splattered on the back of your theoretical spacecraft." Meteor impacts, although in fact a serious issue for voyages of this nature, are not discussed in the passage.

4. According to the passage, which of the following will present the most difficult challenge for humans attempting interstellar space travel?

A. Achieving velocities near the speed of light
B. Withstanding the acceleration necessary for traversing interstellar distances
C. Maintaining clean air and water on a journey that could last centuries
D. Accommodating the effects of relativistic time dilation
E. Enabling the humans on board to survive during the journey

ANSWER: E   The passage states: "Keeping a crew alive on the way turns out to be the trickiest part of all." This is a fair approximation of statement E.

5. According to the information given in the passage, if two 20-year-old twins lived on earth, and one of them left on a journey for Alpha Centauri at very close to the speed of light, then managed to survive the journey and return to earth having aged 40 years during the journey, what could she expect to find upon her return to earth?

A. Her great-grandmother
B. Her twin at the age of 20
C. Her twin at the age of 40
D. Her twin at the age of 60
E. Her twin's great-grandchildren

ANSWER: E   The passage states: "If Mr. Einstein was right about relativity . . . then time slows down when you approach the speed of light. A person traveling at any velocity near the speed of light will age only days for every week, month, or even year that passes on earth." If the twin on the voyage was traveling at "very close" to the speed of light, we can assume that for her, time slowed down a great deal compared to time as experienced on earth. The twin on earth would most likely have died of old age long before the voyaging twin's return, leaving only the possibility that the earth twin's descendants might be there to greet her returning twin.

6. Which of the following inventions, if it could be perfected and manufactured at a viable cost, would address the most challenges to human interstellar space travel, as presented in the passage?

A. A ram-scoop drive that can accelerate a spacecraft of any size to four-fifths of the speed of light within 24 hours
B. A cold-sleep capsule that essentially halts the passage of time for human inhabitants while protecting them from all physical harm
C. A sustainable biosphere that reliably generates healthy food and automatically cleans air and water
D. A neutrino-based communications system that permits instantaneous communication across any distance without any relativistic time dilation
E. An impervious force field that protects the ship and its inhabitants from radiation, meteor strikes, or hostile alien attacks

ANSWER: B   B addresses all the survival issues handled by C, and in addition its protection "from all physical harm" addresses the radiation mentioned in E and the acceleration problems that are inherent in A. B also protects against the daunting passage of time necessary for interstellar space travel. Based on the information in the third paragraph, the invention in A would not be usable without some other protective invention because humans could not withstand that rate of acceleration. D would be an astounding invention on its own, but it does not address as many of the challenges mentioned in the passage as B. B is the best answer. Why hasn't someone invented this thing yet?

7. The author of the passage most likely mentions "Little Green Men" in the first paragraph for what purpose?

A. To poke fun at the ignorance of most science fiction readers
B. To introduce a daunting challenge that will have to be addressed before human interstellar space travel can become possible
C. To draw a comparison between the attempts of humans to voyage in space and the more successful attempts of other civilizations
D. To draw an amusing distinction between a supposed danger of space travel, as presented in the popular media, and the actual challenges posed by interstellar space travel, as perceived by scientists
E. To suggest that the concept of human interstellar space travel is as much of a myth as the "Little Green Men" that appear in science fiction movies and television programs

ANSWER: D   The passage states: "Forget hostile aliens. According to a forthcoming book by noted astrophysicist Egbert Larson, the intrepid humans who first attempt interstellar space travel will face far more daunting challenges before they ever meet the Little Green Men." While the passage is light in tone, it does not suggest that the aliens are necessarily a "myth," as in E, or that those who believe in them are ignorant, as in A. On the other hand, it does not say that they exist or that humans are likely to contact them, which rules out C. The point of the introduction is that there are more daunting immediate problems than the theoretical risk of alien attacks, so B is out. D captures the essence of the introduction.

8. A wholesale fruit distributor, in an effort to increase its profit margins, has proposed cutting the tops off of the pineapples it ships in order to increase the number of pineapples it can ship in a standard-size truck.

Which of the following, if true, gives the strongest evidence that the fruit distributor's plan will increase its profit margins?

A. Pineapples with the tops cut off have been shown to rot three times faster than uncut fruit.
B. Customers buy whole pineapples in part because of their exotic, spiky appearance.
C. Cutting the tops off of pineapples may inadvertently remove some of the fruit within.
D. The fruit distributor ships primarily to a fruit canning company that has no use for pineapple tops.
E. Pineapple juice has been shown to be an even more potent source of vitamin C than orange or cranberry juice.

ANSWER: D   Answer D suggests that the company can reap the benefits of fuller trucks while bearing no ill consequences from cutting off the tops. Answers A, B, and C all give reasons *not* to cut the tops off. Answer E is irrelevant.

9. A brand of cough syrup comes with a measuring cup attached so that customers can measure the proper dosage. A consultant has pointed out that this cup is unnecessary, since most customers have measuring cups at home. Since the cups increase the cost of packaging the cough syrup and reduce the total number of units that can be shipped in a standard package, the consultant advises that the company can increase its net revenue on this product (total revenue minus total costs) by selling the cough syrup without the measuring cups.

Which of the following, if true, provides the strongest evidence that the company should not follow the consultant's advice?

A. Studies have shown that customers who use cough syrup without a measuring cup frequently take either too little or too much of the medicine, rendering the dosage either ineffective or, in cases of overdose, dangerous.

B. The company has included a measuring cup with each bottle of cough syrup for the last 18 years.
C. Studies have shown that 85 percent of consumers possess at home either a measuring cup, a set of measuring spoons, or both.
D. Many customers neglect to follow the recommended dosage of cough syrup even when the measuring cup is packaged along with the bottle of cough syrup.
E. Shipping the cough syrup bottles without the measuring cups will provide a marginal improvement in the number of cough syrup bottles that can be shipped in a standard package.

ANSWER: A Answer A suggests that there will be consequences from selling the cough syrup without the measuring cup that could hurt the product's sales; if the product is perceived as ineffective or dangerous, fewer people will buy it, and that effect will most likely decrease net revenue.

10. Which of the following, if true, provides the strongest support for the dental floss company's claim that the advertisement is misleading?

A. The dental floss manufacturer is concerned that it will lose market share in the dental health market because the advertisement encourages people to switch from dental floss to mouthwash.
B. The dental floss company claims in its own advertisements that brushing and flossing after every meal is the most effective way to maintain good dental health.
C. Although mouthwash is an effective deterrent to gum disease, it is less effective than dental floss at removing plaque and preventing cavities between teeth.

D. Per usage, mouthwash is three times more expensive than dental floss, if the recommended amounts of both products are used.
E. The dentists who conducted the study on the effectiveness of mouthwash in preventing gum disease obtained their funding for the study from a company that manufactures mouthwash.

ANSWER: C If the advertisement suggests that "people who do not like flossing can now rely solely on mouthwash and brushing to maintain good dental health," but in actuality mouthwash is less effective than flossing at performing certain functions that are important to good dental health, then the advertisement is misleading.

11. Which of the following, if true, most supports the mouthwash company's defense that its advertisement promotes greater public health?

A. Since the dental floss company is protesting the advertisement only to protect its own economic self-interest, it cannot be seen as representing greater public health.
B. Greater public health is best served if people use both mouthwash and dental floss, a combination that has been shown to be more effective than either method used alone.
C. Many people object to flossing because it is painful and causes their gums to bleed.
D. Since, on average, people are twice as likely to use mouthwash regularly as to floss regularly, the advertisement will increase the number of people who take effective action against gum disease, a serious public health problem.
E. Gum disease has been proven to have links with the early onset of heart disease, one of the top three threats to public health in terms of mortality.

ANSWER: D   If the advertisement does increase the number of people taking effective preventive measures against gum disease, then it is serving the public health. This argument is vulnerable to the criticism that the public health benefits of the ad are offset by the increased likelihood of plaque and cavities between teeth of people who stop flossing, but answer D is still stronger than any of the alternatives.

12. An electrical appliance company has submitted a new model of washing machine for stress and durability testing. After the conventional round of tests, 26 of the 90 machines tested no longer functioned. Observing these results, the company determined that the washing machine model was acceptable for the consumer market.

Which of the following, if true, most strongly supports the company's decision regarding the washing machine?

A. When the number one rated washing machine was submitted for stress and durability testing, 96 out of 100 machines were still functioning at the end of the test.
B. Because of the extreme stress of the testing process, any model that has more than two-thirds of its machines functioning at the end of the test process is considered sufficiently durable for the consumer market.
C. Most consumers will tolerate a washing machine that functions only 64 times out of 90 attempts.
D. Although the model tested is less durable than other models on the market, its projected price is considerably lower than that of the most durable models.
E. The electrical failure that brought down most of the 26 washing machines that ceased functioning could probably be avoided if the machine were redesigned.

ANSWER: B   B suggests that the observed results of the durability testing are well within the acceptable range for tests of this sort; by this same standard, the washing machine model would have failed the test if 30 or more machines had stopped working.

13. Having accounted for only 13 percent of the student body at Northlake High, students who attended Megalopolis Middle School dominate the Northlake High student government.

A. Having accounted for
B. With
C. Despite having been
D. Although accounting for
E. As

ANSWER: D   The underlined passage should suggest that the dominance of student government by a group representing a small minority of the total student body is contrary to expectations, thus C or D. The past tense of C, however, does not agree with the present tense "dominate" used later in the sentence, so D is the best choice.

14. Because the key witness died just prior to the start of the trial, Detectives Mack and Smith were not able in determining the extent of administrative corruption.

A. Detectives Mack and Smith were not able in determining the extent of
B. therefore the detectives, Mack and Smith, were unable to determine the extent of
C. Mack and Smith, the detectives, were not able of determining the extent to
D. Detectives Mack and Smith were not able to determine the extent of
E. the extent was unable to be determined by Detectives Mack and Smith of

ANSWER: D   The "were not able in determining" of A and the "were not able of determining" in C are unidiomatic, so A and C are out. The passive voice of E—"unable to be determined"—is stylistically inferior to the active voice used in B and D, so E is out unless there are more serious problems with B and D. The use of "therefore" in B is redundant following the "because" at the beginning of the sentence, so B is out. D is the clearest and most standard of the options.

15. Health Department statistics demonstrate that children <u>reading high on glucose with family histories of diabetes</u> are twice as likely as the general population to develop diabetes.

A. reading high on glucose with family histories of diabetes
B. with high glucose readings whose families have a history of diabetes
C. with high glucose readings and who have a diabetic history in the family
D. having high glucose readings and also having histories of diabetes in their family
E. with a history of diabetes running in the family and with high glucose readings

ANSWER: B Answer B is the clearest and most concise formulation of the intended statement. The construction "reading high" in A is awkward; C is incorrect because "a diabetic history" is awkward; D is incorrect because "having high glucose readings" is stylistically inferior to "with high glucose readings"; E is less concise than B.

16. Medical experts have amassed evidence concluding that users of smokeless tobacco <u>be more prone to heart disease, hypertension, and mouth cancers</u> than people who do not use smokeless tobacco.

A. be more prone to heart disease, hypertension, and mouth cancers
B. are proner to heart disease, hypertension, and mouth cancers
C. are more prone to heart disease, hypertension, and mouth cancers
D. experience heart disease, hypertension, and mouth cancers at heightened rates
E. suffer heart disease, hypertension, and mouth cancers at a higher risk

ANSWER: C "be more prone" (A), "are proner" (B), and "at heightened rates than" (D) are all grammatically incorrect, while statement E does not really make sense; statement C is the clearest and most standard wording.

17. Chef Sylvia Bostock's eclectic offerings at her new restaurant, Sylvia's, range from an Asian-inspired tuna tartelette in a soy-ginger

demiglace <u>with</u> a succulent cowboy rib-eye served atop a small mountain of fried onions.

A. with
B. to
C. in addition to
D. and
E. and to

ANSWER: B The idiomatic construction here is "{subject} ranges from X to Y." B completes the construction.

18. The governing board of the new league has modified its rules so that preexisting teams can stay together even though <u>not all their members meet the new minimum age requirement</u>.

A. not all their members meet the new minimum age requirement
B. the new minimum age requirement has not been met by all their members
C. not all their members have met the new minimum age, as required
D. all their members have not met the new minimum age requirement
E. all their members do not meet the new minimum age requirement

ANSWER: A A is grammatical and idiomatic, so it is the best choice. A is preferable to B because B uses the passive voice and because the present tense used in A, "not all . . . meet", corresponds better with the preceding verb phrase "can stay together" than the past tense used in B. A is preferable to C because A uses the present tense and because the final phrase, "as required" in C is somewhat awkward. D and E are incorrect because they imply that no one meets the requirements, rather than just some of the members.

19. Since 1960, the fast-growing town of Hotstone, Arizona, has drawn water from the Gray River, which feeds Lake Mudfish. If the town's water use continues to grow at its present rate, in about 20 years the water level of Lake Mudfish will inevitably decrease to the point that it can no longer support its biologically fragile population of fish.

The prediction above is based on which of the following assumptions?

A. As the town's water requirements grow, it will not be able to meet those requirements by drawing on water sources other than the Gray River.
B. Since 1960, the lake's population of fish has become more biologically fragile.
C. The amount of water that the lake loses to evaporation each year will increase over the next two decades.
D. There are multiple sources of water besides the Gray River that feed into Lake Mudfish.
E. The town of Hotstone will be able to reverse its trend of increasing water use if it implements an aggressive water conservation program.

ANSWER: A **If the town could meet its water requirements from sources other than the Gray River, then the depletion of Lake Mudfish would not necessarily be "inevitable"; since the prediction states that it is inevitable, statement A is an assumption upon which the prediction is based.**

20. Public protests can cause even the most powerful companies to change their policies. For example, an activist group recently staged a demonstration in front of the HydraBore corporate headquarters to protest the company's use of the chemical Ectomazathol. Within three months of the demonstration, HydraBore replaced Ectomazathol in its production plants with another chemical.

Which of the following, if true, casts the most doubt on the connection between the public protest and the decision of the company to change chemicals?

A. Preliminary studies show that the new chemical may be more carcinogenic than Ectomazathol.
B. The recently introduced chemical that is replacing Ectomazathol is less expensive and more effective in its industrial application than Ectomazathol.
C. HydraBore devoted no publicity efforts to announce its switch from Ectomazathol to the new chemical.
D. As protests against HydraBore have become more frequent, the company has subsequently increased its public relations budget.
E. The activist group that staged the demonstration has been linked to illegal acts of theft and sabotage within other corporate headquarters.

ANSWER: B **If B is true, then the company had sufficient reason to switch to the new chemical without taking the public protest into consideration.**

21. A recent spate of art thefts at a major museum has led to a drastic increase in the insurance premiums that the museum must pay to insure its collection. Many art fans are concerned that the museum, which traditionally has charged no entrance fee, will be forced to charge a high entrance fee in order to pay for the increased insurance premiums.

Which of the following, if true, would most alleviate the concern of the art fans that the museum will be forced to charge high entrance fees?

A. Law enforcement officials recently apprehended the Belgian Bobcat, a notorious art thief who has been linked to at least 20 art heists.
B. Citing a dispute with the insurance company over the terms of its coverage, the museum has chosen to cancel its insurance policy.
C. The majority of visitors to the museum are schoolchildren, who could not reasonably be expected to pay a high entrance fee.
D. The museum pays for the majority of its total expenses from its large endowment, which is earmarked specifically for purchasing new art.
E. The museum recently installed a state-of-the-art burglar alarm system that will make future thefts almost impossible.

ANSWER: B **If the museum has canceled its insurance policy, it will not have to pay the increased premiums, so the stated reason for charging a high entrance fee will no longer be valid.**

22. Which of the following, if true, best completes the passage below?

The traditional view of Homer is that of a blind bard who wrote down the epic poems known as the *Iliad* and the *Odyssey* in the eighth century B.C.E. We know now, however, that this picture cannot be true. The language used in the epic poems contains elements of the Greek language dating from the twelfth to the eighth centuries B.C.E., but the Greek writing system was not developed until the late seventh century, when it was used to record clerical notes. A more accurate statement regarding Homer, therefore, is that, if he existed, he most likely _____.

    A. wrote the poems down in the fifth century B.C.E., using a preexisting oral tradition of Greek epic poetry.

    B. was involved in the recording of clerical notes in Greek in the seventh century.

    C. composed the poems orally in the eighth century and then dictated them to a scribe in the late seventh century.

    D. composed the poems orally in the twelfth century, using a predecessor of the Greek language.

    E. composed the poems orally in the eighth century, using elements of preexisting Greek epic poetry.

ANSWER: E **The statement in the passage that the "language used in the epic poems contains elements of the Greek language dating from the twelfth to the eighth centuries B.C.E." suggests that the poem was probably composed in the eighth century, using preexisting poetic material. If "the Greek writing system was not developed until the late seventh century," then the poem must have been composed orally if it was composed in the eighth century, because it could not have been written down at that time. The mechanism described in C is vaguely plausible, although it is very unlikely that a person who composed poems in the eighth century would be alive to dictate them in the late seventh century. E is the best answer.**

23. Of the following, the most appropriate title for the passage above would be:

    A. The Elgin Marbles: Timeless Symbols of the Glory That Was Greece

    B. The Role of Great Museums in the Preservation of Cultural Artifacts

    C. Repatriation of Cultural Treasures: The British Museum's Dirty Little Secret

    D. The Value of Cultural Treasures in Defining National Identity

    E. A Curious Curator: Lord Elgin and the Rise of the British Museum

ANSWER: C **The main subject of the passage is the debate over the repatriation of cultural treasures; the passage states that the subject is not widely noted by the outside world, hence "secret"; and the passage presents the British Museum in a negative light, hence "dirty little secret."**

24. The third paragraph plays what role in the passage?

    A. It summarizes all the points expressed in the first two paragraphs.

    B. It raises new arguments that expand on those previously expressed.

    C. It suggests a possible area for useful research in the future.

    D. It rejects the arguments expressed in the first paragraph.

    E. It provides concrete evidence against arguments expressed in the second paragraph.

ANSWER: E **The example of the Elgin Marbles is used to poke holes in the arguments of museum curators expressed in the second paragraph.**

25. The situation involving the repatriation of the Elgin Marbles to Athens is most similar to which of the following?

    A. A Native American tribe in Oregon requests that a museum in Chicago return some ceremonial masks that could help in fundraising efforts to build a proposed museum in Portland.

    B. The nation of Peru in South America threatens the nation of Ecuador with military action if Ecuador does not hand over various gold artifacts of the Inca Empire, which originated in Peru.

    C. The National Archeology Museum of Cairo in Egypt requests that the Louvre return eight mummies from the time of Ramses the Great for the Cairo Museum's new exhibit hall dedicated to artifacts from Ramses' court.

D. The nation of Greece requests the nation of Turkey to provide Greek archeologists with free access to ancient Greek sites on the Ionian coast of Turkey, and to transfer any cultural artifacts found there to the National Archeology Museum in Athens.

E. A museum in Baton Rouge, Louisiana, requests that the Texas History Museum in Austin, Texas, send the original "Lone Star" flag to Baton Rouge for a new exhibit entitled, "Texas: Our Neighbor to the East."

ANSWER: C   In both C and the description of the Elgin Marbles issue in the text, there is an existing museum, presumably capable of both protecting and preserving cultural artifacts, that is seeking the return of cultural treasures to display in a newly created space among relevant cultural context.

26. What is the purpose of the final sentence of the passage?

A. To express pride in the cultural treasures of Athens

B. To refute the argument that more people can see the Elgin Marbles at the British Museum than at the Acropolis

C. To comment on the relative number of tourists at two of Europe's most famous tourist attractions

D. To express concern that the large number of tourists on the Acropolis will damage the Elgin Marbles, should they be returned

E. To provide an appropriate end to a rousing debate

ANSWER: B   The sentence specifically addresses one of the arguments against repatriation of the Elgin Marbles, i.e., that more people can see the sculptures in the British Museum.

27. The author's attitude toward museum curators who oppose the repatriation of cultural treasures is best summarized as what?

A. Righteous indignation

B. Bemused sarcasm

C. Seething anger

D. Condescending approval

E. Grudging admiration

ANSWER: A   The author's tone is certainly critical, as seen in terms such as "robbed" and "so-called art experts" and in the argument as a whole. The author's hostility to the museum curators does not rise to the level of "seething anger," however, and only one of the sentences ("evidently, the quantity of viewers. . .") could accurately be described as "bemused sarcasm," whereas the tone of the entire passage could be characterized as "indignant."

28. Which of the following, if true, would best support the position taken by the advocates of repatriation, as expressed in the first paragraph?

A. Of seven gold Inca statues sent from the Field Museum in Chicago to the National Archeology Museum in Lima, Peru, four were stolen within six months of being put on display.

B. Mummies taken from the dry heat of Egypt and relocated to the damp climate of London have shown disturbing signs of decay.

C. Operating a first-rate art and archeology museum is financially unfeasible for most developing nations, which face a difficult enough challenge feeding their people.

D. A type of sculpture from central Africa appears dull and nondescript in a museum setting, but when placed in the region of its origin can clearly be seen to replicate the colors and shapes of local rock formations.

E. British colonists in India in the nineteenth century felt that it was their right to claim the nation's artistic treasures as their own in exchange for importing the benefits of a modern industrial society.

ANSWER: D   The passage states, "Advocates of repatriation have argued that cultural treasures should be returned to their nations of origin, both because of basic fairness and because the artwork and cultural artifacts in question are best understood within their local context." The African sculptures in question are clearly easier to understand within their local context.

29. According to government health statistics, <u>Americans born before 1925 develop obesity by the age of 65 only 8 percent of the time, but 35 percent of those born since 1950 did so by age 35.</u>

   A. Americans born before 1925 develop obesity by the age of 65 only 8 percent of the time, but 35 percent of those born since 1950 did so by age 35.

   B. Only 8 percent of Americans born before 1925 developed obesity by the age of 65; if they are born since 1950, 35 percent develop obesity by the age 35.

   C. Only 8 percent of Americans born before 1925 developed obesity by the age of 65; of those born since 1950, 35 percent developed obesity by the age of 35.

   D. Obesity develops by the age of 65 in only 8 percent of Americans born before 1925, and by 35 by the 35 percent born since 1950.

   E. Of Americans born before 1925, only 8 percent of them have developed obesity by the age of 65, but 35 percent of those born since 1950 do by the age of 35.

ANSWER: C A is confusing, both because of its wording and because of its confusion of tenses: "develop" and "did so." B and E also mix tenses. The presentation of facts in D is confusing, and its use of the present tense is inappropriate for data that concern the past. C is the best answer.

30. In his groundbreaking work on special relativity, Albert Einstein displayed an intellectual boldness in the face of a reluctant scientific establishment that was <u>not unlike that of Galileo Galilei, who refused</u> to accept the intellectual limits placed on him by the censors of the Church.

   A. not unlike that of Galileo Galilei, who refused

   B. like Galileo Galilei and his refusal

   C. not unlike Galileo Galilei, who refused

   D. like that of Galileo Galilei for refusing

   E. as that of Galileo Galilei, who refused

ANSWER: A B and C are incorrect because they erroneously compare Galileo Galilei to Albert Einstein's intellectual boldness. D fails to

make clear whether Albert Einstein or Galileo is doing the refusing. E is incorrect because "like" rather than "as" should be used to compare two noun phrases. A is the best answer.

31. <u>The rising of the rate</u> of tardiness among MegaTech employees has generated concern among management that the employees are not sufficiently focused on increasing shareholder value.

   A. The rising of the rate

   B. Rising rates

   C. The rising rate

   D. Because of the rising rate

   E. Because the rising rate

ANSWER: C A is less idiomatic and concise than C. B is incorrect because "rates" does not agree in number with "has generated." The "because" in D and E turns the first clause into a sentence fragment. C is the best choice.

32. Increasingly over the last few years, corporations involved in patent litigation <u>have opted to settle the lawsuit rather than facing</u> the protracted legal expenses of a court battle.

   A. have opted to settle the lawsuit rather than facing

   B. have opted settling the lawsuit instead of facing

   C. have opted to settle the lawsuit rather than face

   D. had opted for settlement of the lawsuit instead of facing

   E. had opted to settle the lawsuit rather than face

ANSWER: C A is incorrect because it employs a nonparallel construction with "to settle" and "facing." In B, "have opted settling" is unidiomatic. D and E both incorrectly use the past perfect tense ("had opted"), which is inappropriate because the introductory clause "over the last few years" implies that the action in question began in the past and has continued into the present; past perfect is used for actions that terminated in the past. C is the best answer.

33. The ManStop, Boston's hot new men's clothing store, offers a selection that <u>is on range from</u> conservative pin-striped suits for that day at the office to stylish cashmere pullovers for that night on the town.

A. is on range from
B. ranging from
C. ranges to
D. ranges from
E. having ranged from

ANSWER: D   The idiomatic construction here is "{subject} ranges from X to Y." D completes the construction.

34. An agricultural cooperative wants to sell more of its less popular vegetables, zucchini in particular. A consultant has suggested that the cooperative's farmers should attempt to market a purple form of zucchini instead of the conventional green form, because people generally dislike green-colored vegetables.

Which of the following, if true, casts the most doubt on the accuracy of the consultant's assertion?

A. Broccoli and green peas, which are both green vegetables, are among the most popular vegetables in the country.
B. Grapes and eggplants, which both have purple skin, are popular among consumers of all ages.
C. Summer squash, a yellow-colored cousin of the zucchini, is one of the most popular summer vegetables.
D. Green tomatoes are far less popular than red tomatoes.
E. A chewing gum company reports that its purple-colored grape gum is less popular than its green-colored sour apple flavor.

ANSWER: A   Answer A offers evidence that directly counters the consultant's statement that people do not like green vegetables. E provides weak support for the idea that a green food could be more popular than a purple one, but the difference between gum and vegetables is sufficiently distinct to make A the stronger answer.

35. Homely Hotels has a customer loyalty program in which for every four nights a customer spends at a Homely Hotel, he or she receives a coupon good for one free night at any Homely Hotel. Recently people have begun selling these coupons on the Internet for less than the cost of a night at a Homely Hotel. This marketing of coupons has resulted in decreased revenue for the Homely Hotel chain.

To discourage this undesirable trade in free-stay coupons, it would be best for Homely Hotels to restrict:

A. The number of coupons a customer can receive in one year.
B. Use of the coupons to the specific hotel in which they were issued.
C. The valid dates of the coupons to only the month immediately following the date of issue.
D. Use of the coupons to the recipient or people with the same last name.
E. Use of the coupons to Homely Hotel franchises that charge an equal or lesser nightly rate than the franchise that issued the coupon.

ANSWER: D   Answer D presents a substantial impediment to unauthorized trade in the coupons, while still retaining the customer loyalty benefits for which the program was presumably created. The other answers either fail to address the unauthorized trade in a meaningful way or significantly reduce the value of the customer loyalty program.

36. An American manufacturer of space heaters reported a 1994 fourth-quarter net income (total income minus total costs) of $41 million, compared with $28.3 million in the fourth quarter of 1993. This increase was realized despite a drop in U.S. domestic retail sales of space-heating units toward the end of the fourth quarter of 1994 as a result of unusually high temperatures.

Which of the following, if true, would contribute most to an explanation of the increase in the manufacturer's net income?

A. In the fourth quarter of 1994, the manufacturer paid its assembly-line workers no salaries in November or December because of a two-month-long strike, but the company had a sufficient stock of space-heating units on hand to supply its distributors.

B. In 1993, because of unusually cold weather in the Northeast, the federal government authorized the diversion of emergency funding for purchasing space-heating units to be used in the hardest-hit areas.

C. Foreign manufacturers of space heaters reported improved fourth-quarter sales in the American market compared with their sales in 1993.

D. During the fourth quarter of 1994, the manufacturer announced that it would introduce an extra-high-capacity space heater in the following quarter.

E. In the third quarter of 1994, a leading consumer magazine advocated space heaters as a cost-effective way to heat spaces of less than 100 square feet.

ANSWER: A Answer A describes a situation in which costs would be substantially decreased because of the savings on worker salaries, but also in which revenues could remain substantially the same because preexisting stock was on hand. The described situation provides a plausible explanation for the observed financial results.

37. Archeological excavations of Roman ruins on the Greek island of Crete show that securing control over the maritime trade routes of the Eastern Mediterranean was a primary goal of the Romans, <u>as it was of the Greeks</u> in preceding centuries.

A. as it was of the Greeks
B. like that of the Greeks
C. as that of the Greeks
D. just as the Greeks did
E. as did the Greeks

ANSWER: A A is the only response that makes clear that the goal was what the Romans and Greeks had in common. B and C lack clear referents for "that." D and E fail to make clear exactly what the Greeks "did." A is the best answer.

38. The family's mood, which had been enthusiastic at the beginning of the trip, sank as the temperature <u>has risen, dramatically, but not enough for calling</u> off the whole trip.

A. has risen, dramatically, but not enough for calling
B. has risen, but not dramatically enough to call
C. rose, but not so dramatically as to call
D. rose, but not dramatically enough to call
E. rose, but not dramatically enough for calling

ANSWER: D The verb form "has risen" is supposed to describe an action simultaneous with "sank," so it should be in the same verb form as "sank," and so "rose" is a better verb form for this sentence; this excludes A and B. C inaccurately implies that the sinking mood itself could call off the trip; D and E correctly suggest that the sinking of the family's mood is a possible justification for calling off the trip. Between D and E, D is preferable because the construction "not . . . enough to call off" is more concise and forceful than "not . . . enough for calling off." D is the best answer.

39. Although no proof yet exists <u>of the electromagnetic disturbances observed being the results of nuclear weapons testing,</u> diplomats are treating the situation with utmost delicacy.

A. of the electromagnetic disturbances observed being the results of nuclear weapons testing
B. regarding the observed electromagnetic disturbances having been the results of nuclear weapons testing

C. that the electromagnetic disturbances observed were the results of nuclear weapons testing

D. that nuclear weapons testing resulted in the electromagnetic disturbances having been observed

E. that the electromagnetic disturbance observed were resulting from nuclear weapons testing

ANSWER: C The construction "proof exists that *x* was *y*" is more idiomatic and direct than the constructions in A and B: "proof exists of *x* being *y*" or "proof exists regarding *x* having been *y*"; consequently, C is preferable to A or B. D incorrectly suggests that the observation of disturbances was the result of the nuclear testing, rather than the electromagnetic disturbances themselves. E contains an error in verb-subject agreement with the construction, "disturbance . . . were." C is the best answer.

40. Hip dysplasia is more common among German Shepherds <u>than</u> dogs of other breeds.

A. than
B. than is so of
C. compared to
D. in comparison with
E. than among

ANSWER: E The idiomatic construction used here is "more common among *x* than among *y*," as in answer E. Answer A leaves open the illogical possibility that hip dysplasia among German shepherds is a more common phenomenon than the existence of other breeds of dogs. B lacks parallelism, and C and D are unidiomatic.

41. <u>The only lucid arguments printed in the newspaper concerning the new bond proposal was put forth by the high school principal who wrote a series of letters to the newspaper's editor.</u>

A. The only lucid arguments printed in the newspaper concerning the new bond proposal was put forth by the high school principal in a series of letters to the newspaper's editor.

B. The principal of the high school wrote a series of letters to the newspaper's editor that put forth the only lucid argument concerning the new bond proposal that was printed in the newspaper.

C. In a series of letters to the newspaper's editor, the principal of the high school put forth the only lucid argument concerning the new bond proposal to be printed in the newspaper.

D. The high school's principal's series of letters to the newspaper's editor lucidly put forth the only arguments concerning the new bond proposal to be printed in the newspaper.

E. Putting forth the only lucid arguments concerning the new bond proposal to be printed in the newspaper, the series of letters to the newspaper's editor were written by the high school's principal.

ANSWER: C C presents the most idiomatic and clearest statement of the facts. A contains a subject-verb disagreement with "arguments . . . was." B implies that the bond proposal, rather than the letters, was printed in the newspaper. D also has a subject-verb disagreement, because "series" is a collective noun and technically should take a singular verb, "series . . . puts forth" instead of "series . . . put forth"; the multiple possessives in D also make it awkward and hard to follow. The organization of information in E is confusing, and the passive construction leaves the natural subject of the sentence, the principal, as the object of a preposition at the end of the sentence. C is the best choice.

Answers and Explanations

1. In the figure above, is $AB > BC$? (*Note*: Figure not necessarily drawn to scale.)

(1) $AB > CD$
(2) $(AD - AB) > (AD - BC)$

ANSWER: B Statement (1) tells us nothing about the relationship of AB to BC, so the answer cannot be A or D. Statement (2), however, tells us that AB must be a smaller number than BC. This gives us sufficient information to answer the question in the negative, so the answer is B. Note that it does not matter whether the answer to a Data Sufficiency question is yes or no; it only matters that you have sufficient data to answer the question.

2. A box contains 90 jelly beans, of which some are orange, some are purple, and some are black. How many black jelly beans are in the box?

(1) There are 27 orange jelly beans.
(2) There are twice as many purple jelly beans as orange jelly beans.

ANSWER: C (1) alone is not sufficient, because there could be 6 or 60 black jelly beans in the jar. (2) alone is not sufficient, because there could be 1 orange and 2 purples, or 20 oranges and 40 purples. But (1) and (2) together tell us there are 27 orange jelly beans, 54 purple jelly beans, and therefore 9 black jelly beans.

3. Is 3^x greater than 100?

(1) $9x = 36$
(2) $\dfrac{1}{3^x} > 0.01$

ANSWER: D To be able to answer this question, we need to know a numerical value for x, because any numerical value will give a value for 3^x that is either greater or less than 100. (1) gives the value of 4 for x, so it is sufficient ($3^x = 81$; it is not greater). (2) can be restated as $100 > 3^x$, so 3^x cannot be greater than 100, and (2) is sufficient to answer the question.

4. How many more dogs than cats are in the veterinarian's office?

(1) There is a total of 30 dogs and cats in the office.
(2) The number of cats is the square root of the number of dogs.

ANSWER: C Statement (1) alone is insufficient because it does not give the breakdown between dogs and cats of the 30 animals. Statement (2) alone is insufficient because the pair of numbers described could be 2 and 4, 3 and 9, 4 and 16, and so on. When the two statements are combined, however, there is only one pair of numbers that can match both statements: 5 and 25. That is sufficient information to answer the question.

5. If p is a positive integer, and $p \neq 0$, is $\dfrac{p^2 + p}{2p}$ an integer?

(1) p is an even number.
(2) p is a multiple of 3.

ANSWER: A One way to verify this is to plug in even numbers; the results soon show that the result is always half of p plus ½, which is never an integer. You could also simplify the equation to $\dfrac{p+1}{2}$, and since an even number plus 1 is always an odd number, dividing the sum by 2 will never produce an integer. So statement (1) alone is sufficient. Statement (2) results in integers if p is an odd multiple of 3, but in nonintegers if p is an even multiple of 3, so this statement alone is not sufficient.

6. A certain prosthodontist specializes in implanting gold and silver teeth in his patients' mouths. He charges $650 for a gold tooth and $325 for a silver tooth. If his total fees for implanting gold and silver teeth last week were $15,925 in total, and he implanted five more gold teeth than silver teeth, how many teeth in total did he implant over the week?

A. 31
B. 32
C. 33
D. 34
E. 35

ANSWER: A It is probably easiest to approach this question by plugging in the available answers and seeing which one works. If it was 31 teeth (answer A), for example, then we know that the doctor implanted 18 gold and 13 silver. $18 \times \$650 + 13 \times \$325 = \$15,925$, so A is the answer.

7. What is the ratio of 3/7 to the product 3(7/3)?

A. 3:7
B. 1:3
C. 3:21
D. 1:7
E. 3:49

ANSWER: E 3(7/3) can be restated as 7. If you multiply 7 times both numbers to get rid of the fraction in 3/7, you get 3 and 49.

8. If the average (arithmetic mean) of a and b is 110, and the average of b and c is 160, what is the value of $a - c$?

A. −220
B. −100
C. 100
D. 135
E. It cannot be determined from the information given

ANSWER: B Restate both statements as equations: $a + b = 220$ and $b + c = 320$. Subtract the second equation from the first and you get $a + b - b - c = 220 - 320 = a - c = -100$.

9. A travel company wants to charter a plane to the Bahamas. Chartering the plane costs $8,000. So far, 18 people have signed up for the trip. If the company charges $300 per ticket, how many more passengers must sign up for the trip before the company can make any profit on the charter?

A. 7
B. 9
C. 13
D. 27
E. 45

ANSWER: B $8,000 divided by $300 per person means that the company must book 26.67 passengers to make a profit, so in practice this means 27 passengers. 27 required minus 18 already booked means that the company must find 9 more passengers.

10. If $x^2 + 9x - 3 = 3x^2 + 2x(4 - x)$, then $x^2 =$

A. 2
B. 3
C. 4
D. 9
E. 16

ANSWER: D The statement $3x^2 + 2x(4 - x)$ can be restated as $x^2 + 8x$. Thus, the original equation can be restated as $x = 3$, so $x^2 = 9$.

11. The pilot of a small aircraft with a 40-gallon fuel tank wants to fly to Cleveland, which is 480 miles away. The pilot recognizes that the current engine, which can fly only 8 miles per gallon, will not get him there. By how many miles per gallon must the aircraft's fuel efficiency be improved to make the flight to Cleveland possible?

A. 2
B. 4
C. 12
D. 40
E. 160

ANSWER: B   For an aircraft with a 40-gallon tank to fly 480 miles, it must average at least $480/40 = 12$ miles per gallon. $12 - 8 = 4$.

12. A circle graph shows how the MegaTech corporation allocates its Research and Development budget: 14% microphotonics; 24% home electronics; 15% food additives; 29% genetically modified microorganisms; 8% industrial lubricants; and the remainder for basic astrophysics. If the arc of each sector of the graph is proportional to the percentage of the budget it represents, how many degrees of the circle are used to represent basic astrophysics research?

A. 8°
B. 10°
C. 18°
D. 36°
E. 52°

ANSWER: D   First, determine what percentage of the budget is devoted to basic astrophysics: $14 + 24 + 15 + 29 + 8 = 90$, so 10% is left over for astrophysics. There are 360° in a circle, so multiply the 10% by 360/100 and you get 36°.

13. If $x + y = 36$, what is the value of xy?

(1) $y - x = 14$
(2) $y = 2x + 3$

ANSWER: D   (1) alone is sufficient; add the two equations together and you get $2y = 50$, so $y = 25$ and $x = 11$. (2) alone is sufficient, because if you plug the equation into the question, you get $x + 2x + 3 = 36$, or $3x = 33$, so $x = 11$ and $y = 25$.

14. A hotdog vendor sold $45 worth of hotdogs at lunchtime Tuesday. Each hotdog cost $1.50. What percentage of his day's stock of hotdogs did the vendor sell at lunchtime?

(1) The vendor started the day with 120 hotdogs.
(2) The vendor sold twice as many hotdogs at dinnertime as he sold at lunchtime.

ANSWER: A   From the information given in the passage, we can determine that the vendor sold 30 hotdogs at lunchtime. To determine the percentage of the total stock sold, we need to know the total stock of hotdogs. (1) provides this number, while (2) does not, so the answer is A.

15. For real numbers a, b, and c, is $ab = bc + 3$?

(1) $ab = 3b$
(2) $b + 3 = c$

ANSWER: C   To answer this question, the statements have to prove either that the equation above is true or that it cannot be true. (1) alone is insufficient; it allows the equation to be restated as $3b = bc + 3$, which could be true or not true depending on the values of b and c. (2) alone is insufficient; it allows the equation to be restated as $ab = b^2 + 3b + 3$, which could be true or not true depending on the values of a and b. If the two are combined, the equation can be restated as $3b = b^2 + 3b + 3$, which can be restated as $b^2 + 3 = 0$. Since b is a real number, b^2 has to be either a positive number or 0, in which case $b^2 + 3 = 0$ cannot be true. Therefore, the equation must be false.

16. What is the number of male employees at the factory?

(1) If the factory were to hire 150 more employees and 2/3 of them were female, the ratio of male to female employees would be 8:3.

(2) The factory has at least twice as many male employees as female employees, and it employs at least 150 females.

ANSWER: E (1) alone is insufficient because if we do not know the total number of either male or female employees, the ratio cannot give us a definitive number for either male or female employees. (2) alone is insufficient because any number of females over 150 and any number of males over 300 could match the conditions. Combining the two statements limits the number of possibilities somewhat, but there are still many different numbers of male and female employees that could meet the stated conditions.

17. An engineer designed a ball so that when it was dropped, it rose with each bounce exactly one-half as high as it had fallen. The engineer dropped the ball from a 16-meter platform and caught it after it had traveled 46.5 meters. How many times did the ball bounce?

A. 5
B. 6
C. 7
D. 8
E. 9

ANSWER: A You can approach this problem by just adding up the bounces. It falls 16 m, then bounces 8 m and drops 8 m (now it has traveled 32 m), bounces 4 m and falls 4 m (40 m), bounces 2 m and falls 2 m (44 m), bounces 1 m and falls 1 m (46 m), bounces 0.5 m and is caught by the engineer. That was 5 bounces.

The following two questions refer to the following diagram:

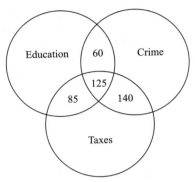

A newspaper polled 1,000 likely voters about which of the following issues, if any, played an important role in their decision-making process for an upcoming election: education, crime, and/or taxes. Of the voters surveyed, a total of 495 named education, 490 named crime, and 440 named taxes. In the figure above, the overlapping areas between two circles represent the people who named only those two items; the overlapping area between the three circles represents those people who named all three issues.

18. What percentage of those polled named only education or only crime but no other issue?

A. 25.5%
B. 31.5%
C. 39%
D. 55%
E. 98.5%

ANSWER: C First, you need to determine the number of people who named only crime and only education: crime only = 490 − (60 + 125 + 140) = 165; education only = 495 − (60 + 125 + 85) = 225; 165 + 225 = 390. 390 is 39% of 1,000.

19. How many of the 1,000 people polled responded "none of the above" to the questions?

A. 140
B. 110
C. 80
D. 20
E. 0

ANSWER: B To determine this answer, you need to group all of the respondents so that they appear in only one group; i.e., you need to determine how many people named crime, education, or taxes only, then add those numbers to the numbers of people who named two or three issues, and then subtract the sum from 1,000. Crime only = 490 − (60 + 125 + 140) = 165; education only = 495 − (60 + 125 + 85) = 225; taxes only = 440 − (85 + 125 + 140) = 90. Add up the totals: 225 + 165 + 90 + 60 + 140 + 85 + 125 = 890. 1,000 − 890 = 110.

20. The equation $\frac{R-3}{28} = \frac{S+8}{35}$ relates the values of two linked currencies, where R is the value in dollars of one currency and S is the value in dollars of the other currency. Which of the following equations can be used to convert dollar values from the R currency to the S currency?

A. $S = \frac{5R - 47}{4}$

B. $S = \frac{4R + 47}{5}$

C. $S = \frac{5R + 17}{4}$

D. $S = \frac{4R - 17}{5}$

E. $S = \frac{5R}{4} - 12$

ANSWER: A You can simplify the equation by multiplying 7 times both sides, which results in the equation $\frac{R-3}{4} = \frac{S+8}{5}$, which can be restated as $5R - 15 = 4S + 32$, which can be restated as $S = \frac{5R - 47}{4}$.

21. If x is a positive number and ½ the square root of x is the cube root of x, then $x =$

A. 64
B. 32
C. 16
D. 4
E. 1

ANSWER: A The fastest approach to a question like this is probably to plug in the answer choices and see which one fits. If $x = 64$, then 1/2 of the square root is 4, which is also the cube root of 64, so A is the answer.

22. If Josh, Doug, and Brad have a total of $72 between them, and Josh has three times as much money as Brad but only three-fourths as much as Doug, how much money does Doug have?

A. $8
B. $9
C. $27
D. $32
E. $36

ANSWER: E If Brad has B dollars, then Josh has $3B$ and Doug has $4B$. Their combined amount of $8B$ equals $72; $B = \$72/8 = \$9$, so Doug has $36.

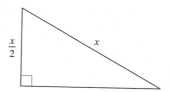

23. The flat triangular lot depicted above is available for development. If $x + \frac{x}{2} = 150$ meters, what is the area of the lot in square meters?

A. 125
B. $150\sqrt{3}$
C. 1,500
D. $1,250\sqrt{3}$
E. $2,500\sqrt{3}$

ANSWER: D You can tell from the statement $x + \frac{x}{2} = 150$ that $x = 100$ meters, and since one of the legs of the right triangle is $\frac{x}{2}$ and the hypotenuse is x, you can tell that this is a 30–60–90 triangle, and the legs of the triangle are then 50 and $50\sqrt{3}$. The area of a triangle is one-half base times height, so $\frac{(50)(50\sqrt{3})}{2} = \frac{2,500\sqrt{3}}{2} = 1,250\sqrt{3}$.

24. For any numbers w and z, $w \cdot z = w^3 z (8 - w^2)$. If both z and $w \cdot z$ are positive numbers, which of the following could be a value of w?

A. 9
B. 3
C. 0
D. −2
E. −9

ANSWER: E   The most direct approach here is probably to plug in the answers and see which one gives a positive value for $w \cdot z$. A and B are out because $(8 - w^2)$ results in a negative number while $w^3 z$ is positive, C is out because 0 is not a positive number, D is out because $w^3 z$ is negative while $(8 - w^2)$ is positive; only E meets the conditions, because both $(8 - w^2)$ and $w^3 z$ are negative, yielding a positive value for $w \cdot z$.

25. $\dfrac{\frac{1}{4} + \frac{1}{5}}{\frac{1}{8}} =$

A. $\dfrac{2}{5}$

B. $\dfrac{9}{20}$

C. $\dfrac{9}{8}$

D. $\dfrac{9}{5}$

E. $\dfrac{18}{5}$

ANSWER: E   The fraction is the same thing as $\dfrac{\frac{9}{20}}{\frac{1}{8}} = \dfrac{72}{20} = \dfrac{18}{5}$.

26. Last year's receipts from the sale of greeting cards during the week before Mother's Day totaled $189 million, which represented 9 percent of total greeting card sales for the year. Total greeting card sales for the year totaled how many million dollars?

A. 17,010
B. 2,100
C. 1,890
D. 1,701
E. 210

ANSWER: B   If 189 million = 9 percent of the total, then 189/9 = 21 million = 1% of the total, and therefore the total sales were 21 million × 100 = 2,100 million.

27. What is the value of $5x^2 - 1.9x - 3.7$ for $x = -0.3$?

A. −4.72
B. −3.82
C. −3.58
D. −2.68
E. 0.57

ANSWER: D   The equation $5(-0.3 \times -0.3) -1.9(-0.3) -3.7 = 0.45 + 0.57 - 3.7 = -2.68$.

28. Two cyclists are racing up a mountain at different constant rates. Cyclist A is now 50 meters ahead of cyclist B. How many minutes from now will cyclist A be 150 meters ahead of cyclist B?

(1) 5 minutes ago, cyclist A was 200 meters behind cyclist B.
(2) Cyclist A is moving 25% faster than cyclist B.

ANSWER: A   To answer this question, we need to know how much faster cyclist A is moving than cyclist B. (1) gives us this information, because we know that cyclist A gained 250 m on cyclist B in 5 minutes, so he is traveling 50 m/minute faster; (1) is sufficient. (2) is insufficient, because their relative rate of motion is useful here only if it can be converted into actual measures of meters over time, which (2) cannot.

29. Is integer x divisible by 48?

(1) x is divisible by 16.
(2) x is divisible by 12.

ANSWER: C   (1) alone is insufficient because the set of numbers divisible by 16 contains some numbers divisible by 48 (e.g., 48, 96), but also some numbers not divisible by 48, such as 16, 32, and so on. (2) alone is insufficient for the same reason. If the two statements are combined, the set of numbers divisible by both 16 and 12 are all divisible by 48; plug in numbers to verify that this is true. It works because 48 is the lowest common multiple of these two numbers.

30. Is $3 < \sqrt{x} < 5$?

(1) $x < 20$
(2) $x > 5$

ANSWER: E   (1) alone is insufficient, because x could equal 1 or 16, which give different answers to the question. (2) alone is insufficient, because x could equal 16 or 64, which give different answers to the questions. The statements combined are still insufficient, because x could equal 16 or 6, which give different answers to the question.

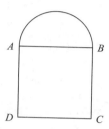

31. The figure above shows the shape of a brick patio. If arc AB is a semicircle and $ABCD$ is a square, what is the perimeter of the patio?

(1) The radius of the semicircle described by arc AB is 4.
(2) The perimeter of the square $ABCD$ is 32.

ANSWER: D   (1) alone is sufficient because the radius of the semicircle is sufficient to give both the circumference of the semicircle (πr) and the length of one of the sides of the square ($2r$). The perimeter of the whole unit then is the circumference of the semicircle plus the lengths of three sides of the square. (2) alone is sufficient, because the perimeter of the square is sufficient to give the length of a side ($P/4$), and then the radius of the semicircle is half of the length of a side of the square.

32. A call to Rosie's Psychic Hotline costs $5.99 for the first 2 minutes and $1.99 for each additional minute. Stuart called the hotline for x minutes, where x is an integer. How many minutes long was the call?

(1) The total charge for the call was $11.96.
(2) The charge for the last 3 minutes of the call was $0.01 less than half the total cost of the call.

ANSWER: D   (1) alone is sufficient because the only way to arrive at a charge of $11.96 is with the initial charge of $5.99 for two minutes plus $5.97 for three additional minutes at $1.99 each; 5 minutes. (2) alone is sufficient, because the only time for which the statement is true is

5 minutes; the easiest way to determine this may be to plug in different numbers of minutes and see which one works. If the last 3 minutes cost $1.99 per minute, then the last 3 minutes cost $5.97. This is one cent less than $5.98, which is half of the cost of a 5-minute call, $11.96.

33. If Z is represented by the decimal $0.W7$, what is the digit W?

(1) $Z > \frac{2}{3}$
(2) $Z > \frac{9}{10}$

ANSWER: B   (1) alone is insufficient because Z could be 0.67, 0.77, 0.87, or 0.97. (2) alone is sufficient, because the only decimal Z that will meet the conditions is 0.97.

34. If a cube has a volume of 125, what is the surface area of one side?

A. 5
B. 25
C. 50
D. 150
E. 625

ANSWER: B   The length of a side of a cube is the cube root of its volume; the cube root of 125 is 5. The area of a side is the square of its length, so $5 \times 5 = 25$.

35. An investor bought 200 shares of stock in ABCD company in 1990. By 1992, the investment was worth only $\frac{2}{3}$ of its original value. By 1995, the 200 shares were worth only $\frac{1}{2}$ of their value in 1990. By what percent did the value of the investment drop from 1992 to 1995?

A. $16\frac{2}{3}\%$
B. 25%
C. $33\frac{1}{3}\%$
D. 50%
E. $66\frac{2}{3}\%$

ANSWER: B   This may be easiest to approach by plugging in actual values. If the 200 shares were worth $300 in 1990, then they were worth only $200 in 1992 (2/3) and $150 in 1995 (1/2). A loss of $50 from $200 is a 25% drop.

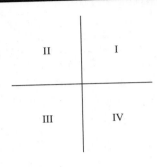

II | I

III | IV

36. In the rectangular quadrant system shown above, which quadrant, if any, contains no point (x, y) that satisfies the equation $x^2 - 2y = 3$?

A. none
B. I
C. II
D. III
E. IV

ANSWER: A   The equation describes a parabola facing upward that crosses the y-axis

at $-3/2$; therefore, it passes through all four quadrants. You can plug in points from each quadrant to verify.

37. Which of the following cannot be the median of five positive integers a, b, c, d, and e?

A. a
B. $d + e$
C. $b + c + d$
D. $\dfrac{b + c + d}{3}$
E. $\dfrac{a + b + c + d + e}{5}$

ANSWER: C   The median is the number that is numerically in the middle of a group. C is the answer because the sum of any three out of five numbers must be larger than the median, because even if it is the three smallest numbers, those numbers will include the median among them. You can confirm that all of the other options are possibilities if the variables equal 1, 2, 3, 4, 5.

Answers and Explanations

---

1. Companies that advertise on television complain that digital television recording (DTR) services make it possible for consumers to watch television programs without viewing the commercials that these advertisers have paid the television networks to broadcast. The DTR service providers respond that their services may actually help the advertisers, because without their service, many consumers would not have been able to watch the programs—or the commercials in them—in the first place.

Which of the following, if true, offers the most support to the advertisers' claims that the DTR services are currently hurting their businesses?

A. Even the best commercials are usually less entertaining than the programs that consumers choose to watch for themselves.

B. DTR services charge such high rates that only a small percentage of consumers subscribe to them.

C. The average per-second cost of advertising on television has risen every year for the past two decades.

D. More than 90 percent of subscribers to DTR services opt to use a setting that automatically edits out commercials.

E. DTR services alter the television viewing experience by allowing customers to view the program of their choice at the time of their choosing.

ANSWER: D   Answer D suggests that the defense stated by the DTR services providers works only in theory, not in practice. If most subscribers to these services are automatically avoiding all commercials, the companies that have paid to broadcast advertising messages to these viewers are going to get less of a return from their advertising investment, which will hurt their businesses.

2. When airlines were deregulated in the 1970s, the average price of a ticket was $135. Three decades later, the average price is $275, there are twice as many in-air collisions, fliers in small markets are at the mercy of predatory carriers, and air rage is at an all-time high. It is time to re-regulate the air travel industry.

All of the following statements, if true, weaken the above argument except for which statement?

A. Because of inflation, a $275 ticket today is actually 10 to 20 percent less expensive than a $135 ticket was in 1975.

B. Deregulation has increased the choices available to fliers in terms of both time of flight and carrier.

C. Airlines are currently flying more than five times as many passenger miles per year as they did in 1975.

D. Compared with passengers in large urban areas, passengers in small markets pay, on average, twice as much per mile flown on domestic flights because their airports are generally served by fewer airlines.

E. Psychologists have been able to determine no connection between the deregulation of the airline industry and the onset of increased levels of air rage.

ANSWER: D   All of the other choices weaken the argument, whereas D supports the argument's contention that "fliers in small markets are at the mercy of predatory carriers."

3. Skilled blacksmiths who could forge useful items out of iron used to play a central role in American life. The onset of industrialization and the mass production of iron products, however, have made the blacksmith's traditional role mostly obsolete. Still, there will always be a job available for a good blacksmith.

Which of the following, if true, provides the most support for the conclusion that a job will always be available for a good blacksmith?

A. Many people are willing to pay considerably more for tools hand-crafted by a blacksmith than for tools created by a machine.
B. Blacksmiths cannot produce iron products with the speed or consistency of machines.
C. Blacksmiths traditionally apprenticed to a master blacksmith for seven or more years before entering business independently.
D. The cowboy never would have conquered the West without the horseshoes crafted by blacksmiths.
E. As skilled craftsmen, blacksmiths traditionally served as community leaders throughout North America and Europe.

ANSWER: A This answer explains how blacksmiths would still be able to find work despite their relative disadvantages in the modern age.

4. When unscrupulous people shoplift, a vicious cycle results. Retailers must raise their prices in order to make up for the lost sales, and the higher prices encourage more people to shoplift. This vicious cycle hurts honest consumers worst of all, because they have to pay higher prices.

The vicious cycle described above could not happen unless which of the following is true?

A. Shoplifters usually steal only items that they need but cannot afford.
B. Retailers do not take shoplifting losses into account when they initially set their prices.
C. The best way for retailers to address shoplifting is by punishing shoplifters to the fullest extent of the law.

D. Some people would shoplift no matter how low retailers set their prices.
E. It costs retailers more to pay security guards to prevent shoplifting than just to absorb the cost of occasional losses due to theft.

ANSWER: B If statement B is not true, then retailers would not raise their prices after shoplifting occurred, and the vicious cycle as described could not happen.

5. When Brad offered his old wooden desk at a garage sale, no one bought it, even though he offered it for only $10. When he offered it at the local auction house, however, someone bought it for $850.

Which of the following, if true, best explains why Brad was able to sell the desk for a high price at the auction while he could not sell it for a much lower price at the garage sale?

A. Brad advertised that the proceeds of the garage sale would benefit a local charity, while he made no such claims for the proceeds from the auction.
B. One of the legs of the desk was shorter than the other three, producing an unbalanced writing surface.
C. The auction house specializes in selling antique furniture, which is generally valued more highly than the discarded furniture sold at garage sales.
D. Brad insisted that anyone who bought the desk had to use it as an actual workspace.
E. Prospective buyers at auctions are often more interested in the auction process than in the items up for bid.

ANSWER: C C suggests that the desk, when sold through the auction house, was marketed and valued as an antique rather than as discarded furniture, and was thus perceived as a more valuable item than it had been at the garage sale.

6. Four Dynacorp Optimall Omniprocessors were shipped in the fourth quarter, <u>and it brought</u> to 13 the number of these ultra-high-capacity processors shipped during the year.

A. and it brought
B. by bringing
C. and brings
D. having brought
E. bringing

ANSWER: E The gerund form in E conveys the intended meaning that the action of the second clause was simultaneous with the main action of the first clause. A and C both require singular subjects in the first clause that do not exist. B does not make sense in the context of the sentence, and D incorrectly uses the future perfect, since the action in the second clause cannot logically have been completed before the action in the first clause.

7. After his 1962 season, in which he set a record for on-base percentage, Mitch McAlister left his old team and signed with the Springfield <u>Argonauts, with an annual salary of $550,000 and was the</u> highest salary in professional baseball at that time.

    A. Argonauts, with an annual salary of $550,000 and was the
    B. Argonauts, earning $550,000 per year and it was the
    C. Argonauts for a yearly wage of $550,000, being the
    D. Argonauts, with annual pay of $550,000 per year, which was the
    E. Argonauts for an annual salary of $550,000, the

    ANSWER: E A incorrectly implies that Mitch McAlister was the highest salary. B has no clear referent for "it." The construction "$550,000, being the . . ." in C is unidiomatic. The construction "annual pay . . . per year" in D is redundant. E is the best answer.

8. Nile perch, voracious predators that will eat anything smaller than themselves, <u>are natives of northern Africa but were introduced to Tanzania's Lake Victoria in a foolhardy attempt during the 1960s of boosting</u> the local sport-fishing industry; since their introduction, these sturdy fish have decimated most other aquatic species in the lake.

    A. are natives of northern Africa but were introduced to Tanzania's Lake Victoria in a foolhardy attempt during the 1960s of boosting
    B. are native in northern Africa but were introduced to Tanzania's Lake Victoria during the 1960s as foolhardy attempts to boost

    C. are native to northern Africa but were introduced to Tanzania's Lake Victoria during the 1960s in a foolhardy attempt to boost
    D. had been native to northern Africa but during the 1960s were introduced to Tanzania's Lake Victoria in a foolhardy attempt to boost
    E. are native to northern Africa but were introduced to Tanzania's Lake Victoria as a foolhardy attempt of boosting

    ANSWER: C A, in stating that the Nile perch in Lake Victoria "are natives of northern Africa," could be read to imply that the fish currently there are personally natives of northern Africa, which based on the timeline in question is almost certainly untrue; also "attempt . . . of boosting" is less idiomatic than "attempt . . . to boost." In B, "native in" is unidiomatic, and it implies that the fish themselves are "foolhardy attempts," rather than the *introduction* of the fish. D, by using the past perfect "had been native," implies that the fish is no longer native, which seems unlikely given that it is a "sturdy fish." E, like B, identifies the fish rather than the introduction as "a foolhardy attempt." C is the clearest and most idiomatic answer.

9. No giant squid has ever survived in captivity because these giant animals of the <u>deeps require extremely high water pressure for the purpose of maintaining its</u> internal osmotic balance.

    A. deeps require extremely high water pressure for the purpose of maintaining its
    B. deep requires extremely high water pressure to maintain its
    C. deep require extremely high water pressure in order to maintain their
    D. deeps requires extremely high water pressure so that it can maintain its
    E. deep require for maintenance extremely high water pressure for their

    ANSWER: C A is incorrect because "for the purpose of maintaining" is unidiomatic and the singular "its" modifies the plural "animals." B incorrectly uses the singular "requires . . . to maintain its" when "animals" is the subject. D also incorrectly treats the subject as singular. In E, it is unclear what "maintenance" refers to. C is the best answer.

10. The state medical review board is considering a new regulation <u>that physicians practicing in state facilities with past malpractice suits having been filed against them are required to disclose any such suits to prospective patients.</u>

A. that physicians practicing in state facilities with past malpractice suits having been filed against them are required to disclose any such suits to prospective patients

B. that requires physicians practicing in state facilities disclose any past malpractice suits filed against them to prospective patients

C. to require physicians with past malpractice suits filed against them and who practice in state facilities to disclose these to prospective patients

D. for physicians that practice in state facilities requiring them to have disclosed to prospective patients past malpractice suits filed against them

E. requiring physicians who practice in state facilities to disclose to prospective patients any past malpractice suits filed against them

ANSWER: E   A is flawed because it is redundant to say of the malpractice suits both that they are "past" and "having been filed"; also, it is unclear whether the "filed against them" refers to the physicians or the state facilities. B fails to include "to" before "disclose." In C, it is unclear what "these" refers to. D illogically suggests that the physicians must "have disclosed . . . past suits" to "prospective patients"; attempting to regulate past behavior in this way is a particularly ineffective form of regulation. E is the clearest statement of the facts; it is somewhat flawed in that it leaves open the reading that the malpractice suits could have been filed against the prospective patients, but a logical reader could easily make the judgment from context that "them" refers to the physicians. E is the best answer.

11. Our criminal justice system is inherently flawed because it relies on amateur juries of decent citizens, who lack the perspective to understand the criminal mind. To have an effective criminal justice system would require professional juries, who would be able to deal with these criminals in a way that gets results.

The argument above depends on which of the following assumptions?

A. Professional jurors will be more reliable than amateur jurors because they will not attempt to avoid jury duty.

B. Professional jurors will not be burdened by the biases against race, gender, and religion that amateur jurors bring into the courtroom.

C. Dealing with criminals in a way that gets results requires an understanding of the criminal mind.

D. No amount of professional training can impart the perspective of the criminal mind necessary to run an effective criminal justice system.

E. Jurors possessing the perspective to understand the criminal mind are unfit to serve on a jury, because they are likely to be criminals.

ANSWER: C   The passage states that amateur juries are inherently flawed because the jurors do not understand the criminal mind, and it states that a professional jury would be able to deal with criminals in a way that gets results, so the logical connection is that jurors who understand the criminal mind will be able to get results. This argument also relies on the assumption that professional jurors will possess the perspective to understand the criminal mind, but since that statement is not included among the answers, C is the best choice.

12. Advertisement: The most flavorful olives in the world are kalamata olives. The more kalamata olives used to make a bottle of olive oil, the more flavorful the oil, and no company buys more kalamata olives than Zorba's Olive Oil. Therefore, when you buy Zorba's Olive Oil, you're buying the most flavorful olive oil available today.

The reasoning presented in the advertisement is flawed because it overlooks the possibility that:

A. Not all of Zorba's competitors use kalamata olives in their oil.

B. Zorba's sells more olive oil than any other company.

C. The most flavorful olive oil is not necessarily the best olive oil.
D. Because of bulk discounts, Zorba's pays less per kilogram of kalamata olives than does its competitors.
E. The number of kalamata olives harvested every year is far less than the number of Spanish olives harvested every year.

ANSWER: B The advertisement just says that Zorba's buys more kalamata olives than any other company; it does not say that it uses more kalamata olives per bottle. If Zorba's sells more olive oil than any other company, it is entirely possible that one or more of Zorba's competitors use more kalamata olives per bottle.

13. The cypress trees of the Louisiana wetlands are threatened by the exploding population of nutria, a type of South American rodent introduced into the area in the 1930s in hopes of starting a nutria fur industry. Unfortunately, no one wanted the fur, and now the rodents number in the millions. A park ranger has suggested introducing the South American jaguar, the nutria's natural predator, into the Louisiana wetlands as a way to control the nutria population.

Which of the following, if true, casts the most doubt on the ranger's plan to introduce jaguars as an effective way to control the nutria population?

A. Past attempts to control the nutria population through traps and poison have resulted in limited and temporary population reductions.
B. A program in Florida found that the best way to conserve the root systems of wetland trees such as cypresses is to surround the trees' roots with tough plastic barriers.
C. The jaguar is a large and deadly predator that, if introduced, could kill livestock, pets, or even humans that it encounters in the Louisiana wetlands.
D. During the past year an unusually cold winter killed an estimated 35 percent of the nutria population in the Louisiana wetlands.
E. The South American jaguar is a predator of the ferret, which is currently the chief predator of the nutria in the Louisiana wetlands.

ANSWER: E Answer E suggests that the introduction of the jaguar will reduce one of the existing checks on the nutria population, which could in fact make the problem worse. None of the other answers specifically address the effectiveness of this particular plan.

14. Which of the following best expresses the purpose of this passage?

A. To explain how a loophole in the Clean Air Act allows power plants to avoid compliance with emissions restrictions
B. To raise awareness of the problems caused by sulfur dioxide emissions from coal-burning power plants
C. To argue against a specific implementation of the Clean Air Act that relates to greenhouse gas emissions
D. To argue that companies should not exploit a loophole in the Clean Air Act concerning an atmospheric pollutant
E. To advocate the passage of a new Clean Air Act that places limits on sulfur dioxide emissions

ANSWER: D A and B address only limited parts of the passage. C could be a strong answer except that it mentions "greenhouse gas emissions," which are not actually mentioned in the passage. E is incorrect because the passage never suggests the passage of a new Clean Air Act, only a more rigorous enforcement of the current one. D best captures the themes of the passage.

15. The author's tone can best be described as which of the following?

A. Angry and subjective
B. Calm and objective
C. Analytic and ambivalent
D. Grim and self-satisfied
E. Tentative and biased

ANSWER: A The use of loaded terms such as "dragged its heels," "tricks and loopholes," and "underhanded" suggests that the author has an emotional involvement with the subject that could be described as angry; the author also clearly has a point of view on the subject, so he or she is subjective. None of the other choices offers a more accurate description.

16. The author most likely begins and concludes the passage with questions for what reason?

A. To suggest possible areas for current and future research
B. To pose a question that is answered in the body of the passage, and then to formulate a question that arises naturally out of the discussion.
C. To gain the readers' attention and encourage their agreement with the arguments in the passage.
D. To suggest through rhetorical questions that the problems described in the passage do not actually have answers.
E. To test the readers' knowledge of the material discussed in the passage.

ANSWER: C   The goals described in C—gaining the readers' attention and securing their agreement—are two of the roles that questions can serve in expository writing. In this passage, the first question aims to draw the reader in by posing a question to which most readers will respond "yes," and the final question asks the reader to agree with the key argument of the passage, i.e., that power companies should not exploit these loopholes in the Clean Air Act.

17. According to information given in the passage, which of the following statements presents the most accurate comparison of an average ton of coal from Wyoming with an average ton of coal from the Appalachian range in West Virginia?

A. The former is cheaper and has higher sulfur content than the latter.
B. The latter is found closer to the surface and contains more sulfur than the former.
C. The former can help coal-burning power plants meet limits on sulfur dioxide emissions and costs more than the latter.
D. The latter generates more energy per pound of coal than the former.
E. The former is found closer to the surface than the latter and helps coal-burning power plants meet limits on sulfur dioxide emissions.

ANSWER: E   The passage states: "Many power plants have even complied with the emissions limits *and* reduced their operating costs by switching from high-sulfur Appalachian coal to the low-sulfur coal produced in Western states such as Wyoming and Idaho. Western coal is not only cleaner than Eastern coal, but also, because it is generally closer to the surface, as much as 30 percent less expensive to extract." Therefore, the former—i.e., the coal from Wyoming—is less expensive, closer to the surface, and lower in sulfur than the latter— i.e., the coal from West Virginia. A, B, and C present inaccuracies in this comparison, while the information in D is not addressed in this passage.

18. According to the information given in the passage, sulfur dioxide emissions are linked to all except which of the following phenomena?

A. Reduced visibility in the eastern United States
B. Damage to the ozone hole
C. Increased rates of asthma
D. Acid rain
E. Damaged forests

ANSWER: B   The passage mentions all of the other answer choices as consequences of sulfur dioxide emissions, but it does not mention the ozone hole.

19. In the fourth paragraph, the passage mentions the "400 power plants" for what purpose?

A. To provide concrete evidence that many power plants have complied with the Clean Air Act provisions without undergoing ruinous financial hardship
B. To demonstrate the size and influence of the energy industry in the United States
C. To demonstrate that only a fraction of the power plants in the country have complied with the Clean Air Act, while hundreds of others have avoided compliance through tricks and loopholes
D. To demonstrate that companies can both comply with the Clean Air Act and achieve reductions in their operating costs by employing new, more efficient technologies
E. To suggest that those companies that have not complied are in the minority

ANSWER: A   The passage states: "Since 1977, more than 400 power plants across the country have managed to comply with the restrictions and are still making money." This statement comes immediately after a presentation of the industry argument that compliance with the Clean Air Act causes undue financial hardship; this statement is intended as a direct refutation of that claim.

20. Which of the following statements, if true, would provide the strongest argument for a utility company spokesman wishing to refute the arguments expressed in the passage?

A. Over the last decade, the energy industry has funded an environmental initiative that has planted more than 200,000 new trees.

B. The dangers of acid rain to human health have been wildly exaggerated by environmental extremists who seek to scare the general public.

C. The specifications of the Clean Air Act, although well intentioned, in practice require power plants to adopt less efficient technologies that increase emissions of atmospheric pollutants other than sulfur dioxide that have been linked to equally serious problems.

D. A substantial upgrade to a coal-burning power plant that includes the installation of sulfur dioxide scrubbing equipment can cost hundreds of millions of dollars, although companies can often recoup most of these costs over the following years as a result of efficiency benefits from the upgrade.

E. The scientific data upon which the Clean Air Act was based have not been corroborated by the scientists at the Center for Atmospheric Truth, a research group funded by a consortium of energy companies.

ANSWER: C   C suggests that the specifications that the passage argues companies should follow in order to clean the air might actually have the opposite effect, and could make the air less clean. If true, this would undermine the entire argument of the passage. A and B are defenses for energy companies but do not fundamentally undermine the argument in the passage. The information presented in D probably weakens the energy industry's argument more than it helps it. And statement E does not say that the scientific data are *false*, only that a group with financial ties to the energy industry (and, hence, probably biased) has not corroborated those data. C is the best answer.

21. Although he played several musical instruments <u>while being a child</u>, Maestro Macintosh did not begin playing the piano until he was 23 years old.

A. while being a child
B. as a child
C. as in childhood
D. at the time of his childhood
E. at the time when he was a child

ANSWER: B   A is unidiomatic, and C does not make sense in the context of the sentence. D and E both suggest that there was a single time when he was a child, rather than an extended period. B is the clearest and most concise choice.

22. Unless the conservator can find a way to protect the photographs in the archives from light and air, these precious historical documents <u>have deteriorated and will continue to do so</u> both in color and in fine detail.

A. have deteriorated and will continue to do so
B. will continue to deteriorate
C. have been and will continue to deteriorate
D. will continue to deteriorate, as they already have,
E. will be deteriorating yet more

ANSWER: B   The sentence begins with "Unless," so the verb in the underlined passage should take the form "unless a happens, then b will happen." A, C, and D make statements declaring that the photographs have deteriorated in the past, but these statements are not warranted by the rest of the sentence. C and E properly suggest that unless conditions are changed, an ongoing process will continue; E, however, is worded in a very awkward way. B is the best choice.

23. Under SEC guidelines, a company in this situation is required either to submit revised financial statements or that they withdraw their plans for a public stock offering.

A. that they withdraw their plans
B. to withdraw its plans
C. that it withdraw planning
D. to have been withdrawn from their plans
E. it should withdraw its plans

ANSWER: B The answer should form a parallel construction with "to submit" because it is part of an either . . . or construction. B and D are the only infinitive constructions, and of these two, B is by far the more standard answer.

24. Unless I am greatly mistaken, any apparent connection between my dog and the destroying of your petunias is purely coincidental.

A. connection between my dog and the destroying of
B. connection between my dog and the destruction of
C. connection of my dog with the destruction of
D. connection between my dog and the destroying to
E. connection from my dog with the destruction to

ANSWER: B There are two issues here: first, the proper construction is "connection between . . . and"; second, "the destruction of" is more standard than "the destroying of." Answer B is the only answer to present both constructions correctly.

25. Nutritionists say that you cannot eat enough fruits and vegetables, arguing that it provides nutrition essential to health.

A. that it provides nutrition
B. that they provides nutrition
C. they provide the nutrients
D. it provides the nutrients
E. that they provide the nutrients

ANSWER: E The answer should contain the construction "arguing that . . .," and the pronoun and verb should agree in number with "fruits and vegetables," therefore "they provide"; answer E is the only choice to present the wording properly.

26. In theory, the Habbendorf rotary engine could be a great racing engine, but in practice, it is not. The reason is that the available fuels do not have sufficient octane to obtain maximum performance from the engine.

The answer to which of the following questions would be most relevant to evaluating the adequacy of the explanation given above for why the Habbendorf rotary engine is not a great racing engine?

A. If the Habbendorf rotary engine were to operate at maximum performance levels, how would its performance compare to that of an engine recognized as a great racing engine?
B. At what level of octane in its fuel does the Habbendorf rotary engine achieve maximum performance?
C. What levels of speed, acceleration, and efficiency must an engine display in order to be considered a "great racing engine"?
D. Could a Habbendorf rotary engine be modified so that it is able to achieve maximum performance with the fuels currently available?
E. If a car equipped with a Habbendorf rotary engine were to race against a comparable car equipped with a great racing engine, by how much would the performance of the great racing engine surpass that of the Habbendorf rotary engine?

ANSWER: A The explanation given in the passage relies on the assumption that if the rotary engine could obtain maximum performance, then it would be a great racing engine. Answer A directly questions that assumption. The question in E is incorrect because it focuses on whether or not the rotary engine is a great racing engine, rather than on the explanation given in the passage. The question in D goes outside the scope of the explanation given in the passage, and B and C do not directly address the given explanation.

27. Government deregulation of the long-distance telephone business has resulted in increased competition among telephone carriers, thus resulting in lower prices for consumers. This process, however, will ultimately result in lower-quality service for consumers, because as the telephone carriers drop their prices to compete with one another for customers, they will be forced to cut corners on nonessential items like customer service.

Which of the following, if true, casts the most doubt on the argument that government deregulation of the telephone business will result in lower-quality customer service?

A. Technological advances have decreased the cost of providing long-distance telephone service to less than one-half of its cost prior to deregulation.
B. In a customer survey regarding the electric utility business, another industry that recently went through deregulation, surveyors found that customer dissatisfaction with service was 30 percent higher than prior to deregulation.
C. Customers have listed poor customer service as their number one reason for switching from one long-distance telephone service provider to another.
D. Some companies have decreased the cost of customer service by installing automated telephone response systems that eliminate the need for expensive live employees.
E. The greatest competition for long-distance telephone service providers will come not from traditional telephone companies, but from cellular telephone service providers.

ANSWER: C   Answer C directly challenges the assumption made in the passage that market forces will drive telephone companies to cut corners on customer service in order to cut costs, because C implies that market forces will give these companies at least as much of an incentive to improve customer service as to cut costs. None of the other answers challenge this assumption. The cost savings mentioned in A and D do not actually give the companies any incentive to devote more resources to customer service.

The next two questions refer to the following passage:

A pharmaceutical company tested a new painkiller on 1,000 lab rats that were fed large doses of the painkiller for a two-month period. By the end of the experiment, 39 of the rats had died. The company concluded that the painkiller was sufficiently safe to test on humans.

28. Which of the following, if true, provides the most support for the pharmaceutical company's conclusion?

A. The amount of painkiller fed to the rats was substantially greater, in relation to body mass, than the dosage any human would take under normal circumstances.
B. Because of the different body chemistry of humans and rats, some compounds can be dangerous for rats but safe for humans, and vice versa.
C. Tests of this same painkiller on dogs showed that 3 out of 50 dogs developed lesions on their livers during the course of the experiment.
D. The researchers found that during the experiment, the rats showed a significantly lower sensitivity to pain than rats do under normal circumstances.
E. In an experiment of this length with this number of rats, it is not unusual for up to 50 rats to die during the experiment for reasons unrelated to the experiment itself.

ANSWER: E   If it is normal for up to 50 rats to die, then the death of 39 rats does not in itself suggest that the new drug is inherently unsafe. Answers A and B help explain why the rats died, but they do not give strong evidence that whatever killed the rats would not be equally dangerous for humans.

29. Which of the following, if true, would cast the most doubt on the pharmaceutical company's conclusion?

A. Fifteen of the 39 dead rats were later found to have died of a rare form of liver cancer that is generally seen in only 1 out of 600,000 lab rats.

B. The director of the experiment, although a respected scientist, is not a medical doctor, and therefore will not be able to continue as director of the experiment once it switches from animal to human trials.

C. Although the painkiller in question has been shown to block certain forms of pain, its duration of efficacy is less than that of other painkillers currently on the market.

D. Human trials of another drug produced by this pharmaceutical company were called off after 30 out of 1,000 rats died of heart failure during the animal testing phase of the experiment.

E. The pharmaceutical company is eager to introduce new drugs to the market because its best-selling product, a drug that reduces blood pressure, will soon lose its patent protection.

ANSWER: A   A disproportionately high percentage (about 1 in 60 versus 1 in 600,000) of rats developing a rare and lethal form of liver cancer during a drug trial should be cause for considerable alarm. If the drug's effect on rats is in any way comparable to its effect on humans—and if it is not, why test it on rats in the first place?—then the drug is clearly unsafe to test on humans.

30. Which of the following would make the most appropriate title for this passage?

A. The Long Way Home: *Ulysses* and *Finnegan's Wake*

B. James Joyce, *Ulysses*, and the Battle against Censorship

C. The Works of James Joyce, Ireland's Literary Genius

D. The Hidden Value of James Joyce's Great Novels

E. A Portrait of James Joyce as a Young Man

ANSWER: C   The passage addresses all of Joyce's great works, and it focuses on why his works are considered to be so brilliant, so C is a fitting title. A, B, D, and E focus on more limited topics that are partially addressed in the passage but are not its main theme.

31. Based on the information in the passage, which of the following would be the most accurate statement about *Dubliners* and *Finnegan's Wake*?

A. *Dubliners* contains one of the greatest short stories in the English language, and *Finnegan's Wake* is the greatest story in the English language.

B. Many of the chief characters in *Finnegan's Wake* were earlier introduced in *Dubliners*.

C. The linguistic experimentation of *Dubliners* paved the way for the "night language" of *Finnegan's Wake*.

D. *Dubliners* is a longer book than *Finnegan's Wake*.

E. *Dubliners* is a more accessible book than *Finnegan's Wake*.

ANSWER: E   The passage identifies *Dubliners* as "Joyce's most accessible work," while it says that *Finnegan's Wake* "employs its own 'night language' of puns, foreign words, and literary allusions," so it is safe to say that *Dubliners* is the more accessible work. There is not sufficient support in the passage for answers A through D.

32. Joyce's works helped introduce all except which of the following literary elements into modern English literature?

A. Narration through second-person address

B. Novel structure based on real-time chronology

C. Linguistic experimentation

D. Literary realism concerning physical reality

E. Stream of consciousness

ANSWER: A   The passage never mentions second-person address. There is support for all of the other answers in the passage: B—"The structure was unique: Joyce recreated one full day in the life of his protagonist"; C—" The novel . . . employs its own 'night language' of puns, foreign words, and literary allusions";

D—"Joyce mentions everything that happens to Bloom—including thoughts, bodily functions, and sexual acts—providing a level of physical actuality that had never before been achieved in literature"; E—"Joyce employed a then-revolutionary technique called stream of consciousness."

33. According to the passage, in what year was Joyce born?

A. 1880
B. 1882
C. 1885
D. 1902
E. 1914

ANSWER: B   The passage states: "In 1902, at the age of 20, Joyce . . ."

34. The author most likely mentions James Joyce's childhood, family, and education to serve what purpose?

A. To suggest that he had to write in order to make a living
B. To suggest that he became a writer because of his father's influence
C. To provide the background and cultural context for his literary work
D. To provide evidence that his literary genius was present when he was a child
E. To explain his opposition to Catholicism and socialism in his later life

ANSWER: C   The first paragraph states: "Young James attended Dublin's fine Jesuit schools, which gave him a firm grounding in theology and classical languages—subjects that appeared repeatedly in his later work. The story of his early life and his intellectual rebellion against Catholicism and Irish nationalism are told in the largely autobiographical novel *A Portrait of the Artist as a Young Man*." These statements provide substantial support for C. None of the other answers receives strong support in the text.

35. Who is the most likely intended audience for this passage?

A. Insurance professionals at a company seminar
B. University professors of English literature at a symposium on twentieth-century Irish playwrights

C. High school students in Ireland studying their nation's traditional folklore
D. College students studying twentieth-century English literature
E. Elementary school students studying the *Odyssey*

ANSWER: D   The educated but generalist tone of the article makes D the best answer. B is incorrect because a passage intended for English professors would probably have a more academic tone, and in any event the passage describes Joyce's novels and makes no mention of plays; C is incorrect because the passage says nothing about folklore; and E is incorrect because the passage is too advanced for most elementary school students, and because the *Odyssey* is mentioned in the passage only tangentially.

36. Which of the following can be inferred about Joyce's attitude toward Catholicism as practiced in Ireland at the end of the nineteenth century?

A. He felt that it repressed intellectual freedom and individual expression.
B. He viewed it as the central component of the Irish national psyche.
C. He feared that it was impeding the Irish nationalist movement.
D. He felt that it forced him to leave Dublin for Paris, Trieste, Rome, and Zurich.
E. He believed that Dublin's Jesuit schools provided the finest education in all of Ireland.

ANSWER: A   The passage mentions "his intellectual rebellion against Catholicism" and "the paralyzing social mores of middle-class Catholic life"; A captures these sentiments better than any of the other answers. There is insufficient support for B and C, D is incorrect because the passage never says that Catholicism forced him to leave Ireland, or indeed that he was forced to leave (and why travel to Paris, Trieste, and Rome to flee Catholicism?); and E is incorrect because it is too strong a statement and it is not focused on the topic of the question.

37. Many doctors direct their patients to name-brand drugs, but smart consumers know that <u>generic drugs cost half as much as buying name-brand drugs.</u>

A. generic drugs cost half as much as buying name-brand drugs

B. buying generic drugs costs half as much as name-brand drugs

C. generic drugs cost half as much as name-brand drugs

D. buying generic drugs cost half as much as buying name-brand drugs

E. to buy generic drugs costs half as much as buying name-brand drugs

ANSWER: C The correct answer should relate the cost of "generic drugs" to the cost of "name-brand drugs," or "buying generic drugs" to "buying name-brand drugs"; in any event, the constructions should match. C and D are the only answers that provide appropriate parallel constructions, but D makes a grammatical error by using a plural verb, "cost," with a singular subject, "buying." C is the correct answer.

38. Usually found in pools of stagnant water or mud, <u>crawfish are esthetically unappealing arthropods, except if they are boiled, at which point</u> it yields a tasty treat.

A. crawfish are esthetically unappealing arthropods, except if they are boiled, at which point

B. crawfish are esthetically unappealing arthropods, but after a proper boiling

C. the crawfish is an esthetically unappealing arthropod, in contrast to after being properly boiled

D. the crawfish is an arthropod that does not appeal esthetically, but subsequent to having been boiled properly

E. the crawfish is an esthetically unappealing arthropod, although after a proper boiling

ANSWER: E The final clause, "it yields a tasty treat," calls for a singular subject in the underlined passage, so A and B are out. Between C, D, and E, the wording of E is the clearest and most standard. E is the best choice.

39. While the new health insurance regulations may be onerous for large corporations, <u>it can potentially be disastrous for small business owners, who</u> in many cases will have to lay off employees in order to pay for the extended coverage.

A. it can potentially be disastrous for small business owners, who

B. they are potential disasters for small business owners, since

C. potentially they will be disastrous for small business owners, whom

D. for small business owners it is a potential disaster, because

E. they are potentially disastrous for small business owners, who

ANSWER: E Since the passage refers to "regulations" plural, the underlined passage should use a plural pronoun; thus A and D are out. "Who" is the only grammatically acceptable word to lead into the final clause of the sentence, so E is the answer.

40. <u>After leaving the Pentagon, MacTaggart could have profited from his connections with defense contractors, but he refused to do so.</u>

A. After leaving the Pentagon, MacTaggart could have profited from his connections with defense contractors, but he refused to do so.

B. MacTaggart could have profited from his connections with defense contractors after leaving the Pentagon, but he refused to do it.

C. MacTaggart could have profited after leaving the Pentagon from his connections with defense contractors, but he refused to do so.

D. Having left the Pentagon, MacTaggart could have used his connections with defense contractors to profit, but he refused to do it.

E. Refusing to profit from his connections with defense contractors, MacTaggart could have done so after leaving the Pentagon.

ANSWER: A A is grammatically and stylistically acceptable. In answers B and D, it is not entirely clear what the final "it" refers to. Answer C implies that MacTaggart left the Pentagon from his connections, which does not make sense, and in E it is unclear from "could have done so" whether this refers to profiting or refusing to profit.

41. Product marketing jobs at MegaCorp are difficult to fill because they require specialized skills, <u>demand great responsibility, but also</u> barely any vacation time.

    A. demand great responsibility, but also
    B. great responsibility, and also
    C. great responsibility, and with
    D. carry great responsibility, and
    E. carry great responsibility, and offer

ANSWER: E   A is incorrect because "vacation time" requires a verb before it in this construction. Either each item in the list of three must take the verb "require" or each must have its own verb. D is incorrect on the same grounds. B and C could be correct if all three items take "require," but in the context it does not make sense for "barely any vacation time" to be the object of "require." Only E makes sense and is grammatically correct.

Answers and Explanations

1. Sam is training for the marathon. He drove 12 miles from his home to the Grey Hills Park and then ran 6 miles to Red Rock, retraced his path back for 2 miles, and then ran 3 miles to Rock Creek. If he is then n miles from home, what is the range of possible values for n?

A. $1 \le n \le 23$
B. $3 \le n \le 21$
C. $5 \le n \le 19$
D. $6 \le n \le 18$
E. $9 \le n \le 15$

ANSWER: C   To find the maximum and minimum range for his distance from home, assume that he traveled either directly toward his home or directly away from his home. The range then is between $12 + 6 - 2 + 3 = 19$ for the maximum, and $12 - 6 + 2 - 3 = 5$ for the minimum, so C is the answer.

2. Amber works 20 days a month at d dollars per day for m months out of the year. Which of the following represents her monthly pay?

A. $\dfrac{m}{20d}$
B. $20d$
C. $\dfrac{10md}{6}$
D. $\dfrac{20d}{m}$
E. $20md$

ANSWER: B   The passage states that she works 20 days a month at d dollars per day, so $20d$ is her monthly pay.

3. There are 450 birds at a small zoo. The number of birds is 5 times the number of all the other animals combined. How many more birds are there than nonbird animals at the zoo?

A. 400
B. 360
C. 270
D. 180
E. 90

ANSWER: B   If the 450 birds are 5 times the number of nonbird animals, then nonbirds $= 450/5 = 90$. $450 - 90 = 360$ more birds than nonbirds at the zoo.

4. If x, y, and z are positive integers, and $4x = 5y = 6z$, then the least possible value of $x + y + z$ is

A. 15
B. 28
C. 37
D. 42
E. 60

ANSWER: C   The least common multiple of 4, 5, and 6 is 60, so the numbers are $x = 15$; $y = 12$; $z = 10$; $15 + 12 + 10 = 37$.

5. Three hundred multiples of three are picked at random, and three hundred multiples of four are picked at random. Approximately what percentage of the six hundred selected numbers are even?

A. 100%
B. 75%
C. 66%
D. 50%
E. 33%

ANSWER: B All multiples of four are even, and half of the multiples of three are even; since they each make up 50% of the 600, the combined percentage is approximately 75%.

Score	Number of students
92	4
91	6
?	3
83	7
71	5

6. The incomplete table above shows a distribution of scores for a class of 25 students. If the average (arithmetic mean) score for the class is 83, what score is missing from the table?

A. 75
B. 77
C. 81
D. 84
E. 86

ANSWER: A If the average score for the class is 83, then the sum of all 25 students' scores will be $83 \times 25 = 2,075$. The sum of the scores for the 22 students for whom we have scores is $368 + 546 + 581 + 355 = 1,850$. So the three students' scores must make up the difference between 2,075 and 1,850; $2,075 - 1,850 = 225$; $225/3 = 75$.

7. $\dfrac{(5^2)(2^6)(3^4)}{72^2} =$

A. $\dfrac{5}{2}$

B. $\dfrac{25}{3}$

C. 25
D. 50
E. 150

ANSWER: C 72^2 is the same thing as $(8 \times 9)^2$, which is the same as $(2^3 \times 3^2)^2$, which is the same as $(2^6)(3^4)$; consequently, everything factors out of the fraction except 5^2, which equals 25.

8. What is the value of y?

(1) $y^2 + 8y + 16 = 0$
(2) $y < 0$

ANSWER: A (1) alone is sufficient because the equation can be restated as $(y+4)(y+4) = 0$, so $y = -4$. (2) alone is insufficient because there are infinite negative numbers that meet the condition.

9. The integer x is how much greater than 4?

(1) $\dfrac{1}{10^x} = 0.000001$

(2) $10^x = 1,000,000$

ANSWER: D Both (1) and (2) are sufficient, because in both cases the answer is that $x = 6$, and therefore x is 2 greater than 4.

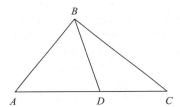

10. In triangle ABC above, if $\angle BAD$ and $\angle ADB$ have measures of $2n°$, and if $\angle ACB$ has a measure of $n°$, what is the length of side AB? (Figure not necessarily drawn to scale.)

(1) $n = 25°$
(2) $CD = 4$

ANSWER: B (1) alone is insufficient because it offers no information about any lengths in the triangle. (2) alone is sufficient; the crucial principle to remember here is that an exterior angle of a triangle—such as $\angle ADB$—is equal to the sum of the remote interior angles of the triangle, in this case triangle BDC. Thus, $n + \angle CBD = 2n$, or $\angle CBD = n$. Since sides of a triangle opposite angles of identical degree are of identical length, BD is the same length as CD, or 4. By this same principle, BD and AB are of identical lengths, so AB is also 4.

11. A dairy farmer has two milk pails, M and P. Milk pail M is 1/3 full. How much milk is in P relative to M?

(1) If M is poured into P, P will be full.
(2) Milk pail P is smaller than M.

ANSWER: E   (1) alone is insufficient, because M could be the same size as P and 2/3 full to start with, or it could be 1/3 the size of P and empty to start with. (2) alone is insufficient, because it tells us nothing about the relative amounts of milk. If the statements are combined, there is still no clear answer, because M could be 2/3 the size of P and 1/2 full to start with, or it could be 1/3 the size of P and empty to start with.

12. Is y between 1 and 2, exclusive?

(1) y^2 is less than y
(2) $y^2 + y$ is between 1 and 2, exclusive

ANSWER: D   (1) alone is sufficient because the only values for y in which y^2 is less than y are if y values between 0 and 1, so the answer is "no." (2) alone is sufficient because there is no value of y between 1 and 2, exclusive, for which this statement is true [the value 1, which is excluded in the question, gives the result 2, which is excluded in statement (2)], so the answer is "no."

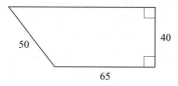

13. What is the perimeter of the figure above? (Note, figure not necessarily drawn to scale.)

A. 155
B. 185
C. 220
D. 235
E. 250

ANSWER: E   To determine the length of the unmeasured side, divide the figure into a rectangle with length 65 and a right triangle. If the height of the triangle is 40 and the hypotenuse is 50, then by the Pythagorean theorem the other leg is 30; the top segment of the rectangle is 65 like its opposite side, so the unmeasured side is 30 + 65 = 95. The perimeter is the sum of the sides: 95 + 40 + 65 + 50 = 250.

14. In a certain growth fund, 3/5 of the investment capital is invested in stocks, and of that portion, 1/3 is invested in preferred stocks. If the mutual fund has $846,000 invested in preferred stocks, what is the total amount of money invested in the fund?

A. $1,974,000
B. $2,538,000
C. $3,264,000
D. $3,826,000
E. $4,230,000

ANSWER: E   If 846,000 is 1/3 of the total amount in stocks, then $846,000 \times 3 = 2,538,000$ invested in stocks. If 2,538,000 is 3/5 of the total, then multiply 2,538,000 times 5/3 to get the total amount in the fund: 4,230,000.

15. $(3^2+1)(81^2+1)(9^2+1)(3^2-1)=$

A. 81^4+1
B. 9^9-1
C. $3^{16}-1$
D. $3^{32}-1$
E. $3^{96}+1$

ANSWER: C   This question at first appears to be a monster, but you can simplify the statements by reordering them and stating all of the exponential numbers as powers of 3: $(3^2-1)(3^2+1)(3^4+1)(3^8+1)$. Then, you can scan through the answers and realize that $3^{16}-1$ is equal to $(3^8+1)(3^8-1) = (3^8+1)(3^4+1)(3^4-1) = (3^8+1)(3^4+1)(3^2+1)(3^2-1)$, which is the same as the statement in the question.

16. If the area of a circle is 81π, then the diameter of the circle is

A. 9
B. 18
C. 36
D. 9π
E. 18π

ANSWER: B   The formula for the area of a circle is πr^2. Therefore, the radius of this circle is the square root of 81, or 9. The diameter is twice the radius, so 18.

17. A standard Veggiematik machine can chop 36 carrots in 4 minutes. How many carrots can 6 standard Veggiematik machines chop in 6 minutes?

A. 36
B. 54
C. 108
D. 216
E. 324

ANSWER: E If a standard Veggiematik can chop 36 carrots in 4 minutes, then it can chop $36/4 = 9$ carrots in 1 minute. 6 machines working for 6 minutes will chop $6 \times 6 \times 9$ carrots $= 324$ carrots.

18. $\dfrac{(0.0063)(0.117)}{(0.03)(0.007)(0.0003)} =$

A. 117,000
B. 11,700
C. 3,900
D. 1,170
E. 390

ANSWER: B Rather than multiplying the numbers out by brute force, try to simplify the statement; it can be restated as:

$\dfrac{(0.0063)(0.117)}{(0.000000063)}$, which is equal to $100,000(0.117)$, which is equal to 11,700.

19. In a sample of patients at an animal hospital, 30 percent are cats and 60 percent are not dogs. What fraction of those patients who are not cats are dogs?

A. $\frac{1}{7}$
B. $\frac{1}{3}$
C. $\frac{2}{5}$
D. $\frac{3}{5}$
E. $\frac{4}{7}$

ANSWER: E For simplicity, assume that there are 100 animals. Of these 30 are cats and 70, therefore, are not cats. If 60 percent of the animals are not dogs, then 40 percent are dogs. If 40 of the noncat animals are dogs, then 4/7 of those patients who are not cats are dogs.

20. Two dogsled teams raced across a 300-mile course in Wyoming. Team A finished the course in 3 fewer hours than did team B. If team A's average speed was 5 miles per hour greater than that of team B, what was team B's average speed, in miles per hour?

A. 12
B. 15
C. 18
D. 20
E. 25

ANSWER: D You could solve this algebraically, or you could just plug the numbers into the statements in the question and see which one fits the facts. If you start from E, 25 mph, then team B will finish the 300-mile course in 12 hours while team A, at 30 mph, will finish the course in 10 hours; this does not meet the 3-hour difference described in the question. If B travels at 20 mph and A travels at 25 mph, then they will finish the course in 15 and 12 hours, respectively, which meets the 3-hour difference. D is the answer.

21. In a club for left-handed people that also admits the ambidextrous, are more than 1/3 of the members ambidextrous?

(1) Exactly 50 percent of the male members of the club are ambidextrous.
(2) The number of females in the club is exactly 1 fewer than half the number of male members.

ANSWER: C (1) alone is insufficient, because it leaves out the female members of the club. (2) alone is insufficient, because it says nothing about the percentage that is ambidextrous. When the statements are combined, it becomes clear that at least 1/3 of the members must be ambidextrous, because males make up at least 2/3 of the membership. Plug in numbers to verify: if there are 2 male members and no female members, then 1 is ambidextrous, which is greater than 1/3; if there are 1,000,000 male members in the club, then at least 500,000/1,499,999 total members are ambidextrous, which is greater than 1/3.

22. If $a \neq 0$, is b greater than zero?

(1) $a + b = 10$
(2) $ab = 24$

ANSWER: C   (1) alone is insufficient because either a or b could be a negative number, e.g., (12, –2), (–2, 12). (2) alone is insufficient, because a and b could both be negative or both be positive, e.g., (–2, –12), (2, 12). If both statements are combined, we know that both a and b must be positive, because if they were both negative, statement (1) would be impossible. The answer to the question is "yes."

23. A truck driver wants to load as many identical cylindrical canisters of olive oil as can fit into the 3-meter × 4-meter × 9-meter storage space of his truck. How many canisters can he load into the truck?

(1) Each canister has a volume of $62,500\pi$ cubic centimeters.
(2) The height of each canister is four times the radius.

ANSWER: C   To determine the maximum number of canisters that can fit in the truck, you need to know the diameter and height of the canisters. (1) alone is insufficient, because the volume of the canisters does not tell you the dimensions; as an extreme example, each canister could have that volume and be 10 meters high, in which case none could fit in the truck. (2) alone is insufficient because each canister could have a radius of 1 meter and a height of 4 meters, or each canister could have a radius of 0.1 m and a height of 0.4 m. If the statements are combined, there is only one set of dimensions that matches the statements. The volume of a canister is $\pi r^2 \times$ height, so $62,500\pi = 4\pi r^3$. This yields the result that $r = 25$ cm and height $= 1$ m, but note that you don't have to do the onerous calculations; once you know that you could derive the radius, and thereby the height, you know that you could then answer the question.

| x | y | y | x |

W ⌊   ⌋ Z

24. In the figure above, what is the length of *WZ*? (Note, figure not necessarily drawn to scale.)

(1) $xy = 64$
(2) $x^2 = y^2$

ANSWER: C   (1) alone is not sufficient, because x and y could be any numbers that multiplied together make 64; remember, you cannot assume that figures are drawn to scale, so (x, y) could be (8, 8) or (1, 64). (2) alone is insufficient, because it gives no information about what x or y equal. The two statements combined are sufficient, because there is only one number that matches the conditions: $x = y = 8$ (you do not have to consider the possibility of negative values here, since the question talks about lengths, and neither x nor y can be a negative length in the figure as drawn).

25. Over the course of a year, a certain house appreciated in value by 10 percent while the house next door decreased in value by 10 percent as a result of foundation damage. At the end of the year, the reduced price of the second house was what percentage of the increased price of the first house?

(1) The amount by which the first house increased in value was half as much as the amount by which the second house decreased in value.
(2) At the end of the year, the second house was worth $70,000 more than the first house.

ANSWER: A   (1) alone is sufficient; it allows you to infer that the initial value of the second house was twice that of the first house, so if x is the initial value of the first house and y is the initial value of the second house, y can be expressed as $2x$. At the end of the year, the ratio of revised values of the second house to the first was $1.8x{:}1.1x$, which can be expressed as a percentage as 164 percent. (2) alone is insufficient, because there are many values of both houses for which the statement could be true.

26. Of 40 applicants for a job, 32 had at least 5 years of prior work experience, 24 had advanced degrees, and 16 had at least 5 years of prior work experience and advanced degrees. How many of the applicants had neither 5 years of prior work experience nor advanced degrees?

A. 0
B. 2
C. 4
D. 8
E. 16

ANSWER: A   To solve this problem, you need to divide the applicants into four exclusive groups that do not overlap. The 16 with both experience and degrees are the first group; we can subtract the 16 from the 24 with advanced degrees to determine that 8 have advanced degrees but not 5 years of experience, and we can subtract the 16 from the 32 with experience to determine that there are 16 applicants with 5 years of experience but no advanced degrees. We can then subtract these three groups from the total pool of 40 applicants to determine how many lack both experience and advanced degrees; $40 - 16 - 16 - 8 = 0$, so there were no such applicants among the 40.

27. If $a \neq 0$, and $a - \dfrac{3a^2 - 15}{a} = \dfrac{b}{a}$, then $b =$

A. $(5-a)(3+a)$
B. $(3-a)(5+a)$
C. $2a^2 - 15$
D. $-3a^2 + a - 15$
E. $15 - 2a^2$

ANSWER: E   If you multiply a times both sides of the equation, you get $b = a^2 - 3a^2 + 15 = 15 - 2a^2$.

$$\begin{array}{r} 2\Delta 7 \\ \times \varnothing 14 \\ \hline 80{,}698 \end{array}$$

28. If Δ and $\varnothing$ represent single digits in the correctly worked computation above, what is the value of Δ times $\varnothing$?

A. 6
B. 10
C. 12
D. 15
E. 18

ANSWER: D   It is probably easiest to determine the values of Δ and $\varnothing$ by plugging in values, which is ugly, but there are ways to simplify your computations. If you look at the answer choices, you will see that 8 and 7 are not factors of any of the choices, so you do not need to try them. Also, if you examine possible values for $\varnothing$, you might realize that $\varnothing$ has to be greater than 2 because $200 \times 200 = 40{,}000$, which is much less than 80,698, so $\varnothing$ is probably 3 or 4, since $200 \times 300 = 60{,}000$ and $200 \times 400 = 80{,}000$. Neither 3 nor 4 is a factor of answer B, 10, so you can eliminate that answer. Plug in the corresponding values of the other answer choices for $\varnothing$ and Δ: A: (3, 2); C: (3, 4) and (4, 3); and D: (3, 5); you will find that D, 15, is the only answer with factors that will make the computation work properly, so D is the answer.

29. A retailer sells 5 shirts. The first 2 he sells for $64 and $39. If the retailer wishes to sell the 5 shirts for an overall average price of over $50, what must be the minimum average price of the remaining 3 shirts?

A. $49.00
B. $49.67
C. $50.00
D. $51.33
E. $55.50

ANSWER: A   For the average price of 5 shirts to be over $50, the total price of the shirts must be at least $250. 250 minus the sum of the two sold shirts $(64 + 39 = 103)$ equals 147. $147 divided by 3 equals $49.

30. The MegaTek Corporation is displaying its distribution of employees by department in a circle graph. The size of each sector of the graph representing a department is proportional to the percentage of total employees in that department. If the section of the circle graph representing the manufacturing department takes up 72° of the circle, what percentage of MegaTek employees are in manufacturing?

A. 20%
B. 25%
C. 30%
D. 35%
E. 72%

ANSWER: A 72° divided by 360° equals 0.2, therefore the sector is equal to 20% of the total.

31. If $x * y = (2x - y)/(2y - x)$ for all integers x and y, then $(-5) * 2 =$

A. −12
B. $\frac{-4}{3}$
C. $\frac{-8}{9}$
D. $\frac{4}{3}$
E. 12

ANSWER: B The equation
$[(2 \times -5) - 2]/[(2 \times 2) - (-5)] = -12/9 = -4/3.$

32. If x, y, and z are positive integers and $x^2 = y^2 + z^2$, which of the following must be true?

I. $x > z$
II. $x = y + z$
III. $y^2 + z^2$ is a positive integer

A. I only
B. II only
C. III only
D. I and II only
E. I and III only

ANSWER: E Statement I must be true, because if all three variables are positive integers and $x^2 = z^2$ plus the square of another positive integer, then x has to be greater than z; plug in numbers to verify. III must be true because the square of a positive integer is always a positive integer, and $y^2 + z^2$ is equal to the square of a positive integer (i.e. $= x^2$). II does not have to be true because if you square both sides of $x = y + z$ you get $x^2 = y^2 + 2yz + z^2$, which does not agree with the original statement.

33. If M is a set of five numbers p, q, r, s, and t, is the range of numbers in M greater than 5?

(1) The average (arithmetic mean) of p, q, r, s, and t is 5.
(2) $p - r > 5$.

ANSWER: B (1) alone is insufficient, because the spread of numbers could be 1, 1, 1, 1, 21 or 5, 5, 5, 5, 5. (2) alone is sufficient, because it states that the range between p and r is greater than 5, so the range of M, which includes p and r, must be greater than 5 as well.

34. Of the 3,600 registered voters in Smith County who took part in the county referendum on altering the property tax exemption, 2,400 were Democrats and 1,200 were Republicans. What was the total number of female voters who voted in favor of the exemption?

(1) The number of female Democrats who voted in favor of the exemption was three times the number of female Republicans who voted in favor of the exemption.
(2) The 150 male Republicans who voted in favor of altering the exemption represented 2/5 of all Republicans who voted in favor of altering the exemption.

ANSWER: C (1) alone is insufficient because it gives no actual numbers to work with. (2) alone is insufficient because it says nothing about the number of female Democrats who voted in favor. If the statements are combined, we see that if 150 male Republicans was 2/5 of the Republican total in favor, then 225 female Republicans voted in favor ($150 \times 3/5$), and 675 female Democrats voted in favor (225×3), and so 900 female voters voted in favor ($225 + 675$).

35. Is the value of $x^3y - x^2y^2 + xy^3$ equal to 0?

(1) $x = 0$
(2) $y = 0$

ANSWER: D   Either statement alone is sufficient, because both x and y are included in every number in the question, so if either is equal to 0, then the whole statement is equal to 0.

36. Is the positive integer y a prime number?

(1) $80 < y < 95$
(2) $y = 3x + 1$, where x is a positive integer

ANSWER: C   (1) alone is insufficient because the range mentioned contains both prime numbers (e.g., 83, 89) and nonprime numbers. (2) alone is insufficient because it provides both prime (e.g., 7, 13) and nonprime values for y. If the statements are combined, they are sufficient, because none of the numbers that meet both criteria (82, 85, 88, 91, and 94) are prime numbers (91 is 13 × 7).

37. What is the area of square floor X?

(1) The perimeter of the floor is a whole-number multiple of 10.
(2) The diagonal of the floor measures $5\sqrt{2}$.

ANSWER: B   (1) alone is insufficient because the perimeter could be 10, 20, 30, and so on. (2) alone is sufficient, because the diagonal of a square, which cuts the square into two 45–45–90 triangles, will be the length of a side times $\sqrt{2}$. Thus, if the diagonal equals $5\sqrt{2}$, then the sides are each 5 in length, and the area then is the square of the side, or 25.

Answers and Explanations

1. The passage is primarily concerned with which of the following?

A. Evaluating the merits of the Electoral College system as a means of protecting federalism

B. Examining the impact of the Twelfth Amendment on the history of the American presidency

C. Disputing the validity of the American democratic process

D. Presenting arguments regarding the best way to elect the president of the United States

E. Comparing arguments regarding the nature of democratic processes

ANSWER: D The passage is entirely concerned with presenting arguments for and against the Electoral College and other systems of electing the American president, so D is the best answer. Answers A and B are too limited in their scope, E is too general, and C is both too general and mostly off topic, since neither of the congressmen suggests that the democratic process is "invalid."

2. Which of the following best describes the structure of the passage?

A. It presents a critique of an institution, then provides a defense of that institution, and then offers possible compromises between the two positions.

B. It presents an argument, lists problems with that argument, and then ultimately refutes the argument.

C. It discusses both sides of a controversial topic and then chooses the side with the stronger arguments.

D. It analyzes flaws in a traditional institution and then provides a series of steps to remedy the flaws.

E. It presents two competing viewpoints and then shows the logical errors in both positions.

ANSWER: A The first two paragraphs are concerned with criticizing the Electoral College system, the third paragraph defends it, and the fourth paragraph suggests three alternative means of reform that would have effects in between those of the current system and a purely popular direct election.

3. From the information provided in the paragraph, what can be inferred about the election of 1892?

A. Its result was disputed on the grounds that smaller states had a disproportionate influence on the outcome.

B. The winner of the election received more popular votes than his opponent.

C. The winner-take-all system of state electoral votes led to a decisive majority for the winner in the Electoral College.

D. Reforming the Electoral College system was an issue of contention in this election.

E. This election led to the formalization of the Electoral College by the Twelfth Amendment.

ANSWER: B The passage states: "there have been four presidential elections in which the candidate who won the Electoral College actually lost the popular vote: 1824, 1876, 1888, and 2000." Logically, therefore, in all of the other elections, the winning candidate won the popular election. The passage does not supply strong support for any of the other answers; note that C is incorrect because the passage states that the system could help create decisive majorities, not that it actually did so in 1892.

4. Hastings's response to Markham's argument that the history of the American government "shows that it [the Electoral College] is doing something right" would most likely be which of the following?

A. Under the current system, each voter in Alaska has proportionately three times as much voting power as each candidate in Florida.

B. We do not know whether or not the American government would have been equally stable had the president been elected by a direct popular election since the beginning.

C. If the candidate who lost the popular election won the presidency four times in 200 years, there is something wrong with the system.

D. Maintaining a strong federal system is less important than upholding the principle that each vote should count equally.

E. A process that maintained the Electoral College but removed the winner-take-all system would substantially reduce the disenfranchisement that occurs under the current system.

ANSWER: C   C directly challenges Markham's statement by using a historical example to refute Markham's point that the system is doing something right. Answers A, D, and E are all statements that Hastings might reasonably make, but they are less relevant to the specific historical argument mentioned in the question; answer B, because of its hypothetical nature, is a weaker statement than C.

5. According to the passage's presentation of Markham's sentiments regarding federalism, which of the following systems for electing the president would be most objectionable to him?

A. An Electoral College system identical to the one currently in use

B. An Electoral College in which each state's number of electors was based strictly on population, but the winner-take-all system was maintained

C. An Electoral College in which each state's number of electors was based strictly on that state's number of members of Congress, but in which the winner-take-all system was replaced by a divided electoral vote proportional to the state's popular vote

D. A direct popular election in which the votes from citizens of smaller states were given more weight than citizens from larger states

E. A direct popular election

ANSWER: E   The passage reads: "Third, the current system of allocating electors helps protect the interests of small states, which would be largely neglected in favor of large states if the Electoral College were based entirely on population. Protecting these states' rights is essential to upholding the principle of federalism (in which the states and the federal government maintain distinct powers)." Therefore, any system that reduces the influence of smaller states, or that reduces the influence of states as a whole in the election process, would run counter to Markham's sentiments regarding federalism. By these criteria, answer E would be the most objectionable, since it both reduces the influence of smaller states and removes the role of states entirely from the electoral process.

6. Which of the following examples from international politics, if true, would give Markham the most support in his argument against Hastings?

A. A nation in Africa that modeled its government on the American governmental system after achieving independence from a European colonial power recently entered into a civil war that has effectively ended any true democratic processes.

B. The ancient city-state of Athens had a form of direct popular election in the fifth century B.C.E., but this government fell as a result of the Peloponnesian War that Athens fought against Sparta.

C. A South American nation that deposed its long-standing military dictatorship and instituted in its place a democratic government with a president elected through a direct popular election has experienced both economic growth and improved relations with the international community.

D. A nation in Central Europe that recently changed its government from a long-standing parliamentary monarchy to a government led by a popularly elected premier was recently thrown into chaos when the popularly elected premier declared a dictatorship.

E. The system of proportional power sharing by the members of the European Union has resulted in a number of thorny disputes between member states that will probably grow more severe as new nations from Eastern Europe enter the EU.

ANSWER: D D describes a situation in which a government changed a long-standing governmental system and experienced political instability as a result; this parallels the implication in Markham's statement, "the Electoral College system, whatever its flaws, has resulted in a stable democratic government for more than 200 years"; Markham implies that a change in the system might endanger that stability. A is problematic for Markham because the African nation became unstable after adopting the American system; B is irrelevant because the government evidently fell because of external, rather than internal, changes; C is an argument in favor of direct popular elections; E does not provide a clear parallel to any of Markham's arguments, although it appears to be an argument against federalism.

7. According to the information given in the passage, which of the following statements about Florida and South Dakota is most accurate?

A. Florida is a larger state in area than is South Dakota.

B. South Dakota has a larger population than Florida.

C. The ratio of members of Congress to electors in the Electoral College is lower for the state of Florida than it is for South Dakota.

D. South Dakota has more members of Congress per voting-age citizen than Florida does.

E. A higher percentage of the voting-age population in South Dakota exercises its constitutional right to vote than is observed among the voting-age population of Florida.

ANSWER: D The second paragraph says "each state's number of electors is the same as its number of members of Congress," and the following statistics showing that South Dakota and several other small states have a combined number of electors the same as Florida but with a combined population only one-third that of Florida suggest that D has to be true. A is not addressed in the text (and is untrue), B and C are both contradicted by the text (the ratio of members of Congress to electors is the same 1:1 ratio for each state), and E is not addressed in the text.

8. Although it has not been confirmed <u>such proteins in whole milk are inducing in children under 12 months milk allergies</u>, most pediatricians advise waiting until the child is one year old before introducing whole milk into his or her diet.

A. such proteins in whole milk are inducing in children under 12 months milk allergies

B. that under 12 months the proteins in whole milk can induce milk allergies in children

C. of proteins in whole milk inducing milk allergies in children under 12 months

D. , the proteins in whole milk can induce milk allergies in children under 12 months

E. that the proteins in whole milk can induce milk allergies in children under 12 months

ANSWER: E The proper construction to use here is "it has not been confirmed that . . ." B and E use this construction, but B incorrectly implies that the proteins, rather than the children, are under 12 months. A is awkward and confusing, the construction "confirmed of . . ." in C is unidiomatic, and the phrasing in D does not make sense with the rest of the sentence.

9. The tango club, which appeared moribund five years ago, has picked up a new <u>step; its numbers are now three times more than</u> when the club president decided to bring in a live band.

A. step; its numbers are now three times more than

B. step; its numbers are now three times greater than

C. step, their numbers now threefold that which they had been

D. step; now with numbers three times greater than

E. step, now with three times the number they had

ANSWER: B A is incorrect because the club doesn't have "more numbers of members," it has "greater numbers of members"; B makes the clearer comparison. The subject of the sentence is the singular "tango club," so the plural pronoun "they" in C and E is incorrect. The construction "now with numbers" in D is unidiomatic, because the phrase lacks a verb to make it sensibly follow the first clause. B, which forms a complete independent clause, is the best answer.

10. During the bronze sculpture boom of the late 1950s, more than 20 tons of bronze were shipped to the SoHo district of Manhattan <u>so as they might sculpt</u> countless bronze statues, busts, abstract shapes, and whimsical figurines.

A. so as they might sculpt

B. in order that they might be sculpted into

C. so that there could be sculpted

D. for the sculpting of

E. such that they could be sculpted into

ANSWER: D A incorrectly suggests that the tons of bronze might sculpt themselves. B and E are awkwardly worded, and their suggestion that the "tons" rather than the "bronze" will be sculpted is somewhat confusing. C is unidiomatic. D is the most concise and idiomatic choice.

11. <u>James Watson, who later headed the Human Genome Project, along with Englishman Francis Crick discovered the double helix in 1953, the basic structure of DNA, when the two were young scientists.</u>

A. James Watson, who later headed the Human Genome Project, along with Englishman Francis Crick discovered the double helix in 1953, the basic structure of DNA, when the two were young scientists.

B. The double helix, the basic structure of DNA, was discovered in 1953 by two young scientists, the Englishman Francis Crick and James Watson, who later headed the Human Genome Project.

C. The basic structure of DNA, the double helix, was discovered in 1953 by the Englishman Francis Crick and James Watson, later head of the Human Genome Project, two young scientists.

D. The Englishman Francis Crick and James Watson, later heading the Human Genome Project, were the young scientists who discovered the basic structure of DNA in 1953, which was the double helix.

E. The basic structure of DNA, the double helix, was discovered by James Watson, later head of the Human Genome Project, along with another of two young scientists, the Englishman Francis Crick, in 1953.

ANSWER: B A implies that 1953 may have been the basic structure of DNA. In C, the phrase "two young scientists" dangles at the end of the sentence with no clear referent. In D, the "which" has no clear referent, and it could be interpreted to read that the double helix was the structure of DNA only in 1953. The information is presented less logically in E than in B, because it makes the most sense to mention that there were two scientists prior to naming either of them, and because it would be clearer if the date of discovery and the verb "discovered" were paired more closely in the sentence. B presents the clearest statement of the facts.

12. Atmospheric scientists in recent years have observed increasing concentrations of chlorofluorocarbons in the tertiary layer of the stratosphere, <u>findings consistent with the documented growth in chlorofluorocarbon emissions from industrial activity</u>.

A. findings consistent with the documented growth in chlorofluorocarbon emissions from industrial activity

B. which are consistent with the documented growth in chlorofluorocarbon emissions from industrial activity

C. a finding consistent with growth in chlorofluorocarbon emissions from industrial activity, as documented

D. finding documented growth consistent with chlorofluorocarbon emissions from industrial activity

E. which findings are consistent with industrial activity's documented growth in chlorofluorocarbon emissions

ANSWER: A **A is idiomatic and makes clear that the "findings" in the second clause refers to the "observed increasing concentrations" in the first clause. B has no clear referent for "which." In C, it is unclear from the dangling "as documented" what exactly has been documented. In D, it is unclear what is meant by "finding documented growth"; they could "document growth" if they published their findings, or they could find "documented growth" if they were looking through documents, but this latter scenario does not agree with the field observations described in the first clause. In E, "which findings are consistent" is unidiomatic. A is the best choice.**

13. The medical board, <u>concerned by the drop in insurance payments and the failure of the accounting department to obtain</u> the anticipated funds, resolved to pursue legal action against the insurance company.

A. concerned by the drop in insurance payments and the failure of the accounting department to obtain

B. concerning the drop in payments by insurance and the failure of the accounting department to obtain

C. because of its concern for the dropping insurance payments and the accounting department's failure at obtaining

D. in its concern that the drop in insurance payments and the failure of the accounting department to obtain

E. being concerned about the drop in insurance payments and the accounting department failing to obtain

ANSWER: A **A presents the information in the clearest and most idiomatic way of all the answer choices. B does not make sense in the context of the sentence. In C, "failure at obtaining" is not idiomatic. The "concern that . . ." structure in D is never completed; it is concerned that the drop and the failure will do what? In E, "being concerned about the drop" is not idiomatic.**

14. The number of violent crimes committed in the greater metropolitan area of Sao Paolo, Brazil, <u>more than doubled</u> from 1975 to 1990 by the influx of drugs.

A. more than doubled

B. increased by more than twice

C. increased more than two times

D. was increased more than double

E. was more than doubled

ANSWER: E **The clause "by the influx of drugs" at the end of the sentence means that the verb in the phrase should be passive, since the sentence specifies that the actor of the sentence is "influx"; therefore, A, B, and C are incorrect because their active verb forms do not agree with this final clause. The construction "increased more than double" in D is not idiomatic. E is the best answer.**

15. One of the biggest threats to a company's productivity is absenteeism. Studies have shown that companies with in-house child-care programs see fewer absences among their employees who are parents than companies without such programs. Therefore, many companies could boost their productivity by starting in-house child-care programs.

Which of the following, if true, most weakens the above argument?

A. Companies that reimburse outside child-care programs actually see less absenteeism among working parents than companies with in-house programs.

B. In-house child-care programs create distractions for nonparents that can harm their productivity.

C. Absenteeism is not a serious problem for companies that impose harsh penalties on employees who miss work.

D. Studies have shown that employees with children are more likely than those without children to remain in the same job for more than five years.

E. Potential employees generally view companies with in-house child-care programs as more desirable places to work than companies without such programs.

ANSWER: B This answer undercuts the argument that companies can boost their productivity by starting in-house child-care programs by showing a way in which such programs can also decrease productivity.

16. A taxi driver purchased four tires of the Toughgrip brand for his cab. Within six months of his purchasing these tires, three of them suffered irreparable blowouts. Despite the poor track record of these tires, the driver replaced all three of the damaged tires with new Toughgrip tires.

Which of the following, if true, does NOT support the driver's decision to replace the damaged tires with new Toughgrip tires?

A. Toughgrip tires are the only tires the driver can afford.

B. The driver feels obligated to buy tires from his brother, who sells only Toughgrip tires.

C. One of the tires was slashed by a rival driver, while the other two blew out in traffic because of material defects.

D. The Toughgrip Company offered to replace all of the tires free of charge because the tires were covered under a 60,000-mile warranty.

E. The taxi company for which the driver works has endorsed Toughgrip as the official tire of the company's cars.

ANSWER: C All of the other answers provide an explanation for the driver's decision, while answer C provides a reason for him *not* to have purchased more Toughgrip tires.

The following two questions are based on the following passage:

An automaker is facing financial difficulties. The vice president of marketing has determined that the root of the company's problems is low brand loyalty. The vice president proposes, therefore, that the company begin an aggressive advertising campaign focused on children aged from three to eight years. By securing strong brand recognition with this demographic, he argues, the company will have an advantage when these customers reach an age when they can buy cars.

17. Which of the following, if true, provides the strongest support for the vice president's proposal?

A. Federal law prohibits the advertising of alcohol or tobacco on any medium for which the primary audience is under 21 years of age.

B. Children aged three to eight, even if they had the money to purchase a car, will not legally be able to drive one for several years.

C. The cost of advertising on children's programs is comparable to the cost of advertising on adult special-interest programs.

D. Focus groups have consistently observed that the automaker's brand is associated with "tradition" and "older" drivers.

E. Studies have shown that lifelong customers of certain products, such as particular brands of toothpaste or peanut butter, frequently credit their brand loyalty to exposure to the product at an early age.

ANSWER: E Answer E gives reason to believe that the vice president's proposal to aim car advertisements at children may result in greater brand loyalty when those children become car buyers. It is not a perfect analogy, because the products mentioned are consumer products that a child could experience directly, but E is the only one of the answers to support the logic of the argument.

18. Which of the following, if true, raises the most serious doubts about the vice president's proposal?

    A. Studies have shown that children are an important factor in the car-buying decision for 75 percent of parents with children under 18 years of age.
    B. The financial difficulties facing the company will result in the company's declaring bankruptcy within five years if the difficulties are not addressed effectively.
    C. The company's most recent advertising campaign, focused on the theme of "Rev up your life," has received positive ratings from the demographic aged 18 to 29.
    D. Children are accustomed to viewing ads for car toys while watching their favorite television programs, so ads for actual cars will appeal to them.
    E. The vice president who made the proposal has only one year of experience in the automotive industry, but has spent more than 20 years in the financial services and children's entertainment industries.

    ANSWER: B If the financial difficulties will bankrupt the company within five years, then an advertising campaign that is unlikely to bear fruit for at least another ten years will not be able to help the company, and will most likely distract attention from more effective solutions.

19. Based on the tone and content of the passage, the author of the passage is most likely which of the following?

    A. An automotive engineer writing to his company management

    B. An enthusiast of automotive history writing to the editors of a car magazine
    C. A college engineering student writing to a car manufacturer
    D. A history professor writing to a television producer of historical documentaries
    E. An environmental activist writing to the editors of a newspaper

    ANSWER: B The first line states, "Given all the coverage that the emergence of hybrid cars has received in your pages in recent months"; the reference to "pages" suggests that the author is addressing the editors of a publication, meaning that we can rule out A, C, and D. B and E are both plausible, but B is the stronger answer because the focus of the article is more historical than environmental, and because the content is more likely to be of interest to readers of a car magazine than to readers of a newspaper.

20. The purpose of the article could best be summarized as which of the following?

    A. To correct a mistaken impression about the performance of gasoline-electric hybrid cars
    B. To educate readers about the economic and technological potential of hybrid cars
    C. To refute a factually inaccurate statement made previously in the publication regarding the history of hybrid cars
    D. To acquaint readers with the history of gasoline-electric hybrid cars
    E. To educate readers about technological innovations at the dawn of the automotive age

    ANSWER: D D captures the basic theme of the passage. A and C address issues that are not addressed in the article, and B and E address only limited parts of the passage.

21. According to the passage, electric and hybrid cars failed to capture the American automotive market in the early twentieth century because of what factor?

A. The improvement in cost and performance of gasoline-powered cars
B. The superior fuel efficiency of hybrid cars
C. The substandard performance of steam-powered cars
D. Consumer fear of being electrocuted by gasoline-electric hybrids
E. Government subsidies for gasoline- and coal-powered cars

ANSWER: A   The passage states: "The cause of their [electric and hybrid cars] decline was the spectacular improvements in the cost and performance of gasoline-powered cars."

22. According to the information given in the passage, which of the following best characterizes the different motivations behind the earliest experiments with gasoline-electric hybrids and the experiments going on in modern times?

A. The earliest experiments with hybrids sought to improve the fuel efficiency of electric engines, while modern experiments seek to improve the performance of gas-burning engines.
B. The earliest experiments with hybrids sought to improve the fuel efficiency of gas-burning engines, while modern experiments seek to improve the performance of electric engines.
C. Modern experiments with hybrids seek to improve the fuel efficiency of gas-burning engines, while the earliest experiments sought to improve the performance of electric engines.
D. Modern experiments with hybrids seek to improve the cruising range of gas-powered cars, while earlier experiments sought to improve the handling and safety of electric cars.
E. The earliest experiments with hybrids sought to combine the power of steam with the efficiency of electricity, while modern experiments seek to combine the efficiency of electricity with the power of gas.

ANSWER: C   A reverses the goals, while B reverses the chronology. The "handling and safety" in D are not addressed in the passage, while the combination of electricity and steam in E contradicts the information about the earliest hybrids given in the passage. C is the best answer.

23. The passage lists which of the following as a reason for the resurgence of interest in the gasoline-electric hybrid engine?

A. The onslaught of fast and inexpensive internal combustion cars from Ford, General Motors, and Buick
B. Advances in battery performance and electricity transfer
C. The Iranian hostage crisis of 1979
D. Dramatic improvements in computer technology
E. The oil crisis of 1973

ANSWER: E   The passage states: "Continuing performance improvements in internal combustion engines and inexpensive gas pretty much kept hybrids buried until the oil crises of 1973 and 1979 gave Americans a reason to start thinking about fuel efficiency."

24. Which of the following examples of business and technology bears the most similarity to the history of the hybrid car, as presented in the passage?

A. American aerospace companies in the 1960s created working prototypes of supersonic passenger aircraft that could complete intercontinental flights in half the time of conventional aircraft, but these projects were canceled because of concerns that the high-altitude craft posed too great a threat to the integrity of the ozone layer.
B. Although oil companies first attempted deep-sea drilling in the Gulf of Mexico in the 1930s, these deep-sea projects could not compete with land-based drilling projects until advances in drilling technology and the rising price of oil made deep-sea drilling economically viable in the late twentieth century.
C. Automakers in the 1980s, after concluding that the average driver could not be relied on to use seat belts

consistently, chose to adopt airbags as a standard safety feature.

D. Lighter-than-air craft, such as Zeppelins, made up a substantial part of total air traffic in the early twentieth century, but they rapidly fell out of favor after airplanes proved to be a faster and safer form of transportation.

E. Although railroads carried more than 90 percent of all land-based commercial cargo in the United States in 1910, by 1980 railroads had been surpassed by trucks in total cargo carried, because of the greater speed and flexibility offered by the heavy truck as compared with the railroad.

ANSWER: B B describes a type of technology—deep-sea drilling—that existed early in the century, was generally disregarded for decades because of competitive pressures, but benefited from a resurgence of interest as a result of technological developments and the rising price of oil. None of the other choices offer this pattern of initial interest, fall from favor, and resurgence that is seen in the history of hybrid cars.

25. Based on the information given in the passage, which of the following can be inferred about an electric-gasoline hybrid car in 1950?

A. It would have been difficult to find a power supply for such a car.

B. Its acceleration would have been roughly comparable to that of a gasoline-burning car that cost less than half as much as the hybrid car.

C. It would have been viewed as "the car of the future."

D. Its performance would have been limited by contemporary battery technology.

E. Had it been produced, it would have sold more than 35,000 units per year.

ANSWER: D The passage states: "Dramatic improvements in electronics . . . during the 1990s, however, finally made the hybrid a reality. Advances in battery performance and, most importantly, computer-guided electric power transfer created a car that could drive

like a regular car . . ." The implication is that hybrid cars were previously unable to drive like regular cars at least in part because of deficiencies in battery technology.

26. Drug use among teens concerns many people in California. Advocates of the "Stop Drugs Now" program, which was piloted in public schools in five California counties last year, argue that the program should be used throughout the state to decrease drug use among teenagers.

Which of the following statements, if true, would most strengthen the argument of the advocates of "Stop Drugs Now" that the program should be expanded statewide?

A. School programs are far less important than parental messages in influencing a teenager's decision to use drugs.

B. Drug use among teens in the five counties where the "Stop Drugs Now" program was piloted has been dropping steadily for over a decade.

C. Teenagers at the public schools where the "Stop Drugs Now" program was piloted reported higher average levels of drug use than did teenagers at private schools in the same counties where the program was not piloted.

D. There is evidence that teenagers who start smoking at an early age are more likely to experiment with illegal drugs than teenagers who do not smoke.

E. The percentage of teenagers who reported using drugs at the schools where the "Stop Drugs Now" program was piloted dropped more in the last year than in any other year over the last decade.

ANSWER: E This answer is the only one that suggests a direct deterrent effect of the "Stop Drugs Now" program on drug use in the schools in which it was piloted.

27. A car manufacturer periodically discounts certain car models to its dealers to coincide with intensive advertising campaigns focused on those cars. After analyzing the results of this program, the manufacturer found that sales of the discounted cars was strong, but it also concluded that it could reap greater profits if it did not hold promotions in this way.

Which of the following statements, if true, best accounts for the manufacturer's conclusion about profitability?

A. Some consumers worry that discounted cars are more likely to be defective.
B. The car manufacturer had not been effective in controlling the production costs of the cars, and these rising costs ate into the manufacturer's profits.
C. Although dealers requested large numbers of the cars at discounted prices, they generally sold the cars at the normal retail price, thereby keeping more of the profit for themselves.
D. Many consumers buy large-ticket items, such as cars, only when they are on sale.
E. The manufacturer's intensive advertising campaign did not sufficiently emphasize the cars' high levels of performance on road tests.

ANSWER: C   Answer C suggests that if the dealers were able to sell the discounted cars at full price, the manufacturer could have sold the cars to the dealers at full price as well, and kept more of the profit from each car for itself.

28. Advertisement:

We at Vesuvius Vacuums always give our customers what they deserve, and they deserve the very best. That's why we use only SuperTec air filters.

Which of the following, if true, most undermines the argument expressed in the advertisement?

A. In a test of three leading air filters, the SuperTec air filter performed at the same level as one of the filters and at a higher level than the other.
B. The SuperTec air filter is the only kind of air filter that will fit in the model of vacuum sold by Vesuvius Vacuums.
C. In a national study by a prominent consumer group, Vesuvius Vacuums gained a "superior" rating for product quality.
D. The customers of Vesuvius Vacuums have expressed no preferences concerning the type of air filter used in the product.
E. The specific air filter used in a given vacuum makes only a small difference in the long-term performance of that vacuum.

ANSWER: B   This answer suggests that Vesuvius uses SuperTec filters in its products not because they are the best, as the advertisement implies, but because they are the only type of filter that will fit into the Vesuvius model of vacuum.

29. Oil is a nonrenewable resource, whereas sunshine is limitless. So why not run cars on solar power? Because a car powered by solar collecting panels would be fine on a sunny day, but as soon as the sun went behind a cloud, the car would no longer function.

Which of the following is presupposed in the argument against running a car on solar power?

A. Solar power is cleaner than fossil fuels, and it involves less geopolitical risk.
B. In most of the northern hemisphere, it can be expected that more than 150 days a year will be cloudy.
C. No system exists for storing solar energy for a car's use when the car is not in direct sunlight.
D. No one has yet introduced a commercially viable process for mass-producing solar cells that convert more than 10 percent of incoming sunlight into usable energy.
E. Consumers accustomed to the rapid acceleration of gasoline-powered cars will not accept the weak acceleration of solar-powered cars.

ANSWER: C   If a system existed for storing solar energy for a car's later use, the objection raised in the passage that a car would stop running "as soon as the sun went behind a cloud" would no longer be valid.

30. Chauncy, <u>like most bulldogs, has</u> a fondness for meat and gravy.

   A. like most bulldogs, has
   B. as most bulldogs, have
   C. like many bulldogs, have
   D. like most bulldogs, having
   E. as with many bulldogs, has

   ANSWER: A   **A is grammatically sound and idiomatic. B and C incorrectly use the plural verb "have" with the singular noun "Chauncy." D creates an incomplete sentence. E is not idiomatic because "as" is not appropriate for comparing two nouns.**

31. Last season, oranges from South Florida were <u>as bountiful as, if not more bountiful than, oranges</u> from the normally more bountiful northern region.

   A. as bountiful as, if not more bountiful than, oranges
   B. equally bountiful, if not more so, to oranges
   C. as bountiful, if not bountifuller, than oranges
   D. so bountiful, and maybe more bountiful, than oranges
   E. as bountiful, if not more bountiful, as oranges

   ANSWER: A   **The proper construction for relationships of equality is "as . . . as," while the proper construction for relationships of greater and smaller is "more . . . than." Answer A, although perhaps unwieldy sounding, is grammatically correct, whereas all of the other choices use improper constructions.**

32. Every lawyer knows that it is difficult to prove culpability in technically complicated lawsuits <u>if there is a lack of some expert to testify</u> about the complicated technical aspects.

   A. if there is a lack of some expert to testify
   B. unless there will be an expert who might testify
   C. should there be no testimony from an expert
   D. without an expert's testimony
   E. lacking some expert to testify

   ANSWER: D   **"If there is a lack of some" is not standard English usage. Answer D is the most concise and standard way to frame this construction.**

33. To be a great salesman <u>requires strong personal skills, the ability to think fast, and demands</u> a can-do attitude.

   A. requires strong personal skills, the ability to think fast, and demands
   B. requires strong personal skills, the ability to think fast, and
   C. requires strong personal skills, demands the ability to think fast, and
   D. requiring strong personal skill, an ability to think fast, and demands
   E. demands strong personal skills, an ability to think fast, but with

   ANSWER: B   **To maintain parallel constructions, each item in the list of three must either be the object of the first verb or have its own verb; A, C, and D are incorrect on these grounds. D also doesn't make sense. E is incorrect because it does not make sense to use "but with" to contrast the previous positive attributes with a complementary positive attribute. B is clear and grammatically correct.**

34. The tremendous insight of Einstein was that the passage of time does not appear the same <u>while standing still as it does to a person traveling</u> at a substantial portion of the speed of light.

   A. while standing still as it does to a person traveling
   B. to a person standing still as to a person traveling
   C. to a person who is standing still as a person who is traveling
   D. while standing still as to traveling
   E. to a person standing still as to a person who travels

   ANSWER: B   **A fails to specify whose point of view is being contrasted with that of a person traveling at near-light speed. C implies that the first person is "standing still as a person," which makes no sense. D makes no sense. E uses nonparallel constructions: "standing" and "travels." B is the best answer.**

35. Professor Markham's theory fails to explain the extent <u>to which savings from personal income has shifted</u> to short-term bonds, money-market funds, and other near-term investments by the instability in the futures market.

A. to which savings from personal income has shifted
B. of savings from personal income that has been shifted
C. of savings from personal income shifting
D. to which savings from personal income have shifted
E. to which savings from personal income have been shifted

ANSWER: E **A and D both incorrectly use the active voice for "has/have," which does not work with the phrase "by the instability" later in the sentence; A also incorrectly uses the singular form "has" for the plural noun "savings." B makes the same error in number, and C also uses the active voice. The construction "explain the extent of savings" in B and C is less idiomatic than the construction "explain the extent to which savings" in E. E provides the clearest and most idiomatic statement.**

36. <u>Approximately $120 billion in venture capital is estimated as having poured into technology stocks during the late 1990s, creating</u> a valuation bubble that burst in 2000.

A. Approximately $120 billion in venture capital is estimated as having poured into technology stocks during the late 1990s, creating
B. During the late 1990s approximately $120 billion in venture capital is estimated to have poured into technology stocks and created
C. During the late 1990s it is estimated that there was approximately $120 billion in venture capital that was poured into technology stocks, creating
D. It is estimated that during the late 1990s approximately $120 billion in venture capital poured into technology stocks, creating
E. It is estimated that there was approximately $120 billion in venture

capital that poured into technology stocks during the late 1990s and created

ANSWER: D **Answers B and C are incorrect because they imply that the estimation took place during the 1990s, not during the present. A is inferior to D because "estimated as having poured" is unidiomatic; E is inferior to D because it is less concise and because the ending of E could imply that the estimation refers to the creation of the bubble as well as to the $120 billion. D is the best answer.**

37. Jim Smyth may be a charismatic speaker, but it seems to be counterproductive to have a high school dropout as mayor in a town <u>where illiteracy functionally affects 37 percent of the electorate.</u>

A. where illiteracy functionally affects 37 percent of the electorate
B. in which functionally the electorate is 37 percent illiterate
C. where 37 percent of the electorate are functionally illiterate
D. which has 37 percent of the electorate functionally illiterate
E. where, of the electorate, 37 percent of them functionally are illiterate

ANSWER: C **A and B are incorrect because "functionally" should modify "illiterate" to agree with standard usage. Of C, D, and E, C is the clearest and most standard of the choices.**

38. The decline in the price of biotech stocks has hurt many institutions that had invested heavily in biotech companies. Last year the state university added 200,000 shares of a biotech stock to its holdings. The stock in question has declined in value by more than 90 percent over the last 12 months. The college, however, did not purchase the stock, but received it as a gift. Therefore, the price decline will not harm the university's finances.

Which of the following, if true, casts the most doubt on the conclusion that the price decline of biotech stocks will not harm the university's finances?

A. The biotech sector is volatile; some stocks that lose 90 percent of their value in one year may regain all of their value and more in the following year.

B. The university needs to pay capital gains taxes only on a stock sale that results in a gain; stocks sold at a loss will incur no tax penalty.

C. Although the biotech sector is down, the overall health-care sector, in which the university has invested heavily, is up for the year.

D. The biotech company in question has a promising new drug in development that could revolutionize the treatment of type II diabetes.

E. The university began construction of a new laboratory last year that the provost had expected to pay for with the proceeds from the sale of the biotech stock in question.

ANSWER: E   If the university initiated large capital expenditures with the expectation of selling the biotech stock at 10 times its current price, then once the stock falls in price, the university will be forced to raise that money from somewhere else; in all likelihood, this will harm the university's finances.

39. A city councilman has proposed a controversial new plan to increase city revenues from the parking places downtown. He has proposed that instead of charging $1.20 per hour for parking in these spots, the city should make all parking spots five-minute loading zones, and then assess $15 parking fines on anyone who parks in the spots for more than five minutes.

Which of the following, if true, provides the strongest argument that the councilman's plan will not increase the city's revenue?

A. A system that promotes parking fines will anger citizens, and they will consequently vote the councilman out of office if the plan goes through.

B. The city owns only 14 parking spots in the downtown area.

C. The costs of assessing and collecting the parking fines will surpass the revenues likely to be collected from the new plan.

D. Ray's parking garage, the only competition for the city-owned parking places downtown, charges $18 per day for its parking places.

E. It has been observed that on an average day, approximately three different cars park in each of the city-owned parking spots downtown.

ANSWER: C   If the plan actually loses money for the city, as suggested in answer C, there is no way that it can increase the city's revenue.

40. Over the last five years, Eagle Trust Bank has seen the number of its retail customer accounts drop by over 40 percent. Over this same period, the price of Eagle Trust stock has increased by more than 80 percent. This phenomenon has perplexed certain investors, who believe that a bank's stock should drop if its number of customer accounts drops.

Which of the following, if true over the last five years, best accounts for the observed movement in the price of Eagle Trust stock?

A. Two years ago Eagle Trust was investigated by the Securities and Exchange Commission for accounting irregularities, but last year the company was cleared of all charges.

B. Eagle Trust recently implemented a highly publicized program for no-fee home mortgages.

C. Eagle Trust is in the process of switching its customer base from retail customers to commercial customers, which now account for over 75 percent of the bank's revenues.

D. There have been many aggressive new entrants into the retail customer banking business over the last five years.

E. Eagle Trust is known for offering one of the best employee benefits packages in the industry.

ANSWER: C   Answer C provides a plausible explanation of why Eagle Trust could lose 40 percent of its retail customers but still see appreciation in its stock price; a switch to commercial customers both explains the reduction in retail customers and provides a new source of revenue to replace that presumably lost from the retail business, and this new revenue could have caused the rise in the stock price.

41. Recent scientific studies have proven that ulcers are caused, at least in part, by the heliobacter bacterium. Dr. Redding has hypothesized that a natural way to prevent and cure ulcers is to eat large amounts of raw broccoli, which contains potent organic compounds that are beneficial to gastric health.

All of the following statements support Dr. Redding's hypothesis, EXCEPT:

A. It has been shown that people who consume raw broccoli on a regular basis have a 65 percent lower chance of developing ulcers than do the general population.

B. One of the organic compounds found in broccoli has been shown to have an antibiotic effect on the heliobacter bacterium.

C. Dr. Redding conducted a study in which groups of patients suffering from ulcers either ate large quantities of broccoli or ate a diet that included no vegetables; several of the patients who ate the large quantities of broccoli showed marked improvement in their conditions.

D. Broccoli is one of the most potent dietary sources of antioxidants, the organic compounds shown to combat the free radicals that are thought to cause cancer.

E. Test animals with chemically induced ulcers showed some signs of improvement when raw broccoli was incorporated into their diets.

ANSWER: D   The answer provides no link between broccoli and a cure for ulcers; while anticancer properties are certainly a powerful argument for eating broccoli, they are not mentioned as part of Dr. Redding's hypothesis.

QUANTITATIVE						VERBAL				
1.	(A)	(B)	(C)	(D)	(E)	1.	(A)	(B)	(C)	(D)	(E)
2.	(A)	(B)	(C)	(D)	(E)	2.	(A)	(B)	(C)	(D)	(E)
3.	(A)	(B)	(C)	(D)	(E)	3.	(A)	(B)	(C)	(D)	(E)
4.	(A)	(B)	(C)	(D)	(E)	4.	(A)	(B)	(C)	(D)	(E)
5.	(A)	(B)	(C)	(D)	(E)	5.	(A)	(B)	(C)	(D)	(E)
6.	(A)	(B)	(C)	(D)	(E)	6.	(A)	(B)	(C)	(D)	(E)
7.	(A)	(B)	(C)	(D)	(E)	7.	(A)	(B)	(C)	(D)	(E)
8.	(A)	(B)	(C)	(D)	(E)	8.	(A)	(B)	(C)	(D)	(E)
9.	(A)	(B)	(C)	(D)	(E)	9.	(A)	(B)	(C)	(D)	(E)
10.	(A)	(B)	(C)	(D)	(E)	10.	(A)	(B)	(C)	(D)	(E)
11.	(A)	(B)	(C)	(D)	(E)	11.	(A)	(B)	(C)	(D)	(E)
12.	(A)	(B)	(C)	(D)	(E)	12.	(A)	(B)	(C)	(D)	(E)
13.	(A)	(B)	(C)	(D)	(E)	13.	(A)	(B)	(C)	(D)	(E)
14.	(A)	(B)	(C)	(D)	(E)	14.	(A)	(B)	(C)	(D)	(E)
15.	(A)	(B)	(C)	(D)	(E)	15.	(A)	(B)	(C)	(D)	(E)
16.	(A)	(B)	(C)	(D)	(E)	16.	(A)	(B)	(C)	(D)	(E)
17.	(A)	(B)	(C)	(D)	(E)	17.	(A)	(B)	(C)	(D)	(E)
18.	(A)	(B)	(C)	(D)	(E)	18.	(A)	(B)	(C)	(D)	(E)
19.	(A)	(B)	(C)	(D)	(E)	19.	(A)	(B)	(C)	(D)	(E)
20.	(A)	(B)	(C)	(D)	(E)	20.	(A)	(B)	(C)	(D)	(E)
21.	(A)	(B)	(C)	(D)	(E)	21.	(A)	(B)	(C)	(D)	(E)
22.	(A)	(B)	(C)	(D)	(E)	22.	(A)	(B)	(C)	(D)	(E)
23.	(A)	(B)	(C)	(D)	(E)	23.	(A)	(B)	(C)	(D)	(E)
24.	(A)	(B)	(C)	(D)	(E)	24.	(A)	(B)	(C)	(D)	(E)
25.	(A)	(B)	(C)	(D)	(E)	25.	(A)	(B)	(C)	(D)	(E)
26.	(A)	(B)	(C)	(D)	(E)	26.	(A)	(B)	(C)	(D)	(E)
27.	(A)	(B)	(C)	(D)	(E)	27.	(A)	(B)	(C)	(D)	(E)
28.	(A)	(B)	(C)	(D)	(E)	28.	(A)	(B)	(C)	(D)	(E)
29.	(A)	(B)	(C)	(D)	(E)	29.	(A)	(B)	(C)	(D)	(E)
30.	(A)	(B)	(C)	(D)	(E)	30.	(A)	(B)	(C)	(D)	(E)
31.	(A)	(B)	(C)	(D)	(E)	31.	(A)	(B)	(C)	(D)	(E)
32.	(A)	(B)	(C)	(D)	(E)	32.	(A)	(B)	(C)	(D)	(E)
33.	(A)	(B)	(C)	(D)	(E)	33.	(A)	(B)	(C)	(D)	(E)
34.	(A)	(B)	(C)	(D)	(E)	34.	(A)	(B)	(C)	(D)	(E)
35.	(A)	(B)	(C)	(D)	(E)	35.	(A)	(B)	(C)	(D)	(E)
36.	(A)	(B)	(C)	(D)	(E)	36.	(A)	(B)	(C)	(D)	(E)
37.	(A)	(B)	(C)	(D)	(E)	37.	(A)	(B)	(C)	(D)	(E)
						38.	(A)	(B)	(C)	(D)	(E)
						39.	(A)	(B)	(C)	(D)	(E)
						40.	(A)	(B)	(C)	(D)	(E)
						41.	(A)	(B)	(C)	(D)	(E)

QUANTITATIVE

1. (A) (B) (C) (D) (E)
2. (A) (B) (C) (D) (E)
3. (A) (B) (C) (D) (E)
4. (A) (B) (C) (D) (E)
5. (A) (B) (C) (D) (E)
6. (A) (B) (C) (D) (E)
7. (A) (B) (C) (D) (E)
8. (A) (B) (C) (D) (E)
9. (A) (B) (C) (D) (E)
10. (A) (B) (C) (D) (E)
11. (A) (B) (C) (D) (E)
12. (A) (B) (C) (D) (E)
13. (A) (B) (C) (D) (E)
14. (A) (B) (C) (D) (E)
15. (A) (B) (C) (D) (E)
16. (A) (B) (C) (D) (E)
17. (A) (B) (C) (D) (E)
18. (A) (B) (C) (D) (E)
19. (A) (B) (C) (D) (E)
20. (A) (B) (C) (D) (E)
21. (A) (B) (C) (D) (E)
22. (A) (B) (C) (D) (E)
23. (A) (B) (C) (D) (E)
24. (A) (B) (C) (D) (E)
25. (A) (B) (C) (D) (E)
26. (A) (B) (C) (D) (E)
27. (A) (B) (C) (D) (E)
28. (A) (B) (C) (D) (E)
29. (A) (B) (C) (D) (E)
30. (A) (B) (C) (D) (E)
31. (A) (B) (C) (D) (E)
32. (A) (B) (C) (D) (E)
33. (A) (B) (C) (D) (E)
34. (A) (B) (C) (D) (E)
35. (A) (B) (C) (D) (E)
36. (A) (B) (C) (D) (E)
37. (A) (B) (C) (D) (E)

VERBAL

1. (A) (B) (C) (D) (E)
2. (A) (B) (C) (D) (E)
3. (A) (B) (C) (D) (E)
4. (A) (B) (C) (D) (E)
5. (A) (B) (C) (D) (E)
6. (A) (B) (C) (D) (E)
7. (A) (B) (C) (D) (E)
8. (A) (B) (C) (D) (E)
9. (A) (B) (C) (D) (E)
10. (A) (B) (C) (D) (E)
11. (A) (B) (C) (D) (E)
12. (A) (B) (C) (D) (E)
13. (A) (B) (C) (D) (E)
14. (A) (B) (C) (D) (E)
15. (A) (B) (C) (D) (E)
16. (A) (B) (C) (D) (E)
17. (A) (B) (C) (D) (E)
18. (A) (B) (C) (D) (E)
19. (A) (B) (C) (D) (E)
20. (A) (B) (C) (D) (E)
21. (A) (B) (C) (D) (E)
22. (A) (B) (C) (D) (E)
23. (A) (B) (C) (D) (E)
24. (A) (B) (C) (D) (E)
25. (A) (B) (C) (D) (E)
26. (A) (B) (C) (D) (E)
27. (A) (B) (C) (D) (E)
28. (A) (B) (C) (D) (E)
29. (A) (B) (C) (D) (E)
30. (A) (B) (C) (D) (E)
31. (A) (B) (C) (D) (E)
32. (A) (B) (C) (D) (E)
33. (A) (B) (C) (D) (E)
34. (A) (B) (C) (D) (E)
35. (A) (B) (C) (D) (E)
36. (A) (B) (C) (D) (E)
37. (A) (B) (C) (D) (E)
38. (A) (B) (C) (D) (E)
39. (A) (B) (C) (D) (E)
40. (A) (B) (C) (D) (E)
41. (A) (B) (C) (D) (E)

QUANTITATIVE						VERBAL					
1.	(A)	(B)	(C)	(D)	(E)	1.	(A)	(B)	(C)	(D)	(E)
2.	(A)	(B)	(C)	(D)	(E)	2.	(A)	(B)	(C)	(D)	(E)
3.	(A)	(B)	(C)	(D)	(E)	3.	(A)	(B)	(C)	(D)	(E)
4.	(A)	(B)	(C)	(D)	(E)	4.	(A)	(B)	(C)	(D)	(E)
5.	(A)	(B)	(C)	(D)	(E)	5.	(A)	(B)	(C)	(D)	(E)
6.	(A)	(B)	(C)	(D)	(E)	6.	(A)	(B)	(C)	(D)	(E)
7.	(A)	(B)	(C)	(D)	(E)	7.	(A)	(B)	(C)	(D)	(E)
8.	(A)	(B)	(C)	(D)	(E)	8.	(A)	(B)	(C)	(D)	(E)
9.	(A)	(B)	(C)	(D)	(E)	9.	(A)	(B)	(C)	(D)	(E)
10.	(A)	(B)	(C)	(D)	(E)	10.	(A)	(B)	(C)	(D)	(E)
11.	(A)	(B)	(C)	(D)	(E)	11.	(A)	(B)	(C)	(D)	(E)
12.	(A)	(B)	(C)	(D)	(E)	12.	(A)	(B)	(C)	(D)	(E)
13.	(A)	(B)	(C)	(D)	(E)	13.	(A)	(B)	(C)	(D)	(E)
14.	(A)	(B)	(C)	(D)	(E)	14.	(A)	(B)	(C)	(D)	(E)
15.	(A)	(B)	(C)	(D)	(E)	15.	(A)	(B)	(C)	(D)	(E)
16.	(A)	(B)	(C)	(D)	(E)	16.	(A)	(B)	(C)	(D)	(E)
17.	(A)	(B)	(C)	(D)	(E)	17.	(A)	(B)	(C)	(D)	(E)
18.	(A)	(B)	(C)	(D)	(E)	18.	(A)	(B)	(C)	(D)	(E)
19.	(A)	(B)	(C)	(D)	(E)	19.	(A)	(B)	(C)	(D)	(E)
20.	(A)	(B)	(C)	(D)	(E)	20.	(A)	(B)	(C)	(D)	(E)
21.	(A)	(B)	(C)	(D)	(E)	21.	(A)	(B)	(C)	(D)	(E)
22.	(A)	(B)	(C)	(D)	(E)	22.	(A)	(B)	(C)	(D)	(E)
23.	(A)	(B)	(C)	(D)	(E)	23.	(A)	(B)	(C)	(D)	(E)
24.	(A)	(B)	(C)	(D)	(E)	24.	(A)	(B)	(C)	(D)	(E)
25.	(A)	(B)	(C)	(D)	(E)	25.	(A)	(B)	(C)	(D)	(E)
26.	(A)	(B)	(C)	(D)	(E)	26.	(A)	(B)	(C)	(D)	(E)
27.	(A)	(B)	(C)	(D)	(E)	27.	(A)	(B)	(C)	(D)	(E)
28.	(A)	(B)	(C)	(D)	(E)	28.	(A)	(B)	(C)	(D)	(E)
29.	(A)	(B)	(C)	(D)	(E)	29.	(A)	(B)	(C)	(D)	(E)
30.	(A)	(B)	(C)	(D)	(E)	30.	(A)	(B)	(C)	(D)	(E)
31.	(A)	(B)	(C)	(D)	(E)	31.	(A)	(B)	(C)	(D)	(E)
32.	(A)	(B)	(C)	(D)	(E)	32.	(A)	(B)	(C)	(D)	(E)
33.	(A)	(B)	(C)	(D)	(E)	33.	(A)	(B)	(C)	(D)	(E)
34.	(A)	(B)	(C)	(D)	(E)	34.	(A)	(B)	(C)	(D)	(E)
35.	(A)	(B)	(C)	(D)	(E)	35.	(A)	(B)	(C)	(D)	(E)
36.	(A)	(B)	(C)	(D)	(E)	36.	(A)	(B)	(C)	(D)	(E)
37.	(A)	(B)	(C)	(D)	(E)	37.	(A)	(B)	(C)	(D)	(E)
						38.	(A)	(B)	(C)	(D)	(E)
						39.	(A)	(B)	(C)	(D)	(E)
						40.	(A)	(B)	(C)	(D)	(E)
						41.	(A)	(B)	(C)	(D)	(E)

	QUANTITATIVE						VERBAL				
1.	(A)	(B)	(C)	(D)	(E)	1.	(A)	(B)	(C)	(D)	(E)
2.	(A)	(B)	(C)	(D)	(E)	2.	(A)	(B)	(C)	(D)	(E)
3.	(A)	(B)	(C)	(D)	(E)	3.	(A)	(B)	(C)	(D)	(E)
4.	(A)	(B)	(C)	(D)	(E)	4.	(A)	(B)	(C)	(D)	(E)
5.	(A)	(B)	(C)	(D)	(E)	5.	(A)	(B)	(C)	(D)	(E)
6.	(A)	(B)	(C)	(D)	(E)	6.	(A)	(B)	(C)	(D)	(E)
7.	(A)	(B)	(C)	(D)	(E)	7.	(A)	(B)	(C)	(D)	(E)
8.	(A)	(B)	(C)	(D)	(E)	8.	(A)	(B)	(C)	(D)	(E)
9.	(A)	(B)	(C)	(D)	(E)	9.	(A)	(B)	(C)	(D)	(E)
10.	(A)	(B)	(C)	(D)	(E)	10.	(A)	(B)	(C)	(D)	(E)
11.	(A)	(B)	(C)	(D)	(E)	11.	(A)	(B)	(C)	(D)	(E)
12.	(A)	(B)	(C)	(D)	(E)	12.	(A)	(B)	(C)	(D)	(E)
13.	(A)	(B)	(C)	(D)	(E)	13.	(A)	(B)	(C)	(D)	(E)
14.	(A)	(B)	(C)	(D)	(E)	14.	(A)	(B)	(C)	(D)	(E)
15.	(A)	(B)	(C)	(D)	(E)	15.	(A)	(B)	(C)	(D)	(E)
16.	(A)	(B)	(C)	(D)	(E)	16.	(A)	(B)	(C)	(D)	(E)
17.	(A)	(B)	(C)	(D)	(E)	17.	(A)	(B)	(C)	(D)	(E)
18.	(A)	(B)	(C)	(D)	(E)	18.	(A)	(B)	(C)	(D)	(E)
19.	(A)	(B)	(C)	(D)	(E)	19.	(A)	(B)	(C)	(D)	(E)
20.	(A)	(B)	(C)	(D)	(E)	20.	(A)	(B)	(C)	(D)	(E)
21.	(A)	(B)	(C)	(D)	(E)	21.	(A)	(B)	(C)	(D)	(E)
22.	(A)	(B)	(C)	(D)	(E)	22.	(A)	(B)	(C)	(D)	(E)
23.	(A)	(B)	(C)	(D)	(E)	23.	(A)	(B)	(C)	(D)	(E)
24.	(A)	(B)	(C)	(D)	(E)	24.	(A)	(B)	(C)	(D)	(E)
25.	(A)	(B)	(C)	(D)	(E)	25.	(A)	(B)	(C)	(D)	(E)
26.	(A)	(B)	(C)	(D)	(E)	26.	(A)	(B)	(C)	(D)	(E)
27.	(A)	(B)	(C)	(D)	(E)	27.	(A)	(B)	(C)	(D)	(E)
28.	(A)	(B)	(C)	(D)	(E)	28.	(A)	(B)	(C)	(D)	(E)
29.	(A)	(B)	(C)	(D)	(E)	29.	(A)	(B)	(C)	(D)	(E)
30.	(A)	(B)	(C)	(D)	(E)	30.	(A)	(B)	(C)	(D)	(E)
31.	(A)	(B)	(C)	(D)	(E)	31.	(A)	(B)	(C)	(D)	(E)
32.	(A)	(B)	(C)	(D)	(E)	32.	(A)	(B)	(C)	(D)	(E)
33.	(A)	(B)	(C)	(D)	(E)	33.	(A)	(B)	(C)	(D)	(E)
34.	(A)	(B)	(C)	(D)	(E)	34.	(A)	(B)	(C)	(D)	(E)
35.	(A)	(B)	(C)	(D)	(E)	35.	(A)	(B)	(C)	(D)	(E)
36.	(A)	(B)	(C)	(D)	(E)	36.	(A)	(B)	(C)	(D)	(E)
37.	(A)	(B)	(C)	(D)	(E)	37.	(A)	(B)	(C)	(D)	(E)
						38.	(A)	(B)	(C)	(D)	(E)
						39.	(A)	(B)	(C)	(D)	(E)
						40.	(A)	(B)	(C)	(D)	(E)
						41.	(A)	(B)	(C)	(D)	(E)

QUANTITATIVE						VERBAL				
1.	(A)	(B)	(C)	(D)	(E)	1.	(A)	(B)	(C)	(D)	(E)
2.	(A)	(B)	(C)	(D)	(E)	2.	(A)	(B)	(C)	(D)	(E)
3.	(A)	(B)	(C)	(D)	(E)	3.	(A)	(B)	(C)	(D)	(E)
4.	(A)	(B)	(C)	(D)	(E)	4.	(A)	(B)	(C)	(D)	(E)
5.	(A)	(B)	(C)	(D)	(E)	5.	(A)	(B)	(C)	(D)	(E)
6.	(A)	(B)	(C)	(D)	(E)	6.	(A)	(B)	(C)	(D)	(E)
7.	(A)	(B)	(C)	(D)	(E)	7.	(A)	(B)	(C)	(D)	(E)
8.	(A)	(B)	(C)	(D)	(E)	8.	(A)	(B)	(C)	(D)	(E)
9.	(A)	(B)	(C)	(D)	(E)	9.	(A)	(B)	(C)	(D)	(E)
10.	(A)	(B)	(C)	(D)	(E)	10.	(A)	(B)	(C)	(D)	(E)
11.	(A)	(B)	(C)	(D)	(E)	11.	(A)	(B)	(C)	(D)	(E)
12.	(A)	(B)	(C)	(D)	(E)	12.	(A)	(B)	(C)	(D)	(E)
13.	(A)	(B)	(C)	(D)	(E)	13.	(A)	(B)	(C)	(D)	(E)
14.	(A)	(B)	(C)	(D)	(E)	14.	(A)	(B)	(C)	(D)	(E)
15.	(A)	(B)	(C)	(D)	(E)	15.	(A)	(B)	(C)	(D)	(E)
16.	(A)	(B)	(C)	(D)	(E)	16.	(A)	(B)	(C)	(D)	(E)
17.	(A)	(B)	(C)	(D)	(E)	17.	(A)	(B)	(C)	(D)	(E)
18.	(A)	(B)	(C)	(D)	(E)	18.	(A)	(B)	(C)	(D)	(E)
19.	(A)	(B)	(C)	(D)	(E)	19.	(A)	(B)	(C)	(D)	(E)
20.	(A)	(B)	(C)	(D)	(E)	20.	(A)	(B)	(C)	(D)	(E)
21.	(A)	(B)	(C)	(D)	(E)	21.	(A)	(B)	(C)	(D)	(E)
22.	(A)	(B)	(C)	(D)	(E)	22.	(A)	(B)	(C)	(D)	(E)
23.	(A)	(B)	(C)	(D)	(E)	23.	(A)	(B)	(C)	(D)	(E)
24.	(A)	(B)	(C)	(D)	(E)	24.	(A)	(B)	(C)	(D)	(E)
25.	(A)	(B)	(C)	(D)	(E)	25.	(A)	(B)	(C)	(D)	(E)
26.	(A)	(B)	(C)	(D)	(E)	26.	(A)	(B)	(C)	(D)	(E)
27.	(A)	(B)	(C)	(D)	(E)	27.	(A)	(B)	(C)	(D)	(E)
28.	(A)	(B)	(C)	(D)	(E)	28.	(A)	(B)	(C)	(D)	(E)
29.	(A)	(B)	(C)	(D)	(E)	29.	(A)	(B)	(C)	(D)	(E)
30.	(A)	(B)	(C)	(D)	(E)	30.	(A)	(B)	(C)	(D)	(E)
31.	(A)	(B)	(C)	(D)	(E)	31.	(A)	(B)	(C)	(D)	(E)
32.	(A)	(B)	(C)	(D)	(E)	32.	(A)	(B)	(C)	(D)	(E)
33.	(A)	(B)	(C)	(D)	(E)	33.	(A)	(B)	(C)	(D)	(E)
34.	(A)	(B)	(C)	(D)	(E)	34.	(A)	(B)	(C)	(D)	(E)
35.	(A)	(B)	(C)	(D)	(E)	35.	(A)	(B)	(C)	(D)	(E)
36.	(A)	(B)	(C)	(D)	(E)	36.	(A)	(B)	(C)	(D)	(E)
37.	(A)	(B)	(C)	(D)	(E)	37.	(A)	(B)	(C)	(D)	(E)
						38.	(A)	(B)	(C)	(D)	(E)
						39.	(A)	(B)	(C)	(D)	(E)
						40.	(A)	(B)	(C)	(D)	(E)
						41.	(A)	(B)	(C)	(D)	(E)